To Duncan

on the occasion of his retiral - May '89
with every good wish for the future —
From,
his 'old pal' (+ brother-in-law)

Albie

THE
GREIG–DUNCAN
FOLK SONG COLLECTION

THE
GREIG–DUNCAN
FOLK SONG COLLECTION

Volume 3

Songs 347–706

EDITED BY

PATRICK SHULDHAM-SHAW, EMILY B. LYLE
AND PETER A. HALL

Published by Aberdeen University Press
for the University of Aberdeen
in association with the School of Scottish Studies
University of Edinburgh

First published 1987
Aberdeen University Press
A member of the Pergamon Group
© University of Aberdeen 1987

The financial assistance of the Scottish Arts Council
and the Aberdeenshire Educational Trust,
in the publication of this Volume is gratefully acknowledged

ISBN 0 08 030391 9

Printed in Great Britain
The University Press
Aberdeen

ACKNOWLEDGEMENTS

The manuscripts of the songs collected by Gavin Greig and James B. Duncan in the early years of the twentieth century are in Aberdeen University Library. They have been edited and prepared for publication from within The School of Scottish Studies of the University of Edinburgh. Both universities acknowledge with gratitude the assistance of the Scottish Arts Council which has given substantial support on both the editorial and publishing sides of the work. A generous and very welcome grant from the imaginatively conceived Glenfiddich Living Scotland Awards scheme has allowed work to proceed on the final phase of the project, and Volume 8 will be especially indebted to this source. We continue to derive valued encouragement from the interest shown by the families of Gavin Greig and James B. Duncan and of the singers from whom they collected, and we would like to express our gratitude; Nan and John Argo are additionally warmly thanked for a further financial contribution to the project. We are also very grateful to the Aberdeenshire Educational Trust for a grant towards the cost of publication, and to the Carnegie Trust for the Universities of Scotland for a grant towards the cost of travel.

An expression of the value placed on the project by folksingers, which resulted in a much appreciated increment to the funds, was a benefit ceilidh held in Portobello Town Hall featuring Ewan MacColl and Peggy Seeger with The Whistlebinkies, The Thistle and Shamrock Ceilidh Band, Margaret and Martyn Bennett, and Nancy Nicolson. Our thanks go to all of these, and to the organisers, of whom we may single out Hamish Henderson and Robin Morton for special mention, and to Edinburgh District Council which gave the use of the hall and also a donation.

Looking back, we recall with gratitude the major grants which allowed the project to be established, from The British Academy, The Carnegie Trust for the Universities of Scotland, The Institute for Advanced Studies in the Humanities at the University of Edinburgh, The Moray Endowment Fund of the University of Edinburgh, The Pilgrim Trust, and The Ralph Vaughan Williams Trust. It is with deep regret that we record the death in the spring of 1986 of two scholars of vision who gave unflagging support to the project from its inception: Professor Bertrand Bronson and Professor William Beattie. Both men will be remembered for their courtesy and humour equally with their scholarship.

Looking ahead, we are pleased to acknowledge substantial backing from the General Council Trust of the University of Edinburgh. This most welcome additional support will speed us forward towards the completion of the project.

E.B.L.

P.A.H.

CONTENTS OF VOLUME 3

SONG TITLES

Page No.

Songs of Home and Social Life

INTRODUCTION TO VOLUME 3

This volume has been prepared jointly by Emily B. Lyle and Peter A. Hall, and the late Patrick Shuldham-Shaw is also named on the title-page since, as first editor of the collection, he laid the foundation of the whole edition. In 1984, the project moved on to a fresh footing by which Emily B. Lyle became general editor of the collection while other scholars took responsibility for separate sections. This scheme has made it possible for work to go forward on a broad front and Volumes 4, 5, and 6, which are being edited respectively by Andrew R. Hunter, Adam McNaughtan, and Elaine Petrie, are all in an advanced state of preparation. Greater financial resources than ever before are now being released for the early stages of production. The improved new method that this permits was adopted while Volume 3 was in process, and the reorganisation entailed has led to some delay in the short term. However, the advantages of the streamlining, carried through by Dr David Hewitt in the role of production manager for the project, are likely soon to make themselves evident through the steady appearance of future volumes.

The principles underlying this edition are detailed in the introductions to Volumes 1 and 2, but a few points will be mentioned again here. It is the intention of the edition to make available the tunes and words of the songs collected by Gavin Greig and the Reverend James B. Duncan, mainly in Aberdeenshire, in the early years of this century, together with the collectors' notes and comments. The name of the singer or source is given after each song version, and the initial G or D is added to indicate from which part of the joint collection, Greig's or Duncan's, the version is derived. The handwritten music is reproduced from the collectors' manuscript books, and the printed music has been converted to staff notation from the sol-fa in the manuscript collection. In the notes, a cross-reference is frequently given to an occurrence of the song in question outside the present collection, preferably in a major printed source, but there is no intention of compiling an exhaustive list of occurrences. Nor is it normally any part of the plan of this edition to supply editorial comment, but an exception is made in the case of songs having a particular association with the North-East of Scotland where the collection was made. In the present volume, which is especially rich in local songs, the annotation on the farm songs has not been confined to the notes but takes the form of an introductory study of "Farm Life and the Farm Songs" by Peter A. Hall. In the case of local material, both Greig and Duncan were inclined to include in their collections pieces of verse not intended for singing, and a number of items of this kind appear in this volume.

The entire collection is scheduled to appear in eight volumes, of which the last will include commentaries and full indexes. The actual process of the compilation of the collection and the biographies of the singers will be the subjects of special study. Anyone who can supply information is urged to get in touch with the editors and join the growing group of people who are participating in the venture of making available this major collection, which is of importance to Aberdeenshire, to Scotland, and to the world at large. Our warm thanks go to those who have helped us in the preparation of the present volume.

Emily B. Lyle   Peter A. Hall
Edinburgh   Aberdeen

FARM LIFE AND THE FARM SONGS

Peter A. Hall

The nineteenth century farm workers, known as farm servants in Scotland, who were responsible for the folk songs which open this volume, were hired for six month or one year periods to work on the farms. The time between hirings was, in the mid nineteenth century North-East, predominantly six months and the hiring was generally called feeing. The songs reflect the life in this respect, as in many others, and the opening of several of the pieces (e.g. 347, 356, 386)[1] details the feeing procedure which took place in the months of May and November.

The day of the feeing market was the only holiday for the farm servants and the actual process of feeing was marked by particular rituals on the part of both master and servant. "Unmarried servants were hired for a six month term at the feeing fairs. A lad looking for a place usually wore a plait of straw in his button hole, or pinned to the side of his bonnet. This he removed when he had agreed with his new employer. When a man had accepted an offer, he was given a shilling as 'arles' – and he was in duty bound to report to his new master."[2]

"Ellon Fair" (353) gives a good account of the hiring, including the drinking which usually accompanied the event. During his six month stay the servant received his keep, with payment on completion of the term. Wages were low; the average annual pay in Aberdeenshire and Banffshire ranged from £10.71 to £11.75 for unmarried farm servants in 1843, i.e. between £5 and £6 for the six month term. Boys and women were paid at lower rates,[3] typically £1 for a herd and £4.10 for a boy doing general farm duties.[4] Wages did not change greatly for the younger workers in the next decades, for Jimmy MacBeath records feeing before the First World War for £4 and £5 in his first two six month terms, although older men seem to have become a little better off, with a fully-fledged foreman having £18, or more rarely £20.[5]

During the six month term the farm servant was usually housed in some part of the farm buildings, the "chaumer". Meals and some of the leisure activities took place in the farm kitchen and this system was therefore known as the chaumer or kitchie system. The bothy system, which was uncommon in the North-East though well known in other parts of Scotland, had servants living in a separate outhouse and feeding themselves with rations supplied by the farmer.[6] Once feed the servant was expected to report to the farm for work on the next day and the agreement had the force of contract so that the farmer could, if he wished, deploy the law, but this was rare. In the latter half of the nineteenth century, it became so common for servants to renege on the bargain that special fairs, called "rascal fairs", were held for servant and master to make new agreements.[7] As well as bargaining over wages the servants would try to ascertain something of the working conditions from the farmer, but it was a common complaint that the farmers deceived the workers on these matters.[8] The horsemen were particularly concerned about the condition of the horses, both because this would affect the horseman in his work and because it indicated the disposition of the farmer towards man or beast (347).

There was widespread middle-class disapproval of the arrangements for the hiring of the farm crews and this centred on the feeing markets, notorious for their drunkenness and sexual licence. The prejudice against these markets was shared by a few workers,[9] but Ian Carter makes a strong case for the benefits of the feeing system to the farm servants, pointing out that the hiring fairs were not the disorderly chaos that was commonly supposed, and that it was not the case that hiring was done merely on the grounds of physical appearance.[10] Farmers and workers made use of the same markets at each term, and if they did not know each other personally they would often have second-hand recommendation and general reputation to go on. The constant flitting, one of the abiding features of the servants' lives, developed with agricultural improvement and the end of payment in kind associated with the remnants of feudalism: "As payment in cash came into practice, farm servants became a much more nomadic class, moving from one farm to another every six or twelve months."[11]

It is clear that the movement from one farm to the next did not always follow dissatisfaction with the position but was part of the servants' life style, and in respect of this, it is significant that the majority of the servants were young and unmarried, and not looking towards a secure or permanent future in agricultural employment.

North-East agriculture was based upon the growing of grain for local subsistence and the raising of young cattle for markets outside the area. Turnips were widely grown to feed the cattle,[12] and common grains were oats and bere, a form of four row barley which was hardier and required a shorter growing season than the commoner plant of its type.[13] The rotation of crops was completed by years in which the ground was put to grass or used as pasture, variations depending on the type of farming being pursued, or the condition of the soil,[14] barley, pease and potatoes being grown in parts of the region. Grain was threshed with flails, or, on the larger farms, with threshing mills, which used water or horse power, and it was common for the horseman to thresh before he went off to plough.[15] Further separation of the grain from the chaff was achieved by winnowing. This involved blowing the grain with a hand turned fan, while other workers in the team fed the machine or collected the products.

The most important job on the farm was that of horseman, for ploughing occupied more than half of the working days in the year. As well as this horses were used for other tasks, like carting and harrowing. Each horseman had his own pair of horses and would work with them and be responsible for their feeding and grooming. Outwith the servants and the farmer, the horse are the most commonly mentioned subject in the songs of the farm servants. They were also one of the major capital costs in farming and the work revolved around making the best use of them. When daylight hours permitted, the working day extended to ten hours with a break in the middle for the midday meal.[16] There are songs detailing this routine (421) and others pointing up the farmers' insistence upon the full ten hours at all times and in all weathers (356, 357). The servant's week was six days, with no half day holiday on Saturday.

The conditions of employment on the farm form not just the background to the songs, but frequently the very subject matter of the pieces, a central theme being the relationship between the farm servant and his master, the farmer. The farmer is called "tyrant" in one piece (359), and equally uncomplimentary epithets in others (356, 357, 358, 364, 365, 384, 386, 387). One common cause of this discontent was the harassment of men known as "hashing". A number of songs characterise this treatment of the the men as inhuman work machines (353, 358). "Drumdelgie" (384) is sometimes given the title "The Hash of Drumdelgie", and in it the men are set to work at threshing and then winnowing before daylight, and when daylight comes they are turned out to plough in the snow. In this song the hard hearted task master is the grieve rather than the farmer himself.

A large farm might have a grieve or foreman to act as director of the daily work. A grieve was the more senior and acted in most respects in the place of the farmer, while the foreman, the senior man and first horseman, was an intermediary conveying the farmer's orders to the men. As with the farmers themselves, one of the main complaints against the grieve was that he hashed the men (384, 386). Sometimes, much to the men's relief, he was not as hard-hearted as the farmer would have liked (372), but an incompetent grieve could expect sympathy from neither farmer nor men (360), for the welfare of all depended upon his expertise (408). In one song the farmer makes the first man up in the morning foreman for the day, saving on the extra pay due to the position, and stressing that he was merely a *primus inter pares* (396).

Where the foreman or grieve might be in a slightly equivocal position there was no doubt that the farmer's wife was seen as one in authority and open to the same critical sallies as the farmer himself. She was in charge of the women whether they were out workers or employed in the farm kitchen and she used her powers assiduously. "The mistress was in the habit of holding a sort of judicial or inquisitorial convocation with her woman servants, and which was nicknamed 'the court-martial'."[17] One of her functions was to keep the men out of the women's sleeping quarters at night (316).

Because farmers often waited till they were older and set up in a farm before they married, it was common to find wives considerably younger than their husbands. This in turn led to numbers of widows left with a farm to run and they were treated with no great respect or gallantry by the authors of these verses (373).

At the opposite end of the scale from the farmer and his wife, was the young boy of thirteen, like Alexander Mitchell, who started as a "little loon" doing the easiest jobs on the farm. He became the "big loon" using a single horse for carting work and rose from these lowly beginnings to third horseman, with his own pair of horse, and then, by the age of nineteen, to second horseman.[18] As often happened, he left farm service at an early age, in Mitchell's case twenty-two. A very few farm servants eventually got employment as grieve, in charge of the whole farm operation. Elevation to this position was the only way in which a servant could stay as an employee in agriculture and very few were able to achieve this. In Aberdeenshire in 1861, only one servant in twenty-nine was a grieve.[19] Most, like Mitchell, had to go elsewhere to better themselves, or even have jobs which allowed them to marry.

On the larger farms, the general tasks were specialised into categories and the ploughmen fitted into a hierarchy of their own. Thus there might be a grieve, first, second and third ploughman, cattlemen and orraman. Status was important and the horesmen were the aristocrats of farm service, ploughing and carting being such an important part of farm work, so that the horseman's position served as the first step on the ladder of promotion to foreman or grieve. This prestige was underpinned by the Horseman's Word and the general pride in a man's horses which was made public in the ploughing matches, notable events in the farming calendar (422 to 427), with prizes for such things as grooming as well as efficient and straight ploughing.[20]

The Horseman's Word was a secret association, which aimed to endow its members with magical powers to control the horses they worked with. The main recorded activity of the cult was the initiation ceremony which the new members underwent in their late teens, at the time when they were first learning to work with a pair of horse. The ceremony involved the bringing of gifts by the initiates, including whisky which was drunk during the bacchanal that followed.[21] The new members were instructed in various incantations including the phrase known as the Horseman's Word, which varied from place to place but was often "both in one".[22] The cult is only mentioned in one song, "Nicky Tams",[23] by the platform entertainer, G.S. Morris, a composition which circulated after Greig and Duncan had made their collection. The late appearance of information concerning the Horseman's Word, both in song and from other sources, far from indicating its lack of importance, suggests that it was kept as a closely guarded secret during the nineteenth century, while it had a significant part to play in the farm servant's social life. It has been seen as an early form of trade union,[24] although the suggestion has been discounted by sources close to the participants.[25] Trade Unions did not appear until the formation of the Aberdeenshire Agricultural Labourers' Association in 1872, and that did not survive more than a few months.[26] Another attempt in 1886 resulted in the setting up of the Scottish Farm Servants' Union which did last to the end of the century, but was a town-based organisation in the North-East, with little impact in rural areas. The more successful union begun by Joe Duncan in 1912 relates to changed conditions in rural employment,[27] and post-dates our songs.

As well as the horsemen there were orramen who did odd jobs about the farm and were sometimes older men now unable for the physically demanding ploughing. Cattlemen or cow bailies were often as highly paid as horsemen but their status was not as great.[28] The sense of hierarchy among the servants is well represented in the songs,[29] with "South Ythsie" (355) giving nine verses to the inventory of farm workers, starting with the foreman. Similar rosters of the farm squad are to be met with in other songs (372, 389, 399, 400).

The farm crew was a tightly knit and self sufficient community whose structure, character and concerns are remarkably well documented in the songs, and whose evolution had much to do with the history of agricultural improvement, particularly with the rather special course it took in the North-East. Improvement was late in coming to the North-East, at least as a comprehensive alteration,[30] despite the early efforts made by such famous names as Elizabeth Mordaunt, the Earl of Haddington and Archibald Grant of Monymusk,[31] all in the first half of the eighteenth century. The early importance of the North-East was overshadowed by that of other regions in the early nineteenth century,[32] for although there was a will to improve, the means to do so were not present.

One of the main obstacles to improvement in the area was the absence of good roads, both to transport produce out and to bring in materials like lime necessary with the new methods. As late as 1794 there were considerable difficulties for wheeled traffic and it was common to transport goods by pack horse or sledge in some areas.[33] Satisfactory roads, apart from military constructions, did not appear in Scotland until turnpikes were built, and in Aberdeenshire most roads of this type were not constructed until the first quarter of the nineteenth century (459, 460).[34] Agriculture was still so backward in the late eighteenth century that famine was a constant threat, with the bad harvest of 1782 a notable example.[35]

Such disasters speeded up the adoption of new methods,[36] among them the use of the horse-drawn plough. The old Scotch plough required a team of oxen of up to twelve to pull it (430) and two men to work it, one leading or goading and the other holding the stilts.[37] There was a saving in the numbers of animals to be kept with the new machine, and a reduction in manpower, but greater skill was required in the handling of the horse, so that the ploughman became a skilled hand and as such his status rose. Advantages of the new plough were the greater effectiveness of the ploughing and the reductions in breakdown that had occurred with the old wooden plough. The old oxen plough was universal in the 1770s, common as late as 1792, and still in use in the Garioch in 1811,[38] and in the parish of Culsalmond in 1815 and 1816.[39] In 1812 it was still being used to break rough ground in lowland Banffshire,[40] and oxen were sometimes employed along with horses, as in the late 1850s bothy ballad, "Drumdelgie" (384).

Improvement also had its effect on harvest, which as well as being the culmination of the farm year, was a most important social event particularly in terms of courtship (406). The harvest crew was composed of farm workers, along with many temporary employees from the district (401), drawn from a wide variety of occupations.[41] In the eighteenth century, the grain had been cut with the sickle, or reaping hook, most commonly wielded by women, followed by a male bandster, who tied up the sheaves with a straw band (407). From 1805 onwards the scythe came into use in the North-East.[42] The cutting with this larger implement was done by the best men, with women as gatherers and the younger men binding and stooking. The region was in the van in the use of the new method, because its efficiency required a smaller team and harvest labour was scarce, for, unlike agricultural areas further south, Aberdeenshire did not attract harvest workers from other parts, but supplied crews for the earlier harvests in the Lothians (404). Although the nature of its organisation changed, the harvest remained an important social event, which continued to be celebrated in verse and song (408 to 412).

The most significant change in the first half of the nineteenth century, and certainly one which affected the mass of the poorer people, was the engrossment of farms. The new methods were more efficient when practised on a larger acreage and the capital costs this entailed were only possible for the better-off farmer, who was willing to take a long term risk. Very often these costs were underwritten by the landlord who accepted a low rent in the early part of the lease in order to make greater gains later, but this was accompanied by a ruthless pruning of tenants so that only the most efficient survived. The reorganisation of the Gordon estates in the 1830s, after the succession of the fifth Duke in 1827, is a good example of the process, in the way that it affected Drumdelgie, the farm from which one of our best known bothy ballads comes. The farmer, William Grant, held Upper Drumdelgie in 1830, and in 1833 Backside of Drumdelgie was transferred to him from Alex Symon so that he came to tenant the largest farm in the parish of Carnie.[43] As a three hundred acre farm, Drumdelgie was extensive for Aberdeenshire, only 7 per cent being as large as this in the 1850s.[44] The majority of farms which can be indentified in the bothy ballads are large for the North-East, i.e. farms employing five or more farm servants; only 7.7 per cent of the area's farms had more than five in 1881.[45]

Engrossment in other parts of Scotland led to the displacement of the previous tenants and subtenants to become landless labour available for hire,[46] but the situation was somewhat different in the North-East because of the large amount of waste land available for development under the new improved farm methods. In the eighteenth century, even in the immediate vicinity of Aberdeen, there had been large tracts of "uncultivated and barren Country".[47] The cultivation of marginal land proceeded unabated until the 1880s,[48] and there are numerous reports of the improvement of such lands during the early nineteenth century, particularly from outlying parishes. While this increased the population of small crofters, precisely the opposite effect was produced by the incorporation of small holdings into the larger farms.[49] The two tendencies worked in harmony because the larger farms that were being created needed the labour pool supplied from the crofts and the crofters needed the employment on the large farms. Crofters' children went as hired labour and crofters themselves supplied day labour and extra hands at busy times like the harvest. This relationship between the small farm labour pool and the large farm labour requirement remained roughly stable in the years 1840 to 1880,[50] the period of composition of most bothy ballads. Neither was the economic interdependence of farmer and crofter a new relationship, for the system had operated in a broadly similar way before improvement, and the changeover was often gradual.[51] The conversion of payment in kind to money meant that many of those that had been subtenanting crofters now became farm servants, for at least part of their lives. The loss of the older home industries of handloom weaving, stocking knitting and distilling helped to undermine the subsistence economy, and many faced the equally unwelcome choices of clearing new land, farm labour or emigration.

The farm servants came from the crofting community and brought with them the values of that society, values which were frequently in conflict with the interests of the larger tenant farmers. The reluctance of the workers to accept some of the consequences of their changed circumstances was reflected in the songs composed by the servants. Many of these express discontent on the specific subjects of food (347, 356, 360), hard work (353, 387), long hours (372, 386) and the early start of working hours (384, 389), but more often than anything else the attitude of the farmer to his servants is the major point at issue.

It was the practice of farmers to have a set of rules which they read to the servants on their arrival at the farm and the resentment these provoked was considerable. The lines in 348 "Jock o' Rhynie" (A3), might be taken to sum up the position of the servant who could bear everything but the farmer's attempt to exercise control over him:

> Rynie's wark is ull to work
> An Rynie's wages is bit sma
> Rynie's laws they're double strick
> An that dis grieve me worst of a'.

Often the farmer's authority is exercised in matters not related to work. He attempts to dominate every aspect of the farm servant's life and expects total compliance so that nothing interferes with the servant as a working machine (356, 386).

There was, of course, good reason for the iron rule of the farmers. These men were themselves under considerable pressure. They were often from the same background as their servants and they had been promoted by landlords from small farms to the larger amalgamated holdings because they had espoused the new improving ways. Such farmers could only survive by driving their men mercilessly and even then they often fell by the wayside. Daniel Skinner, once the farmer at Earlsfield, and identified by one source as the original of the "scranky black farmer" (357), documents his struggles from his beginnings as a farm servant. He was displaced when rents rose and consequently made many shifts, tenanting eight different farms in thirty-five years.[52]

Another factor in the alienation between farmer and servant was the difference in age. The middle-aged masters were in control of a workforce of unmarried men and women, many of them in their late teens, only a step beyond adolescence. The employers often tried to exercise control over the behaviour of their workers. Servants resented such interference with their private lives and clearly thought it was no business of the farmer to meddle in such matters. A number of songs relate these attempts to regulate the servants' morals (356, 381, 384), and many allude to interference with the sexual conduct of the servants (316, 376, 404). Allied to this were the endeavours by the farmers to promote social distinction between themselves and their workers, such attempts being treated in the songs with derisive humour (372, 381, 417).

One facet of the social division which is frequently commented on in the songs is the separation of servants and farmer's family for meals (373, 391). The social historian Malcolm Gray finds changes in the eating arrangements a good indicator of the social situation:

> Now master and servant were drawing apart. Farmhouses would have a parlour as well as a kitchen and the tenant would not take his food in the kitchen. Some servants continued to receive their meals in the kitchen, but for others there was further banishment from the intimacy of the farmhouse.[53]

The final isolation mentioned here was the result of the bothying system, seldom used in the North-East. The bothy was unpopular in the area and this was, at least in part, a reason for its rarity. At their greatest period of popularity in the North-East, bothies held only 5 per cent of the hired single men, and this mostly close to the main bothy area to the south.[54]

The stress laid on this dislike of the bothy, and on the difference between it and the usual arrangement, the "chaumer" or "kitchie" system, has been dismissed as hair-splitting.[55] There is, however, no doubt about its significance in the nineteenth century North-East. The Poor Law Commissioners found the chaumer popularly favoured in 1843,[56] and in the considerable controversy over illegitimacy after the 1851 census the bothy system was blamed,[57] clear evidence that the difference in the two types of accommodation was well understood and perceived as significant. Comments by former farm servants, both for and against, indicate a similar appreciation of the distinction between chaumer and bothy.[58] It is curious that the term "bothy ballad" should have become attached to North-East song, but it is in fact a late development and it is significant that Greig does not use the term, but prefers the description "ploughman songs".[59] Ford seems to have been the first to use the term in print and, following its widespread popular currency and its continued use by academics, we will retain the title for those songs relating the farm servant's experiences during his six month term (347 to 400).[60]

Dislike of the bothy system serves to sum up the rejection by the farm servants of the social ethos of the larger farm, and a wish to continue the values they had been brought up with: "Servants' conceptions of appropriate social relations between a farmer and his farm servants were based on their experience of family farms and smaller capitalist farms."[61] The songs give the servants' view of the desired behaviour, dictated by what Ian Carter calls the "kindly relations" that should exist within the community, and should be observed by employers.[62]

By giving the farm servants' perspective, the bothy ballads are valuable historical documents to set alongside the much more readily available improvers' opinions. The latter, of course, saw the resistance to improvement, and the social changes involved, in a very different light:

> Those in the possession of small farms are generally, from habit and the want of education, very much confined in their ideas. ... Farmers of this description are, for the most part, so much attached to the old system practised by their forefathers, that, insensible to the advantages which might be derived from a change of practice, it is with the utmost difficulty they can be prevailed upon to adopt any mode of improvement different from that to which they have been so long accustomed.[63]

Such sentiments are readily encountered and we rarely meet the opposing interests and social values that are expressed in the bothy ballads. There is, however, one work of fiction which has a similar tone – the novel *Johnny Gibb of Gushetneuk* by William Alexander, himself originally a farm servant. Set in the 1840s, it shows its disapproval of the Birses of Clinkstyle by giving them the same vices that characterised the farmers we meet in the songs – puffed up social pretension and an interfering paternalism coupled with niggardliness.[64]

In the strife between farmer and servant it would seem that the former had all the advantages of economic strength and links with other powerful interests. Resistance to the social change by farm servants was centred on the use, by them, of customs and practices rooted in the rural culture,[65] and this was particularly true in respect of feeing. The significance of the institution of the feeing market lies in the way it was used by the servants, i.e. in their customary practice rather than the institution itself. That it was customary practice rather than limited individual self-interest can be gauged from the attempts to account for the habit of constant flitting. Those close to farm servants tend to say that it was done "almost for the hell of it"[66] or, of a particular servant, that he shifted "just because he wanted a change".[67] The common habit of changing place each term was not of direct economic benefit, for wages were controlled by outside forces of production and the workers' opportunities to leave farm service for better-paid work in other economic sectors.[68]

Moving farm was however very effective in reducing the degree of control exercised by the farmer. A system of permanent employment on one farm would have given the employer considerable power over the worker and ensured a degree of deference in the social sphere. But with a largely new set of employees each six months the farmer had to begin anew to impose compliance, which explains the significance of the regulations that were read to each servant at the outset of his term. The servant's knowledge that he could move on at the next term allowed him considerable latitude in behaviour, and even if sacked he could get work as a day labourer. The choice at each feeing left him in control of the situation, both in reality and psychologically, an important point in terms of the servant's self image. Moreover, the choice was often liable to be a collective one and in the extreme case this led to the clean toon when the whole farm crew decided to leave an unpopular master, as a body.[69] This type of joint decision was, however, informal, and not the outcome of the opposition of combinations of farmers and servants which would have been to the former's advantage. The ultimately individual nature of the feeing set each farmer on his own, and indeed in competition with others, neutralising his greater ability to organise in a group.

The bothy ballads reflect the central importance of the feeing procedure in their outline. In the ideal case they start with the feeing market and finish with the leaving of the farm for the next market. Many of the pieces open with the feeing (353, 366, 372, 378), others finish with the term end (360, 383, 384), and many more have both features (347, 351, 356, 357, 376, 381, 389, etc.). The songs are structured according to the farm servants' behaviour and so the characteristics of the songs are not just formal devices but arise out of the farm servants' actions, reinforcing and serving to validate them. While being directed at the reputation of a single farmer they operate against all farmers, by describing customary behaviour which generalises individual action.

The changes brought about by agricultural improvement were well established by the mid century and it was at this time that the first bothy ballads emerged (348, 349, 356, 384). These songs, which include some of the most popular, belong to the parishes of Carnie, Rhynie and Kennethmont, all in the west of Aberdeenshire, so that more than a third of the song versions of bothy ballads collected by Greig and Duncan came from this area. This western district around Strathbogie can be seen as the cradle of the bothy ballad, with its high density of these songs and all the likely early examples. The corollary of this, that later dated instances come from other areas, is also true, for the six that can be dated to a period after 1861 all lie to the east of the Strathbogie area (353, 360, 372, 373, 378, 441). A further four (316, 386, 387, 390) are very probably late in date and also eastern, so that a pattern emerges of the diffusion of the bothy ballads from a centre in Strathbogie.

In parallel to the movement of the songs, the 1851 Census shows a substantial west to east migration of farm servants in thirteen parishes in the west of Aberdeenshire and Banffshire,[70] suggesting a cause and effect relationship between population dispersal and the arrival of the new song form, as well as accounting for some of the characteristics of the genre. In particular, the influx from the west helps to explain the Gaelic cultural contributions that have been identified in the music,[71] and in other formal and linguistic features.[72] The Irish style that has been detected in the songs,[73] seems more likely to have been a Celtic influence of Highland origin, there being a negligible Irish immigration into the area, either in the form of permanent residents, or of temporary harvest workers.[74]

Some authors have previously linked the bothy ballad with agricultural improvement and the lifestyle of the farm servants, in the North-East,[75] and the general coincidence in time and geographical area is highly persuasive. The changes in farm practice and technique bore directly upon the farm servant's life in that it involved him in a number of new skills, particularly associated with the management of horses and their use in ploughing. This was reflected in their gain in status and financial reward. A similar, though less prestigious change applied to cattlemen, with women, boys and older men being relegated to a lower level in the servant hierarchy. The reduced workforce allowed farms to compete in the market but a consequence of this greater competition was the need to make full use of the manpower resources and therefore to have a much tighter organisation of farm work, which in turn gave rise to the conflict that sparked the songs.

A number of factors brought to an end the era that gave rise to the bothy ballads. The system of employment of farm servants rarely offered them a permanent position,[76] and improvements in rural communications, particularly with the railway expansions of the 1880s,[77] drew population towards the urban centres, so that Aberdeen showed its greatest increase at this time.[78] Labour scarcity, which started in the 1870s, became acute in the 1880s,[79] and mechanisation greatly increased.[80] The agricultural depression of the 1870s had its important impact on fatstock prices in the North-East a decade later,[81] and, with the other factors referred to, led to reorganisation of rural labour hiring and farm servant housing.[82] Not surprisingly the song culture, which was so closely linked to the hiring practices, changed at the same time.

The last of the bothy ballads of the old pattern are from the 1880s (372, 374), and although certain features are carried over into some of the local harvest songs (408 to 412), they lack both the emotional tone and the structure of the older pieces. By the beginning of the present century another form of rural song had emerged. The best and earliest author of these was George Bruce Thomson, and Greig showed his interest by printing Thomson's songs.[83] The best known, 630 "McGinty's Meal-an-Ale", is now well established in oral tradition and the differences between it and the earlier bothy ballad are instructive. The density of dialect is much greater, for it is a surprising characteristic of the older songs that they have less dialect than is found in the local everyday speech of the singers.[84] The emotional ambiance of the songs by newer authors like Thomson, G.S. Morris and Willie Kemp, is much more benign, as befits the changed social situation of North-East life.

Because the bothy ballad was the response in song to the social conditions in nineteenth century North-East rural society, it died when those conditions disappeared, or rather, new pieces were no longer composed and the existing songs were absorbed into the folk song repertoire, to be collected by Greig and Duncan a generation later. Although a few were recorded from former farm servants, many had already passed outside that immediate community to survive apart from their original local associations; as some do to this day. Many must have perished because their too specific features made them incomprehensible to those without the necessary local knowledge. We must be grateful that we have this collection, which preserves so many that might otherwise have been unknown to us.

NOTES

1   Numbers in brackets refer to songs in *The Greig-Duncan Folk Song Collection*.

2   Hamish Henderson, *Scottish Tradition* 1 "Bothy Ballads", notes with record (Tangent Records, TNGM 109).

3   Figures from Ian Levitt and Christopher Smout, "Farm Workers' Incomes in 1843", in *Farm Servants and Labour in Lowland Scotland 1770-1914*, ed. T.M. Devine (Edinburgh, 1984), p. 173.

4   Alexander Mitchell, *Recollections of a Lifetime* ([Edinburgh], 1911), pp. 13, 29, 38-9, and 45.

5   Peter Hall, "Jimmy MacBeath", *Chapbook* vol. 3, no. 2 (1966), p. 6.

6   Alexander Fenton, "The Housing of Agricultural Workers in the Nineteenth Century", in Devine, p. 188.

7   William Alexander, "The Peasantry of North-East Scotland", *United Presbyterian Magazine* 1 (1884), 428.

8   James Taylor, *Eleven Years at Farm Work* (Aberdeen, 1879), p. 53.

9   James Allan, "Agriculture in Aberdeenshire in the Sixties", *The Deeside Field* 3 (1927), 33. Appearing in a magazine with a middle-class circulation, these opinions may not be typical of farm servants.

10   Ian Carter, *Farmlife in Northeast Scotland, 1840-1914: The Poor Man's Country* (Edinburgh, 1979), p. 148.

11   Alexander Fenton, "Farm Servant Life in the 17th-19th Centuries", *Scottish Agriculture* 44 (1965), 282-3.

12   James Anderson, *General View of the Agriculture and Rural Economy of the County of Aberdeen* (Edinburgh, 1794), p. 66.

13   George Skene Keith, *A General View of the Agriculture of Aberdeenshire* (Aberdeen, 1811), p. 247.

14   Keith, p. 238.

15   Anderson, p. 80.

16   Hall, "Jimmy MacBeath", p. 3.

17   Taylor, p. 39.

18   Mitchell, p. 29.

19   Carter, *Farmlife*, p. 108.

20 Keith, p. 225, suggests that the ploughing matches helped to improve the standards of tillage.

21 Hamish Henderson, "The Ballad, the Folk and the Oral Tradition", in *The People's Past*, ed. Edward J. Cowan (Edinburgh, 1980), p. 84.

22 Alexander Fenton, *Scottish Country Life* (Edinburgh, 1976), p. 224.

23 George S. Morris, "A Pair of Nicky Tams", in *Kerr's "Buchan" Bothy Ballads*, book 2 (Glasgow), pp. 2-3.

24 Carter, *Farmlife*, p. 156.

25 Henderson, "The Ballad, the Folk and the Oral Tradition", p. 103.

26 Gwenllian Evans, "Farm Servants' Unions in Aberdeenshire from 1870-1900", *Scottish Historical Review* 31 (1952), 29.

27 Joseph H. Smith, *Joe Duncan: The Scottish Farm Servants and British Agriculture* (Edinburgh, 1973).

28 John R. Allan, *Farmer's Boy* (London, 1925, rep. 1975), p. 96.

29 Francis Collinson, *The Traditional and National Music of Scotland* (London, 1966), p. 148.

30 Malcolm Gray, "North-East Agriculture and the Labour Force, 1790-1875", in *Social Class in Scotland: Past and Present*, ed. A. Allan MacLaren (Edinburgh, 1976), p. 86.

31 William Alexander, *Notes and Sketches Illustrative of Northern Rural Life in the Eighteenth Century*, with an introduction by Ian Carter (Finzean, 1981), p. 33. The first edition was published in 1877.

32 R.C. Boud, "Scottish Agricultural Improvement Societies, 1723-1835", *Review of Scottish Culture* 1 (1984), pp. 74-7. Taking the existence of Agricultural Societies as an indicator of active improvement, Boud shows there to be six North-East societies out of a total of fourteen in 1723-84, but only twelve out of one hundred and thirty-six in 1723-1835.

33 John Patrick, *The Coming of Turnpikes to Aberdeenshire* (Aberdeen, 1984), pp. 4-5.

34 Alexander, *Northern Rural Life*, p. 80.

35 Alexander, *Northern Rural Life*, p. 56.

36 Keith, in *A General View*, p. 275, gives the disastrous harvest of 1782, known locally as "the snowy hairst", as the stimulus to widespread improvement. The manuscript autobiography of Alexander Bisset of Artannies in the North of Scotland Library, Aberdeen, provides details of this harvest for a specific farm.

37 Fenton, *Scottish Country Life*, p. 213.

38 Keith, *A General View*, p. 227.

39 Alexander, *Northern Rural Life*, p. 40.

40 David Souter, *General View of the Agriculture of the County of Banff* (Edinburgh, 1812), p. 127.

41 Carter, *Farmlife*, p. 63.

42 Fenton, *Scottish Country Life*, p. 59.

43 Gordon Castle MSS (1826), GD44 SEC53, Rentals and Factors MS, Scottish Record Office, Edinburgh. The 1861 Census shows that the farm later increased to six hundred acres (Cen. E.B., Cairnie, 1861).

44 Carter, *Farmlife*, p. 109; calculated from table 4.9.

45 Carter, *Farmlife*, p. 107; calculated from table 4.7.

46 Fenton, *Scottish Country Life*, p. 225.

47 Alexander Carlyle, *Journal of a tour to the North of Scotland*, ed. Richard B. Sher

(Aberdeen, 1981), p. 17. The journal was written in 1765.

48 Ian Carter, "The Peasantry of Northeast Scotland", *The Journal of Peasant Studies* 3 (1976), pp. 160-2.

49 Census reports in 1821 and 1831, for the parishes of Chapel of Garioch, Tough, Leochel Cushnie and Rhynie and Essie, mention, "increase in population attributed to the cultivation of waste lands", and ascribe this to "vaste improvements in agriculture". Decreases in Drumblade for 1841 are attributed to the incorporation of farms. See *Census of Great Britain, Population Studies, 1821, 1831, 1841.*

50 Carter, "The Peasantry of Northeast Scotland", pp. 158-9.

51 Gray, *North-East Agriculture*, p. 94.

52 Daniel Skinner, *The Autobiography of Daniel Skinner, Farmer, Earlsfield* (Inverurie, 1929).

53 Malcolm Gray, "Farm Workers in North-East Scotland", in Devine, p. 14.

54 Alexander Fenton, "The Housing of Agricultural Workers in the Nineteenth Century", in Devine, p. 208.

55 David Kerr Cameron, *The Ballad and the Plough: A Portrait of the Life of the Old Scottish Farmtouns* (London, 1978), p. 119.

56 Ian Levitt and Christopher Smout, *The State of the Scottish Working-Class in 1843* (Edinburgh, 1979), p. 71.

57 T.C. Smout, "Aspects of Sexual Behaviour in Nineteenth Century Scotland", in MacLaren, pp. 65-6. The Rev. Dr James Begg led a campaign against the bothy system in the 1850s and 1860s.

58 For the bothy system: Taylor, *Eleven Years*; against: Allan, "Agriculture in Aberdeenshire", p. 33.

59 Greig uses the term "ploughman songs" in both *Folk-Song in Buchan* and Ob. and distinguishes them from other rural pieces like harvest songs (see note to 347 "The Barnyards o' Delgaty"). His use of the term "bothy ballad" for a song from further south, 377 "The Bothy Lads o' Forfar" (see note to version A), suggests that he was well aware of the lack of bothies in the North-East.

60 See Robert Ford, *Vagabond Songs and Ballads of Scotland* (Paisley, 1899), p. 19, where "Jamie Foyers" is called a bothy ballad; cf. the use of the term "bothy song" for "The Weary Farmers" at p. 251. Ord, p. 1, uses "bothy-song" as a synonym for "folk-song". Of recent writers, Francis Collinson, *The Traditional and National Music of Scotland* (1966), p. 147, argues for using "bothy ballads" specifically for songs of farm life, while Ian Carter, *Farmlife* (1979), p. 3, sees them as belonging to the farm servants, and David Buchan, *The Ballad and the Folk* (London, 1972), p. 262, relates them to matters encountered in a term's feeing.

61 Carter, *Farmlife*, p. 107.

62 Carter, *Farmlife*, p. 5.

63 Souter, *General View*, p. 110.

64 William Alexander, *Johnny Gibb of Gushetneuk* (Aberdeen, 1871).

65 Ian Carter, "Unions and Myths: Farm Servants' Unions in Aberdeenshire, 1870-1900", in Devine, p. 223.

66 Cameron, p. 83.

67 Hamish Henderson, "John Strachan", *Tocher* 5 (No. 36-7), 414.

68 Ian Levitt and Christopher Smout, "Farm Workers' Incomes in 1843", in Devine, p. 168.

69 Alexander, *Johnny Gibb*, p. 101; Carter, *Farmlife*, p. 152.

70 Analysis, for 1851, of the farm servants on farms with more than five workers in thirteen parishes in the west of Aberdeenshire and Banffshire shows that, while 24% moved west, 10% moved east. The parishes used were Cairnie, Huntly, Gartly, Rhynie, Kennethmont, Forgue, Drumblade, Insch, Culsalmond, Glass, Botriphnie, Mortlach, and Cabrach. See Peter A. Hall, "Folk Songs of the North-East Farm Servants in the Nineteenth Century" (M. Litt. thesis, University of Aberdeen, 1985), p. 72.

71 Gavin Greig, *Folk-Song in Buchan*, p. 57.

72 Hall, "Folk Song", p. 112.

73 Patrick Shuldham-Shaw, "The Greig-Duncan Folk Song Manuscripts", *New Edinburgh Review* (1973), 5.

74 William Howatson notes in "The Scottish Hairst and Seasonal Labour 1600-1870", *Scottish Studies* 26 (1982), 26, that there is little evidence of Irish immigrants penetrating north of the Tay, where Highland migrants remained the most significant incoming harvest workers. The North-East was to a large extent self sufficient in harvest labour.

75 Buchan, ch. 19 "The Bothy Ballads"; Carter, *Farmlife*.

76 Gray, *North-East Agriculture*, p. 100.

77 *The Railways of Scotland: Papers of Andrew C. O'Dell*, ed. R.E.H. Mellor (Aberdeen, 1984), p. 24.

78 Andrew C. O'Dell, "Population Changes", in *The North-East of Scotland: A survey prepared for the Aberdeen Meeting of the British Association for the Advancement of Science, 1963*, ed. A.C. O'Dell and J. Mackintosh (Aberdeen, 1963), p. 194.

79 Gray, *Farm Workers*, p. 21

80 Carter, *Farmlife*, p. 119.

81 T.M. Devine, "Scottish Farm Labour in the Era of Agricultural Depression 1875-1900", in Devine, p. 243.

82 Fenton, "The Housing of Agricultural Workers", p. 205.

83 Ob. 134, 136, 138, and 144.

84 Hamish Henderson, "*At the Foot o' Yon Excellin' Brae*: The Language of Scots Folksong", in *Scotland and the Lowland Tongue*, ed. J. Derrick McClure (Aberdeen, 1983), p. 113.

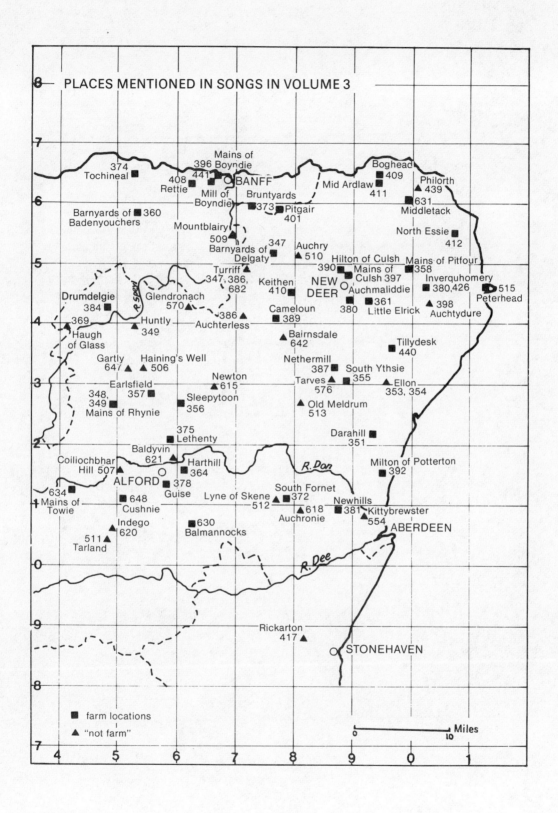

PLACES MENTIONED IN SONGS IN VOLUME 3

8

7

Tochineal 374

Mains of 396 Boyndie
441
Rettie 408
Mill of Boyndie
BANFF
Bruntyards
Boghead 409
Mid Ardlaw
411
Philorth 439

6

Barnyards of 360
Badenyouchers

Pitgair 373
401
Middletack 631

Mountblairy
509
Barnyards of
Delgaty 347
Auchry 510
Hilton of Culsh 390
Mains of Pitfour
North Essie 412

5

Drumdelgie 384
Glendronach 570
Turriff
347, 386, 682
Keithen 410
NEW DEER
Mains of Culsh 397
Auchmaliddie 358
Inverquhomery 380,426
Peterhead 515

369
386
Auchterless
Cameloun 389
Auchmaliddie
380 361
Little Elrick
398 Auchtydure

4

Haugh of Glass
Huntly 349
Bairnsdale 642
Tillydesk 440

Gartly 647
Haining's Well 506
Nethermill 387
South Ythsie 355

Earlsfield 357
Newton 615
Tarves 576
Ellon 353, 354

3

348, 349
Mains of Rhynie
Sleepytoon 356
Old Meldrum 513

375
Lethenty
Darahill 351

2

Baldyvin 621
Harthill 364
Milton of Potterton 392

Coiliochbhar Hill 507
ALFORD
Guise 378
Lyne of Skene 512
South Fornet 372
Newhills 381
Kittybrewster 554

634
Mains of Towie
Cushnie 648
Auchronie 618
ABERDEEN

1

Indego 620
Balmannocks 630

511 Tarland

0

R. Dee

9

Rickarton 417
STONEHAVEN

8

■ farm locations
▲ "not farm"

Miles
0   10

7

4   5   6   7   8   9   0   1

ABBREVIATIONS IN VOLUME 3

(a) Abbreviations referring to the Greig-Duncan Collection

Reference numbers indicate locations in Aberdeen University Library. The letters G and D, standing for Greig and Duncan, indicate whether the item concerned relates to Gavin Greig or James B. Duncan or to both.

Alexander	2 vols. from Robert Alexander. 998/2/1/1-2. (D)
Argo	A collection of notebooks etc. held in trust by the general editor for Mr and Mrs John Argo. (G)
Argo-Duncan	1 vol. (shorthand) from William Argo, William Duncan, and Alexander Duncan. 998/2/11. (D)
Bain	1 vol. (shorthand) from John Bain. 998/2/2. (D)
Bm	1 vol. *Traditional Ballad Tunes*. 785. (G & D)
Bw	5 vols. *Ballads*. 776-80. (G & D)
Dm	1 vol. *Folk-Song Airs of the North-East*. 786. (D)
Dw	6 vols. (shorthand). *Folk-Song Words of the North-East*. 998/1/3-8. (D)
Folk-Song in Buchan	Presidential address, 15 December 1905, printed in *Transactions of the Buchan Field Club* 9 (1906-7), 1-76; see also under Ob. (G)
Garioch	1 vol. (shorthand) from George Garioch. 998/2/4. (D)
Gillespie	1 vol. from Mrs Margaret Gillespie. 788. (D)
Gm	4 vols. *Folk-Music*. 705-8. (G)
Gw	64 vols. *Folk-Songs. (Words)*. 711-74. (G)
Harper	A collection of letters to Duncan and other papers from Mrs Harper. 998/7/1. (D)
Last Leaves	*Last Leaves of Traditional Ballads and Ballad Airs*, ed. Alexander Keith (Aberdeen, 1925). (G & D)
Last Leaves MS	Draft material for *Last Leaves*. 790.1-6. (G & D)
Lyall	2 vols. from Mrs Lyall. 998/2/6/1-2. (D)
Mackay	2 vols. (shorthand) from Alexander Mackay. 998/2/7/1-2. (D)
Misc.	1 vol. *Folk Song Miscellanea*. 998/1/9. (D)
Ob.	A series of one hundred and eighty articles entitled "Folk-Song of the North-East" which appeared weekly in the *Buchan Observer* between 3 December 1907 and 6 June 1911 with the exception of 5 January 1909, 8 June 1909, 14 February 1911, and 11 April 1911. The set of articles was published in a limited edition (Peterhead, 1909-14) and this was reproduced in *Folk-Song in Buchan and Folk-Song of the North-East* by Gavin Greig, with a foreword by Kenneth S. Goldstein and Arthur Argo (Hatboro, Pa., 1963). (G)
Robertson,	
Letters to Duncan	A collection of letters sent by Bell Robertson. 998/15/1-50. (D)
Song Notes	2 vols. 790.2/1-2. (D)

Troup	2 vols. (shorthand) from Alexander, George and Isaac Troup. 998/2/8/1-2. (D)
Walker	1 vol. from Mrs Walker. 998/2/9. (D)
Wallace	1 vol. (shorthand) from William Wallace. 998/1/10. (D)

(b) Other abbreviations

BL	British Library
Carpenter	The collection of folk plays and folk songs made by James M. Carpenter, c. 1930, deposited in the Library of Congress, Washington, D.C. In Britain, microfilm copies are held by the University of Sheffield, The English Folk Dance and Song Society, and The School of Scottish Studies.
Cen. E.B.	Census Enumerator's Book.
Child	Francis James Child, *The English and Scottish Popular Ballads*. 5 vols. (Boston and New York, 1882-98; rep. New York, 1965).
Christie	W. Christie, *Traditional Ballad Airs*. 2 vols. (Edinburgh, 1876-81).
Edwards	D.H. Edwards, *One Hundred Modern Scottish Poets*. 16 vols. (Brechin, 1880-97).
Folk-Song Journal	*Journal of the Folk-Song Society*.
Ford	Robert Ford, *Vagabond Songs and Ballads of Scotland*. New edition. (Paisley, 1904).
Glen	John Glen, *Early Scottish Melodies* (Edinburgh, 1900).
Graham	G.F. Graham, *The Songs of Scotland*. 3 vols. (Edinburgh, 1848-9).
Hogg	James Hogg, *The Jacobite Relics of Scotland*. 2 vols. (Edinburgh, 1819-21).
Johnson	James Johnson, *The Scots Musical Museum*. 2 vols. (Reproduction of 1853 edition, Hatboro, Pa., 1962; original publication of songs, 6 vols., 1787-1803, and of Stenhouse's "Illustrations", 1839).
Kennedy	Peter Kennedy, *Folksongs of Britain and Ireland* (London, 1975).
Kinsley	James Kinsley, *The Poems and Songs of Robert Burns*. 3 vols. (Oxford, 1968).
Laws	G. Malcolm Laws, Jr. Letters A-I, *Native American Balladry* (Philadelphia, 1950); letters J-Q, *American Balladry From British Broadsides* (Philadelphia, 1957).
L.C.	The Lauriston Castle Collection in the National Library of Scotland.
Lyric Gems	John Cameron, *Lyric Gems of Scotland*. 2 vols. (London, n.d.).
Madden	The Sir Frederic Madden collection of broadsides in Cambridge University Library.
McNaughtan	List of Poet's Box song sheets in the Mitchell Library, Glasgow, compiled by Adam McNaughtan.
Middleton	*Middleton's Selection of Humorous Scotch Songs* and *Middleton's Second Collection of Humorous Songs* (Charles Middleton, Aberdeen, n.d.).
Milne	John Milne, *Buchan Folk Songs* (Banff, 1901), reprinted from *The Banffshire Journal*, 12 and 19 February 1901.

National Choir	*The National Choir*, vol. 1 intro. by John Stuart Blackie, vol. 2 intro. by Frederick Niecks (Paisley, [1891-1900]).
OED	*The Oxford English Dictionary*, ed. J.A.H. Murray *et al.* (Oxford, 1888-1933).
Opie	*The Oxford Dictionary of Nursery Rhymes*, ed. Iona and Peter Opie (Oxford, 1952).
O'Neill	*O'Neill's Music of Ireland*, ed. Francis O'Neill (Chicago, 1903).
Ord	John Ord, *Bothy Songs & Ballads of Aberdeen, Banff & Moray, Angus and the Mearns* (Paisley, 1930; rep. Edinburgh, 1974).
Petrie	*The Complete Collection of Irish Music as noted by George Petrie*, ed. Charles Villiers Stanford (London and New York, 1906).
Rogers	Charles Rogers, *The Scottish Minstrel* (Edinburgh, 1870).
Rymour Club Miscellanea	*Miscellanea (Transactions) of the Rymour Club.* 3 vols. (Edinburgh, 1911-28).
Sharp	*Cecil Sharp's Collection of English Folk Songs*, ed. Maud Karpeles. 2 vols. (London, 1974).
SND	*The Scottish National Dictionary*, ed. William Grant and David Murison (Edinburgh, 1931-76).
Songs of the North	*Songs of the North*, ed. A.C. Macleod and Harold Boulton (London, [1885]).
Stenhouse	William Stenhouse, "Illustrations of the Lyric Poetry and Music of Scotland"; included in Johnson.
Whitelaw, *Songs*	*The Book of Scottish Song*, ed. Alexander Whitelaw (Glasgow, 1844).
V.R.	Valuation Roll.

GLOSSARY OF RECURRENT SCOTS WORDS IN VOLUME 3

aboon, abune, abeen, above
acht, aucht, eight
adee, to do
ae, one
ahint, behind
aiblins, perhaps
ane, een, one
anent, over against, opposite
arles, payment made at hiring, earnest
athwart, athwort, across
atween, between
ava, at all
awat, indeed, I am sure
bailie, cattleman
bairn, child
ban, curse
bannock, flat oatmeal cake
barkit, hit, skinned, tanned
batter, paste, glue
bawbie, babie, ba-bee, small coin
bear the gree; bear the bell, take the prize
belly in, eat voraciously
ben, inside, through, inner part of the house
bere, bear, coarse form of barley
besom, heather broom
bide, stay, endure
big, build
biggin', building
birse, bristle
blate, bashful, foolish
blaw, boast
blether, bluter, talk foolishly, senseless talker
blink, glance, give an affectionate look, cheat
body, person
boll, bou, bowaye, grain measure, 140 lbs
boodie, ghost
bothy, quarters for farm workers
bou'd, beet, had to, was forced
bowie, bowl
brae, hill, slope

braw, bra', fine, handsome, splendidly
bree; barley bree, liquid, stock; whisky
breeks, breekies, trousers
brig, bridge
brook, soot
brose, oatmeal with water
browst, brewst, brewing
brunt, burned
busk, get ready, dress
but; but and ben, outer room, kitchen; two-roomed cottage
byre, cowshed
ca, drive, be driven, bring home, hawk, search, call
cadger, itinerant dealer
caff, cauf, chaff
callant, lad, boy, fine man
caller, fresh
can, knowledge
cankered, ill tempered
canny; cannily, careful; carefully
cantie, cheerful, lively, pleasant
cap, caup, wooden dish, cup
cast, remove, toss
cauldrife, cold, indifferent
chaumer, farm workers' sleeping place
chiel, man, lad
clap, pat, caress
clash, blow, crash
claw, scratch, scrape, beat
cloot, patch, piece of cloth
Clootie, the devil
cogie, cog, couge, bowl
coorse, wicked, foul (of weather)
cooter, coulter
coup, overturn, upturn
couth, couthie, agreeable, comfortable
crack, talk, gossip, conversation
crater, creature, person
creel, basket

creesh, grease

crook, pot-hook

crouse, croose, cruse, proud, bold, confident, cheerful

crummie, cow with crooked horns, name for pet cow

cry, call

cuddy, donkey

cuttie; cutty goon, short, short tobacco pipe, short spoon; short pipe

daffin', courting

daft, foolish

dame, daem, deem, young unmarried woman

darg, day's work

dawd, lump

dawt, fondle

deave, annoy, bore

deuk, duke, duck

dicht, wipe

ding; dang, strike; struck, fell heavily and continuously

dirl, spin

divot, turf

doited, old, enfeebled

dominie, schoolmaster

doo, dove

dook, doak, duck, wash

dother, daughter

douce, quiet

doup, rump

dram, glass of whisky, small drink of liquor

dree, suffer

drouth, thirst, particularly for strong drink

drouthy, thirsty, drunken

dub; dubby, puddle; muddy

duds; duddy, clothes, rags; ragged

dunt, thud, hit

dyke, dykie, wall

ear', eir, early

eelie, oil

eident, diligent

ell, yard

ellison, awl

ettle, try

ewie wi' the crookit horn, whisky still

farin', food

farles, flakes, quarters, scones

fash, trouble, inconvenience

Fastern's Even, Shrove Tuesday

fauld, enclosure

feck, greater part

fee, servant's wages

feel, fiel, fool, foolish

feer; feerin', fearin', make the first furrow; first furrow

fegs, faith!

feint, fient, fent, devil

ferlie, marvel

fess, fesh; fice, fessen, fetch; fetched

fidge, fidget

fike, fyke, fuss, have an affair

firlot, fourth part of a boll

fleg, scare

flyte; flaut, scold, engage as poets in a contest of mutual abuse; scolded

forbye, besides

forrit, forward

fou, fu, drunk

fouth, plenty

fraimt, fremt, framed, unfamiliar, stranger

fup, whip, snatch

fur, furrow

fyles, sometimes

gab, gabbie, mouth

gaed, went

gang, ging, gyang, go, walk

gar, cause, oblige

gate, gait, way, road

gaud, stick for driving animals

gavel, gable, buttocks, bundle of cut corn before it is bound into a sheaf

gawpie, fool

gear, goods, equipment

gey, rather

gie, give

gilp, splash

gin, if

girn, complain

girnel, girnal, chest for storing meal, granary

glaiket, stupid

glebe, minister's land

gled, glead, kite, hawk

gleg, keen, smartly

gley'd, squint-eyed, twisted

gloamin', twilight

gowk, fool

graith, harness, tackle

grape, fork

greet; grat, weep; wept

grieve, overseer

groat, coin, hulled grain

grumphy, pig

guidman, gudeman, goodman, head of a household, husband

guise, happening, custom, trick

hain, preserve, save, spare

hairst, harvest

halflin, haflin, lad

hap, cover

hash, excessive pressure of work

haud; haud me on-thocht lang, hold, keep; keep me from wearying

haugh, haughie, piece of level ground

hawkie, halkie, cow, especially one with a white face

heelster gowdie, head-over-heels

heuk, heuck, sickle

hinmost, hinmaist, last

hodden; hodden gray, homespun; wool of natural colour

howdie, midwife

howe, low-lying ground

hummel, hummle, humlie, hornless cow

hup, call to an animal to increase speed or turn to the right

hurl, drive, wheel

ilka, ilk, each, every

ill, difficult

inower, within

intil, into

into, in

jink, dodge

jo, joe, sweetheart

jouk, crouch, duck, ducked

kaim, kame, comb

kebbuck, a whole cheese

keek, peep

ken, know

kep, keep, catch

kilt, tuck up

kirk, church

kirn, kyirn, harvest celebration

kist, chest

kite, belly

kittle, tricky

knot, lump

knowe, hill, knoll

kye, cows, cattle

lane, leen, self, alone

langsyne, long ago

lave, rest

laverock, lark

lawin, reckoning

lead, convey, cart in, bring in harvest

leal, leel, faithful, honest

leas, leys, untilled ground

lees me on, lea's me on, I love

leuch, laughed

lift, sky

limmer, rascal, loose or vile woman

lingle, strap, waxed thread used by shoemakers

lippen, trust

loan, pasture

loon, loun, boy, youth

loup, leap, jump

lout, bend

low, flame

lowse, unyoke

lucky, wife, woman, Mrs

lug; lugey, ear; with a handle or handles

lum, chimney

maun, must

meat, mate, food, feed

mell, hammer

mind, take notice, pay attention, remember

mirkie, cheerful

mischanter, mishanter, mischance, piece of ill-luck

mouter, mooter, muter, multure

muckle, meickle, large

murlan, narrow-mouthed basket

mutchkin, pint or smaller measure

nainsel', yer nainsel', one's self; yourself

neeps, turnips

neiper, neighbouring

neist, next

neive, nive, neivefu', fist; handful

neuk, corner

nickum, rascal

niffer, exchange

no, not

noddle, head

nout, nowte, cattle

od, God

ook, oock, ouk, week

or, before, until

orra; orra loon, odd, unoccupied; odd job
    man

owrecome, refrain, chorus

owsen, ousen, oxen

oxter, armpit

pad, depart, leave, travel on foot

parkit, put or reared in field

pawkie, shrewd, shrewdly

penny fee, wages

pickle, puckle, small amount

pig, jar

plack, small coin

pleuch, plough

pliskie, trick

poke, pock, pockie, bag, small sack

pottage, oatmeal porridge, breakfast

pouch, pocket

pow, head

pree, taste, kiss

puddock, frog, toad

quarrel, make a quarrel with

queets, ankles, fetlocks

quintra, country

raips, ropes

rare, good, pleasing

rattle, crash, blow

rax, stretch, reach

reamin, frothing, foaming

red up, sort out, clean up, make smart

reek; ricky, smoke; smoky

reerie, clamour

rig, strip of land

ring, strike (of clock)

rive; riven, pull apart, tear, split; cracked

roch, rough

rock; rockin', distaff or spindle; convivial
    gathering originally for spinning

roset, resin

roup, auction

row, roll, wrap

ruck, ruckie, stack

rug, pull, draw

rung, stick, cudgel

sair, ser; sairin, serve; serving

sark, shirt, chemise

sauch, saugh, willow, rope of twisted willow
    withes

saunt, saint

scaith, skaith, injury, harm

scranky, lean, scraggy

scunner, disgust, boredom, revolting person

shackle, wrist

shalt, sheltie, shetland pony

sharny, smeared with dung

sharp, sharpen, whet

shear; shore, shure, cut, reap; cut, reaped

shearer, harvester

shiel, shiell, sho'el, shovel

shoon, sheen, shoes

showd, shoud, swing, waddle

sic, siccan, such

siccar, sicker, sure

siclike, such

siller, money

sin, son, sun, sunny

sit, set, suit

skelp, smack, run vigorously

skirl, shriek, cry

sliddery, slippery

smiddy, smeddie, smithy

smore, choke

snap, gobble up

sneeshin, sneechon, snuff, pinch of snuff

snod, tidy

snotter, burnt wick

sonsy, jolly, sturdy

sough, murmur, whirring or slapping sound

souter, shoemaker

sowans, dish made from oatmeal husks

spark, nip of spirits, splash of mud

speir, speer, spear, ask

sprots, rushes, small sticks

squeel, schule, school

stag, stagie, styagie, young horse, stallion

staw, sta, stole

steer, stir, bustle

stirk, stirkie, young bullock
stoit, styte, walk, stumble, saunter
stook, shock of cut sheaves
stot, bullock
stoup, tankard
straucht, straight, straighten
sweer, sweir, reluctant
swither, be undecided, state of agitation
sye, strain
syne, then
tak, take, lease
tane, the one
tattie, potato
teel, tool, equipment
teem, toom, empty
tent, tint, notice, care
term, period of employment
teuch, tough
thack, thatch
theets, theats, traces
thole, suffer, put up with
thraw; thraw his face, turn, twist, throw; grimace
thrawn, twisted, perverse
tine, tyne, lose
tinkler, tinker
tither, the other
tocher, dowry
tod, fox
toddle, make one's way unhurriedly
toon, farm, farm buildings, town
trig, neat, smart
tyke, tykie, dog
twa-three, two or three, a few
unco, uncouth, very, unusual, strange

wae worth, a curse upon
wag, go to and fro, brandish
wame, wime, belly, stomach
want, lack
wardle, world
ware, spend
wat, wyte; a wat, I wyte, know; indeed, I am sure
waucht, wachtie, gulp, draught
wean, child
wear awa, slip away, pass away, die
weary; weary fa, weary on, miserable, troublesome; the devil take
wee, small
whang, slice
whiles, sometimes
wile, lure, choose, while
win; win free; win up, get, earn, gather in; escape; rise
wizzen, wissen, wizand, throat
wrack, vrack, wreck
wrocht, vrocht, worked
wuddy, woody, gallows
wyne, wine, call to oxen to turn to left
wyner, the lead ox on the left
wyte, blame, know
yerd, yeard, yird, ground, earth
yill, ale
yoke, harness, get to work, start
yon, that, those
yowe, ewe
Yule, Christmas, festive season about Christmas and New Year

SONGS OF THE COUNTRYSIDE

THE BARNYARDS O' DELGATY

A

Barnyards o' Delgaty.

In New-Deer pairish I was born, a child of youth to Methlick came,

And gin ye doot me to believe The session clerk will tell the same.

Liltin a die toorin a die, Liltin a die toorin ae.

a	b
The Barnyards of Delgaty	**Jock o' Rhynie**

1 At New Deer parish I was born
A child of youth to Methlic came
And gin ye doot me to believe
The session clerk will tell the same.

2 Good education I have got
And I have learned to read and write
My parents they were proud of me
My mother in me took delight.

3 To bide upon my father's farm
That was never my intent
I loved the lasses double weel
And aye the weary drap o' drink.

4 As I cam in by Netherdale
At Turra market for to fee
I met in wi a thrifty Scot
Fae the Barnyards o' Delgaty.

1 In New Deer parish I was born
A child of youth to Methlic came
And if ye doubt me to believe
The session clerk will tell the same.

2 Good education I hae got
And I hae learnt to read and write
My parents they were fond o' me
My mother in me took delight.

3 To bide upon my father's farm
That was never my intent
I like the lasses double weel
And aye the weary drap o' drink.

4 It was aboot a term time
I went to Turriff for to fee
I met in wi' Thrifty Scott
Frae the Barnyards o' Delgaty.

5 He promised me twa as guid horse
As was in a' the country roon
But when I gaed to the Barnyards
I found they were but skin and bone.

6 Meg Macpherson made my broth
Her and me we cudna gree
First a mote and then a groat
And aye the ither gilp o' bree.

Song No. 347

5 From that place I steered my course
   And to the Highlands I did go
   I did engage wi' Rhynie there
   A half year's servant for to be.

6 To haud the ploo and saw the corn
   It was the wark I took in han'
   Baith weet and dry, baith eer and late
   It soon did tire me o' the fremt.

7 Rhynie's wark was ill to work
   And Rhynie's wages were but sma'
   Rhynie's laws were double strict
   And that did grieve me warst o' a'.

8 I can drink and no be drunk
   And I can fecht and nae be slain.
   I can coort my neighbour's lass
   And aye be welcome to my ain.

9 Jeannie Rhynie made my bed
   Lay doon atween me and the wa
   Straiket doon my curly pow
   Said "Buchan laddie come awa."

7 From that place I steered my course
   Unto the Highlands I did go
   I did engage wi' Rhynie there
   A half year's servant for to be.

8 To haud the ploo and thrash the corn
   That wis the wark I took in han'
   Both wet and dry, both ere and late
   It soon did tire me o' the frem't.

9 Rhynie's wark was ill to work
   Rhynie's wages they were sma
   Rhynie's laws were double strict
   And that did grieve me worst ava.

10 Rhynie is a Highland place
   It disna suit a lowland loon
   Rhynie is a cauld clay hole
   It's far frae like my father's toon.

11 I thought within my inward hert
   If my parents would but look on me
   And come and tak me frae the frem't
   A better bairn I would be.

12 I was sair abused and badly used
   And grieved were they to see the same
   They came and took me frae the frem't
   And pat me to the school again.

13 But woe be to my inward hert
   For it would never them obey
   Both wet and dry, both ere and late
   My fancy led me far astray.

14 Sunday when I gang to the kirk
   Mony a bonny wife I see
   Sitting by her husband's side
   Wha mony a nicht has lien wi me.

15 Jeanie Riach made my bed
   Lay doon atween me and the wa'
   Straiket doon my curling locks
   Says Buchan laddie come awa.

16 But noo my candle is burn't deen
   The snotter o't has brunt me sair
   I'm listed into King Geordie's crew
   Adieu sweet girls for evermair.

JOHN McALLAN — G

4

B

Barnyards o' Delgaty.

In New Deer parish I was born, A child of youth to Methlick came;
And if you do mis-doot me, The session-clerk will tell the same.
Liltin adie turin adie, Liltin adie turin ae.

1   In New Deer parish I was born,
     A child in youth to Methlick came;
     And if you doubt me to believe
     The session-clerk will tell the same.
       Lintin adie toorin adie,
       Lintin adie toorin ae.

2   Good education I did get,
     And I did learn to read and write,
     My parents they did me admire,
     My mother I was her whole delight.

3   But as the years they did roll on,
     My dad and me could not agree,
     I loved the lasses double weel,
     And aye the drap o' barley bree.

4   Fae Methlick parish I cam' fae
     To Turra market for to fee,
     When I met in wi' drucken Scott   [drunken
     Fae the Barnyards o' Delgaty

5   When I arrived at the Barnyards,
     The sicht o' things near upset me,
     We had nae tools to work oor wark,
     Oor beddin' it was unco wee.

6   Oor cairts they were all in a wrack,
     Oor harrows scarce a teeth ava;
     Oor ploos they were a lump o' roost,
     And handles they had nane ava.

7   Oor horses they were unco thin,
     The auld gray meer she widna ca;
     The auld Jock horse lay in the theets,
     And clawed his legs in spite o' a'.

8   But when the turnips we got in,
     Oor horse a' parkit ane and a',
     And we to Turriff on Saturday went,
     And jolly we got ane and a'.

9   When I went to the church on Sunday,
     Mony's the bonnie lass I see,
     Sit shyly by her daddie's side,
     And winkin' owre the pews to me.

10 I can drink and nae be drunk,
     I can fight and nae be slain,
     I can coort my neebor's lass,
     And aye be welcome to my ain.

JOHN MOWAT — G

5

C
The Barnyards o' Delgaty

To the tune of 348 *Jock o' Rhynie* A

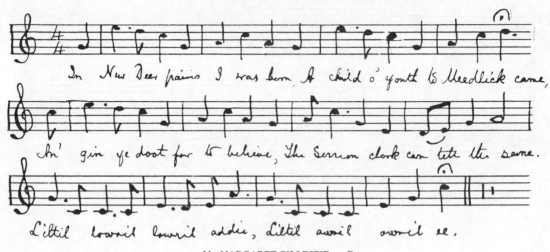

In New Deer pairis I was born, A child o' youth to Meedlick came,

An' gin ye doot for to believe, The Session clerk can tell the same.

Littil lowril lowril addie, Littil owril owril ee.

Mrs MARGARET GILLESPIE — D

D

The Barnyards.

Lillie tooral ooral adie, Lillie tooral ooral ee.

JAMES GREIG — G

E

The Barnyards o' Delgaty.

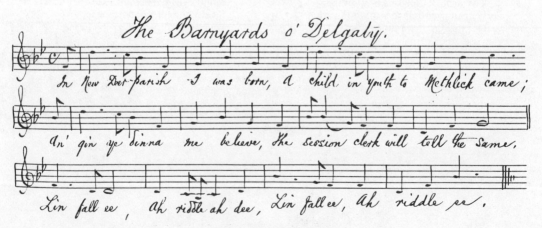

In New Deer-parish I was born, A child in youth to Methlick came;

An' gin ye dinna me believe, The session clerk will tell the same.

Lin fall ee, Ah riddle ah dee, Lin fall ee, Ah riddle ee.

JOHN JOHNSTONE — G

F

The Barnyards o' Delgaty.

SAM DAVIDSON – G

G

The Barnyards

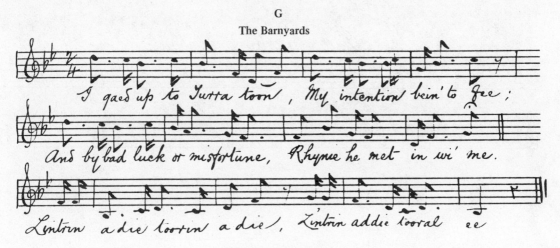

I gaed up to Turra toon, My intention bein' to fee;

And by bad luck or misfortune, Rhynie he met in wi' me.

Lintin a die toorin a die, Lintin addie tooral ee

ARTHUR BARRON – G

H

Barnyards o' Delgaty

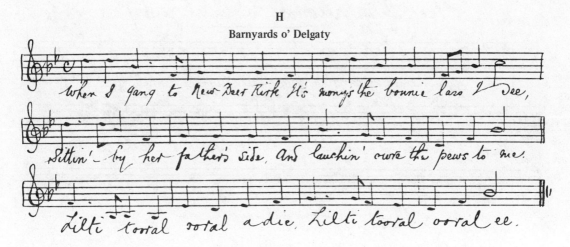

When I gang to New Deer Kirk It's mony's the bonnie lass I see,

Sittin' by her father's side, And lauchin' owre the pews to me.

Lilti tooral ooral a die, Lilti tooral ooral ee.

Mrs FOWLIE – G

7

I

The Barnyards o' Delgaty.

WILLIAM CARLE – G

J

The Barnyards o' Delgaty.

JAMES WILL – G

K

The Barnyards o' Delgaty.

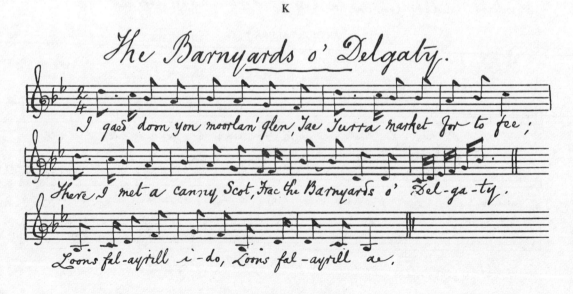

I gaed doon yon moorlan' glen, Tae Turra market for to fee;

There I met a canny Scot, Frae the Barnyards o' Del-ga-ty.

Loons fal-ayrill i-do, Loons fal-ayrill ae.

GEORGE BRUCE THOMSON – G

L

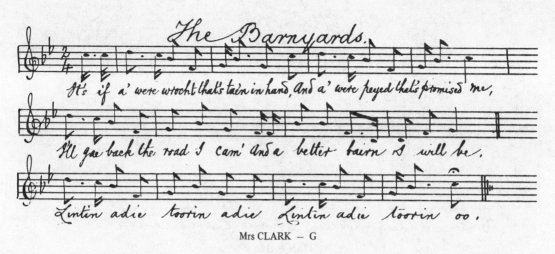

The Barnyards.

It's if a' were wrocht that's taen in hand, And a' were peyed that's promised me,

I'll gae back the road I cam' And a better bairn I will be.

Lintin adie toorin adie Lintin adie toorin oo.

Mrs CLARK — G

M

The Barnyards

As I gaes in by Netherdale To Turra market for to fee,

I met in wi' a fairmer chap At the Barnyards o' Delgaty.

Lintin lowrin, lowrin, lowrin, Lintin lowrin' lowrin' lee

Lintin lowrin, lowrin lowrin, Lintin lowrin lowrin lee

ALEX MILNE — G

N

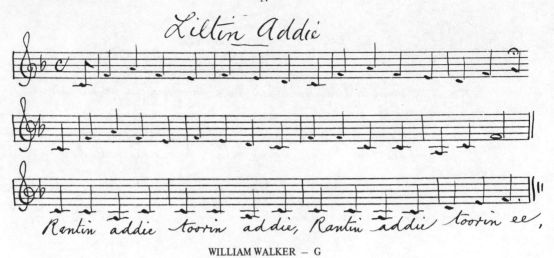

Liltin Addie

Rantin addie toorin addie, Rantin addie toorin ee,

WILLIAM WALKER – G

O

The Barnyards o' Delgaty

1   As I gaed up to Porter Fair
Turra market for to fee
I there met wi' a mierky chiel
Frae barn yards o' Delgaty.
Liltin aran aran addie
Liltin aran aran ee.

2   He promised me the ae best pair
I'd ever set my een upon
Fan I gaed hame the beasties baith
Was fent a thing but skin an bane.

3   My jobie at the Barnyards
It was to ca' the second pair,
But fan I saw the beasts an graith
I a'most got the flittin share.

4   The auld black horse sat on his doup
The auld fite mear lay on her wime
An' a' that I could hup an' crack
They wadna rise at yockin' time.

5   Meg Macpherson maks my brose
But her an me we canna gree
First a moat an syne a knot
Fyls nathing but a gilp o' bree.

6   But yet when I gang to the kirk
There's mony a bonnie lassie there
Prim sittin by her daddy's side
Wad make me welcome to his lair.

7   I can drink an nae be drunk
I can feight an nae be slain
I can coort anither's lass
An aye be welcome to my nain.

8   My can'le noo it is brunt oot
The snotter's fairly on the wain
So fare ye weel ye Barnyards
Ye'll never catch me here again.

JOHN MILNE – G

P
Buchan Prodigal

1 Jeannie Riach makes my bed,
   Lies doon atween me and the wa',
   And straikin' back my curly locks,
   Says, Buchan laddie, come awa'.

2 Meg Macpherson is our cook,
   But her and me we canna gree,
   . . . .
   . . . .

3 In the mornin' we get brose,
   As muckle's we can belly in,
   Willie Ritchie maks them,
   An' I wyte he disna mak' them thin.

4 I gang into the kirk on Sunday,
   Mony's the bonnie lass I find
   Sittin' by her husband's side,
   That mony a nicht has lain by mine.

ALEXANDER ROBB — G

Q
The Barnyards o' Delgaty

1 In New Deer parish I was born,
   A child in youth to Methlic came
   And if ye doubt or disbelieve
   The session clerk will tell the same.
     Lilt-all lara lara laddie,
     Lilt all lara lara lee
     Lilt-all-lara lara laddie,
     Lilt all lara low I lie.

JOHN MILNE — G

11

JOCK O' RHYNIE

A

Jock o Rynie

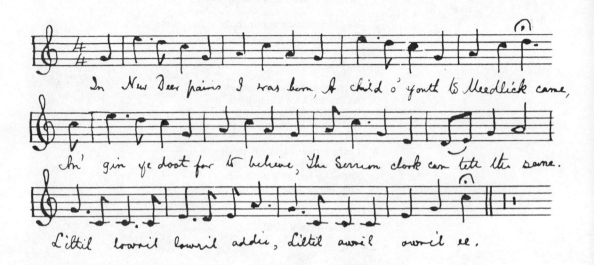

1   In New Deer Paaris I wis born
A child of youth to Methlic came
An gine ye dout for to believe
The session clerk can tell the same.
Lilt til our ril our ril addie
Lilt til our ral our ral 'ee.

2   At Rynie I shore my first hairst
Near to the fit of Ben-achie
My master wis richt ull to sit
But laith wis I to loose my fee.

3   Rynie's wark is ull to work
An Rynie's wages is bit sma
Rynie's laws they're double strick
An that dis greive me worst of a'.

4   Rynie it's a caul clay hole
It's far fae like my father's toun
Rynie it's a hungry place
It disna suit a lowland loun.

5   I' the mornin we get brose
As muckle's we can belly in
An Andrew Dickie stee'rs them roun
I wite he disna stee'r them thin.

6   For weel like I the drap o drink
An sae de I the cup o t'ee
I like the lasses double weel
An that's the thing that's ruin't me.

7   But I can drink an nae be drunk
I can fight an no be slain
I can court my neebour's lass
An aye come welcome to my ain.

8   Jeanie Reach made my bed
Lay down atween me in the w'aa
An straket down my curly locks
Said Buchan laddie come awa.

9   Sair I've wroght an sair I've focht
An I hae won my penny fee
But I'll gang back the gate I came
An a better bairn I will be.

Mrs MARGARET GILLESPIE — D

B
Rhynie's Jock

In New Deer pairish I was born, A child in youth to Methlick came; gin ye doot me to believe, this Sorrin clerk will tell this same. Lilt ill loor il airil addy, Lilt ill loor il air-il dy.

R.D. REID – D

C

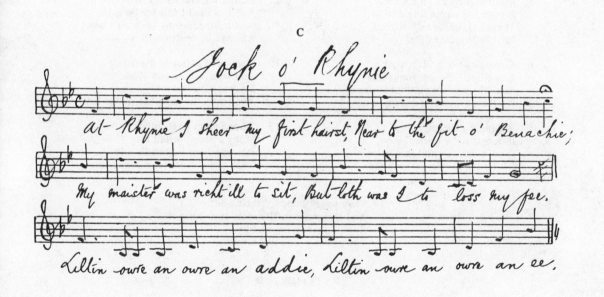

Jock o' Rhynie

At Rhynie I sheer my first hairst, Near to the fit o' Benachie; My maister was richt ill to sit, But loth was I to loss my fee. Liltin owre an owre an addie, Liltin owre an owre an ee.

Rev. JAMES B. DUNCAN – G

D
Jock o' Rhynie

1 In New Deer pairis I was born,
   A child o' youth to Meedlick came,
   And gin ye doot me to believe,
   The session clerk will tell the same.
    Lil a lowril lowril addie,
    Lil a lowril lowril ee.

2 My frien's is peer baith far and near,
   The truth to you I'll shortly tell,
   Johnny Riddell is my name,
   But ye may ca' me Frolic Fair.

3 I have got good education,
   I've been learned to read and write,
   My father was richt fond o' me,
   My mother in me took delight.

4 But to view the country I was fond,
   A common servan' I did fee,
   Sair against my father's will,
   He thocht to mak a man o' me.

5 Into the Hielan's I did steer,
   A common servan' there to be,
   There I did engage wi' Rhynie,
   I got little meat or fee.

6 Rhynie's work is ill to work,
   And Rhynie's wages is but sma',
   And Rhynie's laws is double strick,
   It's that that grieves me worst ava.

7 Rhynie is a Hielan' place,
   It deesna suit a lowlan' loon,
   It's a' owre wi' caul' clay holes,
   It's far fae like my father's toon.

8 If a' were wrocht that's teen in hand
   And a' was paid that's promised me,
   I'll gae back the rade I came
   And a better bairn I will be.

9 Jeannie Riach made my bed,
   Lay doon atween me and the wa'.
   And straikit doon my curly locks,
   Said, "Buchan laddie, come awa."

10 It's noo my can'le has gone oot,
   And the snotter o't has brunt me sore,
   And I'll return to my father's toon,
   And lament for folly evermore.

11 I can drink and nae be drunk,
   And I can fight and nae be slain,
   And I can coort my neebour's lass,
   And aye be welcome to my ain.

12 Weel like I a drap o' drink,
   And weel like I a cup o' tea
   I like the lasses doubly weel,
   And that's the thing has ruined me.

13 When I go in to Meedlick kerk,
   Mony a bonny wife I see
   Sitting by her husband's side
   That mony a nicht has lien wi' me.

14 They weer ribbons o' their heid,
   And they weer ruffles roon' their knee,
   But wi' them I daurna fike,
   The parson's laws is a' sae strick.

Mrs TAYLOR — D

E

1   In New Deer parish I was born
A child of youth to Methlick came
And if ye dinna me believe
The session clerk will tell the same.

2   Rhynie it's a Highland place
It doesna suit a lowland loon
Rhynie it's a cauld clay hole
It's far frae like my father's toon.

Miss ANNIE SHIRER — G

F

Jock o' Rhynie

1   It's New Deer pairish I was born in
A child of youth to Methlick came
An gin ye doot me to believe
The session clerk could tell the same.

2   We get brose in the mornin'
As muckle's we could belly in
Johnnie Dickie steers them roon
An' faith he disna mak them thin.

Mrs DUNCAN — G

G

1   Rhynie is a cauld clay hole,
It's far frae like my father's toon,
Rhynie is a cauld clay hole
It disna suit a Buchan loon.

GEORGE WATT — G

THE PRAISE O' HUNTLY

A

The Praise o' Huntly

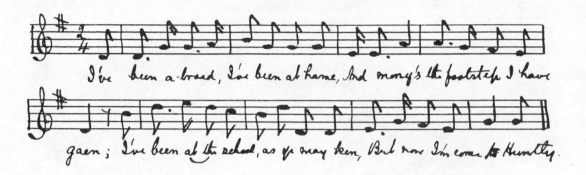

1 I've been abroad, I've been at hame,
   And mony's the footstep I hae gaen,
   Been at the school, ye may weel ken,
   But noo I'm come to Huntly.

2 With Mr Stephen I did agree,
   To work to him for meat and fee,
   And win my bread right honestly,
   Like others in that country.

3 But just 's the sun the world goes roon',
   I fell in love wi' girlies o' the toon,
   And they ca'd me a clever loon,
   And bade me stay at Huntly.

4 The lassies a' were fond o' me,
   I sang to haud them aye in glee,
   But the ne'er a sang had I to gie
   But aye the praise o' Huntly.

5 But Mistress Stephen did me advise
   To rove nae mair but to be wise,
   Make my father's house my only choice,
   And leave the bonny toon o' Huntly.

6 But if I were to leave that toon,
   My comrades a' wad me disown,
   Which causes me to tak a fee
   Near by the bonny toon o' Huntly.

7 But when the term cam and I was free,
   I stepped about at liberty,
   I gaed doon by the back o' Benachie
   To see the Buchan gentry.

8 I stepped aboot at liberty,
   Till Jock o' Rhynie fell in wi' me,
   He spiered if I wad tak a fee,
   And leave that Buchan gentry.

9 He said on me he'd not impose,
   If I wad work but a pair o' horse,
   And stay aside the Tap o' Noth
   As others in that country.

10 "I'm nae a child, as you may see,
   And what I want I mean to learn,
   I'll haud your plough and sow your corn
   Wi' ony in your country."

11 When my parents saw I was engaged,
   At me they were in a very great rage,
   My clothing they kept for a pledge,
   Sent me away quite empty.

12 But when they saw that I was gone,
   And knew not whether I'd die or droon,
   My clothing after me they came,
   But sore they were to hunt me.

13 But stop and I'll tell ye ere a' be deen,
   I'll be mair wiser than I hae been,
   I'll read my bible, hain my sheen,
   Gang nae mair on the country.

WILLIAM WALLACE – D

B
Jock o' Rhynie

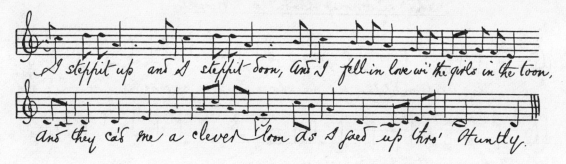

a
Jock o' Rhynie

b

1 When I did leave my father's toon
I kent na weel whether I wad dee or
[droon
But I steppit up by Benachie
And I left the Buchan gentry.

2 When Jock o' Rhynie and me did agree
They saw that better wadna be
My clothes they soon sent after me
Right angry was to want me.

1 I stepped up and I stepped doon
And I fall in love wi' the girls in the toon;
And they ca'd me a clever loon
As I gaed up through Huntly.

3 I stepped up and I stepped doon
And I fell in love wi' the girls o' the toon
And they ca'd me a clever loon
As I gaed up thro' Huntly.

2 When Jock o' Rhynie and me did agree
They saw that better widna dee,
My clothes they soon sent after me
Richt grieved were they to want me.

4 But ye'll maybe think that I'm a bairn
But what I want I'll weel fit to learn
I'll hold your ploo thro' all your fairm
As others in your country.

J.W. SPENCE — G

17

C

The Bonny Toon o' Huntly.

It's Mistress Stephen did me advise To rove no more but to be wise, And make my father's house my choice And gang nae mair to Huntly.

1 It's Mistress Stephen did me advise,
   To rove no more but to be wise,
   And make my father's house my choice
   And gang nae mair to Huntly.

2 But I told her that wadna do,
   My parents wadna look on me,
   . . . .
   . . . .

3 I'm not a fool nor yet a bairn,
   But what I want and I mean to learn,
   To hold your plough and sow your corn
   Wi' ony in your country.

GEORGE GARIOCH – D

D

Jock o' Rhynie

As walkin' at my liberty Jock o' Rhynie fell in love wi' me, An' he bade me such a fee, An' leave the bonny toon o' Huntly.

Mrs WALKER – D

18

E
Jock o' Rhynie

1   I stept aboot at liberty
     Till Jock o' Rhynie fell in wi' me;
     He said, My man, will ye tak' a fee,
     And leave the bonnie toon o' Huntly?

2   I said, My man, I'm but a bairn,
     But what I want I mean to learn,
     I'll hold the ploo, and saw the corn,
     Wi' ony in your country.

3   But Mrs Stephen did me advise
     To read my bible and be wise,
     And make my father's house my choice,
     And to gang nae mair to Huntly.

4   The lasses o' Rhynie socht a sang frae me,
     It wis to keep their herts in glee;
     But fient a ane had I to gie
     But aye to the praise o' Huntly.

5   Rhynie's toon is cauld clay holes,
     It's far frae like my father's toon;
     Rhynie's land is cauld clay holes,
     It disna suit a lawland loon.

Mrs SIM — G

F

1   O I've been abroad an I've been at hame,
     An I've been at squeel as ye may weel ken
     I made my father's house my nain
     Whilst staying in the bonnie toon o' Huntlay.

2   When Jock o' Rhynie got word o' me
     He tried a' his airts to gar me fee,
     Wi' little thought I did agree
     An' left the bonnie toon o' Huntlay.

3   But Rhynie's it's a cauld clay hole
     An' Rhynie's laws are ill to thole
     There's nae coorse days on Rhynie's roll
     It's nae lik the bonnie toon o' Huntlay.

JOHN MILNE — G

G
Jock o' Rhynie

1 I've been at hame and I've been abroad
And mony's the footsteps I hae trod
I've been at school as ye may learn
And now I'm gone to Huntly.

2 The lasses o' Huntly they sair vexed me
To give them a song to keep them in glee
But the fent a ane had I them to gie
But the praise o' the bonnie toon o' Huntly.

Source unrecorded — G

350

TIRED O' WORKIN' LYAUVIE'S BRAES

1 Tired o' workin Lyauvie's braes,
An' tired o' gaun to Imphm's toon,
I'll gang back to Peterhead,
An' there I'll get my penny fun'.

Mrs LYALL — D

20

DARRAHILL

A

1 The horses they were poorly fed
A feed of corn once a day,
And ither twice got neeps and chaff,
To gar them snap their puckle strae.
Lintinadie, etc.

Mrs SANGSTER — G

B

Darahill

1 Dara bade me seek a fee,
And I did seek frae him the same,
He says, Lad your wages is too high,
But I'll gie you the sax pound ten.

2 When I gaed hame to Darahill
To work the wark I took in han',
The horse they werena very guid,
The harness was na worth a d——.

3 Dara was a curious chiel,
And that I kent when I gaed hame,
For deil a word o' sense he spak
But aye the ither "Like ye ken".   [as you know

4 He pat me owre to Smiddyburn,
To ploo upon yon rocky hill,
It was the thing I bou'd to dee
But sair sair against my will.

5 The only thing I do remark
. . . .
. . . .
Raither mony neeps and kail.

6 In the mornin' we get brose,
As mony's we can belly in,
Ondra Dickie steers them roon,
And faith he never maks them thin.

7 Another thing I do remark,
We never get a drink o' ale,
But I'll gae back to Yokieshill,
And there I canna tell the tale.

8 The Buchan Fairs is drawin' nigh,
And doon to them it's we will steer,
In hopes to find some better place,
For d—— the waur we dinna fear.

JOHN JAFFRAY — G

C

Darahill

1 When I was fee'd to Darahill,
It was at a local Buchan fair,
Dara slyly put it on,
Said, Lad would you tak' a fee.
Liltin adie toorin adie,
Liltin adie toorin a.

2 Dara bade me seek a fee,
And I did seek frae him the same;
He said, Lad, the wages is ower high,
But I'll gie you the sax-poun'-ten.

3 When I gaed hame to Darahill,
To work the wark I took in han',
The horses they were aul' and stiff,
And the tackle wisna worth a hang.

4 Among ourselves we hae some grudges,
Ower mony neeps and kail;
Ither things we dee remark —
We never hae a drink of ale.

5 Maggie Dickie makes the brose,
And aye she makes the gued to me,
First a mote and then a knot,
And aye a ither splash o' bree.

6 But the term time is coming on,
But oh it's lang o' coming O,
To lat away the sharney deem,
And hame the dandy 'oman O.

Correspondent in Johannesburg — G

D

Darra Hill

1 When I gaed hame to Darra Hill
I was fee'd at Hallow Fair
When I gaed hame to Darra Hill
It was to drive the second pair.

2 Noo Darra was a curious chiel
An' that I kent when I gaed hame
The never a word o' sense got I
When aught gaed wrang I got the blame.

3 The horses are but poorly fed
A feed o' corn ance a day,
An' neeps an' caff the ither twice
To gar them snap their puckle strae.

4 An' in the mornin' we got brose
As muckle's we could belly in,
An' Anra Dickie steered them roun'
An troth he didna mak them thin.

5 When I gaed on to . . . .
To ploo upon yon rocky hill
I did the wark I took in han'
But sair sair against my will.

6 Anither half year's comin' roun'
An' Buchan Fair will seen be here
We'll maybe get a better place
But fient a waur, o' that I'm seer.

CHARLES MURRAY — D

E

1 Daras took me till a tent,
   And Daras callèd for a dram,
   He clappit the shillin' in my han'
   Says, Lad come hame as seen's ye can.

2 Daras bade me seek a fee
   And I the same did seen lay on,
   He said The wages is rather high
   But I'll gie you the sax poun' ten.

3 When I gaed hame to Darashill
   To work the wark I took in han'
   His horses wisna vera guid,
   And his harness wisna worth a damn.

4 In the mornin' we get brose,
   As muckle's we can belly in,
   And Jamie Ritchie mak's them,
   And fegs he disna mak' them thin.

ALEXANDER ROBB — G

F

Darahill

1 When I engaged to Darahill
   'Twas doon in a Buchan Fair
   The work that I did tak' in hand
   It was to work the second pair.

GEORGE WATT — G

DARRA

Darrahill

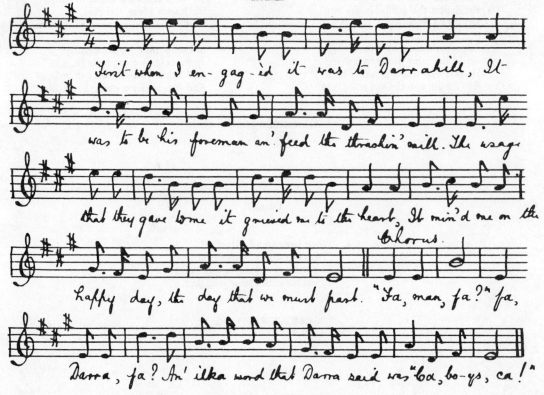

1   First when I engagèd, it was to Darrahill,
    It was to be his foreman, and feed the thrashing mill.
    The usage that they gave to me, it grieved me to the heart,
    It min'd me on the happy day, the day that we must part.
      "Fa, man, fa." Fa, Darra, fa,
      And ilka word that Darra said was aye "Boys, ca'."

2   They put me in a bothy, to mak my brose my leen,
    Gied me a kettle and a cap, a flagon and a speen,
    A little wee bit hamlicky, a cheerie like to fa',
    And a bowie for to haud my meal, my plenishin' is but sma'. [household equipment

3   "Come, ye loons, and lowse your buits as lang as ye hae time,
    For in this hoose ye daurna sit ahin' the oor o' nine.
    Come, ye loons, ye've lien owre lang, ye hinna time to yoke,
    Ye hinna time to tie your buits and far less time to smoke."

4   Darra he has a wifikie and likewise dothers three,
    And yon servant girlie that I am often wi';
    But I'll gae back again the lassie for to see,
    And I winna spier aul' Darra's leave, for me he winna see.

5   Darra he's a corn-dealer and he does ship it a',
    And he's well kent in Aberdeen for "Aul' Darra Fa".

WILLIAM ARGO – D

ELLON FAIR

A
Ellon Fair

1 'Twas in the merry month of May
When flowers had clad the landscape gay
To Ellon fair I bent my way
With hopes to find amusement.

2 A scrankie chiel to me cam near
And quickly he began to spier
If I wid for the neist half year
Engage to be his servant.

3 I'll need you as an orra loon
Four poun' ten I will lay doon
To you, when Martimas comes roon
To close out your engagement.

4 Five shillings more will be your due
If you to me prove just and true
But that will be referred to you
By my good will and pleasure.

5 An' to a tent he then set sail
And bade me follow at his tail
He callèd for a glass o' ale
Therein to keep us sober.

6 Said he "A saxpence noo my loon
I freely will to you lay doon
Threepence for ale I will pay soon
An' threepence buys my farin'." [food

7 When I went hame to my new place
An' at the table showed my face
It's to the brose they said nae grace
The time wis unca precious.

8 Although our usage was but scant
Of wark we never kent nae want
And aye to cairry on the runt
The fairmer cried: "Come on lads".

9 An' when the hairst it did come roon
It's to a scythe I hid to boun'
Likewise to draw the rake aroon'
To keep the fields in order.

Mrs BRUCE — G

B

1 . . . .
. . . .
But that will be referred by you
To my good will and pleasure.

2 I said A shilling pray give me
As arle money now to be   [earnest
And help me onward on the spree
Afore I leave the market.

3 Our ale it was but unco sma
And sometimes we got nane ava
Then Adam's wine to damp oor maw   [water
We gladly took a share o't.

Miss BELL ROBERTSON — G

ELLON MARKET

A

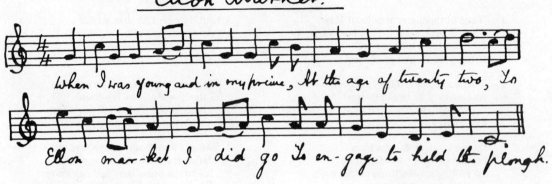

Ellon Market.

When I was young and in my prime, At the age of twenty two, To Ellon mar-ket I did go To en-gage to hold the plough.

1 When I was young and in my prime,
  At the age of twenty two,
  To Ellon market I did go,
  To engage to hold the plough.

2 It was on the road, as it was long,
  I met in with other two,
  They asked me to take a glass,
  As friends would wish to do.

3 We drank our glass, and on did pass,
  On a Hallow Market day
  We three did engage to an aul' man
  To keep his nowt in strae;

4 To plough his land and reap his corn;
  Our fee it was but sma',
  For thirteen poun' paid a' oor fee
  The day we cam awa.

5 It was at the term when we gaed hame,
  We were no boun' till a day,
  We gaed owre till the barnyard
  To thrash the puckle strae.

6 It was thump for thump aye after thump
  O' a' that we could draw;
  And we turned it owre and owre again,
  Oor maister made the straw.

7 Fin mornin' cam, the aul' wife comes oot,
  She was nowise unco braw;
  She brought a pint of richt good ale,
  And gaed among us a'.

8 When eating time it did come roon',
  The brose cap served us a',
  And oor maister sat doon side by side,
  And did the brose cap claw.

9 But noo the warld's turned upside doon
  Wi' maisters, men, an' a';
  Some toons hae gotten a thrashin' mill,
  And some hae gotten twa.

10 There's horse-mills and water-mills,
   But the steam mill beats them a',
   For she thrashes the corn and fills the secks,
   And blaws the cauf awa.

11 The servan's they're nae far ahin',
   But they want their gigs till ca',
   Wi' great lang beards hingin' owre their chin,
   Like a common turnip shaw.   [top

12 It's lang may the fairmers reign,
   For it's him that rules us a',
   When work gets less and money scarce,
   We winna gang sae braw.

WILLIAM PHILIP — D

26

B
Ellon Fair

1 When I was young and in my prime
   My age was twenty two
   To Ellon Market I did go
   To engage to hold the ploo.

2 And on the road as it was lang
   We met wi' other two
   So we a' gaed in to hae a glass
   As friends are wont to do.

3 We took a glass and on did pass
   On a Hallow Market day
   Then we a' engaged wi' the same auld man
   To keep his beasts in strae.

4 To thrash his corn and ploo his lan'
   Oor wages were but sma'
   So thirteen poun' paid a' oor fees
   The day we cam awa.

5 . . . .
   . . . .
   We turned it owre and owre again
   And the auld man made the strae.

6 When the breakfast hour cam roon
   Ae dish saired us a'
   The maister he stood side by side
   And he did the brose cap claw.

7 But noo the warld's turned upside doon
   Wi' maisters men and a'
   At ilka toon there's a threshin' mull
   And some o' them hae twa.

8 There's horse's mulls and water mulls
   And steam mulls best o' a'
   They thresh the corn and fill the sack
   And blaw the cawf awa.

Miss HELEN BRUCE — G

C
Ellon Market

1 When I was young and in my prime
   My age was twenty-two
   To Ellon market I did gyang
   To engage to haud the ploo.

2 But noo the warld's turned upside doon
   For masters, men and a'.

3 There's horse's mulls and there's water mulls
   But the stem-mulls best ava
   For she winnies the corn and fulls the secks
   And blaws the cauf awa.

Source unrecorded — G

27

SOUTH YTHSIE

A

Little Ythsie

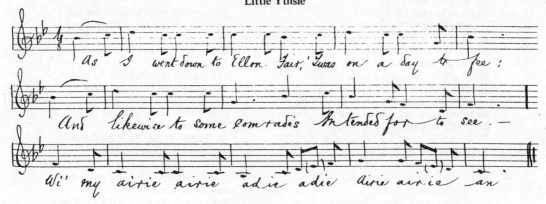

As I went down to Ellon Fair, 'Twas on a day to fee:
And likewise to some comrades Intended for to see. —
Wi' my airie airie adie adie airie airie an

JAMES MURISON — G

B

South Ythsie.

When I these verses did mak' up To haud me on-thocht lang-
I was ploughing in the Chapel park Among the turnip land ----
Wi' my airie idle-dee umti adie airie idle dee ee -----

ARTHUR BARRON — G

C

South Ythsie

1 As I went down to Ellon Fair
   Ance on a day to fee,
   Likewise an opportunity
   My comrades for to see.
     Wi my airy eddle dum dady um
     My eddle dum dair a lee.

2 And steerin' thro' the market
    An auld neebor chanced to see;
    And when I stept up to him
    He asked was I to fee?

3 He told me he was leavin',
    Likewise his neebor tee;
    He said the grieve did want a hand,
    And he thocht that I would dee.

4 He stept up unto the grieve,
    Says, "Here's a man to fee,
    I think he'll suit ye very weel,
    If wi' him ye can agree."

5 He told to me some of the work
    That I would have to do;
    He said I would have little else
    But cart and hold the ploo.

6 He asked at me my wages,
    What they were gaun to be;
    So in a short time after
    Wi' him I did agree.

7 I did engage wi' Johnnie Gray
    The year o' fifty-one,
    Jist for to work his hinmost pair,
    And be his little man.

8 Now to South Ythsie I am bound,
    The term bein' past;
    And trudgin' thro' the Chapel howe
    I cam' to it at last.

9 Straucht to the stable I did go,
    My horses for to view;
    They were a handsome pairie,
    A chestnut and a blue.

10 So on the followin' mornin'
    We a' gaed to the ploo';
    But lang ere it was lowsin' time
    Sae sair's she gart me rue.

11 I held at her wi' a' my micht,
    And cam' but poorly on;
    The ither twa did lauch at me,
    And at me they got fun.

12 But I complained unto the grieve
    That she widna lay the fur;
    He said, "There is a new ane
    Jist ready to gang for."

13 Noo I've got hame my new ane,
    She pleased me unco weel;
    And I do think I am a' richt, —
    I've got a better teel.

14 We hae a gallant foreman,
    His name is Jamie Watt;
    And for to drag the horses on
    Indeed he isna slack.

15 Oor second man is Davidson;
    Indeed to tell the truth,
    It's I do like him very weel,
    He is a jolly youth.

16 And I mysel' the third man,
    My name it is Forsay,
    And I do my endeavour
    Their orders to obey.

17 The neist comes Willie Duncan,
    He's ready wi' a jest;
    Sometimes he doth work orra wark,
    Sometimes the orra beast.

18 We hae a topsman bailie,
    And Wallace is his name;
    He does his cattle off in style
    When he tak's doon his kaim.

19 Likewise we have another one,
    Oor orra beasts to sort,
    And sometimes in the mornin'
    To the barn doth resort.

20 Likewise we have a little boy
    Oor eerants for to go;
    And when he's on an unco road
    Indeed he is some slow.

21 Likewise we have a housekeeper
    Our victuals to prepare,
    And everything that's in the house
    To keep into repair.

22 And likewise we have got a grieve,
    He is a quiet man;
    But for to tell the plain truth.
    His wark he canna plan.

23 Noo I hae wrocht this winter through,
    It's into fifty-twa,
    Still thinkin' on the month o May
    That I micht win awa'.

24 At last the market it has come,
    And I am fee't again;
    I'm going back to Brackley;
    They call him Mr Bean.

25 Noo the twenty-sixth has come,
    It is the term day;
    I'll tak' my budgets on my back, —
    Fareweel to Johnnie Gray.

WILLIAM FORSYTH – G

SLEEPY TOON

A

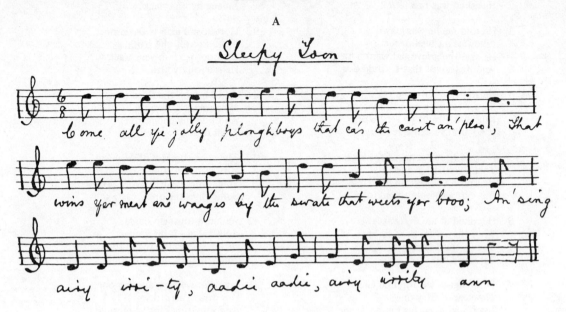

Sleepy Toon

Come all ye jolly ploughboys that ca's the cairt an' ploo, That wins yer meat an' wages by the swate that weets yer broo; An' sing airy irri-ty, aadie aadie, airy irrity ann

1 Come all ye jolly ploughboys
That ca's the cairt an' ploo,
That wins yer meal and wages
By the sweat that weets yer broo.
An sing airy irrity addie, addie
Airy irrity aun.

2 For I am one o' yer brethren
The cairt an' ploo I ca',
I'm a wanderer thro' this warl
Chasin' fortune's slippery ba'.

3 It happened at last Whitsunday
I tired o' my place
I went to Clatt for to engage
My fortune for to chase.

4 I met wi' Adam Mitchell
An to fee we did presume
He's a fairmer in Kennethmont
And lives at Sleepy Toon.

5 If you and me 'ill agree, he says
Ye'll have the fairest play
For I never bids my servan's work
Above ten oors a day.

6 Ye'll work weel in a gweed day
When 'ts bad ye shall work none
A reg'lar diet you shall have
An' yer wages when they're won.

7 Yer rules they are in reason, sir
I hae but little doot
An if a' be true that ye do say
I think the place will suit.

8 So there I bound myself to him
An' thocht to live content
But when I gaed hame to Sleepy Toon
I shortly did repent.

9 'Twas early in the mornin'
We cam to Sleepy Toon
He ranked us in good order
To lay the turnips doon.

10 He ranked us in good order
And to work we did repair
But to keep us hard at labour
Was all his toil and care.

11 I yoked my cairt to drive the dung
So did my neebour Nowes
When a rattlin' thunder shower cam' on
And the order was to lowse.

12 We did obey the order
    Nor longer did remain
    But we never had the fortune
    To lowse for rain again.

13 The rain was still increasin'
    The son was at the mill
    Awa' for meal, auld Adam said
    Yer bellies for to fill.

14 The meal was very weet wi' rain
    But soon the day it breaks
    And next order was to go and scrape
    Yer dinner fae the secks.

15 We never will deny, we says
    What work ye put us to
    But to eat the scrapin's o' yer secks
    Is what we'll never do.

16 Seein' we was determined
    He then pronounced a threat
    He would gar them bake it through the dry
    But still it was to eat.

17 Next order was to yoke at five
    An' work as lang's we see
    Oh no ye're not in reason, sir,
    Denièd ye must be.

18 Will ye deny what I comman',
    Ye scoondrels that ye are
    Oh yes we bargained for ten oors,
    Deny them if ye daur.

19 It's ye will leave the toon, he says,
    And that just instantlie
    We will, gin ye find leisure
    To gie's oor penny fee.

20 You don't deserve yer wages
    For all that you have done
    Ah then we don't deserve to leave
    Before that they are won.

21 Next order was to bed at nine
    And never leave the toon
    For every time you go away
    You shall be fined a croon.

22 My neebour was fined mony a croon
    But never lost the he'rt
    An' I mysel' was fined a note   [pound
    For hurlin' on my cairt.

23 We never minded what he said
    But always took the pass
    We gaed whiles for tobacco
    And whiles to see oor lass.

24 And when he found us oot at last
    He raised some dreadfu' ramps   [outbursts of
    He bann'd and swore at us and ca'd us temper
    Twa most cursèd scamps.

25 An ilka day he hurried on
    The hills and valleys rang
    We never got a moment's peace
    For's everlastin' tongue.

26 He wid mak a famous lawyer
    To set him on a shelf
    He has the knack to licht upon
    The cheap side for himself.

27 But the term is drawin' nigh
    An' we will a' win free
    An' wi' this weary fairmer
    Again we winna fee.

28 Noo Martimas is come at last
    I bid ye all adieu
    Ye sons and dochters auld an' young
    Likewise old Adam too.

29 Whoever he be that fills my room
    I pity much his case
    He'll work him hard by nicht and day
    An' bann him till excess.

30 Noo we are set at liberty
    An' free from bondage chain
    An' we will a' be welcome back
    To Donside again.

JAMES HIGH — G & D

B
Sleepy Toon

To the tune of *Speculation* from the same singer

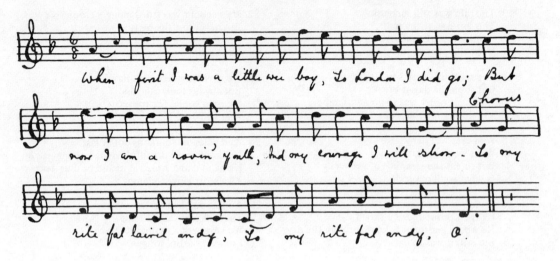

1   It fell aboot a Whitsunday,
    Fan tirin' o' my place,
    I went up through Clatt, a' for to fee,
    And my fortune for to chase.
    And sing airy irrity ah dee,
    And sing airy irrity ann.

2   I met in wi' Adam Mitchell,
    To fee we did presume,
    He's a fairmer in Kennethmont,
    And lives at Sleepy Toon.

3   "If you and me we do agree,
    Ye'll be the foremost man;"
    So he handed me a shillin',
    Says, "Come hame as seen's ye can."

4   "If ye work weel in a good day,
    In a bad ye shall work none,
    A regular diet you shall have,
    And your wages when they're won."

5   'Twas on a Monday's mornin'
    I landed at Sleepy Toon;
    So he ranked us in gran' order,
    The turnips to lay doon.

6   He started me to drive the dung,
    Likewise my neebour Knowles
    When a rapid thunder shoor cam on,
    And the order was to lowse.

7   The rain was still increasing,
    From work we did refrain;
    But we never had it in our poor
    To lowse for rain again.

8   The rain it then went over,
    The son was at the mill,
    It was for meal, auld Adam said,
    Oor bellies for to fill.

9   . . . .
    . . . .
    The order was to go and scrape
    Our dinner fae the seck.

10 "I'll ne'er refuse fat e'er is right,
    Fan that I'm told to do,
    But to eat the scrapins o' your seck
    Is the thing I'll never do.

11 And fan we return to Alford vale,
    We'll make the glass gang roon',
    And we'll tell them o' the usage
    We got at Sleepy Toon.

ALEXANDER MACKAY — D

C

Sleepytoon.

'Twas on a Monday morn-in' I gaed to Sleepy-toon,
He ranked us in guid ord—er The turnips till lay doon.
And sing, airie ittitie, arrie ittitie, airie ittitie an O.

1
    . . . .
He's a fairmer in Kennethmont,
Lives owre at Sleepytoon,
Sing airie ittitie, arrie ittitie,
Airie ittitie an O.

2   'Twas on a Monday mornin'
     I gaed hame to Sleepytoon,
     He ranked us in guid order,
     The turnips tull lay doon.

3   A pair o' blues they led the van,
     So nimbly as they go;
     And a pair o' broons that follows them,
     That never yet said no.

4   A wee bit shalt that ca's the neeps,
     And oh, but it is sma';
     And Balchers he'll declare tae you,
     It's stronger than them a'.

5   The order wis tae bed at nine,
     And never leave the toon;
     And ilka time we gaed fae hame
     We'd be fined half-a-croon.

6   I never minded what he said,
     But always took the pass,
     Sometimes tae buy tobacco,
     Sometimes tae see my lass.

7   But noo the term is drawin' near,
     And seen we'll a' win free,
     And we'll gang doon tae Jeannie Low's,
     And hae a jolly spree.

8   Gin we were doon at Rhynie's Muir,
     And garin' the gless gang roon,
     We will tell them o' the usage
     We got at Sleepytoon.

JOHN JOHNSTONE and CHARLES WALKER — G

D

Sleepy Toon

1 Come, all ye jolly ploughmen
  That ca's the cairt and plough,
  That wins your meat and wages
  By the sweat that weets your broo.
  An' sing airie eeritie addie,
  An' sing airie eeritie an.

2 For I am one o' your brethren,
  The cairt an' pleuch I ca',
  I'm a wanderer through this world,
  Chasin' fortune's sliddery ba'.

3 It happened at last Whitsunday
  I tirèd o' my place,
  An' I went up to Clett to fee,
  My fortune for to chase.

4 So I met in wi' Adam Mitchell,
  An' to fee we did presume,
  He's a fairmer in Kennethmont,
  An' lives at Sleepy Toon.

5 "If you an' me 'ill agree," he says,
  "Ye'll have the fairest play,
  For I never bids my servan's work
  Above ten oors a day."

6 "Ye'll work weel in a gweed day,
  When it's bad ye shall work none,
  A reg'lar diet you shall have,
  An' your wages when they're won."

7 "Your rules they are in reason, sir,
  I hae but little doot,
  An' if a' be true that ye do say,
  I think the place will suit."

8 So I bound myself to him,
  An' thocht to live content,
  But when I cam hame to Sleepy Toon,
  I shortly did repent.

9 'Twas early in the mornin'
  We came to Sleepy Toon,
  An' he ranked us in good order
  To lay the turnip doon.

10 So I began to drive the dung,
  So did my neebour Nowes,
  Till a rapid thunderstorm cam on,
  And the order was to lowse.

11 So we obeyed the order,
  No longer did remain,
  But we never had the fortune yet
  To lowse for rain again.

12 The rain was still increasin',
  His son was at the mill;
  It was for meal, old Adam said,
  Oor bellies for to fill.

13 The meal was very weet wi' rain,
  But soon the day did break,
  The order was to go and scrape
  Our dinner fae the secks.

14 "We never will refuse, sir,
  What work ye pit us to,
  But to eat the scrapin's o' your secks,
  Is fat we'll never do."

15 When he saw we was determined,
  He then pronounced a threat:
  "I'll make them bake it through the dry,
  But still it was to eat."

16 "Ye'll yoke at five o'clock," he says,
  "An' work as lang's we see;"
  "Oh no, ye're not in reason, sir,
  Denièd you must be."

17 "Oh then ye'll leave the toon," he says,
  "And that just instantly;"
  "Yes, if ye wad tak the leisure, sir,
  To gie's wir penny fee."

18 "Ye don't deserve your wages
  For all that you have done;"
  "Then we don't deserve to leave the toon
  Before that they be won."

19 "Will ye deny what I comman',
  Ye devils that ye are?"
  "Oh yes, we bargained for ten oors,
  Deny them gin ye daur."

20 He gave orders for bed at nine,
And never leave the toon,
"For every time ye go away,
Ye shall be fined a croon."

21 My neebour was fined mony a croon,
But never lost the hert,
And I was fined a note mysel'
For hurlin' on my cairt.

22 We never mindit fit he said,
But still we took the pass,
Sometimes gaed for tobacco,
And files to see wir lass.

23 But when he found it oot at last,
He raised some dreadful ramps,
With, "The devil tak ye till himsel'
For twa infernal scamps."

24 And ilka day he hurried on
The hills and valleys rang,
We never got a moment's rest
For his damned eternal tongue.

25 He would mak a famous lawyer
To set him on a shelf,
For he has the luck to light upon
The cheap side for himself.

26 Whoever they be that fills our room,
I pity much their case,
For he'll work them hard baith night and day,
And damn them till excess.

27 But Mairtimas it's comin' here,
I'll bid ye all adieu
To sons and daughters, aul' and young,
Likewise old Adam too.

28 But now we're set at liberty,
And free from bondage chain,
And we are always welcome back
To Donside again.

CHARLES EWEN — D

E

Sleepytoon

1   I happened at last Whitsunday
I tired o' my place
And I gaed up to Insch to fee
My fortune for to chase.
And sing errie erritty adie a'
Sing errie erritty an'.

2   I met in wi' Adam Mitchell
To fee we did presume
He's a fairmer in Kennethmont
Lives ower at Sleepytoon.

3   "If you and I agree" he says
"You'll have the fairest play
For I never bid my servants work
Above ten hours a day."

4   If a' be true ye tell to me
I think the place will suit
Guid faith I think I'll gang wi' you
But ye are an ugly brute.

5   'Twas on a Monday mornin'
I gaed hame to Sleepytoon
He ranked us out in good order
To lay his turnips down.

6   I was put to drive oot dung
Likewise my neighbour Knowles
But soon the rain it did come on
And we got the call to lowse.

7   The rain it still increasèd
The son was at the mill
For meal, old Adam Mitchell said
Our bellies for to fill.

8   The rain has now gone over
The day again doth break
And our next orders was to scrape
Our dinner from the sacks.

9   We'll ne'er refuse dear Adam
The thing you put us to,
But to eat the scrapins o' your sacks
Is a thing we'll never do.

Song No. 356

10 Do ye refuse what I command
   Ye scoundrels that ye are
   Ye are bargained for ten hours a day
   Refuse them if ye daur.

11 But if the one thing winna dee
   The ither I can try
   I'll go and get the kitchen girl
   To mix it through the dry.

12 The order was to bed at nine
   And never leave the toon
   And for every time we left the toon
   We'd be fined half a croon.

13 Mony a crown have I been fined
   But never lost the heart
   And my neighbour he was fined a pound
   For turnin' up a cart.

14 We never heeded Adam
   Sometimes we took the pass
   Sometimes to buy tobacco
   Sometimes to see our lass.

15 But noo the term's come at last
   The trifle safely won
   And we'll awa to Rhynie muir
   And call a glass o' gin.

16 When we are ower in Alford
   We'll gar the glass gang roon
   And we'll tell them o' the usage that
   We got at Sleepytoon.

17 We'll maybe see Old Adam yet
   Jist at his dish o' brose
   And we'll gie 'im our pocket napkin
   To dicht his snuffy nose.

J. W. SPENCE — G

F

Sleepy Town

1 'Twas on a Monday mornin'
   I gaed hame to Sleepytown
   An' he ranked us in good order
   To lay the turnips down.

JOHN ORD — G

THE SCRANKY BLACK FARMER

A

The Tap o' the Garioch.

Up from the low country my course I did steer To the parish o' Kinnethmont you shortly shall hear;

Their customs & fashions to me a' seemed new, My rapid proceedings full sore did I rue,

1 Up from the low country my course I did steer
To the parish o' Kinnethmont you shortly shall hear;
Their customs and fashions to me a' seemed new,
My rapid proceedings full sore did I rue.

2 At the place called Earlsfield we a' did appear,
From various places some far and some near,
From the parish o' Rothes, Grange, Mortlack, and Keith,
Likewise Aberlour, Rothiemay, and Fordyce.

3 Tho' the wind it does beat and the rain down does pour,
Yon hungry black farmer down on us did glower.

4 He called us to the leadin' whenever he desired,
An' thro' the long day none daur say they were tired,
While the Sun travelled round the terrestrial ball,
The harness from our horses did never down fall.

5 No breathing we get from the time that we rise
Till the absence of daylight does seal up the skies.

6 It's now I'm arrived at thirty and one,
An' I've served all the various descriptions of man,
But of all the taskmasters that e'er I did see,
Ane like yon black farmer ne'er glowert upon me.

7 But the day's nigh approachin', the time's comin' on,
That from this black farmer we a' must be gone,
An' I'm going back to my own native shore
Tenthins and to one if you e'er see me more.

8 So farewell Rhynie and farewell Clatt,
For I hae been in ye baith early and late,
It's I hae been in ye baith sober and fou,
So farewell Rhynie, I bid you adieu.

9 It's farewell to the Garioch and adieu to you all,
Likewise to yon farmer in the lan' o' Leithhall,
Bonnie Jeannie maun travel, bonnie Bawbie also,
An' it's back to the beyont o' Montgomery we'll go.

ALEXANDER ROBB – G

B

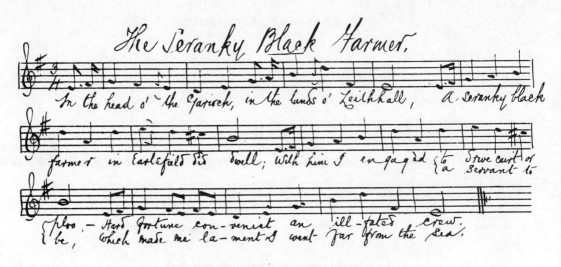

The Skranky Black Farmer.

In the head o' the Gariock, in the lands o' Leithhall, a skranky black farmer in Earlsfield did dwell; With him I engaged {to Drive cart or / a servant to} {ploo, / be,} — {Hard fortune con-veniet an ill-fated crew. / Which made me la-ment I went far from the sea.}

1 In the head o' the Gearry in the lands o' Leath Hall,
   A skrankie black farmer in Earlsfield did dwell
   Wi him I engaged a servant to be,
   Which makes me lament I went far fae the sea.

2 I engaged wi' this farmer to drive cart and plough
   Hard fortune conveniet an illfated crew
   I one of the number which causes me rue
   That ever I attempted the country to view.

3 In the head o' the Gearry we all did appear
   From various countries some far and some near
   From the parish of Kenethmont, Kilmarnock, Keen Keith
   From Aberlour, Rothiemay and Fordyce.

4 The harvest in our country is both early and late
   And all kinds of drudgery of course we do get
   Our wages are rough and our ale is but pale
   It's the brown bree o' Mollashes that we get for ale.

5 It is early in the morning we rise to the yoke
   The storm nor the tempest can never make us stop
   While the rain it does beat and the rain it down pours
   And still yon black farmer he on us does glower.

6 But the day is expiring and the day it will come
   From various countries we all must be going
   Bonnie Jeannie must travel, bonnie Babie also
   Back to the beyone o' Montgomery must go.

7 So farewell Rhynie and adieu to you Clatt
   For I have been wi' you both early and late
   Both early and late, both empty and fou,
   So farewell Rhyne, I'll bid you adieu.

8 So farewell Babie and adieu to you a'
   Likewise to the farmer that lives at Leathhall,
   For to serve this black farmer I'm sure it's nae sport
   And I will be going to my bonnie sea-port.

Mrs CLARK — G

38

C

The scranky black farmer.

In the pairish o' Kinnethmont In the lands o' Leithhall, A scranky black farmer &c

J.W. SPENCE — G

D

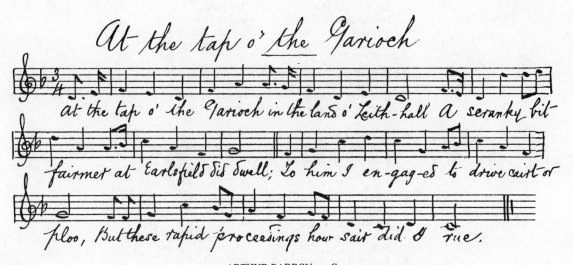

At the tap o' the Garioch

At the tap o' the Garioch in the lands o' Leith-hall A scranky bit fairmer at Earlsfield did dwell; To him I en-gag-ed to drive cairt or ploo, But these rapid proceedings hour sair did I rue.

ARTHUR BARRON — G

E

In the lands o' the Garioch in the muirs o' Leithhall, A scranky black farmer in Earlsfield did dwell; oor usage is roch & oor ale is but sma' There's naething but weel throats lads, Haste ye awa'

J. NAAMAN — G

39

F

The Scranky Black Farmer

1   Up from this low country my course I did steer,
To the parish o' Kennethmont, as soon ye shall hear,
To the top o' the Garioch and the lan's o' Leith-hall,
A scranky black fairmer in Earlsfield did dwall.

2   Wi' him I engagèd a servant to be,
Which makes me lament I went far fae the sea.
Wi' him I engagèd to drive cairt and plough;
Hard fortune convenin' an ill-gettit crew.

3   Early in the mornin' we all did appear,
Fae the various countries, some far and some near,
Fae the top o' the Garioch, Grange, Mortlach, and Keith,
And from Rothiemay, Aberlour, and Fordyce.

4   We all to the yoke while the sun travels roon',
The teckle from our horses we never ball doon.
There's no rest for us, i' the mornin' we rise,
Till the absence o' daylicht does seal up the skies.

5   Early in the mornin' we go to the yoke,
No tempest nor storm does make us to stop,
While the wind doth outbeat and the rain down does pour,
And still yon black fairmer he roars oot for more.

6   The harvest in this country 'tis both ere and late,
And all kinds o' drudgery in coorse we do get,
Our work it is hard, and our ale it's but sma',
There's nothing but dry throats, lads, "Haste ye" for a'.

7   But had I been tractable when I was young,
This muckle-feetit fairmer might hae never on me rung; [domineered over me
I slighted my grammar and that I did do,
And my rapid proceedings full sair do I rue.

8   Years I've now livèd both twenty and one,
And been tried before a' description o' man.
Bit a' the taskmasters I ever did see,
One like yon black fairmer never glowrèd on me.

9   But the time duly end and the day duly come
When we to our own countries we a' must be gone,
Bonny Bawbie maun travel, and Jeannie also,
And back to the beyon' again Montgomerie maun go.

10   Farewell, bonny Bawbie and Jeannie and a',
And adieu to the fairmer o' the lan's o' Leith-hall;
To sair yon black fairmer I'm sure it's nae sport,
And so we'll be gone to yon bonny seaport.

Mrs TAYLOR — D

G
The Scranky Black Farmer

1   Up from that low country my course I did steer
     To the parish o' Kennethmont ye shortly shall hear
     Till the heid o' the Garioch, in the lands o' Leithhall
     A black scranky fairmer in Yirlsfield did dwell.

2   To the place called Yirlsfield we all did appear
     From some various countries, some far and some near
     From the parish o' Rothes, Grange, Mortlach and Keith
     Likewise Aberlour Rothiemay and Fordyce.

3   Early in the mornin' we rise to the yoke
     No storm nor no tempest can make us to stop
     The wind it does blow and the rain it does pour
     Still the black farmer it's on us does glower.

4   The tackle from our horses they never down fall
     Till the sun it goes round the terrestrial ball
     Our usage is rough and our ale it is sma'
     Broon bree of molasses lads, haste ye for all.

5   The fashion in this country is to work ear' and late
     All kinds of trudgery in course we do get
     No breathin' we have from the mornin' we rise
     Till the absence of the sun doth seal up the skies.

6   I've arrived at the age of thirty and one
     And the half of my time is now past and gone
     But by all the taskmasters I ever was wi'
     None like this black fairmer ever glowered on me.

7   If I had been tractable when I was young
     This mucky feet fairmer never ower me had rung
     I slighted my grammar and that did I do
     And this rapid proceeding sore do I rue.

8   But the time is expiring and fast going on
     And from this strange country we all must be gone
     Farewell to ye Betsy and Jean also
     For back to Aboyne and Montgomery I maun go.

Mrs SIM — G

THE GREEDY GLED O' MAINS

There Lives a Farmer

1　There lives a farmer in this place
　　His name ye nead na speire
　　Weel kent o'er a' the quintra side
　　For greed o' wark an' gear.

2　For weet or dry oor wark we ply
　　Awat he disna hain's
　　Keep up your whack an' dinna jauck　　[slack
　　Cries the greedy gled o' Mains.

3　On crafter bodies roon' aboot
　　He aften gies a caw　　　　[pays a visit to
　　An' buys their bits o' stirkies cheap
　　By haudin' on the jaw.

4　Poor silly folk wi him to yock　　[have dealings
　　They want his crafty brains
　　Grab a' ye can is aye the plan
　　Wi' the greedy gled o' Mains.

JOHN MILNE — G

YE'RE NOW ON BOGIESIDE

Bogieside

1　Assist me all ye muses for to compose a song
　　'Tis of a tyrant farmer near Gartly did belong.
　　An' while we were his servants oft times to us he said
　　Come drive them on some smarter, ye're now on Bogieside.

2　We did drive on his horses till they were out of breath
　　They were fitter for the tannerie than for to be in graith
　　For want of corn they did lie hard and he with us did chide
　　And he swore we had neglected them upon sweet Bogieside.

JOHN ORD — G

THE BARNS O' BENEUCHES

A

J.W. SPENCE – G

B

The Barns o' Beneuches or Kempie

1. My friens ane an a' I'll sing you a sang
   If ye a' haud your weeshts it winna tak' me lang   [keep quiet
   It's aboot a mannie Kempie, he's a caird tongued fang   [abusive lout
   For he rages like a deevil in the mornin'.

2. He's a wee little mannie wi' a fern tickled face
   A' the days o' yer life ye never saw sic a mess
   Ye wid swear he hid deserted frae some tinkler race
   Afore they had got a' wakened in the mornin'.

3. At the Barnyards o' Beneuches he has long been a grieve
   But come May the 26th he has to pad I believe
   For he's sieged at his men, till his maister's gien him's leave   [stormed
   So he canna get them up in the mornin'.

4. But when he doth rise ye never heard sic a soun'
   For he'll siege you and damn you like ony dragoon
   His lang caird tongue you'd hear't roun' the toon   [scolding
   Afore he gets his breakfast in the mornin'.

5. Dinna gang to the Barns if ye wish to be weel
   A' the days o' your life ye ne'er saw sic a chiel
   He'll treat you to a breakfast o' buttermilk an' meal
   Wi' a drink o' soor ale in the mornin'.

6. We get beef bree whiles weel seasoned wi' reek
   Wi' three seeds o' barley an' the smell o' a leek
   If you're nae pleased wi' that he'll neen o' yer cheek
   But he'll put you frae his toon in the mornin'.

7   But if e'er sic a thing as a row should arise
    My friens ane and a' tak tent and be wise   [notice
    Keep quietness if you can or the wife will rise
    Dancing mad on her stockings in the mornin'.

8   Twas ae mornin in March juist as near as I can
    She cam' swearin fae the blankets we'd bad used her man
    Wi her sark tail wiggle waggle into the close she ran
    Dancin' mad on her stockins in the mornin'.

9   For a lang caird tongue she's the worst that I ken
    Lord bless me! sic a mornin' may I never see again
    Five or sax naked bairnies a' rinnin' but and ben
    Cryin' "Od mammie's mad in the mornin."

10   Says she to the shepherd "Ye're nae freen o' mine
    For a' body kens ye're a caird Hielan' thing
    You tauld them doon at Brunan I gaed milk to the swine
    And you soor ale to your porridge in the mornin'."

11   But it's May the twenty saxt will be here in a crack
    An' we'll a' leave the Barns never mair to gang back
    We'll gang blithely doon the road like an ill tongued pack
    Singin' Kempie he can follow in the mornin'.

12   Now my name I will reveal if sic a thing I ever hid
    It's but the country clype I'll ne'er deny, gweed forbid   [gossip
    My neighbours a' that ken me weel they ca' me feel Jock Wid
    Sae we'll up an' leave the Barns in the mornin.

JOHN WIGHT — G

361

MAINS O' ELRICK

1   'Twad be a crime, shame, and disgrace,
    To hear the people say,
    That the folk o' Little Elrick
    Works upon the Sabbath day.

Mrs MARGARET GILLESPIE — D

REID HOOSE

1   Reid Hoose it is a fairm toon
It stands upon a knowe
Ye maybe ken the fairmer o't
For he's a muckle yewe.

Miss ANNIE SHIRER — G

THE BENTON CREW

1   They gang to the markets jist in flocks,
Wi' a weel-trimmed hat and a braw topcoat,
For to fee a braw new flock
Hame to the Benton crew, man.

2   Bow-houghed Johnnie fae Heartshill,   [bandy-legged
May the deevil get him in his . . . .
And drive him thro' a brunstane mull,   [brimstane
For he's ane o' the Benton crew, man.

ALEXANDER ROBB — G

BENTON

1 To little Benton I did fee
In Rhynie feein' fair;
It wis to be the foremost one,
To work the foremost pair.

2 I scarcely wis a week come hame
When I did plainly see
The little mannie Benton
And I could not agree.

3 Like many of my calling
I soon began to find
That Benton's study ever was
His servants for to grind.

4 Oftentimes he laid a snare
To catch me in a flaw
The Banton thocht I wis a hen
To cooer when he wid craw.

5 The craw jist o' the Banton cock
It might surprise some men;
But weel could I withstand each shock
And I loot the Banton ken.

6 From time to time the simmer past,
Wi' strife and scoff and jeer;
The days to me like months did seem
Beneath the Banton sneer.

7 But harvest it did now come on
To cut we did repair;
I from the Banton sought a scythe
To cut his corn there.

8 A pair o' scythes in time was brought
And I did grip to mine
The Banton he did quickly say, —
Ye are before your time.

9 Benton in a passion flew
Says, I shall mak' you blithe
To cut jist all the corn through
Wi' an auld roosty scythe.

10 Take home the new scythe, he did say
And bring your auld scythe here;
His orders I did soon obey
And home for her did steer.

11 I soon did bring the roosty scythe
And doon to him I threw;
The Banton he did not look blithe
It made him thraw his mou'.

12 For twa three days I idle went
I widna work a jot
Benton quickly did repent
And back my new scythe got.

13 Cutting being over
And leading weel begun
The Banton thocht he wid get me
Away from him to run.

14 It's to the Banton I stuck fast
As fast as ony brier;
I made him pay me every plack
Or he of me got clear.

15 Come listen all ye plooman lads
That do intend to fee, —
If you go to serve the Banton cock,
Ye'll rue as weel as me.

16 The Banton cock will crowsely craw
When servants gings new hame;
But wi' the cock there's nane can live ava,
Unless a cock that's game.

Mrs SIM — G

FRAE THE MARTIMAS TERM

1 Frae the Martimas term in the year .   .   .   . twa
Till Whitsunday's wind blew a half year awa.

Miss BELL ROBERTSON — G

NETHERTHIRD

A

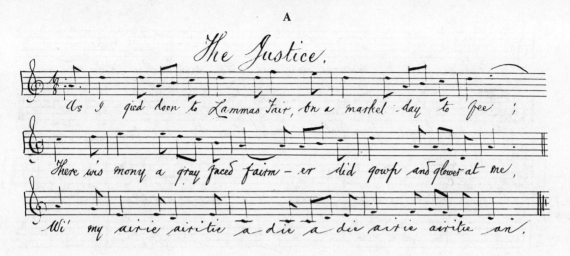

The Justice.

As I gied doon to Lammas Fair, On a market day to fee;
There wis mony a gray faced fairm-er did gowp and glower at me,
Wi' my airie airitie a die a die airie airitie an.

1   As I gied doon to Lammas Fair,
On a market day to fee;
There wis mony a gray faced fairmer
Did gowp and glower at me.
Wi' my airie airitie adie adie
Airie airitie an.

Miss LIZZIE CRIGHTON — G

B

Netherthird

1   As I gaed up through Lammas fair
Ance on a day to fee
Mony a grey-faced fairmer
That day did look at me.

JOHN ORD — G

NETHERHA'

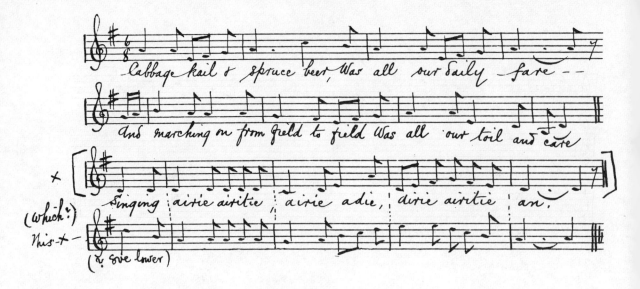

1 The cookmaid and the cowboy,
  Likewise his gallant grieve,
  He has brought them owre the Cairnamount
  For aught that we believe.
    Singing airie airitie, airie adie,
    Airie airitie an.

2 Cabbage kail and spruce beer,
  Was all our daily fare
  And marching on from field to field
  Was all our toil and care.

J. W. SPENCE — G

THIS IS HALLOWEVEN

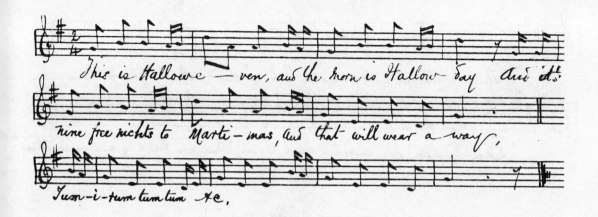

This is Halloweven,
And the morn is Hallowday
And it's nine free nichts to Martimas,
And that will wear away.
Tum-i-rum tum tum etc.

[clear, non-inclusive

Rev. JAMES FORREST — G

369

THE GLASS MARKET

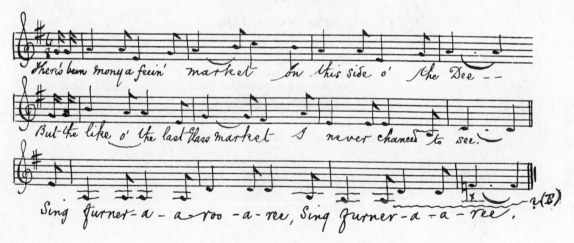

1 There's been mony a feein' market
On this side o' the Dee
But the like o' the last Glass Market
I never chanced to see.
Sing furner-a-a-roo-a-ree,
Sing furner-a-a-ree.

Rev. GEORGE BIRNIE — G

BRANNAN FAIR O' BANFF

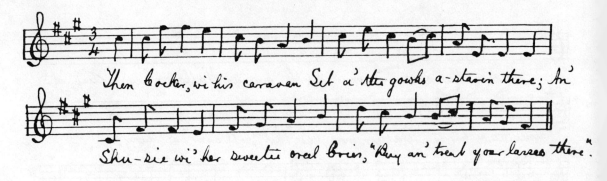

1   Then Cocker, wi his caravan
     Set a' the gowks a-starin there;
     An' Shusie wi' her sweetie creel
     Cries, "Buy an' treat your lasses there".

     Mrs MARGARET GILLESPIE — D

371

THERE WAS A FAIR

1   There was a fair into the toon,
     The lads and lasses a' were boun,
     Wi' glancin buckles o' their shoon,   [shining
     An' floories i' their waistcoats.

     Mrs GREIG and Miss ELIZABETH GREIG — D

JOHN BRUCE O' THE FORNET

A

J.W. SPENCE – G

B

John Bruce o' the Forenit

1. Ae Martmas term I gaed to the fair
   To view the sweet lassies and sniff the fresh air
   And feed wi' a mannie to ca' his third pair
   And his name's Johnnie Bruce o' the Forenit.

2. Fin I gaed hame tae this man John Bruce
   He lived o'er at Skene in a blue sklaitet hoose
   A guid hertit mannie but he lookit some cross
   Fin I gaed hame tae the Forenit.

3. The first Sunday morning were tempered at ease
   Fin oot cam' auld Johnnie wi' a flagon o' grease
   Tae rub oor horse legs frae the queets tae the knees
   They're a' cripple nags at the Forenit.

4. The heat o' the horse syne melted the grease
   An oot there cam' a swarm o' fleas
   Says we tae oorsel's It's the Plague o' the Fleas
   Sent doon on the lads at the Forenit.

5. There's tae oor gaffer a cannie auld man
   He'll neither swear at ye, curse nor damn
   There's nae eneuch o' the deevil in him
   For auld Johnnie Brisee o' the Forenit.

6. Here's tae oor foreman he comes frae Balquine
   His name is McGilvry he wrocht on the line
   He meats his horse weel, bit he hauds on the twine
   For the wark's aye ahin' at the Forenit.

7. Here's tae oor second lad a sturdy young chiel
   He sticks tae his wark and it sets him richt weel
   Bit he wisna lang hame fin he seen seemed to yield
   Tae auld Johnnie Brice o' the Forenit.

8   Here's tae oor third's man tae rant and tae reel
     Some half o' a poet some half o' a feel
     But the lasses are roon him they like him sae weel
     That he'll seen hae tae gang frae the Forenit.

9   Here's tae oor baillie, he comes frae Kinniard
     A little wee mannie and scant o' a beard
     For coortin the lasses he aye seems prepared
     And sortin' his stots at the Forenit.

10   The loon he wis feed tae advance and retire
     Atween the neep park an the auld coo byre
     But he wisna lang hame fin he seen seemed to tire
     Wi' auld Johnnie Brice o' the Forenit.

11   Here's tae oor dochter the Rose o' the Lane
     She plays the piano, and whyles wi' the men
     She gaes thro' the close rinnin tae be keepit again
     By the rovin' young lads o' the Forenit.

12   On Sunday tae the kirk she wears a fite veil
     And a yaird o' her goon ahin her does trail
     An her hair tied up like my horse tail
     Tae charm the lads at the Forenit.

13   The weather bein' bad, and the hairst bein' late
     Ae fine Sunday mornin' a ruckie we led
     The rest o' the day we gid tae oor bed
     An prayed for oor sins at the Forenit.

14   The hairst bein' deen and the weather bein' bad
     We wis a' turned oot wi' a pick and a spad
     He tore aff his jacket the auld nickum gaed mad
     Hurrah for John Bruce o' the Forenit.

Miss ANNIE SHIRER — G

C
Johnnie Bruce o' the Fornet

1   Twas at the Whitsunday term I gaed to the fair
     To view the fair lasses and get the fresh air,
     When a mannie he engaged me to ca' his third pair,
     They ca'd him Jock Bruce at the Fornet.

2   When I gaed hame to the mannie Jock Bruce,
     He bides owre in Skene in a blue-slated hoose,
     Though keen in the fair, he looked unco douce   [driving a hard bargain; pleasant
     When I gaed hame to the Fornet.

3   This cunnin' aul' deevil was temptin' to tease,
     The first Sunday mornin' wi' a flagon o' grease,
     "Grease all your horse legs frae the queets to the knees,
     For they're all cripple naigs at the Fornet."

4 The heat o' their legs soon melted the grease,
When out of the house came a swarm o' fleas
Says I to mysel', "It's the plague o' the fleas
Come doon on the young lads o' the Fornet."

5 Leslie being foreman, he comes from Balquhain,
He once was a navvy and wrocht on the line,
He fed his horse weel, but he held on the twine,
For the work was ahin' at the Fornet.

6 Tough being second, a strappin' young chiel,
To do his work it does suit him weel,
But he wasna lang hame when he thocht he would heel,
And never look back to the Fornet.

7 'Twas I being third for to romp and to reel,
A bit o' a poet and comical feel,
The lasses aroon' they did like me weel
But we'll soon win awa frae the Fornet.

8 We hae a bit baillie, they ca' him Kincaid,
A little wee mannie wi' a scunt o' a baird,
For coortin' the lasses he often preferred,
Though he sortit the stots at the Fornet.

9 We hae a bit loon to advance and retire
Frae the neep park and the aul' coo byre,
But he wasna lang hame when he thocht he would tire,
And never look back to the Fornet.

10 We hae a bit kail cook, she was no great deal,
She made our brose as hard as hail,
I think I could have done better mysel'
To aul' Jockie Bruce at the Fornet.

11 Jock Bruce had a daughter, the flower of the glen,
She played the piano, and whiles with the men,
She ran oot the close to be keppit again
By the rovin' young lads at the Fornet.

12 To the kerk ilka Sunday she wears a lang veil,
A yard of her dress behind her does trail,
She ties up her hair like my horse's tail
To charm the young lads at the Fornet.

13 The hairst being late, and the weather being bad,
He turned us oot wi' the pick and the spade,
He tore his aul' jacket, and nearly gaed mad,
And he danced and damned at the Fornet.

14 The hairst come on, wi' a scanty feed,
The first Sunday mornin', a ruck it was led,
And the rest of the day we lay in our bed
And prayed for our sins at the Fornet.

Miss BARBARA RAE — D

D

John Bruce

1   Last Martmas term I went to the fair
To view the sweet lasses and snuff the fresh air
I fee'd wi' a man to ca his third pair
They ca' him John Bruce at the corner.

2   Fan I gaed hame to that man John Bruce
He lived up at Skene in a blue sklated hoose
Sae keen in the fair but he leuket sae douce
Fan I gaed hame to the corner.

3   The first Sunday mornin' oor temper to tease
Oot cam aul' Johnnie wi' a flagon o' grease
Says Ye'll rub yer horse legs frae the queets to the knees
For they're a' cripple nags at the Fornet.

4   The heat o' the horses soon melted the grease
And oot o' their legs cam a swarm o' fleas
Thinks we to oorsels It's the plague o' the fleas
Sent doon on the lads at the corner.

5   And here's to oor gaffer a canny aul' man
He'll neither curse ye, swear nor damn
There isna enough o' the deevil in him
For aul' Johnnie Bruce at the corner.

6   Here's to oor foreman, he comes frae Balquhin
His name is McGilvray and he wrought on the line
He feeds his horse weel but he hauds on the twine
For the wark's aye ahin at the corner.

7   Here's to oor second a big sturdy chiel
He's gweed at his wark and it sets him richt weel
But he wisna lang hame till he soon seemed to yield
To auld Johnnie Bruce at the corner.

8   Noo here's to our third ane to ramp and to reel
Some pairt o' a poet, some half o' a feel
But the lasses a' roon 'im a' like him sae weel
That he'll seen win awa frae the corner.

9   Here's to oor bailie, he comes frae Kinaird
A little wee mannie, braw scant o' a beard
For courtin' the lasses he's aye been prepared
And sortin' his stirks at the fornicht.

10   The loon he was feed to advance and retire
Atween the neep park and the auld coo byre
But he wisna lang hame or he soon seemed to tire
O auld Johnnie Bruce at the corner.

11   And here's to the daughter, the flower o' the glen
She plays the piano and sports wi' the men
And rins oot o' the close to be kepit again
By the roving young lads at the corner.

12 At the kirk on Sundays she wears a lang veil
And a yard o' her dress ahin her does trail
And her hair is tied up like my horse tail
To charm the lads at the corner.

13 The hairst wis back and the weather wis bad
And ae Sunday mornin' a ruckie we led
And the rest o' the day we lay in oor bed
To pray for oor sins at the corner.

14 The hairst bein' back and the weather bein' bad
We a' set oot wi' a pick and a spade.
He tore off his jacket, the auld deevil gaed mad
Hurrah for John Bruce at the corner.

Miss BELL ROBERTSON — G

E

John Bruce o' the Fornet

1 Ae Martinmas term I gaed to the fair
To view the braw lasses and get the fresh air
I feed hame to a mannie to ca' the third pair
They ca him John Bruce o' the Fornet.

2 When I gaed hame to this man John Bruce
He bides doon in Skene in a blue slatit hoose
He's the king o' the fair but he looket sae douce
When I gaed hame to the Fornet.

3 On Sunday mornin wi' a flagon o' grease
The surly auld dievel some temper did ease
Says Rub your horse legs frae the queets to the knees
For they're a' cripple nags at the Fornet.

4 Here's to oor gaffer a gude auld chiel
Neither curses nor sweers nor looks half grim
There's nae eneuch o' the devil in him
For auld John Bruce o' the Fornet.

5 Here's to the foreman, he comes frae Aboyne
He was ance a navvy and worked on the line
He treats his horse weel but he hands on the time
For the wark's a' ahin' at the Fornet.

6 Here's to the second lad a stout strappin chiel
At his wark it sits him richt weel
We wasna lang hame when he thocht he wad heel   [run away
Frae auld Jeck Bruce o' the Fornet.

7 Here's to the third lad a rant and a reel
A bit o' a poet, some half o' a feel
But the lasses a' roon but they like him sae weel
He will soon win awa frae the Fornet.

55

8   Here's to oor baillie, they ca' him Hinny Aird
A little wee mannie some scanty o' a beard
At coortin' the braw lasses he wad rather be preferred
Afore sortin' the stots at the Fornet.

9   He feed a little loonie to advance and retire
Between the neep park and the cow byre
He wisna lang hame till he seemed to tire
O' auld John Bruce o' the Fornet.

10   Here's to oor dother, the floo'er o' the glen
She plays the piano sometimes wi' the men
Comes oot o' the close to be keepit again
By the rovin lads o' the Fornet.

11   Here's to oor kail cook, she's nae great deal
She maks the brose as hard as a heel
I think I could near dee as weel mysel'
To auld John Bruce o' the Fornet.

12   The hairst being begun we was scantily fed
Ae Sunday mornin' a ruck it was led
The neist sax days we a' lay in oor bed
And prayed for oor sins at the Fornet.

13   The hairst bein' back and the weather being bad
He turned us a' oot wi' a pick and a spad
He tore aff his jacket the auld nickum he gaed mad
And he damned and he swore at the Fornet.

E. FORSYTH – G

F

Johnnie Bruce o' the Fornet

1   I gaed to the market to get a bit fee,
A shochlin' bit mannie he comes up to me,   [shuffling
I gae a bit glint wi' the tail o' my e'e –
"Ay – jist Johnny Bruce o' the Fornet!"

2   I feed wi' the mannie to work the third pair,
For twel' poun' ten, nae a farthing mair,
And a shilling o' arles was a' he could spare,
He's a gae hard nut, is the Fornet!

3   Johnstone the foreman, he cam fae Balquhine,
He eence was a navvy and vrocht on the line,
But now he has teen to the crackin' o' twine,
And works the first pair at the Fornet.

4   And he has a dother, the pride o' the glen,
She plays the piano and coorts wi' the men,
And rins through the close to be keppit again,
By the rovin' blades o' the Fornet.

R.D. REID – D

A

Lucky Duff.

Come all ye jolly young men, And listen unto me ---

And dinna gang to Bruntie's toon The lasses for to see ---

For Lucky she's a wily ane, And she does watch the toon --

And ilka ane that she does catch, And he is fined a croon ---

JOHN QUIRRIE — G

B

Bruntie's

1 All ye rovin' young men com listen unto me,
Never gang to Bruntie's toon the lasses for to see.
Old Luckie she's a wily ane, and she does watch the toun,
And ilka lad that she does catch they are just fined a croon.

2 'Twas on a Tuesday evenin' as I was told by one,
A laddie gyaun to see the girls wi' them to get some fun
Auld Luckie growin' restless, she rose out over her bed,
And there she found a young man with her servant maid.

3 So quickly she did bolt the door, to keep it firm and fast,
And after five o'clock did ring the men appeared at last.
Crying for an open door but Luckie says, Na, na,
Ye'll need to change your road the day and to the entry go.

4 O na na, says the foreman, the brose will hardly work,
If we go to the entry we'll need the knife and fork.
But as it's only breakfast time we shan't be ill to please,
We'll take tea or coffee, butter, eggs, or cheese.

5 But if you will not open the door, the keys that ye can keep
And we'll gang till our beds again, and take another sleep.
But one of them they steppit up and sent the door in,
Good mornin', cries the prisoner, and he was obliged to run.

6 Auld Luckie she's a Christian, as ye dae likely ken,
   And she must hae a regular hoose, within the but and ben.
   Altho' she be a Christian there's one thing she'll forget
   And that's to gie the horses their sufficient meat.

7 Eight bushels a-week amongst the five is all that they dae get,
   And sometimes in the evening they get a taste o' bait.
   But it's composed o' chaff and straw and keeps them aye sae thin,
   The men they a' do swear to me the beens will cut the skin.

8 Now fare ye weel to Luckie noo and fare weel evermore
   If she goes up the high road she'll get a lockit door.
   She'll need to change her course I doot or gang where devils dwell,
   For there she can quarrel and fight in the lowest room o' h — .

A. FOWLIE — G

374

TOCHINEAL

Tochieneal

1 Come a' my young lads, ye'll mak haste and be ready
   For May twenty saxt will be here in a crack.

2 Aucht wives in a house wi' a brick separation
   I dinna nane think it will dae very weel,
   For their tongues are sae ready for to gie provocation
   There'll be nae contentment at aul' Tochineal.

JOHN ORD — G

MONYMUSK

A

As I gaed doon by Monymusk, And doon by Alford vale, A sad misfortune happened to me, Which I dinna think shame to tell Lilti du uriddle ee,

Lilti du uriddle ee,

1   As I gaed doon by Monymusk,
    And doon by Alford vale,
    A sad misfortune happened to me,
    Which I dinna think shame to tell.
        Lilti du uriddle ee,
        Lilti du uriddle ee.

JAMES F. DICKIE — G

B

1   I think it is an awful thing,
    It would provoke a saint, —
    The servant lassie aye gets the lads,
    Fin the gentry they maun want.

Miss ANNIE SHIRER — G

BETWEEN STANEHIVE AND LAURENCEKIRK

A

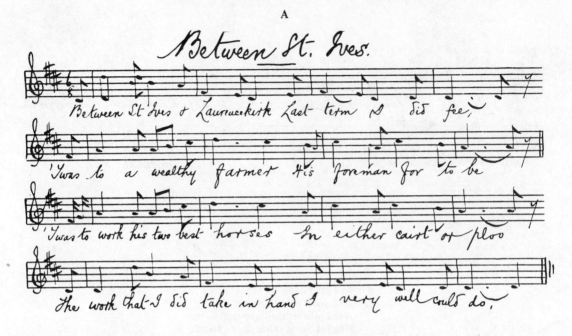

Between St. Ives.

Between St Ives & Laurencekirk Last term I did fee,
'Twas to a wealthy farmer His foreman for to be
'Twas to work his two best horses In either cairt or ploo
The work that I did take in hand I very well could do,

M.J. HILL – G

B

1   It was to Hillhead of Cairness last term I did fee;
And wi' yon wealthy fairmer his foreman for to be;
To work his twa best horses in harra, cairt or ploo;
The work which I did take in hand I very well could do.

2   I worked my horses carefully, and did my maister please,
Till some rants o' fun I did kick up which did his temper tease;   [romps
The courtin' wi' his servant girl is what he's come to know,
And I want to let the word o' this throughout the country go.

3   One night into the stable on tryst I met her there,
On purpose for to get some fun, some guid advice to gie her;
The maister he got word o' this, to the stable he cam' o'er;
And he's gien baith o' us oor leave richt o'er the stable door.

4   It's nae upon the maister that I lay all the blame;
It's upon the maiden o' the place, yon high respected dame;
It is the maiden o' the place, nae lads cam' her to see;   [farmer's daughter
She couldna see sic afa fun atween the lass and me.

5   So, come all ye jolly plooman lads, and try and mend this faut,
It's to the maiden first that ye maun court and dawt;
For if ye court the servant lass, and gang the maiden by,
Ye may be sure and very sure your terms is drawing nigh.

6   But the times are turnin' unco hard when coortin' is a crime,
For it's been in the ward since Guid kens hoo lang syne;
But at yon big hoose ayont the burn it's clean forbidden there;
So it's feein' wi' yon wealthy lad I bid you a' beware.

ANDREW DUNBAR — G

C

Between Stanehive and Laurencekirk

1   Between Stanehive and Laurencekirk at Martinmas I did fee
'Twas wi' a wealthy farmer to work I did agree.
His foremost horses for to work 'twas all I got to do
And I could manage that right well in either cairt or ploo.

2   I worked my horses carefully and did my master please,
Excepting to some bits of pranks I did his temper tease;
And the courting of the servant girl I'm bound to let you know,
For I mean to let the cause of this throughout the country go.

3   One night into the stable we happened to go there,
Expecting for to hae some lark a guid advice to gie 'er
But my master he got word o' this, to the stable he came on
And he has given us baith our leave just at the stable door.

4   It's nae the master of this toon that I lay a' the blame,
But it is the maid at that big hoose, that high-respected dame.
She knew I had my sweetheart which grieved her sore to see,
The happy moments that we spent between that girl and me.

5   Come all ye jolly ploughboys that want to mend the fault,
Be sure and court the maiden first and gae'r what you can't;
For if you court the servant first and at the maiden try
Ye may be sure the term for you is now just drawing nigh.

6   Surely the times are now hard up since courting's called a crime,
For it has been practeesèd God only knows the time.
But at yon big toon abeen the road it is forbidden there
And when ye gang to yon big toon I'll bid ye aye beware.

WILLIAM FORSYTH — G

D

Between Stonehive and Laurencekirk

1   Between Stonehive and Laurencekirk, last term I did fee
Twas with a wealthy farmer, his foreman for to be
To work his twa best horses was what I had to do
A task that I could manage weel, both in the cart and ploo.

2   I wrought his horses carefully, and did my master please,
Excepting some bits runts o' fun, that did his temper tease,
Until the month of January as you may well believe
For courtin' wi' the servant girl, we both did get our leave.

3   It was one night in the stable, on tryst I met her there
On purpose for to have some fun, and guid advice to gie her.
Our master hearing of the same, he quickly has come o'er
And he has given us both our leave, out of the stable door.

4   But it's not upon my master, that I lay all the blame
It is the maiden of the place, that high respected dame
Since no sweetheart to her did come, it grieved her heart to see
The happy moments that was spent between my love and me.

5   O sirs, I think that times are hard when coortin's ca'ed a crime
For it has been practised noo, Gude kens for fu' lang time
But yon big toon abeen the road it is forbidden there
To feeing wi' yon wealthy lad I bid you all beware.

JOHN MILNE — G

E

1   Between Stonehive and Laurencekirk
Wi' a fairmer I did fee,
And to work his twa best horses
Wi' him I did agree.

Miss ANNIE SHIRER — G

THE BOTHY LADS O' FORFAR

A
The Bothy Lads o' Forfar

1   It's ten pair upon our place,
And ten strong able men;
It takes five o' us to light a fire,
And five o' us to scran.   [scrounge
    O Earm, O Dearm,
    Fal the diddle Earm,
    O Earm, O Dearm,
    Fal the diddle ee.

2   Ae nicht we were in the tattie hoose,
Our creels were nearly fu',
When Tattie Jock cries oot, —
Hi' lads, you're nearly fu'.

3   It's ten policemen being sent for,
But only nine did come;
They werena fit to turn us about,
We were so able men.

4   It's Jocky being among us,
The blithest one I saw,
He had to leave his country,
'Cause he couldna stand the law.

5   It's now our summons' come,
And now our sentence' passed;
It's sixteen years' hard labour.
It's all the time at last.

6   As we sat on the top o' the coach,
I heard the coachboy say,
'Twas a pity to see such able men
Rolled down to Botany Bay.

7   But when we arrive at Botany Bay,
We'll send some letters home,
And tell our parents all our hardships
Since we left our native home.

JAMES M. TAYLOR — G

B

1   Ye'll hae heard o' Tattie Jock,
Likewise o' Mutton Peggie?
They had a fairm inower into Fife,
And the name o' it was Craigie.

2   And on the fairm they kept ten pair,
Likewise ten able-bodied men;
When five cam' in to licht the fire,
The ither five gaed oot tae scran.

D.R. McKENZIE — G

THE GUISE O' TOUGH

A

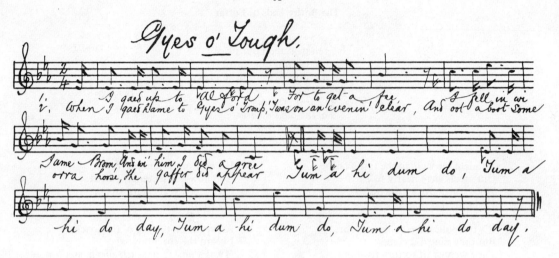

Gyes o' Tough.

1. When I gaed up to Alford, For to get a fee, I fell in wi
2. When I gaed hame to Gyes o' Tough, 'Twas on an evenin' clear, And oot aboot some

Jame Broon, And wi' him I did agree, Tum a hi dum do, Tum a
orra hoose, the gaffer did appear

hi do day, Tum a hi dum do, Tum a hi do day.

1   I gid up tae Alford
     For to get a fee
     I fell in wi Jamie Broon
     And wi' him I did agree.
         Tum a hi dum do,
         Tum a hi do day,
         Tum a hi dum do,
         Tum a hi do day.

2   I engaged wi Jamie Broon,
     In the year o' ninety-one
     Tae ging hame an ca' his second pair,
     And be his orra man.

3   When I gaed hame tae Gyes o' Tough,
     'Twis on an evening clear
     And oot aboot some orra hoose,
     The gaffer did appear.

4   I'm the maister o' this place,
     And that's the mistress there
     And ye'll get plenty cheese and bread,
     And plenty mair tae spare.

5   I sat and ate cheese and breed,
     Till they did roon me stare
     And fegs I thoucht it wis time,
     Tae ging doon and see my pair.

6   Fin I gaed tae the stable,
     My pairie for to view
     Fegs they were a dandy pair,
     A chestnut and a blue.

7   On the followin' mornin',
     I gaed tae the ploo,
     But lang, lang or loosin' time,
     My pairie gard me rue.

8   My ploo wisna workin,
     She widna throw the fur
     The gaffer says There's a better ane,
     At the smiddy tae ging for.

9   When I got hame the new ploo,
     She pleased me unka weel
     But I thoucht she wid be better,
     If she hid a cuttin wheel

10   I wrought awa' a month or twa,
     Wi' unka little clatter
     Till I played up some nasty tricks,
     And brook the tatty-chapper.   [potato-masher

11   The gaffer he got word o' this,
     And orders did lay doon
     That if I did the like again
     He wid pit me frae the toon.

12 We hiv a gallant bailie,
   And Wallace is his name
   And he can fair red up the kye,
   When he taks doon the caimb.

13 We hiv a little bailie,
   And Jamieson is his name
   And he's gane doon tae Alford,
   And raised an ava fame.

14 He's gane doon tae Charlie Watt,
   For tae get a dram
   But lang, lang or I won doon,
   The laddie couldna stand.

15 We hiv a gallant kitchie lass,
   And Simpson is her name
   And for tae tell her pedigree
   I railly wad think shame.

16 She dresses up on Sunday,
   Wi' her heid abeen the level
   Wi' twa raw o' ivory
   That wad scare the vera devil.

17 Now my song is ended
   And I won't sing any more
   And if ony o' ye be offended,
   You can walk outside the door.

M. J. HILL – G

B

When I gaed to the sta—ble My pairie for to view—— To my ey die ow die ey die ow die reydie doo a dee.

JAMES ANGUS – G

C

The Guise o' Tough

1   As I gaed up tae Alford
For to get a fee
I fell in wi' Jamie Broon
And wi' him I did agree.
Dum a hie dum doo,
Dum a hie dum dae
Dum a hie dum doo,
Dum a hie dum dae.

2   I engaged wi' Jamie Broon
In the year o' ninety one
Tae gang and ca' his second pair
And be his orra man.

3   Fan I gaed hame tae Guise o' Tough
'Twas on an evenin' clear
An' oot aboot some orra hoose
The gaffer did appear.

4   He says I'm the maister o' this place
And that's the mistress there
And ye'll get plenty cheese and breid
And plenty mair tae spare.

5   I sat and ate at cheese and breid
Till they on me did stare
An' fegs I thocht that it wis time
Tae gang and see my pair.

6   I gaed intae the stable
My pairie for to view
An fegs they were a dandy,
A chestnut and a blue.

7   On the followin' mornin'
I gaed tae the ploo
But lang lang or lowsin time
My pairie gard me rue.

8   My ploo she wisna workin weel,
She widna throw the fur
The gaffer said there wis a better ane
At the smiddy tae gang for.

9   Fan I got hame my new ploo
She pleased me unco weel
But I thocht she wid be better
If she hid a cuttin' wheel.

10   I wrocht awa a month or twa
Wi' unco little clatter
Till I played up some nesty tricks
And broke the tattie chapper.

11   The gaffer he got word o' this
And orders did lay doon
That if ever I did the like again
He'd pit me fae the toon.

12   We hae a gallant bailie
And Wallace is his name
An' he can fair redd up the kye
Fin he tak's doon the kaim.

13   We hae a little bailie
And Jamieson's his name
And he's gaen doon tae Alford
And raised an awfu' fame.

14   He's gane doon tae Charlie Watt's
For tae get a dram
But lang, lang or I gaed there
The laddie couldna stan.

15   We hae a gallant kitchie lass
And Simpson is her name
And for tae tell her pedigree
I really wid think shame.

16   She dresses up on Sunday
Wi' her heid abeen the level
Wi' twa raw o' ivory
Wid scare the very d— .

17   Now my song is ended
And I won't sing any more
And any of you are offended
You can walk outside the door.

Miss KATE MITCHELL — G

GEORDIE WILLIAMSON

1   As I gaed up tae Aikey Fair
Twas on a day tae fee
I met in wi' Geordie Williamson
Wi' him I did agree.
   Hoch on, yankee doodle,
   Yankee doodle dee.

2   When I gaed hame tae Geordie's
Twas on a nicht sae clear
When oot aboot some orra hoose
The gaffer did appear.

3   Gang ye awa up tae the hoose
And get some cheese and breid
For that ye needna spier,
I'm the gaffer o' this toon,
And this the mistress here.

4   Twa or three weeks did pass by
Wi' unco little clatter
Till I began my orra pranks
And broke the tattie chapper.

5   We had a little bailie,
His name was called Jim
He aye ran roon and roon the toon
And made an awful din.

6   We had an auld gardner
His name was called Ned
He ran upon twa oxter staffs
He had a broken leg.

7   We had a big kitchie woman
Her name I think was Jean
She hadna haen her maidenhood
In the place where it should hae been.

8   Ae day as we gaed tae the plough
We chanced tae pass her by
And a' her orra ornaments
Made the chestnut for to shy.

9   She thocht she wis an awful swell
Wi' her heid abune the level
And a double row o' false teeth
To fleg the devil.

Miss ANNIE SHIRER — G

I LEFT INVERQUHOMERY

1   I left Inverquhomery and gaed to New Deer
To plunge in the bogs wi' a bull and a steer.

2   Auchmaliddie cam' to me and bade me ca awa
But deil care o' that the pleuchie gaed in twa,
The owsen gaed hame wi' the half o' the vrack
And he followeed aifter wi' the lave on his back.

JOHN JAFFRAY — G

NEWHILLS

A

Newmill

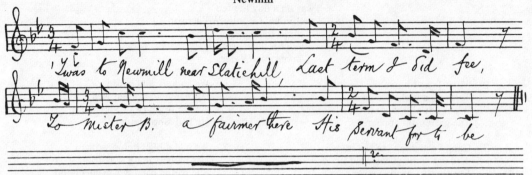

'Twas to Newmill near Slatiehill, Last term I did fee,
To Mister B. a fairmer there His servant for to be

1 It was to Newmill near Slettiehill
Last term I did fee
To Mr B. a farmer there
His servant for to be.

2 I hadna been a week come hame
Till I did plainly see
The tables they were rather bare
They were none suit for me.

3 The bread was thick, the brose was thin
And the broth they were like bree
I chased the barley roon the plate
And a' I got was three.

4 So unsuccessful was my search
My spoon I then threw doon
The knife and fork were seldom seen
But in the carpet room.

5 Our humble cot as you may see
And it stands bleak and bare
And the chuckie hoose stands west a wee   [hen
For to complete the square.

6 And Mr Langnecks is a man
Who can both cheat and lee
And tries to put his servants off
Withoot their penny fee.

7 And he wad sell his chaff and stra
The black silk goons to buy
He wad sell the water in his dam
If any one wad buy.

8 Three hundred stones of hay we cut
And drank three quarts of beer
Two and sixpence was the cost
Oor medicine wasna dear.

9 Oor mistress she the silk goons wore
As true as I do say
And orders to the master gave
To give us every day.

10 When we were to the barn sent
To raip and draw the straw
She at the keyhole o' the door
To hear what we might say.

11 And when her daughters were with us
She did them well regard
And always kept her eye on them
Till twelve o'clock at night.

12 Ae day my horse did lose a shoe
While grazing on the lea
And I was put to seek the same
The feck o' one whole day.

13 Wi' blessed hand and happy fit   [lucky foot
The shoe I then did find
And safely to my master brought
To ease his troubled mind.

14 Now fare ye weel Mr Langnecks
And to your daughters three
But the turkey hen that lives her lane
I think I'll let her be.

15 And fare ye weel Mr Langnecks
Nae langer will I bide
And I will steer my course again
Back to bonnie Deeside.

ALEXANDER ROBB – G

B

Newmill.

'Twas to Newhills, near Sclatie Mills, Last term I did fee;
To Mr. — B. — a farmer there His servant for to be;

JOHN MOWAT — G

C

Sclatie Mill.

The breid was thick, the brose was thin, The broth they war like bree;
I chased the barley roon the plate, An' only gat bit three.

Mrs MARGARET GILLESPIE and GEORGE F. DUNCAN — G

D

Newmill

1 It was to Newmill near Sklatyhill
  Last term I did fee
  To Mr. B. a farmer there
  His servant for to be.

2 I hadna been a week come hame
  Till I did plainly see
  The tables they were rather bare
  They were nae suit for me.

3 The breid was thick the brose was thin
  And the broth they were like bree
  I chased the barley roon the plate
  And a' I got was three.

4 So unsuccessful was my search
  My spoon I then threw doon
  The knife and fork was seldom seen
  But in the carpet room.

5 Oor humble cot as you may see
  And it stands bleak an' bare
  And the chuckie hoose stands west a wee
  For to complete the square.

6 And Mr Langneuks is a man
  Who can both cheat and lee
  And tries to put his servants off
  Withoot their penny fee.

7 And he wad sell the chaff and strae
  The black silk goons to buy
  He wad sell the water in the dam
  If ony ane wad buy.

8 The hinder stack of hay we sent   [last
  We drank three quarts of beer
  Two and sixpence was the cost
  Oor medicine wasna dear.

9 Oor mistress she the silk goon wore
  As true as I do say
  And orders to the master gave
  To give us every day.

10 When we were to the barn sent
   To raip and draw the strae
   She at the keyhole o' the door
   To hear what we might say.

11 And when her daughters were with us
   She did them well regard
   And always kept her eye on them
   Till twelve o'clock at night.

12 One day my horse did lose a shoe
   While grazing on the lea
   And I was put to seek the same
   The feck o' one whole day.

13 Wi' blessed head and happy fit
   The shoe I then did find
   And safely to my master brought
   To ease his troubled mind.

14 Now fare ye weel Mr Langneuks
   And tae your daughters three
   But the turkey hen that lives her lane
   I think I'll lat her be.

15 And fare ye weel Mr. Langneuks
   Nae langer will I bide
   And I will steer my course again
   Back to bonnie Deeside.

Source unrecorded — G

382

STRALOCH

1 All you that are at liberty, I pray you all draw near,
  And listen to my story, it's what you soon shall hear.
  It was at the last Martinmas, I went unto the fair,
  I did engage wi' Straloch, to work the second pair.

Source unrecorded — G

ON THE 16th O' OCTOBER

a

On the 16th October in the year 58,
I went to the ploo, nae doots to haud straucht,
Mysel' in good humour, my horses the same,
I ploo'd till eleiven, and then I cam' hame,
Gaed Nell and Nansy some corn to eat,
An' syne took a besom and swypet my feet.   [wiped
Then to the barn I quickly withdrew,
To bundle some straw, but oh, what a stew!
When denner was over to the stable we went,
To clean up oor horses it was oor intent.
Oor orders fae Dawson for plooin' again,
Nae sinsheen, but cloody and some draps o' rain.
Noo my day's wark is finisht, and I'll hae a smoke,
An' I'm boun' for my bed, for it's past nine o'clock.

b

On the 16th o' October

On the saxteent o' October, the year 68,
I gaed to the ploo, 'twas for to haud straucht;
Mysel' in good humour, my horses the same,
I ploo'd till eleevin, an' syne I cam' hame;
Gied Mallie and Jessie a bit o' a treat;
I syne took a besom an' swypet my feet.

Rev. JAMES FORREST — G

DRUMDELGIE

A

Drumdelgie

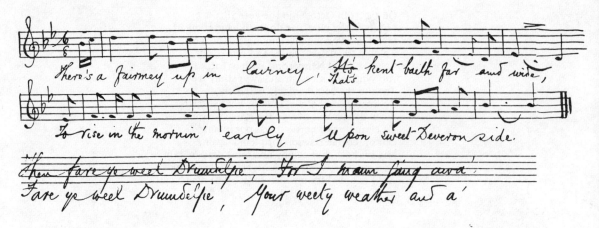

1 There's a farmie up in Cairnie,
   That's kent baith far and wide,
   Tae rise i' the mornin' early
   Upon sweet Deveronside.

2 At five o'clock we quickly rise,
   And hurry doon the stair,
   To get oor horses a' weel corned,
   Likewise to straught their hair.

3 Then after that we usher oot
   Intae the kitchen goes,
   To get some breakfast for oorsels,
   Which is generally brose.

4 We've scarcely got oor brose weel supped
   And gien oor pints a tie   [laces
   When the gaffer shouts Hallo, my lads
   The hour is drawin' nigh.

5 The mill gaes on at sax o'clock
   To gie us a strait wark
   And sax o' us we mak' to her
   Or ye could wring oor sark.

6 And when the water is put aff
   We hurry doon the stair,
   To get some quarters thro' the fan
   Till daylight does appear.

7 When daylight it begins to dawn
   The sky begins to clear
   The gaffer shouts Hallo my lads
   You'll stay nae langer here.

8 There's sax o' you'll gae to the plough
   And twa can ca the neeps,
   And the oxen they'll be after you
   Wi' stray raips roon their queets.

9 Oh when we a' were gyaun oot
   And drivin' oot tae yoke,
   The snaw dang on sae thick and fast
   That we were like to choke.

10 The snaw dang on sae thick and fast
    The plough she widna go
    And cairtin' it commenced again
    Amid the frost and snow.

11 Oor horses bein' but young and sma'
    The shafts wid hardly fill
    And after not the saddler lad   [needed the whip
    To pit them up the hill.

12 But we will sing oor horses' praise,
    Though they be young and sma'
    For they mak' a feel o' their neiper toons [show
    That gang sae bonnie and braw.   up

13 Sae fare ye weel Drumdelgie
    For I maun gang awa'
    Sae fare ye weel Drumdelgie
    Your weety weather and a'.

14 Fare ye weel Drumdelgie,
    I bid you all adieu,
    I leave ye as I got ye —
    A damned unceevil crew!

W. MASSIE — G

B
Drumdelgie

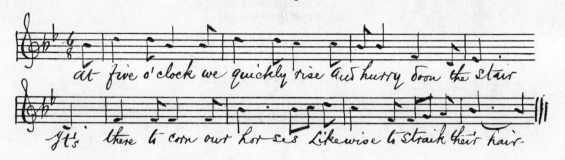

At five o'clock we quickly rise And hurry doon the stair

It's there to corn oor horses Likewise to straik their hair.

1 At five o'clock we quickly rise
And hurry doon the stair
It's there to corn oor horses
And likewise straik their hair.

2 After workin half an hoor
To the kitchen each one goes
There to get his breakfast
Which is generally brose.

3 After we have swallowed them
And gien our pints a tie
The foreman cries Hullo my lads,
The hour is drawin' nigh.

4 At sax o'clock the mull's put on
To gie us a' some wark
It taks four o' us to mak to her
Till we could wring oor sark.

5 The daylicht it begins to peep
And the sky begins to clear
The foreman he cries oot, "My lads
We can stay nae langer here.

6 "First and second will ca' the grain
Third and fourth gang to the ploo
Fifth and six will ca' the neeps
And the orra men will full and poo."

7 Pittin on oor harness
And turnin' oot to yoke
The snaw dung on sae very hard
That we were like to choke.

8 The frost had been sae very hard
The ploo she widna go
And sae, oor cairtin' days commenced
Among the frost and snow.

9 Our horses they were young and sma'
The shafts they didna fill
And they aften not the saddler
To help them up the hill.

10 But we will praise oor horses
Altho' they be but sma'
For they'll outshine Shevado's anes
That tip the road sae braw.   [trip along

GAVIN GREIG Jr — G

C
The Big Toon in Carnie

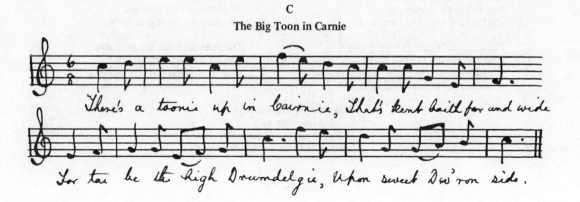

There's a toonie up in Cairnie, That's kent baith far and wide

For tae be the High Drumdelgie, Upon sweet Dev'ron side.

73

Song No. 384

1 There's a placie up in Carnie,
   It's kent baith far and wide
   To be the high Drumdelgie
   Upon swet Dever-side.

2 It's twa oh you will gang tae the plough
   The rest had tae the nips
   The owsen the'll be after you
   When they eat up there nips.

Mrs WALKER — D

D
Drumdelgie

To the tune of 378 *The Guise o' Tough* B

1 Come all ye jolly ploughman lads
   And listen unto me
   And I'll sing a sang to you
   Wi muckle mirth and glee.
   Wi' my tiedy owdy,
   Eidy owdy, eidy, owdy, aye.

2 We brawly rise at five o'clock
   We hurry doon the stair
   For to gie wir horses corn
   And brawly straucht their hair.

3 Four o' you'll gang tae the plough
   And twa'll gang tae the neeps
   And the owsen they'll be after you
   When they get on their theets.

4 The snaw dung on sae very hard
   The plough it widna go
   Then the cairtin it began
   Through the frost and snow.

5 The beasties bein' sae very sma'
   The trams they hardly filled
   And they often not the saddle
   For tae help them up the hill.

6 Fare ye weel Glen Bervy
   For I maun gang awa
   But ye'll tak the shine out o' Reid's horse,
   Though they be but young and sma.

JAMES ANGUS — G

E

Drumdelgie

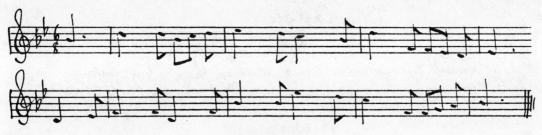

Miss H. RAE — G

F

Drumdelgie

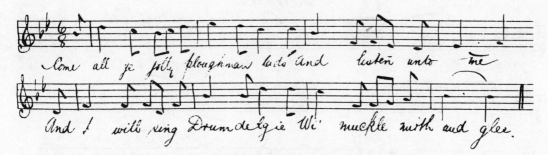

Come all ye jolly ploughman lads And listen unto me

And I will sing Drumdelgie Wi' muckle mirth and glee.

ALEX MURISON — G

G

Drumdelgie

ARTHUR BARRON — G

H

Drumdelgie.

H. ANGUS — G

I

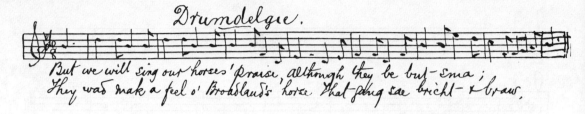

Drumdelgie.

But we will sing our horses' praise, although they be but sma;
They wad mak a feel o' Broadland's horse That geng sae bricht & braw,

JAMES GREIG — G

J

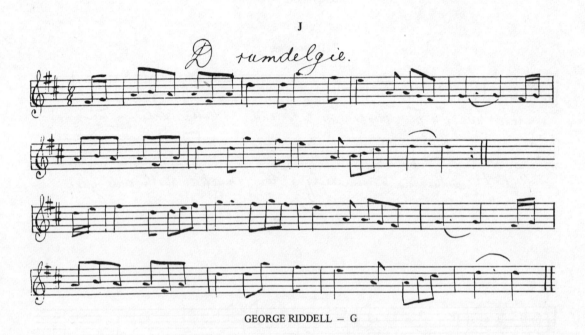

Drumdelgie.

GEORGE RIDDELL — G

K

Drumdelgie.

At six o' clock we quickly rise And rumble doon the stair . . .

It's there to corn oor horses, Likewise to comb their hair

Wi' my airie iddle dum dadium, a riddle dum dayril ae

J. DUNLOP — G

L

W. McC. SMITH — G

M

J. SCOTT SKINNER — G

N

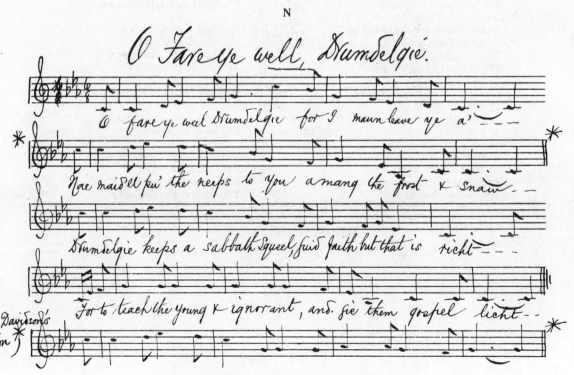

DAVID THOMSON and Miss VIOLET DAVIDSON — G

77

O
Drumdelgie

1   Come all ye jolly hireman lads,
Whatever that you be,
And we will sing Drumdelgie
Wi' muckle mirth and glee.

2   A farmer up in Cairnie,
He's kent baith far and wide,
To be the biggest Drumdelgie
On a' sweet Deveronside.

3   The farmer o' that muckle toon
He is baith hard and sair
The coorsest day that ever blaws
The servants got their share.

4   At five o'clock we quickly rise
And hurry doon the stair;
To get oor horses a' weel kaimed
And likewise straucht their hair.

5   . . . . we then
Into the kitchen goes,
To get some breakfast for ourselves,
Which is generally brose.

6   Gin we get a' oor breakfast
And gie oor pints a tie,
The overseer cries, Hullo my boys,
The hour is drawing nigh.

7   At sax o'clock the mull's put on
To gie us a' straight wark
There's eicht o' us does mak' to her
Till ye could wring oor sark.

8   Frae six o'clock till nearly eight
There is no interval,
There's twelve o' us gets wark at her
At a' that we can sprawl.   [struggle

9   As seen's the mull she is put off,
We hurry up the stair
To get some quarters thro' the fan
Till daylight does appear.

10   As seen's the skies begin to clear
The daylight does appear
The overseer cries, Hullo my lads,
Ye'll stay no longer here.

11   There's eicht o' you'll gang to the ploo,
And twa to ca' the neeps,
And the oxen they'll be aifter you
When they ate oot their neeps.

12   Puttin' on oor harness,
And drivin' oot to yoke,
The snaw blew on so very thick
That we was like to choke.

13   The snaw blew on so very thick
The plough she wadna go,
And then the cairtin' did commence
Among the frost and snow.

14   Our horses bein' but young and sma'
The shafts they didna fill,
They often noat the saddler
To draw them up the hill.

15   But we will praise oor horses
Altho' they be but sma',
They made a feel o' the Brodlin horse
That gaed mair full and braw.

16   We maun neither curse nor ban,
It is oor maister's law,
And gin ye speak profanely
Ye'll jist be putten awa'.

17   We'll gang doon to Huntly town
And get upon the spree,
And then upon the country
Oor lasses for to see.

18   So fare ye weel Drumdelgie,
For I maun gang awa',
Fare ye weel Drumdelgie,
Your coorse weather and a'.

ALEXANDER GLENNIE — G

P
Drumdelgie

1 Come all ye jolly plooman lads
   And listen unto me
   And I will sing Drumdelgie
   Wi' muckle mirth and glee.

2 There's a farmer up in Cairness
   It's kent baith far and wide
   That muckle toon Drumdelgie
   Upon sweet Deveron side.

3 At five o'clock we quickly rise
   And hurry doon the stair
   To get oor horses corned
   Likewise to straucht the hair.

4 Then hauf an oor amang oor horse
   We to the kitchen goes
   To get some breakfast for oorselves
   Which is generally brose.

5 And when the breakfast is put owre
   We gie oor pints a tie
   The overseer cries oot "My lads
   The hour is drawin' nigh."

6 At sax o'clock the mill's put on
   To gie us a' stricht wark
   And sax o' us to mak' to her
   Till you could wring oor sark.

7 Frae sax o'clock till nearly aucht
   There's ne'er an interval
   There's ten o' us gets wark at her
   At a' that we can spaul.

8 When the water is put aff
   It's up the stair we steer
   To get some quarters through the fan
   Till daylicht does appear.

9 And when the sky begins to clear
   And daylight does appear
   The overseer cries oot "My lads
   We'll stay nae langer here.

10 "Sax o' you'll gang to the ploo
   And twa'll ca' the neeps
   And the ousen they'll be after you
   When they get on their sheats."

11 Putting on oor harness
   To get them on to yoke
   The snaw blew so very thick
   That we were like to choke.

12 The horses being baith young and sma
   The shafts they widna fill
   They often need the saddler
   To drive them up the hill.

13 The snow blew on so very thick
   The plough she widna go
   We had to start the cartin'
   Among the frost and snow.

14 But we will praise oor horses
   Though they be young and sma'
   They tak the shine aff Broadlins
   That gang sae neat and braw.

15 We'll gang doon to Huntly
   And we'll get on the spree
   And syne we'll cross the country
   Oor lasses for to see.

16 So farewell Drumdelgie
   For I am gaun awa'
   So farewell Drumdelgie
   Your weetie weather and a'.

Mrs THOM — G

Q
Drumdelgie

1 Come all ye jolly ploughman lads
Come listen until me
I will sing Drumdelgie
Wi' muckle mirth and glee.

2 There's a farm up in Cairnie
It's kent fae far and wide
To be the hash o' Drumdelgie
On bonnie Deveron side.

3 Five o'clock that we do rise
And hurry doon the stair
To get the horses a' weel corned
And likewise straucht their hair.

4 Then we a' leave the stable
And to the kitchen goes
To get some breakfast for oorselves
Which is generally brose.

5 But we've scarcely got oor breakfast
And gi'en oor pints a tie
When the gaffer he says: "Noo my lads
The time is drawin' nigh."

6 At sax o'clock the mill goes on
Which gars us a' start wark
And acht o' his gets wark at her
Till we could wring oor sark.

7 Acht o' his gets wark at her
Jist a' 'it we can sprawl
Fae sax o'clock till nearly acht
Withoot an interval.

8 And when the water is put off
We hurry up the stair
To get some quarters through the fan
Till daylight does appear.

9 When the day begins to dawn
The sky begins to clear
The gaffer he says: "Noo my lads
We'll stay nae langer here.

10 "Sax o' you gang to the ploo
And four gang to the neeps
The oxen they'll be after you
When they ate up their neeps."

11 Then throwin' on the harness
And drawin' to the yoke
The storm cam on sae very fast
That we were like tae choke.

12 The storm cam on sae very fast
The plough she wadna go
So we had to start the cartin'
Amid the frost and snow.

13 Oor horses were sae young and sma
The shafts they hardly fill
They aften needs the saddler
To drive them up the hill.

14 But we maun praise oor ain horse
Altho they be but sma
They mak' a fule o' Broadland's horse
That goes sae keen and braw.

15 Drumdelgie keeps a Sunday school
And faith I think he's richt
To teach the bairns a' the truth
And show them Gospel licht.

16 But fare ye weel Drumdelgie
When I am gaun awa
Fare ye weel ye muckle toon
Coorse weather and a'.

JAMES MORRISON — G

R

Drumdelgie

1 Come all ye servants far and near
Come listen unto me,
An' I'll sing you Drumdelgie
Wi' muckle mirth and glee.

2 The maister o' yon mickle toon
He is baith hard and sair,
The cauldest day that ever blaws
His servants have their share.

3 As soon's the water is put off
Then up the stair we rin,
To get some quarters throw the fan
Till daylight does come in.

4 They sometimes no't the saiddler
To help them up the hill.

5 For they mak' a feel o' Broadlan's horse
That gang sae full and braw.

6 We maun neither curse nor ban,
It is oor maister's law,
An' gin we speak profanity
We'll a' be pitten awa'.

7 But we'll go up to Huntly,
An' we'll get on the spree,
Then out upon the country
Our lasses for to see.

8 Fare ye well, Drumdelgie,
Nae langer will I bide,
An' I am gaun the road I cam'
To bonnie Bogieside.

ALEXANDER ROBB — G

S

Drumdelgie

1 O ken ye o' Drumdelgie's toon
Where a' the crack lads go
Strabogie braw in a' her boun's
A bigger canna show.

2 We pelt nae there wi wearie flail
The lang dark mornin' through
Oor mullie seen macks strae enough
To fill its hungry moo.

3 The gaffer lang afore daylight
Comes roon an' cries Hullo
Hullo my boys ye've got your grub
It's time to yock the ploo.

4 Thr'll aught o' you gae to the ploo
An' twa will caw the neeps
An' ye owsen loons ye'll follow tee
When ye get on your theets.

JOHN MILNE — G

81

T

Drumdelgie

1 There's a farmer up in Cairnie,
   He's kent both far and wide
   To beat the drum at Delgaty
   On bonny Deveron side.

2 There's six o' you will gae to the plough,
   And twa will ca' the neeps,
   The ousen will be after you
   When they get on their theats.

ALEXANDER DUNCAN — D

U

1 Syne after workin' half an hour,
   To the kitchen each one goes;
   It's there to get oor breakfast,
   Which is generally brose.

Source unrecorded — G

385

THERE'S A SET O' FARMERS HERE ABOUT

1 There's a set o' farmers here about,
   The like o' them ye winna get
   'Tween Mormond and the sea, man.

2 But to the farmer here's a toss,
   That uses well his men and horse,
   And carries on the wark wi' force,
   To win the penny fee.

3 They yoke at sax and lowse at ten,
   And then at twa they do the same;
   At sax at nicht comes whistlin' hame,
   And that's the boy for me.

Miss BELL ROBERTSON — G

SWAGGERS

A

Swaggers.

Come all ye jolly ploughmen lads that whistles thro' the fair, Beware o' gaun to Swaggers, He'll be at Porter Fair;

He'll be aye lauch-lauchin', It's he'll be lauchin' there, And he'll hae on the blithest face in a' Porter Fair.

1   Come all ye gallant heroes I pray you'll have a care
    Beware o' meetin' Swaggers, he'll be in Porter Fair
    He'll be aye lauchin, he'll be aye lauchin there
    An' he'll hae on the blithest face in a' Porter Fair.

2   Wi' his fine horse and harness sae weel's he gar ye true
    But if you come to Auchterless so sair's he'll gar ye rue
    He'll be aye fret frettin', he'll be aye frettin' there
    And he'll gie you regulations that's worn threadbare.

3   He will tell you o' some plooin' match that's nae owre far awa'
    And gin ye clean your harness boys ye'r sure to beat them a'
    For my tackle's gained the prize before at every country show
    And if you do lat it fall back you'll be thocht little o'.

4   There's a pair o' blues that leads the van, so nimbly as they go
    A pair o' browns that follows them that never yet said no
    A wee bit shalt that ca'as the neeps an o' but it is sma
    It's Swaggers will declare to you it's stronger than them a'.

5   Now Swaggers in the harvest time will have too much ado
    To twa three o' the jovial lads that drives his cart and ploo
    But he'll gang on some twenty where people doesna him ken
    And he'll engage some harvest hands and bring them far frae hame.

6   He will tell them a fine story how little is to do
    And getting them for little fee is a' his pride I true
    He'll be aye laugh, laughing, he'll be aye laughing there
    And he'll hae on the blithest face in a' Porter Fair.

7   He will say unto the foremost man Keep aye the eident grin
    And dinna lat the orra lads stan idle at the end
    For I pay you all good wages and so you must go on
    And when you are not able there's another when you're done.

8   He will say unto the girlies when they are going back
    Step hardy up my girlies, gie them nae time to sharp
    But now the cuttin's over and we must try to lead
    And mony a curious plan he'll try for to come muckle speed.

9   But syne the wind and rain comes on and dabbles a' oor stooks   [bedraggles
    And we must run from field to field for to get them replaced
    And when that we go to the raipes he'll get up wi' a brawl
    Play in the twine my girlies you're sure to beat them a'.

10   But now the sheaves are all got in and formed in the stack
       And syne the windy days are come when we must hunt the brock   [badger
       We must hunt the brock my boys wi' mony a frown and fret
       And Swaggers cries "Come on my lads, it's like for to be wet."

11   But now the thack is all put on, the ricks have got a snod
       The harvest hands wi' bundles big when they must pad the road
       They must pad the road my boys and wander through the snow
       And they hae sworn a solemn oath they'll ne'er come back ava.

12   Martmas it will be here, my fee into my pouch
       So merrily as I will sing, in I were oot o' the tyrant's clutch
       For he is the baddest master that ever I did serve
       And if ye'll no believe me ne'er mind my observe.

JOHN MOWAT – G

B

Swaggers.

Come all ye jolly ploughman lads that warbles thro' the fair, Beware o' gaun to Swaggers, He'll be at Porter Fair,
He'll be aye lauch lauchin', It's he'll be lauchin' there, And he'll hae on the blithest face he a' Porter Fair.

1   Come all ye jolly ploughman lads that whistles thro' the fair,
      Beware o' gyaun to Swaggers, he'll be in Porter Fair.
      He'll be aye lauch-lauchin', it's he'll be lauchin' there
      And he'll ha'e on the blithest face in a' Porter Fair.

2   He'll tell ye a fine story sae little's ye'll hae adee
      And aye he'll call the ither gill – get them for little fee;
      And aye he'll call the ither gill until he get ye fou,
      And gin ye gang to Swaggers sae seen's he'll gar ye rue.

3   He'll tell ye o' some plooin' match that isna far awa',
      And gin ye clean your harness weel ye're sure to beat them a';
      For it has gained the prize before at a' the country shows
      And gin that ye lat it fa' back ye'll be thocht little o'.

4   It's a pair o' blues that leads the van, sae nimbly as they go
      A pair o' broons that follows them who never yet said no.
      A wee bit shiltie ca's the neeps and oh it is but sma'
      But Swaggers he will gar ye trew it's stronger than them a'.

5   It's Swaggers in the harvest time, he's got too much to do,
      A twa three jovial laddies that ca's the cairt and ploo;
      But he'll gang on some twenty miles where people disna him ken,
      And there he'll fee his harvest hands and bring them far frae hame.

6   He'll tell them a fine story sae little's ye hae adee,
     And aye he'll call the ither gill get them for little fee;
     And aye he'll call the ither gill until he get ye fou,
     And gin ye gang to Swaggers sae seen's he'll gar ye rue.

7   He says unto the foreman Keep aye the steady grin,
     And dinna lat the orra lads stan' idle at the en';
     For I pay ye a' good wages and so ye must get on,
     And gin ye binna able there's another when ye're done.

8   He says unto the girlies as they are comin' back
     Come on my girls go hardy up ere they get time to sharp.
     But now the cuttin's ended and we're begun to lead
     And mony's the curious plan we try for to come muckle speed.

9   But now it is all in and formed in the stack
     And now the windy days are come when we maun hunt the brock
     When we maun hunt the brock, my boys, when we maun hunt the brock,
     And aye he cries, Come on my boys, I fear it will ding on.

10 Now the harvest's ended and the fee into our pouch
     Sae merrily as we'll tramp the road we're oot o' the tyrant's clutch.
     Sae merrily as we'll tramp the road for we're oot o' the tyrant's clutch
     And we'll gang nae mair to Swaggers sae sair's he gars ye rue.

ALEX MURISON — G

C

Swaggers.

A pair of blues that leads the van, sae nimble as they go,
A pair of broons that follows them that never yet said no.
A little shaltie ca's the neeps, And she is wondrous sma',
But Wattie he declares to me She's stronger than them a'.

Miss M. RITCHIE — G

D
Swaggers

1   Come all ye jolly ploughboys, that whistle through the glen,
    Beware on going to Swaggers, for he'll be at Porter Fair.
    He'll be aye lauch lauchin', he'll be aye lauchin' here,
    An' he'll hae on the blithest face, in a' Porter Fair.

2   Wi' fine horse and harness, sae sair he'll gar ye true,
    Bit fin ye come to Auchterless, sae sair's he'll gar ye rue.
    He'll be aye fret frettin', he'll be aye frettin' there,
    He'll tell ye his regulations, they're growin' unco bare.

3   A pair o' blues that leads the van, sae nimbly as they go,
    A pair o' broons that follows them, that never yet said no.
    The aul' black shalt that ca's the neeps and oh it is but sma',
    But an ye believe fat Swaggers says, it's stronger than them a'.

4   Swaggers in the harvest time, he's got so much to do,
    Wi' twa or three jovial laddies, that ca's his cairt and ploo,
    That he'll ging on some twenty mile, far people dinna him ken,
    An' he will engage his harvest han's, an' bring them far frae hame.

5   He'll say unto our foremost man, Keep aye the steady grin,
    An' dinna lat the orra lads stan' idle at the hin;
    I pay ye a' guid wages, so now ye must get on,
    An' gin ye binna able, there's anither when ye're done.

6   He says unto our girlies, as they are goin' back,
    Mak' haste ye an' get on, my girls, gie them nae time to sharp.
    Bit noo the cuttin's over, an' we maun try to lead,
    An' mony a queer plan's been tried for to come muckle speed.

7   Bit noo the sheaves they are all in, and formèd into stacks,
    An' noo the windy days is come, when we maun hunt the brock,
    When we maun hunt the brock, my boys, wi' mony a fraul an' fret,
    An' Swaggers he will say Come on, it's like for to be weet.

8   But Martinmas is worn on, my fee's into my pouch,
    An' merrily, merrily as I sing, I'm oot o' the tyrant's clutch.
    He is as bad a maister as ever I did sair,
    An' gin ye dinna me believe, never mind ye this observe.

Mrs DUNCAN — G

E

Swaggers

1 Come all ye swaggering heroes
I pray ye have a care
Beware o' going to Swaggers
For he'll be in Porter Fair.

2 He'll be aye lauch lauchin'
He'll be aye lauchin there
And he'll hae on the blythest face
In a' Porter Fair.

3 Wi his fine horse an harness
As he will gar ye true
But when ye gang tae Auchterless
Sae sair he'll gar ye rue.

4 He'll be aye fret frettin'
He'll be aye frettin there
He'll show ye a' his regulations
They're worn threadbare.

5 A pair o' broons they lead the van
Sae nimbly as they go
A pair o' blacks come after them
That never yet said no.

6 A wee bit shaltie ca's the neeps
An oh! but it is sma'
But Swaggers he'll declare to you
'Tis stronger than them a'.

7 He will tell you o' some plooin' match
That isna far awa'
And gin ye clean yer harness richt
Ye're sure to beat them a'.

8 For they always gained the prize before
At every country show
And gin ye lat that fa back
Ye'll be thocht little o'.

9 But Swaggers in the harvest time
Has got too much ado
For his twa three laddies
That ca' his cairts and ploo.

10 Sae he'll gang on some twenty miles
Where people dinna him ken
And he'll engage some harvest hands
And bring them far frae hame.

11 He'll say unto the foreman
Keep aye the steady grin
And never lat the orra lads
Stan idle at the en'.

12 For I pay ye a' gude wages
And sae ye maun get on
And when ye arena able
There's anither when ye're dune.

13 He says unto the girlies
As they are comin back
Come hurry up my lassies
Gie them nae time to sharp.

14 But now the cutting's ended
And we maun try to lead
And mony's the curious plan he's taen
For to come muckle speed.

15 But now the sheaves are all in
And formèd in the stack
The windy days are comin' on
When we maun hunt the brock.

16 When we maun hunt the brock brave boys
Wi' many a fret and frown
An' Swaggers says: "Come on my lads
It's like for to ding on."

17 And when that we gang to the raips
He gets up wi' a bawl
Say: Come my girls ply in the twine
Ye're sure to beat them all.

18 Now the harvest's ended
And likewise a' made snug
The harvest hands wi' bundles big
They now must pad the road.

19 They now must pad the road, brave boys,
Amang the frost and snow
And they hae sworn a solemn oath
They'll ne'er come back ava!

JOHN WIGHT — G

F

Swaggers

1 Come, all ye jolly ploughmen
That goes to Porter Fair,
And be aware o' Swaggers,
He's aye sure to be there.

2 He'll be aye lauch, lauchin',
He'll be aye lauchin' there,
And he'll hae the blithest face
In all Porter Fair.

3 He tells them o' a ploughing match
That's nae that far awa,
Says that, "If ye clean yere harness well,
Ye're sure to beat them a'.

4 "For they always gained the prize afore
At ilka public show,
And if ye lat it now fa' back,
Ye'll be thocht little o'."

5 A pair o' broons they lead the van,
Sae nimbly as they go,
A pair o' blues that follows them,
They never yet said No.

6 A wee bit shaltie ca's the neeps,
And oh bit it is sma',
But Swaggers he does curse and swear
It's stronger than them a'.

7 Noo the cutting, it is done,
And we maun try to lead,
And mony a plan does Swaggers try
To gar's come muckle speed.

Mrs BEATON — D

G

1 He'll be aye lauch lauchin',
He'll be aye lauchin' there;
And he'll hae on the blondest face
In a' Porter Fair.

2 Wi' his fine horse and harness,
As he will gar ye true;
But when ye gang home to Auchterless,
Sae sair he'll gar ye rue.

3 He'll be aye fret frettin',
He'll be aye girnin' there;
He'll tell ye a' his regulations —
They are worn thread bare!

Correspondent in *The People's Journal* — G

H

Swaggers in Porter Fair

1   A pair o' blues they lead the band, sae nimble as they go,
    A pair o' blacks they follow them, that never yet said No;
    An' a wee bit shalt that ca's the neeps, an' oh, it's wondrous sma',
    But Swaggers he'll declare to you, it's stronger nor them a'.

WILLIAM DUNCAN — D

I

Swaggers

1   He says unto his foremost man,
    Keep aye a steady grin,
    An' dinna lat the orra lads
    Fa' back aboot the ein.

2   For I pay ye a' gweed wages,
    An' ye maun carry on,
    And fan ye arena fit for that,
    There's anidder fan ye're done.

3   But noo the leadin' it is deen,
    The stooks are in the ruck,
    And we maun man the rakes, my boys,
    And gang and hunt the broke.

4   A wee bit shaltie ca's it hame,
    An' tho' it be but sma',
    Aul' Swaggers will declare to you
    It's stronger than them a'.

ALEXANDER ROBB — G

NETHERMILL

Nethermill, Tarves

1　It was about the term time
　When servants change their place,
　As I went down to Ellon Fair
　My fortune for to chase.
　　Tirim fal de dal de dal,
　　Tirim fal de dido;
　　Tirim fal de dal de dal,
　　Tirim fal de dee.

2　There was a farmer in this place
　He sought me to engage,
　It was na for his fancy man,
　Nor yet to be his page.

3　And when he sought me to engage
　And told me all his plans
　He said, "I have my foreman,
　Ye'll be my second man."

4　It was to work his horses,
　Likewise to hold his ploo,
　But when that I went hame to him,
　Sae sairly as I did rue.

5　For early the next morning,
　'Twas sair against my will,
　When our grieve cam' to our sleeping-place
　Demanding us to the mull.

6　Away down to the mull we go,
　And kindles up a light,
　And then we put the water on
　And wrought wi' all our might.

7　And when the thrashing it was o'er,
　And faith it was na sport,
　And we to the stable go
　To gie our horse a sort.

8　And when that Swaggers he cam' round,
　To gie us out the line,
　He had the watch into his han'
　Just looking for the time.

9　"At seven ye'll gang to your brose,
　At eight ye'll gang and yoke,
　And work away as fast's ye can,
　For men's nae easy got.

10　"Ye'll clean your horses unco well,
　Likewise your harness too,
　And faith, my lads, ye winna stan'
　When ye gang to the ploo."

11　And when that we gang to the neeps
　It's still they cry for mair,
　For drivin' at them ilka day
　There is na time to spare.

12　Faith I'm sure it would gar you laugh
　To hear him rowte and roar,　　[bawl
　And tear and twist his fuskers
　And rin frae door to door.

13　"My horseman lads, ye winna stan',
　Be ye will ca awa;
　And let us get the plooin' tee
　Ere we begin to saw.

14　"And when the sawin' does begin
　It's I will saw the seed,
　And full't up in my leisure hour,
　Just in the time I need.

15　"Ye bailie lads, ye'll gie's a hitch,
　Your master for to please,
　For if ye dinna labour hard
　Your temper he will tease."

16　Now all ye servant laddies,
　I fear ye'll get a gull,　[be taken advantage of
　If ye engage wi' Swaggers
　To gang to Nethermill.

17　And now my song it's at an end,
　I think I'll let ye be;
　But gang ye engage wi' Swaggers,
　The truth o' this ye'll see.

WILLIAM FORSYTH – G

I'VE SAIR'D WI' MEN

1   I've sairt wi' men that eased me well   [made me comfortable
     Wi' men that tried to skin
     I've cuttit many a sair hairst
     Alang the Ythan rin.   [valley

2   At muckle big Baldwhinachie
     A quintra in itsel
     At Haddo on the brae top,
     And low St John's Well.

3   At Upper an Neither Mill,
     At Raxton and Sheithin
     But the like o' the Aucheddly
     My fit was never in.

JOHN MILNE – G

CAMELOUN

A
a
Cameloun

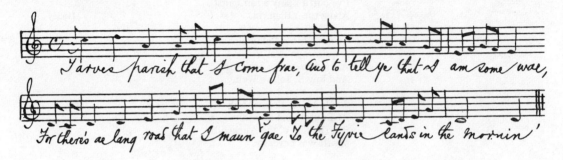

1   It's Tarves parish that I come frae
     And to tell you that I am some wae   [rather sad
     For there's ae lang road that I maun gae
     To the Fyvie lands in the mornin'.

2   At Cameloun I did arrive
     A pair of horses for to drive
     And ilka morn to rise at five
     And ca' the fan in the mornin'.

3   I hadna weel begun to sleep
     When the foreman he began to creep
     And oot o's bed he sprang to's feet
     Cries "Losh boys rise for it's mornin'."

4   To ca' the fan they set me tae
     Which I began richt cannily
     And took a look fu' they wid dee
     In the Fyvie lands in the mornin'.

5   We hae a bailie stoot and stark   [strong
     It sets him weel to work his wark
     But owre his heid he's drawn a sark
     As lang's himsel' in the mornin'.

6   I hadna long been at the ploo
     When I began to couck and spue   [retch
     The nicht afore I'd been some foo
     Sae I had a dowie mornin'.   [woeful

7   Tarves parish is lang and wide
     Tarves parish is fu o' pride
     But in this cauld corner I'll nae langer bide
     Gin I had Whitsunday mornin'.

b
Cameloun

1   It's Tarves parish that I cam frae
     And to tell you that I am some wae
     For there's a lang road that I maun gae
     To the Fyvie lands in the morning.

2   At Cameloun I did arrive
     A pair o' horses for to drive
     And ilka mornin' to rise at five
     And ca' the fan in the mornin'.

3   I hadna weel begun to sleep
     When the foreman laddie began to creep
     And oot o's bed he sprang till's feet
     Cryin' Losh boys rise for it's mornin'.

4   To ca' the fan they set me tae
     Which I began richt cannily
     And took a look hoo they wad dee
     In the Fyvie lands in the mornin'.

5 We hae a bailie stoot and stark
   It sets him weel to work his wark
   And owre his heid he's drawn his sark
   As lang's himsel in the mornin'.

6 Oor kitchie cook she's nae great dale [deal
   I think I wad dee as weel mysel
   For she maks oor bread as green as kale
   To the Fyvie lads in the mornin'.

7 Oor dairy maid she is some shy
   At the bailie laddie as she gangs by
   Just gain' awa to milk her kye
   By gray daylight in the mornin'.

8 The winnyin' past and the fan by set
   The foreman says we'll hae some meat
   At the head o' the table he's taen his seat
   Says "Losh boys, ate for it's mornin'."

9 Ye'll yoke your horses as fast as ye may
   The foreman unto me did say
   You'll get a ploo upon yonder brae
   That'll please right weel in the mornin'.

10 But I hadna lang been at the ploo
   Till I began to couck and spew
   The night afore I'd been some fou
   So I had a dowie mornin'.

11 He said I didna my horses ken
   And on me he laid the blame
   But I let him ken I'd been frae hame
   In the Fyvie lands in the mornin'.

12 I ca'ed him a stupid ass
   Bade him come forrit wi' my brass [forward; money
   And awa frae his toon I'd tak my pass
   Thro' the Fyvie lands in the mornin'.

13 Fyvie parish is lang and wide
   Fyvie parish is full o' pride
   But in this cauld corner I'll nae langer bide
   Gin I had Whitsunday morning.

J. W. SPENCE – G

B

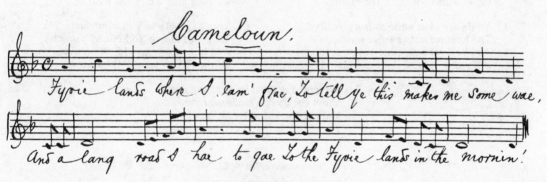

Fyvie lands where I cam' frae, To tell ye this makes me some wae,
And a lang road I hae to gae To the Fyvie lands in the mornin'.

GAVIN GREIG Jr – G

C

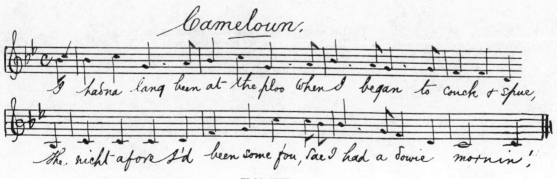

I hadna lang been at the ploo When I began to couch & spue,
The nicht afore I'd been some fou, Sae I had a dowie mornin'.

W. MASSIE – G

Song No. 389

Cameloun.

WILLIAM WATSON — G

E

1 At first when I to Camel's cam'
They a' cried oot Here's oor new man
And a-gazin' at me they a' began
At the Fyvie's lan's i' the mornin'.

2 Fin nine o'clock began to ring
The foreman fae his cheer did spring
Says awa tae our beds we maun gang
Or we winna wun up i' the mornin'.

3 Ye'll yoke your horse as fast's ye may
The foreman unto me did say
And ye'll get a pleuchie oot owre the brae
It'll please ye weel i' the mornin.

4 He says I didna my horses ken
And on me he laid a' the blame
But I let him ken that I'd been frae hame
In the Fyvie lands i' the mornin.

5 It's I caed him a stupid ass
Bade him came forrit wi' my brass
An awa' fae his toon I wad tak my pass
Wi' richt guid wull i' the mornin.

6 Young Camel's he's a clever chiel
They sent him on to Kemnay's schule
And he brought his eddication weel
To the Fyvie's lands i' the mornin.

7 And noo I've tauld ye clear and fair
About the Fyvie's lands sae rare
And gin ony ane aifter me inquire
Ye can tell them I left i' the mornin.

Source unrecorded — G

F

1 The winnyin' bein' past and the fan by set,
The foreman says, We maun ha'e meat
At the heid o' the table he's ta'en his seat,
Sayin' Eat boys, eat for it's mornin'.

2 . . . .
. . . .
Ye'll get yer pleugh lyin' ower on the brae
And tak' that chielie wi' ye i' the mornin'.

Dr NICOL — G

JAMIE BROON

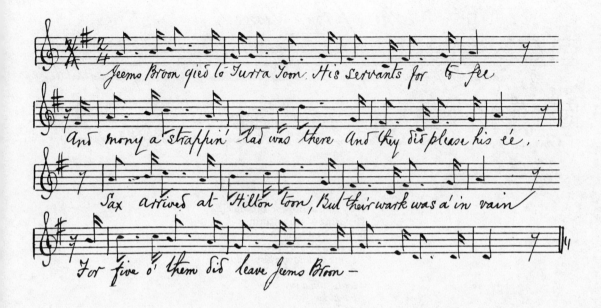

1 Jeems Broon gied to Turra Toon, his servants for to fee
And mony a strappin' lad was there and they did please his e'e.
Sax arrived at Hilton toon, but their wark was a' in vain
For five o' them did leave Jeems Broon . . . . . .

ARTHUR BARRON — G

THE WEARY FAIRMERS

A

The Term Time.

They sing aboot the Broomielaw, They sing o' lan's alairm, But the best sang that e'er was sung, Was sung aboot the Term

Come a radie um a row dow, Radie um a ree, Radie um a row dow, Fal al lee.

1   They sing aboot the Broomielaw,
They sing o' lan's alairm,
But the best sang that e'er was sung,
Was sung aboot the term.
    Come a radie um a row dow,
    Radie um a ree,
    Radie um a row dow,
    Fal al lee.

2   The term time is comin', lads,
And we will a' win free,
And wi' the weary fairmer
Again we winna fee.

3   First there comes the market,
And then there comes the term,
So a' ye weary fairmers
Dinna be alairmed.

4   They'll tap ye on the shouther
And say "Lad are ye to fee?"
And they'll tell ye a lang story
Perhaps it's a' a lee.

5   He'll pit his han' intae his pouch
And he'll pu' oot a shillin',
And he'll say the siller's unco scarce,
Eh! the leein' villain!

6   They'll tell ye every jot o' work
That ye hae tae perform,
But then when ye gang hame tae them
There'll be a ragin' storm.

7   On cauld kail and pitawtis
They feed ye like a pig,
When they ait at their tea and toast
Or hurl i' their gig.

8   Wi' broad-tailed coats and Quaker hats
And whups below their airm
They dunt and ride on horseback
When they get a fairm.

9   Wi' broad-tailed coats and Quaker hats,
And spurs upo' their heels,
Altho' ye ca' the country roon
Ye winna get sic chiels.

10   And noo my sang is ended,
A warnin' tak' frae me,
And wi' the weary fairmer
Be sure and dinna fee.

SAM DAVIDSON — G

B

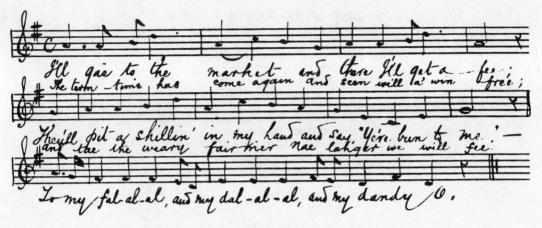

I'll gae to the market and there I'll get a fee;
The toom-time has come again and seen will la' win free;
They'll pit a shillin' in my haud and say "Ye're bun to me,"—
and tae the weary fair nae langer we will fee.
To my fal-al-al, and my dal-al-al, and my dandy O.

Mr MELVIN — G

392

POTTERTON

A

1   At the big toon of Potterton
    There was neither watch nor clock;
    It was porridge time, and sowen time,
    And — Come, lads, yoke.

2   Awa' with yer taties,
    Your sowens, and yer kail;
    Yer ill-baken breid,
    And yer soor-brewn ale.

3   Wi' cauld kail and tatties
    Ye feed us like a pig;
    While ye drink tay and toddy,
    And hurl in yer gig.

Miss ANNIE SHIRER — G

B

1   The folk o' the muckle toon o' Rora
    Hae neither watch nor clock;
    But pottage time, and sowen time,
    And yoke, boys, yoke.

Miss BELL ROBERTSON — G

COME A' YE BUCHAN LADDIES

1 Come a' ye Buchan laddies,
  And listen to my sang,
  And I'll tell ye o' the news
  That's come frae Aberdeen.

2 Hoo Tully's men ha'e gained the day,
  And Tully's lost it clean;
  Hoo stinkin' sowens and buttermilk
  Ha'e forced his men awa.

Dr MITCHELL — G

THERE'S NAE LUCK AT TULLO'S TOON

1 The maiden queen o' buttermilk
  She couldna get a man,
  To be revenged on the male sex,
  She tried the soor milk plan.
    There's nae luck at Tullo's toon,
    There's scarcely meat ava,
    There's stinkin' sowens an' buttermilk,
    They force the men awa.

WILLIAM DUNCAN — D

THE GOODMAN'S SONG

  Wine wine wine awa',
  Halkie's ane and humlie's twa
  Wine wine wine awa.
Gin ye mak' my parach thin
I'll gar a' yer owsen rin;
Gin ye mak' my parach knotty   [lumpy
I'll leave yer lan baulky.   [unploughed
  Wine wine wine awa,
  Halkie's ane and humlie's twa,
  Wine wine wine awa.

Miss BELL ROBERTSON — G

396

MAINS O' BOYNDIE

1 If ye want to learn high farmin'
Come ye to Beenie's big toon
It takes fourteen pair an' some orra
To work it the haill year roon.

2 There's nae chiel here cawed a foreman
To earn a muckle big pay
The lad that yocks first in the mornin'
He's foreman for the day.

3 To see's keepin' cut on the hairst rig
We ficher nane their wi' the heuck   [do not fiddle
The scythe slashes mair doon in ae day
Than ye'd shear wi' a heuck in an oock.

4 We're aye scant o' dishes in hairst time
Parboiled tawties comes loose in the cairt
Whilst a hole in the grun makes a cappie
That hauds broth or milk till we're sairt.

JOHN MILNE – G

397

MAINS O' CULSH

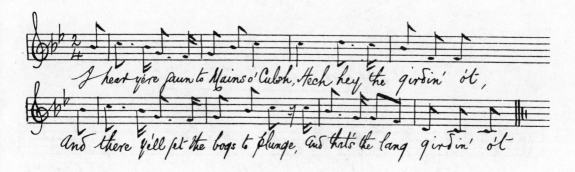

1 I hear ye're gyaun to Mains o' Culsh,
Hech, hey, the girdin' o't;
And there ye'll get the bogs to plunge,
And that's the lang girdin' o't.

2 I hear ye're gettin' a muckle fee
Ye'll maybe get as muckle adee.

3 It's in the mornin' he will rise,
And on the loan ye'll hear his cries.

4 I think my boys ye micht hae been in the yoke
It's half an hoor past sax o'clock.

5 Just as I gaed thro' the close,
Loanie's folk was yokin' their horse.

6 But Loanie's folk's nae rule to me,
They aye get some ither thing adee.

7 He said he wadna keep me anither year,
I learned his bairns to curse and sweer.

8 Indeed I think he's warst himsel'
He'll curse and damn them a' to hell.

9 But noo I'm gaun to Nethermeer
And there to work the merchant's meer.

ALEX MURISON – G

99

LAMACHREE AND MEGRUM

A

ALEX MILNE — G

B

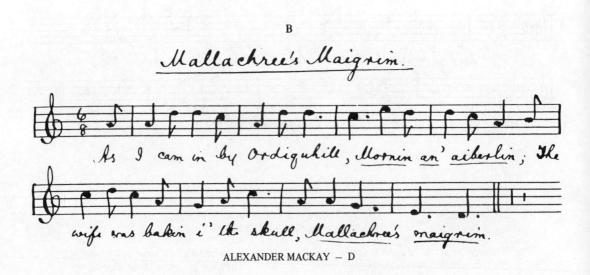

ALEXANDER MACKAY — D

C

Lamachree and Megrum

1 When first I gaed to saire the fremt
    Lamachree and Megrum,
  It was to Auchtiedoor I skeemt
    Auld grey Megrum.

2 The auld guidewife smokes in the neuck
    A-orderin at the throwder cook.   [muddled

3 The nist, I gade to Middlethird
    A better's nae aboon the yeard.

4 I there got buttered bread and cheese
    An oil to keep my sheen in grease.

5 I took a turn at Yoakieshill
    The teuchest plase I e'er gaed till.

6 A hurb to hack and hash the loons, [good for nothing;
    There's nae his like in Buchan's loons.   overwork

7 I hear ye're gaun to Mains o' Culsh
    There ye'll get the boys to plunsh. [for "bogs to plunge"

8 In the mornin' or ye rise
    He's on the loan wi' mony cries.

9 Get's up my boys it's sax o'clock
    And Loanie's men are a' ayoke.

JOHN MILNE — G

D

Lamachree and Megrum

1 First I gaed to Tyrie school,
    Lamachree and Megrum;
  They a' took me to be a feel,
    Aul gray Megrum.

2 I gaed up into Saut Wards,
    It was to get a game at cards.

3 Geordie Burnett began to flyte,
    For brakin' his tobacco pipe.

4 He got up and hit at me,
    It lichtit jist into my e'e.

5 Gin it hadna been for my clergy coat,
    I'd gien him anither knock.

6 I gaed up to Aberdour,
    I got lasses three or four.

7 Betty Barbour was fu' keen,
    She had twa bonnie blinkin' e'en.

8 I gaed up to Skelmande,
    It was to gather berries blae.

9 I gaed to the burn to tak' some trout,
    They barred the door and held me oot.

10 But I'll gang hame and mind my skweel,
    They will nae mair ca' me a feel.

Mrs CHALMERS — G

E

Lamachree and Megrum

1   First fin I cam' to Tyrie School,
     Lamachree and Megrum,
  The lasses thoucht I was a fool,
     Aul gray Megrum.

2   I gaed up to Braeside,
  The lasses there they bade me bide.

3   They bade me bide my brose,
  'Twad help my legs to fill my hose.

4   I gaed up to Aberdour,
  There I got lasses three or four.

Miss BELL ROBERTSON — G

399

MARAFRAY

1   There is a toon oot frae Montrose
  It stands upon a brae
  And the name that it gangs under
  They ca' it Marafray.
     Sing aeri-iritie adie man
     Sing iriti andi kay.

2   The foremost pair aboot oor toon
  They sweer they are the best
  But gin they had the roons to gang
  They'd be as bad's the rest man.

3   The seed time is comin' on
  When we maun look alive
  But they thought they wid get Jip to gang in the
  But they got an awfu surprise man.   [machine

4   We hae a grieve aboot oor toon
  They sweer he is the best
  For to plan the wark to tarnish men
  But the paintin' goes up his back, man.

5   Bell Lowe she rises in the mornin
  Wi' a nose sae neat and fine
  She jabbers and curses, habbers and sweers
  Like a donkey gaun wrang in his mind, man.

6   The term time is comin' on
  When we will get the brass
  And we'll gang doon to Jean Lowe's
  We'll hae a partin' glass man.

7   We'll hae a pairtin glass my lads
  Likewise a jovial spree
  And we'll bid farewell to the dairymaids
  We left at Marafree man.

ALEXANDER GREIG — G

400

SOWENS FOR SAP

1 The foremost man o' oor New Tap he works a stallion fine,
   The Lion they do call him, the Lion is his name.
   The little one that goes on him she's swift and spunky too, —
   The sowens for sap at oor New Tap ye'll find it winna do.   [as drink

2 The second pair of oor New Tap they are coonted the best,
   If he forget to clean them he will be sore opprest.
   For if on their legs a speck be found there'll be a Waterloo —
   The sowens for sap at oor New Tap ye'll find it winna do.

3 The third pair o' oor New Tap, the one o' them's a bay
   The little one that goes on him he's true and trusty aye.
   Likewise the man that works them has a cut below his broo, —
   Sowens for sap at oor New Tap ye'll find it winna do.

4 Likewise we hae an orra man he says he comes frae Perth
   He is the drollest shaver that ever lived on earth
   There's never a day wi' Sandy but there is a Waterloo —
   Sowens for sap at oor New Tap ye'll find it winna do.

5 Likewise we hae an orra woman for waitin' on oor nowte,
   Ye widna see the like o' her the country roon aboot
   For she does wear her leggins and snap her brose I troo, —
   Sowens for sap at oor New Tap ye'll find it winna do.

ALEXANDER ROBB — G

PITGAIR

A

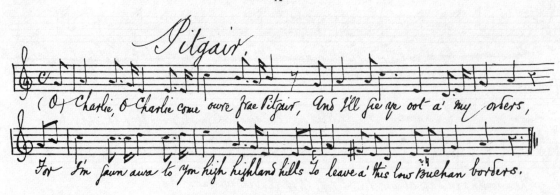

(O Charlie, O Charlie come owre frae Pitgair, And I'll gie ye oot a' my orders,
For I'm gaun awa to yon high highland hills To leave a' this low Buchan borders.

1 Charlie, O Charlie come owre frae Pitgair
Or I gie ye oot a' your orders,
For I'm gaun awa' to yon high Hielan' hills
To leave a' this low Buchan borders.

2 O Charlie, O Charlie, tak' notice what I say
And put every man to his station,
For I'm gaun awa to yon high Hielan' hills
To view a' the parts of the nation.

3 To the lowsin' ye'll pit Shaw, ye'll pit Sandieson to ca'
To the colin ye'll pit Andrew Kindness,
And auld Colliehill he'll feed the mill
And see that he dee't wi' great fineness.

4 Ye'll pit Eppie to the mill and Janet to the cole
And the ither twa men for to carry,
And as for George and Jeck ye'll pit them to the rake
And see that they do not tarry.

5 To the gatherin' o' the hay ye'll pit little Isa Gray,
And wi' her ye'll pit her cousin Peggy
And it's in below the bands it's there ye'll pit your hands
And see that they do it right tidy.

6 It's you Willie Burr ye'll carry on the stir
And ye'll keep a' the young maids a-hoein'
And ye'll tak' care o' Jeck or he'll play you a trick
And will set a your merry maids a-mowin'.

7 And it's you Annie Scott ye'll pit on the muckle pot
And mak' unto them porridge plenty
For yon hungry brosiers that's comin' frae Pitgair   [brose-eaters
They live both bare and scanty.

8 Ye'll tak' little Annie Mack frae the colin' o' the quack   [cutting; bog
To help ye .   .   . the denner for to carry
And at the hour o' one ye will mak' them a' to stan'
At the mull for a moment to tarry.

9 O Charlie, O Charlie, so early's ye'll rise
And see a' my merry men yokin'
And you Missy Pope ye'll sit in the parlour neuk
And keep a' my merry men frae smokin.

JOHN QUIRRIE – G

B

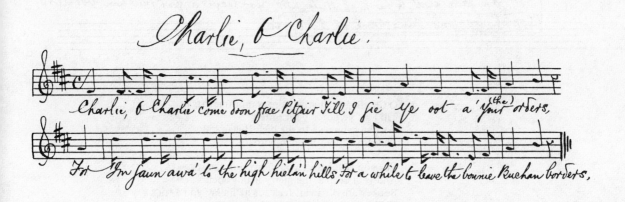

Charlie, O Charlie.

Charlie, O Charlie come doon frae Pitgair Till I gie ye oot a' (the) your orders,

For I'm gaun awa' to the high hielin hills, For a while to leave the bonnie Buchan borders,

1 O Charlie, O Charlie come doon frae Pitgair
Till I gie ye oot a' the orders.
For I'm gaun awa to the high Hielan' hills
For a while to leave the bonnie Buchan borders.

2 Charlie, O Charlie, come notice what I say
And pit every man to his station
For I'm gaun awa' to the high Hielan hills
For to view a' the plains o' oor nation.

3 To the lowsin ye'll pit Shaw, ye'll pit Sandieson to ca'
To the coalin' ye'll pit auld Andrew Kindness
And for auld Colliehill he'll feed the mill
And you'll see that he do it wi great fineness.

4 To the gatherin' o' the hay ye'll pit little Isa Gray
And wi' her ye'll pit her ain cousin Peggy
To gather't wi' their hands and lay't into bands
And you'll see that they do it right steady.

5 And for you Willie Burr ye'll carry on the stir
And ye'll keep a' the lasses a-hoein'
And be aware o' Jeck or he'll play you a trick
And he'll set a' the girlies a-mowin.

6 And for you Annie Scott, ye'll pit on the muckle pot
And ye'll mak' to them pottage plenty
For yon hungry brosers that's comin' frae Pitgair
They're keepit bare and scanty.

CHARLES WALKER – G

C

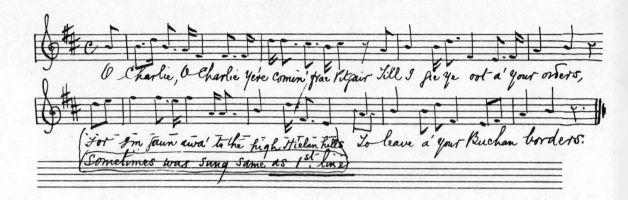

O Charlie, O Charlie ye're comin' frae Pitgair Till I gie ye oot a' your orders,

(For I'm gaun awa' to the high Hielan hills To leave a' your Buchan borders.
(Sometimes was sung same as 1st line)

1   O Charlie, O Charlie ye're comin frae Pitgair
Till I gie ye oot a' your orders
For I'm gaun awa to the high Hielan hills
To leave a' your Buchan borders.

2   For you Willie Burr you'll carry on the stir
And ye'll keep a' the merry maids hoein'
But beware o' sawin' Jeck for he'll play you a trick
He'll set a' your merry maids a-mowin.

3   To the feedin' o' my mill ye'll pit auld Colliehill
And ye'll see hoo he feeds her finely
And to the collin o' the hay ye'll auld Isa Gray
And the rest o' the merry boys a-makin.

4   For you Annie Scott ye'll pit on the muckle pot
And ye'll mak them pottage plenty
For yon hungry brosers they're comin frae Pitgair
And they live a' richt bare and scanty.

Mrs CLARK — G

D

Pitgair

To the tune of 213 *Binorie* A

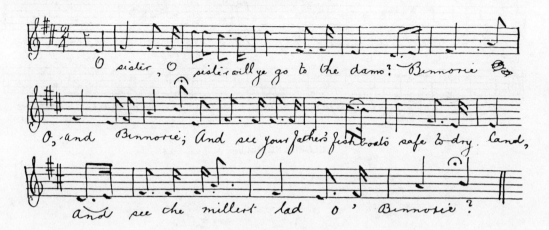

1   O Charlie, O Charlie, ye'll come fae Pitgair,
      Ere I gie ye oot a' my orders;
      For I'm gaun awa to the high Hielan' hills,
      To leave the Buchan borders.

2   O Charlie, O Charlie, sae early's ye'll rise,
      An' see a' my merry men a-yokin',
      An' for you, Missy Pope, ye'll sit in your parlour neuk,
      An' keep a' my lads fae the smokin'.

3   An for you, Annie Scott, ye'll pit on the muckle pot,
      An' ye'll mak them pottage plenty,
      For yon hungry brosiers that's comin' fae Pitgair,
      They live both baire an' scanty.

4   An for you, Geordie Watt, ...
      . . . .
      Tak ye care o' Jeck, or he'll play you a trick
      Or he'll set some o' oor fair maids a-mowin'.

      Mrs MARGARET GILLESPIE — D

E

Come o'er frae Pitgair

Oh Charlie, oh Charlie come o'er fae Pitgair. Ill I gae ye oot o'yer or-ders. For

I'm gaen awa to you high Highland hills To vies a' the bonne Buchan Borders

GEORGE RIDDELL — G

F

Pitgair

O Charlie, o Charlie, ye'll come fae Pitgair, And I'll gae ye oot o' yer orders; For

I'm gaun awa to the high Hielan' nills, For to view i' the Buchan borders.
(leave ?)

Mrs GREIG — D

G
O Charlie, O Charlie

1 O Charlie, O Charlie, come ower to Pitgare
An' I'll gie ye oot a' yer orders
For I'm gaen awa' a while fae ye a'
An likewies the low Buchan borders.

2 O Charlie, O Charlie, mind well what I say,
And put every man to his station
Haud the lads weel at their wark an auld Maggie Park
Winna scrimp them o' ale nor ration.

3 For a forman ye'll get Shaw, ye'll get Sannieson to caw
For a third ye'll get Andrew Kindness
Gar auld Collyhill aye feed the threshing mill
For he'll do it wi' the greatest o' fineness.

4 To the gaitherin' o' the hay you'll put little Annie Grey
An' likewies her cousin Peggie
And the sheaves below the band they will dress them wi' their hand
And ye'll see that they do it steady.

JOHN MILNE — G

402

LIKEWISE WE HAE A HOOSEMAID

1 Likewise we hae a hoosemaid
She's no jist vera bra'
She wears her hair oot owre the croon
To scare the lads awa.

2 As sure's I'm here I near forgot
To mention toothless Annie
Her vera face wad fleg the rats
Fae oot o' Newton's gelly O.   [garret

Source unrecorded — G

109

OOR FAIRM TOON

A

Oor Fairm Toon

1 My wife's awa frae hame the nicht, and sae I've jist come doon
   To tell ye a' the ongauns at oor fairm toon.   [goings on
   We hae a foreman and a second man, a bailie and a loon,
   And they're queer folk the fee'd folk at oor fairm toon.

2 We hae a strappin' kitchie lass at oor fairm toon,
   And for a beauty she would pass at ony fairm toon.
   She maks oor mait and cleans the plates, they ca' her Betsy Broon,
   And the lads a' comes to see her frae the neiper fairm toon.

3 We rise up in the mornin' at oor fairm toon
   There's little time for snorin' at oor fairm toon.
   We gae awa in to oor brose, they're whiles stiff to gae doon,
   But it's a' that we are offered noo at ony fairm toon.

4 We hae some new improvements at oor fairm toon,
   'Mang machinery and implements at oor fairm toon.
   We hae a braw new thrashin' mull and an engine cas her roon
   We're deein' oor ain thrashin' noo at oor fairm toon.

5 We hae things for biggin' rucks upon up at oor fairm toon,
   Instead o' couters they hae screws for steerin' them roon'.
   The chiels they jist sit on o' them and they ploo roon and roon,
   We'll shortly hae the plooin' deen at oor fairm toon.

6 But it's time that I wis wearin' hame to oor fairm toon,
   For the nicht it's unco black like for the want o' a moon.
   And if I bide lang oot at nicht my wife she'll claw my croon,
   Ye little ken fat it is to be at oor fairm toon.

JOHN JAFFRAY – G

B

1 We hae a gran' kitchen deem at oor fairm toon,
   Ye canna get the like o' her a' roon and roon.
   She mak's the meat and bakes the breid wi' ony roon and roon,
   And a' the lads come coortin' her frae the neist fairm toon.

W. CRAIGHEAD – G

THE LOTHIAN HAIRST

A

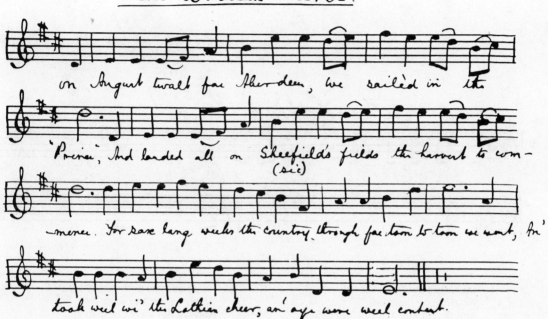

The Lothian Hairst.

On August twalt fae Aberdeen, we sailed in the 'Prince', And landed all on Sheefield's fields the harvest to com—
(sic)
—mence. For sax lang weeks the country through fae toon to toon we went, An' took weel wi' the Lothian cheer, an' aye were weel content.

1   On August twalt from Aiberdeen we sailed upon the "Prince",
      And landed all on Sheefield fields, the harvest to commence.
      For sax long weeks, the country through, from toon to toon we went,
      And took weel with the Louthian cheer, and aye were weel content.

2   Oor gaffer, Willie Mathieson, fae sweet Deeside he came;
      Oor foreman came fae that same place, and Logan was his name.
      O' brisk young lads some half a score; oor lasses were but few;
      While Logan herded what he had, and kept a decent crew.

3   I followed Logan on the point, sae weel as he laid it doon,
      Sae nobly as he led the squad ower mony a thistly toon.
      My mate and I got little chance for Logan's watchful eye,
      Oor fancy chaps could get nae chance, auld Logan was sae sly.

4   He cleared the bothy every night before he went to sleep,
      He would not leave behind him one, so strick his rule he keeped.
      And when we lan' at Aiberdeen, he weel deserves a spree,
      A' for the herding us sae weel, from Louthian tumes we're free.

5   But noo the corn is a' cut doon, and we are on the pier;
      Farewell, ye Louthian feather beds, and a' the Louthian cheer.
      Farewell, Mackenzie, Reid, and Ross, and all the joyful crew,
      Chalmers, Shepherd, Logan, Jack, and royal Stewarts too.

6 O' a' the lads that's in oor squad, to take them one by one,
    Commend me to the Deeside lads, for it's them that leads the van.
    And I mysel', a Hielan' lass, wad seek nae better cheer
    Nor a Deeside lad in a Louthian bed, and a nicht as lang as a year.

ALEXANDER MACKAY — D

B

The Lothian Hairst.

1 On August twalt frae Aberdeen
   We sailed on the Prince
   And landed safe on Crawford's Hills
   Oor harvest to commence.

2 For sax lang weeks the country roon
   Frae toon to toon we went
   An' we took right weel wi' the Lothian chiels
   They were aye richt weel content.

3 Oor maister Willie Mathieson
   Frae sweet Deeside he came
   And oor foreman cam frae that same place
   And Logan was his name.

4 I followed Logan on the point
   Sae weel's he laid it roon
   As bravely as he led the squad
   Owre mony's the thristly toon.

5 My mate and I could get nae chance
   For Logan's watchful eye
   And our fancy chaps could get nae chance
   For Logan was so sly.

6 He cleared the bothy every night
   Before he went to sleep
   And did not leave one man in it
   But strict his rules did keep.

7 When Logan comes to Aberdeen
   He weel deserves a spree
   For herdin' o' the Lothian chiels
   Frae the Deeside girls so free.

8 And I mysel a Highland lass
   Will seek nae better cheer
   Than a Deeside bed and a Lothian lad
   And a nicht as lang's a year.

9 Farewell McKenzie, Reid and Rose
   And all our jovial crew
   And our chaumer shepherd, Lothian Jock
   And loyal Stewart too.

10 Come fill a glass and drink it roon
    Before our boat upstart
    That all may safely reach the shore
    And all in friendship part.

J. W. SPENCE — G

C

The Lothian Hairst.

On August Twalt frae Aiberdeen We sailèd in the Prince,

And safe arrived on Shawfield's shore, The harvest to commence.

1 On August twalt frae Aiberdeen
   We sailèd in the Prince,
   And safe arrived on Shawfield's shore,
   The harvest to commence.

2 [My mate and me] could get [no chance]
   For Logan bein' sae sly,
   The Lothian lads could get nae chance
   For Logan's watchful eye.

3 [He cleared the bothy every nicht
   Before he went] to bed
   And scarcely left behind him one
   [But strict his rules did keep.]

4 Of all the lads into our squad,
   To take them one by one,
   Commend me aye to the Deeside lads
   For it's them that lead the band.

5 Here's to McKenzie, [Reid and Rose]
   Is all a joyful crew
   To Chalmers, [Shepherd, Logan Jock]
   Pat Royal Stuart too.

6 Here's I mysel' a highland lass
   Could wish nae better cheer
   Than a Lothian bed and a Deeside lad
   And a nicht as lang's a year.

7 And when we reach to Aberdeen
   He weel deserves a spree
   And a' for the herdin' o' us sae weel
   For the Lothian chiels were free.

ALEXANDER GREIG – G

D

The Lothian Hairst.

On August twalt frae Aiberdeen We Sailèd on the "Prince,"

And landed safe on Shawfield's shore The harvest to Commence,

J. ROBSON – G

E

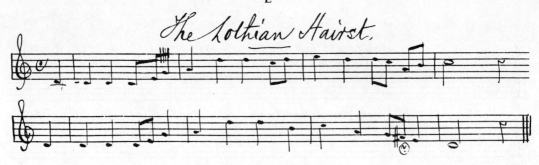

JAMES GREIG — G

F

ARTHUR BARRON — G

G

The Lothian Hairst

1   On August twalt frae Aberdeen we sailed on the Prince
    And landed safe in Jaffer's fields our harvest to commence.
    For sax lang weeks the country roon' frae toon tae toon we went.
    We took richt weel wi' the Lothian chiels and was aye richt weel content.
                                       [took kindly to

2   Our gaffer, Willie Mathieson, frae sweet Deeside he came
    Our foreman came frae that same place but Logan was his name
    We followed Logan on the point and sae weel's he laid it doon
    And sae nimbly as he led our squad o'er mony the thristle toon.

3 My mate and me we had no chance for Logan's watchful eye
My mate and me we had no chance for Logan was so sly
He cleared the bothy every nicht before he went to sleep
And not sae much as one did leave but strict his rules did keep.

4 When Logan comes to Aberdeen he weel deserves a spree
For the herdin' o' us all sae weel in the Lothian manachree
Fareweel, McKenzie, Reid and Rose and the rest o' yer joyful crew
There's Chalmers, Shepherd, Logan Jock and the royal Stewart too.

5 It's I mysel a Hieland lad would wish no better cheer
Than a Lothian lass and a Deeside bed and a nicht as lang's a year.
Come fill our glass and drink it roon before our boat shall start
And may we safely reach the shore and all in friendship part.

Source unrecorded — G

H

Louden Hairst

1 On August twelt from Aberdeen
Away up sailed the Prince;
We landed safe in Jafferedfield
The hairst for to commence.

2 Our master, Willie Mathieson,
From sweet Deeside he came;
Our foreman came fae the same place,
And Logan was his name.

3 For six long weeks and better
From town to town we went.
We took right weel wi' the Lothian chiels,
And aye was weel content.

4 I followed Logan on the point,
Owre mony a thristlie toon;
I followed Logan on the point,
Sae weel's he laid it doon.

5 My mate and me could get nae chance,
For Logan's watchful eye;
My mate and me could get nae chance,
For Logan was sae sly.

6 He cleared the bothy every night
Before he went to bed
. . . .
. . . .

7 Come all ye lads that's in this place,
I'll tak' ye one by one;
Commend me to the Deeside lads,
For it's them that takes the van.

8 Fareweel McKenzie, Reid and Rose,
And all ye joyful crew;
Chalmers, Shepherd, Logan, Jock,
And royal Stewart too.

9 When we do come tae Aberdeen,
We'll be worth a guid fill fou,   [drinking bout
For the keepin' o' us saucy quines   [young women
Frae the Lothian hairst sae free.

10 And I mysel', a Hielan' lass,
I'll seek nae better cheer,
Than a Lothian bed and a Deeside lad,
And a nicht as lang's a year.

JOHN QUIRRIE and FRED WALLACE — G

I

The Lothian Hairst

1 On August twalt from Aberdeen
We sailed on the Prince,
And arrivèd safe on Gaffray's fields
Our harvest to commence.

2 Our gaffer, Willie Morrison,
From sweet Deeside he came;
Our foreman came from that same place,
But Logan was his name.

3 My mate and me co. . . .
For Logan's watchful eye,
Our sporting you . . . .
For Logan was so sly.

4 He clears the bothy every night,
Before he goes to sleep;
He does not leave . . . . .
But strict his . . . . . keep.

5 For six long weeks the country round
Frae toon to toon we went,
We took richt weel wi' the Lothian chiels,
And was aye right well content.

6 I followed Logan on the point,
And so weel as he laid it down,
And so nimbly as he led the squad
Owre mony's the thristly toon.

7 There's I mysel' a highland lass,
Would wish nae better cheer
Than a . . . lad in a Lothian bed
And a nicht as lang's a year.

8 . . . . . drink their health
Afore the boat does start,
And may we safely reach the shore
And all in friendship part.

9 Farewell McKenzie, Reid and Rose,
And all the jolly crew;
Likewise farewell to Lothian Jock,
And royal Stewart too.

10 If Logan comes to Aberdeen,
He well deserves a spree,
For the training of us a sae weel,
And the Lothian rigs so free.

SAM DAVIDSON — G

J

The Lothian Hairst

1 On August twelfth from Aberdeen
We sailed upon the Prince
And landed safe at Clifford's fields
Our harvest to commence.

2 For six long weeks the country roun'
Frae toon to toon we went
And I took richt weel wi the Lothian fare
And aye was weel content.

3 Our master, William Mathieson
From sweet Donside, he came
Our foreman cam frae the same place
An' Logan was his name.

4 I followed Logan on the point
Sae well's he laid it doon
And sae boldly as he's led our squad
O'er mony's the thristly toon.

5 My mate and I could get na chance
For Logan's watchful eye
An' wi' the lads we got nae sport
For Logan was sae sly.

6 He cleared our bothy every nicht
Before he went to sleep
And never left behind him one
But strict the rules did keep.

7 And when we came to Aberdeen
He weel deserves a spree
For the herdin' o' us a' sae weel
From the Lothian lads we're free.

8 Farewell McKenzie, Reid and Rose
And all your jovial crew
An' Logan Jock and Chapman Pratt
And Royal Stewart too.

9 We'll fill a glass and drink it round
Before the boat will start
And may we safely reach the shore
And all in friendship part.

Mrs THOM — G

THE HARVEST SONG

1   Fan the fields are fite and the harvest draws near,
The farmer must then for his shearers repair,
Fae baith toon and country to him they repair,
And a' to try the shearin' o't.
Fae baith toon and country to him they convene,
And a' to the fields they gaither O —
The maister he orders them a' as he thinks fit,
And pits whom he pleases thegither O.

2   Then a' to the hills like fury they go,
And a' to be foremost they do what they do;
Each hates to be hinmost — it is a fine show,
To see the play at the shearin' o't.
But wait ye a while until they begin,
They grow baith tired and weary O;
Until they begin their sairs for to fin'
In the evenin' a battle looks dreary till't.

3   Some cries oot, "My back", and some cries oot, "My airms";
Some cries "Cuttit fingers they do me much hairm";
Some cries oot for heat when the weather is warm,
We'll a' be undone wi' the shearin' o't.
Then oot speaks the maister, "I'm sorry to hear,
Sae mony misfortunes does you befall;
But wait ye awhile till the harvest be done,
There is a time comin' will mak' 'mends for all."

4   Noo lang lookit for it has come at the last,
The corn it is in, and the toil it is past,
They drink and they rant while the day it does last,
There's never a word o' the shearin' o't.
The bandster he now gets the cup in his hand,
"Here's health to my maister sae hairty O,
And to the goodwife that fillit my wime,
And to a' my blithe neebors sae cheery O."

5   Then oot speaks the tailor, "To my needle I'll go
And shape and sew claith to keep oot frost and snow,   [cut to pattern
I'll mend up the old for to hain up the new
And forget a' the toil at the shearin' o't."
Then oot spoke the barnman, "To my barn I will go,
And a' the whole winter I'll bury O   [thresh
Altho' I work sair I stand warm and dry,
And I'll rest men fan I grow weary O."

6   Then oot speaks the ploughman, "To my labour I'll gang,
Thro' win' and thro' weather I'll wag owre the plain,
Until a new crop does cover the lan',
And syne we'll prepare for the shearin' o't."
If ony man wants to know what I am,
I'm a blithe plooman lad lives in Firehall,
Far mony guid hairvest man has gotten his full
O' baith mate and wark and his wage efter all
To reward his toil at the shearin' o't.

Miss BELL ROBERTSON — G

THE BAND O' SHEARERS

A

The Shearin

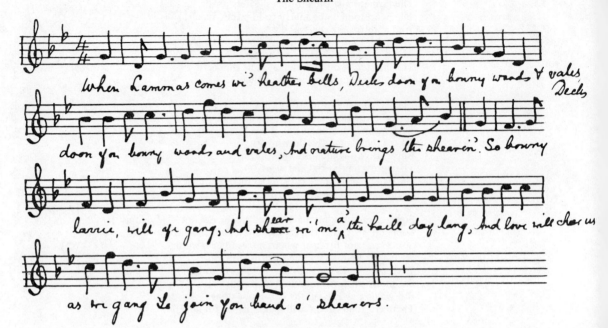

1 When Lammas comes, with heather bells
  Decks down yon bonny woods and vales,
  Decks down yon bonny woods and vales,
  And nature brings the shearin'.
    Bonny lassie, will ye gang
    And shear wi' me the haill day lang,
    And love will cheer us as we gang
    To join yon band at the shearin'.

2 It's if the weather be too hot,
  I'll cast my waistcoat and my coat,
  I'll cast my waistcoat and my coat,
  When we'll be at the shearin'.

3 And if the thistle be too strong
  For your lily-white hands for to wring,
  With my keen blade and I'll cut them down
  When we'll be at the shearin'.

4 And if the folks do us envye,
  And say there's love 'tween you and I,
  So carelessly as I'll pass you by
  When we'll be at the shearin'.

5 But when the corn is a' weel in,
  It's then our joys and they will begin,
  In some dark corner wi' little din,
  And forget a' the toils o' the shearin'.

6 When the corn is a thackit and some in the barn,
  Then we'll haud the rantin' kyirn,
  We'll drink success to John Barleycorn,
  And ae een that likes the shearin'.

WILLIAM WALLACE – D

B

The Shearing

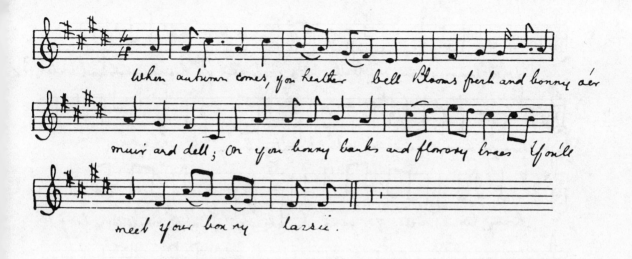

When autumn comes, you heather bell Blooms fresh and bonny o'er muir and dell; On you bonny banks and flowery braes You'll meet your bonny lassie.

1   When autum comes yon heather bell
    Blooms fresh and boney our muir and dell
    On yon bonney banks and flowery braes
    You'l meet your bonney lassie.

2   The thrisle is baith stout and strong
    If to thy lily white hand should do any wrong
    With my keen blad I will cut it down
    While we are at the shearin.

3   And if the people should us envy
    And say there is love between you and I
    We will carlesly pass each other by
    While we are at the shearin.

4   When it's all cut down and his in the barn
    Oh we'll hae money a rantin cairn
    In some dark nook far there's very little din
    Wee'l forget all the toils oh the shearin.

ARCHIBALD KNOWLES — D

C

The Shearing

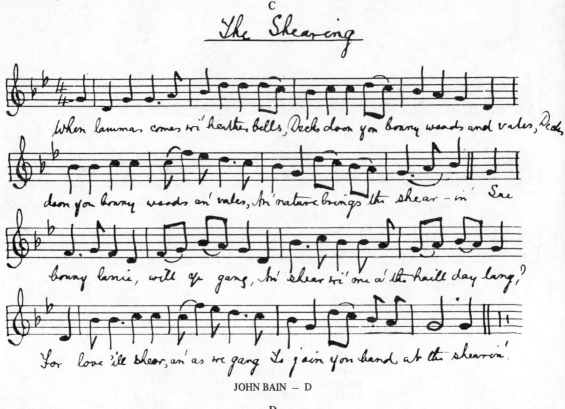

When lammas comes wi' heather bells, Deck doon yon bonny woods and vales, Deck

doon yon bonny woods an' vales, An' nature brings the shear - in' See

bonny lassie, will ye gang, An' shear wi' me a' the haill day lang,

For love 'ill shear, an' as we gang To join you band at the shearin'.

JOHN BAIN — D

D

The Shearin'.

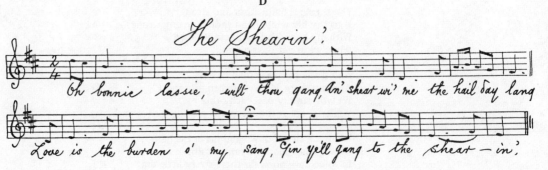

Oh bonnie lassie, wilt thou gang, An' shear wi' me the hail day lang

Love is the burden o' my sang, Gin ye'll gang to the shear - in'.

WILLIAM WALKER — G

E

The Shearin'.

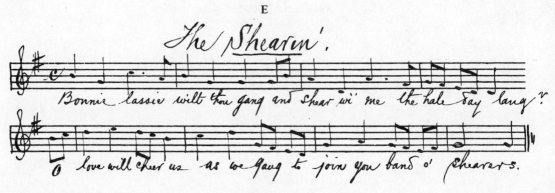

Bonnie lassie wilt thou gang and shear wi' me the hale day lang?

O love will cheer us as we gang to join you band o' shearers.

J.W. SPENCE — G

F

The Band o Shearers

1   When autumn comes wi heather bells
    Bloom bonnie oer yon moorland fells
    And corn that waves in lowland dales
    Is yellow ripe for shearin.
      Bonnie lasssie will ye gang
      An shear wi me the hale day lang
      And love will cheer us as we gang
      To join yon band o sherers.

2 And if the others should envý
    Or say we love, then you an I
    Will pass ilk other slyly bye
    As if we were na care'n.

3 But aye I wi my hook will whang
    The thistles if in prickles strang
    Your bonnie milk white hands they wrang
    When we gang to the shearin.

4 An aye we'll had our rig afore
    An try to hae the shearin o'er
    Sine you will soon forget you bore
    The weary toil o shearin.

5 For then my lassie we'll be wed
    When we hae proof o ither had
    And nae mair need to mind what's said
    When wee'r thegther shearin.

Mrs MARGARET GILLESPIE — D

G

The Band o' Shearers

1 When autumn comes and heather bells
    Bloom bonny owre yon muirland fell
    And corn that waves in lowland dells
    In yellow ripe appearing.

2 My bonny lassie wilt thou gang
    And shear wi' me the hale day lang
    O love will cheer us as we gang
    To join yon bands o' the shearin'.

3 And if the others should envy
    Or say we love then you and I
    We will pass them slyly by
    As if we were na caring.

4 But aye I wi' my hook will whang
    The thistles if in prickles stang
    Your bonny milk white hands they wrang
    When we gang to the shearing.

5 And aye we'll haud our rig of ore
    And fly to hae the shearing o'er
    Syne you will sune forget you bore
    Your neighbour's gibes and jeering.

6 And when we do louse fae the hook
    We will get our supper fae the cook
    We will creep into some canny nook
    And forget a' the toils of the shearing.

7 O then my lassie we'll be wed
    And we will hae a house and bed
    Ah bonny lassie wilt thou gang
    To join yon bands o' shearing.

Source unrecorded — G

H

The Band o' Shearers

1 'Twas on an August afternoon,
When folks could spy the harvest-moon
The lads and lasses gathered roun',
To talk about the shearin'.
I spier'd at Jean if she would gang
And shear wi' me the hale day lang
And join wi' me the merry thrang
A jolly band o' shearers.
  Sae bonnie lassie will ye gang
  An' shear wi' me the hale day lang
  An' love will cheer us as we gang
  To join yon band o' shearers.

2 An' should the weather be ower hot
I'll cast my gravat and my coat
An' help my lass to shear her lot
Amang yon band o' shearers.
An' should the thistles be ower strang
Thy bonnie feet or hands to wrang
I'll swear they'll nae be stanin' lang
To hurt the lassie shearin'.

3 And when our daily task is dune
We'll wander by the rising moon
And string our hearts to love's sweet tune
When comin' frae the shearin'.
And when the harvest days are done
An' slowly sets yon wintry sun
Ye'll be my ain till life is run
Nae mair to join the shearers.

JOHN ORD — G

JOHNNIE SANGSTER

A

1 Of a' the seasons o' the year when we maun work the sairest
The harvest is the foremost time and yet it is the rarest.
We rise as seen as mornin' licht, nae craters can be blyther
We buckle on our finger-steels and follow oot the scyther.   [finger stalls
    For you Johnnie, you Johnnie, you Johnnie Sangster
    I'll trim the gavel o' my shafe for ye're a gallant bandster.

2 A mornin' piece to line oor cheek afore that we gae farder
Wi cloods o' blue tobacco reek we then set oot in order
The sheafs are risin fast and thick and Johnnie he maun bind them
The busy group for fear they stick can scarcely look behind them.

3 I'll gae you bands that winna slip, I'll plait them weel and thraw them
I'm sure they winna tine the grip foo ever weel ye draw them.
I'll lay my leg oot owre the shafe and draw the band sae handy
Wi' ilka straw as straucht's a rash and that'll be the dandy.

4 Some complain on hacks and thraws and some on brods and bruises   [kinks; pricks
And some complain on grippet hips and stiffness in their trowsers.
As soon as we lay down the scythe the pipers yoke their blawvin   [blowing
And in a hint the rabble rook they're owre the lugs wi' twaving. [completely absorbed in
                                                                    the effort

5 Oh lazy wives they hinna skeel for a' their fine pretences
They'll gar ye trow they're never well and loll upon their hinches
They sair themsels afore the lave wi a'thing in profusion
And syne preten' they canna ate their stammacks hisna fushion.   [appetite

6 If e're it chance to be my lot to get a gallant bandster
I'll gar him wear a gentle coat and bring him gowd in hanfu's
But Johnnie he can please himsel' I wudna wuss him blinkit
Sae aifter he has brewed his ale he can sit doon and drink it.

7 A dainty cowie in the byre for butter and for cheeses
A grumphy feeding in the stye wad keep the hoose in greases
A bonnie ewie in the bucht wad help to creesh the ladle
And we'll get tufts o' cannie woo wad help to thick the craddle.

8 . . . .
. . . .
But noo the evenin's wearin' on and we maun cut oor corn
We'll just let a' these matters stan' and settle them the morn.

Foul fa' me but I maist forgot
To tell ye that my name was Scott;
For things like this I'm forced to trot,
I am so silly;
The ither half was made by vote,
And then ca'd Willy.

WILLIAM FARQUHAR (Mintlaw) — G

B
Johnnie Sangster

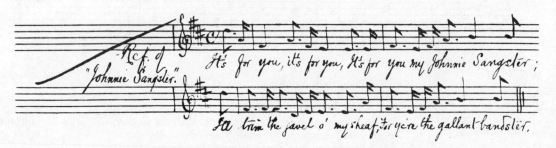

Mrs CLARK — G

C
Jock Sangster

To the tune of *Johnny Lad* from the same singer

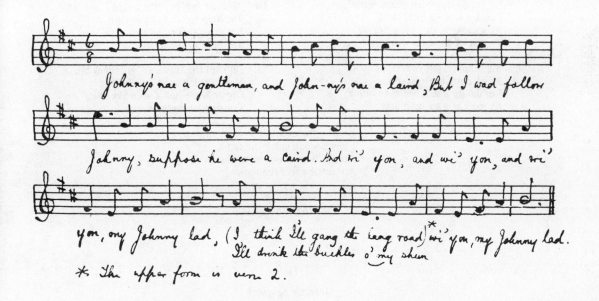

For you, and for you, an' for you, Jock Sangster,
I'll trim the gavel o' my sheaf for you, my gallant bandster.

Mrs MARGARET GILLESPIE — D

D
Johnnie Sangster

1   In a' the seasons o' the year,
     Fin we maun work the sairest,
     The harvest is the only time,
     But still it is the rarest.
      Wi' you my Johnnie, you my Johnnie,
      You my Johnnie Sangster,
      I'll trim the ravel o' my sheaf,
      For ye're a gallant bandster.

2   As soon's the mornin' bit comes in,
     Nae craturs could be blither,
     We buckle on our finger steels
     And follow out the scyther.

3   A mornin' piece to line our cheeks,
     Before 'at we go forder,
     An' clouds o' blue tobacco reek,
     We then set out in order.

4   An' fan the scyther stops his knife,
     Tae sharp his gully gapas,
     The souple joints gets on wi' life,
     But wae be tae the tapies.   [awkward people

5   Dounby the side o' yonder stook
     We a' sit doon sae cozy,
     Wi' barmy cakes an' frothy ale,
     Oor noddle soon gets dozy.

6 It doesna dae sae verra weel,
When lasses tries the speirin',
Bit fin they dinna get the hint,
The lads are lang o' hearin'.

7 Bit Johnnie, ye can please yersel;
I wadna wis' ye blinket,
As soon-as ye dae brew yer ale,
Ye can sit doon an' drink it.

8 Bit Johnnie, gin ye try yer luck,
Be sure an' nae miscarry,
For dandy maids gae a' to muck,
As soon as they do marry.

9 Ye'll gie me twa three gweed milk kye
For butter an' for cheeses,
A grumphy feedin' in the stye
To keep the hoose in greases.

10 Ae ewie feedin i' the bucht
Tae help tae creesh the ladle
Besides a tuft o' bonnie woo'
Tae help to thick the cradle.

11 I'll trim the lamps an' gie them oil,
Mak' a'thing snod an' cheery,
Gin Johnnie had a wife like this,
I'm sure he wadna weary.

12 Bit noo the evenin's wearin' on,
Fin we maun stack the corn,
An' we'll let a' oor maiters stan',
An' sattle them the morn.

Mrs JAFFRAY — D

E

Johnnie Sangster

1 O' a' the seasons o' the year, when we maun work the sairest,
The harvest is the foremost time for yet it is the rarest.
We rise as seen as mornin' licht, nae craters can be blither,
And buckle on oor finger-steels to follow oot the scyther.
For you, it's for you, it's for you, my Johnnie Sangster,
I'll trim the gavel o' my shafe, for ye're the gallant bandster.

2 A mornin' piece to line oor cheek, afore that we gae forder,
Wi' cloods o' blue tobacco reek we a' mairch oot in order.
As seen's the scyther sharps his knife, and stabs his gully gawkie,
The merry lads gaes o' the rig, but woe unto the tawpie.

3 The sheaves are risin' fast and thick, and Johnnie he maun bind them;
And eident aye for fear he stick, can scarcely look behind him.
Doon aside some bit o' stook we set oorsels sae cosie,
And barmy cake and frothy ale to mak' oor noddles doosie.

4 Then ane or twa or maybe three to their fingers yokes a-blawvin,
Twa or three or maybe four a' owre the lugs wi' tchavin.
Some has gaws into their backs, ithers has brods and bruises,
Some compleens on grippet hips, and stiffness in their trousers.

5 Noo, Johnnie lad, tak' my advice, tak' care and nae miscairry,
For dandy deems gaes a' to muck as seen as they get mairriet.

6 They load themsels as seen's they rise wi' a' their fine pretensions,
Syne they say they are nae weel, and live upon their henches.
They load themsels as seen's they rise, wi' a' their fine profession,
Syne they say they canna eat, their stammack has nae fushion.

7   A guid fat hen into the crive, does weel to creesh the ladle,
     A dainty yowie in the bucht does weel to theek the cradle.
     A guid milk coo into the byre does weel to keep the hoose in cheeses,
     A grumphie feedin' in the stye to keep the hoose in greases.

8   Noo Johnnie lad tak' my advice, tak' care and nae be blinket,
     The better ale that ye will brew, the better ye will drink it.

WILLIAM SPENCE — G

F

Johnnie Sangster

1   O a' the seasons o' the year when we man wourk the sairest
     The hairst it is the formist time but yet it is the sarest
     We rise as soon as mornin' light, nae craters could be blyther
     We buckle on our fingerstells an follow on the scyther.
       For you Johnnie, you Johnnie, you Johnnie Sangster
       I'll trim the gavle o' my shafe for yer my gallant bandster.

2   A mornin' piece to line our cheek afore that we gae forder
     Wi' cloods o' blue tobaco reek we then set oot in order
     The sheves are followin' fast an' thick and Johnnie ye man bin' them
     The buisy group for fear they stick can scarcely look behind them.

3   I'll gie ye bands that winna slip I'll plate them weel and thraw them
     I'm sure they winna tine the grip foo ever well ye draw them.
     Sa bang yer knee against the shafe an draw the band sae handie
     Wi' ilka strae as straught's a rash an it will be a dandie.

4   O some complain on backs an strains an' some on broads an brusars
     An' some complain on grippit hips or stiffness in their trousers.
     But as soon as they lay doon the scyth the pipes begins a blawvin
     They ane an' a' forget their dools wi' daffin an wi twavin'.

JOHN MILNE — G

THE HAIRST O' RETTIE

A

JOHN QUIRRIE – G

B

The Hairst o' Rettie

1   I hae seen the hairst of Rettie, ay, and twa three on the throne
    I've heard for sax or seven weeks the hairsters girn and groan.
    But a covey Willie Rae wi' a monthie and a day
    Maks a' the jolly hairster lads gae singin' doon the brae.

2   A monthie and a day my lads, the like was never seen
    It beats to sticks the fastest strips o' Victory's best machine.
    A Speedwell now brings up the rear, a Victory clears the way
    And twenty acres daily yields nor stands to Willie Rae.

3   He drives them roon and roon the fields at what an awfu rate
    He steers them canny oot and in at mony's the kittle gate
    And wiles them safely o'er the clods to mony's the hidden hole
    But he comes by no mishanter if you leave him with the pole.

4   He sharps their teeth to gar them bite then taps them on the jaws
    And when he finds them dully like he brawly kens the cause
    A boltie here, a pinnie there, a little out o' tune
    He shortly stops their wild career and brings the slusher doon.

5   He whittles aff at corners, makes crookit bitties straught
    And sees that man and beast alike are equal in the draught.
    And a' the shavies lying straught and neen o' them agley
    For he'll count wi' ony dominie fae the Deveron to the Spey.

128

6   He's no made up o' mony words nor kent to puff and lee
    But just as keen a little chap as ever you did see
    If you be in search o' harvest work upon a market day
    Tak' my advice be there in time and look for Willie Rae.

7   Now we hae gotten it in aboot, and a' our thingies tight
    We gathered roon that festive board to spend a jolly night
    Wi' Scottish songs and mutton broth to drive all cares away
    We'll drink success to Rettie and a health to Willie Rae.

8   Come all ye jolly Rettie lads a ringin' cheer to a'
    A band o' better working chaps a gaffer never saw
    So eager aye to play their pairt and ready for the brae
    'Twas you that made the boatie row, twas steered by Willie Rae.

ALEX MILNE — G

129

THE BOGHEAD CREW

A

1 Twas in the year 1870,
   On August the 16th day
   From the parish of Longside
   I northward took my way.

2 The mornin' bein' fair and clear,
   I travelled on with speed,
   I was going to be a harvest hand
   On the farm of Boghead.

3 Now I am not a poet,
   Nor yet a learned man,
   But I'll sing a verse or twa
   And spread them as I can.

4 John Macnab oor foremost man,
   He's sturdy, brave, and strang,
   Sae canny's he pits in his scythe
   And carries on the thrang.   [activity

5 His gatherer she cam frae Greenbank,
   Maclennan was her name,
   She was the flooer o' a' oor flock
   A handsome clever dame.

6 And Esselmont he ban' to her,   [bound
   He was a sturdy chiel,
   Ye wadna seen a jollier crew
   Upon a harvest field.

7 Willie Kidd, oor second man
   He filled his berth richt weel,
   He pleased both the girlies,
   The truth I mean to tell.

8 Jean Forsyth she gathered to him,
   Wi' her lovely curly hair,
   I hope they'll meet in wedlock band
   They'll be a slashin' pair.

9 And as for Kidd's bandster
   They ca' him Geordie Grant,
   He's sometimes in a merry mood,
   And sometimes like a saunt.

10 Willie Ritchie and his wife
   Comes next upon the list,
   And they are jist as happy a pair
   As ever wedlock blessed.

11 As for Ritchie's bandster
   We maun mak' some remark,
   He is a deil for pranks and tricks,
   They ca' him Tailor Park.

12 His residence is at Peathill,
   Nae unco far awa,
   And when the shades o' nicht draws doon,
   He northward hame does draw.

13 But early in the morning
   He sets us a' asteer   [stirring
   Likewise he makes the porridge
   And he places them on the fleer.

14 And roon aboot the porridge pot
   The supper did prepare
   The first time that I saw them
   It made me smile and stare.

15 Noo, I mysel comes in the last
   My heart it is richt gled
   To follow up the merry crew
   And wag the hinmost blades.

16 Mrs Sellar she gathers to me
   Alang the bout wi' speed
   And altho' she is nae very big
   She is a gatherer guid.

17 And Jamie Gray he band to her
    The sheaves that she laid doon
    They made him for to thraw his face
    He was only but a loon.

18 Noo Charlie Watt and Davie Gray
    They're in the list you'll find
    They have to march in order
    And trail the rakes behind.

19 And as for Robbie Sellar
    His job it is nae fine
    He's got the beasts to muck and meat
    And likewise ca' the brine.

20 This is a' oor ootdoor folk
    And weel may seem to be
    And as for them that's in the hoose,
    Their number it is three.

21 We hae a jolly maister
    A tall and stately man
    Who can conduct his farm work
    Wi' muckle skeel and can.

22 Although he be a single man
    And lives a rovin' life
    He's never ta'en it in his heid
    For to seek out a wife.

23 We have a jolly female
    Come o' the Gordon race
    Who manages the dairy work
    And fills a mistress's place.

24 She does all her endeavour
    Her master for to please
    And when we were leadin' late at night
    She gied us flint for cheese.

25 When we tried our teeth to it
    It made us fidge and fyke
    We had to gang and brak it sma'
    Wi' stanes upo' the dyke.

26 Eliza Clubb our kitchen maid
    Is handsome neat and tight
    She sang to us some lovely sangs
    When we come hame at night.

ALEXANDER ROBB — G

B

The Boghead Crew.

John Macnab oor foremost man was sturdy stoof and strang,

And sae cannily he pat in his blade and carried on the thrang.

ARTHUR BARRON — G

131

C

The Boghead Crew

The mornin bein' fair and clear, I travelled on wi' speed

I was going to be a harvest hand On the farm of Boghead.

J.W. SPENCE — G

D

The nicht bein' dark & I half drunk, I (traivelled) on wi' speed,
(traiversed)

For to be a harvest hand At the fai-rim o' Bogheid.

WILLIAM CARLE — G

THE KIETHEN HAIRST

1 The hairst began on Keithen's lands
The 17th of September
In the year of 1872
As we may well remember.

2 When Willie Moir with scythe in hand
He quickly led the van
Says Now my lads it's rig and rig
We will sae wha's the man.

3 John Rettie was the second man
He drew the blade with speed
And though the corn was lying flat
He quickly made the head.

4 The ane that cutit third
His name was Jamie Trail
He tried to do his very best
And followed at their tail.

5 Then the gatherers they were next
They were in number three
And better hands upon a field
Your eyes did never see.

6 Jane Robb, she was the foremost girl
The maiden o' Greenness,
She followed hard at Willie's heels
And well deserved her place.

7 Mary Pirie frae the Tuchar howe
A girlie blythe and free
She followed Rettie o'er the fields
And that with mirth and glee.

8 Then Mrs Bain came o'er frae Greens,
A stout and hardy wife.
You would see very few like her
'Tween John o' Groats and Fife.

9 Then Willie Bain and Arthur Brown
They had the sheaves to bind
And Willie Herd frae Turra toon
He set the stooks behind.

10 And Angus Taylor frae New Byth
He was a raker keen
He dragged on frae morn till nicht
And made the fields a' clean.

11 Then Jackie Ross frae Fyvie came,
To keep the beasts in meat
And the farmer he assisted him
I am sure they were a treat.

12 And Betty Duncan and Jean Reid
They were a well-matched pair
They kept the house in proper trim
And thought their task was sair.

13 Although they always busy were
The truth I mean to tell
We always got the best of meat
And plenty of hame brewed ale.

14 Although the weather it was wet
We all got on with glee
Sometime the merriest of the crew
They held a wee bit spree.

15 So noo the hairst is finished up
I have little mair to say
And if you want to know my name
I am Trail from Barbow Brae.

Source unrecorded — G

THE ARDLAW CREW

1   It was in the year 1880
     When I put this in rhyme;
     It's nae concerning things o' auld
     It's aboot the present time.
     Wi' my airy idle tadie um,
     My idle tum taril a.

2   It's nae concerning things o' auld,
     The truth I'll tell to you;
     It's just a verse or twa you'll find
     Aboot the Ardlaw crew.

3   For rhymin's grown sae common noo
     That the like o' me maun try
     To get a verse or twa to clink   [rhyme
     To gar the time pass by.

4   William Michie is our grieve,
     He's a very quiet man;
     He can conduct the jolly crew
     Wi' muckle skill and can.

5   James Sutherland is our foreman,
     His pair is Sharp and Sall;
     He tak's them oot in the mornin'
     A' jist at the first call.

6   He tak's them oot in the mornin',
     A' jist at the first call,
     And gie's them wark frae morn tae nicht
     Till evenin' does doon fall.

7   Sometimes he gaes to the cart,
     And sometimes to the ploo,
     And he must haud the hemp upon the hair
     Or else it wadna do.

8   James Scott he is our second man,
     He's on the list you'll find;
     He drives a pair o' young anes
     And follows tee behind.

9   Sandy Ritchie is our third man,
     Their kickers he can bide,
     He has an iron red and a gallant grey,
     He calls them Bet and Clyde.

10   Clyde and Bet is an able pair,
     And so is Sharp and Sall,
     They have to do the heavy work,
     They are the best among them all.

11   John Howatt is our fourth man,
     His pair is Dash and Ann,
     He follows them through thick and thin,
     He's a knackie little man.   [skilful

12   George Ritchie is our fifth man,
     He drives a pair o' broons,
     He tak's them oot in the mornin'
     And mak's them walk their roons.

13   Sandy Adie is our sixth man,
     He has a chestnut and a broon,
     He follows up the merry crew,
     Upon the Ardlaw toon.

14   James Murison is our orra man,
     He keeps ticht baith close and pens,   [neat; farmyar
     And ony orra job like that,
     Siclike as muck the hens.

15   For me I am first bailie,
     It's a very sharny shift,
     But Whitsunday is comin' roon
     When I can tak' the lift.   [move

16   James Mowat he is our second bailie,
     He suits the berth fu' weel,
     And but and ben the meikle byre
     We gar the barrows wheel.

17   Donald Adie is our third bailie,
     To plan he is nae slack,
     But I am led to understand
     His name is in the tack.   [lease

18   William Mutch he is our fourth bailie,
     New Pitsligo is his hame,
     And he cam' doon to Ardlaw
     Some Irish men to tame.

19   First on the list of the female sex
     Her name is Maggie Broon,
     She has to plan the dairy work
     Upon the Ardlaw toon.

20   Next comes our housemaid,
     Her name is Katie Massie,
     But I canna say meikle aboot her,
     She is only bit a lassie.

21   Maggie Simpson is our kitchen maid,
     She has our kail a-makin',
     But I can plainly tell you
     She's nae jist very takin'.

22 Janet Barron is our out-woman,
    She is on the roll o' ty,
    She has to work the outdoor work,
    And help to milk the kye.

23 But noo our gaffer's leavin',
    And nae langer we can bide,
    So we'll gang to the hirins
    Baith Strichen and Longside.

24 We will traivel up to Strichen toon,
    And then we'll tak' the rails,
    And if they dinna gie's a blast
    We are sure to rug their tails.

25 So fare-ye-well to Ardlaw,
    Nae langer we maun stay,
    We will tak' our budgets on our back
    On the twenty-sixth o' May.

26 Now that is all I've got to say,
    And I hope I've said naething wrang,
    For I jist made it up ae day
    To haud me on-thocht lang.

GORDON McQUEEN — G

412

THE NORTHESSIE CREW

1 As I gaed up to Aikey Fair,
    'Twas for to get a fee;
    A farmer frae St Fergus
    Came steppin' owre to me.

2 This farmer we kent unco weel
    For twa three years and more;
    And soon wi' him I did engage
    As I hae deen afore.

3 Our foreman is a canny chiel,
    Bill Porter is his name;
    To keep us steady at our work,
    I'm sure it is his aim.

4 Charlie Ewen he comes next,
    A bright and rovin' blade;
    He cuts the tares and ca's the neeps,
    First cattleman it is said.

5 I myself a harvest hand,
    My name is Francie Massie;
    So I made this twa three lines
    While workin' at Northessie.

JAMES EWEN — G

MY PLOUGHMAN BOY

1   My laddie is as nice a young man as ere my eyes did see,
    His cheeks they were like roses, and teeth like ivory;
    He had two eyes as black as sloes, and that my only joy
    But go where he will he's my love still, he's my darling ploughman boy.

2   The colour of my laddie's hair was of an auburn brown,
    And with him I would wander from separate town to town,
    And with him I would wander this world round and round,
    But go where he will he's my love still, he's my darling ploughman boy.

3   We both went in the garden to have a while's enjoy,
    He took me in his arms and kissed me tenderly,
    We both sat down upon the grass to have a while's enjoy,
    But go where he will he's my love still, he's my darling ploughman boy.

4   Her father stood at the garden gate to hear what we would say,
    He said he would transport my love and send him far from me,
    He said he would transport my love and deprive me of my joy,
    But go where he will he's my love still, he's my darling ploughman boy.

5   The summer leaves falling with them I make my bed,
    The lilies and primroses they grow beneath my head,
    The juniper tree proves to me and that's my only joy,
    But go where he will he's my love still, he's my darling ploughman boy.

6   Neither to hills nor mountains that I've to seek my sorrow,
    It's for the bonnie laddie that laid his love on me;
    He seldom thinks on me tho' oftimes I think on him
    But go where he will he's my love still, he's my darling ploughman boy.

7   Come fill up the glasses to the brim, let the toast go merrily round,
    There's health to every ploughboy that ploughs and tills the ground,
    When his work is over his home is stirring joy
    And happy happy is the maid that gets the ploughman boy.

SAM DAVIDSON — G

THE JOLLY PLOUGHMAN LAD

1   The jolly jolly ploughman lad goes whistling o'er the lea
There's none in a' the country roun' has a heart sae blithe and free
He loes his bonnie lassie Jean sae tenderly and true
And Jeanie loes the winsome laddie that ca's the cairt and ploo.
    Here's to all Scottish lassies, a' sae bonny blithe and true
    And here's tae a' ye winsome laddies that ca's the cairt and ploo.

2   He rises wi' the mornin licht and he whistles a' the day
The Gadie Rins and Johnnie Cope, Lang Syne and Scots Wha Hae.
And he trysts his bonnie lassie Jean and he prees her rosy moo
For Jeanny loes the winsome laddie that cas the cairt and ploo.

3   Noo Jock and Jean are man and wife Jock whistles a' the same
But his favourites noo are Corn-Rigs and When the Kye Comes Hame,
Their bairnies play at hide and seek in peenies reid and blue   [pinafores
Wha rins to meet their winsome daddie wha cas the cairt and ploo.

4   Noo Jock and Jean are auld and gray, their toiling days are o'er
They smile tae see their halflin lads and lasses three or four
The laddies haud their father's stilts, the lassies milk the coo
And help to cheer the auld man's heart wha caed the cairt and ploo.

JONATHAN ANDERSON — G

THE CARSE O' POMMAIZE

A

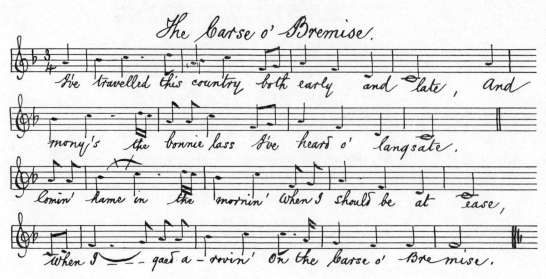

The Carse o' Bremise.

I've travelled this country both early and late, And
mony's the bonnie lass I've heard o' langsate.
Comin' hame in the mornin' when I should be at ease,
When I ___ gaed a - rovin' On the Carse o' Bremise.

1 I've travelled this country both early and late
And mony's the bonnie lassie I've heard o' lansate
Coming hame in the morning when I should be at ease
When I gaed a-roving i' the Carse o' Braemese.

2 The first thing I did when I gaed to your toon
I corned my horses and cleaned them a' doon
My maister aften catches me changing my claes
Says Far are ye gaun i' the Carse o' Braemese?

3 At meal time my mistress often yokes upon me   [joins battle with
Says Laddie ye'd be better gin ye wid lat them a' be
For ye'll mind on that laddie, when ye come to auld age
When I gaed a-rovin i' the Carse o' Braemese.

4 Mony's the time I hae gaen tae your toon
Mony's the time I hae watched the loons
Some darnin' their stockings, some mending their clothes
When I gaed a-rovin i' the Carse o' Braemese.

5 When I gaed to the window to gently sit down
As soon as they heard me, they sprang at my heels
Comin' down the stair naked for want o' their claes
When I gaed a-rovin i' the Carse o' Braemese.

6 Mony's the bonnie lassie I've left for to sigh
Says Fat's come o' the bold rover he's never drawn nigh
We'll gang till wir bed and we'll take a laugh, eh,
For the bold young rover left the Carse o' Braemese.

7   Come all ye lively lads whatever ye may be
Don't take up wi' young women, nor bear their company
For young women they're enticing, when they get on their braw claes
They aye send you a-rovin i' the Carse o' Braemese.

Mrs FOWLIE — G

B
Carse of Pommaize

To the tune of 236 *Erin-go-bragh* B

JAMES ANGUS — G

C
Arline's Fine Braes

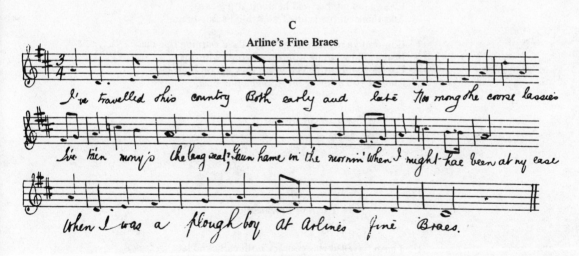

I've travelled this country Both early and late Nae mong the coorse lassies
Sie tän mony's the lang seal? taen hame in the mornin' when I might-hae been at my ease
When I was a ploughboy at Arlines fine Braes.

JAMES EWEN — G

D

The Carse o' Pommaise

1   It's I've travelled this country baith early and late
    And wi' the young lassies I've had a fine seat
    Chatting all the night wi' them when I should have been at my ease
    When I was a ploughboy on Arland's fine braes.

2   It's the first thing I did when I gaed tae yon toon
    Was to corn my horses, syne rub them weel doon
    And aff tae the bothy and shift aff my claes
    And get on a-roving on Arland's fine braes.

3   It's mony's the nicht I've sitten by yon fire
    Sometimes in the barn, sometimes in the byre
    Chatting all the night with them when I should have been at my ease
    When I was a ploughboy on Arlond's fine braes.

4   My mistress and Mollie they've aften told me
    It's I'd been a better laddie if they'd latten me be
    But I'll mind on my roving aye in my auld age
    When I was a ploughboy on Arlond's fine braes.

5   When I go to their window sae gently I kneel
    The girlies when they hear me, they spring tae their heel
    Half naked to their window, ere they get on their claes
    Says Here is the laddie frae Arland's fine braes.

6   It's mony the fair maid I've caused for to sigh
    Says "Where is my laddie, that he never comes nigh
    I'll awa tae my bed and lie doon at my ease
    And think on the laddie frae Arlond's fine braes."

7   Come all ye roving ploughboys take a warning frae me.
    Never follow young women, whatever you dee
    For they will entice you when they get on braw claes
    And set you a-roving on Arland's fine braes.

Miss ANNIE SHIRER — G

E

Earth of Braemese

1   I have travelled this country both early and late
    And wi' the earth lasses I've been mony's the set
    Sitting all the night with them when I should have been at ease
    When I was a roving ploughboy on the Earth of Braemese.

2   The first thing I do when I go to yon town
    Is to corn my horses and groom them well doon
    Then away to the bothy and shift off my clothes   [change out of
    And put on the roving for the Earth of Braemese.

3   Oh, all the day lang as I gae in the yoke
    My mind is containing some evil exploit
    Expecting good prospect when I should hae been at ease
    When I was the roving ploughboy on the Earth o' Braemese.

4   My mither on Yule's day she aften tells me
    I had been a better laddie gin I wad lat them a' be.
    I mind on yon rovin aye, in my auld age
    When I was the ploughboy on the Earth o' Braemese.

5   O it's mony's the time I ha'e sat by the fire
    Sometimes in yon barn and sometimes in yon byre
    Some darning their stockings some mending their clothes
    When I was a roving ploughboy on the Earth o' Braemese.

6   When I go to the window I gently kneel down
    And when they do hear me they spring to their heels
    Half naked to the window before they get on their clothes
    Cries Here comes my laddie from the Earth o' Braemese.

7   Come all ye young lads what ever ye may be
    Never follow young ladies whatever they be
    For they will entice you when they get on their braw claes
    And set you a-rovin' on the Earth o' Braemese.

Source unrecorded — G

F

Arline's Fine Braes

1   I've roved in this country both early and late
    Amongst the coarse lasses and . . . . . .   [bad
    Coming home in the morning when I should have been at ease,
    When I was a young plough-boy on Arline's fine braes.

2   The first thing I did when I gaed to yon toon
    Was to corn my horses and clean them a' doon;
    The master often catches me changin' my claes,
    Says, "Where have you been rovin' on Arline's fine braes?"

3   The mistress at diet-time yokes upon me, —
    "Ye'd be a far better laddie gin ye'd lat them be;
    You will repent it when you come on old days,
    When you went a-rovin' on Arline's fine braes."

4   Mony's the time I sat by yon toon,
    Sometimes in the barn, sometimes in the byre.
    Some darning their stockin's, some mending their claes,
    When I was a young plough-boy on Arline's fine braes.

5   When I go to the window and softly kneel down,
    As soon as they do hear me they spring to their heels,
    Comin' doon the stair half-nakit for want o' their claes
    . . . . . . young rover on Arline's fine braes.

6   Come all ye young plough-boys wherever you be,
    . . . . . . like me give up all false courtship,
    For young women will entice you when they get on their braw claes,
    And send you a-roving' on Arline's fine braes.

SAM DAVIDSON — G

G
Carse of Brindese

1   I have travelled the country both early and late
    And amongst yon Cawder lasses I've had many a lang sit
    Coming hame in the morning when I might been at ease
    When I was a ploughboy on the Carse o' Brindese.

2   The first thing I did when I came to this town
    Was to corn my horses and rub them well down
    But my master often caught me a-changing my claes
    When I was a ploughboy on the Carse o' Brindese.

3   My master at meal times often joked at me
    Says, Seeing you'll no do better I maun just lat you be
    But you'll mind on my words when you come to auld age
    When you were a rover on the Carse of Brindese.

4   Among the bonnie lasses I sat by yon kitchen fire
    Oft times in yon barn oft times in yon byre
    For to leave a bonnie lassie my mind's no at ease
    Unless I am a-roving on the Carse of Brindese.

5   I go to the window and gently do call
    And whenever they hear me they spring to their heels
    Some darning their stockings some mending their claes
    At night as I wander through the Carse of Brindese.

6   Many is the bonnie lassie I hae left here to mourn
    Saying Where is yon merry ploughboy will he ever return
    But we'll go to our beds and sleep at our ease
    Since yon hard-hearted ploughboy has left the Carse of Brindese.

WILLIAM CHEYNE — G

H
Ireland's Fine Braes

1   The first thing I did when I came to this town
    Was to corn my horses and comb them all down
    My master often watched me when changing my claes
    Saying "Where hae ye been, a-roving thro' Ireland's fine braes?"

2   At meal times my mistress often yokèd on me
    Since ye'll dae nae better I may lat ye be
    But ye'll mind o' my words when ye come tae auld age
    For ye'll nae aye be a ploughman on Ireland's fine braes.

3   I've travelled this country both early and late
    And wi' mony glaiked lasses I've taen mony a sate
    Gaun hame in the morning when I micht be at my ease
    When I was a ploughman on Ireland's fine braes.

4   I creep to the windows and gently do kneel
    And when they see me they'll spring tae their heel
    Some darning their stockings, some mending their stays
    When I was a ploughman on Ireland's fine braes.

5   Come a' ye roving young men tak' warning frae me
    And do not trust young weemen where'er ye may be
    For they will entice ye when they tak aff their claes
    And send ye a-roving through Ireland's fine braes.

JAMES CHEYNE – G

416
THE PLOUGHMAN CHIEL AND THE PLOUGHMAN LADDIE

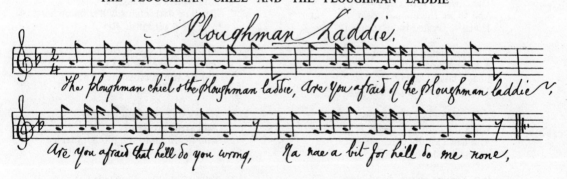

1   The ploughman chiel and the ploughman laddie,
    Are you afraid of the ploughman laddie?
    Are you afraid that he'll do you wrong,
    Na nae a bit for he'll do me none.

Rev. JOHN CALDER – G

THE WOODS OF RICKARTON

A

Whistlin' at the Ploo

1 Come all ye jolly ploughman lads
And listen to my rhyme
The praises o' your bonnie glen
I wad be fain to sing.

2 For I dearly loe the heather hills
And lasses leal and true
That courts the bonnie laddie
That gangs whistlin' at the ploo.

3 The bonnie woods o' Riccarton
I love to wander through
To hear the blackbird whistle
And the cushie coodle-doo   [wood pigeon

4 To see the Cowie winding clear
The cowslips spring so sweet
And to see the bonnie lassie
That I've trysted there to meet.

5 For ilka Jackie has a Jean
A Bawbie or a Nell
I hae a lass I like mysel
Though her name I wadna tell

6 And sae weel's I like to meet her
When the hard day's wark is by
And hae a kindly crack wi' her
At the milkin' o' the kye.

7 But it winna be yon dandy lass
That will win my heart awa'
For she's foul and dirty at her wark
Tho' on Sunday she gangs braw.

8 She needna be sae michty prood
Nor cast her heid sae high
For there's nae a lad in a' the glen
But what wad pass her by.

9 She'll maybe get some fairmer's son
Mair suitin' to her mind
And they can both get married
If they feel so inclined.

10 But he's very welcome to her
And her muckle tocher too
He's free to wear oot my auld sheen
Sin I hae gotten new.

11 But now the harvest's over
And winter's comin' on
The lang dark nichts will soon be here
And we'll get rantin fun

12 Among the lasses in the glen
They're a' sae trig and neat
But we winna cross the Cowie
For fear we weet our feet.

13 Here's success to the fairmer
And great prosperity
And health unto the ploughman lad
That works for meat and fee.

14 I wish the lassie happiness
May she never hae cause to rue
That marries the bonnie laddie
That gangs whistlin at the ploo.

J. W. SPENCE – G

B

a

Riccarton.

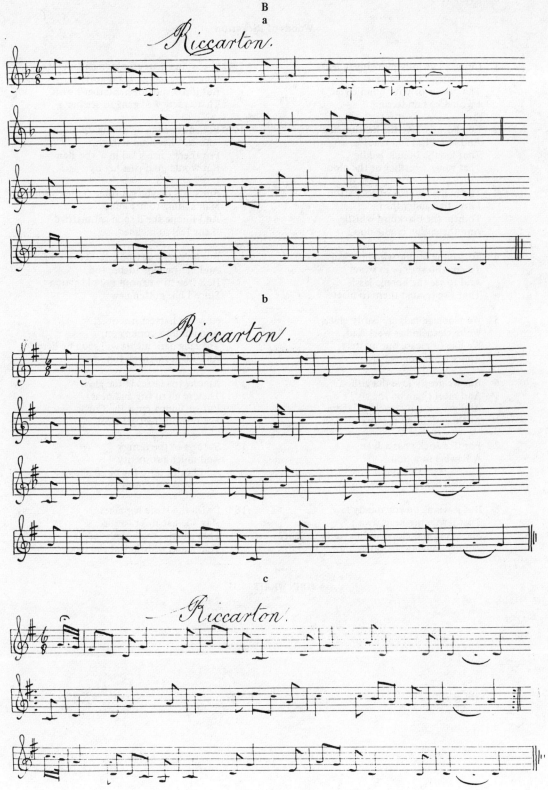

b

Riccarton.

c

Riccarton.

JAMES ANGUS — G

C

Woods of Rickarton

1 Come all ye jolly ploughman lads,
And listen to my rhyme,
The praises of your bonnie glen
I would be fain to sing.

2 For I dearly love the heather hills,
And lasses leal and true,
That loe the bonnie laddie
That gangs whistling at the ploo.

3 The bonnie woods of Rickarton
I love to wander thro'
To hear the blackbird whistle
And the cushie crudle-doo.

4 To see the burnie winding clear,
To cowslip springs so sweet,
And to see the bonnie lassie
That I've trysted there to meet.

5 We plooman lads are hardy chiels,
We're clean and as weel clad,
We like to please our masters
And see our horses fed.

6 But we dearly love the girlies,
And meet them on the sly,
And get a kindly crack wi' them
At the milkin' o' the kye.

7 For ilka Jocky has a Jean,
A Bawbie or a Nell,
I hae a lass I dearly loe
Though her name I winna tell.

8 But it winna be yon dandy lass,
That'll wile my heart awa',
She's foul and clorty at her wark   [dirty
Though Sunday she gangs braw.

9 She widna marry a plooman lad,
'Cause she has a puckle gear,
But if it wisna for her father's cash
There's few wad gang to see her.

10 But she needna be so mighty proud,
And cast her head so high,
For there's nae a lad in a' the glen
But would guid pass her by.

11 But she'll maybe get some farmer's son
Mair suiting to her mind,
And I hope she'll soon get married
If she feel so inclined.

12 But he's very welcome to her
And her muckle tocher too,
He's free to wear out my old shoon
Since I hae gotten new.

13 Now the harvest it is over,
And winter's coming on,
The lang dark nichts will soon be here,
And I'll get wanton fun.

14 Among the lasses in the glen,
They're all so trig and neat,
But we winna cross the Cowie
For fear our feet get weet.

15 Success to the farmer
And much prosperity
And health unto the ploughboy
That works for meat and fee.

16 I wish the lassie happiness,
May she hae ne'er to rue,
That marries the bonnie laddie
That gangs whistling at the ploo.

JOHN WIGHT — G

WE ARE ALL JOLLY FELLOWS THAT FOLLOW THE PLOUGH

A

1 Twas earely one morning by the break oh the day
   The cocks they were crowing the farmer did saw,
   Come rise my good fellows come rise with good will
   Yeer horsess needs something there belles to fill.

2 When six o'clock comes, at breakfast wee meet,
   With beef bread and port boys so heartly eat   [for "pork"
   With a peice in our pocket away then wee go
   To see which of us a strait furr wee can hold.

Mrs WALKER — D

B

The Jolly Fellows Who Follow the Plough

1 It was early one morning at the break of day,
   The cocks were a-crowing; the farmers did say, —
   Come rise, my good fellows, come rise with good will,
   For your horses want something their bellies to fill.

2 When four o'clock comes then up we rise,
   Then into the stable, boys, so merrily flies;
   With rubbing and scrubbing our horses, I vow,
   We are all jolly fellows who follow the plough.

3 When six o'clock comes, at breakfast we meet,
   And beef, bread, and pork, boys, so heartily eat,
   With a piece in our pocket, I swear and I vow,
   We are all jolly fellows who follow the plough.

4 Then we harness our horses and away then we go,
   And trip o'er the plain, boys, as nimbly as does,
   And when we come home there — so jolly and bold,
   To see which of us the straight furrow can hold.

5 Our master came to us and thus he did say,
   What have you been doing boys, this long day?
   You have not ploughed an acre I swear and I vow,
   And you're d——d idle fellows that follow the plough.

6 I stepped up to him and made this reply, —
   We have all ploughed an acre so you tell a d——d lie;
   We have all ploughed an acre, I swear and I vow,
   And we are all jolly fellows that follow the plough.

7 He turned himself round and laughed at the joke,
   It's past two o'clock boys, 'tis time to unyoke;
   Unharness your horses and rub them down well,
   And I'll give you a jug of the very best ale.

8 So come, all you brave fellows, wherever you be,
   Come take this advice, be ruled by me;
   So never fear your masters, I swear and I vow,
   We are all jolly fellows that follow the plough.

JAMES ANGUS — G

THE LAD WHA HAUDS THE PLOO

1 There's some wha like a country life while others prefer the toon
   And some wherever they are placed hae just to cuddle doon   [make themselves
   But ilka place where e'er ye gang in a' the country through   comfortable
   There's nae a blyther lad you'll find than him wha hauds the ploo.

2 He cares na for the biting frost, he cares na for the snaw
   The rain may ding wi' torrents doon yet he sings throughoot it a'
   The sun may burn wi' scorchin heat till the sweat rins doon his broo
   Still nothing seems to daunt the lad wha whistles at the ploo.

3 His horses ken his whistle and his sweetheart kens the same
   She kens his gentle whistle when he ventures near her hame
   True is the ploughman's courtship and there's nane wha ere did rue
   The day they took the gallant lad wha hauds the useful plow.

4 The earth's the ploughman's workshop and his roof the skies aboon
   The stable oft his bedroom when his daily toil is done
   And he sits there wi' his cronies when he's no awa to woo
   For he likes aye near his horses in the hoose or at the ploo.

5 In hoeing time and in harvest he can talk wi' ilka lass
   But his eye is on his horses when they're oot upon the grass
   Unlike most other tradesmen folks his holidays are few
   But he's aye happy wi' his lot for his heart is in his plow.

6 May great success be aye their lot, their labour lightly born
   To plough the ground, to grow the neeps, the tatties and the corn
   And what would Britain do, alas, her prestige wad look blue
   Bereft of a' the gallant lads wha guide the noble plow.

A. ELRICK – G

THE FYVIE PLOUGHMEN

A
The Ploughman Lad

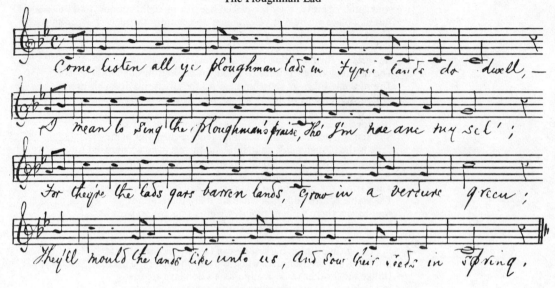

1   Come listen all ye ploughman lads in Fyvie's land that dwell
    I mean to sing the ploughman's praise though I'm nae ane mysel'
    They are the lads makes barren heath grow in a verdure green
    They mould their lands like to the sands and sow their seeds in spring.

2   In summer and in winter months in autumn and in spring
    When going to and from the plough they whistle and they sing.
    Though the winter months be dreary they will brave the winter's blast
    The seeing o' their dearie 'twill warm the winter's frost.

3   The seeing o' their sweetheart is not to be denied
    Nor to such regulations I would not have them tied.
    But I would have you deal justly and not deceivers be
    Nor cheat the bonnie lassie that lays her love on thee.

4   She'll kindly sit doon by your side, her hand laid on your knee
    And sweetly smile into your face, her heart it's a' to thee
    And when you fold her in your arms the time it does beguile
    And when you do embrace her you do forget your toil.

5   To gie the ploughman justice is the thing I mean to dee
    Wi' twa or three exceptions to guide his penny fee.
    The lass that gets a ploughman tho' poor perhaps he be
    She'll never want a sixpence when he has ane to gie.

6   Remember well ye fairmers all there's men as good as thee
    And don't think you're obliging them while that they're serving thee.
    For there's fields of speculation all around as you may see
    And there is emigration to tak' them o'er the sea.

7   Remember then ye fairmers all there's men as good as thee
And if you treat them kindly they will serve you faithfully.
They will do their work wi' pleasure, time will extended be
And you will increase their treasure by largely paying their fee.

SAM DAVIDSON — G

B

The Ploughman Lad

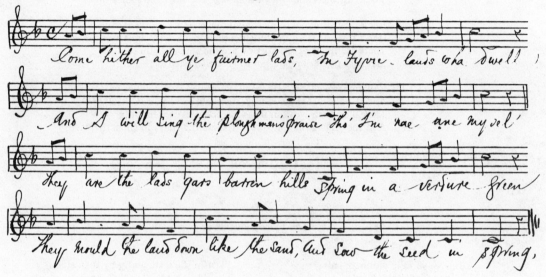

ARTHUR BARRON — G

C

The Ploughmen o' Fyvie

1   Come hither a' ye ploughmen lads that in Fyvie lands do dwell,
And I will sing the ploughmen's praise, tho' I'm nae ane mysel'.
They are the lads gars barren hill turn into verdures green;
They plough the lands like to the sands, and sow their seeds in spring.

2   In summer and in autumn months, in winter and in spring,
In going to and from the plough, they whistle and they sing.
Tho' the winter months be dreary, still they brave the blast,
It's gyaun to see their dearies that warms the winter's frost.

3   It's gyaun to see their dearies, it's nae to be denied,
And for such regulations I widna hae them tied;
But I would hae them to deal justly, and not deceivers be,
Nor cheat the bonnie lassie that lays her love on thee.

151

4   For she will gently sit down by your side, with her hand laid on your knee,
And sweetly smile into your face, says, "Love, it's a' for thee."
And when you take her in your arms, you do the time beguile,
And when you do embrace her, you do forget your toil.

5   To gie the ploughman justice, as I intend to dee,
Wi' twa or three exceptions to spend their penny fee.
The lass that gets the ploughman lad poor although he be,
Shall never want a sixpence as lang as he has ane to gie.

6   To gie the ploughman justice, as I intend to dee,
Twa feeing markets in the year they scarcely mair win free.
Why should their masters quarrell them when they do take a spree?
Twice for their ance they do indulge and taste the barley bree.

7   Remember well, ye farmers all, your men is as good as you;
Don't think that you're obliging them while they are serving thee.
There are fields of speculation around them as you see,
Likewise there's emigration to take them across the sea.

8   Remember well, ye farmers all, your men is as good as ye,
And if you treat them kindly, they will serve you faithfully.
They'll do their work in pleasure, and will contented be
And they'll hae the pleasure o' the lad that pays to them their fee.

SAM DAVIDSON — G

D

The Fyvie Ploughmen

1   Come all ye jolly plooman lads
In Fyvie lands that dwell
I'll sing tae you the plooman's praise
Tho' I'm nae ane mysel'.

2   The plooman lads maks barren lands
Turn into fertile green
They cut the corn in autumn
They sow the seed in spring.

3   In summer and in winter
In autumn and in spring
In gaun and comin frae the yoke
They whistle and they sing.

4   And although the winter nichts be drear
They lively face the blast
In gaun tae see their dearies
It warms them in the storm.

5   In gaun tae see their dearies
It's nae to be denied
And frae such regulations
I widna hae them tied

6   But I'd hae them tae deal justly
And nae deceivers be
Unto the bonnie lassie
That lays her love on them.

7   For she'll sit gently by their side
Her hand laid on their knee
And wi' twa or three exceptions
Wad guide their penny fee.

8   For the girl wha gets a plooman lad
Poor although he be
She'll never want a saxpence
Fin he has ane tae gae.

9   Twa feeing markets in the year
Is a' that they win free
And then their masters quarrel them
Gin they get on the spree.

10   Thrice for their ance they do indulge
And taste the barley bree
But dinna think ye fairmer lads
That they're obligin' you.

11   As lang's there's ither lands tae toil
They winna bide wi you
Tae get a craftie o' their ain
Is what they mean tae dae.

12   And then there's emigration
To tak them owre the sea
Mind this ye fairmers ane and a'
Your men's as guid as you.

13 And gin ye treat them kindly
   While they are servin you
   They'll do your work right justly
   An order will obey
   And then you'll tak a pleasure
   To pey the lads their fee.

Miss ANNIE SHIRER — G

E

The Fyvie Ploughmen

1 Come listen all ye ploughmen lads in Fyvie lands do dwell
   For I mean to sing the ploughman's praise although I'm nae ane mysel'
   They are the lads mak's barren heaths to grow in verdure green
   They plough the land like to the sand and sow their seed in spring.

2 In summer and in autumn months in winter and in spring
   While going to and from the plough they whistle and they sing
   Though winter be dreary they'll wear the winter's blast
   And in seeing of their sweethearts they'll wear the winter's frost.

3 In seeing of their sweethearts they should never be denied
   And to such regulations I would not have them tied
   But to deal justly and no deceivers be
   Nor slight the bonnie lassie that lays all her love on thee.

4 She'll gently set doon by your side wi' her hand laid on your knee
   And sweetly smile into your face for her heart beats all for thee
   The lass that marries a ploughman though poor perhaps he be
   She'll never want a sixpence while he has ane to gie.

5 Come listen now ye farmers all there's men as good as thee
   And if you treat them kindly they'll serve you faithfully
   They'll do their work with pleasure and time attended too
   Or the spirit of emigration will carry them over the sea.

WILLIAM CHEYNE — G

HARROWING TIME

A

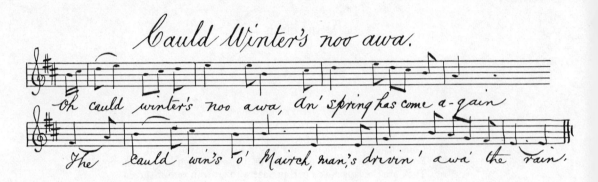

Cauld Winter's noo awa.

Oh cauld winter's noo awa, An' spring has come a-gain
The cauld win's o' Mairch, man's drivin' awa' the rain.

1 Cauld winter's noo awa
An' spring has come again
The cauld wind o' Mairch man's
Drivin' awa the rain.

2 Drivin' awa' the dreary rain
Likewise the frost and snow,
And the hiremen in the mornin'
Are ordered oot to sow.

3 At last we get oor supper
The horses get their hay,
And we meet the pretty girlies
And the milking o' the kye.

4 At the milking o' the kye
And to pree their cherry mou
To hae a banter noo and then
Shak' hans and bid adieu.

5 Noo I intend to en' my sang
And I will end't wi' this
Let the ploughboy get more wages
It is my earnest wish.

6 It is my earnest wish
And it is the ploughboy's due,
For he uphauds both rich and poor
By the handlin' o' the ploo.

Miss LIZZIE CRIGHTON — G

B

Come all ye jolly Ploughboys.

Come all ye jolly ploughboys, It's we maun follow fast,
We're told by our hard master, There is no time to rest...
We're told & in the mornin' We're up to yoke by five -
There's scarce an hour to do o'er the fields our horses we do drive -
(till o'er)

1 Come all ye jolly ploughboys, it's we maun follow fast,
  We're told by our hard master there is no time to rest;
  We're told and in the morning we're up to yoke by five,
  There's scarce an hour till o'er the fields our horses we do drive.

2 We drive them on till twelve o'clock and home to dinner go,
  We scarcely get an hour to rest ere the master cries Holloa.
  The master cries Hallo brave boys it's time to yoke again,
  We'll get it a' well harrowed afore that it come rain.

ANDREW FINDLAY — G

C

Harrowing Time.

The winter it is ov — er, And spring has come again, and the
high winds of Martmas Has driven away the rain. --

Miss H. RAE — G

155

D

C. CLARK — G

E

Harrowing Time

1 Cauld winter's it's all over,
 And the summer comes again,
 And the cauld wind in the month o' March
 Has driven awa the rain.

2 It's driven awa the dreary rain,
 Likewise the frost and snow,
 And the foreman in the morning
 Gets order for to sow.

3 The rest they are the merry ploughboys,
 And they maun follow fast,
 They are bound by their master,
 There is no time to waste.

4 They're taul' they maun be in the yoke
 Each morning strict by five,
 And quickly travel o'er the fields
 Their horses for to drive.

5 And harrow on till twelve o'clock,
 Then home to dinner go,
 A single hour they'll scarcely get
 Till the foreman cries Hullo.

6 The foreman cries, Hullo, my boys,
 It's yoking time again,
 We'll get it a' well harrowed
 Before that it comes rain.

7 We'll harrow on till yon weary sun
 Behind yon hill does hide,
 And then we'll loose our horses,
 And homeward we will ride.

8 And homeward we will ride, my boys,
 To get our horses in,
 We'll clean them a' frae head to heel,
 Their manes and tails we'll kame.

9 And after that the supper,
 And after that we'll hie
 To see some pretty girlies
 A-milking o' their kye.

10 To see some pretty girlies,
 And pree their cherry mou',
 We'll take a loving hour or two,
 Shake hands and bid adieu.

11 And noo I mean to end my sang,
 And I will end wi' this,
 That the ploughman may get mair fee
 For that's my earnest wish.

12 That the ploughman may get mair fee,
 For that's the ploughman's due,
 For he keeps up both small and great
 Wi' sweat of his brow.

Miss BELL ROBERTSON — G

F
Harrowing Time

1 Cauld winter it is now awa,
And spring has come again,
And the cauld dry winds o' March month
Has driven awa the rain.

2 Has driven awa the dreary rain,
Likewise the frost and snow,
So our foreman in the morning
He's ordered out to sow.

3 Then the rest o' us merry ploughboys
We a' maun follow fast,
We are told by our hard master
There is no time to rest.

4 We're told that we must be ayock
Each morning sharp by five,
And quickly ower and ower the rigs
Our horses we must drive.

5 We drive them on till twelve o'clock,
Syne hame to dinner go,
But before the end of one hour
The farmer cries "Hillo".

6 Till the farmer cries "Hillo boys,
It's time to yoke again,
See that ye get it harrit oot,   [harrowed
For fear that it comes rain."

7 So on we drive until the sun
Ahint yon hill does hide,
And syne we lowse our horses tired,
And homewards we do ride.

8 Then homewards we do ride foo keen
To get our horses fed,
We kaim them weel, baith back and heel
Their tails and manes we redd.

9 When that is done, we supper get,
And after that we hie
Awa' to see our pretty girls
A-milkin' o' their kye.

10 Each to see his pretty girlie,
And pree her cherry mou'
Than tak' a flaffin 'oor or twa   [chatting
Shak' hands and bid adieu.

11 So now I mean to end my song,
And I will end it this
May the ploughman get more wages
That is my earnest wish.

12 That is my heartfelt wish I say
It is the ploughman's due,
For he sustains both rich and poor
By the sweat o' his broo.

JOHN MILNE — G

G
The Harrowing Time

1 Cauld winter's awa my boys and spring time's come again
And the cauld win's o' March tae blaw awa the rain
Tae blaw awa the rain my boys, likewise the frost and snaw
And the foreman in the mornin' is ordered out to sow.

2 The rest of our ploughboys must follow him in haste
For we're told by our hard master there is no time to rest
We're told by our hard master to be in the yoke by five
Walking across the fields our horses for to drive.

3 We drive them on to twelve o'clock then home to dinner go.
But we've scarcely got an hour to rest when the master cries Hullo
The master cries Hullo my boys it's yokin' time again
I wid like it a weel harrower before that it comes rain.

4   We drive them on tae yonder knowe till the sun begins tae hide
Then mounting on tae our horseback homeward for tae ride
Homeward for tae ride my boys our horses for tae clean
We clean them a' frae tap tae tae and tails and manes we kaim.

5   After that the supper and after that "hoch hie"
Tae see the bonnie lasses at the milkin' o' the kye
Tae see the bonnie lasses and tae pree their honey mou
Tae bide wi' them an hour or twa shak' hands and bid adieu.

Miss ANNIE SHIRER — G

THE PLOOIN' MATCH

1 The plooman lads at — met
   Some looked bold and some looked blate
   That day there wis mony a drap o' sweat
   Lost amon the ploomen.

2 When they got their tickets oot
   For their rigs they looked aboot
   The clerk to them he gied a shout
   And aff gaed a' the ploomen.

3 A. B. he got number one
   And wi' it tried mony a plan
   Whiles his horse at the en' did stan'
   And thither drew the ploomen.

4 C. D. he got number twa,
   Sae cannily he slippt awa
   His horse and harness looked sae braw
   That day amon the ploomen.

5 E. F. he got number three
   Though a haflin loon wis he
   A pattern he did fairly gie
   Fin he pat up his feerin'.

6 G. H. got number four
   Sae neatly as he turned it ower
   Spectators they at him did glower
   Says Ye'll beat a' the ploomen.

7 I. J. got number five
   He for the first prize sair did strive
   But in the well he took a dive
   That day amon the ploomen.

8 K. L. got number six
   They thocht they hid him in a fix
   But he stack up like lime tae bricks
   That day amon the ploomen.

9 Seven that M. N. did get
   Altho he didna ploo first rate
   Gie him a scythe he'll no be beat
   By ony o' yer ploomen.

10 O. got number eight
    He did his best to mak it right
    He got it up as square and straight
    As ony o' yer ploomen.

11 P. got number nine
    Guid preserv us sic a shine   [commotion
    He forgot tae haud the line
    That day amon the ploomen.

12 Ten that Q. got
    He up the rig jist at the trot
    But R. was on the spot
    Cries Hie it winna dee man.

13 Eleven that S. drew
    His horse weel dresst the rugged two
    But he was awfu' like tae spue
    That day amon the ploomen.

14 The loons they a' ploo'd by themsel
    Pleasure this and that to tell
    They held, they tramped and jumped as well
    As ony o' the ploomen.

15 T. he ploo'd fu' weel
    Tae tak' a prize he didna feel
    Ye ken he's nae a selfish chiel
    Altho he is a plooman.

16 The U. he cam fae New Deer
    Tae tak the prize he had nae fear
    But he got Hey my mannie here
    That day amon the ploomen.

17 V. he wad like a prize
    A bonnie lass is mair his size
    He'll stick to them if he is wise
    And syne he'll be a plooman.

18 The champion ploomen stood the test
    But young W. cam oot best
    And X. grew some lang-faced
    That day amon the ploomen.

19 The judges cam fae far and near
    Tae pit them richt they had nae fear
    But some wad say their sicht wis peer
    That day amon the ploomen.

ALEX MILNE — G

THEN SOME WI PINS

The Ploughing Match

1 Then some wi pins an some wi props
  They a' began a-fearin
  Some o' them seemed to be well pleased
  But some began a-swearin.

2 Some said their rigs were fearfu' tuch
  Some said that theirs was stennie
  The furs wad neither cut nor grip
  Nor yet look square nor bonnie.

3 But in spite o' a' difficulties
  They gaily trudged on   [whisky
  Aft times refreshed wi' mountain dew
  A bannock or a scone.

4 The judges trampit ilk man's rig
  O'er a' its points did grize
  It nearly pauld their wits to tell [perplexed
  Filk rig for ilka prize.   [which

5 Fan ance the prizes were read oot
  They a' gaed toddlin hame
  The unsuccessful's never pleased
  The judges gets the blame.

JOHN MILNE — G

THE TYRIE PLOOIN' MATCH

1 A plooin' match here I'll insert,
  Which may oor ploomen chiels divert,
  Although at rhyme I'm nae expert,
  I'll try my best this mornin'.

2 This match came off in Tyrie parish.
  The ooturn for't was pretty fairish;
  Altho' the day was rather airish,   [cool
  They got het sarks that mornin'.

3 They warlike were, they seemed nae cooards,
  Their ploos a' restin' on their boords,
  Their cooters shinin' sharp as soords,
  In the risin' sun that mornin'.

4 While in a group they a' did stan',
  Their tickets drew wi' anxious han',
  Ilk ane thinkin' he'd be the man,
  As sure's a gun that mornin'.

5 They did their wark in first-rate style,
  Accordin' to their different soil;
  It looked as if they'd a' got oil
  Among their joints that mornin'.

6 Altho' the tenth prize Jamie got,
  The hinmost ane o' a' the lot,
  Jim was well pleased, flung on his coat
  And gaed whistlin' hame that mornin'.

JOHN BURNETT — G

AH, SMILER LAD

1 Ah, Smiler lad, my trusty frien',
   It's guid my pairt to keep ye clean,
   Yer marrow yet I hinna seen   [match
   Amon' them a',
   Yon coast-side lads wad something gien
   We'd hauden awa'.   [kept away

2 Oor pleuchie wi' the clampit beam,
   To lauch at her they thocht guid game,
   They thocht we war owre far frae hame
   Wi' sic a teel;
   But though she wis a wee bit lame,
   She did fu' weel.

3 Yon muckle tearers frae Pitgair,   [furies
   Thocht they wad beat ye clear and fair,
   And flang their heids up in the air,
   To mak' a shaw;
   But faith your heid ye couldna spare
   That wye to thraw.

4 Ye kenned owre weel fat was adee,
   When ye sae mony ploos did see,
   And aye afore ye kept an e'e,
   Straucht to the en',
   And never gaed an inch ajee
   Frae aff the line.

5 Syne when the wark was a' inspeckit,
   And ne'er a faut nor flaw negleckit,
   'Mong sixty ploos we werena bleckit; [beaten
   Though laith to yield,
   At length they owned that naething like it
   Was on the field.

6 And noo yer bed I weel may mak' it,
   Stan' owre a bit and lat me shak' it;
   Your sta' wi' hay I hae weel happit,
   And bait as weel;
   For faith I think ye weel deserve it
   For deein' sae weel.

JOHN MOWAT – G

THE INVERQUHOMERY PLOUGHING MATCH

And now three cheers to Andrew Penny,
For he was first among so many,
From Shannas? Yes, it is the same,
Where he his residence can claim.
The second then they brought to view,
For William Morris it is true;
And it is o'er at Yokieshill
Where he the foreman's place doth fill.
And Alex Cheyne the third made out,
From Middletown you need not doubt,
For it is our proprietor's farm,
Where he can wield the foreman's arm.

. . . .

Then with the judges and some friends,
On whom my interest oft depends,
A social evening we had through,
And parted all a happy crew.

Mrs MOIR – G

DALMUIR PLOUGHING MATCH

1 Come listen a tale I will tell
   Concerning a man who in Dalmuir did dwell
   He is a good ploughman and well may he speed
   From Campsie he came, his name is Will Aikenhead.

2 It happened on the twenty-first of January last
   The date's nae far gane, yet the day is not past.
   In the West Barns of Clyde a ploughing fell
   Every man for a prize did the best for himsel'.

3 Aikenhead, he got up for to get a' things right
   Put his plough in his cart, tied it down tight
   Awa' he did gang wi' his master's gude will
   Some wad rather nae seen him I'll lay ye a gill.

4 The rules were read out just before they began
   A guide to go after the plough or ploughman.
   While the police was there with his stick in his hand
   Crying, Keep aff the ground, can ye no keep the land.

5 Now the ploughers got on, but the first kick-up was
   Young Jamie Park's mear got in a deal o' a fuss.
   The men started it as down the field they did rin
   And frightened the poor beast near out of its skin.

6 It kicked and flung ay, and jumpit aboot
   Till at last they were forced to loose the beast out
   He sent down to Brocks, the milk pony he got
   To make out the day and finish his lot.

7 Two tents were set up to serve out the drink
   It paid them well as you may a' think.
   The day it went round as fast it could slide
   And some got half drunk at the West Barns o' Clyde.

8 Aikenhead was near finished and a' things gaun right
   When an ass of a fellow tried him for to fight
   He said his time wis up and five minutes gane
   He might loose out his horses and gang awa hame.

9 But his watch like himsel wis tellin a lee
   For twa or three pu'ed oot their tickers to see
   And said he had a quarter to finish his bout
   If he manned it in time he would be ploughed out.

10 His guide took the plough, down the field he did rin
   And Will down the field just as fast as he could spin
   Gave a tramp here and there where he thought it had need
   "Well done my man Will" cried out Jamie Reid.

11 Now Will he got finished his time was not out
   When among the ploughmen, there fell out a dispute
   Some said he was wrong and had ploughed the wrong bout
   Some said he was right and they did argue out.

12 They argued, and argued, they cursed and they swore.
   Some tried on poor Willie their vengeance to pour
   But the judges were there, the case to decide
   At that great ploughing match at the West Barns of Clyde.

13 At last they got tired and down to Sandy Reid's went
   And there at the dinner a wee while they spent
   Till auld Jamie Taylor, the prizes did read,
   Some thrawed their faces, some shook their heid.

14 The first, Aikenhead, that's Willie Park's man
   The second the fellow that tried Willie to wrang.
   When the prizes were read the second's father did shout
   That the first and third prizes should be scored out.

15 And now about the old class, my story's near through
   A man from Kilbowrie said the thing that was true
   If Pate had got first he would been out of his breeks
   There wad be nae living wi' him six or eight weeks.

16 And now about the young class I am going to tell
   John Shanks got the first prize, Jim Park got the meer.
   Jim's beast it was young, ay, and easy to fright
   If he'd ta'en ald Billy a' things wad gane right.

17 And for to conclude and finish my song
   I hope that party don't think I've done wrong.
   Aikenhead ploughed himsel' out, I'll leave ye a' tae decide
   At that great ploughing match at the West Barns of Clyde.

F. R. BROWN – G

428

HAWKIE

Hawkie she's a wily beast
And Hawkie winna wide the water
I'll cast aff my hose and sheen
And I'll ca Hawkie owre the water.
Ca Hawkie, draw Hawkie,
Dreel Hawkie owre the water.   [drive with force

Miss BELL ROBERTSON – G

THE HERD LADDIE

A

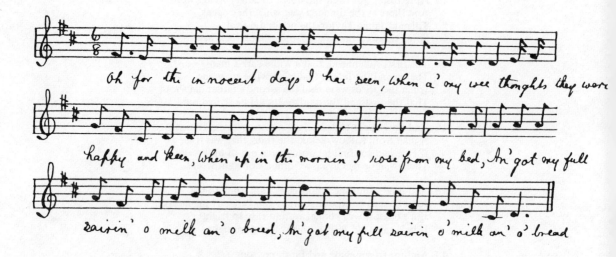

The Herd Laddie

1 O for the innocent days I hae seen
   When a my wee thoughts were happy and keen
   When up in the morning I rose from my bed
   And got my full sairin o' milk and o' bread
      And got my full sairin o' milk and o' bread.

2 Syne aff to the fall an leet oot my nowte
   And O sae merry as they frisket aboot,
   They licked their sleek sides as they went through the Ward
   And lowed a probation o'er a the hale sward.

3 So weel's I min Jeanie was keepin her kye
   An fa was sae heartie as Jeanie and I
   We gaed doon to the stripie that ran in the green
   An puddled till baeth had been dubbed to the een.   [muddied

4 Sae weel as I min how she kiltet her coatties
   To catch the wee minins that ran in the potties   [minnows; holes
   And I mysell the better to ca
   Would have taen aff my breekies an thrown them awa.

5 This fin we were weary an weet to the skin
   We'd gang an spread oot oor weet duds to the sin
   And then to the sinside o' the dyke we wud flit
   An tumle helstergowdie fae the heed to the fit.

6   We spread oot oor plaidies to mak oorsels beds
    And bigged up we hoosies to cover oor heeds
    An fin we creep't in fu canny an sly
    Leet onything licht o' our tail that passed bye.

7   Until that the sun begood hidin his nose
    An then we gaed hame for to get the kail-brose
    A guid dish o' brose wi the kail an the seys   [chives
    The herds are aye hungry new come hame fae the leys.

8   . . . .
    The kail was made ready wi' a wee drap o' reem   [cream
    That set me a-sleepin as seen's they were deen.

9   Syne aff tae my bed I was packit wi speed
    Though crazy my feet an though sleepy my heed
    Aff to my bed I was packit wi speed
    Me an my constant bedfellow the dog.

10 The bed where we lay in it was just so meet
    It scarcely afforded some straw and a sheet
    An lang ere 'twas day the sheet slade awa'
    An left my bare hide to enjoy the straw.

11 An then in the mornin the men thocht a coup
    To tell me the strae it had markit my doup
    But fat war was I for I sleepit as soon
    As though I had lyin in the saftest o' doon.

12 Now these were the days when I had no care
    I was as brown as a tod an as wild as a hare
    I skiffed ower the mountains and snuffed the bluebells
    An pu'd the wild flowers that grew in the vales.

ROBERT ALEXANDER – D

B

The Herd Laddie

1 It's oh for the days and the nights that are gane,
   When a' my thoughts they were happy and keen,
   'Twas up in the mornin' I raise fae my bed,
   And got my full serving o' milk and o' bread.

2 Then I up wi' my plaid, and I doon wi' my tree,
   And awa to the leas I gaed singin' wi' glee;
   I'd a little wee bonnet to haud my heid dry,
   And moggins to wear on my leggies forbye.   [footless stockings

3 I'd gae doon to yon faul', and I leet oot my nout,
   Sae merrily 's they gaed friskin' about;
   They'd gae doon by yon dykeside, and feed on yon sward,
   With loud approbation gave all my full herd.

4 When Jeannie and I were herding the kye,
   O wha was so happy as Jeannie and I?
   We biggèd wee hoosies, and made oorsels beds,
   We biggit wee hoosies, and happit oor heads.

5 We'd gang owre by yon dykeside, by yon hallow flat,
   And tumble owre goudies fae heid to the fit,
   We'd gae doon by yon dykeside, by yon hallow green,
   And puddle till baith o' us were weet to the een.

6 Oh weel do I min' how she preened up her coaties,   [pinned
   To catch the swift minnows that swam in the potties,
   And I mysel', the better to ca,
   I keest aff my breekies an' threw them awa.

7 Then awa to the ringfoolie's nest we wad haste,   [reed bunting
   It was to surprise the wee thing fae its nest,
   The little wee eggies foo speckled and gay,
   We gazed at them a whilie and then ran away.

8 So when we had played us a lang summer day,
   We thought of no ill, and we dreaded no wae;
   For when the bright sun gaed a happy night's close,
   It was then we went hame to oor kail and kail brose.

9 A drappie o' kail and a starnie o' seys   [small amount
   A herdie is needin' new in fae the leys;
   A drappie o' kail and a wee spottie cream
   Would set me a-sleepin' as seen 's I was deen.

10 Then awa to my bed I was packit wi' speed,
    Though crazy my feet and sleepy my heid,
    Awa to the chamer I had to jog,
    Me and my constant bedfellow the dog.

11 The beddie was little, there was naething on it,
    There was naething afforded but straw and a sheet,
    And lang ere daylicht the sheet slid awa,
    And left the poor hide to enjoy the straw.

12 When I rose in the morning, the men had a crack,
    To tell how the bedstrae had markit my back;
    But I was as happy, and sleepit as soon'
    As though I had lien on the saftest o' doon.

13 Oh then was the days when I had no care,
   When brown as a tod and wild as a hare,
   I skipped owre the mountains and pu'd the blue bells,
   And kissed the wild roses that grew in the vales.

WILLIAM WALLACE — D

C

The Herd Laddie.

Oh for the innocent days I hae seen, When a' my young thochties were happy and green, When up in the mornin' and oot o' my bed I got my full sairin' o' milk and o' breed, I got my full sairin' o' milk and o' bread

1   Oh for the innocent days I hae seen!
     When a' my young thochties were happy an' green,
     When up in the mornin' an' oot o' my bed,
     I got my full sairin' o' milk an' o' bread.

2   Then up wi' my plaidie an' doon wi' my tree,
     I gaed owre the leas seen a-singin' wi' glee,
     Sometimes a wee bonnet to haud my heid dry,
     An' moggins to wear on my leggies forby.

3   Awa' to the faulds an' lat oot my nowte,
     Sae merrily's they gaed friskin about,
     They lickit their sidies at the heid o' the sward,
     An' a' my full care was to be a gweed herd.

4   An' wee Jeannie used to be keepin' her kye,
     Oh wha was sae happy as Jeannie an' I?
     We biggit wee hooses to haud oor heids dry,
     Lat onything fa' on the tail that cam by.

5   An' weel do I min' hoo we thocht it a jest
     To scare the wee ring fool aff o' its nest,
     To see the wee eggs in their saft beds o' doon
     . . . . .soon.

6   An' weel dae I min' hoo she kiltit her coaties
To catch the wee minnins that swam in the potties,
An' I mysel to help for to ca',
I keest aff my breekies an' threw them awa.

7   Wi' this we wad spen' a lang simmer day,
We thocht o' nae evil an' dreaded nae wae,
Until the bright sun gaed a-hidin' his nose,
An' seen we gaed hame for the kale an' kale brose.

8   The kail an' kail brose an' a wee puckle seys,
Jist fit for a herdie new in fae the leys;
The kail an' kail brose an' a wee drappie ream
They sent me to sleep as seen's they war deen.

9   When my sleep it was deen, to my bed I wad jog,
Me an' my constant bed-fellow the dog.

10   The bed that I had it was not very meet,
It seldom afforded but straw an' a sheet,
An' lang ere the mornin' this sheet slid awa'
An' left the bare hide to enjoy the straw.

11   The men in the mornin thocht they had a coup,
To tell how the bedstraw had markit my doup,
But little cared I when I sleepit as soon
As though I had lain on the saftest o' doon.

12   But these were the days when I had nae care,
When broon as a tod and wild as a hare,
I skipped owre the meadows an' kiss'd the sweet bells
And pulled the red roses that grew in the dales.

Mrs MARGARET GILLESPIE and GEORGE F. DUNCAN — D

D
Herd Laddie

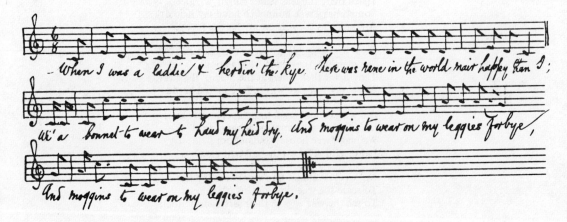

168

1   When I was a laddie and herdin the kye
      There was nane in the warld mair happy than I
      Wi' a bonnet to wear to haud my heid dry
      An' moggins to wear on my leggies forbye.

2   Sweet little Jeannie she herded nearby
      And fa' was sae fain as Jeannie and I
      We went to the burnie that ran in the glen
      And puddled till we war baith weet to the e'en.

3   We made oorsels showds o' the twigs o' the trees
      And bigget birds' nesties oorsels for to please
      Then awa to the heid o' the braes we did flit
      And tumbled owre gowdy frae the heid to the fit.

4   We spread oot our plaidies and made oorsels beds
      And bigget wee hoosies to cover oor heids
      When oor heids they were happit sae cosy and sly
      Lat onything licht on oor tails that cam by.

5   When wearied o' daffin' the lang summer day
      And then we began to tak' hame oor kye.
      As soon as the sun did shut up his nose
      It was then we went home for to get oor kail-brose.

6   Awa to my bed I wis ca'd wi speed
      Tho' sleepy my heid and weary my feet
      Awa to the chaumer I then had to go
      My only bed-fellow being Carlo the dog.

7   The bed where I sleepit was far frae complete
      There was naething afforded but straw and a sheet
      And lang ere the morning the sheet was awa'
      And left the bare hide to enjoy the straw.

8   And then in the mornin' thocht it a coup
      To see hoo the straw had markit my doup
      But it made nae odds aifter for I sleepit as soon'
      As tho' I'd been lyin' on the softest o' down.

9   But oh in that days and hoo little care
      When as broon as a toad and swift as a hare
      I wad skip owre the mountains and pu' the bluebells
      And kiss the red roses that grew in the vales.

ALEXANDER ROBB – G

E

The Herd Laddie.

—I carena for that, for I sleepit as soon as gin I'd been laid on the saftest o' doun.—

Miss M. RITCHIE — G

F

The Herd Loon

When I mind on the innocent days I hae seen, When a' my young thochts they were happy & green, I rase in the mornin' up frae my bed And got my fu' sairin' o' milk & o' breid.

JAMES BREBNER — G

G

1   A wee suppie porridge, and a drappie o' cream,
    And they set me a-sleepin' as sune's they were dune.

Source unrecorded — G

JOCKY AND HIS OWSEN

Twa afore ane,
Three afore five,
First twa and syne twa,
Four comes belyve.   [immediately
Noo ane and than ane,
Three at a cast,
Dooble ane and twice twa,
An' Jocky at the last;
Jenny and her five kye
Fullin' in fast.

Mrs RETTIE — G

HERDIE DERDIE

1   Herdie Derdie, blaw your horn,
    A' your nowt's among the corn;

2   First ane, and syne twa,
    Herdie Derdie beats them a'.

F.R. BROWN — G

COWAYE

Cowaye cowaye
Cut a roadie throw aye
A peck for a firlot
A firlot for a bowaye.

Mr RENNIE — G

THE MUIRLAND FARMER

A

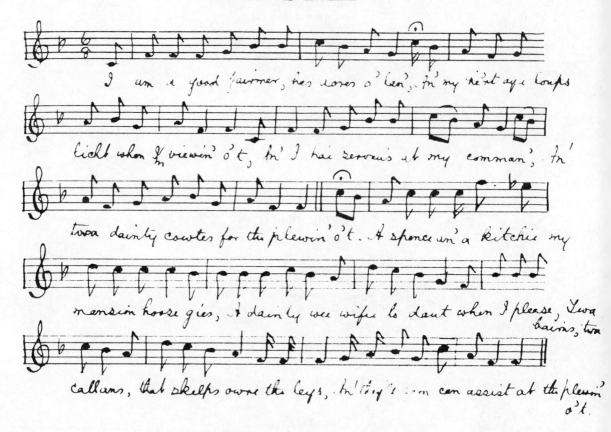

The Farmer.

1. I am a gweed fairmer has acres o lan'
   An my heart aye loups light when I'm viewin o't
   An I hae servants at my comman
   An twa dainty cowts for the plooin o't.

2. A spence and a kitchie my mansion hoose gies   [sitting room
   A dainty we wifie to daut when I please
   Twa bairns, twa callants that skelps o'er the leas
   An they'l soon can assist at the plooin o't.

3. O leeze my lan it's faen to my share   [blessings on
   It taks sax muckle bous for the sawin o't
   I've sax braid acres o' pastur an mair
   An a dainty wee bog for the mawin o't.

4. My farm it lies up on yon sooth slopin hill
   While the sun shines sae bonniely beamin on't
   An by my door rins a clear prattling rill
   Frae the loch where the wild deuks are swimmin on't.

5 While on its green banks in the fine simmer days
  My bonnie wee wifie gangs bleachin her claes
  While on the dear creature with rapture I gaze
  While I whistle an sing at the plooin o't.

6 My farm it's a snug one lies high on yon muir
  The muircocks an plovers aft skirl at my door,
  An when the sky lowers I am sure o' a shower
  To moisten my lan for the plooin o't.

7 Now in this douf days when loud hurricanes blaw
  How snug in the spence we'l be viewin o't
  An jink the rude blast in a rash thackit ha'   [rush
  When the fields there seal't up frae the plooin o't.

8 Syne my bonnie we wifie, the bairnies an me
  Our peat stack and sod stack our Phoebus shall be
  Till Day close the scowl o' its angry ee
  An we'l live in good hopes o' the plooin o't.

9 An noo when to kirk an to market I ride
  My weefare, what needs me be hidin o't
  Wi my braw leather beets shinin black as the slaes
  It tempts me to try the ridin o't.

10 Wi my braw worstit breeks that my granmither span
  They hae been sae vyogie sin I wis a man   [grand
  But noo they're laid by, an I've coft cordivan [soft leather
  An my wife never grudged me a shillin o't.

11 Last towman I selt a four bous o' gweed bere [complete year
  And thankfu I was, for the victual was dear
  I came hame wi my spurs o my heels shinin clear
  I had sae gweed luck at the sellin o't.

ROBERT ALEXANDER — D

B
The Sma' Farmer

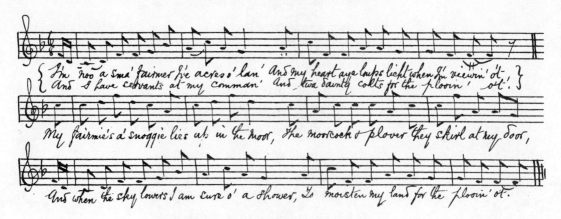

1   I'm noo a sma' fairmer I've acres o' land
    And my heart aye loups licht when I'm viewin o't
    And I have servants at my command
    And twa dainty colts for the plooin' o't.
    My fairmie a' snoggie lies up i' the moor   [tidy
    The moorcock and plover they skirl at my door
    And when the sky lowers I'm sure o' a shower
    To moisten my land for the plooin' o't.

2   My hoosie stands sweet on a south slopin hill
    And the sun shines right brightly beamin' on't,
    And doon by my door stands a clear win
    From the loch where the wild ducks are sweemin' on't.
    On its green banks the sweet summer days
    My wifie trots barefit and bleaches her claes
    And on this dear creature with rapture I gaze
    While I whistle and sing at the plooin' o't.

3   To rank among farmers I hae muckle pride
    But I maun speak high when I'm tellin' o't
    How brawly's I like on my sheltie to ride
    Wi' a sample to show for the sellin' o't.
    Last towmont I sell't a four bows o' guid bere
    And thankfu was I for the victuals was dear
    And I cam hame wi' my spur shinin' clear
    I had sae good luck at the sellin' o't.

4   Now in the damp days when loud hurricanes blaw
    How snug in the spence I'll be viewin o't
    How brawly's I am in my rash-thackit ha'
    When fields are sealed up fae the plooin' o't.
    My spence and my kitchen, my mansion house gay
    My cantie wee wifie to daut when I please
    Twa bairnies twa callants that will skip owre the leas
    And they soon shall assist at the plooin' o't.

5   My cantie wee wifie my bairnies and me
    Oor peat-stack and oor tirr-stack our fame they shall be   [turf-stack
    Until the day close wi the scowl o' his angry e'e
    And we'll rest in good hopes o' the plooin o't.

ALEXANDER ROBB — G

C

The Muirland Farmer.

1   I am a guid farmer, etc.

2   My farm's a trig ane, etc.

3   Last towmon' I saul, etc.

4   Noo hairst time is o'er, etc.

5   Wi' blue worstit buits, etc.

6   My canty wee wifie, etc.

7   Noo welcome gweed weather, etc.

Mrs JAFFRAY (Mintlaw) — G

D

The Aul' Farmer

1   I am an aul' farmer, I've acres o' land
    An' my heart aye loups licht when I'm viewin' o't
    An' I hae servans at my comman'
    An' twa dainty couts for the ploughin' o't.
    I've a kitchen an spence — my mansion hoose gi'es
    An a bonnie wee wifie to daut when I please
    Twa bairnies — twa callants to skip o'er the leas
    They soon will assist at the ploughin o't.

2   My biggin' stan's snug on yon south slopin' hill
    An the sun shines bonnily beamin on't;
    An' past my ain door trots a clear clattrin rill
    Frae the loch where the wil' dukes are swimmin on't.
    Along the clear banks in the clear summer days
    My bonnie wee wifie gangs bleachin' her claes
    An on the dear creature wi' rapture I gaze
    As I whistle an' sing at the ploughin' o't.

3   To rank among farmers I hae mickle pride
     Tho' I mauna speak high when I'm tellin o't
     Fu brawly I'll strut wi' my shelty to ride
     Wi' a sample o' grain for the sellin o't.
     In my blue worset boots that my aul mither span
     I've aft been sae vogie since I was a man
     But noo they're cast bye an I've coft cordowan   [bought
     An' my wife never grudged me a shillin o't.

4   Noo when to the kirk or to market I gae
     My welfare — what need I be hidin' o't —
     Wi' my braw leather boots shinin' clear as a slae
     I'll dink me to try the ridin' o't.
     Last towman I sal' aff four bows o' good bear
     Fu thankfu' was I, for the victual was dear,
     I came hame wi' new spurs on my heels shinin' clear
     I had siccan good luck at the sellin o't.

5   Now hairst time's gane bye — a fig for the laird
     My rent's now secure for the toilin' o't;
     My fields are a' bare an' my crap's in the yaird
     I'm nae mair in doots o' the spoilin' o't.
     Come welcome cauld weather, come win' or come weet
     Come bal rugged winter, come hail, snaw, or sleet.
     Nae mair can ye draggle my crap mang your feet   [bedraggle
     Nor work it mischief at the spoilin o't.

6   An' in the dark days when the hurricans blaw
     How snug in my spence I'll be viewin o't
     An jink the rude blast in my weel thackit ha'
     When fields are sealed up frae the ploughin o't.
     My bonnie wee wifie, my bairnies an' me
     Wi' our peat stack, our turff stack, fu' canty we'll be
     Till day close the sky on its angry e'e
     An' we'll rest in good hope for the ploughin' o't.

7   An' when the year smiles an' the laverocks they sing
     My man Jock and I will be doin' o't
     He'll thrash and we'll toil in the field in the spring
     An' turn up the soil at the ploughin' o't.
     An' when the wee flowers begin for to blaw
     The laverock, the peeseweep, an skirlin' sea-maw   [lapwing; gull
     They'll hiss the black water to Laplan awa'
     An we'll ply the blythe hours at the sawin' o't.

Source unrecorded — G

THE BEAUTY OF BUCHAN

1   Come all my relations with deep lamentations,
     Ye shepherds o' Buchan come listen I pray,
     Let my song be respected since sheep is rejected
     And they from their pastures are banished away.

2   I hae seen our green fountains on wild heathy mountains,
     Wi' flocks all clad over how pleasant were they;
     But now they are lonely for want o' flocks only
     Since the beauty from Buchan is banished away.

3   I hae heard lasses liltin' when met at ewe milkin'
     Each one with her sweetheart in innocent play,
     But now they want leisure to crack wi' their treasure
     Since the beauty frae Buchan is banished away.

4   I hae seen the rams sporting and corams resorting   [groups
     And nothing disturbing their innocent play,
     But now they go mourning both evening and morning
     Since the beauty frae Buchan is banished away.

5   I hae seen the lambs bleating their careful dams weeping,
     To guard them frae Lowrie that made them his prey,
     Now Lowrie is starvin', it's what he's deservin'
     Since the beauty frae Buchan is banished away.

6   I hae seen at sheep shearin' sportin' and jëerin'
     Their sunny white fleeces how pleasant were they,
     But now we maun buy them frae merchants that cry them,
     Since the beauty frae Buchan is banished away.

7   Woe to our gentry, they're ruined a' our country,
     And brought our fine pastures so deep in decay
     Mong hedges and ditches they've spent a' our riches,
     And banished our beauty entirely away.

8   Lament all ye shepherds for want o' your clipherds,
     Wi' sighing and sobbing and sorrow for aye;
     Let my song be respected since sheep is rejected,
     And they from their pastures are banished away.

Miss BELL ROBERTSON — G

435

DEPRESSION

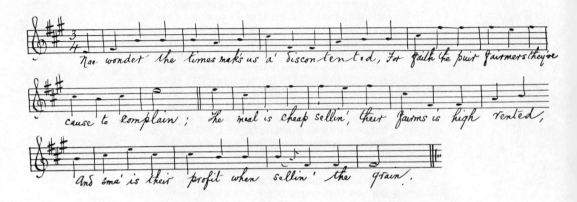

Nae wonder the times mak's us 'a' discontented, For faith the puir fairmers they've cause to complain; The meal is cheap sellin', their fairms is high rented, And sma' is their profit when sellin' the grain.

1 Nae wunner though the times maks us a' discontentet
   For faith the puir fairmers they've cause to complain
   The meal is cheap sellin their fairms high rentit
   And sma is their profit when sellin their grain.

2 Some one thing some other likewise the bad weather
   The craps torn doon wi' the torrents o' rain
   The cattle that's parket will no tak the market
   We'll jist tak them in for a twalmonth again.

3 It's aft hae I heard my auld granny tellin'
   That fairmin in her day — that wid a bin nine —
   There wis plenty o' siller and the meal aye weel sellin
   It made her richt wae when she thocht on langsyne.

4 But this cursed gentry they walk oot on sentry
   They coont ilka plack and babie that they won
   Walks out at their leisure, lies up at their pleasure
   Like Solomon's lilies they card not nor spin.

5 But we'll fill up a nappie and tak a wee drappie   [drinking bowl
   And aye be contented wherever we go
   Nae langer this nation will thole the oppression
   The laird and the factor will get an overthrow.

JOHN MOWAT — G

178

THE FROSTIT CORN

1   Oh I am a young farmer hard set by the frost
     My gude expectations hae sairly been cross't
     My craps that looked weel, they are noo nearly lost
     By thir calamitous mornin's.

2   In the midst o' last simmer it was understude
     That we wad a' haen plenty o' gude halesome fude
     For man and for beast an' we ettled to dae gude   [expected
     But the frost it has backit it sairly.   [harmed

3   An' when that the frost it did gang awa'
     The rain it came on like to ruin us a'
     It rained that lang that it shortened the straw
     An' added aye the mair till the mornin'.

4   But yet for a' that we mauna compleen
     It was so ordered or it ne'er wad hae been
     It's maybe for oor gude tho' that hisna yet been seen
     For to humble oor pride in the mornin'.

5   When things lookit weel a scheme I had laid
     I promised to marry a bloomin' young maid
     To share o' the o'ercome when a'thing was paid   [surplus
     But the frost it has backit it sairly.

6   But my crap as it is, it is noo in the yaird
     And still for the lassie I hae a regaird
     I think that I'll marry her and no pay the laird
     Let him ken there was frost in the mornin'.

7   An' if he should break oot in ragin' an strife
     He may weel tak the year but he'll no tak my life
     If I should hae naething else I will aye hae a wife
     To comfort me in the mornin'.

JAMES CHEYNE — G

THE THRESHERMAN

A

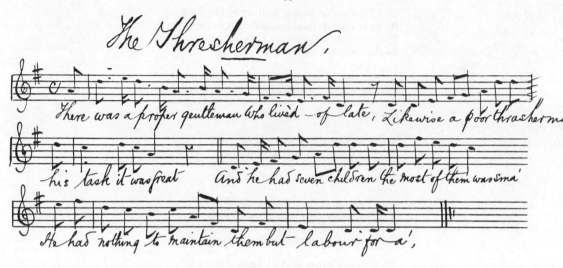

1 There was a proper gentleman who livèd of late,
Likewise a poor thrasherman, his task it was great,
And he had seven children, the most of them was sma
He had nothing to maintain them but labour for a'.

2 One day as the gentleman was going to his work,
Likewise the poor thrasherman was going to his work,
It's ye hae seven children the most of them are sma
And how do ye maintain them so well as ye do.

3 Sometimes to hedging and ditching I go
At other times to harrowing, and some corn I sow,
With my flail in my hand, and some water for my beer
We aye keep the raggit ane ben frae the door.

4 When me and my wife draws thegither in the neuk,
We live like the turtle, we're seldom provoked
We're seldom provoked altho' we be poor
We aye keep the raggit ane ben frae the door.

5 Since I have found you so loving to your wife
There's sixty acres to you during your life.
Since that I have found you so loving full of care,
To you and to you and for ever to your heir.

Mrs MILNE – G

B
The Thresherman

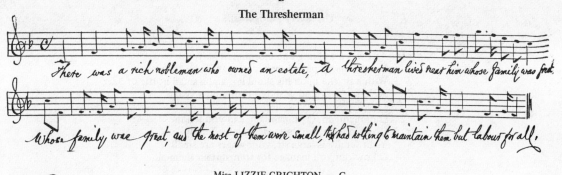

There was a rich nobleman who owned an estate, A thresherman lived near him whose family was great. Whose family was great, and the most of them were small, He had nothing to maintain them but labour for all.

Miss LIZZIE CRIGHTON — G

C

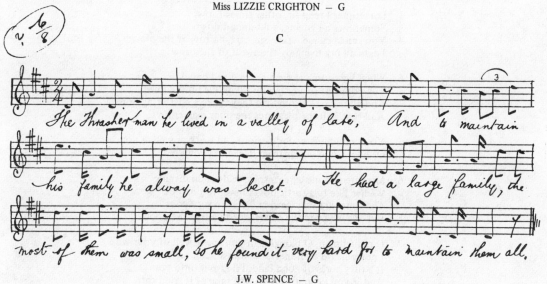

The Thrasher man he lived in a valley of late, And to maintain his family he alway was beset. He had a large family, the most of them was small, So he found it very hard for to maintain them all.

J.W. SPENCE — G

D
The Thresherman

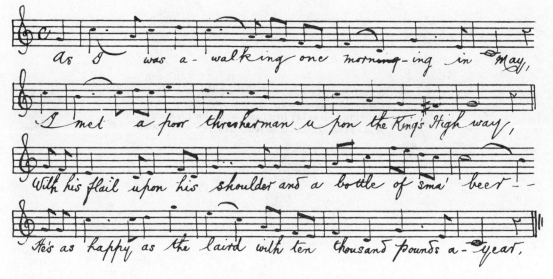

As I was a-walking one morning-ing in May, I met a poor thresherman upon the King's High way, With his flail upon his shoulder and a bottle of sma' beer — He's as happy as the laird with ten thousand pounds a-year.

Mrs STEVENSON — G

E

The Merry Ploughman

1 As I was a-walking one morning in May
  I met a merry ploughman, a-ploughing by the way
  With a scythe upon his shoulder, and a small bottle of beer
  As happy as a lord with ten thousand a year.

2 O ploughman, O ploughman, can you tell me
  How you can maintain such a large family
  Your family is large sir, your wages are small
  O how can you manage for to maintain them all.

3 Sometimes I reap sir, other times I sow
  Sometimes a-hedging, a-ditching I do go
  You canna ca me wrang sir, cart, harrow or the plough
  I earn all my living by the sweat of the brow.

4 When I go home at even as tired as I could be
  The youngest of my family I'll diddle on my knee   [dandle
  And all the rest around me they make a chattering noise
  And that's all the pleasures the poor man enjoys.

5 Your wife must be industrious and work as well as you
  Or how could you manage as well as you do.

6 My wife and me agree sir, we seldom do dispute
  We live like twa turtle doves never to provoke
  The times are very hard and we are very poor
  But aye we keep the messenger awa frae the door.

7 O ploughman, O ploughman you speak well of your wife
  I never heard an honester confession all my life
  It's fifty acres of good land, I'll give it unto you
  And if you keep it well sir, and take of it good care
  It's after you are dead and gone I'll give it to your heir.

WILLIAM SCOTT — G

F

1 Sometimes a-hedging and ditching I go,
  Other times some corn I harrow and sow,
  With my flail in my hand and water for my beer,
  And as cheerful as those that have thousands a-year.

A. MURCAR — G

LORD FIFE

A

Lord Fife.

Good people all, both great & small, Come listen unto me, For I sing the praise of a noble lord In our north country. His like was never in ages past, Nor never will be again; For every acre he does possess, It's called the happy land

1	Good people all, both great and small Come listen unto me For I sing the praise of a noble Lord In our north country.	7	First they'll empty your barn walls The next they'll empty your byre They'll thirdly tirr your back and bed [strip And lastly put out your fire.
2	His like was never in ages past Nor never will be again For every acre he does possess It's called the happy land.	8	But when good Lord Fife's poor tenants come Their property to tell, Go home, he says, possess your place, I'll pay the rent mysel'.
3	Mar Lodge is his summer-seat Duff House it is the same In case you do mistake the man I'll here mention his name.	9	I like to see my tenants thrive With a brisk and prosperous view With a handsome house and a neat clean wife Sing Ba-lelie-loo.
4	So long life to good Lord Fife And happy may he be And while he hath a day to live Enjoy prosperity.	10	Brandy nor rum I cannot drink Wine won't agree with me But while I have two pence on earth I'll drink to him in tea.
5	When ye gang to our petty lairds Your dwelling place to crave And if you give the worth three fold Your asking you may have.	11	His praises I could never set forth The hundered pairt that's due And if you want to know my name It's M. and W.
6	Gin you fall in their arrears I tell you what they'll do They will not leave you horse nor mair Your sheep nor yet your cow.	12	His presence fills each heart with joy, Puts mirth in every eye; You're welcome home oh brave Lord Fife, Your bonnie lands to spy.

13 And so long life to good Lord Fife,
And happy may he be;
And those who does not say Amen,
Ashamed let them be.

Mrs CRUICKSHANK — G

B

1   When to Lord Fyfe his tenants go,
     Their misery to tell, —
     Go home, possess your farms again,
     I'll pay the rent mysel'.

JONATHAN GAULD — G

439

A SONG OF WELCOME

1   Our noble Lord's come to the North,
     To view his bonnie lands o' Florth;
     Come let us join and a' come forth
     And welcome him richt cheery.
       Come bid him welcome ower the seas,
       Mak' cannon roar and bonfire bleeze,
       Let's a unite wi' joy and glee
       And welcome him richt cheery.

2   Frae Florth's sweet vale to Mormond Hill,
     Around by Tyrie and Whitewell,
     Come let us join frae hill and dale
     And welcome him richt cheery.

3   He is a landlord kind and good
     Of generous heart and noble blood,
     Against our foes oft-days he stood
     On battlefield richt cheery.

4   To Egypt's lands he first did go
     'Gainst Frenchmen there, our daring foe
     And bravely did his valour show
     Wi' "Forty-twa" richt cheery.

5   Our hero fought at Waterloo,
     In midst of men whose hearts were true
     And bravely did the French subdue,
     And beat them a' richt weary.

JOHN MOWAT — G

440

THERE'S TILLYDEASK

1   There's Tillydeask, amang the reast
     An Piltochie in the glen
     An the gear an' guide o' that toons
     It a' gaes to Ardgrain.

2   There's Turnerha an' Dudwick's Hill
     They think themsel's nae sma'
     But they canna cope wi Elphin
     For Elphin capes them a'.

JOHN MILNE — G

MULLNABEENY

A
Mullnabeeny

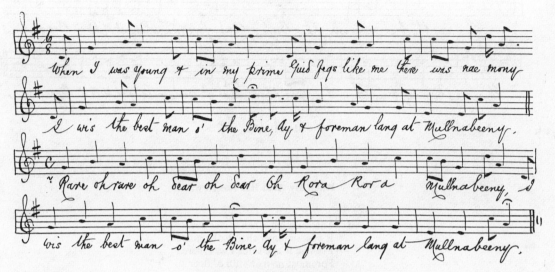

1 When I was young and in my prime,
   Guid fegs like me there wisna mony,
   I was the best man o' the Bine,
   Ay, and foreman lang at Mullnabeeny.
     Rare oh rare, oh dear oh dear,
     Rora, rora, Mulnabeeny,
     I wis the best man o' the Bine,
     Ay and foreman lang at Mullnabeeny.

2 When I engaged wi' Johnnie Mull
   It wis for five poun and a guinea,
   It wis to drive the foremost pair
   Ay and lead their mennies o' Mullnabeeny.

3 When this auld hat o' mine was new
   It cost me mair than half a guinea,
   Mair than fifty years ago
   When at the hash o' Mullnabeeny.

4 Ho, flesher Robb he's but a snob
   Ha, fat's their mennies o' Mullnabeeny?
   The bows o' bere I've carried there
   Wid hae killed their mennies o' Mullnabeeny.

5 Oh for back at twenty one,
   Hip hurrah for Mullnabeeny,
   To ca' blin' Joe the game's but low
   Besides the hash o' Mullnabeeny.
     Rare oh rare, oh dear oh dear,
     Rora, rora, Mullnabeeny,
     Twenty pair when I wis there
     A' at the hash o' Mullnabeeny.

Miss LIZZIE CRIGHTON — G

B

Mill o' Beenie

I was the best man in the Boyne And foreman lang at Mill o' Beenie;

There was twenty pair when I was there, And foreman lang at Mill o' Beenie,

Mrs STUART — G

C

When My Auld Hat Was New

1   This auld hat when it was new
     It cost me mair than half a guinea
     I've had it aye since I was there
     Foremost man at Mull o' Beenie.

Source unrecorded — G

D

1   Ochon for back to Mull o' Beenie —
     Sax pound ten and a guinea;
     Twenty pair fin I was there,
     Hashin' on at Mull o' Beenie.

A. DAWSON — G

442

SA UP AND RISE

Sa up and rise, my merry lads,
For a' maun rise, for a' maun rise.

JOHN MILNE — G

THE BRAES O' BROO

A

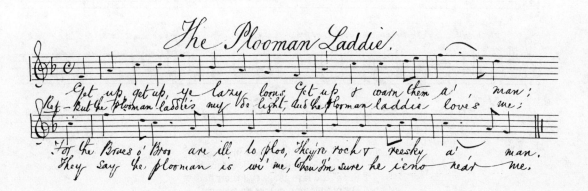

The Plooman Laddie.

Get up, get up, ye lazy loons, Get up & warn them a', man;

Ref - But the plooman laddie's my die light, And the plooman laddie loves me;

For the Braes o' Broo are ill to ploo, They're roch & reesky, a', man.

They say the plooman is wi' me, When I'm sure he isno near me.

1 Get up, get up, ye lazy loons,
 Get up an' waur them a', man,   [get the better of
 For the Braes o' Broo are ill to ploo,
 They're roch and reesky a', man.   [marshy
  But the plooman laddie's my delight,
  And the plooman laddie loves me,
  They say the plooman lad's wi' me
  When I'm sure he is no near me.

2 Oh, he's ta'en up his owsen gaud,
 An' it sets him weel to ca', man,
 He's laid it o'er the owsen bow,
 Says, Scurry, come awa', man.

3 What think ye o' oor ploomen noo,
 Wi' their high-cuttin' ploos and a', man?
 But it wasna sae ance in a day
 When the wooden pleuchie ploo'd a', man.

4 What think ye o' oor fairmers noo
 Wi' their binders ane and a', man?
 But it wasna sae ance in a day
 When the plooman shure it a', man.

5 What think ye o' oor fairmers noo
 Wi' their thrashin' mulls and a', man?
 But it wasna sae ance on a day
 When the plooman threesh it a', man.

6 What think ye o' oor lasses noo
 Wi' their bicycles sae braw, man?
 But it wasna sae ance on a day,
 That widna dee at a', man.

7 It's I will wash my plooman's hose,
 And brush his dubby sheen, man,
 An' I'll maybe be a plooman's wife
 Or a' thae days be deen, man.

WILLIAM WATSON — G

B

The Ploughman Laddie's My Delight

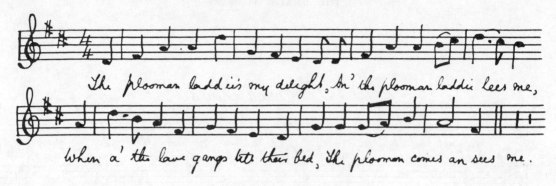

1 The ploughman laddie's my delight
  An the ploughman laddie lees me
  Fin a' the lave gangs tull their bed
  My ploughman comes an sees me.

2 Fat think ye o' our lassies noo
  Their grown a' sae braw
  They widna suit a ploughman's wife
  They winna dea ava.
    But the ploughman laddie's my delight
    The ploughman laddie lees me
    The markest nicht it ever I saw   [darkest
    My ploughman comes an sees me.

3 He taks up his ousen gaud
  It sets him weel to ca'
  An lays it our his ousen bow
  Says "Scurrie come awa."
    For the ploughman laddie's my delight
    An the ploughman laddie lees me
    Fin a' the lave gangs to their bed
    My ploughman comes an sees me.

4 Fat think ye o our lasses noo
  Their parasols an a'
  At kirk or market fin they gang
  Wi a' their ribbons braw.
    But the ploughman laddie's my delight
    An the ploughman laddie lees me
    When his wark is dean at e'en
    It's then he comes an sees me.

5 Bit I will wash my ploughman's hose
  An brush his dubby sheen
  An I'll maybe be my ploughman's wife
  Fin a this days is deen.
    For the ploughman laddie's my delight
    An the ploughman laddie lees me
    Fin a the lave gangs to their bed
    My ploughman comes an sees me.

6   What think ye o our farmers noo
     Their thrashing mulls an a'
     It wisna sae in our young day
     The ploughman threshed the straw.
       Bit I will wash my ploughman's hose
       An brush his dubby sheen
       An I'll maybe be the ploughman's wife
       Fin a this days is deen.

Mrs MARGARET GILLESPIE — D

C

The Plooman Laddie.

1   What think ye o' oor fairmers noo,
     Wi' thrashin' mills and a' that?
     It wasna sae in former days
     When the young men threesh the straw.
       The plooman lad is my delight,
       The plooman laddie loes me;
       When a' the rest gang tae their bed
       The plooman comes to see me.

2   What think ye o' oor lasses noo,
     Sin' they're a grown sae braw?
     They hinna laid a bawbee by
     Sin' they put on the straw.

3   It's I will wash the plooman's hose,
     And I will brush his sheen,
     And I'll maybe be the plooman's wife
     When a' the days are deen.

4   He's ta'en up his owsen gaud,
     Sae weel's he could it draw,
     And he's laid it owre his owsen bow,
     Says, "Shirrie, come awa."

Mrs CORBET — G

D

The Plooman Laddie's my delight.

Miss SANGSTER — G

E

The Plooman Lad.

The plooman lad is my delight, And the plooman laddie loves me;
They say the plooman is wi' me When I'm sure that he isna near me,

Mrs RETTIE — G

F

The Braes o' Broo

1 What think ye o' oor lasses noo
    They're grown a' sae braw man
    They've scarcely laid a bawbee by
    Since they put on the straw man.

2 What think ye o' their fal-da-rals
    Their boas, lang ells twa man
    The craze they've ta'en for foreign furs
    Will scare their lads awa man.

3 I've learned to spin as grannie did
    My ploughman lad to clead man   [clothe
    I'll weave the hose to hap his feet
    The bonnet for his head man.

JOHN MILNE — G

G

The Plooman Laddie

1   The plooman laddie's my delight,
      The plooman laddie loes me,
      Fin a' the lave gang to their bed
      The plooman comes and sees me.

2   It's I will wash the plooman's hose,
      And dry them o'er the door,
      I'll maybe be the plooman's wife
      I've been his lass afore.

3   Oh I will wash the plooman's hose,
      And I will brush his sheen,
      I'll maybe be the plooman's wife
      Fin a' this days is deen.

      Miss BELL ROBERTSON — G

444

IT WASNA SAE

1   We hae nocht but stamfern horse   [stumbling
      To toil our grun ava,
      When they come to a lairy place   [boggy
      They falter like to fa'
      The bonnie humlies did see that
      They shortly toiled it a'.

2   Our fairmers a' are grown sae big
      Wi' thrashin' mills and a',
      It wasna sae in my young days
      When the ploomen thresh the straw.

      Miss BELL ROBERTSON — G

THE PLOOMAN LADDIE

A

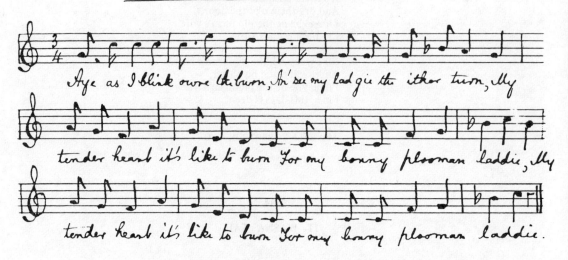

The Plooman Laddie.

Aye as I blink owre the burn, An' see my lad gie the ither turn, My
tender heart it's like to burn For my bonny plooman laddie, My
tender heart it's like to burn For my bonny plooman laddie.

1 Aye as I blink owre the burn,
  And see the lad gie the ither turn,
  My tender heart it's like to burn
  For yon bonny plooman laddie.

2 The plooman he comes doon the toon,
  Wi' his twa horses ringlin' roon',   [jingling
  The plooman he's a merry loon,
  He whistles aye fan he sees me.

3 The plooman he's baith neat and trig,
  O' middle size, though he bena big,
  I love the plooman above all trade,
  He's a bonny plooman laddie.

4 But I'll cast off my goon o' green,
  And I'll put on my bonny broon,
  In a bed o' straw we'll baith lie doon,
  And I'll clap my plooman laddie.

5 The plooman he says noo he's mine,
  And he smells to me like a buss o' thyme.   [clump
  An' he can kiss me when he thinks time,
  And prove himsel' a plooman.

Mrs LYALL — D

B

The Plooman Laddie.

1 The plooman he comes doon the toon,
   Wi' a' his rings a' ringlin' roon,
   The plooman he's a merry loon,
   He whistles aye when he sees me.

2 I would hae got the merchant into yonder shop,
   But a' his goods they're nae worth a groat,
   The chiel himsel' he's but a sot;
   And I'm for my plooman laddie.

3 I would hae gotten the miller into yonder mill,
   The smell o' the dust would hae done me ill,
   I love the plooman and aye will dee, —
   I'm for a plooman laddie.

4 I would hae got the smith into yonder smiddy,
   But the smiddy coom would hae ruined me, [soot
   I love the plooman and aye will dee,
   And I'm for my plooman laddie.

5 It's I'll tak' aff my goon o' green,
   And I'll put on my goon o' broon,
   On a bed o' strae we'll baith lie doon,
   And I'll clap my plooman laddie.

CHARLES DAVIDSON — G

C

I micht hae gotten.

1 I might of gotten the miller of yonder mill
 But the smell of dist wad hae deen me ill
 I love my ploughman, I love him still
 I love my ploughman laddie.

2 I might of gotten the gairner of yonder tree
 But the smell of time would of sickened me
 I'll love my ploughman until I dee
 I love my ploughman laddie.

Mrs SANGSTER and Miss SANGSTER — G

D

Mrs MILNE — G

E

The Plooman Laddie

1 As my plooman lad gangs roon the toon,
 Wi' a' his irons hangin' roon;
 An' oh he is a bonnie loon,
 He whistles aye when he sees me.

2 I love the smith and the smiddy tee,
 But the smiddy coom widna do wi' me,
 I love the plooman, his hert is true,
 The bonnie plooman laddie.

3 I got a merchan' frae yonder shop,
 But I'm sure his goods wisna worth a groat,
 And for himsel' he's a drucken sot,
 But I love my plooman laddie.

4 When I gang oot and gang tae the stack,
 And hear the whip gie the ither crack,
 My very hert is like to brak,
 For the bonnie plooman laddie.

5 When I gang oot and look o'er the burn,
 And see the ploo gie the ither turn,
 I'm sure my hert is like to burn
 For the bonnie plooman laddie.

6 I had a father and a mother good,
 And of my beauty they were prood,
 But they hae turned their back on me,
 Because I love the plooman laddie.

7 The plooman lad, bein' nae far away,
 He heard all his bonnie love did say, —
 Cheer up your hert, love, and ye'll be mine,
 And ye'll be the plooman's dearie.

8 Gin that day week she was a bride,
 And gin that day fortnicht she was wed,
 And sae happy as she is in ae bed laid,
 And she's gotten her plooman laddie.

9   I've gotten my plooman puir eneuch,
     And puir as ever cam' frae the pleuch,
     But I love my plooman, and he loves me,
     He's my bonnie plooman laddie.

Miss K. MORRICE — G

F

1   When I look up and owre the burn
     And saw the plough gie the ither turn
     My tender heart is like to burn
     For yon bonnie plooman laddie.

2   I will wash his dubby breeks
     And I will brush his sheen
     And I'll maybe be the plooman's wife
     Ere a' my days be deen.

Mrs CORBET — G

446

MY LOVE'S A PLOOMAN

My love's a plooman, & follows the ploo, I promised to him and I'll keep it true; I promised to him, and I'll never rue The lovin' o' the plooman laddie.

1   My love is a ploughman and follows the plough
     I promised to him and I'll keep it true
     I promised to him and I'll never rue
     The lovin' o' the ploughman laddie.

Mrs SANGSTER and Miss SANGSTER — G

THE PRAISE OF PLOUGHMEN

A

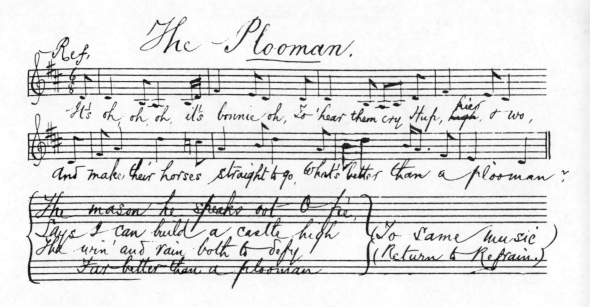

It's oh, oh, oh it's bonnie oh
To hear them cry Keep back and Wo
And make their horses straight to go
What's better than a plooman.

1 The mason he speaks oot "O fie"
Says "I can build a castle high
The win' and rain both to defy
Far better than a plooman."

2 O mason dinna crack sae croose,   [talk so
We own that ye can build a hoose confidently
But fae the king doon to the moose
Depends upon the plooman.

3 The miller he speaks oot fu' weel
Says I do grind the corn for meal
Says I do grind the corn for meal
For to maintain the plooman.

4 O miller ye should haud yer jaw   [keep quiet
Go home and look to your call wa'
There widna muckle dust doon fa'
If it werena for the plooman.

ALEXANDER ROBB – G

B

The Praise of Ploughmen

1   Ye lads and lasses a' draw near
I'm sure it will delight your ear
And as for me I'll no be sweir
To sing the praise o' ploomen.
The very king that wears the crown
And brethren of the sacred gown
And dukes and lords of high renown
Depend upon the ploomen.
   Oh happy is the plooman's joe
   To hear the plooman cry, Hie wo,
   And make the horse so straight to go
   The gallant merry plooman.

2   The gardener he cries out wi' speed
I'm sure I was the first man made
And I was learned the gardener trade
Before there was a plooman.
Oh gardener lad it's true you say
But how long gardener did you stay
I'm sure it was just scarce a day
Ere ye became a plooman.

3   The blacksmith he says I hear news
Do I not make your iron ploughs
And fit the coulter for its use
Or there would be nae ploomen?
Oh blacksmith we must all allow
That you can mak' an iron plough
But you would never get that to do
If it were not for the plooman.

4   The mason he cries, Ho, ho, fie
Do I not build your castles high
The wind and rain for to defy
Far better than the plooman?
Oh mason ye may build a house
And fit it for its proper use
But from the king unto the mouse
Depends upon the plooman.

5   The miller he speaks out wi' glee
Do I not sit at the mill e'e
And grind the corn food for thee
Far better than the plooman?
Oh miller ye may haud your jaw
And sit and look at your mill wa'
And see if dust frae it wid fa'
If it were not for the plooman.

6   The souter he cries out Hurrah
Do I not make boots and shoes right braw
For to defend baith frost and snaw
That's worn by the ploomen?
You may mak' boots and shoes wi' speed
Wi' last and leather, birse and thread
But where's the meal for to be breid
If it were not for the plooman.

7   The tailor he cries out wi' haste
I pray if this don't mak' a jest
Oh I can mak' coat, trews and vest
Far better than the plooman.
Oh tailor ye may mak' braw clothes
But where's the meal for to be brose?
Ye might close up both mouth and nose
If it were not for the plooman.

8   Success to ploomen's wages crown
Let ploomen's wages never come down
And plenty in Scotland abound
By the labour o' the ploomen.

JOHN MOWAT — G

197

C
Britain's Isle

1   The people o' my native isle
    And you that lives in Britain's isle
    May fortune lang upon you smile
    By the labours o' the plooman.

2   Many knichts, baith lairds in vain
    Wi' brushed boots and glancing canes
    Wha think themsels nae sheep sma banes
    Lives by the labouring plooman.

Mr FINNIE — G

D
The Labours o' the Plooman

1   O millert, ye may haud yer jaw
    For ye wad lick a clean mill wa';
    Faur wad ye get corn to mak yer meal,
    An it werena for the plooman.

Mrs MARGARET GILLESPIE — D

THE PAINFUL PLOUGH

A

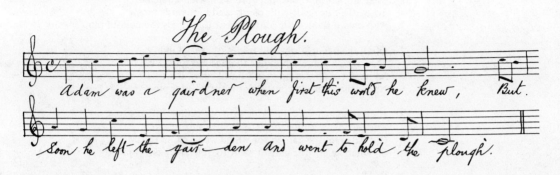

The Plough.

Adam was a gairdner when first this world he knew, But Soon he left the gairden And went to hold the Plough.

P.R. GORDON — G

B

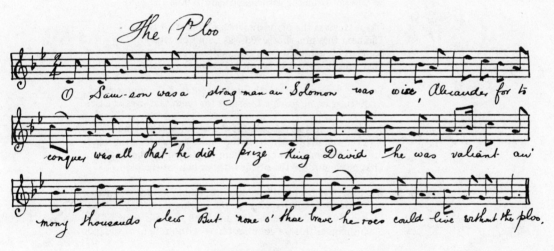

The Ploo

O Samson was a strong man an' Solomon was wise, Alexander for to conquer was all that he did prize King David he was valiant an' mony thousands slew But none o' thae brave heroes could live withoot the ploo.

GEORGE RIDDELL — G

C

The Painful Plough

1   Come all ye jolly ploomen of courage stout and bold
That labours all the winter thro' rain wind and cold
To clothe our fields with plenty and barnyards renew
And crown them with contentment that holds the painful ploo'.

2   Of all the occupations and trades of every kind
Through all inaurate nations there is not one you'll find
So useful in its station you'll find I speak it's true
Nor is there one so constant as is the painful ploo.

3   Hold plooman says the gardener your calling I despise
For each man for his living upon his trade relies
Old Adam in the garden for which we've cause to rue
So when he left the garden went to hold the painful ploo.

4   Hold gardener says the ploomen count not your trade like ours
For walk ye through the garden and view the early flowers
See every curious border and pleasant walks review
There is not such peace nor pleasure performed by the ploo.

5   Old Adam in the garden was sent to keep it right
But tell me how long stayed he for I think scarce one night.
He did eat none of his labour but what was noo his due
So was put from the garden and sent to hold the ploo.

6   Old Adam was the plooman when plooin' first began
The next that him succeeded was Cain's eldest son
Some of his generation his calling does pursue
That bread may not be wanted, I mean the painful ploo.

7   You see the wealthy merchant that trades to far countries
And brings home foreign treasures for them that lives at ease.

8   Tea, sneechon, and tobacco they're useful in their kind
And they're all brought from the Indies by virtue of the wind.
And yet the man that brings them must own to what is true
That he cannot sail the ocean without help of the ploo.

9   We must have beer and biscuits, rice, pudding flour and peas
To fill our jolly sailors when on the roaring seas
Likewise we must have candles and rope and sails anew
Such things as this we could not have without help of the ploo.

10 Nor could our own tradesmen live if we consider't right
The mason, smith, and tailor, the weaver and the wright.
The miller has no corn to grind nor could he take his due
But him and thousands you will find lives by the painful ploo.

11 I hope there's none offended at me for singin' this
For it is not intended for to be ta'en amiss
If you consider't rightly you'll find I speak it's true
All trades that I have mentioned lives by the painful ploo.

Miss ANNIE SHIRER — G

D

The Ploughman and the Gardener

1 O ploughman, says the gardener, count not your trade with ours,
   Go, walk ye thro' the garden, and view the early flowers;
   Go, view each curious border, and every walk just view,
   There is not such peace nor pleasure performèd by the plough.

2 O gardener, says the plooman, no calling I despise,
   As each man for his being upon his trade relies;
   Old Adam was a gardener, when first the world he knew,
   But he soon left his garden and went to hold the ploo.

3 Old Adam was a plooman when plooin' first began,
   And the next that him succeeded was Cain his eldest son
   Some of his generation yet this calling doth pursue,
   That bread may not be wanted around the painful ploo.

4 Samson was a strong man, and Solomon was wise,
   Alexander loved to conquer, it being all his prize;
   King David was a valiant man, and many a thousand slew,
   But there's none of all those brave men could live without the ploo.

5 Behold our bakers in the streets who daily doth supply
   Our cities with great plenty of bread with wheat and rye
   Appear as white as angels whilst in their golden line,
   This cakes would get nae flour to bake if 'twerena for the ploo.

6 Likewise the wealthy merchant that ploo the raging seas,
   To bring home foreign dainties, for those who live at ease.
   They must have beer and biscuits, rice puddins, flour and peas,
   To feed the jolly sailors that ploo the ragin' seas.

7 And yet the man that brings them he'll own to what is true,
   They're a benefit to England, by virtue o' the ploo.

A. ROTHNIE — G

E

The Painful Plough

1 Come all ye joyful ploughboys with courage stout and bold
   That labours all the winter through stormy winds and cold.
   To crown the fields with plenty their barnyards to renew
   And crown them with contentment that holds the painful plough.

2 Friend gardener to the ploughboy, Count not your trade with ours
   Come walk ye through this garden and view these early flowers
   And all these curious borders these pleasant walks review
   There is not much peace and pleasure can by formed by the plough.

3 Friend ploughboy to the gardener Do not our trade despise
   For each one for his living doth on our trade rely
   If it weren't for the ploughboy both rich and poor would rue
   So we are all depending on the painful plough.

4 Behold the wealthy merchants that ploughs the raging seas
 That brings home foreign treasures for them that leaves at ease.
 Who brings silks from the Indies and fruits and spices too
 These are all brought to England by virtue of the plough.

5 Behold the men that bring them will own to what is true
 They cannot plough the ocean without the painful plough
 They must have bread and biscuits, rice, pudding, flour, and peas,
 To feed their jolly sailors that plough the raging seas.

6 I hope there is none offended at me for singing this
 For it never was intended to be taken amiss.
 If you will consider rightly what I have said is true
 That we are all depending upon the painful plough.

T. ROGER – G

THE LADDIE THAT HANDLES THE PLOO

A

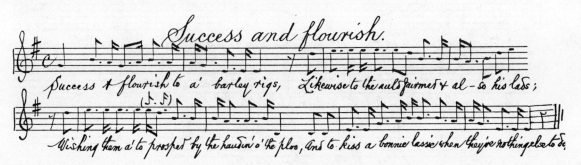

Success and flourish to a' barley rigs
Likewise to the auld fermer and also his lads.
Wishing them a' to prosper by the haudin' o' the ploo.
And to kiss a bonnie lassie when they've nothing else to do.

1   The mason he's a laddie that's prood o' his post
    In't hidna been the mason we wid a' hae dee't wi frost.
    But fat aboot the mason? He wid hae little for to do
    If it warna for the bonnie boy that handles the ploo.

2   The smith he's a laddie that's a' smeer't wi' brook
    An' when he sees a bonny lass sae canty's he dis look
    He kisses her, an' claps her, and ca'es her his doo
    Bit he's far fae like the bonnie boy that handles the ploo.

3   The sooter he's a laddie that works wi' his awl
    In't hidna been the souter we wid a' hae dee't wi' caul.
    The sooter's like the lave, he wad hae little to do
    In't warna for the bonnie boy that handles the ploo.

4   The millert he's a laddie that's a' smeert wi' dist
    An' fin he meets a bonnie lass he wad gie her a kiss
    But the miller's like the lave he wad hae little for to do
    In't werena for the bonnie boy that handles the ploo.

5   The tailor he's a laddie etc.

6   The jiner etc.

Mrs DUNCAN — G

B
Trades

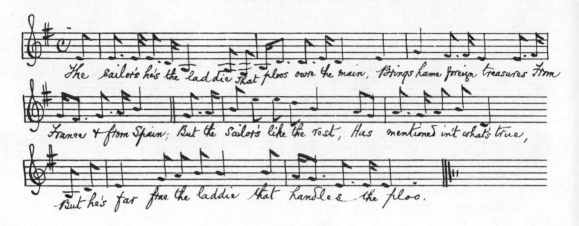

The sailor's he's the laddie that ploos owre the main, Brings hame foreign treasures From France & from Spain; But the sailor's like the rest, Has mentioned in't what's true, But he's far frae the laddie that handles the ploo.

1   The miller he's the laddie that's aye in a steer
    Wi' twa three auld wifes aye on the fleer
    But the miller's like the rest, he'd have little to do
    If twerna for the laddie that handles the ploo.

2   The sailor he's the laddie that ploos owre the main
    Brings home foreign treasures from France and from Spain
    But the sailor's like the rest, has mentioned in it what is true
    Still he's far frae like the laddie that handles the ploo.

J. McBOYLE — G

C
The Laddie That Handles the Ploo

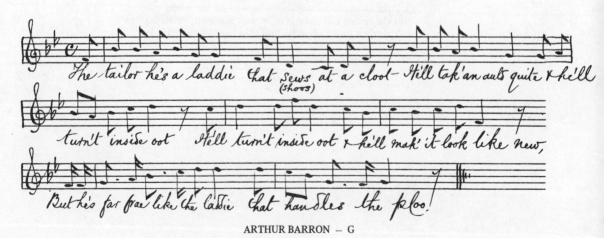

The tailor he's a laddie that sews at a cloot He'll tak' an auld quite & he'll (shoos) turn't inside oot He'll turn't inside oot & he'll mak' it look like new, But he's far frae like the laddie that handles the ploo!

ARTHUR BARRON — G

204

D

The Laddie that Handles the Ploo

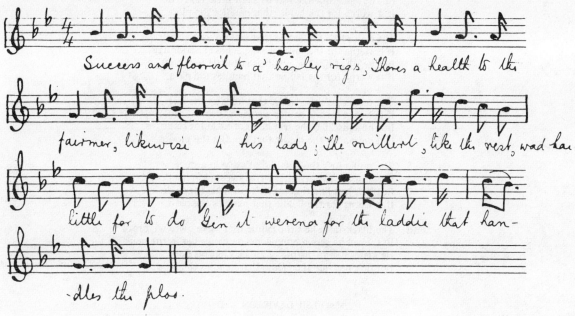

Success and floorish to a' barley rigs, There's a health to the fairmer, likewise to his lads; The millert, like the rest, wad hae little for to do Gin it werena for the laddie that han--dles the ploo.

Mrs LYALL — D

E

Health to the Farmers.

Success and floorish to a' barley rigs! Here's a health to the farmers, likewise unto their lads; For I wish them a' success for the haudlin' o' the ploo, And for kissin' bonnie lasses when they're nothing else to do.

Rev. JOHN CALDER — G

F

The Laddie That Handles the Ploo

1 The teacher he's the laddie that handles the pen
 If it werna for the teacher we couldna sign oor name
 But he's just like the rest he's got little for to do
 If it werna for the laddie that handles the ploo.
  Success an' floorish tae a' barley rigs
  Health unto the fairmer success unto the ploo
  Aye success to the haudin' o' the ploo
  An kissin' bonnie lassies fan they've na ither thing to do.

2   The mason he's the laddie that builds on the wa'
    If it werna for the mason we wid a dee wi' cauld
    But he's just like the rest he's got little for to do
    If it werna for the laddie that handles the ploo.

3   The tailor he's the laddie that maks a' oor claes
    If it werna for the tailor we'd gae naket a' oor days
    But he's just like the rest he's got little for to do
    If it werna for the laddie that handles the ploo.

4   The souter he's the laddie that handles the awl
    If it werna for the souter we wid a' dee wi' caul
    But he's just like the rest he's got little for to do
    If it werna for the laddie that handles the ploo.

5   The miller he's the laddie that's aye in a steer
    Wi' four an' twenty auld wives sweepin in his fleer
    But he's just like the rest he's got little for to do
    If it werna for the laddie that handles the ploo.

6   The blacksmith he's the laddie that's aye owre wi' brook
    But when he sees a bonnie lass he hauds her in the neuk
    He kisses her an' claps her an' ca's her his doo
    But he's nae like the laddie that handles the ploo.

Miss ELSIE DAVIDSON — D

G

Tradesman's Song

1   The mason he's a laddie that's proud o' his post
    Gin it werna for the mason we would a' dee in frost.
    But he like the rest would get little for to do
    Gin it werna for the laddie that handles the plough.
     Success and ploughrace to a' barley rigs
     Here's health unto the farmer likewise unto his lads
     Wishin them to prosper by the handling o' the plou
     And the kissin o a bonnie lassie when there's nothing else to do.

2   The wright he's a laddie that handles the plane
    Gin it werna for the wright we wid a dee in rain.
    But he like the rest would get little for to do
    Gin it werna for the laddie that handles the plough.

3   The souter he's a laddie that handles the awl
    Gin it werna for the souter we would a' dee in cauld.
    But he like the rest would get little for to do
    Gin it werna for the laddie that handles the plough.

4   The smith he's a laddie that's aye owre wi brook
    But when he meets a bonnie lass he gies a blythsome look
    He kisses her and claps her, gies her aye promise true
    But he's far frae like the laddie that handles the plough.

Miss DUNCAN — G

H

The Laddie That Handles the Ploo

Success and flourish to all barley rigs
Here's t' the fairmer, likewise unto his lads
For I wish them great success to the han'lin' o' the ploo
And the kissin' o' the lasses when there's nothing else to do.

1 The mason he's a laddie that's prood o' his post
Gin it warna for the mason we wad a' dee wi' frost
But the mason like the rest wad get little for to do
Gin it warna for the laddie that handles the ploo.

2 The joiner he's a laddie that handles the plane
And when he meets a bonnie lass he mak's her think he's fain   [loving
He mak's her think he's fain, but ah she's sure to rue
For he's nae like the laddie that handles the ploo.

3 The smith he's a laddie that's aye smeared wi' brook
And when he meets a bonnie lass he gies a mirky look
He gies a mirky look but ah he's far frae true
And he's nae like the laddie that handles the ploo.

JAMES M. TAYLOR — G

I

1 The mason he's the laddie is proud o's post,
Gin it werena the mason we wid a' dee in frost;
But the mason's like the lave, he has little for to do
Gin it werena the laddie that handles the ploo.

2 The wright he's the laddie that handles the plane,
And fan he meets a bonnie lass he maks her true and fain,
But the wright's like the lave, he has little for to do
Gin it werena the laddie that handles the ploo.

Miss BELL ROBERTSON — G

J

1 The millert is a laddie that's aye in a steer,
Wi' twa or three auld wives dancin' on the fleer,
But the millert, etc.

JONATHAN GAULD — G

COME, ALL YE JOLLY PLOOBOYS

The Plooman

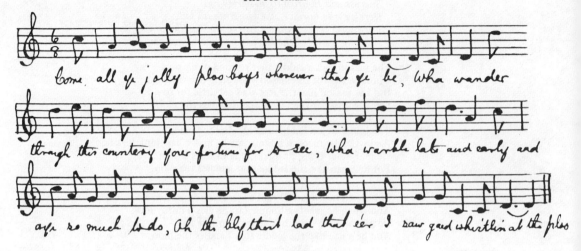

1 Come, all ye jolly ploughboys wherever that ye be,
That ramble through this countery your fortune for to see,
Wha warble late and early and aye so much to do,
Oh the blythest lad that e'er I saw gaed whistlin' at the ploo.

2 Oh the plooman he's a clever lad, he's aye sae neat and trim,
He daurna lowse before his time for a' the rain and win',
While the stormy win's do beat, and the rain down doth pour,
A' the time the jolly ploughboys for through the lan' doth score.   [scour, move swiftly

3 When drivin' in the yoke, at the harrows, cairt, or ploo,
Or drivin' in the thrashin' mill, a sang he'll bring in view,
Some bit cheery lilt he'll sing his spirits to revive;
Oh the plooman he's a clever chiel, his work wi' him will thrive.

4 There are several airts that man can do of high respect and low,
But to keep the teeth fae roosting is the handlin' o' the ploo;   [rusting through
The plooman works for rich and poor, for people great and sma,   lack of use
And awat he is the blythest lad that is amang them a'.

5 The masons they stan' wondrous big upon yon scaffold high,
And noo and than they'll gie a smile as the plooboy does pass by.
But what can they dee but chap a steen and lay it on the wa'?   [tap
And when there comes a shoor o' rain, like sheep they rin awa.

6 The souter he sits wondrous big oot ower upon yon stool,
And noo and than when he thinks lang, the leather he will mell.   [is bored
He'll rug it and he'll tug it and he'll tear it wi' his teeth,
And then he'll send it off to wear upon the ploughboy's feet.

7 The blacksmith he's a hero bold, he beats at iron and steel,
His face is always ower wi' brook, as black's the very deil;
It's seldom that the blacksmith can get ower much ado,
Yet he's the fittest hand to trim the irons o' the plough.

8   The miller his a usefu' trade, few could his labour want;
      If it werena for the miller, oh oor bannocks would be scant;
      But miller tee, though that he be, his happer would rin dry,
      If it werena for the sacks o' corn the plooboy does supply.

9   The soldier he's a hero bold, let folk say what they will,
      He fights for his countery, likewise his enemies kill;
      The soldier and the ploughboy, if they're offended sore,
      Oh what would our poor nation do, oh if they were no more?

WILLIAM WALLACE — D

451

COMMEND ME TO THE PLOOMAN

The Plooman

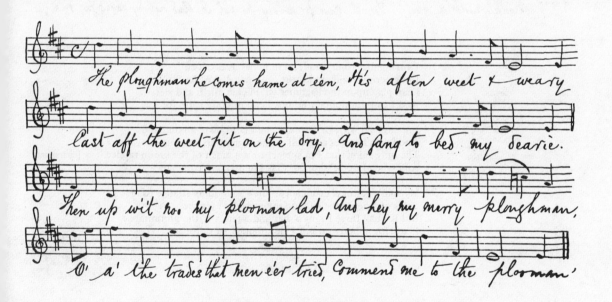

1   The ploughman he comes hame at e'en,
    He's aften weet and weary
    Cast aff the weet pit on the dry,
    And gang to bed my dearie.
      Then up wi't noo my plooman lad,
      And hey my merry ploughman,
      O' a' the trades that men e'er tried,
      Commend me to the plooman.

Miss ANNIE RITCHIE — G

THE MILLER O' STRALOCH

A

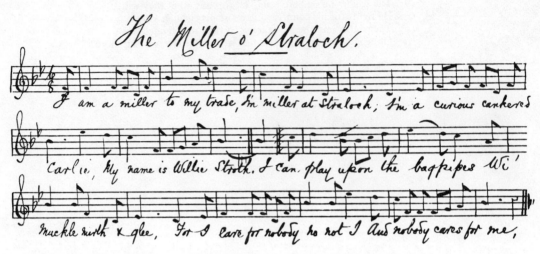

1 I am a miller to my trade, I'm miller at Straloch
  I'm a curious cankered carlie, my name is Willie Stroth.
  I can play upon the bagpipes wi' mickle mirth and glee
  And I care for nobody no not I and nobody cares for me.

2 I'm engaged with Dr Ramsay, he's laird owre all our land
  And when he does give call to me I am at his command.
  The only thing that I'm subject to is a pinch of the broon rappee   [coarse snuff
  And when I do fa' short o' that I'm no good company.

3 My mill's got new machinery, she's something strange to me
  She's of a new construction my eyes did ever see.
  But if I had three roons o' her and a pinch o' the broon rapee
  I care for nobody no not I and nobody cares for me.

ALEXANDER ROBB – G

B

The Wee Millar

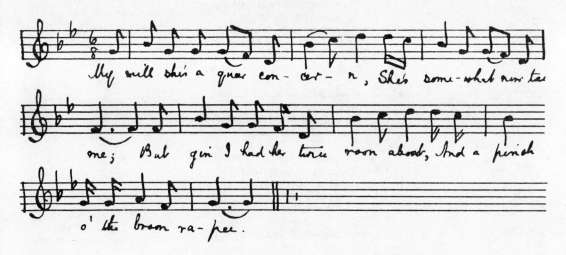

1 I am a little wee millirtie
   An' I sometimes gang on the spree
   But I care for nobody no not I
   Since nobody cares for me.

2 My mill she's a queer concern
   She's somewhat new to me
   But gin I had her twice roond aboot
   An' a pinch o' the broon rapee.

Mrs LYALL – D

C

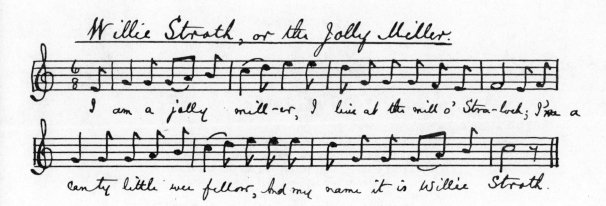

1 I am a jolly millar
 I live at the mill o Straloch
 I'm a canty little wee fellow
 My name is Willie Stroth.
  I care for nobody no not I
  An nobody cares for me
  The only thing I am subject to
  Is a pinch o the brown rapee.

2 I'm engaged wi Mister Ramsey
 He's laird o a the land
 An when that he does call on me
 I am at his command.

3 Some people say he's quarrlesome
 But he never quarreled me
 An what care I what any say
 If him and I agree.

Mrs MARGARET GILLESPIE — D

D

The Miller of Straloch

Rev. JAMES B. DUNCAN — G

E

The Miller of Straloch

1 I am a jolly wee miller come frae the Mill o' Straloch,
 And if you do not know me, my name is Willie Stroth
 I play upon my bagpipes wi' muckle mirth and glee,
 And I care for nobody, no, not I, since nobody cares for me.

2 When first that I came here about I had too much ado,
 For binding corn and shearing grass, both late and early too;
 But now my harvest's ended, and I'm in my millie,
 I care for nobody, no, not I, and there's nobody cares for me.

3 I'm engaged to one, Mr. Ramsay, the laird of a' oor land,
   And when that he does call me, I am at his command;
   Some people say he's quarrelsome, but he never quarrels me,
   So I care for nobody, no, not I, there's nobody cares for me.

4 My mill's got new machinery, she is quite strange to me,
   She is of a new invention as ever my eyes did see;
   But gin I had her twice gaen roon, and a pinch of the Brown Rappee,
   I would care for nobody, no, not I; there's nobody cares for me.

5 I'm nae gien up to drinkin', for it never troubles me,
   Nor is there one of the female sex would keep my sleep frae me;
   But there's one thing I am subject to is a pinch of the Brown Rappee,
   And when that I'm deprived of it then surely I maun dee.

6 Wi' carryin' heavy burdens my back's inclined to boo,
   Wi' carryin' heavy burdens my back's near broken in two;
   And nature has formed my eemist lip to kep the sneeshin' bree;   [upper; snotter
   So I care for nobody, no, not I, there's nobody cares for me.

JOHN WIGHT — G

F

The Miller o' Straloch

1 I am a jolly miller come frae the mill o' Straloch
   And if you do not know me my name is Willie Stroth.
   I play upon my bagpipes wi' muckle mirth and glee
   And I care for nobody, no not I, and there's nobody cares for me.

2 First when I cam here aboot I'd too much for to do
   For binding corn and shearing grass both late and early too
   But now the harvest's over and I'm in my millie
   So I care for nobody, no not I, there's nobody cares for me.

3 I'm engaged to one Mr Ramsay the laird o' a' oor lan'
   And when that he does call on me I am at his command.
   Some people say that he's quarrelsome but he never quarrels me
   So I care for nobody, no not I, there's nobody cares for me.

4 My mill's got new machinery she is quite strange to me
   She is of a new invention as ever my eyes did see
   But gin I had her ance or twice gaen roon and a pinch o' the broon Rappie
   I will care for nobody, no not I, since nobody cares for me.

5 I'm nae gien up to drinkin' for it never troubles me
   Nor is there one of the female sex would keep my sleep from me
   But there's one thing that I'm subject to is a pinch o' the broon Rappie
   And when that I'm deprived o' it then surely I maun dee.

6 Wi' carryin' heavy burdens my back's inclined to boo
   Wi' carryin' heavy burdens my back's near broken in two
   And nature has formed my eemest lip to kep the sneeshin bree
   So I care for nobody, no not I, and nobody cares for me.

J. W. SPENCE — G

453

MERRY MAY THE MAID BE

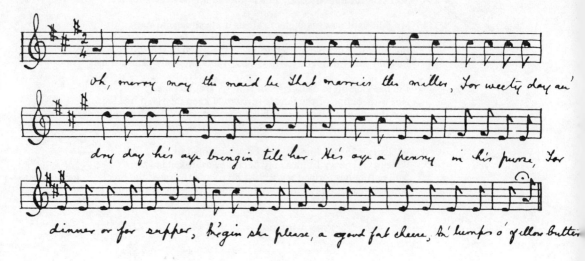

1 Merry may the maid be that marrys the miller
   For weety day an dry day he's aye bringing tull her
   His aye a penny in his purse for dinner an for supper
   An gin she please a good fat cheese an lumps o yellow butter.

2 When Jamie first did w'oo me I spear'd what wis his callin
   Fair maid says he O come an see, ye're welcome to my dwalling
   Tho I wis shy yet I could spy the truth o what he told me
   An that his house wis warm an couth an room in it to hold me.

3 Behind the door a bag o meal an in the kist was plenty
   Of good hard cakes his mither bakes an bannocks werna scanty
   A good fat sow a sleeky cow was standing in the byre
   While lazy puss wi mealy mouth wis play'n at the fire.

4 Good signs are these my mither says an bids me tak the miller
   For weety day an dry day he's aye bringing tull her
   For meal an maut she disna want nor onything that's dainty
   An now an than a kecklin hen to lay her eggs a plenty.

5 In winter when the wind an rain blaws o'er the house an byre
   She sits beside a clean hearth stane before a rousing fire
   With nut-brown ale he tells his tale which rows him our fu nappy   [intoxicated
   Who'd be a king a petty thing when a miller lives sae happy.

Mrs MARGARET GILLESPIE – D

THE DUSTY MILLER

A

The Dusty Miller

1 Hey the dusty millar an his dusty coat
He will win a shillin e'er he spend a groat
Dusty was the coat, dusty was the colour
Dusty was the kiss that I gat fae the millar.

2 Hey the dusty millar an his dusty sack
Leeze me on the callin fills the dusty peck
Fills the dusty peck, brings the dusty siller
I wid gie my coatie for the dusty millar.

Mrs MARGARET GILLESPIE – D

B

1 Hey, the dusty miller, ho! the dusty miller!
Weel fares the lass that gets a dusty miller
Dusty was his coat, dusty was his colour,
Dusty was the kiss that I gat frae the miller.

2 Lease me on the calling brings the dusty siller
Weet day and dry day he's aye bringin' till her.

3 Fills the dusty pockie o' the dusty siller.

WILLIAM FORBES — G

C

The Dusty Miller

JAMES HARDIE — G

D

Hey the Dusty Miller

1 Hey, the dusty miller, and his dusty pock,
He will win a shillin' ere he spend a groat.
Dusty was his coat, and dusty was his colour,
Dusty was the kiss that I got frae the miller.

2 Hey the dusty miller, and his dusty peck;
Leeze me o' the callin' fills the dusty seck;
Fills the dusty seck that brings the dusty siller;
I wad gie my coatie for the dusty miller.

Miss BELL ROBERTSON — G

THE CROOK AND PLAID

A

1   I winna lo'e the laddie that ca's the cart an pleugh
    Although he may be constant an tho' he may be true
    For he that has my bosom to fondest love betrayed
    Is my faithful shepherd laddie that wears the crook an plaid.
        For he's aye true to his lover
        Aye true to his lover
        Aye true to me.

2   At noon he leans him down upon the high an heathy fell
    An views his flocks beneath him a-feeding in the dale
    An when he sings the sangs o love the sweetest ever made
    O how happy is the lad that wears the crook an plaid.

3   He pu's the bells o heather red the lilies flower so meek
    Ca's the lily like my bosom an' the heath bell like my cheek
    His words are soft an tender as the dew frae heaven shed,
    An ne'en can charm me like the laddie that wears the crook an plaid.

4   Beneath the flowery hawthorn tree wild growing in the glen
    He meets me in the gloman gray when ne'en on earth can keen
    An leel an tender is his heart beneath the spreading shade
    An weel he keens the way I trow to row me in his plaid.

5 When the dews begin to fall, an the gloman shades draw on
   When the stars come stealing through the sky an the kye are in the loan
   He whistles through the glen sae sweet my heart is lighter made
   To keen the laddie hameward hies wha wears the crook an plaid.

6 The youth o many riches may to his fair one ride
   An w'oo across a table his mony titled bride
   But we will woo beneath the tree where cheeck to cheeck is laid
   O nae wooer's like the laddie that rows me in his plaid.

7 To own the truth o faithful love what heart wid no comply
   Since sure love gies mair happiness than aught aneath the sky
   When love is in the bosom the heart is ne'er afraid
   Sae through life I'll lo'e the laddie that wears the crook an plaid.

Mrs MARGARET GILLESPIE – D

B

The Crook and the Plaid

1   If lassies love the laddies they surely should confess
    For every lassie has a lad she lo'es aboon the rest
    He's dearer to her bosom whatever be his trade
    And thro' life I'll lo'e the laddie that wears the crook and plaid
      For he's aye true to his lover
      Aye true to his lover
      Aye true to me.

2   He climbs the mountains early his fleecy flocks to view
    He spies the little laverock spring out frae 'mang the dew
    His faithfu' little doggie sae frolicsome an' glad
    He follows aye the laddie that wears the crook and plaid.

3   He pu's the bloomin' heather, he pu's the lily meek
    Ca's the lily like my bosom, the heather like my cheek,
    His words are aye sae tender, my heart is aye sae glad,
    There's nae wooer like the laddie that wears the crook and plaid.

4   It's doon beside the hawthorn that blooms in yonder dale
    I met him in the gloamin' far frae the noisy gale,
    His words they war sae tender, my heart it was sae glaid,
    For he kens the wye to row me sae cosy in his plaid.

5   To such a faithfu' lover, oh who would not comply,
    True love gives greater pleasure than aught beneath the sky.
    If love be in your bosom your heart can ne'er be sad
    Sae thro' life I'll lo'e the laddie that wears the crook and plaid.

GEORGE F. DUNCAN — D

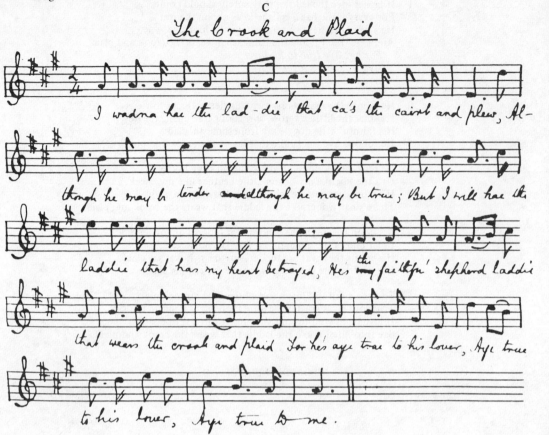

The Crook and Plaid

C

I wadna hae the lad-die that ca's the cairt and pleugh, Although he may be tender and although he may be true; But I will hae the
laddie that has my heart betrayed, His the faithfu' shepherd laddie
that wears the crook and plaid For he's aye true to his lover, Aye true
to his lover, Aye true to me.

Mrs LYALL – D

D

The Crook & Plaid.

I winna love the laddie that ca's the cart & pleugh, Tho' he should own that
tender love that's only felt by few. For he that has this bosom a' to
fondest love betrayed Is the faithfu' shepherd laddie that wears the crook & plaid
For he's aye true to his lassie, Aye true to his lassie Aye true to me.

Miss ANNIE RITCHIE – G

220

E

The Crook and Plaid

JAMES ANGUS — G

F

1   I wadna hae the laddie that drives the cairt and ploo —
Although his heart be tender — although his heart be true
But I'll hae the laddie that hath my heart betrayed
He's a faithful shepherd laddie that wears the crook and plaid.
He's aye true to her lover —
He's aye true to me.

Source unrecorded — G

456

THE COUNTRY CARRIER

1   I am a country carrier,
A jolly soul am I
I whistle from morning till evening,
All troubles I defy.

ALEXANDER ROBB — G

JIM THE CARTER LAD

A

Jim the Carter Lad.

1 My name is Jim the carter lad, a jolly block am I
   And I am aye contented let the weather be weet or dry.
   I snap my fingers at the snow and whistle at the rain
   I've braved the storms for many a day and can do so again.
       Then crack, crack goes my whip, I whistle and I sing
       As I sit upon my waggon I'm as happy as a king.
       My horse is always willin and for me I'm never sad
       There's none can lead a jollier life than Jim the carter lad.

ALEXANDER ROBB – G

B

Jim the Carter Lad

1 My name is Jim the Carter, a jolly lad am I
   I always am contented be the weather wet or dry.
   I snap my fingers at the snow and whistle at the rain
   I've braved the storm for many a day and can do so again.
       Crack, crack goes my whip, I whistle and I sing
       As I sit upon my waggon I'm as happy as a king.
       My horse is always willing and for me I'm never sad
       There's none can lead a jollier life than Jim the Carter Lad.

2 My father was a carrier many years ere I was born
   He used to rise at daybreak and go his rounds each morn.
   He'd often take me with him especially in the spring
   I loved to sit upon the cart and hear my father sing.

3   I never think of politics or anything so great
     I care not for their high-bred talk about the church or state.
     I act aright to man and man and that's what makes me glad
     You'll find their beats an honest heart in Jim the Carter Lad.

4   The girls they all smile on me as I go driving past
     My horse is such a beauty as he jogs along so fast.
     We've travelled many weary miles by happy days we've had
     There's none can use a horse more kind than Jim the Carter Lad.

5   But now I'll bid you all goodnight, tis time I was away
     My horse I know will weary if I much longer stay.
     To see your smiling faces here it makes my heart quite glad
     I hope you'll grant your kind applause to Jim the Carter Lad.

JAMES ANGUS — G

C

Jim the Carter Lad

1   My name is Jim the Carter, a jolly cock am I
     I always am contented be the weather wet or dry.
     I snap my fingers at the snow, I whistle at the rain
     I've braved the storm for many a day and may do so again.
      Crack crack goes my whip, I whistle and I sing
      I sit upon my wagon, I'm as happy as a king.
      My horse is always willing, 's for me I'm never sad
      None can lead a jollier life than Jim the Carter Lad.

2   My father was a carrier many years ere I was born
     He used to rise at daybreak and go his rounds each morn.
     He often took me with him especially in the spring
     O I loved to sit upon the cart and hear my father sing.

3   I never think of politics or anything so great
     I care not for their high-bred talk about the church and state.
     I keep aright to man and man and that's what makes me glad
     You'll find there beats an honest heart in Jim the Carter Lad.

4   The girls they all smile on me as I go driving past
     My horse is such a beauty and he jogs along so fast.
     We've travelled mony a weary mile and happy days we've had
     For none can treat a horse so well as Jim the Carter lad.

5   So now I'll bid you all goodnight, it's time I was away
     I know my horse will weary if I much longer stay.
     To see your smiling faces it makes my heart feel glad
     So I hope you'll give your kind applause to Jim the Carter Lad.

JOHN WIGHT — G

THE TOLL BAR

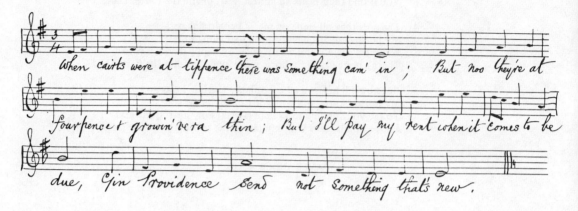

1   When cairts were at tippence there was something cam' in;
    But noo they're at fourpence and growin' vera thin;
    But I'll pay my rent when it comes to be due,
    Gin Providence send not something that's new.

Mrs BARRIE — G

459

BOYNDLIE ROAD

1   The year 1803
    Our gentlemen did all agree
    To make a live road o'er the lea
    Out through the haughs o' Boyndlie.

2   Howbeit they never laid the plan
    Till Mr. Forbes bought the lan',
    Till Mr. Forbes bought the lan'
    That joins to Upper Boyndlie.

3   Forbes o' Pennan gae a shout
    That he would turn the road about;
    Our esquires then made a dispute
    About the roads o' Boyndlie.

4   Forbes o' Boyndlie got his will
    To take it by the Mirrel Hill;
    Contractors then did try their skill
    To make the roads o' Boyndlie.

5   White and Taylor and Sam Rose
    They fought like soldiers to their foes,
    And hewed them down wi' sturdy blows
    To make the roads thro' Boyndlie.

6   Munro he boldly led them on,
    And wishing that the work was done,
    Wi' hammers and mells they broke the stone
    To make the roads thro' Boyndlie.

7   Stout McLean, but than McLee,
    And Sawney Campbell, a' the three,
    Wis boarded owre a file wi' me
    Fan it wis near their border.

Miss BELL ROBERTSON — G

THE BUCHAN TURNPIKE

A

1   'Twas in the year auchteen hun'er and aucht
    A road thro' Buchan was made straucht
    And mony a Hielan' lad o' maucht
    Cam' owre the Buchan border.

2   There was some in tartan, some in blue
    And weskits o' a warlike hue
    And werna they a strappin crew
    To put the road in order.

3   Ye'll ken oor foreman Sandy Joss
    I fear puir man he's gotten the loss
    I doot his purse'll seen turn boss   [empty
    If he work lang on oor border.

ALEXANDER ROBB — G

B

JOHN JOHNSTONE — G

C

The New Turnpike

1 Twas in the year auchteen hunner and aucht
   A road through Buchan was made straught
   When many a Hieland lad o' might
   Cam owre the Buchan border.

2 Twixt Peterhead and Banff auld toon
   It twines the knowes and hollows roon'
   Ye scarce can tell its ups frae doon
   It's levelled in sic order.

3 The Hieland and the Lowland chiels
   Cut down the knowes wi' spads and shiells
   And bored the steens wi' jumping dreels
   To get the road in order.

4 And many a hup, and many a ban,
   Got cartin' horse and lazy man,
   For foo and teem and aye they ran
   To push't a bittie forder.

5 Chiel Chalmers he frae Strichen cam,
   Wi' ae black horse as bold's a ram
   Nae ane could match him in the tram
   He made a braw recorder.

6 The Meerisons, the Waughts and Giels
   Were swack and willing working chiels
   Sae weel's they banged the barrow steels   [shafts
   To gar the road gae forder.

7 The road's as smooth's a harrowit rig
   Wi' stankies on ilk side fu' trig   [ditches
   And ilk bit burn has now a brig
   Where earst we had to ford 'er.   [formerly

8 This turnpike it will be a boon
   To a' the quintra roon and roon
   And let folk gae and come frae toon
   Wi' easedom and wi' order.   [comfort

9 On fit ye're owre it free to stray
   But if a beast ye chance to hae
   At ilka sax miles ye maun pay
   For gaun a bittie forder.

10 The writer's name gif ye should spier   [if
   I'm Jamie Shirris frae New Deer
   A name well kent baith far and near
   I dwell near the road's border.

JOHN MILNE — G

D

The Buchan Road

1   In aughteen hunner an aught
    A road through Buchan was made straught
    When mony a Hiland lad o' maught
    Cam o'er the Buchan border.

2   The Hieland an' the Lowland chiels
    Cut doon the knows wi' spads an' sheels
    An' bored the steens wi' jumpin' dreels
    To lat the road gae forder.

3   An many a hup an many a ban
    Got cart an horse an' lazie man
    For foo an' teem an aye they ran
    To get the road in order.

4   The Meerisons, the Weghts and Geels
    Were swack and willian workin' chiels   [active
    Sa weel's they bang'd the barrow wheels
    To mack a braw recorder.

JOHN MILNE — G

E

In the Year Auchteen Hunner an' Aucht, or, The Road-Makin'

1   In the year auchteen hunner an' aucht
    The roads through Buchan were made straucht
    . . . .
    To pit the roads in order.

2   The thieves into my hoose they cam',
    An' to my leathern bags they ran,
    An' oot o' them they filled their han',
    An' sert them oot o' order.

Mrs MARGARET GILLESPIE — D

F

1   Fair oot owre the hills an' doon thro' howes
    The roads through Buchan were made like bows.

WILLIAM DUNCAN — D

THE SMITH'S A GALLANT FIREMAN

A

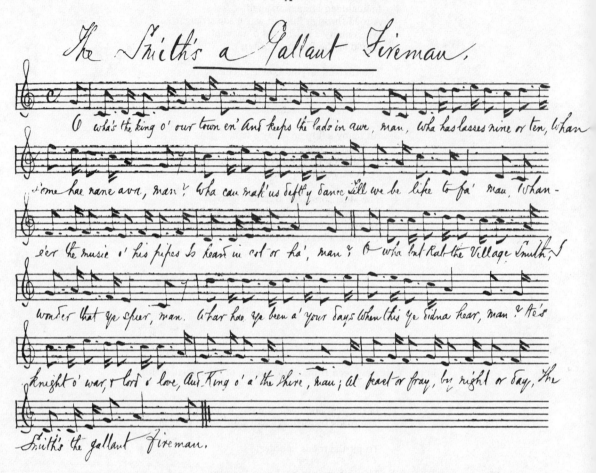

JOHN HARRISON — G

B
The Smith's a Gallant Fireman

1 O wha's the king o' oor toun en', and keeps the lads in awe man?
Wha has lasses nine or ten when some hae nane ava man?
Wha can make us deftly dance till we be like to fa' man,
Whane'er the music o' his pipes is heard in cot or ha' man?
O, wha but Rab, the village smith? I wonder that ye speir, man;
Whar hae ye been a' your days whan this ye didna hear man?
He's knicht o' war an' lord o' love an' king o' a the shire man
At feast or fray, by nicht or day the smith's a gallant fireman.

2 O wha can spend or spare a plack an aye hae twa behind it
Gie a frien' a helpin han' an' never care to mind it?
Wha for honour's sacred cause an' honest independence
Like steadfast rock wad daur the shock o' a' the warl's vengeance?
O Rab's the man wi' heart and han', tho' clad in rude attire man;
Stern resolve an' iron nerve nae mair does he require man.
He bends the bars o' iron and steel as gin they were but wire man
Dependin' aye upon himsel' — the smith's a gallant fireman.

3 O wha wad be a lordling's slave — a thing withoot a name man?
Wha wad beg frae ither folk what he micht hae at hame man?
Wha wad squander a' his gear an' syne gie fate the blame man
The growin' grass aboon his grave micht turn red wi' shame, man.
Let folk deride an' ca' it pride — be't mine to still aspire man;
He that winna wale the road deserves to dree the mire man;
Let moral dignity and worth your heart and soul inspire man
Let's honour pay whar honour's due — the smith's a gallant fireman.

Mrs GORDON — G

C
The Smith's a Gallant Fireman

1 Lang, lang wad I want ere I had a hireman,
Lang, lang wad I want ere I had a hireman,
Lang, lang wad I want ere I had a hireman,
O' a' the trades that man can try, the smith's the gallant fireman.

Rev. JAMES B. DUNCAN — D

JOHN BUCHAN, BLACKSMITH

1 Dear John, my plough is come to hand
And shall be paid upon demand
But still I think she's rather grand
For my course
And then our cursed staenny land
Will gie ir sic totens.

2 But Lord man, had ye seen the steer
Of men and boys come to see 'er
The very old wives to spier
The keas about her
And blacksmith's measured a' her gear
Beam, stilt and culter.

3 But let them use their utmost power
And stand, and gape and stare and glower
Though they should measure twelve-months four
It is all a farce
In end they'll spit and gie it owre
And claw their —— .

4 Her every joint is so exact
And a her stricken so compact
And a so strong yet she may brack
No man can tell
But still although she gang to wrack
Auld iron will sell.

5 The very bruts that's yokit at her
Is goin' sae saucy the gate
They will not stop to mak their
At head or en'
And neighbours swear they are grown fat
And out o' ken.   [unrecognisable

6 As sure as night brings on the moon
As sure as bruts wear hoof and horn
As sure I'll grow mair bear and corn
And far mair straw
And laugh the neighbour carls to scorn
Baith ane and a'.

7 Your arly works of iron and steel
Declars you o' a blessing still
And then the own spinning wheel
You put thegither
Secures you o' a blessing till
Frae your auld mither.

8 Your iron works are turned sae rife
Down thro' firth and owre to Fife
That should you still improve their life
It will be seen
That ye will make iron wife
Or a be done.

9 But sic hard luck that'll now be thine
You'll get a role mair to mine
You'll allow me to devine
I'll gie my warron
That ye shall get the bonniest guest
That steps by Caron.

10 But dimly wi' ilk light hizzie
That wi' daft duds their heids are dizzie
Far wi' sic sonnet the deil's aye lesey   [tale; lying
To get them you nicket   [cheated
Instead then of a desent Lizzie
You've ae ill breet.   [creature

11 But you that studies stock rains
Kens a the blots and a' the blains   [sores
And all every other that stains
The human life
It will not cost you muckle pains
To wile a wife.

12 Give my kind love to your mamie
And to your sister ane an a'
And to your love tho' far awa
She may be frae you.
You'll get nae mair o' my foul sang
So God be wi you, I am yours.

13 Johnny if it be your will
Step owre the gate to Mungamill
Gie my kind wishes to my Will
And or ye leave that
I hope he'll treat ye wi' a gill
Of his Glenlivet.

WILLIAM WALKER — G

THE MASONS

A

The Mason Lads

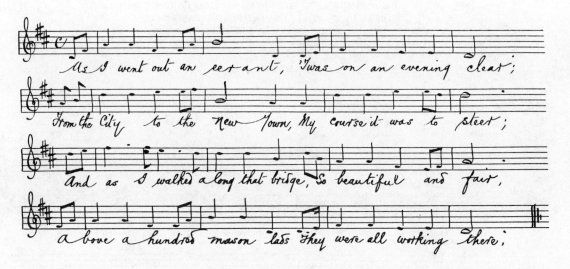

As I went out an eerant, 'Twas on an evening clear;
From the City to the New Town, My course it was to steer;
And as I walked along that bridge, So beautiful and fair,
Above a hundred mason lads They were all working there.

1   As I went out an eeran' it was on an evenin' clear
From the city to the new toon my course it was to steer
And as I walked along that bridge most beautiful and fair
Above a hundred mason lads they were all working there.

2   It being six o'clock at night and the sun was going down
And to their habitations every mason lad was bound
And when I viewed that mason lads I really much admired
To their respected dwellings each man he doth retire.

3   And when I viewed that beautiful bridge it really made me stand
To see how they do trample on the works of their own hand
And for to walk along that bridge and crime they thought it none
From the city to the new town where carriages runs along.

4   I said My generous mason lads your praises I will tell
If I were a boy as I am a girl I would be one myself.
But since I am a maid so young and still a single life
I hope to be entitled a mason's wedded wife.

5   I am a maid of fortune of fifteen thousand pounds
And for this generous mason lad I'll freely lay it doon
Though I be high in parentage and he of a low degree
As long as I have an hour to live his loving wife I'll be.

6   When I go to my window and on the same looks owre
To see that beautiful buildings I really much admire
With their turrets and their primlets which they have built so high
Their primlets and their brazen tops near reaching to the skies.

7   Ye blacksmiths and ye founders that work into the fire
Your curious occupations I really much admire
Ye silversmiths and goldsmiths and refiners of fine gold
If it werna for the mason lads ye would all die with cold.

8 I dearly love our printers for they are crafty men
   If it were not for our printers who would be scholars then?
   For the king unto the cobbler and men of high estate
   If it were not for our printers of course we would look blate.

9 So now my song is ended I hope there's no offence
   And since I've got no more to say I will lay down my pen.
   I will lay by my pen just now and no more verses sing
   So now my song it's ended by all God save the King.

JOHN MOWAT – G

B
The Freemasons

1 As I went oot an eeran' 'twas on an evenin' clear
   From the city to the new toon my course it was to steer
   And as I walked along the bridge most beautiful and fair
   Above a hundred mason lads they were all working there.

2 This beautiful bridge which they have built it really made me stand
   To see how they do trample on the work of their own hands
   But they have built it so secure and crime they think it none
   From the city to the new toon the carriage it runs along.

3 It was at six o'clock at night the sun was going down
   And to each habitation every mason lad was boun'
   And when I viewed the mason lads I really much admire
   As they to their respective dwellings each one he does retire.

4 When I go to my window and at the same look o'er
   To see the beautiful building I really much admire
   With their struts and their primlets which they have built so high
   With their turrets and their brazen tops all reaching to the sky.

5 I am a maid of fortune near sixteen thousan' pounds
   And for this generous mason lad I'd freely lay it down
   Though he be mean of parentage and I of high degree
   As long as I've an hour to live his loving wife I'd be.

6   Ye blacksmiths and ye founders that works into the fire
     Your curious occupations I really much admire
     Ye silversmiths and goldsmiths and refiners of fine gold
     If it had not been for oor mason lads ye would all died of cold.

7   I dearly love our soldiers for they have gone so far
     They have gone to the Indies to fight our bloody war.
     To face our mortal enemy and keep us from our foe
     If it had not been oor soldiers our buildings would be low.

8   I dearly love oor printers for they are crafty men
     If it had not been oor printers we'd been no scholars there.
     From the king unto the cobbler and men of high estate
     If it had not been oor printers oor courts they would look blate.

9   Last Sabbath as I went to church to hear the holy band
     A generous man, a tailor, I saw wi' ruffles round his hands.
     Ye masters of all tradesmen and men of high estate
     I pray lay by your ruffles noo noo tailors are so great.

WILLIAM WATSON — G

C

From the City to the New Toon

1   It being six o'clock at night the sun was going down
     Unto their habitations each mason lad was bound
     And when I saw these mason lads it really made me stand
     To see how they would trample on the works of their own hands.

2   Across that [bridge which they have built so strong with stone and lime]
     And for to walk upon the same the masons thinks no crime
     And for to walk upon the same and crime they think it none
     From the city to the new toon the carriages on it run.

3   [I dearly love the mason lad] the truth that I wad tell
     But if I were a boy as I'm a girl I would be one mysel
     [But since I am a] maid [sae young] and still of single life
     [I hope you'll soon entitle me to be a mason's wife.]

4   Though I be a maid of fortune full fifteen thousand pounds
     For this loving mason lad I'd freely lay it down
     Although he be of low parentage and me o' a high degree
     As lang as I've a pound to spend his loving wife I'd be.

5   [I dearly love] our printers [for they are crafty men]
     If it hadna been oor printers our scholars wad been thin.
     [Fae the king unto the cobbler and men o' high estate]
     If it hadna been oor printers of course we'd a' look blate.

6   Last Sabbath as I went to church to hear that holy band
     A generous man a tailor I met with ruffles round his hand
     Now all ye master tradesmen and men of high estate
     I pray lay by your ruffles now when tailors are grown so great.

7   Now since my song is ended I hope there's none offent
     Or if I thought they were offent I wad lay by my pen
     I would lay by my pen and ink and no more verses sing
     Now since my song is ended I'll sing God save the Queen.

Mrs FINNIE — G

D

The Masons.

Mrs MILNE — G

234

E

From the Seatown to the Newtown.

GEORGE RIDDELL — G

F

The Masons

1 As I went oot an eeran' twas on an evenin' clear
   Frae the city to the new toon my course it was to steer
   And as I passed along the road so beautiful and clear
   Aboot a hundred mason lads they were a' workin' there.

2 This beautiful bridge which they have built so strong with stone and lime
   And for to walk upon the same the masons thinks no crime
   And for to walk upon the same and crime they think it none
   From the city to the new toon the carriages on it run.

3 I dearly love the mason lad his praise I would tell
   If I'd been a boy as I'm a girl I would been ane mysel
   But since I am a girl sae young and leading a single life
   I hope you'll soon entitle me to be a mason's wife.

4 I dearly love the sodger lads since they have gone sae far
   Since they have gone to India to fight our bloody war
   To face our mortal enemy and keep us fae the foe
   If it wisna for our sodger lads our buildings wad lie low.

5 Ye blacksmiths and ye founders what works unto the fire
   Your curious occupation I really much admire
   Ye goldsmiths and ye silversmiths refiners of fine gold
   If it wisna for wir mason lads ye wid all die of cold.

6 I dearly love the printer lads for they are crafty men
   Fae the king unto the cobbler fa wid be scholars then?
   Fae the king unto the cobbler and men o' high estate
   If it wisna for the printer lads our courts wad a' look blate.

7 Come all ye master mason lads and men of high estate
   I pray lay by your ruffles now since tailors are grown sae great.

Miss HALL — G

235

G
The Mason Laddies

1   That beauteous bridge that they ha'e made so strong of stone and lime,
     And for to trample on the same the masons think no crime.

2   But since I am so young a girl, and of a single life,
     I hope you will entitle me a loving mason's wife.

3   One day as I went to the church to hear the holy band,
     A generous man a tailor I saw wi' ruffles at his hands;
     All ye that's master builders, and men of high estate,
     I pray lay by your ruffles noo fan tailors are grown so great.

Miss BELL ROBERTSON – G

464

THE BONNIE MASON LADDIE

The Bonnie Mason Laddies

1   Simmer's gaun awa, and the winter's comin' on,
     And the bonnie mason laddies they'll be comin' home,
     Wi' their pockets fu' o' money, and their lasses for to see;
     And the bonnie mason laddie he will marry me.

2   I winna hae the sailor that sails on the sea;
     Nor yet will I the plooman that ploughs on the lea;
     But I will hae the mason for he is a bonnie lad,
     And I'll wash the mason's apron and think it nae degrade.

3   I winna hae the blacksmith that burns a' the iron;
     Nor yet will I the weaver that works the creeshy yarn;   [greasy
     But I'll hae the mason and the mason he'll hae me;
     And the bonnie mason laddie I'll mount the scaffold wi'.

Miss BELL ROBERTSON – G

THE MASON LADDIE

A

The Mason Laddie

To the tune of *Johnny Lad* from the same singer

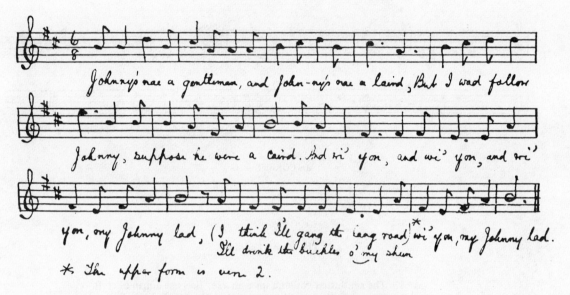

Johnny's nae a gentleman, and John-ny's nae a laird, But I wad follow

Johnny, suppose he were a caird. And wi' yon, and wi' yon, and wi'

yon, my Johnny lad, (I think I'll gang the lang road) wi' you, my Johnny lad.
I'll drink the buckles o' my sheen

* The upper form is vers 2.

1　Leaning oer a window an looking oer a mound
　I spied a mason laddie who gave my heart a wound
　A wound in a wound an' a deadly wound gave he
　But I wid was his apron gine he would fancy me.

2　I winna hae the minister for a' his many books
　I winna hae the dominie for a' his wily looks
　I winna hae nean o' the twa though they wid fancy me
　But my bonnie mason laddie he bears awa the gree.

3　I winna hae the mautman for a' his muckle sho'el
　Nor yet will I the millar for a his mity meal　　　　　　[infested with mites
　I winna hae nean o' the twa though they sid fancy me
　For my bonnie mason laddie gies up the scaffold hie.

4　I winna hae the ploughman that gangs at the pleuch
　Nor yet will the chaptioner fo he his gear enough　　　　[bailiff
　I winna hae nean o the twa tho they sid fancy me
　For my bonnie mason laddie his stowen my heart fae me.

5　I winna hae the souter that rubs on the shoon
　Nor yet will I the weaver that gingles on the loom　　　　[works his feet
　I winna hae nean o the twa tho they sid fancy me
　For my bonnie mason laddie he bears awa the gree.

6　A smith that canna smeethe an axe is nae a man o craft
　A wright that canna seam a deal can never lay a laft　　　[fit a plank; build a loft
　A lad that canna kiss a lass is nae a lad for me
　But my bonnie mason laddie can kiss an clap tea.

Mrs MARGARET GILLESPIE — D

B

The bonnie mason laddie.

Mrs CORBET — G

C

The Mason Laddie

1   The smith that couldna smee an axe, he's nae a man o' craft
     The vricht that couldna seam a deal, he couldna lay a laft
     The lad that canna coort a lass, he's nae the lad for me
     It's the bonnie mason laddie that I'm gaun wi'.

Source unrecorded — G

FREEMASONS' SONG

1   Behold in a Lodge we dear brethren are met,
    And in proper order together are set;
    Our secrets to none but ourselves shall be known,
    Our actions to none but Freemasons be shown,
      Derry down down, down derry down.

2   Let brotherly love be among us revived,
    Let's stand by our laws that are wisely contrived;
    And then all the glorious creation shall see
    That none are so loving, so friendly as we.

3   The Temple and many a magnificent pile,
    Even buildings now standing within our own isle,
    With wisdom contrived, with beauty refined,
    With strength to support, and the building to bind.

4   These noble structures will always proclaim
    What honour is due to a Freemason's name;
    Even ages to come, when our work they do see,
    Will strive with each other like us to be free.

5   What tho' some of late by their spleen plainly show,
    They fain would deride what they gladly would know,
    Let every true brother these vermin despise,
    And the ancient grand secret keep back from their eyes.

6   Then brethren, let's all put our hand to our heart,
    And resolve from true Masonry never to part;
    And when the last trumpet on earth shall descend,
    Our Lodge will be closed, and our secrets shall end.

JAMES ANGUS — G

THE FREEMASON KING

A

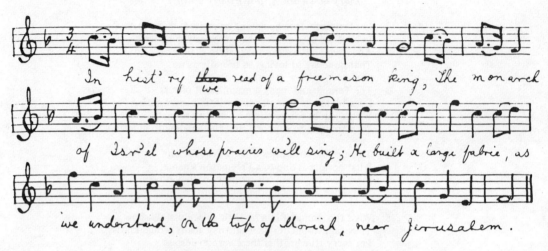

The Freemason King

1 In hist'ry we read of a Freemason king,
   The monarch of Israel whose praises we'll sing;
   He built a large fabric, as we understand,
   On the top of Moriah, near Jerusalem.

2 Says David to Solomon, with a heart full of love,
   "Since we two are chosen by the Powers above,
   Our great Architect in honour you see,
   He gave all this fine pattern in writing to me."

3 It's Solomon being willing to raise this fine plan,
   He numbered all the workmen that were in his land.
   Three score and ten thousand to bear burdens and serve,
   Eighty thousand in the mountains to cut, hew, and carve.

4 Three thousand six hundred he ordered to be
   Masters of the workmen and to oversee,
   And if you'll believe me, I'll tell you what's true,
   He clothèd them all with the orange and blue.

5 Then straight into Tyre a letter did send,
   Beseeching King Hiram for to stand his friend;
   It's Hiram being willing to send him relief,
   He sent that crafty workman called Hiram the brave.

6 He was son to a widow, a daughter of Dan,
   And in every particular you'll find him a man,
   For in all things put to him he did nothing amiss,
   He exceeded them all in the casting of brass.

7 He keest two fine pillars of the image work;
   They spread out their wings for to cover the ark.

GEORGE GARIOCH – D

B
The Building of the Temple

1   In history we read of a Freemason King
He's the monarch of Israel his praises we'll sing
He built a fine fabric as we understand
On the top of Moriah near to Jerusalem.

2   He that slew Goliath in history we find
He purchased the lands to raise his design
He ordered young Solomon he being his son
To raise up this strong work that he had begun.

3   Says David to Solomon with heart full of love
Since we two are chosen by the high Powers above
That great Architecture of honour we see
He gave all this fine patterns in writing to me.

4   Then Solomon in order to raise this fine plan
He numbered the workmen that were in the land
Seventy thousand to bear burdens he then did reserve
80,000 on the mountains to cut, hew and carve.

5   Three thousand six hundred he ordered to be
Masters of workman and to oversee
And if you'll believe me I'll tell you a true
That he clothed them all in orange and blue.

6   Then these crafty workmen the stones they did square
Made ready for building before they came there
Upon proper carriages they were brought down
That in all their fine building not a hammer did sound.

7   Then straightway to Tyre a letter did send
In hopes that King Hiram would stand his friend
And he being willing to send him relief
Sent him that crafty workman called Hiram a bief.

8   He was the son of a widow a daughter of Dan
And in every particular you'll find him a man
In all things put to him he did nothing amiss
He exceeded them all at the casting of brass.

9   He cast two fine pillars would have dazzled your sight.
They were full eighteen cubits as they stood upright
He set one on each side of Solomon's porch
That Israel might see them when they went to church.

10   Such beautiful pillars sure never were cast
Admired by all people that did them by pass
And the place where he cast them is still to be found
In the plains o Jordan among the clay ground.

11   He made a fine cherubim of fine image work
And spread forth their wings for to cover the ark
It stood better there than it did in the field
It was made by Aholiab and by Bahsereel.

12 And the molten sea was eight cubits about
    And the brazen oxen without any doubt
    And the brazen oxen King Solomon did cast
    And many more vessels I'm sure I have missed.

13 When the Queen of Sheba heard of his fame
    Straightway to Jerusalem she instantly came
    For the fame of that King through the nations did pass
    He was the King Solomon grandson of Jess.

14 She proved him with questions according to art
    He told her the secrets that were in his heart
    She being quite amazed like one in surprise
    Such a beautiful building sure dazzled her eyes.

15 Jerusalem's a city with walls great and high
    Admired by all people that does it pass by
    When light against light makes the beauty to shine
    Such a beautiful building sure never was seen.

Mr THOMSON — G

C
The Building of Solomon's Temple

1 In history we read of the Freemason King,
   That Monarch of Israel whose praises we sing;
   He built a large Temple of honour and fame,
   On the top of Moriah, near Jerusalem.

2 He that slew Goliath, in history we find,
   Had laid off the ground and on plans there designed,
   He instructed Solomon, being his son,
   To furnish the strong works that he had begun.

3 Said David to Solomon with a heart full of love, —
   We for this have been chosen by a Power from above;
   Our great Architect of eternal degree,
   Has given all these patterns in writing to me.

4 When Solomon saw how the fabric was planned,
   He numbered all the workmen that were in his land;
   Fourscore thousand on the mountains to cut, hew, and carve,
   Threescore and ten thousand to bear burdens and serve.

5 Three thousand six hundred he ordered to be
   Masters of all these workmen, and to oversee;
   And there uniformly the work to pursue,
   He has clothed them all in the purple and blue.

6 These crafty workmen the stones then did square,
   And for building the fabric did fully prepare;
   Then on proper carriages they were brought round,
   That on the fine buildings no hammer might sound.

7   Then straightway to Tyre he a letter did send,
Beseeching King Hiram there to stand his friend;
And he being willing to give him relief,
Sent him that crafty workman called Hiram Abiff.

8   The son of a widow, a daughter of Dan,
And in every particular he was a great man;
In all exercises he quickly did pass,
And soon excelled them all in the casting of brass.

9   He cast two fine pillars which dazzled their sight,
They were full eighteen cubits while they stood upright,
And were set on the top of King Solomon's porch,
That all Israel might view them as they went to church.

10   Such beautiful pillars their like was ne'er cast,
Admired by all by whom they were passed;
The place where he cast them is still to be found,
In the plains about Jordan upon the clay ground.

11   He cast two fine cherubim of good image work;
They spread forth their wings to o'er cover the ark;
They stood better there than they did in the field,
Aholiab and Bezaleel their forms revealed.

12   The molten sea was eighteen cubits about,
And the brazen oxen without any doubt;
All these the Freemason King cast we are told,
And many more vessels of silver and gold.

13   There was placed on the top of the beautiful pile
Three bright golden rods that no birds might defile;
And the place there to worship our Creator's name
Was all quite laid over with gold of Parvaim.

14   When Phoebus each morning may darkness dispel,
This beautiful building had then appeared well;
When light against light unto three rows did shine,
The view everywhere must have been very fine.

15   Jerusalem's a city with walls great and high,
A wonder to strangers who may pass near by;
It's the top of that vision was there noticed fine,
At the island of Patmos by John the Divine.

16   When the Queen of Sheba had heard of its fame,
Straightway for to view it she instantly came;
She was greatly amazed and filled with surprise,
When the beautiful building had dazzled her eyes.

17   As the fame of the Freemason King far and near
Had been spread through the world, it then would appear,
She proved him with questions about every part,
Till he fully explained the most of the art.

18   When our noble Freemasons in a Lodge all do join,
Each brother is clothed in jewels so fine;
When our right noble Master is placed in his chair,
He governs them all with his compass and square.

19 May he that doth rule in the Temple above,
    Bless all our Freemasons with honour and love;
    Keep Solomon in memory, and Hiram also;
    Come fill up a bumper, we'll taste ere we go.

20 And let us our utmost endeavours all try,
    At last to arrive at the Temple on high;
    Its great Architect there to praise and adore,
    When fabrics on earth we can raise up no more.

Miss BELL ROBERTSON — G

D
The Building of Solomon's Temple

1 Three thousand six hundred was ordered to be
   Masters and workmen and to oversee;
   And if you believe me, I'll tell you it's true,
   He clothèd them all in the orange and blue.

Mrs JOHNSTONE — D

THE RULES OF MASONRY

Freemason's Song

1   Ye people who laugh at Masons, draw near,
    Attend to my ballad without any sneer;
    And if you'll have patience, you shall soon see
    What a fine art is Masonry.

2   There is none but an atheist can ever deny
    But that this art came first from on high;
    The Almighty God here I'll prove for to be
    The first Great Master of Masonry.

3   He took up his compass with masterly hand,
    He stretched out his rule and he measured the land;
    He laid the foundation of earth and sea
    By his known rules of Masonry.

4   Our first father Adam — deny it who can,
    A Mason was made as soon as a man;
    And a fig-leaf apron at first wore he,
    In token of love to Masonry.

5   The principal law our lodge does approve
    Is, that we still live in brotherly love;
    Thus Cain was banished by Heaven's decree,
    For breaking the rules of Masonry.

6   The Temple that wise King Solomon raised,
    For beauty, for order, for elegance praised, —
    To what did it owe all its elegancy? —
    To the just-formed rules of Masonry.

7   But should I pretend, in this humble verse,
    The merits of Freemasons' art to rehearse,
    Years yet to come too little would be
    To sing the praises of Masonry.

8   Then hoping I have not detained you too long,
    I here shall take leave to finish my song;
    With a health to the Master, and those who are free,
    That live to the rules of Masonry.

JAMES ANGUS — G

THE COMPASS AND SQUARE

1 On this lang wished for nicht we are met in grand style
As aft has been done in our famed Scottish isle;
The blessings of freedom and plenty to share,
And walk by the rules of the compass and square.

2 While many in quest of false happiness roam,
Of strife and contention divested we come,
Ourselves to enjoy without trouble or care,
In the straight pathway marked by the compass and square.

3 Let misers with fondness count over their store,
Let pride and ambition triumphantly soar;
For tho' war, the red fiend, o'er the nation does rair   [roar
In peace we will walk by the compass and square.

4 In the bonds of true friendship we meet to pursue
The interests of all with hearts honest and true
In companionship mutual that virtue most rare
We walk by the rule of the compass and square.

5 Our works like our friendship triumphantly stand,
The pride and the glory of every known land, —
Of the works of proud Science what trophies are there
Like those that we rear by the compass and square!

6 What are lands and possessions of silver and gold
Without friendly dwellings to screen from the cold?
And but true Masons such homes can prepare,
By means of their art and the compass and square.

7 From the page of true history it plainly is seen,
That kings and wise prophets Freemasons have been;
And nobles and men with their heads full of lear   [learning
Have deemed it an honour to handle the square.

8 O'er the world, as brothers in concord we live,
For one cannot want while another can give;
Esteemed by the great, and caressed by the fair,
We live by the rules of the compass and square.

9 The Great Architect, who the worlds did frame,
Instructed our sires in the great building scheme,
In the art thus acquired we will aye persevere,
And work by the rules of the compass and square.

10 Here's a health to true Masons, wherever they be;
May others soon learn to be happy as we,
And the time soon arrive when mankind shall dare
To perfect their plans by the compass and square.

F.R. BROWN — G

THE SONS OF LEVI

1 Come all ye knights of Malta, come forth,
In glittering armour shine;
Assist your good and worthy Prince
To protect the ark divine;
For we are the true-born sons of Levi,
Few on earth to us compare;
We wear the black and scarlet garter
On our left breast a blazing star.

2 With trembling steps I slow advanced
Sometimes I knocked both loud and shrill
Until a knight in armour bright
Demanded me what was my will.
For we are the true-born sons of Levi,
Few on earth to us compare;
We wear the black and scarlet garter
On our left breast a blazing star.

3 After some questions being asked,
To which I answered with some fear
They told me neither Turk nor Heathen
Could by any means enter here.
For we are the true-born sons of Levi,
Few on earth to us compare;
We wear the black and scarlet garter,
On our left breast a blazing star.

4 With a cross and star placed on my breast,
And Justice girded my loins all round, –
Always remember the twelve stones
On Jordan's banks are to be found.
For we are the true-born sons of Levi
Few on earth to us compare;
We are the root and branch of David,
That bright and glorious morning star.

5 Noah planted the first garden;
Moses planted the first rod;
He smote the waters for the Egyptians
And turned the Jordan into blood.
For we are the true-born sons of Levi
Few on earth to us compare;
We wear the black and scarlet garter,
On our left breast a blazing star.

6 As Joshua and I passed over Jordan,
These twelve stones we bore along;
It was the twelve Priests and our Grand Master
That moved the ark of God along.
For we are the true-born sons of Levi
Few on earth to us compare;
We wear the black and scarlet garter,
On our left breast a blazing star.

7 There were seven trumpets of ram's horn
Sounded loud before the Ark;
Gilgal it was our resting quarter,
And there we left our holy mark.
For we are the true-born sons of Levi,
Few on earth to us compare;
We are the root and branch of David,
That bright and glorious morning star.

8 Come all you brethren, and join with me,
And bear the cross as I have done;
Come enter into this bright temple
Fitted near Jerusalem.
For we are the true-born sons of Levi
Few on earth to us compare;
We are the root and branch of David,
That bright and glorious morning star.

F.R. BROWN – G

WI' THE APRON ON

A

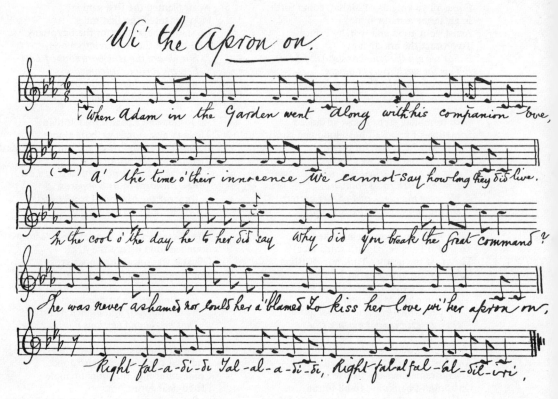

1   When Adam in the Garden went along with his companion Eve,
A' the time o' their innocence we cannot say how long they did live.
In the cool of the day he to her did say, Why did you break the great command?
She was never ashamed nor could she be blamed to kiss her love wi' her apron on.
    Right fal-a-di-di, tal-al-a-di-di,
    Right fal-al-fal-al-dil-iri.

2   Did ye not hear the mason word? 'Twas whispered round the other night.
Silly toys doth us annoy, and puts us in the least affright.
The serpent in Eve as you may say with their black tricks and curious plans
They soon made Adam his folly to see. 'Twas then that he clappit his apron on.

3   It's brethren dear I beg your leave till I do end this simple song,
Five hundred and two both just and true to this Mason Lodge it does belong.
There is five steps that you must learn before the jewels you do put on,
Our Master dear sits in his chair, bless him and his apron on.

MAGGIE WATT – G

B

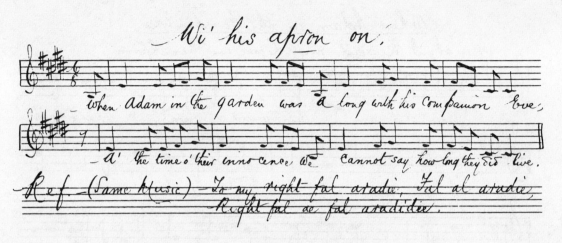

Wi' his apron on.

1 When Adam in the garden was
   Along with his companion Eve,
   A' the time o' their innocence
   We cannot say how long they did live.
     To my right fal aradie, fal al aradie,
     Right fal ae fal aradidee.

2 In the cool of the day He to her did say
   Why did ye break the great command?
   And in a short time they will never mind,
   So then he clapped his apron on.

      Rev. JOHN CALDER — G

C

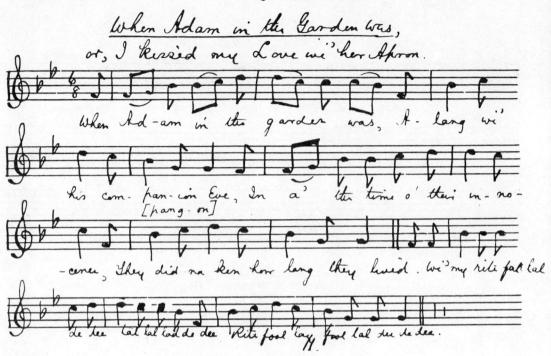

1   When Adam in the gairden was
    Alang wee his companion Eve
    An all the time o their innocence
    They didna ken fou lang they leeved.
      Right fa a fal al dide dee.

2   . . . .
    . . . .
    I was never ashamed fu could I be blamed
    To kiss my luve wee his aperon on.

Mrs MARGARET GILLESPIE – D

D

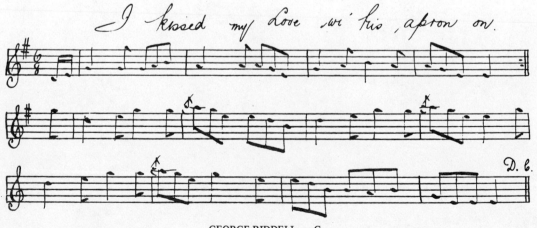

GEORGE RIDDELL – G

250

E
Wi' His Apron On

1 When Adam in the garden was along with his companion Eve,
'Twas in the time of innocence, we do not know how long it was.
The serpent slee so cunningly wi' his dark tricks and curious can
He soon made Adam his folly to see. It was then that he clapt his apron on.
Light faladit, talaladadie, lit fala falairalee.

Miss BELL ROBERTSON — G

472

THE PLUMB AND LEVEL

Adam and Eve, or The Plumb and Level

1 When Adam ruled the world, with an order from the ground,
And with his beauty spoose, both stout, in Eden's happy land,
To pass the hour they formed a bower to shade them from the weather's evil,
And his worship's working plan was to act upon the square and level.
Wack fal de dal lal, fal de dal de dee.

2 They lived in social harmony till madam longed for fruit,
Which was the cause in latter days of many a sad dispute,
And this, you know, when things stood so, which being the cause of many an evil,
And the bit she went out one morning for to meet the deevil.

Mrs JOHNSTONE — D

THE FREE GARDENER

A

Old Adam Was a Gairner

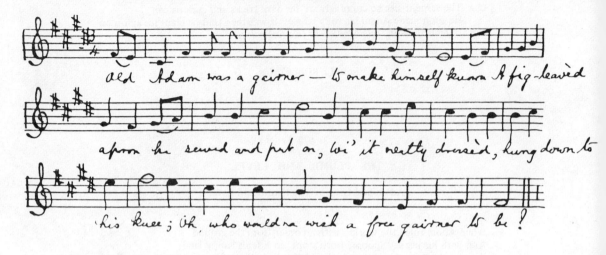

1 Old Adam was a gairner, to make himself known
  A fig-leavèd apron he sewed and put on
  Wi' it neatly dressèd and down to his knee
  And wha wadna wish a free gairner to be.

2 When Eve was created trasported to see
  A garden so neat and a gairner so free
  She said to the gairner "Deal kindly with me
  And I pray you invite me a gairner to be."

ROBERT ALEXANDER – D

B

The Free Gardener

1 Ye sons of old Adam, so noble and brave,
  Ye sons of antiquity, friendly and grave,
  By Heaven's great nature and mother work we,
  Then who would na wish a free gardener to be?

2 It's Heaven's great king our first garden did plant,
  Eastward in Eden where nothing did want,
  With flowers of each nature and first on each tree,
  Then who would na wish a free gardener to be?

3 It's old Adam was the gardener to make himself known,
  A fig-leavèd apron he sewed and put on,
  With it nicely dressèd, hanging down to his knee,
  Then who would na wish a free gardener to be?

4   Old Adam a well-dressèd garden did keep,
    Till the smell of the lilies did lull him to sleep,
    He found a fair wife at the foot of a tree,
    Then who would na wish a free gardener to be?

5   When Eve was created, transported to see
    A garden so neat and a garden so free,
    She says to the gardener, "Deal kindly with me,
    And I pray you'll admit me a gardener to be."

6   Says old Adam, I will tell you my mind very plain,
    That no woman on earth my secrets should gain;
    I early obtained them by Heaven's decree,
    Then who would na wish a free gardener to be?

7   We're noble fellows and our aprons are blue,
    We toil in our garden, we plant and we sow,
    Kings are our companions, how noble are we!
    Then who would na wish a free gardener to be?

8   But Eve she has pressèd on Adam so bold,
    She made him eat the apple, as I have been told;
    She made him go bound when he might have gone free,
    She made him leave the garden a ploughboy to be.

        Mrs BEATON — D

THE SPINNIN' O'T

1   It was ance on a time but I dinna ken fan
     I wisna there at the beginnin' o't
     The sang had been sung by some canty goodman
     A wee pickle tow for the spinnin o't.

2   The stupid auld carlin she loutit sae low
     The ingle wis blinkin' and kindled the tow
     Ere she was aware it was a' in a low
     And that was an ill beginnin o't.

3   I hae keepit a house this twa score o' year
     And a' without tryin' the spinnin o't
     But fou I was sarket foul fa' them 'it spiers
     It was something like the beginnin o't.

Miss BELL ROBERTSON — G

SPINNING RHYME

The wheelie gangs roon, the wheelie gangs roon,
An' aye it casts the ban',
It's nae the wheelie that his the wyte,
It's my unsteady han'.

Mrs LYALL — G

THE WIFE AND HER WEE PICKLE TOW

A

The Spinnin O'ot

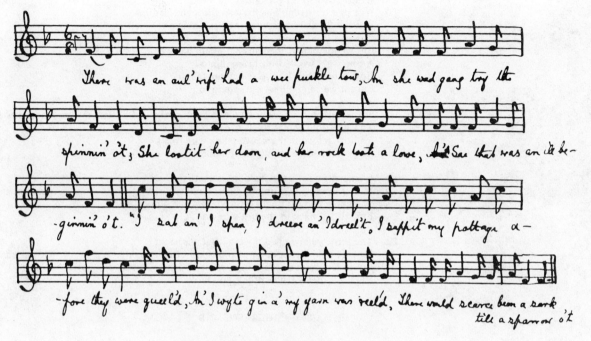

1 There wis an auld wife hid a wee puckle tow
 An she wid gang try the spinnin o't
 She looted her doun an her rope took o low   [went on fire
 Sae that wis an ull beginning o't.

2 She sat an she grat she flaut an she flang
 She threw an she blew she wriggled an' wrang
 She chockit an bocket an cried like the mang   [as if to go mad
 Alas for the weary beginning o't.

3 For never since ever they ca'd as the ca me
 Did sic a mishap an mischanter fa me
 But ye sall get leave to hang an to draw me
 The neist time I try the spinnin o't.

4 I've wanted a sark this sax year an ten
 An this wis to be the beginning o't
 But altho I should want ane as lang again
 I'll never mair try the spinnin o't.

5 I sat an I span I dreve an I drill't
 I supp't my pottage afore they were queeled
 But I wite gine a' my yarn wis reeled
 There wid scarce been a sark tull a sparrow o't.

6 But our wemon no'o-a-days are a' grow so braw
 Some maun hae ae sark an some maun hae twa
 The wardle wis better when nae ane ava
 Had bit a rag at the beginning o't.

7 In the days they ca' yore, auld folks hid bit ane
   Two surcoat sic for the beginning o't
   Of coat raper weel cut by the cast o' their bum
   They never sought mair o the spinnin o't.

8 A pair of grey huggers weel cluitet bi new   [footless stockings
   Wi nae ither lit bit the hue o the ewe   [dye
   Wi a pair o ruff mullins to scuff through the dubs
   Was the fee they sought at the beginning o't.

9 But we maun hae linen an that maun hae we
   An how get we that bit bi spinnin o't
   How can we hae face to seek a big fee
   Except we can help wi the spinnin o't.

10 For we maun hae parlins an mabbies an cocks   [lace; mob-caps; head-dresses
    An some ither things the ladies ca smocks
    An how get we that gine we takna wire rocks
    An pow what we can at the spinnin o't.

11 It's needless for us to mak ony remarks
    Wi our mithers miscooking the spinnin o't   [mismanaging
    She never know'd ought o the good o the sarks
    Frae this a' back to the beginning o't.

12 The three yellow plaidin wis a' that wis socht
    By wire auld farren boddies and that but be bought   [old-fashioned
    For in ilka toun siccan things warna wroght
    Sae little they keen'd o the spinnin o't.

Mrs MARGARET GILLESPIE — D

B

The Rock and the Wee Pickle Tow

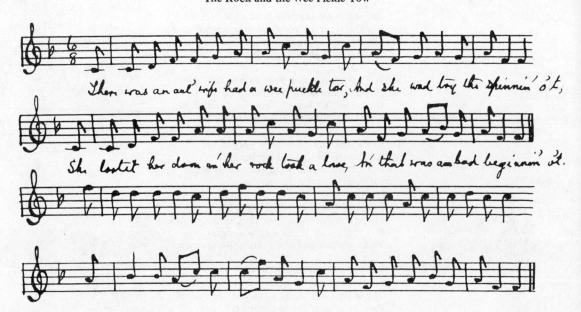

1   There was an auld wife had a we pickle tow,
     And she would try the spinin o't,
     She lootit her doon, and her rock took a low,
     And that was a bad beginnin o't.

2   Quo' Johnie to Nellie, "The week's near an en',
     Tween sewin an' spinnin we've aye got a hame
     And whiles fin t was need we a trifle could lend
     So here's to the auld and beginnin o't."

3   "I've wantit a sark for this aucht year an ten
     . . . .
     But I vow I would want ane for as lang again
     Afore that I try the spinnin o't."

ROBERT ALEXANDER – D

C

The wee puckle tow.

There was an auld wife had a wee puckly, tow, And she wad gae try the spinnin' o't ;
But she chokit & bockit, her rock took a low, And that was an ill beginnin' o't.
She chokit & byockit, she fret & she flang ; She chokit & byockit, she swore let me hang ;
She chokit, she byockit, she swore let me hang, But she never would try the spinnin' o't.

ALEXANDER ROBB – G

257

D

The wife and her wee pickle tow.

There was an auld wife had a wee pickle tow, And she wad try the spinnin' o't
She lootit her rock gang up in a low, And that was a bad beginnin' o't.
She spat ont she - - - - - - -

Rev. GEORGE BIRNIE — G

E

The Rock and the wee Pickle Tow

There was an aul' wife had a wee pickle tow, An she wad gae try the
spinnin' o't, She lootit her doon, an' it took a lowe, An' that was a bad beginnin' o't.

Mrs WALKER — D

THE WEAVER LAD

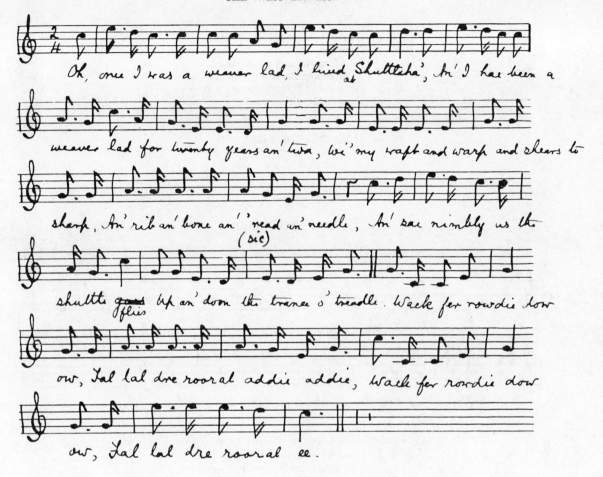

1 Oh once I was a weaver lad, I lived in Shuttleha',
   An' I hae been a weaver lad, for twenty years an' twa,
   Wi' my waft an' warp an' shears to sharp an' rib an' bone an' read an' needle,   [scissors
   An' sae nimbly as the shuttle flies up an' doon the trance o' treadle.
      Wack fer owdie dow ow fal al dre roorel addie addie,
      Wack fer owdie dow ow, fal aldre roorel ee.

2 We'll maybe live to see the time when things'll tak' a come,
   When we'll get notes to buy braw coats and breeks to hap oor bum,
   Fouth a' ale fae cock and pail and reamin' in a luggit bicker,   [bowl; frothing; beaker with handle
   Besides a dish o' gweed fat brose an' iron girds to haud them siccar.   [hoops

Mrs GREIG – D

O, MITHER, ONYBODY!

1 O mither, onybody! onybody!
   O mither, onybody, ither than a weaver!
   A weaver's jist as guid as nane
   A crater worn to skin and bane
   I'd rather lie through life my lane
   Than cuddle wi' a weaver.

Miss BELL ROBERTSON — G

479

THE SHOEMAKER

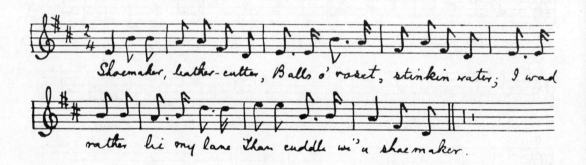

1 Shoemaker, leather-cutter,
   Balls o' roset, stinkin water;
   I wad rather lie my lane
   Than cuddle wi' a shoemaker.

Miss ELIZABETH GREIG — D

MY LOVIE WAS A SHOEMAKER

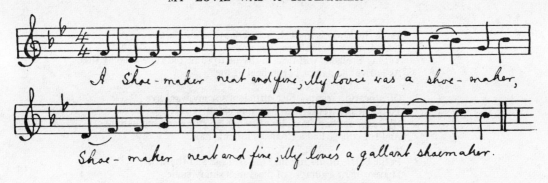

1   A shoemaker neat and fine,
    My lovie was a shoemaker,
    Shoemaker neat and fine,
    My love's a gallant shoemaker.

Mrs MARGARET GILLESPIE – D

THE SHOEMAKER AT HIS LAST

Sair fauld noo, hinnie,
Sair fauld noo,
Sair fauld noo, hinnie,
Sin I ken'd thou.

W. McC. SMITH – G

THE COBBLER

1 Mong the lowly is my lot, scarcely owner of a groat
For a living cobble shoes, peg or sew
Yet my thoughts will flow in rhyme to some old tune keeping time
As I drive the nail or peg in heel or toe.

2 Of education scanty, just sufficient for my want aye
To count my weekly earnings very small
My Latin and my grammar were my lap-stone and my hammer
And for college had a Crispin's humble hall.

3 In the battle of my life mid the struggle and the strife
I have caught a glimpse of pleasure's sunny smile
I have felt the pang of sorrow, know what it is to borrow
And to beg a fellow mortal's leave to toil.

4 Yet I envy not the great of their titles or estate
Nor yet the man of means tho' I am poor
Contented if I'm healthy with my labour if not wealthy
If I keep the ravening wolf from the door.

5 For why should I repine for such things that are not mine
To mar the simple comforts I possess
Be our pleasures small or great let us not grieve at our fate
Discontentment only makes enjoyment less.

6 In our lowly homes obscure let us cherish what is pure
Our pleasures aye be what to virtue tends
To conquer in the fight let us use our lives aright
And our talents for His glory Who them lends.

7 Then may peace and plenty smile with contentment on our Isle
And our shores be kept from war and its alarms
That we sow and reap in peace and be gladdened with increase
While around us be the everlasting arms.

A.M. INSCH — G

DICK DORBIN THE COBBLER

A

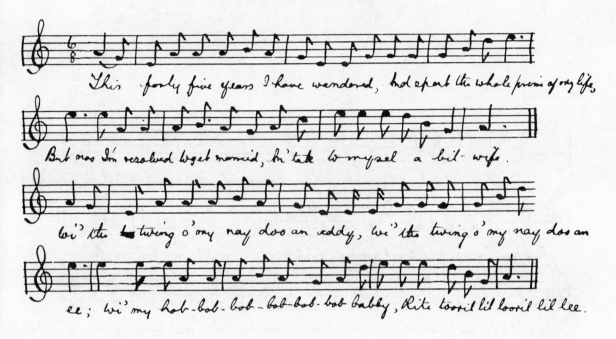

Dick Dorbin the Cobbler

This forty five years I have wandered, And spent the whole prime of my life,

But noo I'm resolved to get married, An' tak to mysel a bit wife.

wi' the turing o' my nay doo an eddy, wi' the turing o' my nay doo an

ee; wi' my hob-bob-bob-bob-bob-bob babby, Rite tooril lil looril lil lee.

1 My name is Dick Dorbin the cobbler
I've servèd my time in Dalkent
They cae'd me an auld fornicator
But noo I'm resolved to repent.
  Wi the turing of my nay do-en-adie
  Wi the turing of my nay do-en-e'e
  Wi my hob-ob-bob-bob-bob-bob-bob o ba-be
  Right tooral al ooral lie-day.

2 This fourty-five years I hae wandered
An spent the whole prime o my life
My pincers my awls an my hammers
I carry them round on my back.

3 This forty-five years I hae wandered
An spent the whole prime o my life
But noo I'm resolved to get married
An tak to mysel a bit wife.

4 (Spoken)   I'll tell what kine o a wife I got.

She was humphy an bumphy an bleary
She was humphy an bumphy an black
A beggar for fechting an scawlin
An her tongue it cried cliperty clap.

5 (Spoken)   I'll tell ye fat wye I got rid o' her.

'Twas early one Monenday's mornin
One mornin before it was licht
I tumbled her into the river
I courts'ly bade her good nicht.

Mrs MARGARET GILLESPIE — D

B
The Souter

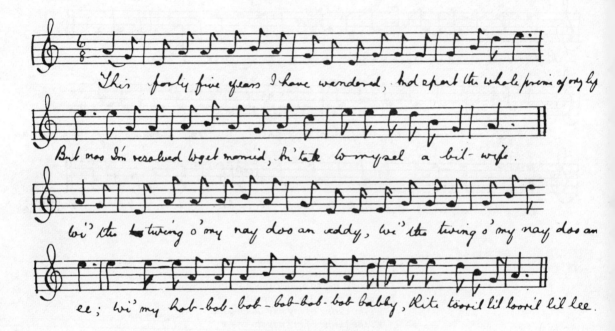

1   My name is Dick Dorbie the cobler
I hae served the best half oh my life
But no I am fairly resolved
Tae take to mysell a bit wife.
   We the turin o my a do a dadie
   We the turin oh my aye do a day
   We my robin dob dobin dob dobin
   We my fall ill ye dome day.

Mrs WALKER — D

C
The Cobbler

1 My name is Dick Doobin, the cobbler
  I served my time in Dunkeld
  They ca me an aul' fornicator
  Bit noo am resolved for tae mond.
    Wi' ma turing ah fan an doo ah di do
    Turing ah fan an doo ah daa
    Wi' ma hob an bob bob an bob bady
    Right toorall all oorall all aa.

2 My auld faither was hanged for sheep stealin'
  My mither was brunt for a witch
  My sister's a lodgin-hoose keeper
  An masel' weel I'm a rare komikal b——h.

3 It's forty-five years have I rambled
  An spent the best o' my life
  But noo I'm resolved tae reform
  An' tak tae masel a bit wife.

4 (Spoken)   A'll tell ye fat like a wife I got.

  She was humpy, she was grumpy
  She was blarney, she was black
  She's a limmer for cursin an swearin'
  An' her tongue cries clitterty clack.

ALEXANDER BRUCE — G

THE BOATMAN'S DANCE

1   The spring o' the year is come at last,
    An' the fishing time is gone and past.
    Four an' twenty boatmen, all in a row,
    Sailing on the banks o' the O'io.
        Dance the boatman's dance,
        We'll dance the boatman's dance.
        We'll dance all night till the broad daylight,
        And go home with the girls in the morning.
        Ree-oh, the boatman O,
        Sailing on the river o' the O'io.
        Ree-oh, the boatman O,
        Sailing on the seashore, O'io.

2   The boatmen dance, and the boatmen sing,
     The boatmen can do everything.
     I never saw a pretty girl in all my life
     But what would hae been a boatman's wife.

3   The boatman he's a lucky man,
     There's none can do as the boatman can.
     When the boatman comes on shore,
     He spends all his money and he works for more.

Mrs MARGARET GILLESPIE — D

THE BONNIE FISHER LASS

A

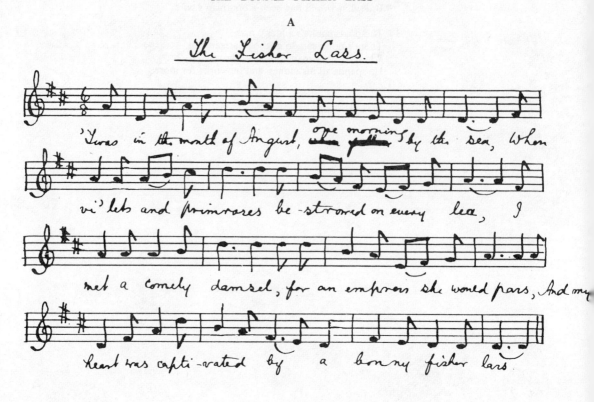

1 'Twas in the month of August, one morning by the sea,
When vi'lets and primroses bestrowed on every lea,
I met a comely damsel, for an empress she would pass,
And my heart was captivated by a bonny fisher lass.

2 "Good morning to you, fair maid," I unto her did say,
"Oh why are you so early here, where are you going this way?"
"I am going to the sea, kind sir, so I pray do let me pass,
For to get my lines in order," says the bonny fisher lass.

3 "I am going to the rocks, kind sir, some missels for to pick,
No matter whether it rain or snow, the bait we have to get,
And we must lend a helping hand, and his pardon we will ask,
And we'll jog along our journey," says the bonny fisher lass.

4 Her petticoats they were sae short, and tied above her knee,
Her handsome legs and ankles they quite delighted me,
Wi' her rosy cheeks and her yellow hair they on me did compass,
With her creel she trudges daily, does this bonny fisher lass.

5 "My father's on the ocean wide, a-toilin' in his boat,
And for to gain a livelihood, and oft-times he's afloat,
And when he does return home he lovingly will grasp
Into his aged bosom his hardy fisher lass.

6   "And when a storm arises, I'm out upon the pier,
I stand and watch sincerely, for I'm in dread and fear
Lest he should meet with a watery grave and be snatchèd from our grasp,
Then we'd wander broken-hearted," says the bonny fisher lass.

JOHN BAIN — D

B
The Bonnie Fisher Lass

SAM DAVIDSON — G

C

JAMES ANGUS — G

D
The Fisher Lass

1   Twas in the month of August one morning by the sea
     When violets and primroses were strewed on every lea
     I met a pretty damsel for an empress she would pass
     My heart was captivated by a bonnie fisher lass.

2   The petticoats she wore were short and tight above her knee
     Her handsome legs and ankles, how they delighted me
     Her rosy cheeks and yellow hair so neatly they compared
     With her creel she trudges daily, doth the bonny fisher lass.

3   "Good morning to you fair maid" I unto her did say
     Oh why are you so early or where are you going this way?
     I am going to the rockland, sir, oh pray now let me pass
     For to get my lines in order, said the bonny fisher lass.

4   I am going the rocks behind, sir, some mussels for to pick
     No matter whether it be snow or rain the bait we have to get
     But I will lend a helping hand, for your pardon I will ask
     So I'll go along my journey said the bonny fisher lass.

5   My father's out on the ocean wide there toiling in his boat
     And for to make a livelihood he often goes afloat
     And when he doth return again so lovingly he will grasp
     In his bosom, his charming fisher lass.

6   When the storm arises I out upon the pier
     I stand and watch sincerely for I must dread and fear
     Lest he should meet with a watery grave and be smashed from my grasp
     So I would wander broken-hearted said the bonnie fisher lass.

Mrs FOWLIE — G

486

A KING CANNA SWAGGER

1   A king canna swagger,
     An' get drunk like a beggar,
     Nor be so happy as I.

WILLIAM WALKER — G

COME ALL YE TRAMPS AND HAWKERS

A

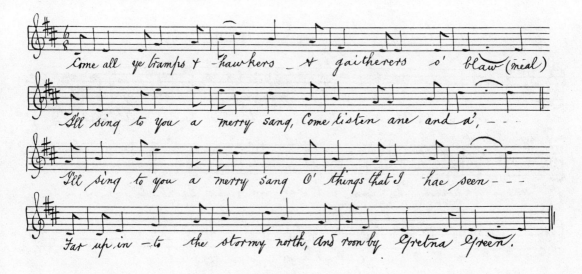

Come all ye tramps & -hawkers _ & gaitherers o' blaw (meal)
I'll sing to you a merry sang, Come listen ane and a', ---
I'll sing to you a merry sang O' things that I hae seen ----
Far up in -to the stormy north, And roon by Gretna Green.

JAMES ANGUS — G

B

The Jolly Beggar

1   Come all ye tramps and hawkers, and gie tae ithers a blaw,
    Wha tramps the country roon and roon, come tae me ane and a';
    An' I'll tell ye o' some rovin' tales in things that I hae seen,
    Far up into the stormy north, and south by Gretna Green.

2   I hae seen Ben Nevis aye towrin' to the moon;
    I've been thro' Crieff and Callender, and by the bonnie Doon,
    An' through the weary dreary sichts o' places ill tae ken,
    An' thro' the nests and silvery tides o' Urquhart's fairy glen.

3   Loch Lomond and Loch Katrine they've baith been seen by me;
    The Don, the Spey, and many more wha hastens to the sea.
    Dunrobin Castle by the way I nearly had forgot,
    An' through the cairney marks the hoose o' Johnny Groat.

4   I sometimes think intae mysel' when trudgin' on the road,
    Upon my back an empty box, my face as broon's a toad,
    Wi' lumps o' cake and tatie scones, and cheese and braxy ham   [meat of
    Nae thinkin' on the road I'm gaun, nor yet the road I cam'.   diseased sheep

5   I'm happy in the summer time, beneath the bright blue skye,
    Nae thinkin' in the mornin' at nicht where I'm tae lie,
    In barn or byre or anywhere or down among the hay
    An' if the weather does permit, I'm happy every day.

JAMES MORRISON — G

THE BEGGING

A

To the Beggin' I will go.

By a' the trades that man can try, The beggin is the best; For when a man is weary, he can sit doon an' rest. To the beggin I will go, will go, To the beggin' I will go.

1   O a' the trades that ane can try
    The beggin is the best
    For when a man is weary
    He can sit doun an rest.
        To the beggin I will go, will go,
        To the beggin I will go.

2   First I maun hae a meal puoke
    Baith big an fitly made
    Will haud a least a firlet
    Wi room for beef an bread.

3   Syne I'll go to the cobbler
    An gare him sole my sheen
    Wi at least twa inch o solin
    An clootit our abeen.   [covered on top

4   An I'll gang to a greasy cook
    An buy an auld hat
    Wi twa or three inches roun about
    Glittern our wi fat.

5   And I'll gang to a tailor
    Wi a wab o hooden grey   [coarse wool
    An gaur him mak a greatcoat
    Tae cover me night an day.

6   An I'll gang tae the turner
    An gaur him turn a dish
    Will haud at least three chappins   [Scots half
    For less I couldna wish.   pints

7   Then wi my pike staff in my haun
    Last o my beggin stock
    I'll gang unto some lucky wife
    To hansel my new puoke.   [inaugurate

8   Before that I begin my trade
I'll lat my beard grow strang
Nor pare my nails this year an mair
For beggars wear them lang.

9   I'll put nae water on my hauns
As little on my face
For aye the lowner like I am   [humbler
The mair my trade I'll grace.

10   I'll gang an seek my quarters
Before that it be dark
Jist when the gude-man
Comes in fae his wark.

11   Maybe the gude-man will say
Peerman wi hae nae room
Gin a' our folks were in aboot
You'd scarce get in yere thoom.

12   Maybe the gude-wife will say
Peer-man come in-bye
We'll a' hitch close thegether
It's been a caul day.

13   An when they're a' come in aboot
Then I will start an sing
An dee my best to gaur them lauch
An mak a merry ring.

14   An when the gude wife rises up
To mak the brose an kail
Syne I'll tak out my muckle dish
An tramp it fue o meal.   [press

15   Maybe the gude-wife will say
Peer-man pit bye yere meal   [put away
Ye're welcome tea yere quarters
Likewise yere brose an kail.

16   In the mornin I'll no stir
Wha ere to labour cries
Till the theevil on the parritch pot   [stirrer
Will strike the hour to rise.

17   Then I'll twist up my meal pokes
Before I gang away
An maybe the gude-wife will say
Come back our pot to claw.

18   And gin it ever happen
A maariage to be there
I will poer my blisses
Upon the happy pair.

19   An some will gie me bread and beef
An some will gie me cheese
An out among the maariage folk
I'll gither ba-bees.

20   If beggin is as good's I think
I may come back an tell
But if the trade gaes backlins
I'll keep it to mysel.

Mrs MARGARET GILLESPIE — D

Song No. 488

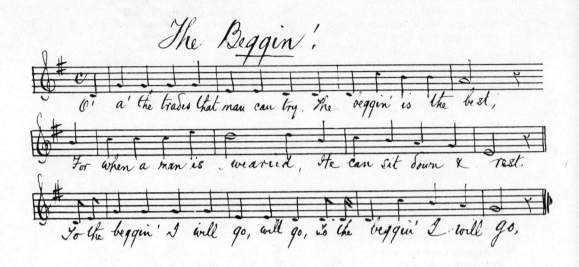

The Beggin'

O' a' the trades that man can try, The beggin' is the best,

For when a man is wearied, He can sit doun & rest.

To the beggin' I will go, will go, to the beggin' I will go,

1 O' a' the trades that man can try
The beggin is the best
For when a man is wearied
He can sit doon and rest.
   To the beggin I will go, will go
   To the beggin I will go.

2 Afore that I dae gang awa
I'll lat my beard grow lang
And for my nails I winna pare
For beggars wears them lang.

3 I will get a meal pock
Made o' the ledder reed
And it will haud twa firlots
And room for beef and breed.

4 I'll gang tull a cobbler
And gar him mak my sheen
Wi' twa three inches roon aboot
A' cloutit owre abeen.

5 I'll gang tull a hatter
And gar him mak a hat
Wi twa, three inches roon aboot
A' glitterin owre wi' fat.

6 At marriage or at market fair
Though it be far or near
I'll mak a point for to be there
For fat ye needna spier.

7 For some will gie me beef and breed
And some will gie me cheese
And roon amo the marriage folk
Will gidder bawbees.

8 Gin I come on as I wid like
I will come back and tell
But gin the trade gans arselins
I'll keep it tae mysel.

L. BREBNER — G

274

C

The Beggin'.

1 Of all the trades that e'er man tried,
   The beggin' is the best,
   For when a body's wearied,
   He can sit down and rest. —
       To the begging I will go, will go,
       To the begging I will go.

2 I'll gang to some souter,
   That cobbles auld sheen,
   Twa three inches o' a clout
   And cobbled owre abeen.

Miss ANNIE RITCHIE — G

D

The Begging.

Of all the trades that man can try, The begging is the best,

For when a man is wearied He can sit doon and rest,

To the begging I will go will go, To the begging I will go.

JOHN MOWAT – G

E

To the beggin' I will go

O' a' the trades that man can try, The beggin' is the best; For

Refrain.

when a man is weary he can sit doon an' rest, To the

beggin' I will go, will go, To the beggin' I will go.

WILLIAM DUNCAN – D

F

The Begging.

Mrs SANGSTER – G

276

G

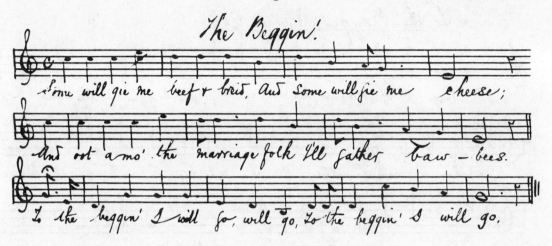

The Beggin'.

Some will gie me beef & breid, And some will gie me cheese;
And oot a mo' the marriage folk I'll gather baw—bees.
To the beggin' I will go, will go, To the beggin' I will go.

JOSEPH BEATTIE — G

H

To the beggin I will go.

GEORGE RIDDELL — G

I

The Begging.

O' a' the trades that e'er I tried, The beggin' is the best;
For when a man gets wearied wi' He can sit doon & rest.
To the beggin' I we will go, go, go, To the beggin' we will go.

Rev. JOHN CALDER — G

J

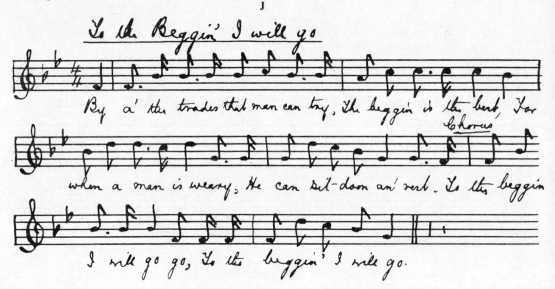

FRANK CHRISTIE – D

K

JAMES ANGUS – G

L

The Begging

1 O' a' the trades that I do ken
   The begging is the best,
   For when the beggar's weary
   He can sit down and rest.
      To the begging we will go, will go,
      To the begging we will go.

278

2 First I maun hae a meal-pock
    O' leather fitly made,
    Will haud at least a firlot,
    Wi' room for beef and bread.

3 Syne I will to the cobbler
    And gar him sort my shoon,
    An inch thick i' the boddom,
    And clouted weel aboon.

4 And I will to the greasy cook,
    Frae him will buy a hat,
    Weel pressed and weather-beaten,
    And glitterin' ower wi' fat.

5 And I will to the tailor,
    Wi' a wab o' hodden gray,
    And gar him mak' a cloak for me
    Will hap me nicht and day.

6 And I will to the turner gang
    And gar him turn a dish
    Will haud at least three chappins
    For less I couldna wish.

7 Then wi' my pikestaff in my hand
    To close my beggin' stock
    I'll go unto some lucky wife
    To hansel my new pock.

8 And yet ere I begin my trade
    I'll let my beard grow lang,
    Nor pare my nails this year and day
    For beggars wears them lang.

9 I'll put nae water on my hands,
    As little on my face;
    But still the lowner-like I am
    The mair my trade I'll grace.

10 And I'll look out my quarters
    Aye lang or it be late;
    At ilka cosy corner
    I'll hae a canny seat.

11 When I come to a farm-toun
    I'll say wi' hat in hand
    Will the beggar man get quarters here?
    Alas I canna stand.

12 It's maybe the guidman will say,
    "Puir man we hae nae room;
    Gin a' oor folks were in aboot
    We couldna lodge your thoom."

13 It's maybe the guidwife will say,
    "O puir man, come inby
    We'll budge a bit and mak a seat,
    It's been a cauldrife day."

14 And when they're a come in aboot
    Then I will start and sing,
    And do my best to gar them lauch
    A' round aboot the ring.

15 And when the guidwife rises up
    To mak' the brose and kail,
    Syne I'll tak' oot my meal dish
    And tramp it fu' o' meal.

16 It's likely the guidwife will say,
    "Puir man, put past your meal,
    Ye're welcome to your brose I'm sure,
    Your breid, ay and your kail."

17 In the mornin' I'll no stir mysel'
    Whae'er to labour cries
    Till the theevil on the parritch pot
    Will strik' the 'oor to rise.

18 When twistin' up my meal-pock
    Before I gang awa',
    It's then nae doot the wife will say,
    "Come back oor pan to claw."

19 If there's a waddin' in a toon,
    I'll airt me to be there,
    And pour my kindest benisons
    Upon the winsome pair.

20 And some will gie me beef and breid,
    And some will gie me cheese,
    Syne I'll slip out among the folk
    And gather the bawbees.

21 And I will gallop out a dance
    Or tell a merry tale,
    Till some guid fellow in my dish
    Will pour a soup o' ale.

22 If beggin' is as guid's I think,
    And as I hope it may,
    It's time that I was oot the gate
    And trudgin' ower the brae.

23 And if I chance to prosper
    I may come back and tell,
    But if the trade goes backlins
    I'll keep it to mysel'.

T. ROGER – G

M
The Begging

1 Oh a' the trades a man can try
The begging is the best
For gin a man is wearied
He can sit doon and rest.
To the begging I will go, will go
To the begging I will go.

2 First I maun get a meal pock
Made o' the leather red
That will haud three firlets weel enough
And room for beef and breed.

3 Afore that I do gang awa
I'll lat my beard grow strang
And for my nails I winna pare
For beggars wears them lang.

4 I'll gang to some greasy cook
And get frae her a hat
Wi' twa three inches o' a rim
And glittering owre wi' fat.

5 Then I'll go to a cobbler
And gar him cobble my sheen
Wi' twa three steeks across my sole
And clouted owre abeen.

6 Syne I'll gang to a turner
And gar him turn a dish
That'll haud three chapins weel enough
For less I widna wish.

7 I'll gang and seek my quarters
Afore that it grows dark
Fan the guidman is new come in
And sattled frae his wark.

8 But maybe the guidwife will say
Peer man we hinna room
For fin a' wir folk come in aboot
Ye'd scarce get in yer thoom.

9 But maybe the guidman 'll say
Peer man come in bye
And a' wedge thegither for
It's been a cauld day.

10 Then I'll tak oot my muckle caup
And tramp it for a meal
And say "Gee me bree to mak my brose
I winna seek yer kail."

11 But maybe the guidwife 'll say
Peer man put by yer meal
Ye'll be welcome to yer brose this nicht
Likewise yer breed and kail.

12 And gin there be a marriage
I'll try for to be there
And pour oot my blessins
Upon the happy pair.

13 Some will gie me breed and beef
And some will gie me cheese
And oot amo' the marriage folk
I'll gather bawbees.

14 And gin there be a minstrel
As they are never scant
Then doon amo' the marriage folk
I'll dance the beggar's rant.

15 Gin I come on as I expect
I will come back and tell
But gin I dinna dae that
I'll keep it to mysel.

Miss BELL ROBERTSON — G

N
The Beggar

1 O' a' the trades that men can try
The begging is the best,
For when a man is wearied
He can sit down and rest.
To the begging I will go, I'll go,
To the begging I will go.

2 Before that I did gang awa
  I'll let my nails grow lang,
  And for my beard I winna shave,
  For beggars wears them lang.

3 I'll gang in to some greasy cook,
  And buy frae her a hat,
  Wi' twa three inches o' a rim,
  And glittering owre wi' fat.

4 I'll gang in to a turner,
  And gar him turn a dish
  That will hold three chapins,
  For I couldna dee wi' less.

5 And gin there be a marriage,
  I'll endeavour to be there,
  And I will pray my blessing
  Upon that happy pair.

6 I'll gang and buy some instruments,
  For I'm sure they are na scant,
  And in amang the marriage folk
  I'll dance the beggar's rant.

7 And some will gie me beef and bread,
  And some will gie me cheese,
  And out amang the marriage folk
  I'll gather bawbees.

8 I'll gang and seek my quarters
  Before that it grow dark,
  Jist when the guidman's new sitten doon,
  Jist new hame frae his wark.

9 But maybe the guidwife will say,
  Puir man we hinna room,
  For when we're a' set roon aboot
  Ye'd scarce get in your thoom.

10 But maybe the guidman will say,
  Puir man come ye in by,
  We'll ca a wedge to gie ye room
  It's been a cauld day.

11 Syne I'll tak oot my muckle dish
  An stap it fu' o' meal
  And say, Guidwife, if ye gie me bree,
  I winna seek your kail.

12 But maybe the guidman will say,
  Puir man pit up your meal
  Ye're welcome to your brose this nicht,
  Likewise your breid and kail.

13 If a' be true that I ha'e said,
  I will come back and tell,
  And if it dinna be that,
  I'll keep it to mysel'.

CHRISTINA ALLAN — G

O

The Begging

1 A' the trades that man can try
  The begging is the best;
  For a man is wearied
  He can sit down and rest.
    To the begging I will go, I'll go,
    To the begging I will go.

2 Before that I do gang awa
  I'll lat my beard grow lang,
  An' for my nails I winna pare,
  For beggars wears them lang.

3 I'll gang to some greasy cook,
  An' buy an auld hat,
  Wi' twa-three inches o' a rim,
  An' glittering o'er wi' fat.

4 I'll gang and seek my quarters,
  Afore that it grows dark,
  Jist when the goodman comes
  In fra his wark.

5 Maybe the goodman will say,
  Puir man, come inby,
  We'll a' sit close thegither,
  It's been a caul' day.

6 Then I'll take out my muckle dish,
  An' tramp it full o' meal, —
  Gin ye gie me bree, goodwife,
  I winna seek your kale.

7 Maybe the goodwife will say,
  Keep in yer pickle meal,
  Ye're welcome to yer quarters,
  Likewise yer brose and kail.

8 Gin a marriage ever chance,
   It happen to be here,
   I will lay my blessing
   On that happy pair.

9 Some will gie me bread and beef,
   Some will gie me cheese,
   An' oot amo' the marriage folk
   I'll gather bawbees.

10 Gin I come on as I do think,
   I'll come back and tell;
   An' gin I dinna dae that,
   I'll keep it to mysel'.

E.G. – G

P
To the Beggin' We Will Go

1 O' a' the trades that man can try
   The beggin' is the best
   For when a man gets wearit
   He can sit doon an' rest.
     To the beggin we will go an' we'll go
     To the beggin' we will go.

2 Afore that I do tak the road
   Or lat my beard grow lang
   An' for my nails I winna pare
   For beggars wears them lang.

3 I'll gang an' seek my quarters
   Afore that it be dark
   An' the gweedman be in aboot
   An' rested fae his wark.

4 Maybe the gweedwife will say
   Peer man we hinna room
   For when we're a' set in aboot
   You'll scarce get in your thoom.

5 But maybe the gweedman will say
   Peer man come in bye
   For we'll gie a hitch thegither
   It's been a cauld day.

6 I'll tak oot my muckle dish
   An' tramp it fu' o' meal
   If ye wad gie me bree this nicht
   I wadna seek your kale.

7 But maybe the gweed wife will say
   Peer man pit up your meal
   For ye will get your brose this nicht
   Likewise your bread an' kale.

8 If there be a mairriage in the place
   It's minstrels will be here
   An' in amang the mairriage folk
   I'll bless that happy pair.

9 Some will gie me beef an' bread
   An' some will gie me cheese
   An' in amang the mairriage folk
   I'll gither bawbees.

10 But if trade gae on as I suppose
   I sall come back an' tell
   But if the trade it dinna dee
   I'll keep it to mysel'.

Miss F. GRANT – D

Q
The Beggin

1   O' a' the trades that man can try
     The beggin' it's the best
     For when a man gets wearied
     He can sit doon and rest.
      To the beggin' I will go, I'll go
      To the beggin' I will go.

2 I'll go into some tailor's shop
    An buy a web o' grey,
    I'll mak' him mak' a cloak o't
    To mak me nicht and day.

3 I'll go into some cobbler's,
    An' mak' him cobble my sheen,
    Two three inches roon aboot
    An' clooted o'er abeen.

4 I'll go into some turner
    An' mak him turn a dish
    It'll haud three chappin'
    For it widna dee nay less.

5 I'll go into some farmer's wife
    An' maybe the guid wife 'll say
    Puir man I hinna room.

6 But maybe the guidman 'll say
    Puir man come in by
    An weel a hands thegither
    For it's been a cauld day.

7 Gin I come on as weel as I wad like to dee
    I'll come back an' tell ye
    But gin I dinna come on sae weel
    I'll keep it to mysel'.

8 I'll tak' my muckle cap
    An tramp it foo o' meal
    Gin e' gie me bree guid wife
    I shidna seek yer kail.

9 I'll go into some greasy cook,
    An buy an aul' hat
    Wi' a' twa three inches roon aboot
    A glitterin' oer wi' fat.

10 Gin a marriage chance to be
    I'll endeavour to be there
    An' some 'll gie me bread and beef
    An' some 'll gie me cheese
    An oot amo the merriage folk
    I'll gider bawbees.

Mrs SMITH — G

R

1 I'll gang unto some tailor,
    Wi' a wob o' grey,
    An' gar him mak' a cloakie o't
    To hap me nicht and day.

Source unrecorded — G

BUY BROOM BESOMS

A

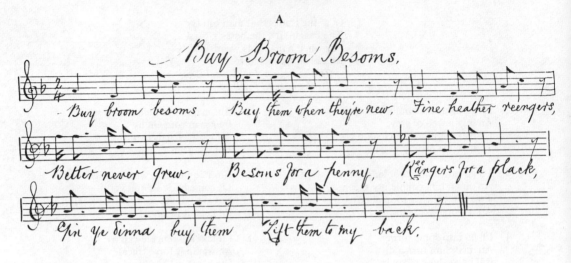

Buy broom besoms Buy them when they're new, Fine heather reengers,
Better never grew, Besoms for a penny, Reengers for a plack,
Gin ye dinna buy them Lift them to my back.

SAM DAVIDSON – G

B

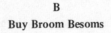

Buy Broom Besoms

1 Buy broom besoms, buy them when they're new,
  Fine heather reenges, better never grew.   [scourers
  Reenges for a penny, besoms for a plack,
  An' gin ye winna buy them, I'll tie them on my back.

WILLIAM DUNCAN – D

C
Buy Broom Besoms

1   Buy broom besoms — wha'll buy them noo?
      Fine heather ranges — better never grew.
      There's ane for a penny, and there's twa for a plack;
      And gin ye winna buy them, come lift them on my back.

Miss ANNIE RITCHIE — G

D
Buy Broom Besoms

1   Buy broom besoms, buy them fan they're new,
      Fine heather rangers, better never grew,
      Besoms for a penny, reengers for a plack,
      Gin ye winna buy them, lift them to my back.

Miss BELL ROBERTSON — G

490

THE SCAVENGERS' BRIGADE

1   We're always upon duty boys in sunshine or in storm
      With our brooms upon our shoulders it's our only uniform
      It's everywhere in street and square we are daily on parade
      As we march in style in Indian file in the Scavengers' Brigade.

Mrs DUNCAN — G

THE PLOUGHBOY'S DREAM

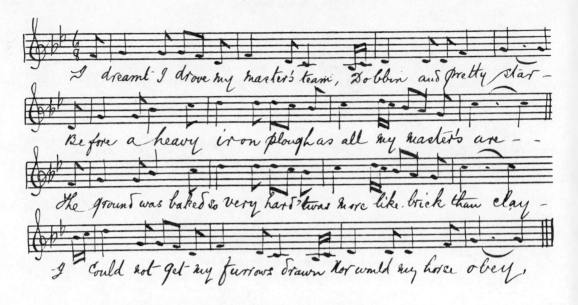

I dreamt I drove my master's team, Dobbin and pretty Star –
Before a heavy iron plough as all my master's are – –
The ground was baked so very hard 'twas more like brick than clay –
I could not get my furrows drawn nor would my horse obey,

1   I am a ploughboy, stout and bold as ever drove a team
    Three years ago I slept in bed and dreamed a fearful dream.
    But tho' 'twas but a dream my boys I have it here in rhyme
    For other chaps to read or sing my rhyme when they have time.

2   I dreamt I drove my master's team, 'twas Dobbin and pretty Star
    Before a heavy iron plough as all my master's are.
    The ground was baked so very hard 'twas more like brick than clay
    I could not get my furrows drawn nor would my beasts obey.

3   The more that I did curse and swear the less my horses did
    Dobbin lay down while pretty Star did nothing else but kick.
    When lo! above me a bright form that seemed to float on air
    With purple robe and snowy wings as angels painted are.

4   "Withhold you cruel wretch" he cried "do not your beasts abuse
    For if the ground were not so hard would they for once refuse?
    Besides I heard you curse and swear as if dumb beasts could tell
    Tho' they don't know there's One that knows your crimes and sins as well."

5   Come all ye jolly ploughman lads, a warning take by me
    Whate'er you do or e'er you think, let kindness your motto be
    And when that this life's toil is o'er all darkly though it seems
    You will bless the day you heard me sing the humble ploughboy's dream.

ARTHUR BARRON – G

THE AULD HORSE'S LAMENT

A

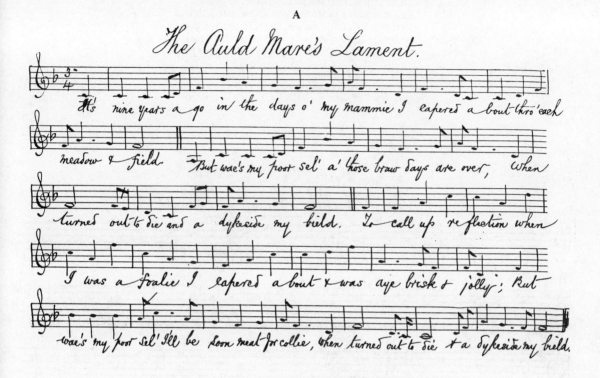

The Auld Mare's Lament.

1 Nine years ago in the days o' my mammie
   I capered about through each meadow and field
   But waes my poor sel' a' these braw days are over
   When turned out to die, and a dykeside my bield.
   To call up reflexions when I was a foalie
   I capered about and was aye brisk and jolly
   But waes my poor sel' I'll be soon meat for collie
   When turned out to die and a dykeside my bield.

2 When young Mr Galloper bought me to ride on
   And he like mysel' was a rambling chiel,
   With spurs my poor sides, there was scarce a bit hide on
   My back wi' the saddle was blistered and beeled.   [sore
   For pleasure he rode in and out at the gallop
   And ilka noo and than he o'ertook me a wallop
   But I flang him fae me ae nicht in the shallop
   And bade him lie there till his humours were queeled.

3 For this the neist day I was saul to a cadger
   Braw niffer thocht I, but I was beguiled
   For he wrought me hard ilka day like a nigger
   Till ye may believe me, my rumple was peeled.
   Hard toiled all the day, scanty fare was my supper
   My drink was the dregs o' some foul stinkin gutter
   And noo when my life's worn oot to a twither
   I'm turned out to die and a dykeside my bield.

4 Ye mortals take warning from this my sad story
  Scarce able to shift for mysel' in the field
  What though my poor neighbours they a' should be sorry
  Their pity affords me ne'er shelter nor bield.
  Lay something in store when ye hae strength and vigour
  Lest old age comes on you the thin chafted nigger
  And then like mysel' ye'll but cut a poor figure
  When turned out to die and a dykeside your bield.

JAMES MACKIE – G

B

The Auld Horse's Lament.

First of all Mr. Gallofret bought me to ride on, And he like mysel' was a ramblin' chiel;

My back in the saddle there was scarce a bit hide on, And my ribs wi' the spurs they were blistered & beeled.

For pleasure he rode forth & home at the gallop, And aye noo & than he o'er-took me a wallop

But I flang him frae me ae nicht in a shallop, And bade him lie there till his humour did queel.

J. McBOYLE – G

C
Old Horse's Lament

1   Young Mr Galop he bocht me to ride on
    And he like mysel was a frolocksome cheil
    My sids we the spurs there wis scarce ony hide on
    My back we the saddle wis riddled and peeld
    And aye oot and in he rad me at the galop
    And noo and than he oertook me a wallop
    Until I aye day threw aff in a shallop
    And bade im lie there till his emmer did qeel.

2   For that the nest day I wis sal till a cadger
    And I never thocht it I hid been beguld.

3   And my drink was the dregs o a foul stinkin gutter
    And noo fan my life's worn oot till a truter
    I'm turnt oot to die and a dykeside's my beyld.

Miss BELL ROBERTSON — D

493

THERE LIVES A MAN IN ARDES TOWN

There Lives a Man

1   There lives a man in Ardes town
    For rarity we hear,
    Wi' little meat and sair wark
    He's killed a guid young meer.

2   He works her hard and hungers her,
    And pines awa her life,
    And deed they say he beats her,
    They say he beats his wife.

3   The wives o' —— they cam' oot,   [denunciation
    Wi' mony sad misca',
    They thocht to get her lifted,   [carried out for burial
    But she gaed ower them a'.   [was out of their control

4   The wives o' Fernie Brae cam' oot,
    To phrase aboot the meer,   [make virtuous speeches
    They wad 'a ta'en her to themsels,
    Gin she had been better gear.

Miss BELL ROBERTSON — G

THE AULD MAN'S MEAR'S DEID

A

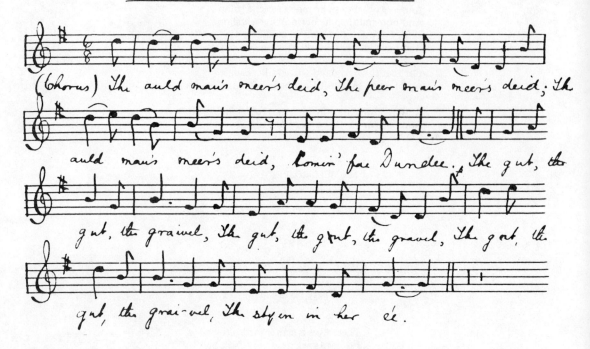

The auld man's mare's de'ed
The peir man's mare's de'ed
The auld man's mare's de'ed
Comin fae Dundee.

1 There wis hay to ca – an lint to lead
A hunder ho'ts o muck to spread   [baskets
An neeps an peats an a' to lead
An yet the jade to dee.   [nag

2 She had the feircie an the fleuk [farcy; diarrhoea
The whugloch and the wanton yeuk   [itch
On ilka knee she had a breuk,   [abscess
What ailed the beast to de'e?

3 The gut the gut the graivel   [gravel
The gut the gut the graivel
The gut the gut the graivel
The sty'en on her e'e.

4 She wis cut lugget, pinch lippet,   [thin lipped
Steel wimed, staincher fitted   [stiff legged
Chanler chaftet, lang necket,   [lantern-jawed
An yet the brute did de'e.

5 The puer man's head's sair
Wi greetin for his auld grey mare
He's like to de'e himsel wi care
An yet the jade to de'e.

6 He's thinkin on the bye gane days
An a' her douce an canny ways
An how his ain guidwife auld Bess
Micht jist as weel been spared.

Mrs MARGARET GILLESPIE – D

B

The Auld Man's Mear's Deid

The aul' man's mear's deid,
The peer bodie's mear's deid,
The aul' mannie's mear's deid,
A mile ayon' Dundee.

1 There was hay to ca and lint to lead,
    A hun'er hotts o' muck to spread,
    And peats and sods and a' to lead, —
    And yet the jaud to dee!

2 She had the gout, the gravel,
    The strangrey and the spavie,
    The brook-boil ahin' her lug,   [swollen gland
    And the pearlin' on her e'e.   [cataract

Miss BELL ROBERTSON — G

DUNCAN MACKALLIKIN

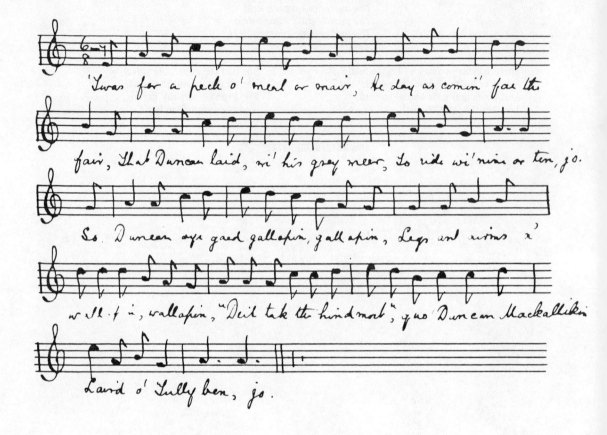

'Twas for a peck o' meal or mair, the day as comin' fae the fair, That Duncan laid, wi' his grey meer, to ride wi' nine or ten, jo.

So Duncan aye gaed gallopin, gallopin, Legs and arms a' wallopin, wallopin, "Deil tak the hindmost," quo Duncan Mackallikin Laird o' Tullyben, jo.

1 Twas for a peck o meal or mair
Aye day as I wis coming fae the fair
That Duncan laid wi his grey mare
To ride wi nine or ten jo.
So off he set a-gallopin gallopin
Legs an arms a-wallopin wallopin
Deil hae the last qo Duncan McCalligan
Laird o Tillie-Ben-Jo.

2 The neist I think wis Tam the wright
But Tammy ne'er go sic a fricht
Fell aff his beast an doun did licht
Upon his nether'en Jo.
But Duncan aye kept gallopin gallopin
Legs an arms a-wallopin wallopin
Lie ye there qo Duncan McCalligan
Laird o Tillie-Ben-Jo.

3 The neist I think wis smithy John
An auld coach horse he rode upon
Its back sae sharp ye'd thought it's bone
In twa wid maist him rent Jo.
But Duncan aye kept gallopin gallopin
Legs an arms a-wallopin wallopin
Are ye ridin on a saw, qo Duncan McCalligan.
Laird o Tillie-Ben-Jo.

4 The wily souter ran like wud   [mad
He stuck fast to Duncan's fud   [tail
Till in the glaur wi awfu thud   [mud
His gallopin a' did end Jo.
But Duncan aye kept gallopin gallopin
Legs an arms a-wallopin wallopin
Lie ye there, qo Duncan McCalligan
Laird o Tillie-Ben-Jo.

5 Hab the millar he wis taen
Wi sic a wamlin in the wime   [squeamishness
Till bouckin rainbows o'er the main   [retching
Nae langer could conten Jo.
But Duncan aye kept gallopin gallopin
Legs an arms a-wallopin wallopin
Dirty brute, qo Duncan McCalligan
Laird o Tillie-Ben-Jo.

6 A wee bit taylor prick the luce   [louse
In settin out he wis fue cruse
He se'en go flyld an filed his truse [frightened; messed his
Before the race did end Jo.   trousers
But Duncan aye kept gallopin gallopin
Legs an arms a-wallopin wallopin
Laurd sic an air, said Duncan McCalligan
Laird o Tillie-Ben-Jo.

7 The baxter neist came at his tail
His fup he handled like a flail   [whip
Through thick an thin he flew like hail
Troth he came right for Ben Jo.   [for "far ben"
But Duncan aye kept gallopin gallopin
Legs an arms a-wallopin wallopin
Deil hae the last qo Duncan McCalligan
Laird o Tillie-Ben-Jo.

8 But Duncan's mare she flew like drift
As fast an sure her feet could lift
At ilka spang she leat a rift   [leap; passed wind
Out fae her hinner end Jo.
But Duncan aye kept gallopin gallopin
Legs an arms a-wallopin wallopin
I've won the meal qo' Duncan McCalligan
Laird o Tillie-Ben-Jo.

Mrs MARGARET GILLESPIE — D

TRUSTY

1   There was a tyke, a tyke o' fame
    An Trusty was the doggie's name
    There nae dog that he wad head
    Although he was o' mastiff breed
    He had a coat o' guid black hair
    For tusk nor teeth he didna care
    O he was valiant, O he was brave
    His coat o' mail, it did him save.

2   But it fell once upon a day
    As tales do tell and folks do say
    Twas said that he did bite an heir
    Which did breed muckle dool and care
    Now neighbours gether a' thegither
    I'm feart that we will hae ill weather
    Come sit an crack wi' ane anither
    I hope you'll pity me — the mither.

3   O M. got up in sad despair
    She rave her duds and tare her hair   [tore
    Her ribbons red, her mutch an toys
    Flew to the air like mild flambeaux.
    Her rock, her beck and her ain body   [stomach
    Flew to the clouds just like a rocket
    She rampaged, raved and swore by God
    That her dear chill wad rin red mad.

4   When to the doctor fast she ran,
    Creed "Ah dear sir, do what you can,"
    She sighed, she raved and cried Ohhon
    O my dear chill, he will be gone
    See him, oh see him, fu he is torn
    He winna live until the morn
    For Death will glack his mutton wi' him.
                       [gratify his desire

5   O wae upon the venimous beast
    To hurt my laddie was nae jest.
    O kill, shot him dead, and gore him
    And hap the deadly yerd out owre him   [earth
    His very inside out O turn him
    And then a' heretic burn him.
    Had I been there I wad hae tore him
    For twenty deaths is owre guid for him.

6   O wha will heir our well worn gear
    We've plenty o't I'm very seer.
    Now wha will heir his duds and lippens
    'Baith stentin strings and many clippens   [stretching
    And wha will heir the pot and ladle
    For we do hae nae grape nor paidle   [gardening fork; hoe
    An wha will heir my warm jerkin
    An clews o' thread wad be a heidle   [balls
    The byken and the button needle   [hook
    An' a'thing that's for ony use
    Our lap board and our noble goose.   [smoothing iron

7   When she her venom a' had spent
    She straight until a Justice went
    Begged her a warrant then wad gie
    That death the doggie's fate might be.
    The honest judge defined the laws
    And telled her it widna do ava
    For to the Shirra ye maun gang
    Ere Trusty ye can shot or hang
    In maybe to the House o' Commons
    He says a law made by the Romans
    Troth maybe to the House o' Lords
    For justice only it affords
    Nae judge nor jury upon earth
    Can gar the doggie gie his aith.

8   And now ye think I might hae dane
    But oh the tear comes to my e'en.
    In sympathy I hired a lad
    Just to haud M—— on gane mad.
    The lad cam round wi' a round spouter
    Wi vengeance he dang something out o' her
    And jest by dint o' skill and speed
    He laid the doggie fairly deed.

9   O that sic death was ever invented
    Nae sooner dane than it was repented
    He winna kill his life I'm seer
    Although he live this hunner year.
    Now neighbours ye'll hear and see
    Ye pitied, ye'll pity me
    The dog is dead for want o' breath
    As true a friend I had on earth.

10 Now wha will keep his master's house
   The cat can only take the mouse
   She's nae a guard to her ain home
   Altho' lang wi' a beast o' fame.
   Now she will keep the byre an' barn
   The green and ony puckle yarn
   An wha will keep the puckle clase   [guard; close, yard
   An fleg awa the nak an pays
   Or wha will ca' the cow and ewe
   For servants true I hae but few.

11 At even when I'm wakin' and weary
   Oh wha will bark an keep me cheery
   For now I hae nae ane to back me
   Hobgoblins dear nae doubt will tak me.
   Comin throw the moor or woodie
   Ilka thing will be a boodie.
   Muirhens they will get up wi' a bicker   [commotion
   I'll fa' for fear I am nae air sick.
   An unsunken spirits — water kelpies
   Will tak me by the tail and skelp me.
   When I had Trusty at my foot
   I didna need to stir a bit
   He ran fu gley to a' thing fearfu'
   And ay cam back right crouse and cheerfu'.

12 But what needs I thus make my moan
   Since faithful Trusty is dead and gone
   Since he's awa I maunna care
   I'm sure I'll never see him mair.
   He's peyed his debt, nae mair aboot it
   Sic lingo we can do withoot it
   The doggie's deid, sae maun the heir
   An M—— maun dee an deil ma care
   Tho' baith were deid, there's nae great scaith
   The dog was better than them baith.

       ALEX MACDONALD – G

TAM GIBB AND THE SOO

A

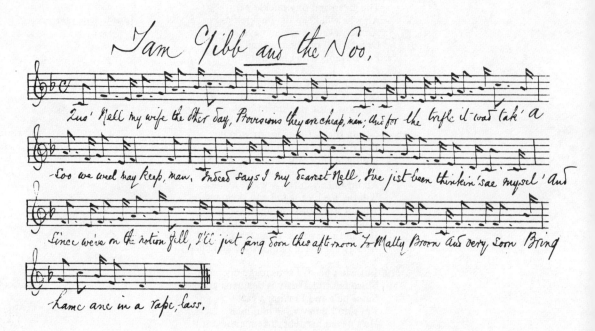

J. NAAMAN – G

B

ARTHUR BARRON – G

C

Tam Gibb and the Soo

1   Quo' Nell my wife the ither day, —
Provisions they are cheap, man,
And for the trifle it would tak',
A soo we weel micht keep, man.
Indeed, says I, my dearest Nell,
I've jist been thinkin' sae mysel',
And since we've on the notion fell,
I'll jist gang doon to Matty Broon
This efternoon, and very soon
Bring hame ane in a rape, man.

2   Sae in my pooch I pat the rape,
And doon to Matty's went, man,
Resolved to hae a guid ane wiled,
Reflections to prevent, man,
As seen's I entered Matty's door,
She blithely met me on the floor,
And kindly questions spiered a score,
About mysel', the bairns and Nell,
Nor can I tell what cracks befell
Ere my eerant it was kent, man.

(Spoken) For ye maun ken Matty and me was auld sweethearts, and in fact were ance near aboot married, had it not been for a confounded auld mither o' hers that pat ill atween's.

3   But when auld stories a' were telt,
And aiblins something new, man,
I fan' 'twas time that I should mak'
Some mention o' the soo, man.
When my eerant I did unfauld,
I fan' the young anes a' were sauld,
But gin I'd like to tak' the auld,
Wi' a' her hert she'd send her cairt,
She weel could spare't, I thanked her for't,
But oot the rape I drew, man.

(Spoken) Na, na, says I, Matty, far be it frae Tam Gibb to pit his auld sweetheart to sae muckle trouble. Here's a bit new rape that I hae brocht, and nae doot the beast will gang the road braw and canny.

4   Sae roon dame grumphy's hinmost leg
The rape I soon did tie, man;
And wi' a supple birken twig
I drave her oot the stye, man.
Wi' Matty straucht I bade guid-e'en,
And briskly to the road we ta'en,
But scarcely fifty yards we'd gane,
When madam soo impatient grew,
And soon, I trow, made me to rue
That her I chanced to buy, man.

5   For bein' o' the female breed,
    She proved a stubborn jaud, man;
    Were I to flay the brute alive,
    She'd aye hae her ain wye, man.
    I wanted east, but she'd be west,
    Or ony wye she liket best,
    And did my brains sae fairly pest,
    Till in my wrath, wi' mony an aith,
    I vowed her skaith, and kicked her baith,
    And gart her squeak aloud, man.

(Spoken) Oh, she was the most positive brute o' a soo that ever was born. She wad neither gang her ain road nor the wye I wanted her. I held on like grim death, and I daresay I wad hae managed her, had it no been for a confounded muckle stane that trippet me, and doon I gaed a' my length amo' the dubs, snap gaed the rope, awa' ran the soo, and, I can tell ye, I never saw anither sicht o't.

6   But tho' pig's flesh it never mair
    Should be my lot to pree, man,
    I vow and swear anither soo
    Will ne'er be bought by me, man.
    As lang's there's herrin' in Loch Fyne,
    I'll ne'er want kitchie while I dine,   [tasty food
    And henceforth bid adieu to swine;
    O' nae sic gear the price I'll spier,
    Nor stan' the sneer and jaunting jeer
    That I frae neebors dree, man.

(Spoken) Faith, I'm no fit to stan't. And the callants are the warst. Od, ye'll see them, as a body gangs alang the street, jinkin' intil a close, and keekin' oot and cryin', — Hey, Tam — hey Tam Gibb — faur's yer soo?

Source unrecorded — G

D
Tam Broon and his Sou

1 Quo Nell my wife the ither day;
   "Provisions they are cheap man
   And for the trifle it wad tak'
   A sou we weel micht keep man."
   "Indeed," says I, "my dearest Nell
   I've jist been thinkin sae mysel'
   But since we've on the notion fell
   I'll jist gang doon to Matty Broon
   This efternoon, and very soon
   Bring hame ane in a rape man."

2 Sae in my pooch I pat the rape
   And doon tae Matty's went man,
   Resolved to hae a guid ane wiled
   Reflections to prevent man.
   As seen's I entered Matty's door
   She blithely met me on the floor
   And kindly questions spiered a score
   Aboot mysel', the bairns, an' Nell
   Nor can I tell what cracks befell
   Or my eeran it was kent man.

(Spoken) Ye ken Matty an me, were aince aul' sweethearts an' we'd
hae been marriet thegither if it hidna been an aul wreck o' a mither o'
mine that pit ill in atween's.

3 An' fan' I got the eeran' taul'
   I fan' ther young anes a' were sal'
   But gin I liked to tak the aul'
   Wi' a' her heart she'd send her cairt
   She weel could spairt, I thanked her for't
   But oot the rape I drew man.

4 Sae round dame Grumphy's hinmist leg
   The rape I seen did tie man
   An' wi' a supple birken twig
   I drew her oot the sty man.
   Frae Matty's stracht I bade gude even
   And briskly tae the road we ta'en
   But scarcely fifty yards did gang
   Till madam sou impatient grew
   An' soon made me to rue
   That her I chanced to buy man.

5 She bein' o' the female breed
   She proved a stubborn gad man
   Were I tae flay the brute alive
   She'd a' her ain road hae man.
   I winted east but she'd hae wast
   Or ony wey she likèd best
   An' did my brains sae fairly paithe
   I ooit her scaith and kicked her baith
   An' gart her squeak aloud man.

(Spoken) But I think I wid hae managed ahin' a' gin't hidna been a
great muckle steen that took my fit and owre I fell, and knap gaed the
rape an' I never saw rape nor nane.

6   As lang's there's herrin' in Loch Fyne
    I'll ne'er wint kitchy fan' I dine
    An' henceforth bid adieu to swine
    O' nae sic gear the price I'll spier
    Nor stan' the sneerin' tauntin gear
    That I fae neighbours drew man.

(Spoken)   The callants said the warst o't. They wad hae been comin'
cheeklin' roon the neuk o' the hoose cryin' "Hie Tam Broon, faur's
your sou man?" Could I be thocht tae stan' that?

Source unrecorded — G

JOHN FOX

1   There lives a man into this place,
      John Fox it is his name;
      And o' a' the ill deen hereaboot
      John Fox he gets the blame.

2   He gaed to Mill o' Tyrie,
      Thinkin' to catch a hen;
      But he has faun intil a trap
      Contrived by wily men.

3   Then oot there spak' ane o' them,
      We'll use the law most strict;
      We'll hae him up to Strichen Hoose,
      Weel tied up in a sack.

4   Then oot there spak' anither o' them,
      There's nae eese for that ava;
      We'll hae him up to Tyrie —
      We hae the civil law.

5   But since it's so that I maun die
      Without either court or session,
      I pray haud aff your bloody hands
      Till I make my confession. —

6   My father frae his infancy
      He was a common thief,
      And he left me this foul napkin
      This day to dicht my teeth.

7   I was mairriet tull a lustich wife   [lusty
      Was ill to please o' diet;
      I never hid her countenance
      But fin she lived in riot.

8   I never hid her countenance
      Fin I gaed empty hame,
      But fin she saw I hidna sped
      She bade me swith begone.   [immediately

9   She never wi'd eat anything
      That ever cam' o' meal,
      But fat lambs, and feather or flesh —
      Inducing me to steal.

10   I gaed to Mill o' Boyndlie
      Thinkin' to catch a ewe,
      But she lap in at Katie's door
      And there I lost my clue.

11   I gaed to Sawney Riddle,
      The carlie o' the hill,
      I took frae him twa gweed fat lambs,
      I did him nae mair ill.

12   I ate a lamb and a half
      Unto my mornin' feast,
      I left till him but the hips o' ane
      His ain fat lamb to taste.

13   I gaed to Mill o' Tyrie,
      Thinkin' to catch a hen,
      But I am catched intil a trap
      Contrived by wily men.

14   All you young lads that are to wed,
      Take warning frae the tod;
      And gin ye marry a lustich wife
      Ye train her wi' the rod.

15   Use her to nae delicacies,
      But sic's becomes your kin;
      And gin Providence upon you smile,
      Increase your diet syne.

Miss BELL ROBERTSON — G

499

FATHER FOX

A

Up, John, Get Up, John

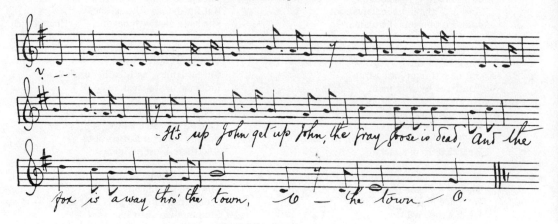

It's up John get up John, the gray goose is dead, And the fox is away thro' the town, O — the town — O.

ARTHUR BARRON – G

B

Up, John, Get Up, John

Up John get up John the gray goose is dead, And the fox is a way thro' the town O, the town O, the town O, And the fox is a way thro' the town O.

Miss M. RITCHIE – G

C

Father Fox

1 As the fox travelled out on a dark wintry night
He prayed that the moon might shine, show him light.

Mrs JAFFRAY – D

302

500

THE HARE'S LAMENT

1   Come all ye poachers far and near
    And to my story pray give ear
    Fa's that to helm ye needna spier
    I'm sure ye hard o' Bashen.

2   Ae night last ook as I went out
    Wi' howmin light I glourt about
    I saw a makin take the rat   [hare; road
    An owre the knowe to Bashon.

3   Goodman said she are you within
    Come to the door, speak to a friend
    To you I'm come to mak my mean
    And bide this nicht wi Bashon.

4   The poachers now are grown so rife
    I'm sure I cannot save my life
    Ere I be shot I'll take a knife
    And end my days wi' Bashon.

5   Ance on a day we didna fear
    Nae dog nor poacher that came near
    Woe's me my sight is nae sae clear
    Have pity on us Bashon.

6   Auld Mause you'r like myself I true
    Ye'r grown right gray about the mous
    And we live lang we'll be sae to
    We'll live and die in Bashon.

7   Make haste and gie consent right seen
    Or roun the know we will convin
    May nae in the moss be in the moss be seen
    Ye bads come all to Bashon.   [hares

8   Nae sand nor war ye needna drive
    We'll toath your young and mak them thrive
    For meat we'll round the country drive
    And come home to Bashon.

9   That fatal day the moss ye crossed
    And chased the poachers to their cost
    Other nor you my life I had lost
    My blessings on you Bashon.

10 My heart was glad to see them rin
    O man they made a devilish din
    Through hills and bogs unto the chin
    And aye they cursed at Bashon.

11 My heart was sair ye needna doubt
    When through the moss they did set out
    Wi an auld plough shilt tied in a cloit [for "stilt"; cloth
    To shut the bodie Bashon.

12 But ye maun thole their jeer and mock
    Wi three gray peats intil a pock   [sack
    Ye thocht it was three of the flock
    But here we are Bashon.

13 Nae doubt auld Mouse we eat the kale
    Sometimes blink the wivies' ale   [bewitch
    Or maybe drives the milking pail
    But a comes to Bashon.

14 Ye hae faults yourself ye ken
    Sometimes ye pay to pounds for ane
    Or swear fouse o a the yoursel to screen
    It maks nae ods to Bashon.

15 I'm sure I never told to ane
    When peats and on sneeshin ye did conven
    Or birns of corn and bear at even   [loads
    Aye true to Bashon.

16 Your only sister fye for shame
    They shot him for I daur name
    But if I kent the rogue to blame
    I wad go and tell to Bashon.

17 Tho Mouse they need not try sic fun
    Wanting siller in their gun
    They might think well ruff upon a dram
    Or shot at in Pat Bashon.   [beat upon a drum

18 Go to the poachers' court outright
    Get mouse black sark round you tight
    Or gin they come to swear you right
    The guise is won wi' Bashon.

19 Ye'll be well paid a twenty pounds
    For information ye maun own
    All the more come ner gint wer stain
    It maks nae odds to Bashon.

20 Our ancient freedom now restored
    We'll dance and sing and lout for sport   [bow
    And scour the braes of all resort
    And aye cam hame to Bashon.

21 We'll have our friend all in the drift
    Dobin Caperfry and Thrift
    Auld Mouse as lightsome in the drift   [carefree
    Any aye come hame to Bashon.

22 Long may you live in healthful guid
    To keep the poachers all in dread
    Ye have been a friendly indeed
    My blessings on you Bashon.

23 Long may you live and when you are dead
Nae shiel nor spade shall hap your head
But nine feet deep of makins guid
A monument to Bashon.

24 He did it trick until a wife
I wadna tell it for my life
Until her breast he held . . .
And ripe the poacher Bashon.   [search

25 I'll take your ain hen from the rest
An nae three pets to make it fest
For fear it dinna well digest
Nor leave it but to Bashon.

26 Auld Mother Mouse, our comrade dear
Thi's ben wur Queen this mony a year
To crave our aid she sent me here
And stay this night in Bashon.

27 It's no bads tells that I am to tell
But face to face speak to yourself.
And let the haries bide themsels   [hares
Aneath the knowes of Bashon.

28 O Bashon man with all your might
Ye'll watch the pertorics day and night [partridges
For fare have we to louge this night   [lodge
But in the plains of Bashon.

Source unrecorded — G

FIN WE GANG UP TAE LONDON

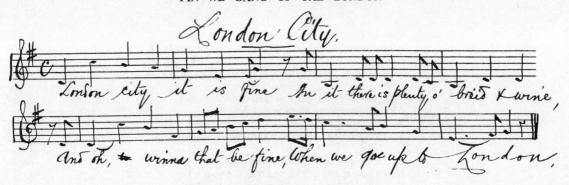

1 The ladies in London say, How do you do?
   Quite well I thank you; how are you?
   Quite well I thank you; how are you,
   Since you came up to London?
       London city it is fine,
       In it there is plenty bread and wine,
       And oh, winna that be fine,
       When we gang up to London?

2 And when the dinner it is o'er,
   The carriage is drawn to the door,
   The coachman he gets on before
   To drive us on thro' London.

3 . . . .
   . . . .
   The mistress paid to her her fee
   And bade her trip to London.

ALEXANDER ROBB — G

502

O JANET BRING ME BEN MY SUNDAY COAT

O Janet Bring Me

1 Oh Janet bring me ben my Sunday coat
   Get a' my hoddens rankit   [ready
   For I'm for London speed of fit
   As sune's my brose is clankit.   [swallowed

2 Ye'll turn up the boddam o' the pot
   Mak ma brogues fu' handy
   For I'm for London speed o' fit
   An' I maun be a dandy.

3 Ye'll bring me ben my cutty pipe
   And a' my snuffy boxes
   I'll break them ere I gang awa'
   They're the father o' the taxes.

4 The nobles o' the Hoose o' Lords
   They're haudin' sic a barkin'
   I think there wud be little ull
   To gie their knobs a jarkin'.

5 The folks will wonder far ye cam fae
   As ye gae up the pave stanes
   Ye'll be lookin' like mortality
   Come out amon' the grave stanes.

GEORGE SHEARER — G

THE BERWICK FREEMAN

1   Here sit I! an old freeman of sixty odd years,
    All my sorrows and joys, all my smiles, all my tears,
    Are bound up with Berwick that old Border town
    Which stands first on the page of Albion's renown.

2   Which of all other spots in the country can say
    Alone independent she stands here today
    She's a nation herself for pray you take heed
    Tis Great Britain and Ireland and Berwick on Tweed.

3   In the days when contention was rife in the land
    How the wave of war surged o'er the spot where we stand!
    How the red blood would course and the dark eyes would gleam
    When Berwick was ever the warrior's dream.

4   But back from the walls the opposing hosts hurled
    She's emerged with a fame that stands first in the world
    You talk about England and Scotland indeed
    'Tis Great Britain and Ireland and Berwick on Tweed.

5   I adore the old town that in centuries past
    Has withstood the rude shock of war's deadliest blast
    Has seen the kings and court beauties in panoplied seats
    While the tramp of mailed thousands has rung through her streets.

6   And now that these days of her glory are o'er
    Shall her children be free as her children of yore
    Aye, as long as her sons live, her bounds round to lead
    Say Great Britain and Ireland and Berwick on Tweed.

7   Come pledge me a glass to my dear native town
    With a long hearty cheer, let it find its way down
    Long may old Berwick flourish, and growl her old bear
    If to touch with her rights any fause loon should dare.

8   Let's drink to her trade, and replenish anew
    To her sons and her daughters so lovely to view
    Come fill to the brim and sing out the God speed
    To Great Britain and Ireland and Berwick on Tweed.

JONATHAN GAULD — G

THE HILLS O' GALLOWA'

A

The Hills of Gallowa'

1 Among the birks sae blythe and gay I met my lassie hameward gaun
   The linties chantit on the lea, the lammies loupit ower the lea
   In ilka howe the sward was mawin', the braes wi' gowans buskit braw   [being mowed
   The gloamin' plaid o' nicht was thrawn oot ower the hills o' Gallowa'.

2 Wi music wild the woodlands rang, and fragrance winged along the lea
   As doon we sat the woods amang, upon the banks o' stately Dee.
   My lassie's arms encircled me and softly slid the hours awa'
   Till dawnin' coost a glimmerin' e'e ootower the hills o' Gallowa'.

3 "It isna owsen, sheep nor kye, it isna gowd it isna gear,
   This lifted e'e wad hae," quo' I, "the world's drumly gloom tae cheer,   [troubled
   But gie to me my lassie dear, ye powers wha row this earthen ba',
   And oh sae blythe's through life I'll steer amang the hills o' Gallowa'.

4 "When gloamin' danders up the hills, and oor guidman ca's hame the yowes
   Wi' her I'll tread the mossy rills ootower the muir meandering rows,
   An' oot among the scroggy knowes, my birchen pipe I'll sweetly blaw
   I'll sing the straits, the straths, the streams, the hills and dales o' Gallowa'.

5 "And when Auld Scotia's heathy hills, her rural nymphs and jovial swains,
   Her flowery wilds and wimpling rills nae mair awakening canty strains
   Where friendship dwells and freedom reigns, where heather blooms and muircocks craw,
   Oh bury me and hide my banes, amang the hills o' Gallowa'."

GEORGE F. DUNCAN — D

B

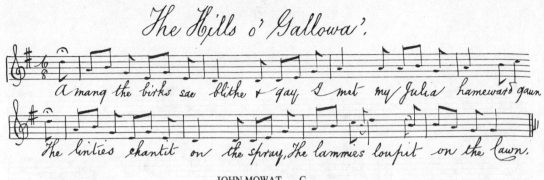

JOHN MOWAT – G

505

THE LAND OF THE WEST

1　O come to the west love O come there with me
　　Tis a sweet land of verdure that springs from the sea
　　Where fair plenty smiles from its emerald shore
　　O come to the west and I'll make you mine own.

2　I'll gaurd you and shield you and love you the best
　　And you'll say there's nae land like the land o the west
　　The south has its roses its bright skies and blue
　　But ours are resplendant with love's own changeful hue.

3　Half sunshine half tears like the girl I love best
　　Oh what is the south to the beautiful west
　　Oh come there with me and the rose on thy mouth
　　Will be sweeter to me than the flowers of the south.

4　The north has its mountains of dazzling array
　　All sparkling with gems in the near setting day
　　Thare the storm king may dwell in the halls he loves best
　　But the soft breathing zephyr he plays in the west.

5　Then come to the west where no cold winds doth blow
　　And thy neck will seem fairer to me than the snow
　　The sun in his gorgeous beams chaseth the night
　　As he rises refreshed in his beauty and might.

6　But where does he go when he seeks his sweet rest
　　Oh where does he go but the beautiful west
　　Then come there with me tis the land I love best
　　This land of my sires tis my own darling west.

Mrs MARGARET GILLESPIE – D

308

HAININ'S WAAL

1 O' a' the drinks that ere I saw
   Liquor or wine or usquebaugh   [whisky
   I ken o' een that's worth them a'
   A wauchtie oot o' Hainin'.

2 Half wye upwuth to Corskie's croon
   Yon stoddert in amo' the broom   [area of green grass
   It's there the caller strype comes doon   [stream
   Sweet trinklin' doon fae Hainin.

3 Its vera gurglin charms the air
   It gars the girse growe bonnie there   [grass
   Though royal purple everywhere
   It's aye pure green at Hainin.

4 I've watched the sheeters on the Twalt
   Aye at the Quarries call a halt
   Tell Gemmie to unpack the shalt
   An' spread their lunch at Hainin.

5 The beastie kens 't as weel as they
   An' taks his full upon the brae
   If he could speak I'm sure he'd say
   "The girse is sweet at Hainin!"

6 The wandrer from his native soil
   Who goeth forth for leave to toil
   Oft finds his inmost thoughts recoil
   And fondly cling round Hainin.

7 In fancy he beholds the spring
   Where lads an' lasses used to sing
   An' mak the vera sklate steens ring
   Wi' hyse o' fun at Hainin.   [height

8 His ardent thoughts awake desire
   To view again his native shire
   And quench his burning homesick fire
   Wi' copious draughts from Hainin.

9 Come then ye lads an' lasses come!
   The bees amo' the heather hum;
   That's Russell's fiddle hark the bum!
   We'll hae a fling at Hainin.

10 An' fan we teyre, sit doon an' sing
   The praises o' this glorious spring
   Nae finer gift can Nature bring —
   O leeze me on thee Hainin.

F. GILRUTH — G

THE HILL O' CALLIVAR

It's noo I'm turnin' auld & my hair is growin' gray, My legs is gettin' feeble I'm sorry for to say, But we will feel out pockets & ca' anither gill, And drink the health o' Scotland yet & Forbes Arms Hotel.

1 If you want to take a walk I'll tell ye where to gang
   Doon by the Brux Brig and as ye gang alang
   Ask her for to be your wife and tak' her at her will
   And tak' her for a ramble on the Callivar Hill.

2 The Hill o' Callivar it is a' clad wi' weeds
   Some pluckin' blaeberries and ithers rollin' stanes.
   The cryin' o' the cuckoo and the roarin' o' the bull
   Wad mak' your heart contented on the Braes o' Callivar.

3 It's noo I'm turnin' auld, my hair is turnin' gray,
   My legs is gettin' feeble I'm sorry for to say;
   But we'll feel our pockets and ca' anither gill
   And drink the health o' Scotland yet and Forbes Arms Hotel.

T. ROGER – G

508

LOCHNAGAR

1 Around Lochnagar where the stormy mists gather,
   Winter presides in his cold icy car;
   Clouds there encircle the forms of my fathers
   That dwell amidst the tempests of dark Lochnagar.

GEORGE GARIOCH – D

MOUNTBLAIRY

1   Mountblairy, oh Mountblairy thy woods and walks are green
Shall ever haunt my memory in many a happy scene
Thy pleasant scenes in after years I'll lovingly review
Mayhap, oh dear Mountblairy when I am far from you.

2   Thy whispering leaves upon the trees can tell a tale I ween
But keep thee ever silent, as silent as you've been
And I will ever love you as time doth softly slide
Mountblairy sweet Mountblairy by bonnie Deveron side.

Correspondent in Stirlinghill — G

510

MONQUHITTER'S LONELY HILL

1   I love Monquhitter's lonely hills
Where waves the purple heather bells
And where the muircock claps his wings
Sae joyfully the lintie sings.

2   In quiet Monquhitter I was born
Ilka neuk o' it I ken
Fra Hattons to Balthangie's burn
Fra Greens, tae Tillymaul's lang glen.

3   The woods and waters o' Auchry
Are bonnie in the simmer time
It is a scene to charm the eye
When trees and flowers are in their prime.

4   Among the trees there is a spot
The loveliest of a' the lot
Sweet, sunny cosy mull a' Pot
Where flowers and virtue never fails.

5   When the gloamin lingers lang
Pleasant there to take a turn
To hear the birdies' evening sang
And see the trouts lap in the burn.

Source unrecorded — G

THE TARLAND LAWS

1 Was ye as far as a' Cromar
Or did our country see man?
We a' do like the truth to speak
Upo' the banks o' Dee man.

2 There's lasses braw baith neat and sma'
So merry brisk and gay man
There's hearty boys that face their foes
An' joyful companies man.

3 Our fertile fields good corn yields
The country roun' to serve man
It's nae Cromar baith near nor far
Will ever beg or starve man.

4 The mountains high which round it lie
Keep aff the stormy win's man
While down below sweet riv'lets flow
Through valleys of all kinds man.

5 So we'll go on to Tarland toon
That joyful place to view man
A weekly fair ye will find there
An' markets not a few man.

6 Ye'll find as good as e'er drew blood
To fight in Tarland toon, man,
Knocks doon their foes wi' hardy blows
An' nobly cracks their croons, man.

7 Doon frae Strathdon ye needna come
To brag nor boast Cromar, man,
Nor Towieside for a' yer pride
For Tarland winna scare man.

8 Ye Locheol Bains may keep your glens
Among your frost an' snaw man
Gin ye come here we'll gie ye cheer
An' chase ye far awa man.

9 Your Deeside boys mak' little noise
They ken oor Tarland laws, man,
An' needna come to brag Cromar
For clubs an' shak' a-fa' man.

10 So let us sing till Sol does spring
On Morven's top so high, man,
An' let us sing till Tarland ring
The praise o' this countrie, man.

11 We'll drink success to George's race
An' to loyal subjects a' man,
To heritors and governors
An' rulers o' the law, man.

12 To farmers a' baith great an' sma
To lads an' lasses braw, man,
Lang may we sing this merry thing
That Tarland wins ye a' man.

JONATHAN GAULD — G

THE BODIES O' THE LYNE O' SKENE

1   Ye powers o' rhyme gie me a lift to string thegither twa'r three line,
About some frien's that I hae here that's lang been guid to me and mine;
Gie me the power to raise a lilt, to show my thoughts and feelings keen,
Wi' gratefu' glee I fain wad sing, the bodies o' the Lyne o' Skene.
    Auld farran canty bodies, better never hae I seen;
    Auld farran canty bodies, dwals into the Lyne o' Skene.

2   Frae Castle Fraser tae Braid Straik I've drawn mony a shinnin' groat;
Kintore and Echt hae aften help'd to brighten up my gloomy lot.
The twa Afflochs, the Terryvales, the bonnie Newton, an' Greystane
May well come ben — they're brithers to the bodies o' the Lyne o' Skene.

3   There's Lauchintilly an' Scrapehard, the blessings of the puir hae won;
An' better folk ye winna get than Drumnaheath and Tillybin —
The Letter gars my spirits glow. In Wardis I fin aye a frien',
An Breamy, kind, may weel compare — wi' bodies o' the Lyne o' Skene.

4   The gardener lads I canna pass, for deeds o' kindness never slack —
Baith auld an' young hae aften help'd to fill my purse an' teem my pack.
The auldest frien' that I hae here, wi' heart like steel, sae true and keen,
Lang may he live to crack and joke wi' bodies o' the Lyne o' Skene.

5   For Craigiedarg, I'll ne'er forget, wi' kindly welcome sets you down —
An' Bervie, Corskie, Waterton shall mingle in my hamely tune.
Back Ward, Blue Park, the merchant's folk, hae ever kind and cantie been —
An' lang may Marshal's humour please the bodies o' the Lyne o' Skene.

6   There's tailors, souters, wrights, an' smiths, like brithers kind hae been to me,
And lealer hearts ye widna fin 'atween the banks o' Don and Dee.
The Fornets gran' I maun bring in 'afore my ravel't rhyme be deen,
An cottage bodies warm my heart like bodies o' the Lyne o' Skene.

7   When frosty fogs bedim the moss, an' little Robin's nearly dumb —
Or storms drive o'er frae Wardis braes, an' roar like thunder o'er the lum;
The tempests sweep the leafless woods, and bend an' brak the firs sae green,
Yet cosh and cosie here I sit 'mang bodies o' the Lyne o' Skene.

8   May health and peace their steps attend, and plenty ever swell their store —
And friendship true and love's warm glow spring in their heart for evermore;
May a' their hopes wi' joy be crown'd, may sorrow never dim their e'en —
The open-handed, kindly-hearted bodies o' the Lyne o' Skene.

9   May corn an' cattle ever thrive, an' kirns an' girnals ne'er gae deen,
An' layin' hens and heavy calves, an' kebbucks like the harvest meen,
An' taty pits like giants' graves, an' kail an' clover ever green,
An' buckin' stacks and towerin' rucks, be ever in the Lyne o' Skene.   [leaning

Source unrecorded — D

AUL' MELDRUM TOON

Oh Cruel

1   Oh cruel were my parents that stole my love fae me
    And cruel was the big big ship, that took him to the sea
    But bonnie was the little boat that brocht him fae his foes
    Though the colour a' had left his cheek and settled on his nose.
      Singin Tooral ooral ooral addie, tooral ooral ae.

2   As we baith cam doon fae Foggielon and in the road by Turra
    We landed at Almeldrum toon, I ocht tae ca't a burra   [ought; burgh
    They're aften scarce o' water there, bit at the still upby
    The ewie wi' the crookit horn never yet ran dry.

3   It's a patriotic tory toon, wi' drams and ither fairin'
    But ay the wye of five o'clock the fizz o' roastin' herrin'
    For salmon, pertrick, grouse or snipe, they hinna muckle favour
    We think a Glesga magistrate wad beat them a' for flavour.

4   Syne in the road there stans a brig faur ance there was a fordie
    And there you'll see a notice stickin' up upon a boordie
    It means the brig is auld and frail and very far fae stoot
    And a loaded engine jist maun gang some ither way aboot.

5   I wish they'd yoke and big thae brigs a little thochty better
    They'll be stoppin neist a bairnie wi' its little perambulator
    The Coonty Cooncil's afa doon on trespasses and sins
    They mith lat ower a bairn but troth ye needna try wi' twins.

JAMES MORRISON — G

THE DEN O' AULDBAR

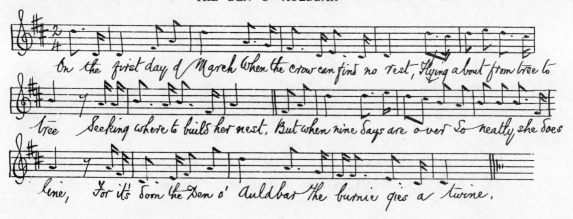

1 On the first day of March when the crow can find no rest,
   Flying about from tree to tree seeking where to build her nest.
   But when nine days are over so neatly she does line,
   For it's doon the Den o' Auldbar the burnie gies a twine.

Rev. JOHN CALDER — G

515

PETERHEAD

1 A busy town was Peterhead
   And work for high and low
   And all was bright from morn till night
   In the days of long ago.

2 The lasses sang from morn till eve
   As loons worked to and fro
   Wages were sure to help the poor
   In the days of long ago.

3 The big ships sailed to catch the whale
   Midst Greenland's ice and snow
   And all were glad, high hopes they had
   In the days of long ago.

4 And when the ships cam home again
   And money bright did flow
   And not a care had any share
   In the days of long ago.

5 The fishermen went out to sea
   And hearty did they row
   No trawlers' beams disturbed their dreams
   In the days of long ago.

6 The mothers sang while babies slept
   "Weel may the boatie row"
   Liners and drifters were unknown
   In the days of long ago.

7 But brave hearts never did give in
   Whatever come and go
   And Peterhead will flourish still
   As in the days of long ago.

J. LEASK — G

516

O CANNY AN' CUTE MEN YE'LL MEET BY THE DEE

1   O canny an' cute men ye'll meet by the Dee
An brave men an' blythe men on Don there may be
But the lads o' auld Ythin o'er a' bear the gree
An the blythest are they that lives nearest the sea.

JOHN MILNE — G

517

O UGIE THO NAE CLASSIC STREAM

1   O Ugie tho nae classic stream
Nae far-famed poet's chosen theme
Though art the licht o' mony a dream
O'er lan an sea
In hearts aft lichted by a gleam
At thought o' thee.

2   Flow on thou bonnie wimplin tide
Though thou hast nane to gar thee glide
Amang the rivers sung wi' pride
To classic ear
They sterling beauties winna hide
They sparkle here.

JOHN MILNE — G

ROTHIEMAY

1   As Deveron rows its waves alang to meet the briny sea
     It sweeps past many a rugged hill and twines through many a lea
     Tho' fair are aft the varied scenes through which it wends its way
     It mirrors back nae fairer spot than bonnie Rothiemay.

2   When Spring tells Winter's weary woods to don their vernal dress
     And bring a sunny smile aince mair to brichten nature's face
     Then gaily on the flowerie banks the lichtsome lammies play
     Oh fresh and sweet seems a'thing then in bonnie Rothiemay.

3   The summer brings a wealth o' flowers an' skies sae blue and fair
     And bounteous autumn seldom fails to scatter plenty there
     And when the winter's icy gems are deckin' ilka spray
     There is nae lack o' loveliness in bonnie Rothiemay.

4   The Millton nestles mang the trees beside the singing stream
     Where ane would think that life should pass as calm as some sweet dream
     The kirk is near an' by its wa's a fair kirkyard they hae
     God's acre is nae wildness in bonnie Rothiemay.

5   The "Hoose" uprears its stately wa's amang the woods sae green
     We're tauld lang syne it shelter lent tae Scotia's fairest queen
     Wha's reign was wrecked by party strife and mony a bloody fray
     I wonder what Queen Mary thocht o' bonnie Rothiemay.

6   The room she used can yet be seen an' strange it seemed tae me
     To gaze fae oot the window there on river field and tree
     An' think perchance here Mary stood in a' her grand array
     And mused upon the loveliness o' bonnie Rothiemay.

7   'Tis dear to me that lovely spot for it was there I spent
     My happy careless childish days sae fu' o' sweet content
     By Deveron side I gaed to school, a bairnie, licht and gay,
     And nature's beauty thrilled me first in bonnie Rothiemay.

8   Oh swiftly past the lesson 'oors an' mony a romping game
     We played in evenin's calm as we a merry band trooped hame
     Fu proud to courtsey if we met the leddy on the way
     Wha aye showed kindness tae the bairns in bonnie Rothiemay.

9   Noo merry playmates like mysel' hae places taen in life
     Some mang the country's rural scenes some in the city's strife
     But leal true hearts whaure'er they be maun fond remembrance hae
     O' happy days of childhood spent in bonnie Rothiemay.

10 There's ane I lo'ed o'er a' the rest, my brother dear tae me
     Tho lang sy[n]e he was ta'en awa he'll ne'er forgotten be
     Oh weel I mind the April morn when still in death he lay
     And I kent first what sorrow meant in bonnie Rothiemay.

11 I whiles thinks hoo it micht hae been had he been livin' noo'
     Ah! manhood wid hae brocht its cares to mar yon sunny brow
     Far better kent the Father wise who didna lat him stay
     But took him to a sinless place fae bonnie Rothiemay.

Song No. 518

12 The years they hinna idle been but workin change on change
    The bairnies in the village school tae me wid a' be strange
    But this I ken whaure'er I roam till memory's powers decay
    My heart will treasure thochts o' youth an' bonnie Rothiemay.

Correspondent in Stirlinghill — G

519

THE GIRLS O' AIBERDEEN

1 My muse sae thrawart mony a day,   [perverse
   Soars blyth on lichtsome wing again;
   Inspired by her I'd fain essay
   To sing aince mair a hamely strain.
   But wha or what my theme shall be,
   I scarce can tell nor can ye ween;
   I'll sing the flowers o' Don and Dee,
   The charming girls o' Aiberdeen.

2 In merry England's sunny clime,
   The girls are unco fair and braw,
   And, basking in their smiles, the time
   I gaily gladly wile awa.
   But, tho' they're braw and bonnie too,
   The Scottish lasses ding them clean
   And far aboon them a' I lo'e
   The charming girls o' Aiberdeen.

3 I loe the lasses ane and a',
   O' ilka country and degree;
   But nane can wile my wits awa',
   Dear girls o' Aiberdeen, like ye.
   My heart ye've stolen, — and kept it too, —
   Thieves, — can ye hope to be forgi'en?
   Alas! ye hae't amang ye noo,
   Ye charming girls o' Aiberdeen.

4 "The Lasses a'!" — I fill my cup
   Wi' guid red wine a glorious draught,
   And freely, blythely, drink it up,
   And to this toast it shall be quaffed:
   "Here's to ilk ane that's woman named
   From lowly lass to crownèd queen,
   Gentle or simple, syb or framed,
   But chief, the girls o' Aiberdeen.

A. H. DUNCAN — G

THE TOON O' ARBROATH

A

The Toon o' Arbroath.

Altho' far awa' frae my ain native heather, An' thoosans o' miles across the blue Sea,

At night when I'm wearied my heart likes to wander To the scenes of my boyhood sae dear unto me.

Ref.
(Same music)

Here's to the sons o' dear auld St. Thomas,
The lasses sae bonnie, sae blythe aye and free,
The auld Abbey ruins, the cliffs and the commons,
The Toon o' Arbroath will be aye dear to me.

Mrs PARLEY — G

B

The Town o' Arbroath

1   It's although far away from my own native heather
And thousands o' miles across the blue seas
At night when I am weary, my mind likes to wander
To scenes of my boyhood, sae dear unto me.
Near the town of Arbroath is my hame and my birth-place
It was there when at school wi' the rest o' the boys
When our lessons were over we played till the gloamin'
It was there I first tasted my life's sweetest joys.
    Then here's to the sons o' dear auld St Tamas
    The lassie sae bonnie, sae blythe and sae free
    The auld abbey ruins, the cliffs and the commons
    The town o' Arbroath will be aye dear to me.

2   It was there where my father and mither baith taught me
To act fair and honest, and to be kindly and free
And to mind there's an eye that watches aboon me
An' sees a' oor actions, wherever we be
It was there I first wooed my ain bonny Mary
Her cheeks like the roses sae lovely and glow
I proposed, she consented, wi' a kiss then we sealed it
Adoon Sittin's e'en where thy burnie doth flow.

3 It's although far away frae my ain native heather
  And thousands o' miles frae my ain native shore
  I am like a true Scotchman nae wash ever fears me
  And now I can boast I hae wealth in galore.
  Wi' the next ship that sails, I will sail for auld Scotland
  And live in the hame that I left lang ago
  And when life's journey's over then I'll die contented
  And sleep my last sleep neath the auld Abbey ruins.

Source unrecorded — G

C

Town o' Arbroath

1 Although far away frae my own native heather
  Thousands of miles across the deep sea
  At night when a-weary my mind loves to wander
  To the days of my childhood so dear unto me.
  The town o' Arbroath is my hame and my birthplace
  It was there I was schooled among the rest of the boys
  And when lessons were over we played till the gloaming
  It was there that I tasted my life's sweetest joys.
   Then here's to the sons of the dear auld St Thomas
   The lassies sae comely, sae frank and sae free
   The auld abbey ruins, the cliffs and the commons
   The toun o' Arbroath will be aye dear to me.

2 It was there that my faither and mither retaught me
  To deal honest and fair, to be upright and free
  And ne'er to forget that there's aye Ane abeen me
  To watch o'er my actions where'er I may be.
  It was there that I courted my ain bonnie Mary
  Her cheeks like the rose and her skin like the snaw.
  I proposed, she consented, we kissed, and we cancelled
  Down by Saten's den where the burnie doth flow.

3 I've lived like an exile since I left auld St Thomas
  I've toiled day and night on a far distant shore
  But like a true Scotchman, my work never failed me
  And now I can boast, I've got riches galore.
  But the next ship that sails I'll go to auld Scotland
  Back to the hame I left long ago
  And when life's journey's over, I'll die there contented
  And sleep the lang sleep neath the auld Abbey ruins.

JAMES M. TAYLOR — G

MY HEART'S IN THE HIGHLANDS

1 My heart's in the highlands my heart is nae here
   My heart's in the highlands a-chasing the deer
   Chasing the wild deer and following the roe
   My heart's in the highlands where ever I go.

2 Farewell to the highlands farewell to the north
   The birthplace o' valour the country of worth
   Where ever I wander where ever I rove
   The hills of the highlands for ever I love.

3 Farewell to the mountains high covered with snow
   Farewell to the straths and green valleys below
   Farewell to the forests and wild hanging woods
   Farewell to the torrents and loud pouring floods.

4 My heart's in the highlands my heart is n'ae here
   My heart's in the highlands a-chasing the deer
   Chasing the wild deer and following the roe
   My heart's in the highlands where ever I go.

Mrs MARGARET GILLESPIE — D

THE HIGHLANDS! THE HIGHLANDS!

My Heart's in the Highlands

1 The Highlands! the Highlands! my whole bosom swells
   To think on the streams rushing down the deep dells.

2 Though bleak be your clime and though scanty your fare
   My heart's in the Highlands, oh! gin I waur there!

3 The Highlands far up yon deep glen
   There's a cosy wee cot wi' a but and a ben,
   There's a deece by the door and my auld mither's there
   Croonin', "Haste ye back, Donald, to leave us nae mair."

Miss BELL ROBERTSON — G

523

MY NATIVE HAME

1 Far far frae thee my native hame across the mountains high
   I canna see the heather hills and glens I used to spy
   But I am blessed wi' memory sweet while fancy fondly strays
   To where the Ythan water rins mang Fyvie's woods and braes.

2 Oh I would like to tread once mair amang the hazel trees
   To rove through Fyvie's woods so fair, inhale the fragrant breeze
   For there, I strayed and wild flowers pu'd in youth's bright early days
   Where smooth the Ythan water rins by yon sweet woodland braes.

3 No black coal pits in my dear land but air aye pure and clear
   Where flowers bedeck on every hand the weary hearts to cheer.
   Where birds salute the spreading birches and warble o'er their lays
   Rejoicing where the Ythan rins through my dear native braes.

Souce unrecorded — G

THE BONNETS O' BLUE

1   I'll sing ye a sang in praise o that land
    Whaur the snaw never melts on her mountains sae grand.
    Whaur the sweet purple heather it covers the bens
    And the thistle grows green in her valleys and glens.
    I'll sing o' that hardy intelligent race
    Wha's valorous deeds time can never efface
    And wha's sires the Romans could never subdue
    I'll sing o' the lads wi the bonnets o' blue.
       Then Hurrah for the tarten the kilt and the plaid
       Then Hurrah for the claymore they wear by their side
       And Hurrah for the hearts aye sae trusty and true
       Success tae the lads wi the bonnets o blue.

2   Wha hasna heard o' the year forty five
    When Charlie for Scotland sae nobly did strive
    And wha hasna sighed for the heroes sae brave
    Wha fought at Culloden a glorious grave
    Their thoosands they offered for Charlie's fair heid
    But they werna the men for the dastardy deed
    They might torture them hang them starve them tis true
    But nae traitors were there mang the bonnets o blue.

3   Ye'll hae heard hoo in Egypt Napoleon the great
    Turned oor brave army on as he thought to their fate
    And hoo fairly bewildered he gazed when he saw
    The gallant advance o' the brave Forty Twa
    And o' hoo that his boasted Invincible corps
    Turned tail at the glint o each gleamin claymore
    And o hoo his auld guardsmen at famed Waterloo
    They ran frae the charge o' the bonnets o blue.

4   Swift was the terrible march o the Gael
    The men wha were never known to fail.
    Hard was the stroke o each trusty claymore
    When relieving Lucknow or avenging Cawnpore.
    King Edward kens aye, kens braw and weel
    That his ain kilty lads are as true as their steel
    And whenever there's dangerous work for to do
    He sends for the lads wi the bonnets o blue.

D.R. McKENZIE — G

THE LAND O' CAKES

1 The land o' cakes, the land o' cakes, mony's the blessing on it;
  Fair fa' the land o' hills and lakes, the bagpipe and the bonnet.
  The country o' the kilted clans, wha cowed the Dane and Roman,
  Wha's sons hae aye the heart an' han' to welcome friends and foemen.
  Then swell the sang, baith lood and lang, till the hills like aspens quiver,
  And fill it up, and toast the cup, "The land o' cakes for ever."

2 Be scorned the Scot within whose breast nae patriot flame is burning,
  Wha kens nae pain frae hame to part, nae joys at back returning.
  For him nae love on earth doth yearn, nae tears in death deplore him;
  He'll hae nae cronach cry nor cairn, wha scorns the land that bore him.

3 While flows the quaich within her glens, and in the halls the glasses,
  We'll toast auld Scotland's honest men, thrice owre her bonny lasses.
  And deep we'll drink to king and kerk, our country and our freedom;
  We've broad claymore and highland dirk, aye ready when we need them.

WILLIAM WALLACE — D

BANNOCKS O' BARLEY MEAL

A

Bannocks o' Barley

To the tune of *The Lass o' Glenshee* from John Duncan

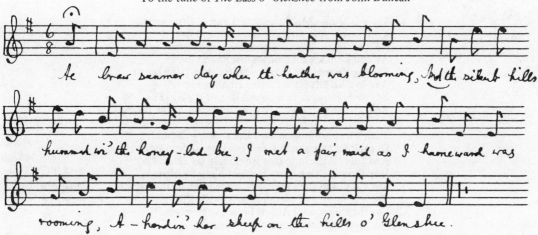

1 An auld Hieland couple sat dune by the ingle,
   While smokin' their cutties an' crackin' awa;
   They spak' o' lang syne, o' their daffin' when single,
   O' the freaks o' their childhood, their auld age, an' a'.

Mrs MARGARET GILLESPIE — D

B

Bannocks o' Barley Meal

1 An auld Hielan' couple sat late by the ingle,
   While smokin' their cutties and crackin' awa',
   They spak' o' langsyne, o' their daffin' when single
   O' the tricks o' their youth, o' their auld age and a'.
   And Donald he braggit o' his bravest o' actions
   When he was a sodger wi' Geordie the Third,
   Hoo his faes fell before him the leader o' actions
   And Donald he grat while his faes bit the yird.
   Sae up wi' your kilties and bonnie blue bonnets,
   Wha when put to their mettle were ne'er kent to fail,
   For a Hielanman's hert is upheld wi' a haggis
   Ay, and weel-buttered bannocks o' barley meal.

2 For Donald an' 's wifie in their broom-covered dwellin'
   Stood far frae the warld its troubles and toils
   My country, he cried, is my hert's dearest treasure
   And Mary thou'rt neist for I lo'e thy saft smiles.
   In the mids o' the moor 'mang the bracken and heather
   Sae far frae the warld its troubles and cares
   The news never entered the snug little dwellin'
   Unless when a packman stept in wi' his wares.

3   The Romans langsyne tried a claucht at oor bannocks   [clutch
The Normans and Danes they tried the same game,
But Donald cam' doon wi' his claymore and crimock
Mauled the maist o' them stark, fleyed the rest o' them hame.
And gin ere they again wad jist try sic a pliskie
She swore by the dirk and the Laird o' Kintail
That she'd pairt wi' her bluid and pairt wi' her whisky
Ay and pairt wi' her bannocks o' barley meal.

4   There is Mungo Macfarlane the Laird o' Drumgarlane
Yon briskie auld carle o' threescore and five
He'll wield his lang airm and gie them a harlin'
Ay and keep his ain grun wi' the glegest alive.
There's Michael the sodger who fought wi' the rebels
And lost his left leg jist a wee ere they ran
But he has got ane o' wud and he gart it play thud
And whenever there's a row Michael's aye in the thrang.

5   Then fill up a bumper, lat's hae a guid waucht o't
Oor mither Meg's mutch be't oor care to keep clean
And foul fa' the loon that would fain lay claucht o't
May Clootie's lang claws haul oot baith his e'en.
She's auld and she's rauchelt, she'll nae bide their scornin', [dilapidated
She will fecht well when put to a battle I'll bail   [guarantee
For she winna want Athole brose in the mornin'
Nor weel-buttered bannocks o' barley meal.

JOHN JAFFRAY — G

527

HIGHLAND HEATHER

1   Some like the red rose, some the white and some the drooping lily
The daisy and forget-me-not may please young maidens silly
But there's a flower abune them a', earth hisna sic anither,
Nae sickly hothouse plant is it but hardy Highland heather.

2   The heather's queen o' mountain flowers, wha ever saw sic anither!
Search roon the world — she beats them a' — the hardy Highland heather!

Miss BELL ROBERTSON — G

THE HIGHLAND LAD

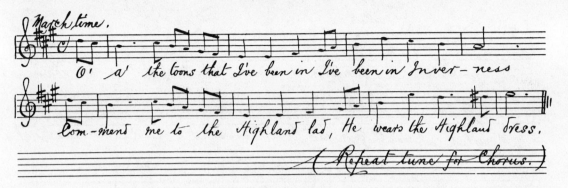

1 O' a' the toons that I've been in
I've been in Inverness
Commend me to the Highland lad
He wears the Highland dress.
    And awa wi' him, awa' wi' him
    And awa' wi' him I'll go
    I'll follow up my Highland lad
    His knees are like the snow.

2 His coat is o' the scarlet
His philabeg is green
Wi' sky-blue ribbons on his head
And ribbons till his e'en.

Miss LIZZIE CRIGHTON — G

DUNCAN MACINTOSH

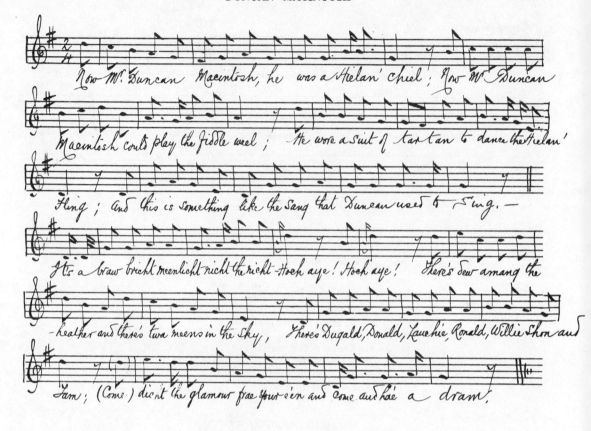

1 Noo Mr Duncan Macintosh, he was a Hielan' chiel
   Noo Mr Duncan Macintosh could play the bagpipes weel
   He wore a suit o' tartan to dance the Hielan' Fling
   And this is something like the sang that Duncan used to sing.
   It's a braw bricht meenlicht nicht, the nicht, oh ay, oh ay,
   There's dew among the heather, there's twa meens in the sky.
   Thus Dougal Donald, Lauggy Ronald Willie Shone and Tam,
   Come dight the glammer off yer kilt and come and hae a dram.

2 Noo Duncan's whiskers they were like, the heather on the braes,
   Duncan fed on tatties, scones, and pottage a' his days
   He liked the lasses well and could dance the Hielan' Fling,
   And when a drap was in his e'e he wid jump aboot and sing.

3 Noo Duncan's gotten a letter frae the Earl o' Aberdeen
   To come and play the bagpipes to His Majesty the King
   And when we reach Balmoral he wid jump aboot and sing
   And His Majesty aboot the place so joyfully did sing.

Mrs CLARK — G

LAUCHIE

A

Lauchie

Her nainsel frae the Hielans cam,
Where many a one had sell't the tram
Her father both herd sheep and lamb
Amongst the Hielant praes man.

But Shentleman a notion took
Oh me, because sae weel I look
And got me teacket the Lowland book
And on me pat praw claes man.

As seen's the Lowland I could speak
And on my knee had gottent a preek
I'll gree wi man who plant the leek
In Lowlands for to work man.

Near han to Glasgow town I'll wrought
And soon a bigger wage me sought
My master rage and wi me fought
Like any Jew and Turk man.

(Spoken) Ho ho! says me you be a very good man, and was told me
you was my master too, but I was told you was a very dam't swinle,
and I was told you that before; — but I will go into Glasgow and the
first one I shall know when I enter the town of Glasgow, pe Allister
Malcolm Voully. Him was a soldier. Him's father keeps the young kye
in our country. "Bless me" said he when he see'd me before, "Lauchie
is this you?" "I" says me "it's me." "When did you see your father
Lauchie?" "O" said me "I seed my father next week." "Did you do any
kind of wrought since you came to town Lauchie?" "Oh yes," says me
"I wrought two weeks in a cabbage kail garner." "Did you travel all the
way Lauchie?" "Oh no" says me "I will come good piece on board a
carrier." "Will you list Lauchie?" "Me wis no carin" says me. "Come
along then."

So now a soldier she was made
And learned to walk in praw parade
She heard a bonnie lady say
She's a braw lad that McSwane's man.

In the rank she always wore
Her ruffled shirt and clean was shaved
Her Major says she's weel behaved
She'll mack a Sergeant fine man.

So now the Sergeant's post she's got
Wi' three strips on the armour coat
It's that the Sergeant does denote
Upon the arm fu praw man.

Her Sergean Major did her teach
A story lang as ony preach
I think it was a cruiting speech
The name they did her ca man.

(Spoken) Come round all you tram heads praw pretty young lads from five to five and a half and to six years old and from thirty to forty feet high. All those that is possessed with a springing spirit and means to shine the army; you will now have the grand oppertunity of entering her Majesty's regiment of forty two Highlandmen, new hame frae the Isle of St Malcolm's in the Western Vengeance, and I will tell you, Shentlemen, that our regiment is commanded by the Hinsiple, Principe, Worshipal, Lord, Duke o' Argyle, King o' the Hielands, and Emperor of all the Europes in Scotland. Now my lads I will not argument any more with you but list if you like and I shall tell you where you shall find me every time. A little ago you shall find neighbour door to a sweep on the one hand, neighbour door to a pal ma cows eating house on the other. If you will no see the great big letters above the door you will see the sow's wing and cow's tail in plates lying in the window. Come up two stairs and there you shall find me, and when you have found me you will have a shilling, a bread and a sheese and two three bottles o' London porter and a new poon egg till petter mates be ready. Where you shall have a calket shoe and a shiny one, a prass buckle to tie her wi', a ruffled shirt, fine black leather neck cloth, and better as a' you shall have a braw new kilt pe far better than going with your legs in pocks all your days. Now my lads I will not argument any more with you, but list if you like and you will get a great pig bounty when you go through the toctor.

> So now she's learned the mans to drill
> To use the sword and musket weel
> Hold up their heids and pe genteel
> And quickly for to traw man.
>
> But some o' them pe awkward prutes
> They gar me raise some angry cruits
> They winna mind their calket foot
> When I maun swear them a' man.

(Spoken) Now my lads you will stand in your raws till I call you all tonicht. Shon Ross, you'r fugul today, you'll come out of the ranks and stood there. Pay contention to your names. Allistir Malcolm Voully. "Amashew." Shon Wright. "Hear Sir." Oh you English prute can you not cry "Amashew" like the rest of our lads? I will put you in the guardman's house tonicht. Neil McKenzie. O Neil, Neil, if I was known you for a leer, I was believe you, but you was in the bad habit of crying "Amashew," whether you was hear or not, for that I will mark you down absent. Now my lads you are to make the grand fire today before your grand sheneral tomorrow, put your right about your left your calket fit formost, shoulder your attention come twa steps to me. That will do fine. Draw your ram rods. O Lauchie McNeil you are no traw at all. Can you no traw that iron stick out o' the preast of your gun and ram it doon her pellie wi' er? I was told you that pefore. Now for the grand pré-sent fire: shoot. O Tougal, Tougal, you are no fugal at all. You shust come out o' the ranks and stood there like a tog. Did you think I was a mice altogether?

[fugleman

> But now McSwane she'll drill no more
> Because you see the wars are o'er
> But should break oot as done before
> There's mony a gallant man still.
>
> That in the continent has fought
> And for their blood their victory bought
> It widna cost herself a thought
> Nor a' her gallant clan man.

JOHN MOWAT — G

B

Macswain

1   Her nainsel fae ta Hielans cam,
    Her mither there she sell't a tram,
    Her father was o'er hoose and lan'
    Amang ta lawlan praes, man.
    She'll herd ta sheep, ta coos an' a'
    Wi' bra claymore an' kilt sae praw,
    Till aff she'll gang through frost an' snaw
    Straucht on to Glasgow toon, man.

2   An when she'll come she'll get some wark
    To build a braw hoose 'mong ta park
    As sure's a gun, her nainsel wark
    Like ony sure Turk, man.

Mrs MARGARET GILLESPIE — D

531

THE HILLS O' TRUMMACH

1   The hills o' Trummach pe ill to clim',
    Pe ill to clim', pe ill to clim',
    The hills o' Trummach pe ill to clim',
    Tre hoey an' tre hoey.

FRANK CHRISTIE — D

THE SONG OF THE EMIGRANT

1   I am lying on a foreign shore and hear the birdies sing
    They speak to me o' auld lang syne an' sunny memories bring
    Oh but to see a weel-kent face or hear a Scottish lay
    As sung in years lang, lang gane by they haunt me nicht and day.

2   My hair ance like the raven's wing — noo mixed wi' siller threads
    Mind me o' ane wha used to sing o' Scotia's valiant deeds
    She sang while I sat at her knee the dear sangs o' lang syne
    Auld Robin Gray and Scots Wha Hae and . . . . sae fine.

3   She sang to me the White Cocade, she sang the Rowan Tree
    There Was a Lad Was Born in Kyle and Bonnie Bessie Lee
    Where is the sang can melt the heart or gar the saut tear fa'
    Like auld Scotch sangs sae dear to me noo that I'm far awa'.

4   I've watched the sun at mornin' rise, strike o'er the lofty blue
    I've watched him yet wi' greedy e'e to whaur he sets again.
    I ken he shines on Scotia's shores tho' far across the seas
    And while I being have I'll sing my native land of thee.

Source unrecorded — G

MY HIELANT HAME

1   Oh for a sprig o' my ain Hielant heather
     That grows wild and free on the tap o' the Ben
     Oh for a crack wi' my father and mither
     In the wee thackit hoosie at the tap o' the glen.

2   Weel dae I mind on the day that we pairted
     I wondered if this was the last I wad see
     O' my faither and mither wha near broken hearted
     Were thinkin' the very same thochts as me.

3   Sair was my thochts when I crossed the wide ocean
     For I had nae friend for to welcome me there
     It's then that ye value a mother's devotion
     When you're far far awa frae her kind love and care.

4   Oh wha could forget the auld folk in the hameland
     Tho' ye may be far frae your ain Hieland glen
     Ye'd miss them when sleepin' as ye wander in dreamland
     Their dear weel-kent faces will come back again.

5   Then oh for a sprig of my ain Hielant heather
     That grows wild and high at the tap o' the glen
     Oh for a crack wi' my father and mither
     In the wee thackit hoose at the tap o' the glen.

JAMES M. TAYLOR — G

THE HIGHLAND SHORE

A

The Highland Shore

1 Ye curious searchers of each narration
   Who can amusement and mirth afford,
   Pray give attention to my relating
   While I sincerely the same record.

2 My youthful days I profusely wasted,
   In hunting, gambling and such pastime
   While women's pleasures I freely tasted
   Which makes me wander thro' foreign clime.

3 When first I parted this blessed region
   And up to London's fair city came
   There I saw madams and crowds of lasses
   Enough to eclipse the rising sun.

4 And I saw madams and crowds of lasses
   And drunken Bacchers they seemed to ring.
   . . . .
   . . . .

5 But do believe me their painted faces
   Are to ensnare us poor wanton slaves
   They hae nae love in their lewd embraces
   And we're all fools to their jilting ways.

6 I spent my money until while it lasted
   Among this gaudy witching train
   And when I saw it was near exhausted
   I slipped to traverse the raging main.

7 A voyage to China was my desire,
   And when the country to me was known
   I thought the country was all on fire
   Such an awful heat in the Torrid Zone.

8 I viewed with raptures of admiration
   Their silver streams and their golden mines
   Their fruitful valleys and rich plantations
   Which nature's beauty so much refines.

9 But had I all the riches of their nation
   I would give it all and as many more
   Once for to taste that sweet sensation
   Which still remains on the Highland shore.

10 Ye madams, Grecians, ye fair Ephesians,
   Your gaudy dresses I do despise,
   Ye Mahommedans, Parthians, and fair Eumod-
   Ye black Chinese and Strateen likewise.   (ians

11 Wi' your surly looks and your greasy faces,
   Dare ye compare ye your tawny hues
   Once to this young and sweet lovely fair one
   Which represents such a one as you.

12 But now I'm crossing the briny ocean
   I'm bound for home if God spares my life
   I'll tell you plainly my settled notion
   My rambling's oer, I'll hae a wife.

13 I'll strive and struggle from exultation
   My native soil to enrich once more
   And by pious works of sweet contemplation
   I'll end my days on the Highland shore.

ALEXANDER ROBB – G

B

Ye Curious Sages

1 Ye curious sages of each narration,
That does amusement and mirth afford,
Pray give attention to my relation
While I sincerely the same record.

2 My golden days I profusely wasted,
In hunting, gaming, and such pastimes,
And other pleasures of which I tasted,
Which made me wander to other climes.

3 I went up to London city
. . . .
. . . .
. . . .

4 There I saw madams in clouds of laces,
Enough to eclipse the rising sun,
With their modest looks and their painted faces,
You would have sworn each was a nun.

5 But their modest looks and their painted faces
Is to ensnare us poor foolish slaves;
There is no love in their false caresses,
But we're all fools to their jilting loves.

6 I spent my fortune while it lasted,
Among the giddy by which it reigns;
And when my money was near exhausted,
I shipped to traverse the swelling mains.

7 A voyage to India was my desire,
And when that clime unto me was known,
The very world seemed all on fire,
There cheatery shines in the Torrid Zone.

8 But all the riches in that nation
I would freely give and thrice as much more
For to taste that sweet recreation
That still remains on the Irish shore.

9 But now I am crossing the briny ocean,
Now bound for home if God spares my life,
And I'll truly tell you my settled notion —
The wars are over, I'll hae a wife.

10 I'll strive and struggle with reformation,
My native soil to enrich once more,
With pious works and sweet contemplation
We'll spend our days on the Irish shore.

Miss BELL ROBERTSON — G

THE LAND O' AMERICA

A

1   You native Scots, and relations all,
     A ploughman's wages is but small,
     I wid advise you ane and a'
     To come to the land of America.

2   There is plenty o' tobacco te smoke and te chaw
     For you in the land o' America.

3   Indian brogues I winna wear,
     Nor yet will I forsake my dear,
     But I'll won gold and buckle braw,
     And I'll come te you te the land o' America.

Mrs WILLOX — G

B
America

1   Yer stinkin' cheese, and yer breid fired raw,
     There's nane o' that in America.

2   The women there they nakit rin,
     They neither learn to card or spin,
     They hae twa short aprons and that is a'
     That the women wear in America.

3   Their lang black hair hangs to their hips,
     Gweed keep us a' oot o' their grips,
     For wi' their teeth they tare us a',
     The Indians o' America.

Miss BELL ROBERTSON — G

C

1   There's plenty o' tobacco and smoke to chew
     Doon in the lands o' America
     And we'll be lairds and ladies a'
     Doon in the lands o' America.

Miss ANNIE SHIRER — G

THE NEW PLANTATION

1   Oh heard ye ever so strange a thing,
      So strange a thing in our nation?
      As that our bonnie laddies are a' gaun awa'
      To plenish the new Plantation.   [stock

2   They sailed up and they sailed down,
      On the tap o' the main ocean,
      Till they saw a level-lyin' lan' —
      They call that their new Plantation.

3   Welcome, welcome ye Scotch lads a'
      Ower the tap o' the main ocean,
      Ye's get fish and ye's get flesh
      And the full food o' oor nation,
      And a bonnie young girlie to cheer ye wi',
      To plenish our new Plantation.

4   They looked to us and we to them,
      We thought them not our fellow,
      Their girlies all we could not love
      Because their skins were yellow.

5   They wore no muslin on their head,
      On their necks they wore no napkin,
      A piece of gold it was beaten broad,
      Was all they had for a napkin.

6   O gin we were home again
      Ower the tap o' the main ocean,
      We sud never come back again
      To plenish their new Plantation.

          Miss BELL ROBERTSON — G

AWA' TAE CYPRUS

A

ARTHUR BARRON — G

B
Awa' Tae Cyprus

1   Oh, I've jist looked in tae see ye, and to bid ye a' guid-bye;
I'm gaun awa' tae a foreign shore, my fortune for to try.
They're starving noo in Scotland, in England and Ireland tae;
I canna bide nae langer here, so now I must away.

(Spoken) It's awfu' times, freens, as shair's death. I've seen whaun a
body could leeve; but no noo-a-days. Losh, I canna get saut tae my
kail. But I'm awa' wi't.

    Fareweel, freens, I maun bid ye a' guid-bye;
    I'm gaun awa' across the seas my wee bit luck to try;
    I canna get as muckle meat here as feed a moose,
    So I'm gaun awa' tae Cyprus to open a public hoose.

2   They tell me that in Cyprus the gold lies at your feet,
And great big diamonds are as thick as causeys on the street;   [cobblestones
I'll never sup nae parritch there, nae mair cauld kail for me,
I'll hae a turkey for my dinner and whusky in my tea.

(Spoken) Fancy what a change that will be, getting real whusky in
your tea, no the fusel oil kind, oh no, but the real stingo. Losh, here
I canna get milk to my parritch. But I'm awa'! Fareweel, Sandy; guid-
bye, Tam. I'm aff!

    Fareweel, freens, I maun bid ye a' guid-bye;
    I'm gaun awa' across the seas my wee bit luck to try;
    I canna get a muckle meat here as feed a moose,
    So I'm gaun awa' tae Cyprus to open a public hoose.

3   Tae gain the favour o' the folk I'll either dance or sing;
    I'll sell them the rare auld stingo, tae mak' them kick and fling;
    And if a fortune I should mak', I'll maybe then come hame,
    Wi' my pouches fu' o' siller, and a Pasha to my name.

(Spoken) Wad it no' be gran' tae come back wi' a Pasha tae my name?
Then see me walking alang Argyll Street. I wadna soil my feet in the
Sautmarket. See the braw leddies admiring my handsome carriage,
even the wee kids crying out, "Crickey, look at so-and-so; he's a
Pasha noo." Oh, I'm aff. Gie us a guid chorus for the last.

Fareweel, freens, I maun bid ye a' guid-bye;
I'm gaun awa' across the seas my wee bit luck to try;
I canna get as muckle meat here as feed a moose.
So I'm gaun awa' tae Cyprus to open a public hoose.

Source unrecorded — G

538

THE NABOB

A

The Traveller's Return

1 In silent times wi' lightly foot I trod on thirty years
   My native land I socht again wi' mony hopes and fears
   Wha kens gin the dear frien's I left will still continue mine
   Or gin I e'er again shall taste, the joys I left lang syne.
   For auld langsyne my frien's, those happy days lang syne
   It gars me think the joys at han' are naething to lang syne.

2 My ivy towers now met my view, where minstrels used to blaw
   Nae frien' cam' oot wi' open arms, nae weel kent face I saw,
   Till Auld Donald tottered to the door, whom I left in his prime,
   An' he grat to see the lad come back he bore about langsyne.

3 I ran thro' ilka weel ken't room in hopes to find frien's there
   I saw the place where ilk ane sat and hung o'er ilka chair
   Till soft oblivion drew his veil across this scene o' mine,
   I steek't the door and sobbed aloud when I thocht on langsyne.

4   A new sprung race o' motley kin' would now their welcome pay
     They shuddered at my gothic walls and wished my groves away,
     Cut, cut they cried yon gloomy tree, lay low yon mournfu' pine,
     Ye ken our father's name grows there, memorials o' langsyne.

GEORGE F. DUNCAN — D

B

Auld Lang Syne.

GEORGE MILNE — G

341

C

When silent Time.

JAMES ANGUS — G

D

The Nabob.

When silent Time and lightly fit had trod on thirty years,

My native home I socht again wi' mony hopes and fears.

wha kens gin those dear friends I left may still continue mine? Or

gin I e'er again should taste the joys of auld lang syne.

ALEXANDER MACKAY — D

E

Silent Time or Traveller's Return

1　When silent time we' lightly foot had trod on thirty years
　　My native land I sought again wi' mony hopes and fears.
　　Wha keens gine the dear friends I left will still continue mine
　　Or if I e'er again shall taste the joys I left lang syne.

2　As I drew near the ancient pile my heart beat a' the way
　　Ilk place I passed seem'd yet to speak o some dear former day
　　Those days that follow'd me afar those happy days o' mine
　　Which made me think the joys at haun were nathing to lang syne.

3　The ivy'd tower now met my view where minstrels used to play
　　Nae friend stepp'd forth wi open hand nae weel keen'd face I saw
　　Till Donald totter'd to the door whom I left in his prime
　　He grat to see the lad come back he bore about lang syne.

4　I ran to ilka weel kent room thinking to find friends there
　　I knew where ilk-ane used to sit and hang oer ilka chair
　　Till soft oblivion threw its veil across this een o' mine
　　Twas only then I could forget the joys I left lang syne.

5　Some pensy chiels a new sprung race did next their welcome pay　　　　[affected
　　Who shuddered at my Gothic wa's and wish'd my groves away.
　　Cut cut they cried those aged elms lay low yon mournfu pine
　　Na na our fathers' names grow there memorials of lang syne.

6　To wean me frae those waefu thoughts they took me to the toun
　　But sair on ilka weel keen'd face I miss'd the youthfu bloom.
　　At balls they pointed to a nymph whom a' declar'd divine
　　But sure her mother's blushing cheeks were fairer far lang syne.

7　In vain I sought in music's sound to find that magic art
　　Which oft in Scotland's ancient lays has thrill'd through a my heart.
　　The sang had mony an artfu turn my ear confess'd twas fine
　　But miss'd the simple melody I listen'd to lang syne.

8　Ye sons to comrades o my youth forgi'e an auld man's spleen
　　Wha midst your gayest scenes still mourns the days he ance has seen.
　　When time has passed and seasons fled your hearts will feel like mine
　　And aye the sang will maist delight that minds ye o lang syne.

Mrs MARGARET GILLESPIE — D

F

The Traveller's Return

1　When silent times wi a light foot, had trode on thirty years,
　　My native land I sought again, in many hopes and fears;
　　Wha kens gin the dear friens I left, will still continue mine,
　　Or gin I e'er again shall meet, the joys I left langsyne.

2　As I drew near my ancient pile, my heart beat a' the way,
　　Ilk place I passed seemed yet to speak of some dear former day;
　　Those days that followed me afar, those happy days of mine,
　　Which made me think the joys at hand, were naething to langsyne.

3   My rugged towers now meet my view, where minstrels used to blaw,
     Nae friends stepped forth wi open arms nae well ken'd face I saw,
     Till Donald tottered out the door, wham I left in his prime;
     And grat to see the lad come back, he bore about langsyne.

4   I ran through ilka weel kenne'd room in hopes to meet friends there,
     I saw where ilk ane used to sit, and hang on ilka chair,
     Till in oblivion's shade I sought, to ease my burden'd min,
     I steeked the door and sobbed aloud as I thought on langsyne.

Miss JESSIE H. McDONALD — D

AULD YULE

1 Ae night frae hame I chanc'd to stray
An' thro' the Braes I took my way;
When near a lonely burn,
Wi' sic chield I did forgether,
As pat me in an eiry swither   [fearful
Gin I wad gang or turn. –
Sae wrinkled oer his gothic face
Sae white his beard to see;
The father o' some ancient race
I thought he needs must be.
His waving locks like silver sheen'd
And seemed to sweep the plain
Whilst cow'ring o'er his staff he lean'd
Beneath the sleety rain.

2 I stood awhile in sad amaze
And did upo' the Carle gaze
An' thought his breath wad fail.
His head he raised when me he spied
"Come near young man" he faintly cried
"An hear my waefu' tale.
My glass you see 's near run o' sand,
I fast approach my end
'Gainst crazy age I canna stand
But 'neath his power maun bend.
Nae beild hae I, nor place o' rest
By a' I'm set adrift
Wi' eild and sorrow sair opprest   [age
A scanty meal to shift.

3 "But whan at first I journey'd here
I welcome gat, an' merry cheer
Baith frae great folks an' sma
An aye the best they could afford
Was quickly set upo the board
To drive ilk care awa.
The smiling maids wi' mothers vi'd,
To entertain the Guest
An' house wi' house fu' kindly tri'd
Wha best end mak' the feast.
Then plenty wi' her open han'
Set trysts to meet me there;
The poorest house in a' the lan',
Had something aye tae spare.

4 "An' ilka night ere I did come
The Ha'ners clean'd, well swept the lum
An a'thing made fu' tight
An' syne upo' the merry morn
Ilk ane was sure to get a horn
O' sowens by candle licht
In which the yellow butter swim'd
So pleasant to the view,
It glanc'd sae bricht, pure gold it seem'd,
Braw tunes were these I trow.
Had Canker then in guise o' frien'
But try'd to shaw his face
The vera dogs wad hunt the fien'
Far frae the happy place.

5 "An' aye into the farmer's Ha'
Mang lads and mony lasses braw
I down sae welcome sat.
There Broth an' Mutton, Beef an' Bac'n
Store o' hens, or cocks or Cap'n
We for our dinner gat.
An' aft a Haggis on a plate
Well season'd up wi' spice
A dish at which none e'er look'd blate
But cleared it in a trice
An' syne the nappy beer g'ed roun'
To pass the gleesome hour;
Wi' prancing like to deeve the town
They danced awa their power.

6 "An' crofters poor, an cottar fock
Altho' they had but little stock
Wid aye some cheer provide
They, kindly souls! wi' honest hearts
Fu' gladly tried to act their parts
At sic a merry tide.
A wee bit beef, a cock or hen
Ged to their scanty pat.
Altho' they were but bare the ben
We this for dinner gat.
And then the childer's heads they'd stroke
An' bless the bonny weens
Or smoke a pipe, or crack a joke,
Right hearty wi' their freens.

7   "And ilka puir auld widow wife
That leads a langsome lanely life
Did brander'd bannocks bake
A pickle maut she'd buy an' brew
Wi' tenty han' the wort she drew   [careful
That neighbours might partake.
Her well-hained kebbuck met the knife
On Yule-day i' the morn
When all boot taste, or else the wife   [had to taste
Wad tak it in great scorn. –
Tho' lasses sair, an' ambry bare   [cupboard
She had to grapple wi'
Net blythe to find that she ance mair
Auld Yule had lived to see.

8   "But sair the guise is alter'd noo,
For which I hae great cause to rue
As lang's I drawn my breath
Nae hope hae I the times will mend
Until I win my journey's end
An' fairly sleep in Death.
Thro' ilka place where I do pass
In a' my weary travel
I scarcely now can get a glass
To cure the gripping gravel.
O' late sae chang'd is Scotland's lot
Frae what I ance hae kent 'er
That for to work the whiskie pat
Her crofters darena venture.

9   "An' beer is now but senseless trash
Tho' hap or wormit maks it harsh   [hop; wormwood
G–d kens it's nae wi' strength;
For ilka wife wha brews it noo
Each art she tries, – I speak o'erbrue
To rax it to the length. –
Nor will ye think the reason strange
How drink is made sae bare
Whan ye sall hear the waefu' change
That's filled my breast wi' care.
A crown the bow o' weel-paid tax
Brought millions to the state
Four crowns an' mair the now do ax
But nane a'maist can pey 't.

10   "Nor can I get a bit o' beef
To cheer my heart sae wrung wi' grief
Good folk hae nane to spare.
A glancing eye upon the pot
To had the broth lang boiling hot
I fear I'll see nae mair.
Now senless water, meat an' saut
Is feck o' a' their cheer
Sin a' that comes o' beef or maut
Is so excessive dear.
Sair pinching belly, back and side,
They sin with barely serve.
Wi' a change at guid Yule tide
They're forc'd to lat me starve."

11   "Waes me!" quo I "poor honest Carle
Dame Fortune sair at you does snarle
In sic a dreary time
To ca' ye forth in sic a seas'n.
Wi' nae a drap to wet your wizz'n
Or bit to fill your wame.
But mang the Knabbs ye was acquanted   [important
What now has bred the turn?   people
Amang them ance ye sa' nae want
Nor had ye cause to mourn,
Their pantries aye sae largely filled
Wi' what befits a table
To share wi' you, if rightly will'd
They sure at least are able."

12   "Alas!" quo he "I had my time
Nor turn'd off for ony crime
But auld an' oot o' fashion.
As now they're sic a novel crew
If aught they see but skyrin' new   [utterly
It puts them in a passion
Then was I forc'd my awls to pack
An' quickly off gae trudging
Nae mair again to venture back
Nor there to seek a lodging
Their like sa wi the times has turned
That 'tis my constant lot
In place o' welcome to be spurn'd
An' ca'ad a senseless sot.

13   "Back sixty years or thereabout
A crazie hand first flang me oot
An' ca'ad me Papist Knave;
An' said they did a sinfu' wrang
For whilk ilk ane deserved to hang
Wha bread and quarters gave.
Wi' sic bland zeal sae blawin up
The wad na lat me rest
Nor wad they gie me bit or sup
By night and day opprest.
Their Holy Sauls thought Heav'n to win
By visage dark an' sour;
Nor think they do a deed o' sin,
To this deficient hour.

14   "Neist cam a callan caad New Style
Bred up in some outlandish Isle
He now diverts the Knabbs.
Frae yont the sea into this part
New Fangle brought him glib and smart
To cheer them wi' his gabs.   [chat
He took my place wi' ill bred speed
An' mang them aye does lodge
He quickly gat the table head
An rules there like a judge.
My best efforts now out o' date
Tho' Mirth an' Wit were mine
Wid frae these gentry win but hate
It was nae sae lang syne.

15 "Yet mang the honest country fock
    I back and fore did brawly trock   [deal
    This forty year an' mair
    Until some ither wicked rogue
    Has o' me played some black a brogue
    That's put me in despair.
    Tis by some cursed magic slight
    The honest country men
    Are sae deprived o' their sight
    That me they dinna ken.
    Their Kalendar ance mair is changed
    The waefu' aughteen Hunder
    Has a' their Rackenings sae deranged
    They'll never cour the wonder.

16 "Sae like the Hermit in a glen
    Nae company but the moorhen
    To cheer me wi' her sang,
    Thus back an' fore hae been tost
    Wi' chillin' winds an' nipping frost
    My days will nae be lang.
    For now the times are fairly past
    That I hae often seen
    Whilk gars the tears rin doon sae fast
    Frae baith my hollow e'en
    The youngsters now may gap an' glower
    When tauld what mirth and glee
    Flash'd round the fire in my best hour
    The like they'll never see."

17 'Twas said when to my sad surprise
    Auld Yule he vanished frae my eyes
    Like Vapour aft did gleam.
    Nae house nor haul then being near
    In ilka limb I shook for fear
    Beside the lonely stream.
    Then wi' my staff try'd to steer
    Me homeward thro' the bogs
    An' wi' a twitch o' them got clear
    By help o' barking dogs.
    The night grew dark, the heavens scowled
    I kent my collie's moan
    He either missed me or he howl'd
    Because Auld Yule was gone.

WILLIAM WALKER — G

347

THE AULD HAT

A

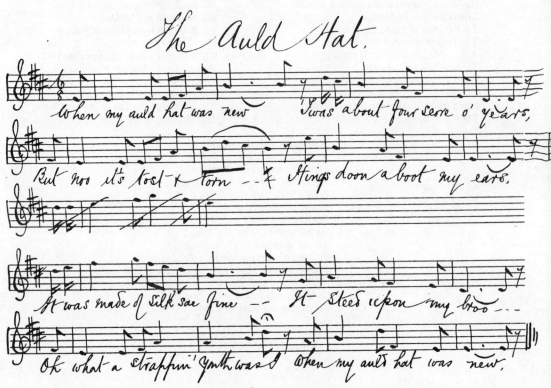

1   When my auld hat was new 'twas about four score o' years
     But noo it's tossed and torn, hings doon aboot my ears.
     It was made o' the silk sae fine, it steed abeen my broo —
     Oh what a strappin' youth was I when my auld hat was new.

2   And when the time o' harvest came and we went oot to shear,
     Awyte we wis made hearty fou wi' brandy gin or beer.
     And when the corn wis ta'en in and bigget in a mou
     Awyte we had a hearty rant when my auld hat was new.

3   It's the goodman at the boord-head he did the table grace,
     And as the servants did come in they rankèd in their place
     And it's the goodwife wi' her eidence to gie every one their due;   [attentiveness
     And that was sae in my young day when my auld hat was new.

4   Oor great goodwives noo "Mistress" gets and they maun hae their tea
     And some o' them wears gowns o' silk as ye may plainly see,
     But it wisna sae in my young day, for that was aye their due,
     A goon sic as their minny span when my auld hat was new.

5   And instead o' a great supper that we'd eest to get before
     They'll gie ye by your portion noo like beggars at the door,
     And it's near their hoose ye daurna gang tho' it be ne'er sae fu';
     But it wisna sae in my young day when my auld hat was new.

Mrs MILNE — G

B

When my auld hat was new.

When my auld hat was new ---'Twas a'bout fourscore years, But noo it's tossed & torn --- flings doon aboot my ears. It was made o' the silk sae fine — It steed abeen my broo--- Oh what a strappin' youth was I when my auld hat was new.

WILLIAM LAWRENCE — G

541

I AM NOW A POOR AULD MAN IN YEARS

When My Auld Hat Was New

1   I am now a poor auld man in years,
    Come listen to my song;
    Provisions they are twice as dear
    As they were when I was young.

T. ROGER — G

THE HAPPY DAYS OF YOUTH

A

1   The happy days of youth they are fast fleeting by
     Old age is coming on with a dark stormy sky.
     Oh, where shall I shelter while the stormy winds do blaw
     Since the happy days of youth they are a' gane awa'.

2   Some say that wisdom comes in manhood's riper years
     But little do they think of the dangers and the cares
     I would gie a' the wealth if any wealth was mine
     For a pleasant summer's morn and a lovely lang syne.

3   It was down among the broom where me and my love met
     The bonnie blooming flowers did bloom around our seat
     The birdies droppèd singing, it was only for a wee
     And they went to their nest in their ain birken tree.

4   The happy days o' youth they canna lang remain
     There is owre muckle mirth and owre little pain
     So farewell to happy youth likewise to mirth and glee
     The young may counter and smile but they are a' gane frae me.

Mrs CLARK — G

B

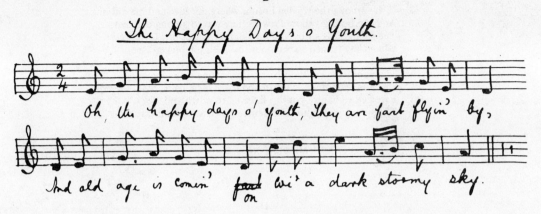

The Happy Days o Youth.

Oh, the happy days o' youth, They are fast flyin' by,

And old age is comin' on wi' a dark stormy sky.

1 O the happy days o youth
   The are fast flying by
   And old age is comming on
   We a dark stormy sky.

2 Oh where shall I shelter
   From that storms when they blaw
   For the happy days o youth
   They are fast gawn awa.

3 I wid gee my wit
   It's gin ony wit were mine
   For a sinny morn
   O bonny aul lang syne.

4 Amongest the bonny yellow broom
   Where my love and I did meet
   And the pretty little flowers
   As they waved about our feet.

5 And the small bird sweetly singing
   It was only for a wee
   Then awa till its nest
   In yon birken tree.

6 Then so farewell happy youth
   Sence ye canna lang remain
   There is oor muckle mirth
   And oor little gain.

7 Then so farewell happy youth
   And the youths o youthful glee
   For the young may coort a smile
   But they are gawn awa fae me.

ISAAC and GEORGE TROUP — D

C

The Happy Days of Youth

1 The happy days of youth, they are fast flying by,
   Old age is coming on wi' a dark and gloomy sky;
   Oh where shall we shelter from the cold winds when they blow?
   For the happy days of youth, they are gan awa.

2 It's said that wisdom comes wi' manhood's riper years,
   Oh little can you tell of its sorrows and its griefs;
   I would give all my wealth, though half the world were mine,
   For ae happy evening of auld lang syne.

3 'Twas among the waving broom where my love and me did meet,
 And the bonny yellow flowers they waved among our feet;
 The small birds stopped their singing, it was but for a wee,
 When they turned to their nest by their ain birken tree.

4 The happy days of youth and they canna lang remain,
 There is owre muckle mirth and owre little pain;
 Farewell to happy youth, farewell to mirth and glee,
 The young may court and smile, but it's gan awa frae me.

Mrs BEATON — D

D
The Happy Days of Youth

1 The happy days of youth are fast fleeting by
 Old age is coming on with a dark stormy sky
 O where shall I shelter when the stormy wind does blaw
 Since the happy days o' youth is a' gane awa.

2 Some says that wisdom comes in manhood's ripe years
 But little do they think of its dangers and its cares
 I wad gie awa my wealth if any wealth were mine
 For a bonny sunny morn of a lovely langsyne.

3 O the bonny waving broom, where me and my love met
 And the bonny blooming flowers that waved round our seat
 The birdies droppit singin, but it's only for a wee
 When they went to their nests in their ain birchen tree.

4 O the happy days o' youth they could not lang remain
 There wis owre muckle mirth and owre little pain
 So farewell to happy days wi' a' their mirth and glee
 The young may court their smiles but they are a' gane frae me.

Source unrecorded — G

SONGS OF HOME AND SOCIAL LIFE

THE FARMER'S INGLE

A
The Farmer's Ingle

1   Let Turks triumph, let tyrants pray
Let poets sing melodiously
Let Turks triumph and poets live single
But my delight's at the farmer's ingle.
    For the farmer's ingle is the place
    Where freedom shines on ilka face
    My wish is while on earth to mingle
    With gude honest people at the farmer's ingle.

2   In winter when the frost and snaw
Drives a' the masons frae the wa'
Your hearts wad warm and your ears wad tingle
To hear the cracks at the farmer's ingle.

3   The British ship's the seaman's boast
Success to the trade's the merchant's toast
The miser for his money does pingle   [work laboriously, drudge
But my delight's in the farmer's ingle.

4   The sailor boldly ploughs the main
The soldier flies o'er heaps of slain
But my wish on earth's ne'er to live single
Here's a bumper to the farmer's ingle.

JAMES CHEYNE — G

B
The Farmer's Ingle

1   When winter's blaws wi' sleet and snaw
Drives a' the fairmers to the ha',
Our heart wid beat and our ears wid tingle
To hear the tales o' the fairmer's ingle.

2   The fairmer's ingle is the place
Where beauty shines in ilka face;
My wish is sure for aye to mingle
Wi' bonny lads in the fairmer's ingle.

Mrs HALLEY — D

544

THE WIND AND THE SNOW

1   The wind and the snow oer the cold world blow
    From the wild raging east to the west
    But noo I'm sitting snug at my warm chimney lug
    And I carena a fig for the blast.

Miss ANNIE SHIRER — G

545

WHEN THE DAY IS ON THE TURN

Glenlivet Song

1   Though the hoose be couth and warm and aye a blazing fire
    The lang nichts o' winter mak's everybody tire
    Mak's every ane to tire an' to fret and to mourn
    An' nathing will content them till the day be on the turn.

2   The fair maid in the evening gaes lichtly wi' her pail
    The cotter sits contented o'er the lingle o' his flail
    The gudewife she is fond to say when scouring out the churn
    We'll a' get fouth o' butter when the day is on the turn.

JOHN ORD — G

356

A WIFE AND A BIGGIN O' YER AIN

1 It's gran' to hae a wifie and a biggin o' yer ain
  Where ye can rest wi' comfort and a balm for every pain
  To hear the birdies coortin on the thack abune your heid
  To sit and smoke your cutty ere ye tak the wye to bed.

2 There's naething can be nicer tho' ye seek frae east to west
  Than that bit sweet and bonnie biggin' whaur the weary fin' a rest
  It is the greatest blessin' that man has ever ha'en
  A wifie trim and couthie and a biggin' o' yer ain.

3 I like to see my wifie wi' the bairnie on her knee
  In the simmer at the doorstep sit lookin oot for me
  The bonnie bairnie dressed wi' his cheekies rosy red
  And his mammie's jist as bonnie as the day that we were wed.

4 Ilk evenin' as I entered my biggin o' my ain
  There's something fresh to cheer me and drive awa all care
  The hearth stane's aye sae bonnie and the grate sae neat and clean
  I ken-na hoo I'd manage if I didna hae my Jean.

5 I've been in lodgings bonnie wi' the brussels on the floor   [carpet
  Wi' curtains on the window and a knocker on the door
  But altho midst wealth and grandeur I hae very often lain
  It wisna half sae cosy as this biggin' o' my ain.

Miss ANNIE SHIRER — G

BOGIE'S BANKS AND BOGIE'S BRAES

1   I hae a housie oh my ain
A kist the but an ane the ben,
An mair nor a the wardle kens
On the bonnie banks oh the Bogie.
Bogie's banks an Bogie's braes
An Bogie's haughs for bleaching claes
An Bogie's banks faur lamies' plays
On the bonnie bonnie banks oh the Bogie.

2   I hae a grannie in the nuk
Whiles at her wheel whiles at her book
An I hae cow an hen an duke
On the bonnie banks oh the Bogie.

3   I hae a laddie leel an true
A strappin cheel we een oh blue
A better never brushed the dew
On the bonnie banks oh the Bogie.

4   Frae Craig tae Huntly weel I ken
I'll twist an twine on haugh an glen
I lenered every stap an stane   [learned
On the bonnie banks oh the Bogie.

5   Let naught put on my grave look down
By Bogie's waters sweetly crown
In yon churchyard an I'll sleep soon
Tis the bonniest bit oh the Bogie.

ROBERT ALEXANDER — D

THE AULD MAN'S SANG

A

The Auld Man's Sang

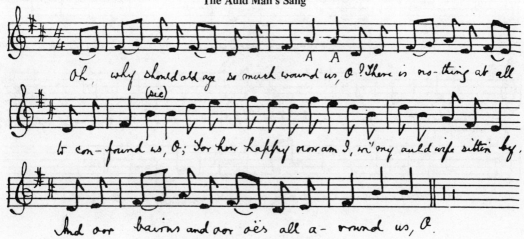

1 O why should old age so much wound us O
   There is nothing at all to confound us O
   For how happy now am I with my auld wife sitting by .
   With our bairns an' our oyes all around us O.   [grandchildren

2 We began in this warld wi' naething O
   An we've jogèd an' toilèd for a'thing O
   We mak use o what we had an oor thankful hearts were glad
   When we got the bit meat an' the claithing O.

3 What though we cannot boast o' our guineas O
   We've plenty o' Jockies an' Jennies O
   And these more interesting are, more desirable by far
   Than a bagfu' o' poor yellow steenies O.

4 We ne'er laid a scheme to be wealthy O
   By means that were cunning or stealthy O,
   But we always had the bliss an' what further could we wish
   To be pleased wi' oorsels an' be healthy O.

5 We have seen mony wandering fairly O
   Of changes that are almost yearly O
   Of rich folks up an' doon baith in country and in toon
   Wha live noo but scrimply an' barely O.   [sparingly

6 In this hoose where we first came thegither O
   Where we've lang been a father an' mither O
   Though not of stane an' lime it will lest us a' oor time
   An' I hope we shall ne'er need anither O.

7 Then why should old age so much wound us O,
   There is nothing in it all to confound us O
   For how happy now am I with my auld wife sitting by
   With our bairnies an' our oyes all around us O.

Mrs LYALL – D

B

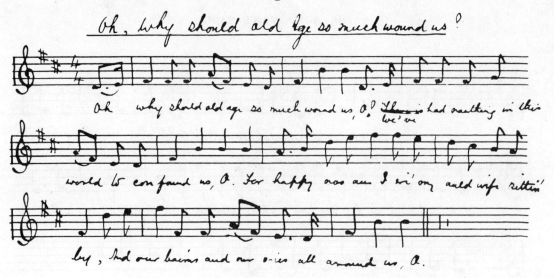

Mrs MARGARET GILLESPIE — D

C

J.A. FOTHERINGHAM — G

D

1 We began in the warld wi' naething O,
An we've jogged on an' toil'd for the aething O,
We made use o' what we had and our thankfu' hearts were glad
When we got the bit meat an' the claithing, O.

JOHN MILNE — G

HAPPY ROON' THE INGLE BLEEZIN'

Happy roon' the ingle bleezin',
Canty we'll be ane an' a';
Blyther still we'll be thegether,
Ere we think o' gaun awa.

1 See the miser and his riches,
   Watchin' ower 't wi' cautious e'e;
   See the sons o' social pleasure
   Spend the nicht in harmony.

2 Frien'ship mak's us tak' a drappie,
   Frien'ship mak's us a' unite,
   Frien'ship mak's us a' fu' canty,
   Frien'ship brought us here tonight.

JOHN BAIN — D

550

THE PRESENT TIME IS OORS

1   Come, let us a' be hearty, boys, the moments we are here,
And banter o'er our earthly joys, they're only twa-three year.
They're only twa-three year, my boys, and maybe only hoors;
So haud a jeering spark aboot, the present time is oors,
Oh, the present time is oors, the present time is oors,
So haud a jeerin' spark aboot, the present time is oors.

2   Awa wi' a yer gaudy shirts, what signifies a show?
For multitudes o' cares and griefs they only prove a foe.
A raggit coat wi' elbucks oot will bang the winter shoo'rs,   [elbows; defeat
So haud a jeerin' spark aboot, the present time is oors.

3   Let ministers say what they will, they'll tell ye this and that,
Sae blithe are we and sae are they when quietly they meet,
When quietly they do sit roon, secure wi' lockit doors,
So merrily they laugh and sing, The present time is oors.

4   They'll bid ye raise yer hopes abeen, and greet where'er ye dwell,
They'll mak' ye lairds ayont the meen, but grip the gless themsel',
But let us learn tae be wise, and pu' the sweetest floo'rs,
Leave thistle leaves to them that please, the present time is oors.

WILLIAM WATSON – G

THIS CRONIES O' MINE

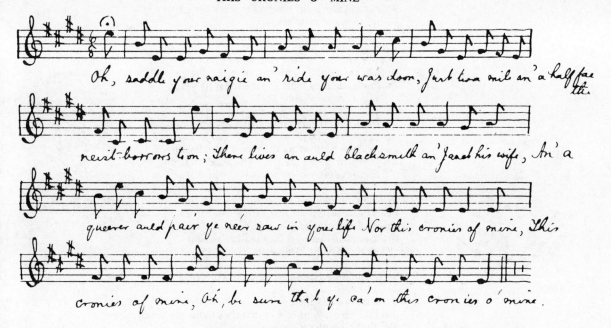

1 Ye'll saddle your naigie and ride yer waes doon
Juist twa mile an a half to the neist borro's toon   [borough
There lives an aul' blacksmith an Janet his wife
An a queerer aul' pair you ne'er saw a your life
    Nor this cronies o mine, this cronies o' mine,
    O be sure that you call them this cronies o' mine.

2 The smeddie you'l ken by the twa trochstanes   [troughs
Wi its auld fashioned biggin and black battered panes
Wi the three iron cleeks that he stack in the wa   [hooks
To tie up wile yads when high customers ca   [unruly old mares
    On this cronie o' mine etc.

3 Up agen his aul' gavel a light ye will view
A tramless cairt or a cooterless plew   [shaftless
An aul' broken harrow, or a brecham ring bent   [horse collar
An mair broken gear than that a to be men't
    By this cronie o' mine etc.

4 Ye'll fin him as I've deen, a trustworthy chiel
Weel tempered wi wit frae the heid to the heel
Wi a soul in his body aul' Nick ne'er could clout
An a spark in his throat 'at was ill to droon oot
    Had this cronie o' mine etc.

5 Twa or three lads fae the toon, they're sure to be there
There's the baldheided butcher wha aye taks the cheer
The queerest o fowk, a amon ane an anither
That e'er in this warl were a clubbit thegither
    A cronies o' mine etc.

6   There is dominie Davie, fu glib i the mou   [voluble
But as like ye will fin the aul' carl blin fu
An the wee barber boddie wi' his wig fu o news
Wha would shave ony chap a the week for a bouse
    A cronies o' mine etc.

7   There is Tam the aul' toon-clerk, he's taen to the pack
But it's naething in bulk to the humph on his back
His legs are a boo'l an his splayfeet sae thrawn   [bow-legged
Troth it's nae easy tellin the road that he's gain
    Tho a cronie o' mine etc.

8   There's Robin the plooman that's cramm'd fu o fun
An gamekeeper Davie wi dog, bag, an gun
The miller wha blythely the pipers can play on
An ye're sure to get fae him "The Miller o' Drone"
    Fae this cronie o' mine etc.

9   Syne aul' brookie his greybeard he's sure for to draw   [blacksmith; jug
Fae a black seety hole that ye'll see in the wa
An ere it be emptied I muckle doot
If the ae chap ken weel fat the ither's aboot
    Wi this cronies o' mine etc.

10   So wi clinkin on hammers an tinklin o tyangs
. . . .
Wi ae thing or anither, ye'll aiblins be deaved
But take care o your breeks that they dinna get sieved
    Wi this cronies o mine etc.

11   An noo my guid freen gies a shack i your han
The night is far spent an wee man be gaun
The laddie will bring doon your naig in a blink
But afore that ye gang let us drink.
    To this cronies o mine, this cronies o mine,
    O they'l mak you richt welcome this cronies o' mine.

ROBERT ALEXANDER – D

SAE WILL WE YET

A

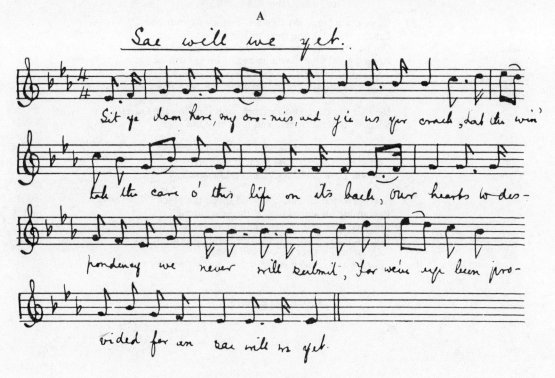

Mrs MARGARET GILLESPIE – D

B

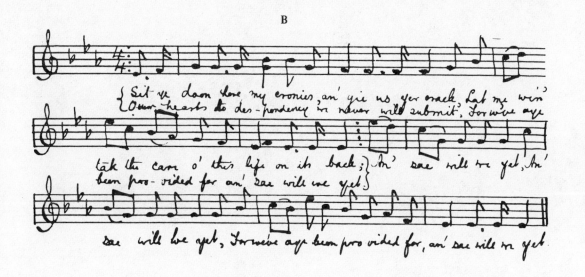

Mrs MARGARET GILLESPIE – D

C
Sae Will We Yet

1   Sit ye doon here, my cronies, and gie us your crack,
Let the wind tak the cares of this life on its back
Our hearts to despondency, we never will permit,
When we fell we aye win up again, an sae will we yet,
    An sae will we yet, I, an sae will we yet
    When we fell we aye got up again, an sae will we yet.

2   Here's a health to Old England, and long live the Queen
Success to her subjects, and long may she reign

    . . . .
Britain's aye been victorious, an sae will she yet.
    An sae will she yet, an sae will she yet
    Britain's aye been victorious, and sae will she yet.

3   Success to the farmer, and God speed the ploo
Rewarding his eident han' a' the year through
For seed time and harvest time we're aye sure to get
For we've aye been providet for, and sae will we yet
    An sae will we yet an' sae will we yet
    For we've aye been providit for, and sae will we yet.

ROBERT ALEXANDER — D

MY AIN FIRESIDE

A

Oor ain fireside.

To bide my langer' it wad be a Sin, For the drinks a' drunk & the siller's a' deen,
the drinks a' deen & the siller's a' peyed, And we'll a' awa' hame to oor ain fireside
To my ain fireside, To my ain fireside, We'll a' awa' hame to oor ain fireside --

Miss ANNIE RITCHIE — G

B

My Ain Fireside

1   Come bonnie lads will ye mount and go
A'm gaun home are ye gaun or no
For the drink is a deen and the lawin is a paid
An' I'm gaun hame tae my ain fireside
　Tae my ain fireside my ain fireside
　For the drink is a deen an' the lawin is a paid
　An' I'm gaun hame tae my ain fireside.

2   To sit langer here it wad be a shame
For siller is scarce an' ill to win
An' we'll aye be the dearer the langer that we bide
An we'll a' sit as cheap at oor ain fireside
　At oor ain fireside, at oor ain fireside
　And we'll a sit as cheap at oor ain fireside
　For we'll aye be the dearer the langer we bide
　And we'll a' sit as cheap at oor ain fireside.

3   My wife she sits at hame her lane
And sittin' sae late she has bleart her e'en
An tae face her in fact I'm amaist afraid
For the kickin' up a row at oor ain fireside
　At oor ain fireside, at oor ain fireside
　For the kickin up a dust at oor ain fireside.

[inflamed

4   But I'll get a bottle an' I'll full't foo
And I'll gae hame I'll tell ye true
I'll tell ye true whatever betide
I'll drink it wi' my wifie at oor ain fireside.

5   First a gless and then a sang
    Then cast aff oor claes tae oor bed we gang
    And I'll cuddle her in my airms like a new made bride
    And crack aboot the joys o' oor ain fireside.

6   Then here's tae ilk weel-thinkin' chiel
    An' fae my heart I wish him weel
    An' tae please his wife he'll aye tak a pride
    An he'll aye be contented at his ain fireside.

WILLIAM SCOTT — G

KITTYBREWSTER

1 She selt a dram — I kent her fine
   Oot on the road to Hilton
   Afore the door there stood a sign
   Ahint a lairack beltin'.   [clump of larch trees

2 The sign tae mak it bright and gay
   Taxed Tinte's best resources
   An ale-stoup and a wisp o' hay
   Farin' for man and horses.

3 Her drawin' was good, but O! her ale
   Twas it that did her credit
   Abeen a' brewsts it bore the bell
   And 'twas hersel that made it.

4 Just twa-three waughts o't wi' a freen
   Oot owre a bargain makin'
   Wad cheer yer hert and licht yer een
   And set your lugs a' crackin'.

5 Her yaird had midden cocks an' game
   And mony a cacklin' rooster;
   She was a canty, kindly dame
   They ca'd her Kitty Brewster.

6 At brewin' time her mashin' tubs
   Hed sic a mauty flavour
   It gart the gabs o' drouthy swabs   [loafers
   Rin ower in langin' slaver.

7 And when the browst was sweet an' new
   It sae slid ower the wissen,
   Ye thocht ye waur in bliss — your pow
   Had sic a pleasant bizzin'.

8 And syne she whanged the kebbuck doon,
   And cakes het frae the griddle
   While some blythe chap struck up a tune
   Upon the merry fiddle.

9 And Kate hersel was never sweer
   If ony one induced her
   Tae fit it deftly on the fleer —
   Kind canty Kitty Brewster.

10 Her kitchen had a fireplace lairge
    A deep recess and cosey
    Wad haud a dizzen in its mairge   [boundary
    A' canty and jocosey.   [cheerful

11 This was a place in winter keen
    For mony a crack political
    When dykers had their day's darg deen
    And state affairs were critical.

12 And sae they managed the debate
    They couldna be correcker
    Had they been ministers o' the State
    Or Chancellors o' the Exchequer.

13 And aye tae fill another jug
    Her Parliament induced her
    By whispering something in her lug
    That pleased kind Kitty Brewster.

14 Alas the change! houses like men
    Have just the time tae live it
    Kind Kitty's canty but and ben
    Is levelled wi' the divot.

15 Nae mair o' mashin maut the smell [brewing malt
    Sets drouthy mou's a-sleverin';
    On yon road-side, ye couldna tell
    Whaur stood the cosey tavern.

16 There's naething now but cattle roups
    And smells o' melted tallow
    Whaur ance were filled the reamin stoups
    To mony a hearty fellow.

17 I fear that they their wits wad tire
    Wi' train and locomotive
    The chaps wha ance at Kitty's shrine
    Pour'd their libations votive.

18 Kate's brewin' craft and spotless fame —
    For nane had e'er traduced her
    We own when Lily Band we name
    Conjoined wi' Kitty Brewster.

JAMES CHEYNE — G

555

THE ALE-WIFE

A

The Ale-wife

1 The ale wife an' her barrelies
The ale wife she grieves me
The ale wife and her barrelies
She'll ruin me entirely.

2 She's ta'en her barrels on her back
Her pint stoup in her han'
An' she's awa tae "Lowrin Fair"
Tae haud a rantin stan'.   [riotous stall

3 But I hae ousen i' the pleuch
An' plenty o' guid corn
Fesh ben tae me anither pint
Tho' I should beg the morn.

Mrs RETTIE — G

B

1 The auld wife and her barrelie,
The auld wife and her gin;
The auld wife and her barrelie
She's ruined me within.

Source unrecorded — G

CRIPPLE KIRSTY

1   It's wha amang ye hisna heard o' weel-kent Cripple Kirsty
    A porter met her in the street and spiert gin she wis thirsty.
    "Oh yes indeed, an' that I am" she smirkin said fu' pawkie
    "And gin ye'll lay yer tippence tae mine we'll hae a wee drap whiskie."
       Sing Fal the dal etc., etc.

2   Quo he "Wi me noo wark is scant an' siller is nae plenty
    Yet when a mornin's caul' and wet to join I am content aye
    Sae he drew tippence frae his spunge a spunge made o' a cat skin   [pocket
    An' ower to Shirras's baith they gied an' called for half-a-mutchin.

3   Kirsty smellt it ere she took her tift an' said twas gweed, she houpit   [drink
    Syne turnt her fingers to the lift an' Lanrick wise did coup it –
    "Well done" quo he – "Fill up" quo she "An lat us hae some mair o't"
    "Na! na!" quo he "ye greedy jade I think ye've got yer share o't."

4   "A weel – a weel if that's the cure then I maun be contentit
    But faith it's done me muckle gweed for I had nearly faintit."
    An noo I hope ye'se gies a ca' some mornin' fin yer thirsty
    An as ye gae by the Fiddler's Close cry in for Cripple Kirsty.

WILLIAM WALKER – G

A WEE DRAP O' WHISKY

A

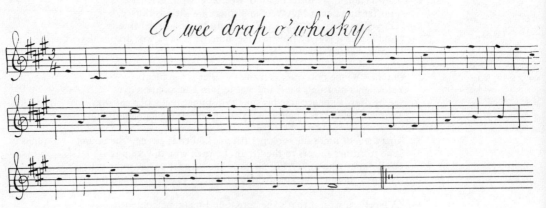

1 A wee drappie whiskey, oh when I am wearied
   Ma blood it will warm, my spirits will cheer
   For when I sit doon, I intend to be merry
   Come fill up a bumper and hand it round here.

2 I can scarce get a hauf oor, oh when I am wearied
   To tell you the truth that I'm vrocht very sore
   My ploo and my lassie is a' my whole pleasure
   We'll both tak' a kiss an' hae a drap more.

3 Contented I sit and contented I labour
   Contented I drink and contented I sing
   I never dispute nor fall oot wi' my neebors
   For that is a mean and a contentious thing.

4 Oh few, very few ever hear me compleenin'
   Though ofttimes the load of oppression I bear
   Oh fat is the use o' a man aye compleenin'
   For aye fan he tastes, he maun hae a drap mair.

5 Come noble waiter, bring in a large measure,
   I mean hauf a mutchkin the best o' the toon
   An' when it is drunken, it's time to be joggin
   We'll gang merrily hame wi' the canniest carl.

6 So good night to you all, I think it's but reason,
   Altho' that the whiskey speaks lood in my ear
   Good night and safe home, till farther occasion
   We'll a' meet in friendship and hae a drap mair.

WILLIAM WATSON – G

B

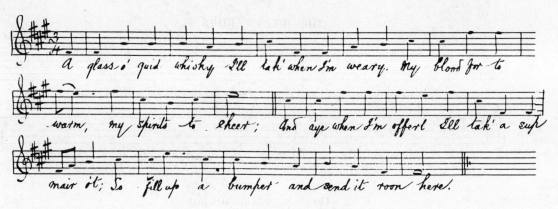

a glass o' guid whisky I'll tak' when I'm weary. My blood for to
warm, my spirits to cheer; And aye when I'm offered I'll tak' a sup
mair o't; So fill up a bumper and send it roon here.

J.W. SPENCE – G

C

A Glass o' Guid Whisky

1   A glass o' guid whiskey I tak' when I'm wearied,
    My bluid for to warm and my spirits to cheer;
    And when I sit down I intend to be merry,
    Come fill me a bumper and send it round here.

2   For I scarcely can get half an hour when I'm wearied,
    To tell you the truth I'm wrought very sore,
    My plough and my dearie they're a' my whole pleasure,
    We baith tak' a kiss, and we'll hae a drap mair.

3   Come in, noble waiter, and bring us more liquor,
    I mean a half mutchkin the best in the town,
    And when it is done it is time to be gaun,
    And wi' the canniest o' care we'll gang toddlin' hame.

4   Say God bless us a', and I think it's nae treason,
    The whiskey begins now to speak in my ear;
    Good nicht and safe home until some other season,
    When we'll a meet in friendship and hae a drap mair.

A. HUTCHEON – G

THE HIELAN' HILLS

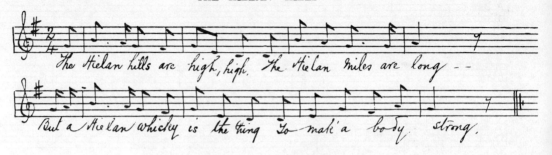

1 The Hielan' hills are high high
   The Hielan' miles are long
   But Hielan' whisky is the thing
   To mak a body strong.

2 She'll tak a glass — be ne'en the waur
   An' maybe she'll tak twa
   An' if she should take six or five
   What business that tae you.

3 Her cuttie pipe is no that bad
   To warm a body's nose
   And a Hielan whisky is the thing
   To paint it like the rose.

Rev. JOHN CALDER — G

JOHN BARLEYCORN

1   There was three kings into the East,
    Three kings both great and high
    And they hae sworn a solemn oath
    John Barleycorn must die.

2   They took a plough and ploughed him down
    Put clods upon his heid
    And they hae sworn a solemn oath
    John Barleycorn was deid.

3   The cheerful Spring cam' kindly on,
    And sho'ers began to fall
    John Barleycorn got up again
    And sore surprised them all.

4   The sultry sun o' Summer came
    When he grew thick and strong
    His heid weel armed with pointed spears
    That no one should him wrong.

5   The sober Autumn entered mild
    When he grew wan and pale
    His bending joints and drooping head
    Showed he began to fail.

6   They took a weapon long and sharp
    And cut him by the knee
    And tied him fast upon a cart
    Like a rogue for forgery.

7   They laid him down upon his back
    And cudgelled him full sore
    They hung him up before the storm
    And turned him o'er and o'er.

8   The wasting hour o' scorching flame
    The marrow of his bones
    But a miller used him worst of all
    He crushed him between twa stones.

9   John Barleycorn was a hero bold
    Wi' noble enterprise
    For if you do but taste his blood
    It will make your courage rise.

10 'Twill make a man forget his woe
    And brighten all his joy
    He'll make the widow's heart to sing
    Tho' the tear were in her eye.

11 Come let us toast John Barleycorn
    Each man a glass in hand
    And may his great prosperity
    Never fail into Scotland.

Mrs SIM — G

A WEE DRAPPIE O'T

A

The wee drappie o't.

It's life is the ~~burden~~ journey we a' hae to gang, And care is the burden we carry alang; But tho' heavy be oor burden & poverty our lot, We're aye happy wi' oor frien' — the wee drappie o't. Owre a wee drappie o't, Owre a wee drappie o't; We're aye happy wi' a frien' owre a wee drappie o't.

1   It's life is the journey we a' hae to gang,
    And care is the burden we carry alang,
    But tho' heavy be oor burden, and poverty oor lot,
    We're aye happy wi' oor frien' — the wee drappie o't.
        Owre a wee drappie o't, owre a wee drappie o't
        We're aye happy wi' a frien' owre a wee drappie o't.

2   Man's troubles they rise day by day as the seas they wash the shore
    But like a glimpse o' sunshine they quickly pass o'er;
    And the weary fate o' man wad appear withoot a blot
    When seated wi' a frien' owre a wee drappie o't.

3   I've seen the trees in winter a' leafless and bare,
    Resembling a man that is burdened wi' care,
    And I've seen the trees in summer wi' their green verdant coat,
    Rejoicing like a man owre a wee drappie o't.

4   When Robin sang the mournfu' strains that man was made to mourn,
    He said there was no pleasure from the cradle to the urn,
    But in his lamentation, I doot he had forgot
    The pleasures and the joys owre a wee drappie o't.

Miss LITTLEJOHN — G

B

A Wee Drapie O't

1   O life is a journey we a' hae to gang
An' care is the burden we carry alang
But tho grief be our portion and poverty our lot
We're happy a' thegether our a wee drapie o't.
     A wee drapie o't, a wee drapie o't,
     We'll aye sit an tipple o'er a wee drapie o't
     But tho grief be our portion and poverty our lot
     We're happy a' thegether our a wee drapie o't.

2   Gae view the birk in winter a' leafless an bare   [birch
Resemblin a man wi a burden o care
But see the birk in summer wi its braw verdant coat
Rejoicing like a man our a wee drapie o't.

3   We're a' met thegether o'er a glass an a sang
We're a' met thegether by special comman'
Free frae a' mean ambition an every evil thought
We're a' met thegether o'er a wee drapie o't.

4   When friendship an truth an gudefellowship reign
An fouk grown auld are made youthfu again
When ilka heart is happy an wardly cares forgot
Is when we're met a thegether o'er a wee drapie o't.

5   Job in his lamentations says man wis made to mourn
That there's nae sic thing as pleasure frae the cradle to the urn
But in his meditation oh! he surely had forgot
The warmth that spreads sae sweetly o'er a wee drapie o't.

6   A wee drapie o't mak's kind hearts agree
Yet a big drapie o't mak's a' true wisdom flee
So ilka chiel that wants to wear an honest man's coat
Maun never ance tak mair than jist a wee drapie o't.

     Mrs MARGARET GILLESPIE — D

C

A Wee Drappie O't

1   Oh life is a journey we a' hae to gang
And care is a burden we carry alang
But though grief be our portion and poverty our lot
We are happy a' thegither owre a wee drappie o't.
     A wee drappie o't and a wee drappie o't
     We are happy a' thegither owre a wee drappie o't.

2   Gae view the birk in winter a' leafless and bare
Resemblin' a man wi' a burden o' care
But see the birk in summer wi' its braw verdant coat
Rejoicing like a man wi' a wee drappie o't.

3 We are a' met thegither owre a glass and a sang
   We are a' met thegither by special command
   Free frae a' mean ambition and frae every evil thought
   We are a' met thegether owre a wee drappie o't.

4 When friendship and truth and gude fellowship reign
   And folk grown auld are made youthful again
   Where ilka heart is happy and a' warldly cares forgot
   Is when we're met thegither owre a wee drappie o't.

5 Job in his lamentation says "Man was made to mourn"
   That there's nae sic thing frae the cradle to the urn
   But in his meditation he surely had forgot
   The warmth that spreads sae sweetly owre a wee drappie o't.

6 A wee drappie o't maks kind hearts agree
   Yet a big drappie o't makes true wisdom flee
   So ilka chiel that wants to wear an honest man's coat
   Maun never ance tak' mair than a wee drappie o't.

Source unrecorded — G

561

WHEN JONES' ALE WAS NEW

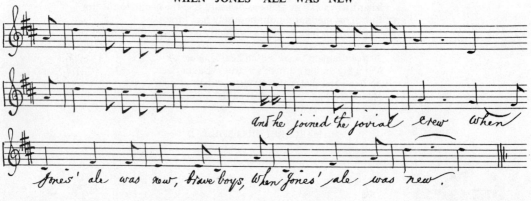

1 . . . .

. . . .

. . . .

And he joined the jovial crew
When Jones' ale was new, brave boys,
When Jones' ale was new.

P.R. GORDON — G

COME, LANDLORD, FILL A FLOWING BOWL

1 Come, landlord, fill a flowing bowl,
   And fill it till't run over
   For this night we'll merry be, be,
   For this night we'll merry, merry be, be,
   And tomorrow we'll get sober.

2 Here's to the lad that courts a lass
   And courts her for his pleasure,
   He's a fool, he's a fool if he marries her
   He's a fool, he's a fool if he marries her
   Without she have some treasure.

3 Here's to the lad that courts a lass,
   And goes to tell his mother,
   He ought to have his head cut off
   He ought to have his head cut off
   And never get another.

Mrs MARGARET GILLESPIE — D

THE COVE THAT SINGS

A

The Cove that sings.

- I'm come to tell ye 'noo --- That I'm the cove that sings ---, oh yes indeed I am --- U-pon my word 'tis true ---. Right ti-tural atidie --- Right ti-tural oo.

ALEXANDER ROBB – G

B

The Cove That Sings

1 No doubts a song you've heard
   How greatly it delights
   It compromises in a word
   The luck of a cove that writes
   But I've a song so true
   For my mind to truth it clings
   And I am going to tell to you
   The luck of a cove that sings.
      O yes I am indeed
      Pon my word it's true
      Ri-te toldrel, oldrel
      Oldrel, oldrel oo.

2 In a garret I served my nobs
   In Earl Street Seven Dial
   My father was a snob
   And my mother she dealt in verbs
   But my mind took higher flight
   I hated lowly things
   Made friends with a cove that writes
   And now I'm a chap that sings.
      O yes I am indeed etc.

3   When at singing I made a start
Some said my voice was fine
I began with the serious parts
But turned to the comic line
For I find that it was best
Some fun it always brings
I gives to the room zest
And it suits the cove that sings.
     O yes it does indeed etc.

4   To a concert, ball or route,
Each night I'm asked to go
With my new tog-rari goes out
And I cut no dirty show
Goes up to the music all right
At the women I sheep's eyes flings
Gets my luish free all the night   [drink
Because I'm the chap that sings.
     O yes I am indeed etc.

5   Each day so well's I fare
On each thing good so fine
In the grub way well I share
For I always go out to dine
And those who ask me so free
Plenty of their friends bring
They come for miles d'ye see
To hear the chap that sings.
     O yes they do indeed etc.

6   When I go to take a room
There needs no talk or stuff
Bout a reference they don't fume
For my word is quite enough
For my money they don't care a sow
The landlady kind looks flings
She's proud to have in her house
A gentleman that sings.
     O yes she is indeed etc.

7   While strolling t'other night
I drop't into a house d'ye see
The landlord very polite
Insisted on treating me
I called for a glass of port
When half a bottle he brings
How much to pay, landlord, says I
O nothing of the sort, says he
As you're the chap that sings.
     O yes you are indeed etc.

8   My song is now 't an end
My story through I've run
And all that I did intend
Was to cause a morsel o' fun
If I succeed all's right
There's a pleasing pleasure brings
And I'll try some other night
The luck of a cove that sings.
     O yes I will indeed etc.

WILLIAM LAWRENCE — G

TAK' ANITHER GILL

1 It's cattle noo are very low, and corn winna sell,
   But we'll aye keep oor spirits up and tak' anither gill;
   And tak' anither gill, boys, and wi' the lasses tig,   [play
   For the fient a ane fell on her back that ever broke a rib.

2 We'll kiss them helter skelter frae the tae lug to the tither,
   And they'll surely ne'er gae greetin' hame, and tell their auld mither.

A. ROTHNIE – G

I'LL TAKE THIS GLASS INTO MY HANDS

1 I'll take this glass into my hands, and drink to all that's here;
   I cannot tell where we may be before another year.
   Some may be wed, some may be dead, some may be lying low;
   Some may be lying on a foreign shore, and know not where to go.

Miss ANNIE SHIRER – G

566

THE SNUFFER'S TOAST

Here's to the nose, and up it goes,
And all that it contains,
It clears the eyes and clogs the nose,
And clarifies the brain;
And it makes the lugs to crack;
And oh it is a capital thing
For ony man to tak'.
                         Amen.

F.R. BROWN — G

567

SNUFFER'S GRACE

Here's my mull and tak' a sneeshin,
Dodsake gie yer nose a creeshin;   [for God's sake
Ye're welcome sid ye snuff a groat,
Yestreen I snuffed a pun and mair o't
The feint a grain o't made me sneeze
In fact it isna worth the cairryin',
If it warna jist to scare flees.

F.R. BROWN — G

TOBACCO PIPES AND PORTER

Tobacco pipes, tobacco pipes, tobacco pipes and porter
Mony ane will sing a sang, but few will sing a shorter.

Miss ANNIE SHIRER — G

THERE WAS FIRST GUID ALE

A

There was first guid ale, and syne guid ale,
And second ale and some;
Thirl the berry and twice as many,
And scour the gate and trim,
Hink-pink, and swats drink   [kinds of weak beer
And guid sma' ale ahin'.

Mrs RETTIE — G

B

There was first guid ale, and syne guid ale,
And second ale and skim,
And hinky-slink and plooman's drink.

ALEXANDER ROBB — G

GLENDRONACH

O potent ally Glendronach,
Thou Prince of the barley bree.

Mrs RETTIE — G

TAM BROON

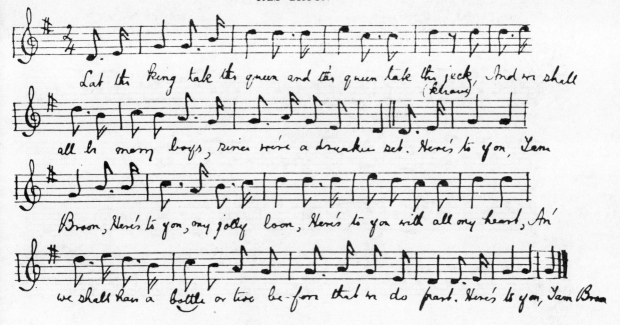

1 Let the king tak the queen, and the queen tak the jeck,
And we shall all be merry boys, since we're a drunken set.
Here's to you, Tam Broon, here's to you, my jolly loon,
Here's to you, with all my heart,
And with you we'se have a bottle or two
Before that we do part;
Here's to you, Tam Broon.

2 Let the jeck tak the ten, and the ten tak the nine,
And we shall all be merry boys, since we are drinking wine.

3 Let the nine tak the eight, and the eight tak the seven,
And we shall all be merry boys, as we go to Newhaven.

4 Let the seven tak the six, and the six tak the five,
And we shall all be merry boys, since we are all alive.

5 Let the five tak the four, and the four tak the three,
And we shall all be merry boys, since we do all agree.

6 Let the three tak the two, and the two tak the one,
And we shall all be merry boys, and end where we began.

ISAAC TROUP – D

I'VE GOT A SHILLING

A

I've Got A Shilling

1 I've got a shilling, a jolly, jolly shilling,
   And I love that shilling as I love my life;
   A penny I will spend, another I will lend,
   And tenpence I'll take home to my wife.
       No pot nor pint shall grieve me,
       Nor no false girl shall deceive me,
       But happy is the girl that shall keep me,
       As I go rolling home.
       Rolling home, rolling home, rolling home,
       As I go rolling home.

2 I've got a tenpence, a jolly jolly tenpence
   And I love that tenpence as I love my life
   A penny I will spend, and another I will lend
   An eightpence I'll take home to my wife.

3 I've got an eightpence, a jolly jolly eightpence
   And I love that eightpence as I love my life
   A penny I will spend, and another I will lend
   An sixpence I'll take home to my wife.

4 I've got a sixpence, a jolly jolly sixpence
   And I love that sixpence as I love my life
   A penny I will spend, and another I will lend
   And fourpence I'll take home to my wife.

5   I've got a fourpence, a jolly jolly fourpence
And I love that fourpence as I love my life
A penny I will spend, and another I will lend
And twopence I'll take home to my wife.

6   I've got a twopence, a jolly jolly twopence,
And I love that twopence as I love my life
A penny I will spend, and another I will lend
And myself I'll take home to my wife.

ROBERT ALEXANDER — D

B

The Shilling

1   I love my shilling, my jolly jolly shilling
I love my shilling as I love my life
A penny I'll spend and another I'll lend
And it's tenpence I'll carry home to my wife.
No merry merry maid shall deceive me
No gill stoups nor pint stoups to grieve me
Sally is the girl that will keep me
When I go rowling home.
Row-row-row-rowling ho-o-ome
Row row row rowling ho-o-me
Sally is the girl that'll keep me
When I go rowling home.

2   I love my tenpence, my jolly jolly tenpence
I love my tenpence as I love my life
And a penny I'll spend and another I'll lend
And it's eightpence I'll carry home to my wife.

3   I love my twopence, my jolly jolly twopence
I love my twopence as I love my life
And a penny I'll spend and a penny I'll lend
And it's nothing I'll carry home to my wife.

WILLIAM SPENCE — G

C

1   Hey my jolly shilling, how my jolly shilling,
I love my shilling as dear's I love my life.
I've a penny for to spend, I've a penny for to lend,
I'll take tenpence home to my wife.
Neither pint stoup nor glass shall grieve me,
And no flashy girl shall deceive me
But happy is the girl that does keep me,
When I go rolling home,
Rolling home, rolling home,
When I go rolling home.

Miss BELL ROBERTSON — G

JOCK GEDDES

1   Jock Geddes on some business bent, to market gaed ae day light-hearted;
    His mither, careful o' her son, saw Jock fu' trig ere he departed.
    But Jock at markets whiles got fou, the place whaur tricky scamps wad trick 'im
    His mither therefore at the door cried oot — Come hame sober noo, ye nickum.
       Braw, braw, tae be weel liket, braw, braw, tae be sae bonnie;
       Braw, cried Jock, it is to be sae muckle thocht o' by sae mony.

2   But Jock as usual soon forgot, the plain injunctions o' his mither;
    The market made him awfu' dry, the cure was whisky — deil anither,
    He met a freen as dry's himsel', and aff they went tae weet their wizzens,
    Glass after glass gaed doon until the total number cam' tae dizzens.
                                        [with their thirst quenched

3   The cronies, slockit, rase tae pairt, and pairt they did in freenly fashion;
    By fegs, says Jock, it's kittle road, I'll hae tae use the utmost caution.
    At twal' o'clock he sleekit hame, he hadna deen his mither's biddin',   [slunk
    He couldna thrive, he tript and fell, wi' a' his length across the midden.

4   Jock jist lay still, fell fast asleep, the drink had fairly stopt his kickin',
    The soo cam' by, first smelt his moo, and likin' that, commenced a-lickin'.
    Hauf-waukened Jock cried oot — Weel, weel, it's my misfortune tae be bonnie;
    What limmer kisses at my mou? Haud aff, hoot dinna tak' sae mony.

5   The curious soo still licket on. Cried Jock, Noo Jean, haud aff, that's plenty;
    Lat Kirsty get a smack or twa, I'm sure ye've gotten mair than twenty.
    I ken I am a weel-faur'd chiel, but dinna get in sic a swither   [good-looking
    I'll lat ye kiss me, but od sake, ye maunna eat me a'thegither.

6   But Jock tae sense cam' roon at last, and, lookin' up, saw Sandy Campbell,
    Ye naisty brute beast, cried Jock, ye'll never mair upon me wammle.   [wallow
    He rase and spat for near an' oor, that soo had played an awfu' plisky,
    The brute was killed that vera day, and Jock has never since ta'en whisky.
       Braw, braw, tae be weel liket, braw, braw, it is, but, bless me,
       Owre weel liket winna dae: I never thocht a soo wad kiss me.

D. LAWSON — G

THE DRUNK MASON

1   A mason who was on the spree went staggering down the street
But still he strove right manfully to keep upon his feet.
Another mason who came round and saw his woful plight
Determined as in duty bound to see him home all right.

2   It was no easy task to do for toilsome was the road
He had to drag the drunk man too and he was no light load
He paused by the hillside to rest and looking to the light
That still was lingering in the west he saw an uncouth sight.

3   He knew it and was not afraid twas someone stealing grain
But turning to his friend he said in a light bantering strain.
Now William you always said Old Nick was sure to come for you
See here he comes to catch you quick, your prophecy comes true.

4   William looked and saw against the light the moving load of grain
Was quickly sobered by the sight though muddled still his brain
As from his lips a startling sound of frantic fear their rang
From off the road with one quick bound across the ditch he sprang.

5   He fell face foremost in the mire, thence rasing many a spark.
But rose and like a flash of fire he vanished in the dark
As Maggie ran to be secure from the infernal crew
So ran poor William always sure Old Nick did him pursue.

6   He did not know what way he went and not a straw cared he
At length with toil and terror spent he reached the Sauchen Tree.
He knocked. A man came to the door and looked out in amaze.

7   For such a guest within the place the man had no desire
So slammed the door right in his face and rushed back to the fire
When William saw his quick retreat he made a horrid din
Attacked the door wi' hands and feet and tried to break it in.

8   Then all the men together came and brought with them a light
And what they then saw was to them a mirth-provoking sight.
It was no monster to devour all clad in robes of fire.

Miss BELL ROBERTSON — G

THE DRYGATE BRIG

Mirren Gibb's

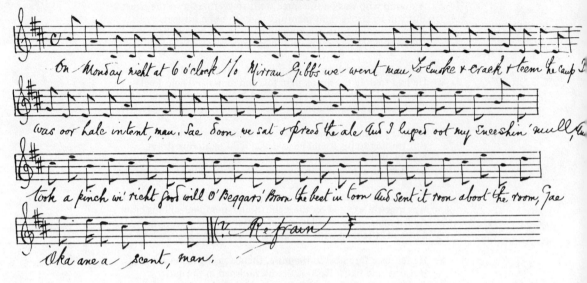

1. On Monday nicht at sax o'clock
   To Mirren Gibbs I went man
   Tae smoke an' crack and teem the caup
   It wis my hale intent man.
   Sae doon we sat, an' pree'd the ale
   An' I lugg'd oot my sneeshin' mull
   An' took a pinch wi' richt guid will
   O beggar's broon the best in toon
   Then sent it roon aboot the room
   Gae ilka ane a scent man.

2. As I cam in by the Drygate Brig
   The win' began tae blaw man
   It fuppit aff my aul grey wig
   And blew it far awa man.

3. Syne hammerin' in the dark man   [walking clumsily
   An bickerin' wi' my staff man   [striking out
   I coupit owre a muckle stane
   An skailt my puckle snuff man.   [spilt

4. Noo wad ye profit by my loss
   Then tak advice frae me man
   An' ne'er lat common sense tak' wing
   On fumes o' barley bree man
   For drink'll heeve a man as high
   As mak his heid maist touch the sky
   But doon he tumles bye-an-bye
   Wi' sic a thud, mang stanes an mud
   An' aft it's guid, but dirt an' bluid
   Be a' he hae tae dree man.

A. RETTIE – G

THE TARVES RANT

A

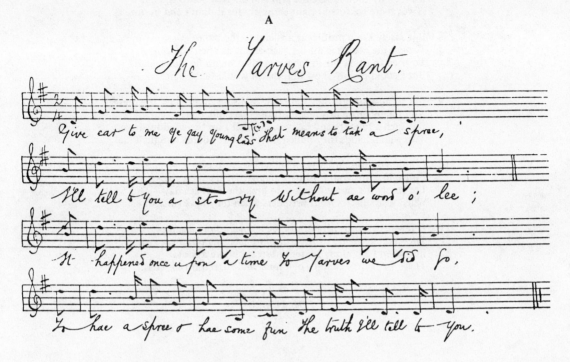

The Tarves Rant.

1 Give ear to me ye gay young lads that means to take a spree,
   I'll tell to you a story withoot ae word o' lee.
   It happened once upon a time to Tarves we did go,
   To have a spree and ha'e some fun, the truth I'll let you know.

2 My name I needna mention it's hardly worth my while
   I dinna mean to ruin mysel' or spend my time in jail
   For I canna work your horses I canna haud your ploo
   Cut nor build in harvest but I can feed a coo.

3 To Tarves we for treacle came we bein' on oor brose,
   Some o' them for boots and shoes, and some o' them for clothes.
   There was as few there that I did know and as few there knew me,
   But there was one amongst the rest who tried to bully me.

4 When we arrived in Tarves to Duthie's we did part
   'Twas there we heard fine music which filled our hearts with glad.
   The man that played the music his name I winna hide,
   He was a gallant ploughboy, they ca'd him Ironside.

5 Away to Philip's we did go to have a little fun
   'Twas there I got ensnarèd with the maiden o' the inn.
   She was a lovely maiden, gey maiden that she be,
   Twa rosy cheeks, twa rollin' eyes, and a lovely maid was she.

6 Drink it was right merriment and drink I think nae shame
   But syne we left the tavern to steer oor course for hame.
   'Twas there I lost my comrades and on them I did cry
   And at that very moment a man in blue cam' by.

7   He told me very quickly if I didn't hold my tongue
He would take me into custody and that before nae lang.
He roughly took me by the arm and dragged me to the inn
'Twas there we fought right earnestly for it didn't end in fun.

8   But surely I'm a profligant a villain to the bone
To tear the coat frae aff his back and it nae bein' his ain.
To tried to shove me in the room his strength he didna spare
But I could plainly show him that it would tak' a pair.

9   But soon assistants they did come and shoved me thro' the door
And I bein' left a prisoner a prisoner to think o'er.
But such a thocht cam' in my mind that I up the window drew
Twa willin' hands they pulled me oot, but I didna like the blue.

10   I think you folk in Tarves a jail will need to get
For to lock up your prisoners and nae lat them escape.
For surely it's an awfu' crime to brak the Sabbath day
When searchin' for your prisoners when they have run away.

11   A few mair words I'll tell to thee it's nae to my disgrace,
They brocht me up to Aiberdeen to mak' me plead my case.
But when I heard my sentence I heard it like a shot,
There was thirty shillin's o' a fine, and fifteen for his coat.

JAMES EWEN – G

B

The Tarves Rant.

Gae, ear to me, you gay young lads that mean to tak' a spree; I'll tell to you a story with-oot a word o' lee; My name I will not mention, it's hardly worth my while, I dinna like to harm mysel', or spend my time in jile.

SAM DAVIDSON – G

392

C

Tarves Rant

To the tune of 417 *The Woods of Rickarton* B

JAMES ANGUS — G

D

The Tarves Rant

1   Gae ear tae me ye gay young lads wha' mean to tak' a spree
    I'll tell to you a story withoot a word o' lee
    My name I will not mention, it's hardly worth my while
    I dinna like to harm mysel' nor spend my time in jile.

2   I canna work your horses nor can I haud the ploo
    Nor cut nor bind in harvest but I can feed a coo.
    Ae day we did to Tarves gang for to hold a spree
    And the truth I will lat you ken.

3   When we arrived at Tarves to Duthie's we did gang
    We got some very fine music which made our hearts feel glad
    The man that played the music his name I winna hide
    He was a gallant ploughman lad they called him Ironside.

4   Some were there for boots and shoes and some were there for clothes
    And he was there for treacle as being on his brose
    Very few were there that I did know and very few knew me
    But there was one amang the rest that tried to bully me.

5   Then down to Mr Philips' we went twas there to get some fun
    But I was so ensnared wi' the maiden o' the inn
    She was a lovely maiden a maiden that she be
    Twa rosy cheeks, twa rolling e'en a pretty maid was she.

6   We sat and drank and merry went, we drank till we thought shame
And then to leave the tavern and steer our course for hame
But I did lose my comrade and on him I did cry
When just at that fair moment the lad in blue came by.

7   "I'll tell to you quite plainly if you dinna hold your tongue
I'll bring you into custody and that before it's long."
He took me roughly by the arm and dragged me to the inn
Twas there we fought in earnest twas nae then in fun.

8   He tried to haul me through the door his strength he couldna spare
But I did plainly show to him that it wad tak' a pair
At last he got assistance and hauled me through the door
Twas there I was made a prisoner and left to think it o'er.

9   Oh surely I'm a profligate, a villain at the bone
To tear the coat from off his back it being not his own
A few more thoughts came to my mind when up the window drew
Twa willing hands did haul me out they did not like the blue.

10   I think the folk in Tarves a jile wad need to get
For to hold their prisoners and not let them escape
I think it is a crime to break the Sabbath day
In searching for their prisoners when they do run away.

11   A few more words I have to say but not to my disgrace
I was ta'en to Aberdeen twas there to plead my case,
When I received my sentence I received it like a shot
Twas thirty shillings for a fine and fifteen for the coat.

12   Now I'll tell you briskly ploughman lads a warnin' tak by me
It's when ye gang to Tarves to get upon the spree
Just buy what you're requiring and steer your course for hame
For when a row arises ye winna get the blame.

Source unrecorded — G

E

The Tarves Rant

1   Give ear to me ye young men that mean to take a spree,
I'll tell to you a story without a word o' lee
My name I winna mention, it's nae worth the while,
I dinna mean to ruin mysel nor spend my time in jail.

2   I canna work your horses, I canna haud your ploo,
Nor cut nor bind in hairst, but I can feed a coo.
It happened on one evening to Tarves we did gang
To hae a spree and get some fun, the truth I'll lat ye ken.

3   When we arrived at Tarves to Duthie's we did go
It was there we got some music that made our hearts feel glad;
The man that played the music, his name I winna hide,
He was a jolly ploughman lad, they ca'd him Ironside.

4 For treacle he to Tarves came, for he was on his brose;
Some was there for boots and shoes and some was there for clothes.
Few was there that I did know, and as few there knew me;
But there was one amongst the rest that tried to bully me.

5 It's then to Philip's we did gang to get a little fun;
I was so ensnarèd wi' the maiden o' the inn.
She was a lovely maiden, the maiden that she be,
Twa rolling eyes, twa rosy cheeks, and a lovely girl was she.

6 We sat and drank in merriment, we sat till we thought shame,
And to leave the tavern, and steer our course for hame.
It was there I lost my comrades, and on them I did cry,
And just at that moment a lad in blue came by.

7 "I plainly tell to you gin ye dinna haud your tongue,
I'll get ye into custody, and that before it's lang."
He's ta'en me roughly by the arm, and led me to the inn,
It was there we fought in earnest, for then it wisna in fun.

8 Surely I am a proligant, a villain at the bone,
To tear the coat from off his back, and it being not his own.
It was to get me till a room, his strength he didna spare,
But I did plainly show to him that it would need a pair.

9 It's soon assistance came to him, they dragged me thro' a door,
And I was made a prisoner, and left to think it o'er.
A few came into my head, and up the window drew,
Twa willing hands they pulled me out, they didna like the blue.

10 I think the folk in Tarves a jail they'll need to get,
For to lock up their prisoners and not let them escape;
For I think it is a sin to break the Sabbath day
Searching for their prisoners while they do run away.

11 A few mair words I've got to say, but not to my disgrace,
To Aberdeen they did me bring, it's for to plead my case.
When I received my sentence, I received it like a shot —
I had thirty shillings for a finè, and fifteen for a coat.

12 Come all ye jolly ploughman lads, that mean to take a spree,
Fan ye gang to Tarves dinna get upon the spree;
Just go and get your eerant, and steer your course for hame,
And when a row does begin ye winna get the blame.

SAM DAVIDSON — G

F

The Tarves Ramble

1 Come all ye jolly hireman lads
And listen unto me
I'll tell to you a story
That's nae a word o' lee.
    Wi a airy airrity aidie, aide
    Airy airrity ann.

2 My name I needna mention
It's hardly worth the while
I am a jolly bailie lad
Near Tarves I do dwell.

3 I canna work your horses
I canna haud the plough
Cut nor build in harvest
But I can feed the coo.

4 It happened on an evening
To Tarves we did go
To get a dram and hae some fun
The truth I'll let you know.

5 When we arrived at Tarves
To Duthie's we did pad
And there we got some music
Which made our hearts right glad.

6 The chap that gave the music
His name I needna hide
He is a jolly ploughman lad
His name is Ironside.

7 Some was there for boots and shoes
And some was there for clothes
But he was there for treacle
He being on his brose.

8 Few was there that I did know
And as few there knew me
But there was one amongst the rest
That tried to bully me.

9 We next to Mr Philip's went
To try and get some fun
There I was sore ensnared
Wi' the maiden of the inn.

10 She was a lovely maiden
If maiden that she be
Twa rosy cheeks, twa rollin' e'en
And a lovely girl was she.

11 We sat and drank and merry were
We drank I think na shame
When eleven o'clock began to strike
We steered our course for hame.

12 It was there I lost my comrade
And on him I did cry
Just at that very moment
A man in blue came by.

13 And he did plainly tell me
If I didna hold my tongue
He would take me into custody
Before that it was long.

14 He tried to drag me to the inn
His strength he didna spare
But I did plainly show to him
That he would need a pair.

15 But surely I am a profligate
A villain at the bone
To tear the coat from off his back
It being not his own.

16 But assistance soon unto him came
They dragged me to the door
There I was made a prisoner
And left to think it o'er.

17 A sudden thought came in my mind
I up the window drew
Twa willing hands did pull me out
That didna like the blue.

18 I think the folks in Tarves
A jail would need to get
For to lock up their prisoners
And nae let them escape.

19 For surely it maun be a sin
To break the Sabbath day
Searching for their prisoners
When they do run away.

20 I've something more to tell you
Which adds to my disgrace
To Aberdeen I was brought up
Just for to plead my case.

21 The judge in passing sentence
I heard it like a shot
There was thirty shillings to pay down
And fifteen for the coat.

22 Now all ye jolly hireman lads
A warning take by me
When you go down to Tarves
Pray don't get on the spree.

23 But get what you are wanting
And steer your course for hame
And when a row it does break up
You winna get the blame.

Source unrecorded — G

ROBIE AND GRANNY

1 Robie and Granny they gaed to the toon
   Atween themsels twa they did spend hauf-a-croon
   For ae gless that Robie drank, Granny drank twa
   And aye the puir body said Pu' Robie, pu'
   Pu', pu', pu', Robie, pu'.

2 Robie and Granny they set awa hame
   And Granny fell into a ditch in the glen
   O Robie, O Robie, oh far am I noo
   I'm intil a ditch wid ye gie me a poo
   Singin Pu' pu, pu, Robie, pu'.

3 Robie heeld at her until he fell back
   Wi' a terrible rattle against a cairt track
   He cursed her and ca'd her an auld drunken soo
   But aye the puir body cried Pu Robie
   Pu' pu', pu' Robie pu'.

Mrs SIM — G

TAKE IT, BOB

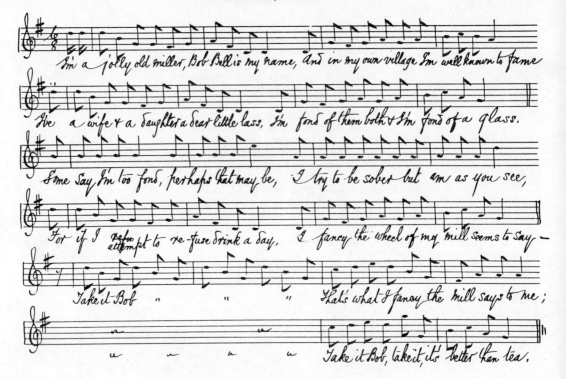

1   I'm a jolly old miller, Bob Bell is my name;
And in my own village I'm well known to fame;
I've a wife and a daughter, a dear little lass,
I'm fond of them both, and I'm fond of a glass.
Some say I'm too fond, well perhaps that may be,
I try to be steady, but am as you see;
For if I attempt to refuse drink a day,
I fancy the wheel of my mill seems to say —
    Take it Bob, take it Bob, take it Bob, take it Bob,
    That's what I fancy the mill says to me;
    Take it Bob, take it Bob, take it Bob, take it Bob,
    Take it Bob, take it, it's better than tea.

2   I tried very oft a teetotaller to be,
My mill is quite right, brandy's better than tea,
And altho' what I say you may all think absurd,
I believe what my mill says is right 'pon my word.
I called on old Jones 'bout some business you know,
He says, Bob a pipe and a glass 'fore ye go;
Now I didn't require it, believe what I say,
For altho' a mile off I could hear the mill say —
    Take it, Bob etc.

3   I dreamt the other night that Bob Bell was no more,
That he died at the age of p'raps forty or more,
And I heard people round me say, drink's done its worst,
But altho' I was dead I was dying with thirst;
A bottle of brandy close by I could see,
'Twas meant for the mourners, it wasn't for me,
But as on my bed still and silent I lay,
In the distance distinctly I heard the mill say —
   Take it Bob etc.

4   Now I'm only up here for a bit of a spree,
My wife thinks it's business, between you and me,
For you know the old saying that never deceives,
What the heart does not see why the eye does not grieve.
I must toddle away, so good-bye to you all,
I hope the next season I'll give you a call;
Don't ask me to drink when I'm going away,
Or I'm certain to fancy I hear my mill say —
   Take it Bob etc.

JAMES IRONSIDE — G

TAK IT, MAN, TAK IT

A

The Mill and the Kiln

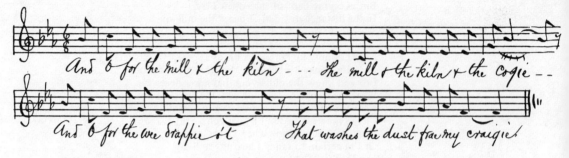

And O for the mill & the kiln --- The mill & the kiln & the cogie --
And O for the wee drappie o't   That washes the dust frae my craigie

ARTHUR BARRON – G

B

Tak It Man – Tak It

1   When I was a miller in Fife
  Losh I thought that the sound o' the happer
  Said "Tak hame a' we flow to your wife   [small quantity of meal
  To help to mak brose to your supper."
  Then my conscience was narrow and pure
  But someway by random it rackit   [stretched
  For I liftet twa neivefu' or mair
  While the happer said "Tak it man – tak it."
    Then hey for the mill and the kiln
    The garlan' and gear for my cogie
    And hey for the whisky and yill
    That washes the dust frae my cragie.   [throat

2   Although it's been lang in repute
  For rogues to make rich by deceivin
  Yet I see that it disna weel suit
  Honest men to begin to the thievin
  For my heart it gaed dunt upon dunt
  Oh I thought ilka dunt it wad crack it
  Sae I flung frae my neive what was in't
  Still the happer said "Tak it man, tak it."

3   A man that's been bred to the plough
  Might be deaved wi' its clamorous clatter
  Yet there's few that would suffer the sough
  After kennin what's said by the happer.
  I whiles thought it scoffed me to scorn
  Saying "Shame! is your conscience no chackit?"
  But when I grew dry for a horn
  It changed aye to "Tak it man – tak it."

4   The smugglers whiles came wi' their pocks
      Cause they kent that I liket a bicker   [beaker, drink
      Sae I bartered whiles wi' the gowks
      Gied them grain for a sup o' other liquor
      I had lang been accustomed to drink
      And aye when I proposed to quat it
      That thing wi' its clapperty clink
      Said aye to me: "Tak it man – tak it."

5   But the warst thing I did in my life
      Nae doot but you'll think I was wrang o't
      Od I tauld a bit body in Fife
      A' my tale and he made a bit sang o't
      I have aye had a voice a' my days
      But for singing I ne'er had the knack o't
      Yet I try whiles just thinkin' to please
      The greedy wi – Tak it man – tak it.

6   Noo miller and I as I am
      This far I can see through the matter
      There's men mair notorious to fame
      Mair greedy than me o' the muter
      For twad seem that the hale race of men
      Or wi' safety the hauf we may mak it
      Hae some speakin' happer within
      That said to them: "Tak it man – tak it."

Source unrecorded – G

580

ALE AND TOBACCO

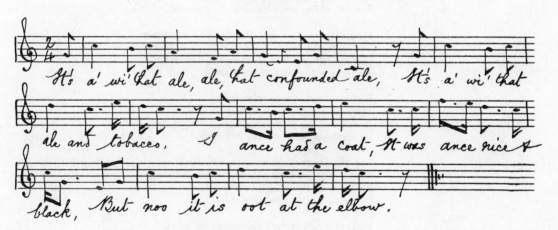

1   It's a' wi' that ale, ale, that confounded ale,
      It's a' wi' that ale and tobacco.
      I ance had a coat, it was ance nice and black,
      But noo it is oot at the elbow.

ARTHUR BARRON – G

DONALD BLUE

A
Donal Blue

To the tune of *Peggy in the Mornin'* from the same singer

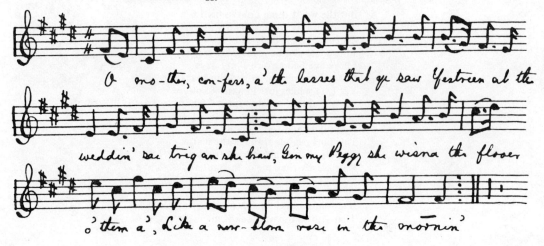

1   My nane's Donal Blue an ye keen me fu weel
    Gine ye straik me canny I'm a quate simple chiel
    Bit gine ye rouse my bleed I'm as rough the very diel
    Wi a claught o yere noodle in the mornin.

2   Bit I'll tell ye o a trick that happned in sooth   [really
    A smith got a wife an she had an unco drouth
    She lik't it sae well an pat sae muckle in her mouth
    She was aften carriet hame in the mornin.

3   It happned ae day when the smith he wis thrang   [busy
    They brought him a wife a wife that coud'na stan'
    He took her on his back an up the stair he ran
    An flung her in the bed till mornin.

4   He fell to his work he wis shoeing at a horse
    They cried Tak in yere wife smith she lien at the cross
    He liftet up his hammer an struck wi sic a force
    He nocket down his study in a fury.   [anvil

5   The diel's in the folk what do they mean ava
    Gine I've ae drunken wife I'm no needin twa
    Bit they cried aye the looder Tak her in fae the sna
    Or she's sure to be de'ed in the mornin.

6   I locket the door took the key in my haun
    An came down the stair, oh wretched man
    This conduct o hers I'm no fit to stan
    I'll list for a sodger in the mornin.

7   So the smith he gid out an' view'd her a' round
    By my sooth an it's her but how did she won doun?
    He hoisted her awa on his back to the room
    Whaur the either wife wis lien soundly snorin.

8 The smith to his surprise coudna tell which wis his
Frae the tap to the tae they were dress'd in a piece
An sae close they resembled each either in the face
He coudna tell which wis his Jeannie.

9 Deil ma care says the smith let them baith lie still
When ance she is sober she'll surely keen hersel.
Now frae that day to this Jeannie never buys a gill
Nor will she wet her moo in the mornin.

Mrs MARGARET GILLESPIE — D

B

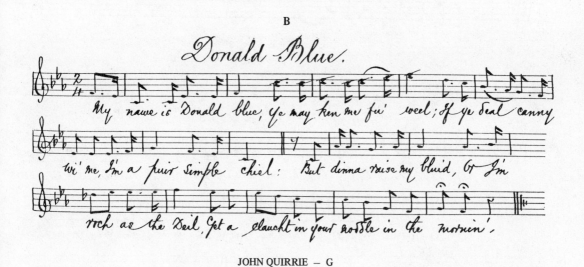

Donald Blue.

My name is Donald blue, ye may ken me fu' weel; If ye deal canny
wi' me, I'm a puir simple chiel: But dinna raise my bluid, Or I'm
roch as the Deil, Get a claucht in your noddle in the mornin'.

JOHN QUIRRIE — G

C

Donal' Blue

My name's Donal' Blue, an' ye kein one fu' weel, Straik me canny wi' the
hair, I'm a quaet simple chiel, But gin ye raise my bleed, I'm as roch's the
werra deil, wi' a claught o' yer noddle in the mornin'.

WILLIAM DUNCAN — D

403

D

J.W. SPENCE – G

E

My name's Donal' Blue, ye may ken me fu' weel, If ye deal cannie wi' me I'm a braw simple chiel; But if ye rouse my bleed I'm as mad as the deil, I wad ding doon a smiddy in the morn - in'.

Mrs DUNCAN – G

F

My name it is Donald Blue, Ye may ken me fu' weel: If ye deal canny with me I'm a puir simple chiel; But if you raise my blood, I'm as fierce as the deil – Get a claught in your noddle in the mornin'.

MAGGIE WATT – G

G

Donald Blue.

C. CLARK – G

H

Donal' Blue.

Oh the deil's i' the folk, what dae they mean ava? I've ae drucken wife an' I'm nae needin' twa;

But aye they cri-èd, Tak' her in frae the snaw, or she'll be dei'd lang afore the morn — ing.

JOHN JOHNSTONE – G

Donal' Blue

I

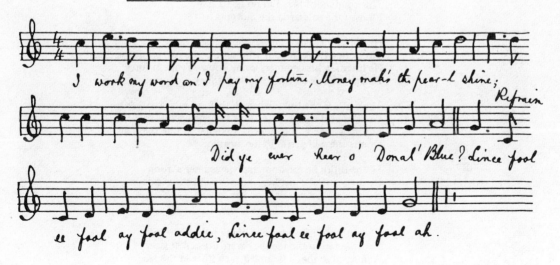

I work my word an' I pay my fortune, Money mak's th' pearl shine;

Refrain

Did ye ever hear o' Donal' Blue? Lince fool

ee fool ay fool addie, Lince fool ee fool ay fool ah.

Mrs LYALL – D

J

Donald Blue

GEORGE RIDDELL — G

K

Donald Blue

1 My name is Donald Blue, ye may ken me fu' well
   I am a canny but a poor simple chiel
   But gin ye pull my beard I'm as rough as the deil
   Gin I get a claucht of your noddle in the morning.

2 But I'll tell you o' a trick that happened in the south
   A smith got a wife that was ill wi' her drouth.
   She liket it sae weel, pat sae muckle in her mouth
   She was often helpit hame in the mornin.

3 So it happened ae day when the smith he was thrang
   They brought to him a wife that wi' drink couldna stan'
   He took her on his back an' up the stair he ran
   And flang her on the bed wi' a fury.

4 He lockit the door brought the key in his hand
   And cam doon the stair crying O bewitched man
   This conduct of hers I'm no fit to stan'
   I'll list for a soldier in the morning.

5 He fell to his wark, he was shoeing at a horse
   They cried "Tak in your wife smith, she is lying at the cross"
   He lifted up his hammer, came doon wi' siccan force
   He knocked doon the study in his fury.

6 The deil's in the folk, what do they mean ava
   Gin I've ae drunken wife, lord I'm nae needin' twa
   But they cried a' the louder, Take her in frae the snaw
   Or else she will perish in the mornin.

7 So the smith he gaed oot and viewed her a' roon
   By my sooth it's just her, but why did she get doon
   He hoisted her awa back to her room
   But there lay the ither lucky snorin'.

8 The smith to his surprise couldna tell his ain wife
   Frae the tap to the tae they were dressed apiece
   And so close they resembled each ither in the face
   He couldna tell which was his Jeannie.

9   Deil ma care, says the smith, let them baith lie still
     When once she is sober she'll surely ken hersel'
     Noo fae that day to this day Jeannie lives another life
     She's the joy of my life in the morning.

Source unrecorded — G

L
Donald Blue

1   My name is Donald Blue ye may ken me fu' weel
     If ye deal cannie wi' me I'm a braw simple chiel
     But gin ye rouse me up I'm as roch as the deil
     Get a clach tae your croon in the mornin'.

2   There was a smith lives awa a bittie sooth
     Wha has a wife that is ill wi' a drouth
     She keepit him sae doon hadden wi' sae muckle tae her mouth   [in
     She wis aften carriet hame in the mornin.   subjection

3   It happened ae day that the smith he wis thrang
     They fice hame a wife tae him, wha for drink culdna gang
     He took her in his airms and he hid her tae her room
     And he laid her on her bed in the mornin.

4   He started tae his wark, he was sheein' at a horse
     When the folk cam cryin "Smith, tak in your wife frae the Cross"
     He up wi' his hammer, cam doon wi' sic a force
     Micht hae knocked doon a smiddy in the mornin'.

5   What devil does the folk mean, what did they mean ava
     Altho' I hae a drunken wife I'm nae needin' twa
     But aye they cried the sairer Tak her in frae the snaw
     Or else she'll be deid lang or mornin'.

6   He buckled up his apron and doon the street he ran
     O it's jist you, fou the deil did you come home
     He took her in his airms an' hid her tae her room
     But there lay the ither lucky snorin'.

7   Noo they were baith clad apiece
     And likewise resembled ither in the face
     And the puir smith himsel didna ken which ane wis his
     He scarce kent the ither in the mornin'.

8   But frae that day tae this Jeannie led anither life
     For noo she's turned oot tae be a clean and sober wife
     And for the smith himsel' she's the joy o' his life
     For he sings like a lark in the mornin'.

Miss ANNIE SHIRER — G

M
The Smith's Drunken Wife

1 The smith is now blessed with a good sober wife
 And aye sin that time she's the joy o' his life
 And he sings like a lark in the mornin'.

Miss BELL ROBERTSON — G & D

THE DRAP O' CAPPIE O

A

The drap o' cappie O.

There lived a wife in oor toon-en, wha loved a drap o' cappie O,
And a' the gear that ever she got she slipt it in her gabbie O.

Mrs SANGSTER — G

B

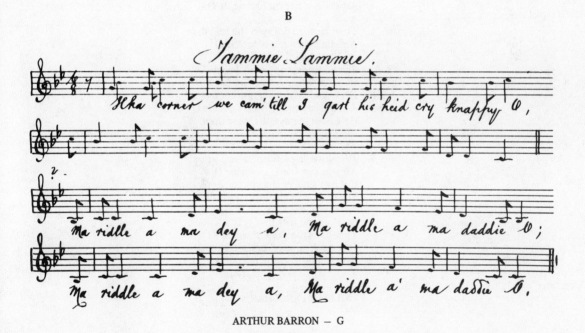

Tammie Tammie.

Ilka corner we cam' till I gart his heid cry knappy O,
Ma riddle a ma dey a, Ma riddle a ma daddie O;
Ma riddle a ma dey a, Ma riddle a' ma daddie O.

ARTHUR BARRON — G

C
The Drap o' Cappie O

1   There lives a wife at our gate en'
     That likes the drap o' cappie O   [ale
     An a' the gear that she can get
     She slips it in her gabbie O.
       My little lamb O doo O
       My little lamb O daddie O.

2   An she has called on her gudeman
     She ca's him Tammy Lammie O
     Bring ben the keys to me gudeman
     An we sal hae a dramie O.

3   It's Tammy being an honest man
     Himsel he likes the drappie O
     It wasna sooner owre his throat
     Than she was in his tappie O.   [reproving him

4   It's he's gane oot to the mill dam
     He's fessen in a pockie O
     He's pitten her in baith head an' feet
     An thrown her on his backie O.

5   Then he gaed doon to the mill dam
     And he's gaen her a dookie O
     An ilka chiel that hid a rung
     Played thump upon her backie O.

6   It's O gudeman ye'll murder me
     An' out my brains ye'll knockie O
     He's gaen her aye the ither thud
     Lie still ye evil buckie O.   [perverse person

7   This wifie lived for nineteen years
     An was aye frank an voggie O   [happy
     But aye sin e'er she got the dook
     She's never ta'en the drappie O.

8   So a' young lads that gets a wife
     That likes the drap o' cappie O
     Just dook them a' in time o' need
     An I'll lend you the pockie O.

WILLIAM FARQUHAR — G

O, FOO WILL I GET HAME

A

1 Ask my feet, and then my noddle,
Brandy rumbles in my wime,
My feet they winna tak the gate,
And O, foo will I win hame?
Aye fu' and seldom sober,
Aye fu' ere I win hame.

2 I got five shillings fae a frien',
To buy a coat to my auldest son,
But the weary drouth cam in my throat,
And I drank it a' ere I wan hame.

3 I've selt the sheen aff o' my feet,
I also sold my spottit gown,
My tartan shawl is in the pawn,
And O, foo will I win hame?

4 I've selt the meal oot o' the kist,
My husband never did me blame,
The mice and rats was blamed for that,
And O, foo will I win hame?

5 To kerk and session I've been summoned,
A' for to gar me think shame,
But the folk hereaboot they a' ken me,
And they ca' me drunken Jeannie Deans.

6 The Allan Water it's too close,
And I will fall into the stream,
I hae a man and bairnies three,
And O, foo will I win hame?

ISAAC TROUP — D

Song No. 583

B

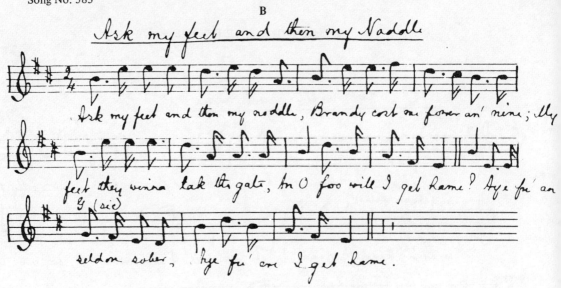

Ask my feet and then my noddle, Brandy cost me fower an' nine; My
feet they winna lak this gate, An O foo will I get hame? Aye fu' an
seldom sober, Aye fu' ere I get hame.

Rev. JAMES B. DUNCAN — D

HOOLY AND FAIRLY

A

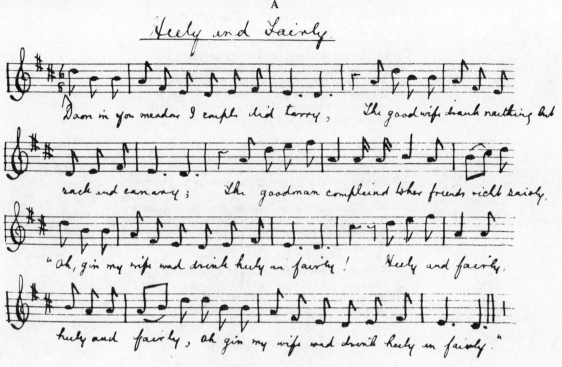

1 Doun in yon meadow a couple did tarry
  The guidwife drank naething bit wine an Canary
  The guidman complained to her friends richt sarely
  Oh gine my wifie wid drink hooly an fairly.   [moderately
     Hooly an fairly, hooly an fairly
     O gine my wifie wid drink hooly an fairly.

2 First she drunk Crummie an sine she drank Gerrie
  An sine she drank my bonnie grey marie
  That carrit me through a the dubs in the glaurie   [mud
  Oh gine my wifie wid drink hooly an fairly.

3 She drank her hose an she then drank her sheen O
  An n'oo she drunken her bonnie new goun O
  She drunken her sark that cover'd her rarely
  Oh gine my wifie wid drink hooly an fairly.

4 Wid she drink bit her ain things I widna much care O
  Bit she drinks my claes that I canna weel spare O
  An when I'm wi my gossips it angers me sairly
  Oh gine my wifie wid drink hooly and fairly.

5 My braw Sunday's coat she his laid it in wad O   [pawn
  An the best blue bonnet that e'rr was on my head O
  At kirk or at market I'm cover'd bit barely
  Oh gine my wifie wid drink hooly an fairly.

6   My bonnie white mittens I wore on my hands O
       Wi her ne'ebours wife she laid them in the pawn O
       My bane headed staff that I liket sae dearly
       Oh gine my wifie wid drink hooly an fairly.

7   I never was fond o wrangling or strife O
       Nor did I deny her the comforts o life O
       For when there's a war I'm aye for a parley
       Oh gine my wifie wid drink hooly an fairly.

8   When there's any money she maun keep the purse O
       If I seek bit a babee she'll scold an she'll curse O
       She lives like a queen while I'm scrimpit an sparely
       Oh gine my wifie wid drink hooly an fairly.

9   A pint wi her cummers I wid her allow O   [friends
       Bit when she sits down the jade she gets fu O
       An when she is fu she is unco camsterrie   [unruly
       Oh gine my wifie wid drink hooly an fairly.

10   When she comes to the street she roars an she rants O
       Has nae fear o her ne'ebours nor minds the house wants O
       She sings up a foul sang like "Up yer heart Charlie"
       Oh gine my wifie wid drink hooly an fairly.

11   When she comes hame she lays on the lads O
       The lasses she ca's them baith bitchs an jades O
       An mysel she ca's an auld cuckle carlie
       Oh gine my wifie wid drink hooly an fairly.

Mrs MARGARET GILLESPIE — D

B

Hooly and fairly

First sh. drank Crummie and then sh. drank Gairie, Then sh. drank my bonnie gray mearie, Carried me off thro' the dub and the lairie, Oh gin my wife wad drink hooly and fairly!

Mrs GREIG — D

C
Hooly an Fairly

1   O neebours what had I ado for to marry
    My wife she drinks brandy an wine o Canary
    An ca's me a niggardly thraw gabbit carlie   [crooked mouthed
    Oh gin my wifie wid drink hooly an fairly.
        Hooly an fairly, hooly an fairly,
        O gine my wifie wid drink hooly an fairly.

2   She feasts wi her kimmers on daintys anew aye
    Aye bowin an smirkin an ditin her mou aye
    While I sit aside an am helpet bit sparely
    Oh gine my wifie wid feast hooly an fairly.

3   To fairs an to bridals to preachin's an a' O
    She gangs sae light heartet an buskit sae braw, O
    Wi ribbons an pearlins it mak's me gang barely
    Oh gine my wifie wid spend hooly an fairly.

4   In the kirk sic commotion last sabbath she made O
    Wi bits o red roses an brest knots o'erlaid O
    The dominie sticket his psalm very nearly   [stopped
    O gine my wifie wid dress hooly an fairly.

5   She's waring an fighting fae mornin till e'en aye
    An if ye gainsay her her e'en glowers sae keen aye
    Then tongue, nive, an cudgel she'll lay on you sairly
    O gine my wife wid strike hooly an fairly.

6   When tired wi her cantrips she lies in her bed aye   [antics
    The wark a' neglect't the house ill upraidd aye   [ordered
    When a' our good neebours are stirring richt early
    O gine my wifie wid sleep timely an fairly.

7   A word o good counsil or grace she'll hear none O
    She bandies the elders an mocks at Mess John O   [bandies words with
    An back in his teeth his ain text she flings rarely
    O gine my wifie wid speak hooly an fairly.

8   I wish I were single I wish I was freed O
    I wish I were doited I wish I wer de'ed O
    Or she in the mouls to dement me nae mair, lay   [earth
    What does it avail to cry Hooly an fairly.
        Hooly an fairly, hooly an fairly
        Aye wastin my breath crying Hooly an fairly.

Mrs MARGARET GILLESPIE — D

JOCK AND MEG

A

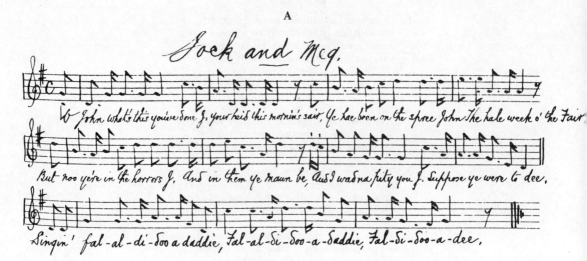

O John what's this you've done J, your heid this mornin's sair, Ye hae been on the spree John the hale week o' the Fair

But noo ye're in the horrors J, And in them ye maun be, And I wadna pity you J, suppose ye were to dee,

Singin' fal-al-di-doo a daddie, Fal-al-di-doo-a-daddie, Fal-di-doo-a-dee,

1   Oh John what's this ye've done John, your heid this mornin's sair
Ye hae been on the spree John the hale week o' the Fair
But noo ye're in the horrors John and in them ye maun be
And I wadna pity you John suppose you were to dee.
    Singing Fal-al-de-doo-a-daddie
    Fal-al-de-doo-a-daddie
    Fal the doo a dee.

2   Ye gang and see the shows John along wi' dandy Katie
And leavin' me in the house to starve wi' neither fire nor meat.
But your race is nearly run John your sportin' days are by
So be grieved for what ye've dane John and really so am I.

3   O Meg, O Meg, be easy Meg ye drink as weel as me
Fa's riven a' yer goon Meg fa's gien ye that blue e'e
And dinna haud me speakin' Meg or I will tell ye mair
The rigs ye carried on Meg the whole week o' the Fair.

4   Fa wis't that raised a row Meg wi' druckin Saunny Gray,
Fa wis't from off to Hight St. Meg was hawlin' you away
Fin ye was in the habble Meg fa wis't that peyed the fee   [mêlée
Ye wid hae been in Bridewell Meg if it hadna been for me.

5   Fa pawned the cups and saucers Meg, fa pawned the pots and pans
Fa pawned the blankits aff the bed come tell me if you can.
To treat your dandy weaver lad ye've stripped the hoose fu' bare
And ye've scarce been ae nicht in your bed the hale week o' the Fair.

6   But the cure is in the harm Meg anither gill bring in
And frae this time to New Year's day Meg we will pit in the pin.   [give up drinking
For we maun noo confess Meg that we've taen oot oor spree
And we will need to try Meg what better we can dee.

ALEXANDER ROBB — G

B

Jock and Meg

Lilti fal al the dadil dum Fal al the dadil dum Fal al the day.

1 Oh John, oh John what's this ye've done yer heidie's mair nor sair
For a' the rigs ye've cairret on the hale week o' the fair
But noo ye're in the horrors John and in them ye shall be
This nicht I widna pity you although ye were tae dee
    Liltie fal al the dadle-dum
    Fal al the dadle dum
    Fal al the dae.

2 Ye've gane through a' the show John alang wi' dandy Kate
Ye've left me stairvin in the hoose awantin' fire and mait
But noo yer race is run John yer sportin' days gone by
I'm sorry for what ye've done John and really so am I.

3 Oh Meg, oh Meg, be easy Meg ye drink as well as me
Fa wist that tore yer goon Meg, fa gaed ye that blue e'e?
Fan ye wis in the hobble Meg fa paid tae you the fee?
You would have been in brindle Meg if it hadna been for me.

4 Far's a' yer cups and saucers Meg, far's a' yer pots and pans?
Yer blankets aff the verra beds ye hae put in the pawn
To treat yer dandy weavers ye've stripped the house quite bare
Ye've scarcely been a nicht in bed the hale week o' the fair.

5 Fa' wist that raised the row Meg wi' drunken Sandy Gray?
Fa' wist in yon back street Meg that hurled you away?
You'll better haud yer tongue Meg for fear I tell ye mair,
For a' the rigs ye've cairret on the hale week o' the fair.

6 To cure us of the horrors Meg another gill we'll join
And then until New Year's Day we will tea-total join
Lang we may confess Meg we hae been on the spree
But we will need to try Meg fu' better we can be.

Miss KATE MITCHELL — G

C

Jock and Meg.

A boot yersel' this mornin, Jock, I'm sure yair heid is sair - The rigs ye carriet on J. the hale week o' the Fair;

But noo yir'e in the horrors J, And in them ye maun be; This nicht I widna pity you, Altho' ye were to dee. -

Singin' Fal al the deedle dee, Fal al the dee,

JAMES BEATON — G

D

Jock and Meg.

Cho.

And sing Fal al idly tidly, Fal al idly tidly, Fal al didee.

JOHN JOHNSTONE — G

E

Jock and Meg

1 About yersel' this morning, John, come, tell me what you think;
The very shirt frae aff your back, you'd pawn for want o' drink;
But ye are in the horrors, John, and in them weel may be;
For this nicht I widna help ye, altho' ye were to dee.
    Singing Fal al deedle deedle,
    Fal al deedle deedle,
    Fal al the dee.

2 Oh John, what's this you've done, John; your head is mourning sair
The rigs you've carried on, John, the hale week o' the Fair;
Your race is nearly run, John, your scorching days is nigh;
And ye are vexed for what ye've done, and really so am I.

3   You went to see the shows, John, alang wi' dandy Kate,
     Leaving me at hame, John, wi' neither fire nor meat.
     There's nae a tavern in the toon but what ye hae been through,
     And wi' them left your siller, John, what care they for ye noo?

4   O Meg, O Meg, be easy Meg, ye drank as weel as me;
     Wha wis't that tore your gown, Meg, wha gied ye that blue e'e?
     Oh dinna gar me speak, Meg, or I will tell ye mair,
     The rigs ye carried on, Meg, the hale week o' the Fair.

5   Whar's a' your cups and saucers, Meg, whar's a' your pots and pans?
     Wha pawned the blankets aff the bed? Come tell me if ye can.
     To treat your jolly weavers, Meg, ye've skinned the house clean bare,
     Ye wisna ae nicht in your bed the hale week o' the Fair.

6   Wha wis't that raised the row, Meg, wi' drunken Sandy Gray?
     When ye wis in the habble, Meg, wha hurled you away?
     When ye wis in the horrors, Meg, wha wis't that paid the fee?
     And ye would a' been in Bridle, Meg, an't hidna been for me.

7   In case o' the horrors, John, anither gill bring in;
     And then until New Year's Day we'll both ca in the pin.
     We maun confess for lang, John, we've carried on the spree;
     But we will need to try, John, an betters we can dee.

Miss ANNIE SHIRER — G

F
Jock and Meg

1   Oh John, oh John what's this you've done my heart is mair than sair
     I ken the rigs you've carriet on the hale week o' the fair
     But now you're in the horrors John an in them ye maun be
     This night I wadna pity you altho' you were to dee.
        Liltie fal-al de dadle dum,
        Fal-al de dadle dum,
        Fal-al de day.

2   You've gane through a' the shows John alang wi' dandy Kate,
     An left me starvin in the hoose for want o' fire and mate
     There's no a tavern in the toon but what you hae been through
     But noo your siller's dane John what care they for you noo?

3   Be easy Meg, be easy Meg, ye drunk as well as me
     Wha wis't that tore your gown Meg, wha gaed you that blue e'e?
     When ye wis in the hobble Meg, wha paid for you the . . . .
     You might have been in brindle Meg, had it nae been for me.

4   Where's a' my cups and saucers, Meg, where's a' my pots and pans?
     The very blankets aff the bed ye hae put in to pawn.
     To treat your dandy weavers, Meg, you've strippit the house quite bare
     You've scarce been ae night in your bed the hale week o' the fair.

5   What wis't that raised the row, Meg, wi' drunken Sandy Grey?
     Wha wist in yon back street, Meg, that hurlt you away?
     Be easy Meg, be easy Meg, nae haud me sayin' mair
     Or I'll tell ye a' the rows ye raised the hale week o' the fair.

6   I think we'll best be friens Meg, an anither gill we'll join,
    An then until New Year's day we will teetotal sign.
    For lang we maun confess, Meg, we hae been on the spree,
    But we maun really try an better we can be.

Miss GEORGINA REID — G

G

John and Meg

1   O John, O John, what's this you've done? your head this mornin's sair;
    Ye hinna been in your bed, John, the hale week o' the Fair.
    Ye've been in the horrors, John, and waur ye canna be;
    I widna pity you, John, altho' ye were to dee.
    To my Fal-al-di-dadie-adie,
    Fal-al-di-dadie-adie,
    Fal-di-do-a-da.

2   O Meg, O Meg, be easy Meg, ye drink as weel as I;
    Wha was't was in the Coogate, Meg, when I was passin' by?
    Noo jist haud your tongue, Meg, nor tempt me to say mair,
    For ye ken the rigs ye carried on the hale week o' the Fair.

3   Wha was't was on the spree, Meg, wi' drunken Sanny Gray?
    Wha was't was in the row, Meg, when haulin' you away?
    Wha was in the row, Meg, wha peyed the fee?
    O you wid been in Bridle, Meg, if it hadna been for me.

4   Wha pawns the cups and saucers, Meg, wha pawns the pots and pans?
    Wha pawns the blankets aff the beds, come tell me if you can?
    To treat your drunken weavers, Meg, ye've robbed the hoose quite bare;
    For ye hinna been in your bed, Meg, the hale week o' the Fair.

5   But there's anither saxpence, Meg, anither gill bring in;
    Frae this day till New Year's Day, Meg, we'll baith put in the pin.
    For it's gin we be na better, Meg, it's waur we canna be;
    But I think we'll need to try, Meg, what better we can dee.

ANGUS MICHIE — G

H

Jock and Meg

1   Oh John, what's this ye've done, John? your heid is mair than sair;
    The sprees ye've cairriet on, John, the hale week o' the Fair.
    There's nae a tavern in the toon but what ye hae been thro';
    Your claes are in the pawn, John, what care they for ye noo?

2   The bawbees are a' deen, John, your pouches are a' teem;
    So ye may grunt and groan, John, what care they for ye? — neen!

3 O Meg, O Meg, be easy, Meg, ye drank as weel as me;
   Fa wis't that tore your shawl, Meg, fa gied ye that blue e'e?

4 Faur is your cups and saucers, Meg, faur is your pots and pans?
   Ye've pawned the blankets aff the bed, – deny it if ye can.
   To treat your dandy weaver, Meg, ye've stript the hoose quite bare;
   Ye hinna been three nichts in bed the hale week o' the Fair.

5 And dinna gar me speak, Meg, or else I will say mair.

6 Your bawbees are a' deen, Meg, your claes are in the pawn;
   Ye've paid for your nicht's fun Meg so ye may grunt and groan.

7 Your race is nearly run, John; your sportin' day is by;
   You're vexed for what ye've done, John, and really so am I.

Mrs INGRAM – G

I
John and Meg

1 Aboot yoursel' this mornin' John, I'm sure your head is sair
   The rigs you've cairried on John the hale week o' the fair
   But noo ye're in the horrors John and in them ye maun be
   This nicht I widna pity you although ye war to dee.
     Singing Fal-lal-de-raddee-taddee
     Fal-lal-de-dee.

2 Oh Meg, oh Meg, be easy Meg, ye drink as weel as me
   Fa' wist that tore your goon, Meg, fa gaed ye that blue ee?
   Fin ye wis in the habble Meg, fa wist that pey'd the fee?
   Ye mith hae been in Bridewell Meg in't hidna been for me.

3 Faur's a' your cups and saucers Meg, faur's a' your pots and pans?
   Ye've pawn't the blankets in the beds so tell me if you can
   To treat your dandy weaver Meg ye've stripp't the hoose quite bare
   And ye hinna been in your bed Meg the hale week o' the fair.

4 . . . .
   Fae this time till New Year's day we'll baith shove in the pin
   And we will need to see Meg fa's carried on the spree
   And we will need to try Meg if better we can dee.

Mrs DUNCAN – G

J

Jock and Meg

1 Your bairnies they're a' ruined, Jock, their claes is in the pawn;
They've paid for your week's sportin', so ye maun grunt and groan.
There's nae a tavern in a' the toon but what ye hae been through;
But noo your money's a' done, Jock, what care I for ye noo?

2 O Meg, O Meg, be easy Meg, ye drink as weel as me;
Fa wis't that tore your goon, Meg, and gied ye that blue e'e?
Fan ye wis in the hubble, Meg, fa paid for you the fee?
Ye wid hae been in brindle, Meg, an it hidna been for me.

3 And lang may we confess, Meg, on haein' been on the spree;
But really we will try, Meg, and better we will be.

J. WILLOX – G

K

1 Wha was't that raised the row, Meg, wi' drunken Sawney Gray
Wha took you frae the High Street, Meg, wha hawled you away
When ye were in the habble Meg, wha was't that pay'd the fee
Ye would hae been in Bridewell, Meg, if it had not been for me.
  Singing Fal-al-al the derry
  Fal al the dee.

JOHN ORD – G

THE BARLEY BREE

A

The Barley Bree

1   Oor auld guidman gaed to the toon, to sell his puckle woo';
    And he cam' back withoot a plack, his noddle reevin' fou;   [blazing
    And on the road he lost his wig, as black as ony slae,
    Besides a plaid I span mysel', the best o' hodden gray.   [wool of natural colour
      Oh, weary on the barley bree, that brings baith skaith and scorn;
      It mak's us tyne oor peace o' min', and wish we'd ne'er been born.

2   Wi' fearfu' bang he oped the door, syne clashed doon by the fire;
    His troosers split frae heid to fit, his han's a' owre wi' mire;
    His cheeks were skarted right and left, wi' fa'in amo' the whins;   [scratched; gorse
    His nose had come against a stane, and he had peeled his shins.

3   Wae's me, I cried, I never thocht that I would live to see
    My ain guidman in sic a plight, – is this your love to me!
    Is this a wye to treat a wife, wha lo'es ye day and nicht;
    The bairns are greetin' in their beds, I'm maist near deid wi' fricht!

4   It's haud your tongue and dinna speak, but keep as quaet's a moose,
    Or than I'll tak' and brak' your backs, and syne I'll fire the hoose.
    Wi' that he tummelt aff the cheer, and fell doon on the rug;
    And there he lay till mornin' gray aside the collie dog.

5   I sleepit nane that leelang nicht, my he'rt was like to brak';
    But there he lay wi' baith his han's firm clasped roon collie's neck.

6   But noo it's altered days, I trow, I'm happier than a queen,
    For ilka day's as blithe as May; we're gettin' snug and bien.   [comfortable, well-off
    And hoo this change has come aboot, I trow ye'll maybe guess, –
    Oor Robin's turned teetotaler, and winna taste a gless.

JAMES THOMSON – G

B

1   Get out, said he, don't speak to me, I'll leave ye a' the morn;
    I'll sell my horse, I'll sell my kye, and a' my wheat and corn.

Miss BELL ROBERTSON – G

JOHNNIE, MY MAN

A

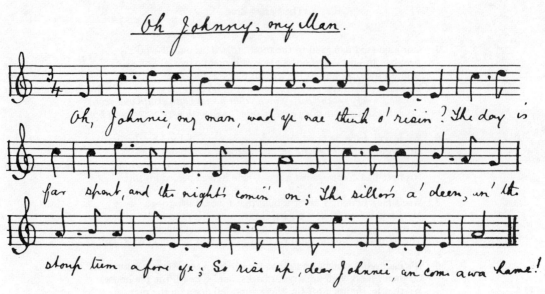

Oh Johnny, my Man.

Oh, Johnnie, my man, wad ye nae think o' risin? The day is far spent, and the night's comin' on; The siller's a' deen, un' the stoup teem afore ye; So rise up, dear Johnnie, an' come awa hame!

1 O Johnie my man wid ye no think on risin
The day is far spent and the nicht's comin on
The siller's a dune and the stoup's teem afore ye
O rise up dear Johnie and come awa hame.

2 Wha's that at the door I hear speakin sae kindly
Is that my wee wifie cae'd Jeanie by name?
O come awa in an tak a wee drapie
I'll rise up content'et an gang awa hame.

3 De'ye no mind my Jeanie when you an I court'et
Nae drink touched were heads nor hunger were mind
We spent the lang nicht mang the sweet scented roses
Was there e're a word Jeanie o going awa hame?

4 O weel do I mine on the days that ye speak o
Those days they are gone an will no come again
I mind on the present O try to ammend it
O rise up dear Johnie an come awa hame.

5 Wid ye no think on hame an the bairnies a' greetin
Nae meal in the barrel to fill their wee wames
While ye sit here drinkin ye leave me lamentin
O rise up dear Johnie an come awa hame.

6 Now Johnie rase up and the door he banged open
Said Woe to you, tavern, that ever I came
My cantie wee wifie has gained my affection
Could I disobey her? No I'll awa hame.

7   Noo Johnie gaes out in a fine summer evening
     Wi his wife an his bairns fu trig an fu braw
     When a wee time ago in rags they were rinnin
     And Johnie in the ale-house wis drinkin it a'.

8   Contented an happy he sits by his ain fireside
     And Jeanie a happier wife there is neane
     Nae mair to the tavern at nicht dis he wander
     But's happy wi Jeanie an his bairnies at hame.

Mrs MARGARET GILLESPIE — D

B

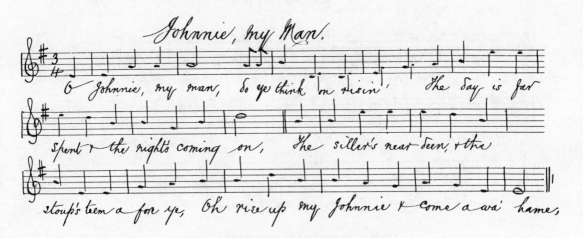

Johnnie, my Man.

O Johnnie, my man, do ye think on risin' the day is far
spent & the nights coming on, The siller's near deen, & the
stoup's teem a for ye, Oh rise up my Johnnie & come awa' hame,

1   Johnnie my man, are you no thinkin' o' risin'
     The day is far spent and the night's comin' on.
     Your siller's neer deen, and the stoup's teem afore ye
     O, rise up my Johnnie and come awa hame.

2   Wha's that at the door I hear speakin' sae kindly
     I think it's the voice o' my ain wifie Jean
     O come in my dearie and sit doon beside me
     For it's time enough yet to gang awa hame.

3   O Johnnie my man, when we first fell a-coortin
     We had naething but love then to trouble oor mind
     And we spent a' oor time mang the sweet scented roses
     And I ne'er thought lang then to gang awa hame.

4   Oh weel dae I mind on the time that ye speak o'
     And weel I remember the sweet flowery glen
     But thae days are past and will never return love
     Sae sit doon beside me and soon I'll gang hame.

5   Oh Johnnie my man oor bairns are a' greetin
     Nae meal in the hoose for to fill their wee wames
     While ye sit here drinkin' and leave me lamentin'
     Oh rise up my Johnnie and come awa hame.

6 Then Johnnie he rose and he banged the door open
   Saying Cursed be the tavern that e'er lat me in
   And cursed be the whisky that made me sae frisky
   So farewell whisky for I'll awa hame.

7 Noo Johnnie contented sits by his ain fireside
   And Jeannie a happier wife there is nane
   Nae mair to the tavern noo e'er does he wander
   But happy wi' Jeannie and bairnies at hame.

Miss GEORGINA REID – G

C

Oh Johnnie, My Dear

1 Oh Johnnie my dear do ye no think o' risin
   The day is far spent and the night's coming on
   Yer siller's a' daen and the till stoup is empty
   Oh rise up my Johnnie and come awa hame.

2 Wha's that at the door that is speakin' so canty
   It is my wee wifie sae weel's I do ken
   Come in my dear lassie and sit doon beside me
   Oh rise up my Johnnie and come awa' hame.

3 The bairnies at hame they're a' roarin' and greetin'
   Nae meal in the barrels to fill their wee wames
   And you sit here drinkin' and me sad lamentin'
   Oh rise up my Johnnie and come awa' hame.

4 Oh Johnnie my dear when we first acquainted
   Nae ale house nor tavern e'er ran in oor minds
   But spent the lang day mang the sweet scented roses
   And ne'er wad we thocht upon gaien awa hame.

5 Oh weel do I mind on that time that ye speak o'
   That days are awa and they'll ne'er come again
   But as for the present we try for to mend it
   O gie's yer hand Jeanie and come awa hame.

6   Then Johnnie got up and he banged the doors open
Says Woe to the day to this tavern I came
And fare ye well whisky that makes me aye tipsy
O gie's yer hand Jeanie and come awa hame.

J.W. SPENCE – G

D

Mrs SANGSTER – G

E

JOHN MOWAT – G

F

O Johnnie my man.

JOHN FOX – G

G

Johnnie my dear.

J. McBOYLE – G

H
Oh Johnnie, My Man

1   O Johnnie, my man, do ye no think o' risin'
    The day is far spent and the nicht's comin' on
    Yer siller's near deen and the stoup's teem before ye
    So rise up my Johnnie and come awa' hame.

428

2   Wha's that at the door, that's speakin' sae kindly
     Tis the voice of my wifie, ca'ed Jeanie by name,
     Come in by my dearie, and sit doon beside me
     It's time enough yet for to gang awa' hame.

3   Don't ye mind on the days when we first fell a-courtin
     We had naething but love then to trouble our mind
     We spent a' oor time mang the sweet scented roses
     And I ne'er thocht it lang then to gang awa hame.

4   O weel do I min' on the time that ye speak o'
     And weel do I min' on yon sweet flowery glen
     But thae days are a' past and will never return love
     Sae sit doon beside me and I'll soon gang hame.

5   Don't ye mind on your bairns, they're a' at hame greetin
     There's nae meal in the barrel to fill their wee wames
     While ye sit there drinkin' and leave me lamentin'
     Oh rise up my Johnnie and come awa hame.

6   Then Johnnie rose up, and he banged the door open
     Saying Cursed be the tavern that e'er let me in
     And cursed be the whisky that made me sae frisky
     Oh farewell whisky for I'm awa' hame.

7   And Jeannie, my dear, your advice will be taken
     I'll leave aff the drinkin' and follow thee hame
     Live sober and wisely and aye be respected
     Nae mair in the alehouse I'll sit doon at e'en.

8   Noo Johnnie gaes oot on a fine simmer's evening
     Wi' his wife and his bairns fu' trig and fu' braw
     Though no long before that in rags they were rinnin'
     While Johnnie sat drinkin' in the alehouse at e'en.

9   Contented and crouse, he sits by his ain fireside
     And Jeannie, a happier wife there is nane
     Nae mair to the alehouse at nicht he does wander
     But he's happy wi' Jeannie and the bairnies at hame.

Mrs THOM — G

I
Johnnie, My Man

1   O Johnnie man bit there's naething will raise ye
     The day is far spent and the nicht's comin on.
     Yer siller's a' deen and yer stoup's teem afore ye
     So rise up my Johnnie and come awa hame.

2   Whose is that sweet voice I hear aye sae lovely
     It is my wee wifie, it's Maggie by name
     Come in by my dearie and sit doon beside me
     And I'll rise up contented and gang awa hame.

3   Oh Johnnie man bit the bairnies is greetin
Nae meal's in the barrel tae fill their wee wames
And fan ye're sittin drinkin' it leaves them lamentin'
So rise up my Johnnie and come awa hame.

4   O Maggie lass when we was first acquainted
Nae hunger or cauld ever troubled our mind
But roved oot the nicht among sweet scented roses
And never a word aboot gaun awa hame.

5   O Johnnie man, but that days is forgotten
That days is awa and will never come again
But gin ye wid walk wisely ye wid aye be respeckit
Gang nae mair tae the alehouse and mak it your hame.

6   So Johnnie got up and the door he banged open
Says O curse on the day that to this tavern I came
So fare ye well whisky for it makes me thirsty
And fare ye well alehouse for I'm awa hame.

7   When Johnnie went out on a fine summer's evening
Wi' wifie and bairnies sae trig and sae braw
An' a wee while before that in rags they were rinnin'
When Johnnie wis sittin in the alehouse at even.

Mrs GRIEVE — G

J

Johnnie My Man

1   Johnnie my man would you nae think o' risin'
The day is far spent and the nicht's comin' on
The siller's a' dane and the stoup's teem before you
O rise up my Johnnie and come awa' hame.

2   Oh wha's at the door that I hear call sae lovely
Tis the voice o' my wee wife Maggie by name
Come in beside me a wee while my dearie
And I'll rise up contented and gang awa' hame.

3   Oh Johnnie man but the bairnies are greetin'
There's nae meal in the barn to fill their wee wames
While ye sit here drinkin ye leave us lamentin'
Oh rise up my Johnnie and come awa hame.

4   Oh Maggie lass when we were first acquainted
Nae hunger or thirst ere cam into oor mind
We strayed out at evening mang sweet-scented roses
And ne'er took a thocht upon gane awa' hame.

5   Oh Johnnie man, but these days are all over
These days are awa' and will ne'er come again
An' ye wad mind on the present and try for to mend it
And gang nae mair to the alehouse nor mak it your hame.

6 Johnnie got up and the door he banged open
   Said Cursed be the day to this tavern I came
   Fare ye weel whisky that makes me richt tipsy
   And fare ye well alehouse for I'm awa hame.

7 Noo Johnnie can get oot on a fine simmer's evening
   Wi' his wife and his bairnies fu' trig and fu' braw
   But a short time before in rags they were rinnin'
   While Johnnie sat a-drinkin' in the alehouse at een.

Source unrecorded — G

K

Johnnie, My Man

1 O Johnnie lad, are ye no thinkin' on risin'?
   The day is a' spent, and the night is comin' on;
   Ye're sittin' here drinkin', and the stoup is teem before ye;
   So rise up, my Johnnie, and come awa' hame.

2 Oh wha is that there that speaks so kind to me?
   It's no my wee wifie called Maggie by name;
   Come sit doon beside me a wee while, my dearie,
   And I'll rise up contented and gang awa' hame.

3 O Johnnie lad, the wee-anes is greetin',
   Nae meal in the barrel to fill their wee wimes,
   While we sit here drinkin' we leave them lamentin',
   Oh rise up, my Johnnie, and come awa' hame.

4 O Maggie lass, when we were first acquainted,
   Nae hunger nor thirst never troubled our mind;
   We spent the lang night among sweet-scented roses,
   And never took a thought of gaun awa' hame.

5 Oh Johnnie lad, that days are forgotten,
   That days are awa' and they'll ne'er come again,
   We'll think on the present and strive for to mend it,
   So gang nae mair to the alehouse nor mak' it your hame.

6 Johnnie's got up and banged the door open,
   Says, Cursed be that alehouse that ever I came,
   Singing, Fare ye weel whisky that oft made me tipsy,
   Sae fare ye weel whisky, and I'll awa' hame.

Miss ANNIE SHIRER — G

431

L
Johnnie, My Lad

1 Hey Johnnie lad, are ye thinkin' o' risin'?
    The day is far spent, and the nicht comin' on;
    When there ye sit drinkin' and leave me lamentin',
    So rise up, my Johnnie, and come awa' hame.

2 O hey Johnnie lad when we were first acquaint,
    Nae hunger nor thirst wad hae troubled my mind,
    When we could walk oot in a fine summer gloamin',
    And never ance thocht o' gaun awa' hame.

3 But oh Johnnie lad, that days are forgotten,
    That days are far spent and they'll never come again;
    But we'll hope for the future and try and dae better,
    So rise up, my Johnnie, and come awa' hame.

4 Oh hey Johnnie lad, the bairnies are a' greetin',
    Nae meal in the barrel tae fill their wee mou's;
    And there ye sit drinkin' and leave me lamentin',
    So rise up, my Johnnie, and come awa' hame.

5 When Johnnie heard this, tae the door he gaed stoopin',
    Says, Wae's to the tavern that e'er I cam' in;
    Says, Farewell whisky, for thee I'm aye thristy,
    I'll nae mair gang a-drinkin' at e'en.

6 Noo Johnnie can walk oot in a fine summer gloamin',
    Wi' his wife and his bairnies fu' neat and fu' clean;
    When nae lang afore they were hingin' in tatters,
    And Johnnie in the alehoose drinkin' at e'en.

Miss ANNIE SHIRER — G

M
Johnnie, My Man

1 The weans are a' greetin'
    Nae meal in the barrel to fill their wee wames
    The siller a' dane and the fire burnt oot,
    So rise up my Johnnie and come awa hame.

2 He's thrown doon the gill stoup, the door he's banged open
    O cursed be the day to your tavern I came
    Surely it's the voice of my wifie called Jeannie by name
    Saying Rise up my Johnnie and come awa hame.

3 Oh dinna ye mind on the days that are gone
    Nae drink hurt oor heads nor hunger oor wames
    But we rowed a' the nicht mang sweet scented heather
    An' neer took a thocht upon gang awa hame.

4 Oh weel div I mind o' the time that ye speak o'
    But that days are awa and they'll ne'er come again
    The bairns are greetin' an' needin' their supper
    So rise up my Johnnie and come awa hame.

Mrs DUNCAN — G

588

COME HAME TO YER LINGLES

To the tune of *Jock Robb* from the same singer

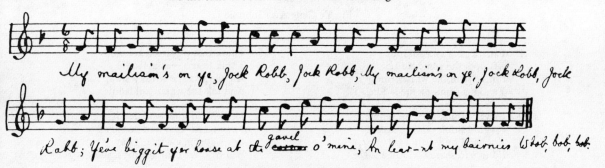

My mailison's on ye, Jock Robb, Jock Robb, My mailison's on ye, Jock Robb, Jock Rabb; Ye've biggit yer house at the gavel o' mine, An learnt my bairnies Whob, bob, bob.

1   Come hame to your lingles, ye ne'er do weel.

2   Better to nae hae a Monday ava.

Mrs MARGARET GILLESPIE — D

FIN YE GANG AWA JOHNNIE

a

Fin Ye Gang Awa Johnnie

1 Fan ye gang awa Johnnie
Aff upo' the spree laddie
Fin ye're in the whisky shop
Ye dinna think on me laddie.

2 I wyte I think on thee Jennie
I wyte I think on thee lassie
An' had I only half a gill
I'd like to share't wi' thee lassie.

3 I widna hae yer drink Johnnie
I widna hae yer drink laddie
For gin ye saw me in the ditch
I winner fat ye'd think laddie.

4 I wid think that ye were fu' Jennie
I wid think that ye were foo lassie
I'd jist think ye'd hauden gey
Muckle o' the liquor to yer moo lassie.

5 Think that o' yersel' Johnnie
Think that o' yersel laddie
An' gie awa the whisky stoup
And tak the water pail laddie.

6 I ken na fu' that wad dee Jeanie
I ken na fu' that wad dee lassie
For water in a winter's day
Wid be owre caul' for me lassie.

7 I'll mak it into tea Johnnie
I'll mak it into tea laddie
Ye'll learn a' oor bairns to drink
And ye'll get a' the bree laddie.

8 Sit up and dicht your ee Jeannie
My story is a lee lassie
For I've resolved that never mair
I'll touch the barley bree lassie.

9 To see you in the street Johnnie
A' dress't in ribbets neat laddie   [stripes
An squeer at ilka lantern post   [loiter
Indeed it gars me greet laddie.

b

1 Ye ken I'm growin' aul' Jeannie,
My bleed, it's growin caul' lassie
The drappie warms me, an' I'm sure
It's cruel o' you to scaul lassie.

Mrs DUNCAN — G

THE BRAW BLACK JUG

A

The Braw Black Jug

Long have I sitten in re-quest of thee, But now since we're met, we both shall agree, But now since ye're sae near my nose, Turn up, black jug, and down he goes, Ye're my braw black jug. Ye are my darling, ye are my jewel both night and morning; Ye're my braw black jug.

1   Long have I sitten in request of thee
      But now since we've met we both shall agree
      And now since ye are sae near my nose
      Turn up black jug and down it goes.
         Ye'r my braw black jug
         And ye are my darling both the night and the morning
         Ye'r my braw black jug.

2   But oft times ye make me pawn my clothes
      And oft times ye make my friends my foes
      But now since ye are sae near my nose
      Turn up black jug and down it goes.

3   And if my wife should me despise
      Oh I would give her two blue eyes
      But if she loves me as I love thee
      Oh what a loveing couple as we would be.

4   And when that I am dead and gone
      I will have it engraven on my grave stone
      I will have it engraven on my grave stone
      Grim death though me from my black jug have torn
         You'r my braw black jug etc.

ARCHIBALD KNOWLES — D

B
Aul' Black Jug

1   Oft times ye've made my friends, my foes
     Oft times ye've made me pawn my clothes
     But since ye've come so near my nose
     Turn up black jug, an' away she goes.
         Ye're my braw black jug
         Oh! ye are my darlin'
         Oh! ye are my jewel baith the nicht an' the mornin
         Aul black jug.

2   If my auld wife should thee despise
     I wad gie into her a pair o' blue eyes
     If my wife lov'd me, as I love thee
     Oh! what a loving couple we would be.

Mrs RETTIE — G

AUL' SANNERS AN' I

A

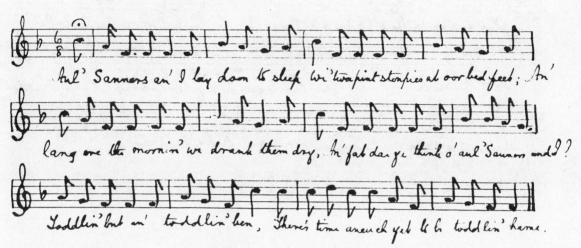

Mrs MARGARET GILLESPIE — D

B

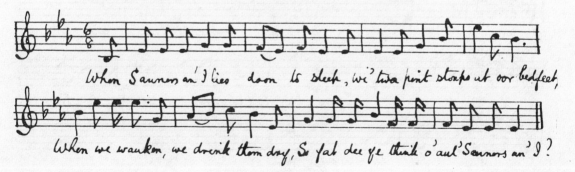

Mrs GREIG — D

THE DROUTHY SOUTERS

A

Mrs WATSON – G

B

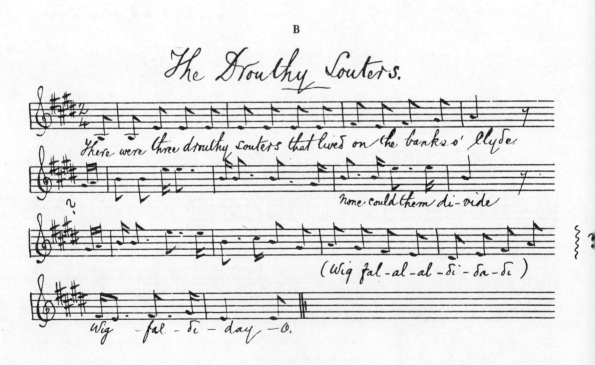

ARTHUR BARRON – G

593

GOOD ALE

A

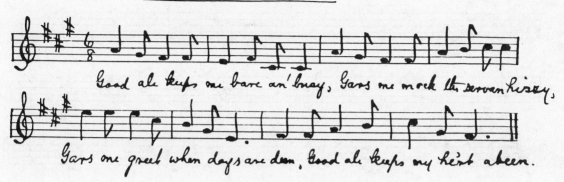

1   Good ale keeps me bare and busy,
      Gars me mock the servan' hizzy,
      Gars me greet when days are deen,
      Good ale keeps my hert abeen.
         Good ale comes, and good ale goes,
         Good ale gars me sell my hose,
         Sell my hose and pawn my sheen,
         Good ale keeps my hert abeen.

2   I have six ousen in a pleuch,
      And they a' rug it weel aneuch;
      He selt them a' just een by een,
      Good ale keeps my hert abeen.

3   He had six children bare and duddy,
      He lived hard to keep them fae the wuddy,
      He jiled them a' jist een by een
      Good ale keeps my hert abeen.

WILLIAM ARGO — D

B

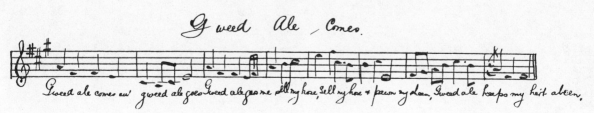

GEORGE RIDDELL — G

THE DRUNKARD'S RAGGIT WEAN

Mrs FINNIE — G

WATTY AND MEG

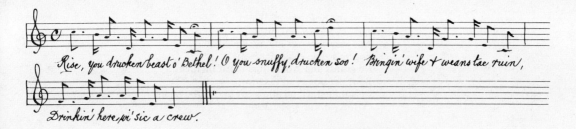

1 Rise, you drucken beast o' Bethel!
   O you snuffy, drucken soo!   [sulky
   Bringin' wife and weans tae ruin,
   Drinkin' here wi' sic a crew.

T.S. TOWERS – G

596

REFORM AND WHIGS

1 O weary Reform and Whigs
That ever they war invented
And wae's me for my ain gudeman
For he's gane clean dementit.
He grunts and groans frae morn till nicht
Boot pensions and taxation
He's ruined wi' meetin's got up for the nicht
O' the workin' population.

2 The feint a turn o' wark he'll do
To save us frae starvation
He leaves the horse tae sort the coo
For he maun sort the nation
There's nocht he'll do but read the news
An' he reads wi' sic attention
That breeks are a' worn thro' in a place
That I'm ashamed to mention.

3 He gaes to publics every nicht
And ilka groat he'll spend it
An' hoo he gets hame when in that plicht
I canna comprehend it
An' then my sons like twa young Hams
Laugh at their drunken faither
As doon in the floor wi' a clyte he slams   [heavy fall
An' o' Reform he'll blether.

4 Before the Whigs began their rigs
He wis a different creature
His e'en were bricht as orbs o' licht
An' fair was ilka feature.
His broo was like the lily white
His cheeks were red as roses
He had a back like Wallace wight   [valiant
And a thicker beard than Moses.

5 Bit noo he's lost his handsome face
An' tint his stalwart figure
His e'en are sunk oot o' their place
An' his nose is growin' bigger
And then guid sake when nicht sets in
He's fushionless as a wither   [pithless; willow
His back sticks oot and his wame's fa'in in
An' he's a' reformed thegither.

6 Oh dinna ye min ma ain guidman
When first we came thegither
How pleasantly life's current ran
Hoo pleased wi ane anither
Time passed away like a Sabbath day
When distant bells are ringin'
Your breath was sweet as new mown hay
And no like a rotten ingin.   [onion

442

7 Jist think what maist ye liket then
 An' see what noo yer brocht to
 And see if we werna far better aff
 Afore Reform was thocht o'.
 For if ye wantit a sark to your wame
 Ye made an awfu' wark man
 But what's to be done wi you noo when ye want
 A wame to pit on your sark man.

8 O! gin ye wad bit tend the ploo
 And mind yer empty pockets
 'Twere better far than drink or read
 Yer e'en oot o' their sockets
 Leave them wha can to mak' the laws
 An' while yer breeks I men' man
 Just lat the nation look to itsel
 An' look ye to your hinder-end, man!

Source unrecorded — G

WEARY ON THE GILL STOUP

A

What a Mischief Whisky's Done

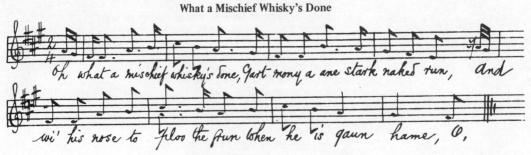

1   What a mischief whisky's done
    Gar't many a one stark naked run
    And wi' his nose to shiel the grun'
    As he is goin' home O.
        Weary on the gill stoup
        The gill stoup, the gill stoup
        My curse upon the gill stoup
        Brings muckle grief at hame O.

2   Drunken Jake he's no much better
    He drinks the whisky like cold water
    And then he sets oot like a hatter
    Oot owre the ragin' main O.

3   Soldier Tam gaed doon the toon
    Gaed doon the toon to draw his pay
    And he met in wi' Soldier John
    And they brocht nae a bawbee hame O.

4   My gudeman gaed to the mill
    Gaed to the mill to buy some meal
    The miller he being on the spree
    They saul the sack gaun hame O.

5   The lasses thinks they are nae richt
    While they lie doon their lanes at nicht
    And day and night their fancies flight
    Sayin' How'll we get a man O.

ALEXANDER ROBB — G

B

Weary on the Gill Stoup

1   Souter Jock, the ither day,
    Gaed doon the street to draw a spae,   [for "his pay"
    He met wi drunken Sauny Grey,
    Brocht nae a bawbee hame O.
        The weary on the gill stoup
        The gill stoup, the gill stoup
        The weary o' the gill stoup,
        Maks muckle grief at hame O.

ROBERT ALEXANDER and WILLIAM DUNCAN — D

ALWAYS ON THE SPREE

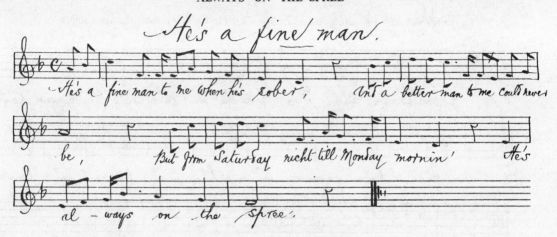

1 He's a fine man to me when he's sober,
And a better man to me could never be,
But from Saturday nicht till Monday mornin'
He's always on the spree.

ALEXANDER ROBB – G

THE FILLIN' O' THE PUNCHBOWL WEARIES ME

To the tune of *He's a Bonnie, Bonnie Laddie That I'm Gaun Wi'* from the same singer

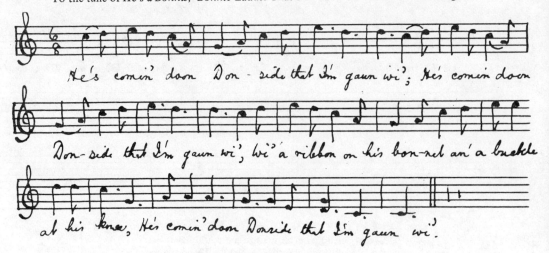

He's comin' doon Don-side that I'm gaun wi'; He's comin' doon
Don-side that I'm gaun wi', wi' a ribbon on his bon-net an' a buckle
at his knee, He's comin' doon Donside that I'm gaun wi'.

1 The fillin' o' the punchbowl wearies me,
    The fillin' o' the punchbowl waries me;
    The fillin' o' the punchbowl, the drinkin' o' the tea,
    And the kissin' o' a bonny lassie cheeries me.

Mrs MARGARET GILLESPIE – D

600

WAE BE TO THAT WEARY DRINK, JOHN ANDERSON, MY JO

A
John Anderson, My Jo

1 John Anderson, my jo John, I wonder what ye mean,
Ye're goin' on the spree, John, and stayin' oot at even.
Ye'll ca' yoursel' to ruin, John, and why should ye do so?
What ails ye noo at hame and me, John Anderson my jo?

2 Ye're going to Lucky Fill the Stoups, ye meet wi' Cooper Will,
Ye sit and booze like silly gowks, and aye the ither gill;
And aye the ither gill, John, till all your money go,
Ah wae be to that weary drink, John Anderson my jo.

3 It's the door is aff the barnie, John, the roof is aff the byre,
And I hae burned them baith, John, and a' for want of fire.
We've neither coo nor yowe, John, it used na to be so,
What ails ye noo at hame and me, John Anderson my jo?

4 But I'll tell you what, John Anderson, gin ye'll advised be,
And join the total abstinence, I'll join along with thee;
So we'll get peace and plenty, nae poverty and woe,
And ye'll nae repent ye gave consent, John Anderson my jo.

5 Jean Anderson, my jo Jean, fair fa' your honest heart,
Ye've sic a coaxing way, Jean, weel hae ye played your part.
So I'll advised be, Jean [*remainder sung together*] and hand in hand we'll go,
And we'll sleep thegither at the foot, Jean [*and* John] Anderson, my jo.

GEORGE GARIOCH — D

B

1 The roof is aff the barn, John, the door's aff the byre;
And we hae brunt them baith, John, and a' for winter's fire.
It's we hae neither cow nor yowe, for a' we ance hid baith,
And there's a curse upon your drap o' drink, John Anderson my jo.

Miss ANNIE SHIRER — G

JOHN BARLEYCORN, MY JO

John Barleycorn

1 John Barleycorn, my jo John when we were first acquaint
   I had money in my pocket John but noo, ye ken I want
   I spent it all in treating John because I loved you so
   And look ye how you've cheated me John Barleycorn my jo.

2 John Barleycorn, my jo John, one of your many ills
   You rob me of my money John which ought to pay my bills
   My creditors upbraid me John why I do use them so
   Which is the cruellest thing ava John Barleycorn my jo.

3 John Barleycorn my jo John, beside your other evils
   You threatened, sir, to frighten me by raising your blue devils
   Sic company I dinna like John from the regions down below
   So dinna try sic tricks again John Barleycorn my jo.

4 John Barleycorn my jo, John of friends ye hae sae many
   But surely ye hae nae forgot on drunken Peter Rennie
   For mony's the merry nicht we've had in sunshine and in snow
   But we three maun ne'er meet again John Barleycorn my jo.

5 It's true he will forswear you for longer time or shorter
   For often ye do gang to him disguised as Mr Porter
   Sic tricks I dinna like John they are so mean and low
   I wad rather see you naked far John Barleycorn my jo.

6 And in the early morning John before that I get up
   I would take you in a tumbler John and gladly drink you up
   We are told to love our enemies John and why should it not be so
   That we take our last and farewell glass John Barleycorn my jo.

7 You are surely turning frail John, when friends upon you call
   Unless it be at certain hours ye can't be seen at all
   And likewise upon Sunday John your face ye winna show
   Unless to some particular folks John Barleycorn my jo.

8 But we will never miss you John suppose ye keep your bed
   For we've plenty of lay preachers in the country in your stead
   Wha deals the spirit largely alike to rich and low
   I hope that it will stand the proof John Barleycorn my jo.

9 And at the feeing markets John, on you we'll turn our backs
   And we will treat the lassies John to Peter Drummond's tracts
   Who will receive them gladly John and read them as they go
   Your days are numbered now on earth John Barleycorn my jo.

A.M. INSCH — G

THE TEETOTAL MILL

1 Two jolly old topers once sat at an inn,
Discussing the merits of brandy and gin,
Said one to the other, I'll tell you what, Bill,
I've been hearing to-day of the Teetotal Mill.

2 You must know that this comical Mill has been built,
Of old broken casks, when the liquor's been spilt,
You go up the steps, and when at the door sill,
You've a paper to sign at the Teetotal Mill.

3 You promise, by signing the paper (I think),
That ale, wine, and spirit, you never will drink,
You give up, as they call it, such rascally swill,
And then you go into the Teetotal Mill.

4 There's a wheel in this Mill that they call "self denial,"
They turn it a bit just to give you a trial;
Old clothes are made new ones, and if you've been ill,
You're very soon cured in the Teetotal Mill.

5 Bill listened and wondered, at length he cried out —
Why, Tom, if it's true what you're telling about,
What fools we must be to be here sitting still,
Let us go and look in at the Teetotal Mill.

6 They gazed with amazement, for up came a man,
With disease and excesses his visage was wan,
He mounted the steps — signed the pledge with good will,
And went for a turn in the Teetotal Mill.

7 He quickly came out the picture of health,
And walked briskly on in the highway of wealth,
And, as onward he pressed, he shouted out still
Success to the wheel of the Teetotal Mill.

8 The next that went in were a man and his wife,
For many long years they'd been living in strife,
He had beat and abused her, and swore he would kill,
But his heart took a turn in the Teetotal Mill.

9 And when he came out, oh how altered was he!
His conduct was changed; and how happy was she;
They no more contended — no, you shan't — yes, I will,
But together they're blessing the Teetotal Mill.

10 Then next came a fellow as grim as a Turk,
To curse and to swear seemed his principal work,
He swore that that morning his skin he would fill,
And, drunk as he was, he reeled into the Mill.

11 But what he saw there, sure I never could tell,
But his conduct was changed and his language as well,
I saw, when he turned round the brow of the hill,
That he knelt and thanked God for the Teetotal Mill.

12 The poor were made rich, the rich were made strong,
    The shot was made short, and the purse was made long,
    These miracles puzzled both Thomas and Bill
    At length they went in for the Teetotal Mill.

13 A little time after, I heard a great shout,
    I turned round to see what the noise was about,
    And a crowd among which were both Thomas and Bill
    Were shouting hurrah for the Teetotal Mill.

JAMES GREIG — G

NANCY WHISKY

A

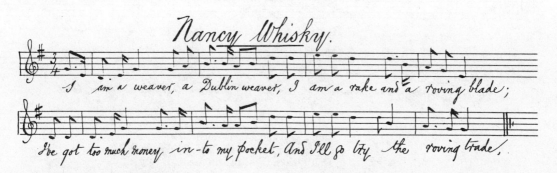

Nancy Whisky.

I am a weaver, a Dublin weaver, I am a rake and a roving blade;
I've got too much money in-to my pocket, And I'll go try the roving trade.

1 I am a weaver, a Dublin weaver
   I am a rake and a rovin blade
   I've got too much money into my pocket
   And I'll go try the rovin trade.

2 As I went down through Dublin city
   Nancy Whisky I chanced to smell
   And I went in for to see my Nancy
   It's seven long years since I loved her well.

3 I went in with hat in hand
   And I asked pardon for being so free
   Nancy Whisky jumped on the table
   You're welcome in young man to me.

4 The more I kissed her the more I loved her
   The more I loved her she on me smiled
   Till Nancy Whisky, till Nancy Whisky
   Till Nancy Whisky did me beguile.

5 Ben came the landlord
   And he asked me for to stay all night
   And Nancy Whisky would bear me compan
   Till tomorrow morning or daylight.

6 It's in the morning when I awoke
   And I found myself in an unca bed
   I tried to rise but I was not able
   For Nancy Whisky held down my head.

7 Ben came the landlord
   And I asked him what was to pay
   Fifty shillings besides cost reckoning
   Come pay it quickly march on your way.

8 I put my hand into my pocket
   Fifty shillings I did pay down
   I put my hand into my pocket
   And all I left was a single crown.

9 As I went up through Dublin city
   Nancy's sister I chanced to smell
   And I went in, spent four and sixpence
   And none remained but a crooked scale.

10 Will I regard this crooked saxpence
   Will I lay it up in a store
   I'll go in have another gill
   And I'll go home and I'll work for more.

11 I'll go home to my old master
   So nimbly as I'll make the shuttle fly
   I'll mak mair by the linen weavin
   Than eer I'll do by this rovin' way.

12 Come all ye weavers, ye Dublin weavers
   Ye linen weavers, where'er ye be
   Don't lay your love upon Nancy Whisky
   Or she'll ruin you as she's ruined me.

JOHN MOWAT — G

B

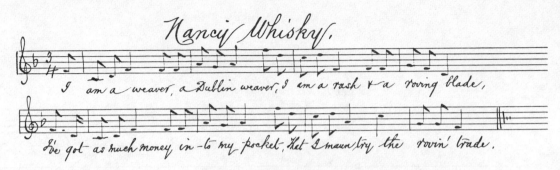

Nancy Whisky.

I am a weaver, a Dublin weaver, I am a rash & a roving blade,

I've got as much money, in-to my pocket, that I maun try the rovin' trade.

1   I am a weaver, a Dublin weaver,
    I am a rash and a rovin' blade,
    I've got as much money into my pocket
    That I maun try the rovin' trade.

2   Down the city as I was walking,
    Oh Nancy Whisky I chanced to meet,
    The more I kissed her, the more I blessed her,
    The more I kissed her the more she smiled,
    Till Nancy Whisky, till Nancy Whisky,
    Till Nancy Whisky has me beguiled.

3   Down the stair came the landlord,
    I asked him for all night to stay,
    And Nancy Whisky to bear me company
    Until the morning I go away.

4   In the morning when I awakened
    I found myself in an unco bed,
    I tried to rise but I was not able,
    For Nancy Whisky held down my head.

5   Down the stair came the landlady,
    I asked her what was to pay,
    Just fifty shillings with bygone reckonings,
    So pay your money and go your way.

6   I put my hand into my pocket,
    And all that money was well paid down,
    All that was left to buy me clothing,
    All that remained was but a crown.

7   Down the city as I was walking,
    Nancy's sister I chanced to smell,
    I went in, spent four and sixpence,
    All that remained was but a scale.

8   I do not value this crookèd sixpence,
    Neither will I lay it up in store,
    But I'll go and call another gill,
    And then go home and work for more.

9   I'll go back to my cotton weaving,
    So quickly I'll make the shuttle fly,
    For I'll make more at the cotton weaving
    Than ere I did by the roving boy.

10 Come all ye weavers, ye Dublin weavers,
Ye cotton weavers, where'er you be,
And take ye care of Nancy Whisky
She'll ruin you as she ruined me.

Miss GEORGINA REID — G

C

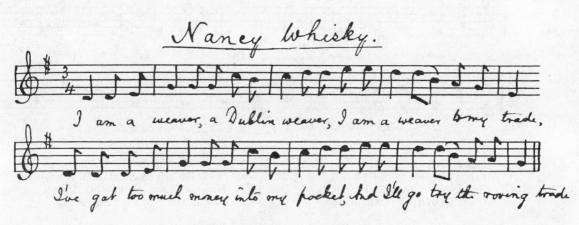

Nancy Whisky.

I am a weaver, a Dublin weaver, I am a weaver to my trade,

I've got too much money into my pocket, And I'll go try the roving trade

1   I am a weaver a Dublin weaver
     I am a weaver to my trade
     I've got too much money into my pocket
     And I'll go try the rovin trade.

2   For fifteen years I've been a weaver
     And all my wages has been well told down
     And I'll go on to Dublin City
     To buy some clothing in that fine town.

3   As I went up through Dublin City
     Nancy Whiskey I chanced to smell
     O Nancy I will go in and see you
     This fifteen years I have loved you well.

4   The more I kissed her the more I blessed her
     The more I kissed her the more she smiled
     Till Nancy Whiskey till Nancy Whiskey
     Till Nancy Whiskey my heart beguiled.

5   In the morning when I awoke,
     I found myself in a stranger bed,
     I tried to rise, but I was not able
     For Nancy Whiskey held down my head.

6   I called then on the landlady
     And asked her what was to pay
     Fifty shillings of bye gone reckoning,
     So pay it quickly and go your way.

7   I paid my bill to the landlady
     With fifty shillings well told down,
     And all remained and all remaineding,
     And all I had was but one crown.

8   As I gid down through Dublin City
     O Nancy's sister I chanced to spy
     I went in and drank four and sixpence,
     And all that remained was a crooked boy.

9   I do not value this crooked sixpence
     Nor will I lay it up in store
     But I'll go in have another gill
     And then I'll go and work for more.

Mrs MARGARET GILLESPIE — D

453

D

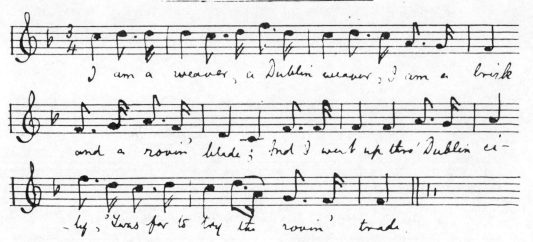

The Dublin Weaver

I am a weaver, a Dublin weaver, I am a brisk and a rovin' blade; And I went up thro' Dublin ci-ly, 'Twas for to try the rovin' trade.

1   I am a weaver, a Dublin weaver,
I am a brisk and a rovin' blade,
And I went up through Dublin city,
'Twas for to try the rovin' trade.

2   As I walked up through Dublin city
'Twas Nancy Whisky I chanced to smell,
Wi' heart and hand I stepped up to her,
'Twas seven lang years since I loved her well.

3   The more I kissed her, the more I loved her,
The more upon me and she did smile;
The more I kissed her, the more I loved her,
Till Nancy Whisky did me beguile.

4   The landlord then he called for reckoning,
The money there I paid it doon;
'Twas thirty shillings had I gone reckoning,
And all remainèd was half a croon.

5   As I walked up through Dublin city,
'Twas Nancy's sister I chanced to smell;
With her I spent twenty ither shillings,
And all remained was a naked scale.

6   I don't regard this crooked sixpence,
Nor will I hoard it up in store,
I'll go to the alehouse, and drink it,
'Twill help me hame to work for more.

7   Noo I'll gang back to my gweed auld maister,
So quick as I'll make the shuttle fly,
For I'll make more by the cotton weaving
Than ever I'll do by this roving way.

8   Now come, all ye weavers, ye Dublin weavers,
Come all ye brisk and roving blades,
I pray tak warning of Nancy Whisky,
For that is the thing has ruined me.

ALEXANDER MACKAY — D

E

Mrs STUART — G

F

It's – I'm a   weaver a Dublin weaver I am a rich & a rakish blade,

I've got some money into my pocket And I think I'll try the rovin' trade.

Mrs CLARK — G

G

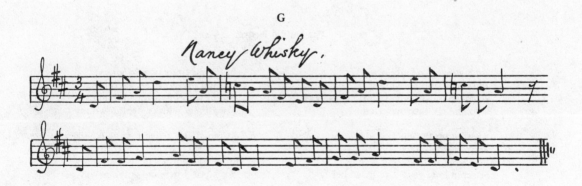

Mrs SANGSTER — G

H
Nancy Whisky

1 I am a weaver, a Dublin weaver
  I am a rough and a rakish blade
  I've got so much money into my pocket
  So I mean to try some rovin trade.

2 I gaed up through Dublin city
  Nancy Whisky I chance to smell
  Says I'll go in and call on Nancy
  It's seven long years since I told her well.

3 The more I kissed her, the more I blessed her
  The more I kissed her, the more she smiled
  The more I blessed her, the more I kissed her
  Till Nancy Whisky did me beguile.

4 The landlady she came down the stair
  Just asking me for all night to stay
  And Nancy Whisky would bear me company
  Until tomorrow when I went away.

5 Early next morning when I awoke
  I found myself in an unco bed
  I tried to rise but I was not able
  For Nancy Whisky held down my head.

6 The landlord he came down the stair
  I asked at him what was to pay
  Fifty shillings of my good reckoning
  Pay down your money and pad on your way.

7 I put my hand into my pocket
  The money all I did pay down
  And all that was left to buy meat and clothing
  It's all that was left was a single croon.

8 I stepped down a little farther
  And Nancy's sister I chanced to smell
  So I went in, drank four and sixpence
  And a' that was left was a crooked scale.

9 Now will I drink this single sixpence
  Or will I lay it by in store
  No I'll go in, call another gill
  And then go home and work for more.

10 I'll go home to my good old master
  So nimbly I'll make the shuttle fly
  For I do more at the cotton-weaving
  Than ever I did in a rakish way.

11 Come all ye weavers, ye Dublin weavers
  Come all ye young men where'er ye be
  And drink nae mair o' Nancy Whisky
  Or she'll do to you as she's done to me.

Source unrecorded — G

I
The Dublin Weaver

1 I am a weaver, a Dublin weaver
  I am a right and a rovin blade
  I've got so much money into my pocket
  I'll go and try the rovin trade.

2 As I went up through London city
  Nancy Whisky I chanced to spy
  And I went in to see my Nancy
  For seven long years I've loved her well.

3 The more I drank her, the more I loved her
  The more I kissed her, the more she smiled
  The more I kissed her, the more she smiled
  Till Nancy Whisky has me beguiled.

4 In the morning when I arose
  I found myself in an unco place
  I tried to rise but was not able
  For Nancy Whisky held down my head.

5 I rapped and called for the landlady
  To see what money I had to pay
  It's fifty shillings O poor stranger
  So pay it down and go your way.

6 I put my hand into my pocket
  And all my money I did pay down
  And all remained, and all remained
  And all remained was but a crown.

7   As I went up through London city
    Nancy's sister I chanced to spy
    And I went in, drank four and sixpence
    And all remained was a crooked scale.

8   It's I will not keep you crooked sixpence
    Nor will I lay you up in store
    But I'll go and ask for another gill
    And then I'll go and work for more.

9   It's I'll go back to my auld master
    And so nimbly's I'll make the shuttle fly
    I'll make more money by the cotton weaving
    Or ere I'll do by the rovin trade.

10   So come all ye weavers, ye Dublin weavers
    Come all ye weavers where'er ye be
    Don't lay your love on Nancy Whisky
    Or she'll ruin you as she's ruined me.

WILLIAM LORIMER — G

J
Nancy Whisky

1   It's fifteen years I've been a weaver,
    And a' my money's been weel paid doon,
    Noo I'll gang on to Dublin city,
    And buy some clothing in that fine toon.

2   As I went up thro' Dublin city,
    It's Nancy Whisky I chanced to smell,
    I swore I would go in and taste her,
    It's fifteen years since I loved her well.

3   Nancy Whisky jumped on the table,
    Says, You're welcome here young man to me;
    Nancy Whisky jumped in the tumbler,
    Says, You're welcome here, young Jack McGhee.

4   I sat and drank her oot o' the tumbler,
    Till I had nocht but pennies three;
    The landlord said, Ye maun be marchin',
    It's closing time, young Jack McGhee.

5   And I went up thro' Dublin city,
    Nancy's sister I chanced to smell,
    . . . .
    . . . .

6   But I'll gang back to my old master,
    And nimbly gar the shuttle fly,
    . . . .
    . . . .

KENNETH SHIRER — G

K
Nancy Whisky

1   I don't regard this crookit sixpence
    Neither will I lay it up in store
    But I'll ging in an' I'll drink a gill o't
    It'll do me home and I'll work for more.

2   When he gaed in to drink his gill
    Nancy's sister I chanced to smell
    Oh I did droon my Nancy Whisky
    In a pint or twa o' ale.

3   Neist mornin' I tried to rise
    But I wisna able
    For Nancy Whisky told doon my head
    Nancy Whisky jumped on the table.

Mrs DUNCAN — G

THE CLEAR CAULD WATER

A

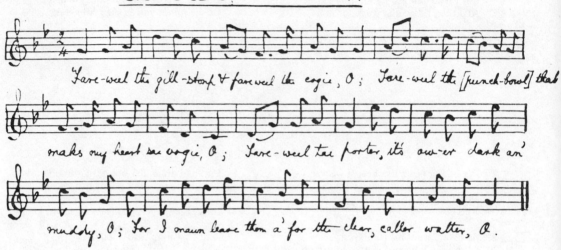

The Clear Caller Watter.

Fare-weel the gill-stoup & fare weel the cogie, O; Fare-weel the [punch-bowl] that maks my heart sae cogie, O; Fare-weel tae porter, it's ow-er dark an' muddy, O; For I maun leave them a' for the clear, caller watter, O.

GEORGE F. DUNCAN — D

B

The Clear Caller Water

1   Fare ye weel, ye ale wives, sae canny as ye clatter, O,   [gossip, chatter
For I maun leave ye a' for the clear, caller water, O.
Fare ye weel to whisky, an' fare ye weel to brandy, O
. . . .

Mrs MARGARET GILLESPIE and WILLIAM DUNCAN — D

C

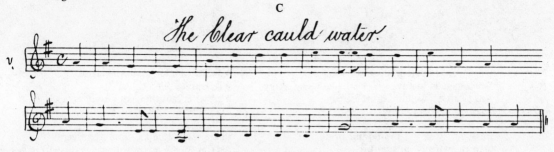

The Clear cauld water.

New Leeds woman — G

D

The Clear Cauld Water, O!

1   Fare-weel my bonnie cog, and fareweel my nappy O,
    And fareweel the broon jug that hauds the reamin' drappie O!
    And fareweel to whisky that maks me sing and clatter O,
    Now I wad leave ye a' for the clear cauld water O!

2   Fareweel ye gillstoups and fareweel to toddy O,
    And fareweel ye ginshops, and a' drunken body O.
    Fareweel ye alewives sae canny's ye can clatter O,
    Noo I wad leave ye a', for the clear cauld water O.

3   Fareweel ye new wine that sparkles fan it's ruddy O,
    And fareweel to porter ye're ower dark and muddy O.
    Fareweel to brandy, ye never made me fatter O
    Noo I wad leave ye a', for the clear caul' water O.

4   Fareweel to ruin and fareweel filthy stews
    Fareweel to intemperance and fareweel ye heavy dues.
    Fareweel ye standard hingin' by a tatter O,
    Noo I wad leave ye a', for the clear caul' water O.

Miss BELL ROBERTSON — G

SCOTCH MEDLEY

1. Was ne'er in Scotlan' heard or seen
   Sic dancin an' deray   [disorderly revelry
   As at Pattie's weddin' on the green
   Tae bonnie Mary Gray.

2. Busk ye, busk ye, my bonnie bride
   Quo the wife ayont the fire
   An' leave the rock an' wee puckle tow
   An' the muckin' o' Geordie's byre.

3. First four and twenty fiddlers came
   Wi' piper Rob th' Ranter
   He made them fain tae follow him
   When he blew up his chanter.

4. Fye let us tae the bridal a'
   Cried bonnie blue eyed Nelly
   And I'll dance whistle o'er the lave o't there
   Wi' the glee'd aul' Earl o' Kellie.

5. Then Bonnie Jean frae Aberdeen
   Cam through the Haughs o' Bogie
   An' Jonnie Faa cam in sae braw
   Wi' dainty Kathrine Ogie.

6. An' Wanderin Willie cam frae mang
   The Birks o' Invermay
   An' Jenny Nettles took the road
   Wi' peer Auld Robin Gray.

7. An' honest Aul' John Anderson
   Cam totterin' doon the hill
   An' Dainty Davie he brought in
   The Lass o' Patie's Mill.

8. Peer Duncan Gray sighed oot an' in
   An' made an unco bather
   An' spak o' Loupin owre the Linn
   If he gotna Maggie Lauder.

9. A tailor cam tae cloot the claes
   Wi' flaes he filled th' ha'
   Bit by ma saul they got a rout
   Frae Duncan an Maggie Macraw.

10. There was Cauld kail frae Aberdeen
    An Caustics frae Strathbogie   [stalks of kail or
    Hurrah for Bannocks o' Barley Meal   cabbage
    An' Whisky in a Cogie.

11. An there was brose an butter tae
    An' muckle store o' lang kail
    Ye micht hae cracked a lowse on Maggie's wime
    She supped sae mony pan kale.

12. The Ewie wi' the Crookit Horn
    The Haggis in a pot
    The Kale Brose o' Aul' Scotland tae
    An Herrin' laid in saut.

13. An' Willie brewed a peck o' maut
    That set them a' a-roarin
    The fiddlers rubbed their fiddle strings
    An' gae them Tullochgorum.

14. Then Heilan folk an' Lowlan folk
    They danced wi' muckle pride
    An merrily danced the Quaker's Wife
    Wi' the Lads frae Erroch side.

15. Puir Johnnie's grey breeks burst the steeks
    An rave up tae the gavel   [stitches
    And Jennie Diver bade them play
    The cattie rode the pedal.

16. An Tibbie Fowler o' the glen
    Tho mony lads were puin at 'er
    The deil a ane wad she dance wi'
    Bit the Braw Lads o' Gala Water.

17. Bit Andra wi' his cutty goon
    He gied her pride a fa'
    The lassie tint her silken snood
    Among the green pea straw.

ALEXANDER BRUCE — G

606

FY, LET'S A TO THE BRIDAL

Fy, let's a' to the bredal An fy, let's a' gang braw, For Jocks to be married to Maggie, The lassie that's nae far awa.

1　Fy let's a to the bridal
　　An we'll get lilting there
　　For Jock's to be married to Maggie
　　The lass wi the gouden hair.
　　An there'll be lang kail an pottage
　　An bannocks o barley meal
　　An there'll be good saut herrin
　　To relish a cogie o ale.
　　　　Fy let's a to the bridal,
　　　　An fy let's a gang braw
　　　　For Jock's to be married to Maggie,
　　　　The lassie that nae far awa.

2　And ther'll be Sandy the souter
　　An Wull wi the muckle moo
　　An ther'll be Tam the bluter
　　An Andrew the tinkler I trew
　　An ther'll be bow-leggit Robbie
　　Wi thumless Katie's guidman
　　An ther'll be blue cheekit Dobbie
　　An Laurin the laird o the land.

3　An ther'll be sou livered Pattie
　　An plookie-faced Watt o the mill　　　　　　　　[spotty-faced
　　An capper nosed Francie an Gibbie
　　That win's in the howe o the hill
　　An ther'll be Alister Sibbie
　　That in wi black Bess mool
　　Wi sneevlin Lillie an Tibbie
　　The lass that sits aft on the stool.

4　An ther'll be Judan Maclowrie
　　An blinkin daft Baby Macleg
　　Wi flea luggit sharney faced Laurie
　　An shangie-moo'd haluket Meg　　　　　　　　[lantern jawed; uncouth
　　An ther'll be happer hipp'd Nancie　　　　　　　[with protruding hips
　　An fairy faced Flowrie by name
　　Muck Maudie an fat luggit Grizzy
　　The lass wi the gouden wime.

461

5 An ther'll be girn again Gibbin
      An his glaikit wife Jenny Bell
      An misle-shinn'd Mungo Macapie   [with blotched legs
      The lad that wis skipper himsel.
      There's lads an lasses an pearlins   [lace
      Will feast in the heart o the ha
      On sybows an reffarts an carlins   [onions; radishes; peas
      That are baith sodden an raw.

6 An ther'll be fadges an brachen   [barley loaves
      An fouth o guid gabbocks o skate   [mouthfuls
      Pow soudie an drammock an crowdie [sheep's head broth; oatmeal; soft
      An caller nowt feet on a plate.   cheese
      An ther'll be partins an buckies   [crabs; whelks
      An whytens an speldins anew   [dried fish
      An singet sheep heads and a haggis
      An scadlips to sup till ye spue.   [thin broth

7 An ther'll be lapper milk cabbocks   [curdled milk cheeses
      An sowans an farles an baps   [buns
      Wi swats an well scraped pinches   [tripe
      An brandy in stoups an' in caps
      An ther'll be meal kail an kustocks   [cabbage
      Wi skink tae sup till we rive   [shin of beef
      An roasts to roast on a brander   [gridiron
      Of flukes that were taken alive.   [flounders

8 Scraped haddocks, wilks, dulse, an tangles [seaweed
      An a mull o' guid sneeshin to pree
      When weary wi eatin' an drinkin
      Wee'l rise up an dance tull we dee
      Fy lat's a till the bridal
      For ther'll be lilten there,
      For Jock's to be married wi Maggie
      The lass wi the gouden hair.

Mrs MARGARET GILLESPIE — D

THE WEDDING

A

Patie's Weddin.

1   Come in man an gie us yer crack,
     I heard ye was owre at the weddin'
     Oh well I wyte man I was that
     And lent them a han' at the beddin'.
     Guidsake, man, and hoo cam' ye on?
     For Patie's a comical body
     And mony a terrible day
     We hae had wi' him coortin' the howdie.
        Right-fal-dreedle-irrel-ay-ae.

2   Come on man I wyte we did weel
     Ye ne'er saw the like o't I'm thinkin'
     For there was baith fiddlin' and dancin'
     And fouth o' guid eatin' and drinkin'.
     It's nae like the weddin's that's noo
     Wi' their bits o' laif breid and some butter
     And twa three cup o' gibbrel o' tae   [for "gibblich", small amount
     Sweetened up wi' a wee pickle sucker.

3   For there there was plenty to eat
     Ay kail man to sup while ye're able
     Forby a guid herty Scots haggis
     To grace up the heid o' the table
     And there was great mountains o' beef
     And a hale buik o' weel roas'n mutton
     And Patie cried "Sirse will ye eat?"
     And Will worriet jist like a glutton.

4   O faith man I almost thocht shame
     O' this great glutton hash that sat next me,
     We had baith to eat oot o' ae plate
     And this was the wye that he fixt me.
     Fan the haggis was a' servit roon
     As muckle as micht weel ser't a dizzen
     I scarce had got liftet my spoon
     Fan he had it a' crammed doon his wizzen.

5   "Preserve's man," quo' I, "is it deen?"
    Quo' Will "Man, I'm fond o' a haggis
    But see, man, yonder's a bane
    And plenty o' mutton and taties.
    Nae fear but we'll a' get oor fill
    For Patie's a braw herty fallow,
    But oh man, the haggis was guid
    For I'm sure that the half o't was tallow.

6   A' gabs noo were eident at wark,
    Like bees in a byke they were bummin'   [hive
    And the meesie o' breath on het kail   [cooling
    And speens on teem plates keepit hummin'
    The veevers gang doon like a shot   [dishes
    Waesooks for the gawkie that lingers   [alas for the fool
    And some that were scuttert for speens   [hindered by
    Were liftin' great dawds wi' their fingers.

7   But Glenraggick was noo a' the cry,
    For he was to play them the fiddle
    Tho' some ane had fulled him sae fou
    He scarcely could gar her play diddle.
    We wid fyles wi' the hair gie a screek
    But as aft wi' the stick come a scrattle   [scratching
    Till the fit gaed awa' frae the cheer,
    And he fell on the fleer wi' a rattle.

8   He swore they had knockit him doon,
    Fan never a body was near him,
    And liftet a great muckle rung
    And startit a-cursin' and sweerin',
    Till Will for to mak' up the peace
    Gaed and filled up a gless o' guid toddy
    Says, "Glenraggick, tak' this and play up
    Till I get a reel wi' the howdie."

9   Sic a Shirrameer never was seen   [noisy rumpus
    Sic hoochin', sic skirlin', sic swingin',
    Some settin', some reelin', some wheelin',
    And some were jist loupin' and flingin'
    Fan o' dancin' they'd a' got their fill,
    Oh then they repaired to the beddin'
    Got fun wi' the mixin' o' legs,
    And that pat an end to the weddin'.

JAMES MORRISON – G

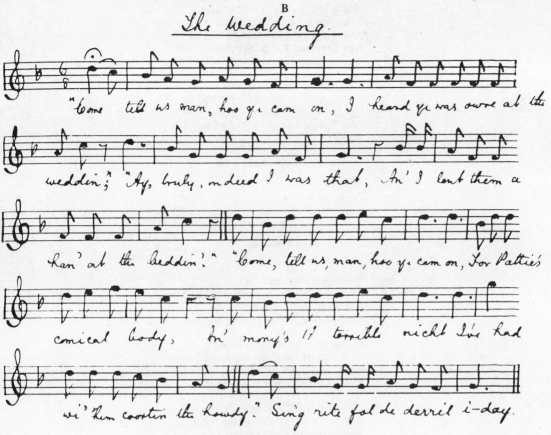

B
The Wedding.

"Come tell us man, hoo ye cam on, I heard ye was owre at the weddin;" "Ay, truly, indeed I was that, An' I lent them a han' at the beddin'." "Come, tell us, man, hoo ye cam on, For Patte's comical body, An' money's i' terrible nicht I've had wi' them coortin the howdy." Sing rite fal de derril i-day.

1 Come tell us man how you cam on
   I heard you was ouer at the weding
   Aye truley indeed I
   An I lenet them a han at the bedin.
   Oh tell us man how ye came on
   For Patey's a comical body
   An money's the terrible night
   I have haid we him courtin the howdie.
   Sing right falde lairl de lay.

2 The haggis wis served us a roun
   As much as might ay sert a dizen
   I scarsley got liftit my spoon
   Fin Will had it a in his wizen.
   Guid preserve me qu I is it dune
   Aie quha Willey I'm fond oh the hagis
   But look up yonder aboon
   There is plenty oh muttin and tatties.

3 Some of them ran for Blin Hughie
   It was for to play them the fiddle
   But some of them filled him sae fue
   That he scarsley quid gar hir cry didle.
   For files wi the hair he played screck
   And files we the hair he played scrattle
   Till awa went the feet fae his chair
   And he fell on his back wi a rattle.

4   Till we dancing they a got their fill
    And syne they began we the singin
    Johney sang Bony Tweed Side
    And Willey sang Hooley and Fairley
    And Tam sang The Banks oh the Clide
    An Jean sang The Auld Druken Carline.

5   Til we singin we a got our fill
    And sine we prepaired for the bedin
    Got fun we the mixin o legs
    And that pit an end to the wedin.

ARCHIBALD KNOWLES — D

C

Patie's Weddin'

1   The haggis wis served aroun',
    I'm sure it micht hae weel served a dizzen,
    Afore I got haud o' a spoon
    They hid it a' rammt in their wizzen.

2   It's nae like the weddins are noo
    Wi' nocht bit some fite breid and butter
    And three cups o' ghibblichie tae,
    Sween't up wi' a wee pucklie sugar.

3   They sent for blin' Hughie,
    And he wis tae play them the fiddle,
    Somebody full't him sae fou,
    He scarcely could gar her ca diddle.

4   For ance he cam' scrape o' the hair
    He twice on the timmer cried scrapple,
    Awa gaed a leg fae a chair,
    And he fell on the fleer wi' a rattle.

J. FAITH — G

608

CUTTIE'S WEDDIN'

A

GEORGE BRUCE THOMSON — G

B

WILLIAM REID — G

THE TINKERS' WEDDIN'

A

The Tinklers' Waddin'

1   In June when broom in bloom was seen,
    An' bracken waved fu' fresh an' green,
    An', warm the sun wi' siller sheen,
    The hills an' dells did gladden, O.

Mrs MARGARET GILLESPIE — D

B

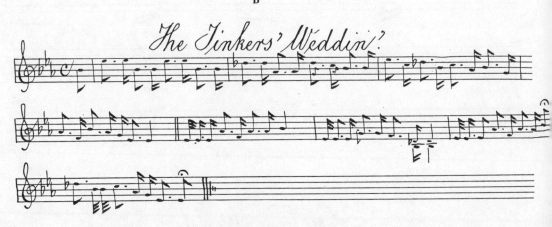

JOHN MOWAT — G

610

THE DONSIDE WEDDING

1   'Twas on the fifth of June, my boys,
     The truth I will make known,
     There stood a merry marriage
     Upon the banks of Don.

P.R. GORDON – G

HEY THE BONNIE BREISTKNOTS

1   There was a bridal in the toun
    And till't the lassies a' were boun
    Wi maunkie facings on their gowns   [calamanco, glossy wool
    And some o them hid breistknots.   [knots of ribbons
       Hey the bonnie breistknots
       Ho the bonnie briestknots
       Blythe an merry were they a'
       When they got on their breistknots.

2   And there was mony a lusty lad
    As ever handled grape on spand
    I wa't their manhood we'el they showed
    At the rufflin o the breistknots.

3   The bride by this time was right fain
    When she saw sae light a train
    She prayed the day micht keep fae rain
    For spoilin o the breistknots.

4   Forth cam the wives a' wi a phrase
    And wished the lassie happy days
    An muckle made they o' her claes
    Especially the breistknots.

5   Forth spak her mither when she saw
    The bride an maidens a' sae braw
    Wi cackling clouts black be ye're f'ase
    Ye've made a bonnie cast o't.

6   Next down their breakfast it wis set
    Some barley lippies o milk mate   [measures
    It leipit them it wis sae het
    As seen's they got a taste o't.

7   Till some frae them the speens they threw
    And sworn that they hid brunt their mo'o
    An some into their cutty blew
    I wat their wull they mus'd not.

8   When ilka ane hid claw'd his plate
    The piper lad he looket blate
    Altho they said that he sude a'te
    I tr'o he lost the best o't.

9   Syne forth they got a' wi a loup
    Owre creels an dales they a' did coup
    The.piper said wi them de'el scoup
    He'd mak a merry feast o't.

10   Syne aff they got a wi a fling
    Each lass unto her lad did cling
    An a' cried for a different spring   [dance
    The bride she soucht The Breistknots.

11   When they tied up the marriage band
    At the bridegroom's hame they neist did land
    Forth came auld Madge wi her split maund [basket
    An breed an cheese a feast o't.

12   She took a quarter an a third
    On the bride's head she gae't a dird   [blow
    Till farles flew athort the yird,
    She pairted roun the rest o't.

13   The bride then by the han's they took
    Twice thrice they led her roun the crook,
    Some said gudewife we'll mak ye brook
    An some great count they cast on't.

14   Some ran to kilns an barns in ranks
    Some sat on dales and some on planks
    The piper lad stood on his shanks
    An dirrle'd up The Breistknots.

Mrs MARGARET GILLESPIE — D

O WHA'S AT THE WINDOW

1 O wha's at the window O wha O wha
 O wha's at the window O wha
 Nane bit blyth Jamie Glen his come sax miles an ten
 To tak bonnie Jeanie awa awa,
  To tak bonnie Jeanie awa.

2 There is mirth on the green an the ha the ha
 There is mirth on the green an the ha
 There's fiddling an flinging an dancing an singin
 Bit the bride's father's gravest ava.

3 It's na that she's Jamie's ava ava
 It's na that she's Jamie's ava
 It maks my heart weary fin a the lave's cheery
 Bit it's jist that she'll aye be awa.

4 O bridal maidens are braw are braw
 O bridal maidens are braw
 But the bride's modest eye an her warm cheek to me
 Wi pearlins an broaches an a.

Mrs MARGARET GILLESPIE — D

THE ROAD TO PETERHEAD

A

GEORGE RIDDELL – G

B

The Road to Peterhead

1 In Buchan as I walked near,
Where Ugie's stream rins smooth and clear,
I went into a house to spier
The road to Peterhead.
But ere I came to find the door,
I ne'er got sic a fright afore
Upon the green there was three score
Of lads and lasses guid.

2 They were a' dancing in a ring,
The piper playing to them a spring,
Oh dear it was a pretty thing
To see them shake their feet.
I got nae time the reason to spier
Till ilk ane cries, "Ye're welcome here."
They took me for another I fear
So down I beet to sit.

3 I found myself in good Longside,
And that same house contained a bride
That made me fonder far to bide
In quarters for the night.
I got a man that told me well
The people's names and where they dwelt
He let me ken as weel himsel',
I am sure he told me right.

4 The bride's young man was Rora bred,
A jolly farmer to his trade,
His sweetheart . . . . maiden staid
I hear she was his choice
Sic bonnie lasses neat and clean,
Some dressed in white and some in green,
I wyte they didna spare their sheen,
The souters may rejoice.

5 The bonnie lads frae the ither side,
Adorned with wit instead of pride,
Was a' made welcome by the bride,
Her bread and ale to try.
It's up and doon and here and there,
Thro' Inverquhomery and everywhere,
The lads and lasses did not spare
To bear her company.

6 Sic bonnie lasses neat and clean,
Some dressed in white and some in green,
And some in yellow they did shine
And mony a different weed
The most of all young maids and men
Was more than seven score and ten,
It was well worth the poet's pains
To write their praise indeed.

7   But it would tak' me ere the morn
    To tell them a' baith heid and horn,
    It's twenty year sin' I was born
    And yet I never saw
    A winter day sae furnishèd
    Wi' husbandmen and men o' trade,
    Wi' souters, wivers, tailors bred,
    For makin' people braw.

8   But hark, I'll tell you other news,
    The bridegroom he sends for his spouse,
    She daurna for her life refuse,
    So we must all remain.
    Then to the church in haste we passed,
    The bridegroom followed at the last,
    Who got the parson to knit fast
    The nuptial knot of love.

9   This binds the husband to his wife,
    To love and cherish a' his life,
    And in obedience free from strife,
    She owns the man her head.
    Then to their dwelling we come all,
    I think Sandhole they do it call,
    A melancholy place to dwell,
    Close neighbours with the dead.

10 The lads and lasses a' were pleased,
    Beside a table linen faced
    The head of which our bride she graced
    Her young men by her side;
    A sumptuous dinner there we got,
    All pipin' it cam' frae the pot,
    A country shearer, by the Scot,
    To treat his bonnie bride.

11 With plenty of oatcakes and ale,
    With fowloo bree, and cabbage kail,   [chicken broth
    With broth and beef we did not fail
    To fill our wimes wi' speed.
    But thing most suprisèd me,
    I thought our wedding would been free;
    But now another thing I see —
    We're sevenpence ower-heid. [at an average rate per item

12 A sixpence did not serve forbye,
    And a' that did not signify
    Among such jovial company
    I thought I wared it weel.
    Then for to dance we tried our can,
    The bridegroom on the bride's young man,
    The maiden on the bride began —
    They call it shamful reel.

13 At 8 o'clock the heel she beats,
    And with modest voice invites,
    The modest folks to take their seats
    And lay the play aside.
    The modest sort syne did obey
    But some were willing for to stay
    In merriment to close the day
    At twelve o'clock at night.

14 But now I must them a' dismiss
    And let the bridegroom clasp and kiss,
    While on his marriage bed of bliss
    We've gotten him laid doon.
    His loving wife clasped to his breast
    By lawful orders frae the priest
    So this concludes our marriage feast
    And I wish they may sleep soun'.

15 My choicest blessings on them rest,
    From this time furth while life doth last,
    As for myself I think it best
    To bid Sandhole adieu;
    And if my song make any grudge,
    To seek me out ye need not budge,
    For at the place where I did lodge
    It's vain to seek me noo.

A.D. – G

C

1   In Buchan as I walked near
    Where Ugie's stream rins quick an' clear
    I went into a house to speer
    The road to Peterhead
    But as I gaed up to the door
    I ne'er got such a fright before
    For on the green there was a score
    O lads and lasses gweed.

473

2 And they were dancin' in a ring
The piper playin' up the spring
Oh but it was a pleasant thing
To see them shak' their fit.
I hadna time the road to speer
Till ilk ane cried Ye're welcome here
They took me for some ither, I fear
And down I be't to sit.

3 I found I was in brave Longside
And that the house contained a bride
Which made me then richt fain tae bide
And quarter there that nicht.

4 I thocht the weddin had been free
But noo anither thing I see
But noo anither thing I see
They are sevenpence a head
A saxpence disna sair forby
But a' that didna signify
Wi' mirth and glee to spen' the nicht
Wi sic a jovial company.

WILLIAM WALKER — G

474

614

SHEELICKS

1 Pey attention tae my sang and I'll tell ye o' a weddin
On the thirty-first o' July at the toon o Sleepy-steadin'
A the countryside wis there for ye didna need a biddin'
Tae the mairrage o' McGinnis tull his cross-eyed pet.
There wis lots o' fun an' frolic tho we hidna a piana
Bit a fluter wi' a niz for a' the earth like a banana
An a piper wi' his chanter in a seck that heeld guana
At the mairrage o' McGinnis tull his cross-eyed pet.
    Tootle tootle gaed the flute, fiddle diddle gaed the fiddle
    They gaed reelin oot an' in agane an' up an' doon the middle
    An they ging-a-ringit roon aboot like sheelicks roon a riddle   [grains of corn
    At the mairrage o' McGinnis tull his cross-eyed pet.

2 A fiddler he cam doon the howe, fae Mains of Butterscottie
An his fiddle it wis cobblt up wi batter glue an potty
If the instrument wis paralyst the fiddler he gaed dotty
At the mairrage o' McGinnis tull his cross-eyed pet.
Aye an syne there wis some singin fae a cheelie ca'd Macara
Tull he tried them wi a versie o a sang they ca Ta-ra-ra
He gaed there upon a bicycle bit hame upon a barra
Fae the mairrage o McGinnis tull his cross-eyed pet.

3 A tinkler wi' a timmer leg he danc't like ane dementit
In the middle o' a fowersome reel he bruk it throu an' tint it
Bit they men't it wi' a barra tram an he gaed hame contentit
Fae the mairrage o' McGinnis tull his cross-eyed pet.
Fin McGinnis yokit tee tae dance ye never saw his marra
'Twid a min't ye on a grubber dancin wi an iron harra
Tull he tum'lt ower the sweetie wife an' landit in her barra
At the mairrage o' McGinnis tull his cross-eyed pet.

4 There wis pottit heed an' herrin reed an jeely on the table
An a rooth o' tatie bannocks near as heich's the toor o Babel   [abundance
There wis roly-polys roon the sides an hens at ilka gable
At the mairrage o' McGinnis tull his cross-eyed pet.
Syne some gaed east an some gaed wast an tee the door wis yarket [wrenched
For the din wis like the skellin' o' a Faisterns Even market
Bit I fell doon an open drain, an baith my shins wis barket
Stytterin hameworth fae the mairrage o' the cross-eyed pet.   [stumbling home

GEORGE BRUCE THOMSON — G

GORDON O' NEWTON'S MARRIAGE

wi' Gordon's plaid the Forbes maid Does now herself a- dorn; Lang
may he wear't, lang may she share't, And love's flame brighter burn! And lang
may oor la-dy fair Be spared 'mong us to shine, May every [= ivy]
sprout and broom still grow As high, as fair's langsyne!

1 My comrades a' baith great an' sma along with me confide
This night our Gordon has brought home a young and bloomming bride.
We welcome her, thrice welcome her with loyal hearts an' true
And may she e'er in years to come our confidence renew.

2 Our tenants a' wi' harmless mirth welcome our lady home
And ever may your grateful hearts still bless the day she came.
An lang lang may our lady fair be spared 'mang us to shine
We'll drink her health in three times three as deen in days langsyne.

3 Wi' Gordon's plaid the Forbes maid does now herself adorn
Lang may he wear't lang may she share't an' love's flame brighter burn.
There gardens fair be perfumed with Sweet William, rue and thyme
May ivy sprout, an' broom still grow as high, as fair's langsyne.

ROBERT ALEXANDER — D

PATIE'S WEDDING

A

Patie's Wedding.

Oh, Patie cam in wi' a sten', Said, "Peace be here in the
(= Petty)
biggin'." "Y'ire welcome, quo' William, "come ben, or it wish it onay
rise to the riggin. Draw in by your seat an' sit doon, An'
tell's your news in a hurry, An' Maggie, y'ell hist an' be deen, Hing
on the pan an' the berry." Rye fal dril lal dril lah, Rye
fal dril lal dril laddy; Rye fal dril lal dril lah,
Fal dril lal dril laddy.

1   O Petty on wedlock was bound
    He dressed himself up with his dicky
    His coat and knee breeches he donned
    An O but he thought himself vauntie,   [smart
    A bonnet nae far fae the new
    An it had a loop an a slittie
    To tie in a ribbon sae blue
    To bob ower the neck o' his coatie
       Ri falderal alderal a
       Falderal alderal adie.

2   O Petty cam in wi a sten   [leap
     Said "Peace be here an the biggin"
     "Ye're welcome" quo' William come ben
     For I wish it may rive to the riggin
     Draw inbye your seat an sit doon
     An tell's your news in a hurry
     An Maggie ye'll haste and be deen
     Hang on the pan wi the berries."

3   "Guidman my news is nae thrang
     Yestreen I was wi his honour
     I took fae him three rigs o' braw lan'
     An I ban mysell under a bonar   [became a tenant
     Goodman, my erran to you
     Is for Maggie to help me to labour't
     I think you may gies your best coo
     For vow, my haudin's bit sober.   [unsubstantial

4   "Petty lad I dinna ken
     But since ye hae speeret at my daddy
     Ye're as weel born as bane   [for "Ben"
     An I canna say but I'm ready
     There's plenty o' yarn an clews
     To mak ye a coat an a gentie
     An plaiden eneuch to be trews
     Gin I get ye I sanna scrimp ye."

5   "O Petty to fordel you this   [supply
     I'll be at the cost o the bridal
     I'll cut you the neck o' a ewe
     That had amaist deed o the side-ill
     That'll make plenty o bree
     Sae lang as the well is na reestit   [dried up
     To a oor gweed neebours and we
     For I think we'll be very weel feastit."

ROBERT ALEXANDER — D

B

Patie's Wedding

As Patie cam up frae the glen, Drivin his wedders be-fore him, He met bonny Meg gangin hame, Her beauty was like for to smore him. I kenna ye ken, bonny Meg, That fun and I's gaen to be married? I rether had broken my leg, Before sie a bargain mis-carried

Mrs JOHN MILNE — D

C

Patie cam' doon the Glen.

GEORGE RIDDELL — G

Song No. 616

Miss H. RAE — G

Patie's Weddin'

1   Patie cam' owre the glen
    Drivin' his wethers before him,
    He met bonnie Meg gyaun hame,
    And her beauty was like to smore him.

2   Says, Dinna ye ken, bonnie Meg,
    That you and I's gyaun to be married
    I'd rather hae broken my leg
    Afore sic a bargain was carried.

GEORGE MILNE — G

617

THE WATERS OF DEE

1 A wedding! a wedding!
    The bride she bides at the bonnie burn en'
    And the bride-groom he bides at the hill of Glenshee
    And he'll never win owre the water o' Dee.

2 The bride and her maiden ga'ed oot to the hill
    But never a stime o' 'im could she see.   [least sight
    Then oot it cam' the bride's young man
    Says "Come in to your dinner as fast as ye can,
    For he'll never win owre the waters o' Dee."

3 Fan they were a' at their dinner
    Fa cam' rap, rap at the gate
    Oot spak' the bride wi' a blythe blinkin' 'ee
    Says, "Foo wan ye owre the waters o' Dee?"

4 "Come saddle my horse, come get me a man
    Mak' a'thing ready as fast as ye can.
    For we have had a day and we sall hae a night"
    And so they were mairriet wi' candle-light.

    Miss BELL ROBERTSON — G

THE CANTIE CARLIE

A

A	B
The Cantie Carlie	**The Cantie Carlie**

1 It fell about the time o' year,
    When neither goud nor warld's gear,   [When] siller [goud]
    Could gi'e a widow man sic cheer,
    As a young wife at e'en.
        There was a Cantie Carlie,
        The lasses lov'd him dearlie;   He loved the lasses dearly
        He said he would brak barlie,   [brak] parly
        If he lay lang him leen.

2 He recollected as he lay
    He was na married to deid clay;
    An' he thought lang, baith nicht and day,
    For a young wife at e'en.
        Fair fa the Cantie Carlie,
        The lasses lov'd him dearlie;
        He said he would brak barlie,
        If he lay lang him leen.

3 Says he, "I hae baith house an' lan',
    And I can also gang an' stan';
    I'll tak my pike staff in my han',
    And try to Aberdeen.
        I'll court the lasses rarely,
        And tell my erran' fairly;
        I winna rise sae early,
        If I had her at e'en."

4 "I'm come to court you, Bell," said he,
    "Therefore I hope you will agree;"   In this I hope we will agree
    "Indeed, I am content," said she,
    "I dream't o' you the streen.
        Fair fa my Cantie Carlie,
        I'll marry my Cantie Carlie,
        He's welcome to brak barlie,   An' wi ma cantie carlie
        He canna lie him leen."   I'll dance a twasome reel.

5   They're booket and proclaim'd wi' speed,
      And O, I wat they had great need;
      Says she, "I ken't it was my creed,
      To get a man ere yeel.
          Fair fa my Cantie Carlie,
          I'll marry my Cantie Carlie;
          Then wi' my Cantie Carlie,
          I'll dance a twasome reel."

6   At length the marriage day appears.
      But Oh, alas! great were their fears,
      I wat they baith shed saut, saut tears:—
      The drift blew wondrous keen, —
          For the day was dreary,
          The bride she was nae cheery,
          The bridegroom he was weary
          Wi' lying lang him leen.

7   He says, "My friends we'll a' convene
      Young men, as brisk as ere was seen,
      To bring my bride frae Aberdeen,
      They'll rin, and winna bide;   Ye'll
          Now lads I am not jokin',   Mak haste an' dinna tairry
          It is a thing provokin',   For I maun haste an' mairry
          And will be very shockin',   For fear that I miscairry
          For me to want my bride."   Or ye bring hame ma bride.

8   Syne Gauger Bent and Rogiehill,
      They baith were guid at pint an' gill;
      An', faith, I wat they had their fill,
      Ere they left Auchronie green;
          For O, the day was dreary,
          An' they were a' grown weary,
          The bridegroom was na cheery
          At th' thought o' lying him leen.

9   "O, gi'e them plenty o' ale saps,   It's cook get up, get ale an' saps
      An' fill them up frae kytes to craps; An' cram the lads fae kytes tae craps
      To gar them big on lasses' taps,   An' gar
      As they bring hame my bride.
          Now, lads, I am not jokin',   For troth
          'T would be a thing provokin',
          An' surely very shockin',   An' wadna it be shockin'
          For me to want my bride."

10 They row their legs wi' straen rapes,   [They] wan
      Magirkies on their heids for caps;   [wool hats Pit gurkies
      They're busked up like twa bees' scapes, [hives Buskit up their backs like twa bee skeps
      And on to Aberdeen.
          The maids they ran to meet them,
          The bride she did salute them;
          And says I winna cheat them,   Quo she
          I'll lie na mair my leen.   He sanna lie him lane.

11 Young men and maidens get a-close,
      And kilt their coats abeen their hose;
      And said, 'We'll now try for the brose,
      Be't fair or foul abeen."
          But O, the day was dreary,
          They a' grew very weary,
          The bride she was na cheery,
          The tears fell frae her een.

12 They puff and blaw, and stamp and stride,
   Indeed they had na will to bide;
   Gin they came to Kinmundy side,
   The drift blew very keen;
     For O, the day was dreary,
     They a' grew very weary,
     The bride she was na cheery,
     The tears fell frae her een.

So noo they're a' oot owre the hill
For win nor widder widna yield
Until she got her eemers queeled
She tint the fooshin' syne
     She was nae mair gallantish
     Nor roch, nor rogue, nor rantish
     Awyte she turned fantish
     She tint the fooshin' syne.

13 The bride cried now, "Tak's on yer backs,
   Or else we'll lodge in Johnny Black's
   They'll say ye are na worth twa placks,
   If ye gang hame yer leen."
     For O, the day was dreary,
     They a' grew very weary,
     The bride she was na cheery,
     The tears fell frae her een.

Quo' she "Noo lads, tak's

They'll think ye are

14 Wi' that the sends tak' to their heels,
   Now, wer'na they twa shamefaced chiels?
   They left the women jist like feels, —
   Kinmundy took them in.
     For O, the day was dreary,
     They a' grew very weary,
     The bride she was na cheery,
     The tears fell frae her een.

Fan they heard this they took their heels

Tae leave the lassies baith like feels

15 As they sat by Kinmundy's fire,
   The sends they tak the road wi' ire,
   And stopp'd at neither pot nore mire,
   T' they reach Auchronie side;
     But O, blate was their meetin',
     The bridegroom he was frettin',
     Sighin', sobbin', greetin',
     He says, "Where is my bride?"

They didna stick at pot nor mire
       [Auchronie] green

16 An' some say this an' some say that,
   The bridegroom raves he kens na what;
   He flet, he spat, an' up he gat,
   He bann'd and gae a grane —
     "Oh what shall I dae now, sirs,
     I swear I'll gar them rue, sirs,
     I fear it's ower true, sirs,
     They've lost her, skin and bane.

But up he gat, an' up he spat
       [gae a] girn
     I wis' it binna true, sirs
     Awyte I'se gar ye rue sirs
     Ye've lost her skin an' birn.

17 "Because my joints are still and aul',
   An' I'm obliged to gang twafaul',   [doubled
   I sent young men were straught and tall;
   I thought they would be keen.
     Young men ha'e but little thrift,
     That stick at either win' or drift,
     To help a needfu' bride a lift,
     That canna lie her leen.

18 "I swear by deil, as well's by sa'nt,
   I will go mad for Bellie Grant;
   My heart it fails, I'm like to fa'nt,
   For fear I lie my leen.
     Young men ha'e little shift or thrift,   [enterprise
     That stick at weet or win' or drift;
     To help a needfu bride a lift,
     Wha cann lie her leen."

19 The Cook now cries, "Sit doun an' dine,
   It's gailie ower, 'tween aucht and nine; [well on
   Gin ye get meat ye'll little tine,
   Tho' ye lie doun yer leen.
      Why mak ye sic a reary,   [disturbance
      Tho' the night be dreary;
      Come eat and drink fu' cheery,
      And syne lie doun your leen."

            Here's guid fat skinks to gar ye lick yer lips
            Livers an' lungs like littluns' hips
            A haggis atween yer han's to grip
            Weel seasoned wi' spice
               They madena mair marearie
               Altho' the day wis dreary
               They ate an' drank fu' cheery
               Awyte they warna nice.

20 The bride by now was well an' warm,
   Kinmundy's fire had been her charm;
   "I think," says she, "we'll get nae harm,
   To try out o'er the hill.
      To bide it mak's a ravel,   [disorder
      And now we're fit to travel;   An' I am fit to traivel
      As lang as we are able,   I've naither gut nor graivel
      We'll just try o'er the hill.   An' neen has better will.

21 "Skipper, wi' your art and skill
   You'll steer our course straught o'er the hill;   Ye'll show's the wye oot owre the hill
   Ye'se get a warm pint and gill,   hearty [pint and gill]
   Upon Auchronie green."   When ye reach Auchronie's green
      Says he, "I'll see you righted,
      Since ye are so benighted
      I think I will be knighted,   I'd think masel beknichted
      To gang wi' you my leen."

22 Upon the hill o' Auchencleich,   As they gaed throu the howe o' Auchin-
   He gasps and glowers, and, wi' a pech,   [pant   It's wi' a stride an' wi' a pech   [lech
   Says, "Look! the road leads through the laigh,   The roadie noo lies down the laich
   So I will try for hame;   [low-lying ground   Quo' he, "I'll try for hame."
      Auchronie ye can see now;"
      The bride says, "Can this be now?"
      Wi' that she's like to flee now,
      I wat she was na lame.

23 She shortly chaps at her ain door;
   The bridegroom he teets through a bore,   [peeps
   And tho' he was near four score   [hole
   Lap like a spainin' lamb.   [springing
      "What's that?" he gae a golly
      "I see twa angels holy,
      Or else, without a folly,
      It is my ain dear lamb."

24 He gae the door a hasty rug
   The bride she then crept in right snug;
   He kissed her syne frae lug to lug,
   And bade her welcome in.
      He says, 'Now sirs, be cheery,
      The night is nae mair dreary,
      I'll kiss till I be weary;
      I'll lie nae mair my leen."

25 He fidges, laughs, and loups like daft,
   And says, "The mill's near on the shaft;
   O for the Parson up the craft! —
   We think he's at Moss-side."
      Then out spake Jamie Carnie,
      "I think the night some starny,
      They're blinking o'er the barny;
      I'll rin and winna bide.

Wi' this the mannie gaed like daft
He thocht the mail was on the shaft

There's twa-three frien's amissin' still
Gauger Bent an' Roger Hill
Gaed for a tryst o' pint or gill
Bit noo they've a' lost heart
      As they gaed owre the Gavel
      The wade up tae the navel
      Awyte they got the gravel
      An' wisna that great scarth.

26 Now Jamie Carnie he comes back,
   And how he sped tells in a crack;
   How Mossie cried, "Ah, shame an' lack
   To use the Parson so.
      Indeed, I think him slighted,
      To tryst him so benighted,
      But now he's hame and righted,
      Your folk may scale and go.

"Ha! ha!" he says, "it's ye may lauch
Tae use the parson so
      He says he has been slichted
      Tae tryst him sae benichted
      Before he got ye richted
      Yer company may skail an' go."

27 "He ventured out, the drift amang,
   His will was good his legs were lang;
   And, best o' a', his faith was strang
   To guard him frae a' harm;
      Sae rin and dinna bide now,
      Gae back and tell the bride now,
      She's come ahin' the tide now,
      And that will mak' alarm."

28 This answer gart auld James look black,
   Cries he, "Its ill upon war's back;
   We'se bed, I car'na half a plack,
   And marry syne the morn."
      The bride said, "Awa na, man,
      It is against the law, man,
      The like I never saw, man,
      Since ever I was born."

Bit this is ill upon waur's back
I doot it garred auld Jeems look black
I'll bed, I carena half a plack
An' mairry syne the morn.

29 "Indeed," says James, "the truth I'll tell,
   Ye needna be sae nice, now, Bell,
   Ye keist a leggin gird yersel',
   Ere ye left Aberdeen."
      This hat her on the sair heel,
      The truth she cou'd na bear weel,
      She was like to bid him fareweel,
      And lat him lie his leen.

[Ye keist] the ylaagan
Since [ye left]

30 "It's rashly said," she then cried out —
   "An' ill it sets your wizzen't snout,
   I hae guid will to thraw't about,
   And gar you lie your leen —
      You ill-faur'd canker'd Carlie,
      You said you lov'd me dearlie;
      You've noo made me a fairlie
      Since I left Aberdeen."

Says she, "Deil speed yer wizen't snoot
Wi' guid will wad I thraw't aboot
Wi' guid will wad I thraw't aboot
An' lat ye lie yer lane.

      [made me a] ferly

But since ye'r like me to beguile
I'll bed wi' keen young Knappie Style
The boy whispered wi' a smile
"Ye sanna lie yer lane."
    Quo' Jeems Low, "What tricks sirs
    For troth ye're wirth yer licks sirs
    Ye'll gie auld Jeems the glaik sirs
    Or a this days be deen.

31 The bride's-maiden, that modest bird,
    Cries, "Mak a shakdoun on the yird,
    Altho' ye want a leggin gird,   [Altho'] we lost oor
    It's neither sin nor shame;
        The bed will haud us a', syne,
        And I'se lie neist the wa', syne,
        The man atween us twa, syne,
        And that's the better schame."

32 Some said it's better to restrain,
    The bridegroom winna ken his ain;
    But others cried, ah, deil be fain!   [But] Jeems Low [cried]
    They'll haud the Carlie warm.
        The company withdraw, now,   [withdraw] seen
        And three instead o' twa, now,   [instead o' twa] seen
        Get in without a flaw, now,   Crap in
        And thought it was nae harm.

33 Neist mornin', being stormy still,   The morn it was driftin' still
    To venture out they had nae will;
    To bide at hame was better still   [better] skill
    Than wade up to the clift.   [to the] clifts
        The bride's now into biggit wa's,
        Ben i' the nook wi' a' her braws;
        Therefore they thought there was nae cause
        To smore amo' the drift.

34 "But as the Kirk, the ring commands,"   "It's tae the Kirk the King commands
    Says James, "We'll go and join our hands,
    For fear we lose our twal pund pawns –   fower [pund]
    Kirk folks hae unco greed.   For Kirk fouk's unco greedy."
        Therefore be still my dearie,   "Oh yes" says she "my deary
        There's nothing needs to fear ye,   There's naething else to fear thee"
        I'll gang tho' I be weary,
        And climb the braes wi' speed."

35 So after twa nights an' a day,   [They] buskit up [to Kirk] to [gae]
    They busk again, to Kirk they gae;
    A new-year gift auld James maun hae,
    A hail buik to him leen.
        And though the man was ance sae stiff,
        To gang to Kirk he had nae pith;
        He's souple in body, limb, an' lith,   [joint
        To get a wife at e'en.

36 The nearest toun that they cam' by,   An' ilka toon
    The folk cam' out with shout an' cry;
    Some shot, some mocked, and some cried fie!   shoot [an' cry]
    The like was never seen!
        He that's gaen' to be wed   The man that's gaun
        Might be the lassie's luckydad, [grandfather [the lassie's] luckiedaid
        Instead o' lyin' in his bed,
        December linked to June.

Song No. 618

37 Forward, still, they do repair
 To Kirk — the Parson's ready there
 To say the word, by grace and prayer,
 Thereby to mak' them one.
  And noo they're join'd in holy bands
  The ring's too wide, fa's aff her hands;
  They carena noo for Kirk nor Pawns:—   [They carena] mair
  And ten month brings a Son.   Gin nine

38 Thus have you heard the merry jest,   Indeed wha wis their happiest guest
 O' what concerns our worthy guest,   Or fa wis there an' fa' shared best
 Wha waited lang and fared the best   There's nane here kens for nane here
 On sic a merry day.   On sic a merry day.   [speired
  Fair fa' the Cantie Carlie,   Fair fa' wir canty carlie
  The bride she lov'd him dearlie;   She's mairried wir canty carlie
  May they get babies yearlie, —   An' they get bairns yearly
  I ha'e nae mair to say.   I hae nae mair tae say.

WILLIAM WALKER — G   WILLIAM WATSON — G

C
The Wanton Carlie

To the tune of *Bonny Glasgow Green* from the same singer

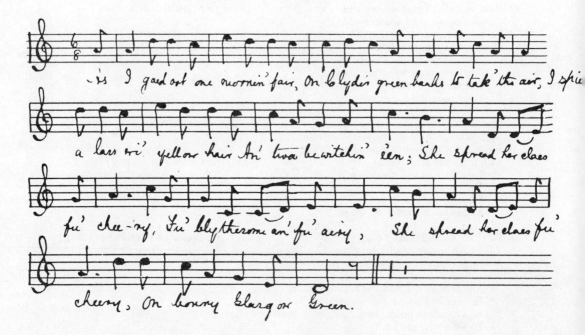

1 Wae a want ye for a carlie,
   Ye said ye lo'ed me darly
   Ye said ye wid brak parly,
   Gin ye lay lang yer leen.
   But weary fa' yer wizened snoot,
   For little o' me I wad thraw't aboot,
   For little o' me I wad thraw't aboot,
   An' lat ye lie yer leen.
       For ye're a wanton carlie,
       A dautit, doitet carlie,   [pampered; old and foolish
       For ye're a wanton carlie,
       That winna lie yer leen.

2 Ye needna be sae saucy, Bell,
   Ye keest the lyaugin-gird yersel,
   Ye keest the lyaugin-gird yersel,
   Ar ye left Aiberdeen.

Mrs MARGARET GILLESPIE – D

D

The Canty Carlie.

An' he's aye my canty carlie,
The lasses like him dearly,
An' I'm feart 'at he brak barley
Gin he lie lang him lane.

1 Ye needna be sae saucy, Bell,
   Ye brak the langen gird yersel',
   Ye brak the langen gird yersel'
   Or ye left Aiberdeen.
       An' he's aye, *etc.*

Mrs JAFFRAY (Mintlaw) – G

E
The Cantie Carlie

1　There was a cantie carlie,
　　He loved the lasses dearly,
　　He swore he would brak' parley
　　Gin he lay lang him lane O.

2　He says, I have baith house and lan',
　　I can also gang and stan',
　　I'll tak' my pikestaff in my han',
　　An' try to Aberdeen O.

3　I'll court the lasses rarely,
　　An' tell my eerant fairly,
　　I winna rise sae early
　　Gin I'd a wife at e'en.

4　He win his legs wi' straw and raips,
　　Put hankies on his heid like skeps,
　　And buskit up like a beeskep,
　　And awa' to Aberdeen O.

5　A'm come to coort you, Bell, says he,
　　Therefore I hope we will agree,
　　Indeed I'm weel content, quo' she,
　　I dreamt o' you yestreen O.

E.G. – G

F
The Cantie Carlie

1　Then oot spak' Jamie Carnie,
　　Says, "I think the nicht's some starnie
　　They're blinkin' owre the barnie,
　　We'll gang an' winna bide."

Mrs RETTIE – G

619

THE WEDDING OF BALLAPOREEN

A

The Wedding o' Bellapereen

1 There was Johnnie McCormack an' Brady O'Lin,
   An' the fat red haired cookmaid that lived at the inn;
   There was Sheelie an' Lawrie the genius
   An' Pat's uncle, old Derby Denis,
   Black Taddy an' crooked McGuinness
   Assembled at Bellapereen.

2 The bride she got up to make an oration,
   An' she charmed all the men with her kind botheration,·
   What profit you'll have if you thrive, sirs,
   You'll be welcome all dead or alive, sirs,

   . . . .
   At this wedding o' Belapereen.

3 The birds they did sing and the asses did bray

   . . . .
   The bride she cam first i' the rear sirs,
   O losh now the captain did swear sirs,
   You're welcome both dead or alive sirs,
   At this wedding o' Belapereen.

Miss ELIZABETH GREIG — D

B

The wedding of Ballaporeen.

Your attention this night to a true Irish bard, With a song ready made, he composed it himself

WILLIAM REID — G

C

The Wedding o' Ballaporeen.

JAMES GREIG — G

D

The Wedding o' Ballyparreen

1   Descend ye chaste nine to a true Irish bard
     You're auld maids to be sure — but he'll send you a card
     To beg you'll assist, a poor musical elf
     With a sang readymade — he'll compose it himself
     About maids, boys, a priest and a wedding
     With a crowd ye could scarce thrust your head in
     A supper good cheer and a bedding
     Which happened at Ballypareen.

2   It was a fine summer morn, about twelve in the day
     All the birds fell to sing and the asses to bray
     When Patrick the bridegroom and Eunich the bride
     In their best bibs and tuckers set out side by side
     Oh the piper played first in the rear, sirs
     The maids blushed, the bridesman did swear, sirs
     Oh losh how the spalpeens did swear, sirs
     At this weddin' at Ballypareen.

3   They were soon tacked together and home did return
     To make merry that day at the "Sign of the Churn"
     When they sat down together a frolicsome group
     Oh, the banks of our Shannon ne'er saw such a group
     There were turf-cutters, threshers and tailors
     With harpers, and pipers and nailers
     There were pedlars, and smugglers and sailors
     Assembled at Ballypareen.

4   There was Brian McDermack, and Shack and his brat
     With Terence and Triscal and platter-faced Pat
     There was Norah McCormack and Brian O'Hinn
     And the fat red-haired cook maid who lived at the inn
     There was Sheilah and Lawrie the genius
     With Pat's uncle, auld Derby Dennis.
     Black Teddy, and crooked McGainns
     All assembled at Ballyporeen.

5   Now the bridegroom sat down to make an oration
     And he charmed all their souls with his kind batheration
     They were welcome he said and he swore and he cursed
     They might eat till they swelled and might eat till they burst
     And the first christening I have, if I thrive sirs
     You'll be welcome all dead or alive, sirs
     To the christening at Ballypareen.

6   The bride she stood up to make a low bow
     But she twittered and fell, she couldn't say how
     She blushed and she stammered the few words she let fall
     And she whispered so low that she bathered them all.
     And her mother cried "What! are you dead child?"
     Oh for shame, if you hold up your head, child
     Tho' sixty I wish I were wed child,
     Oh! I'd rattle auld Ballypareen.

7   Now they sat down to meat, Father Murphy said grace
Smoking hot were the dishes, and eager each face
The knives and forks rattled, spoons and platters did play
And they elbowed and jostled and walloped away
Rumps, shines and fat sirloins did groan, sirs.
Whole mountains of beef were cut down, sirs
They demolished all to the bare bones, sirs
At this wedding at Ballyporeen.

8   There was bacon and greens, but the turkey was spoiled
Potatoes dressed both ways both roasted and boiled
Hog's pudding, red herring, the priest got the snipe
Cauld cannon, pies, dumplin, cod, cow, heel and tripe
And they ate till they could eat no more, sirs.
But the whisky came pouring galore, sirs
Oh, how Terry McManns did roar, sirs
Oh! he bathered all Ballypareen.

9   Now the whisky went round and the songsters did roar
Tim sang "Paddy O'Kelly" Nell sang "Molly Asthore"
Till a motion was made that their songs did forsake
And each lad took his sweetheart their trotters to shake
Then the piper and couples advancing
Pumps, brogues, and bare feet fell a-prancing
Such piping, such figuring and dancing
Was ne'er known at Ballypareen.

10   The maids growing tired and the men growing drunk
The bridegroom grew sleepy and away the bride slunk
Some saddled their garrons, some boxed in the lane
And a pretty black eye, Murphy gave to McKane.
Some knocked down in the dirt were a-crawling
The men roared and the girls fell a-squalling
And some in the ditches were sprawling
Such fun was at Ballypareen.

11   Now to Patrick the bridegroom, and Eunich the bride
Let the harp of Auld Ireland be sounded with pride
And to all the brave guests, young or old, grey or green
Drunk or sober, who jig it at Ballypareen
And Cupid shall lend his wherry
To trip over the conjugal ferry
I wish you may be half as merry
As we were at Ballyporeen.

Source unrecorded — G

620

THE HAUGHIES O' INDEGO

1 'Twas on a Halloweven's day,
   The play begood aboot the sky,   [began
   They took a wallop thro' the ley
   'Po' the haughies o' Indego.

2 The Farquharsons were plenty there,
   The Frasers flocked frae everywhere,
   The Gordons brave they had their share,
   'Po' the haughies o' Indego.

3 The laird o' Echt and piper Skene
   Danced baith bare-headed 'neath the meen,
   An' lads an' lasses on the green,
   'Po' the haughies o' Indego.

4 A greater woe there did betide,
   Miss Catherine Gordon was a bride,
   The laird o' Skene lay by her side,
   'Po' the haughies o' Indego.

5 Some ran aff to the Isle o' Skye,
   Some wanna by the Brig o' Dye;
   The laird he had to France to fly
   Frae the haughies o' Indego.

Rev. GEORGE WILLIAMS — D

CADGER BRUCE

1   The lottery would hae been complete
Had cadger Bruce gane there to see't
Or Jamie Birse the lousy breet
Had he been there in the mornin'.

2   The lottery it's raised muckle din,
It's fired the cadger's auldest sin
An' fouk a' roon by Bauldyvin
They lie nae lang in the mornin'.

3   Tailor Morris o' the Mors
Likewise the man 'at maks the doors
An' smiths an' plewmen a' like boars
Or they got hame in the mornin'.

4   But an' it had been in Cromar
It wouldna been sae vera far
But to ca' awa' ayont Dunbar
Adieu to it in the mornin'.

CHARLES MURRAY — D

DUBBIENEUK

1   In the cauld month o' December
     When aneath a roof we jouk
     Dancie Scot's ta'en up a dancing
     At a place ca'ed Dubbienuck.

2   There came the gardners up frae Florth
     And lads frae Catchiebrae
     There came a souter frae Hairstane
     An lassis frae Pitblae.

3   Auld Jaumie Mackie he was there
     A dainty plouman chiel
     Wi' Betty Forbes at his back
     Could scarcely dance a reel.

JOHN MILNE — G

MARY GLENNIE

1   Mary Glennie she was there
    Dressed up like ony doo
    And aye as she gaed thro' the reel,
    Says Sandy I'm for you.

A. WATSON — G

624

JEAN DALGARNO

1   Miss Jean Dalgarno she was there   [prim
    A maid sae primp an' slim
    And fa think ye gaed hame wi' her
    But Arnot's shoudin sin.

Source unrecorded — G

THE SINGING CLASS

A

1   Joseph Fowlie he was there,
    Goodman o' Cadgiedykes,
    The room was filled or he came in,
    He sat amo' the tykes.

2   Sawners Fenty he was there
    Fleein' like a bird,
    He fuppit oot's psalm-book
    And gae't to Piper Third.

Miss BELL ROBERTSON — G

B

1   . . . . was there,
    . . . .
    And the high notes of Bangor
    Garr'd a' her ribbons crack.

2   Some sang Bangor,
    And some sang bass,
    But bonny Mary Jamieson
    Sang munsy in the ase.

Mrs MARGARET GILLESPIE — D

626

THE AUCHNAIRY BALL

A
The Auchnairy Ball

1   .   .   .   she was there,
   And she was unco nice,
   She had a feestle in her arse,   [commotion
   Wad grun Jamaica spice.

Mrs MARGARET GILLESPIE — D

B

1 Jean Shearer she was there,
   And vow but she was nice,
   She had a tweedle in 'er tail   [wiggle
   'It wad 'a grun spice.

Miss BELL ROBERTSON — G

LANNAGAN'S BALL

A
Laddikin's Ball

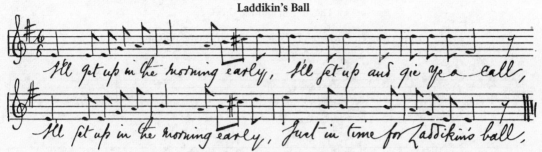

I'll get up in the morning early, I'll set up and gie ye a call,
I'll set up in the morning early, Just in time for Laddikin's ball.

Miss ANNIE RITCHIE — G

B

Lannagan's Ball.

I'll get up in the mornin' early, I'll set-up and gie ye a call,
I'll get up in the mornin' early, Just in time for Lannagan's Ball.

ALEXANDER ROBB — G

628

THE BALL AT DAVIDSON'S

A

The Murlin and the Creel

To the tune of *Errol on the Green* from Mrs Margaret Gillespie

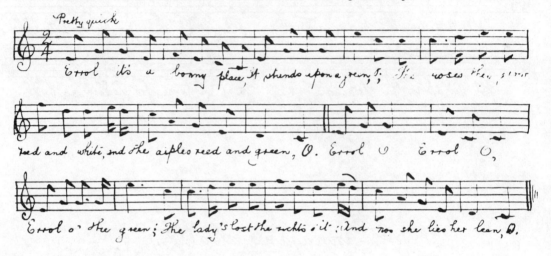

1   If I live anither year,
    And gin my thoom bide hale, O,
    I will buy some Buckie beast,
    And I'll ca' fish mysel', O.

ROBERT CHREE — D

B

The Ball at Davidson's

1   There was a ball at Davidson's
    Just i' the mids o' Lent,
    An' a' the live lang winter nicht
    In mirth an' glee they spent.

2   There was farmer fouk an' thimble fouk   [thimble-riggers
    An' cadgers in great style
    An' several o' the lottery fouk
    Fae Jamie o' the Isle.

3   They did convene at Davidson's
    To get some hens an' bree
    For sic a stormy time it was
    Nae haddocks could they gie.

4   The farmer hasna spirit noo
    They cunna sell their stock
    But the herrin' an' the thimble fouk
    They carry on the joke.

502

5   The cattle they are very flat
     An' little for the grain
     But him that buys the buckie beast
     He's sure to haud his ain.

6   But gin I live anither year
     An' gin my thooms are hale
     I'll buy a bonny murlan thing
     An' carry fish mysel.

7   But an Lizzie would come ou're the gait
     An' Janet an' the creel
     An' Willie an' the cadger's sin
     To dance a cadgers' reel.

CHARLES MURRAY — D

THE SOUTERS' FEAST

A

1 There was a souter and a soo,
   Tanteerie orum.
   And for her birse he kissed her mou,
   Sing howdle ilti orum.

2 The souters they had a feast,
   And wasna that a merry jeest?

3 Souters cam' fae far and near,
   And some o' them ayon New Deer.

4 Some o' them cam' oot o' Turra,
   And some as far's the laigh o' Moray.

5 Ane o' them cam' oot o' Fife,
   Ridin' on a rusty knife.

6 The souters they got a' fou,
   And ane o' them began to spue.

7 He spued some leather and some lasts,
   And sharpit knivies five or sax.

8 Ballies o' roset and broken gless,
   Cam' rattlin' fae the souter's ——

9 And when they thocht the breet was clean,
   He spued a muckle beatin' stane.

10 And when they thocht, etc.

JOHN MOWAT – G

B

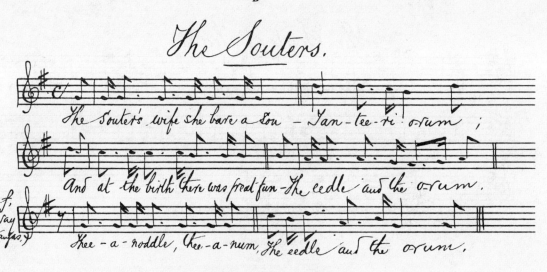

The Souters.

The Souter's wife she bare a son — Tan-tee-ri-orum;

And at the birth there was great fun — The eedle and the orum.

Ref.
ad lib. — say
after 2 stanzas.)

Thee-a-noddle, thee-a-num, The eedle and the orum.

1 The souter's wife she bare a son,
   Tanteerie orum;
And at the birth there was great fun,
   The eedle and the orum;
The souters they wad haud a feast
   Tanteerie orum;
And wasna that a fine jest?
   The eedle and the orum.
   Thee-a-noddle, thee-a-num,
   The eedle and the orum.

2 Souters cam' frae Auld Deer,
And some o' them was gey and queer.
Souters cam' frae Aiberdeen,
And souters cam' frae yont the meen.

3 Souters they cam' hine frae Perth,
And souters cam' frae 'neath the earth.
Souters cam' frae Peterheid,
Wi' fient a teeth in a' their heid.

4 Souters they cam' doon frae Turra,
And souters cam' frae Elgin o' Moray.
Souters cam' frae Aberdour,
Drivin' in a coach-and-four.

5 An ill-faured skyple cam' frae Crimon',   [ugly
A perfect scunner to the women.   wretch
A muckle hypal haveless loon, [uncouth; careless
Frae the Fite Steen cam' hoiterin' doon. [lurching

6 And when they thocht they a' were come,
A cripple breet cam' owre frae Drum,
Ridin' on a cripple mear,
His apron for his ridin' gear.

7 As he cam' past the mou' o' hell,
He saw a barkit hide for sale.
Sae he gaed doon to price the leather
Tail and lugs and a' thegither.

8 He gaed doon they kent nae hoo,
But he cam' up wi' a foul mou'.
Syne a' sat doon until their cheer,
It was the lowmons o' a mear.   [entrails

9 But when wi' feastin' they were fou'
Syne foul mou' began to spew.
First he spewed the rack strap,
And efter that the batter caup.

10 Eleven lasts upon a string,
And after that an ellisin.
A bunch o' birse, a ball o' wax,
And crookit futtles five or sax.

11 And when they thocht that he was clean,
He spewed the turkiss and a stane.   [pair of pincers
Syne when they thocht that he was clear
Up cam' the steel and a' the gear.

JAMES BREBNER — G

Song No. 629

The Souters' Feast.

The Souter's wife she bore a son, Tanlee eerie o rum, ... The, cedle & the orum

Thee a noddle thee a rum, The cedle & the orum.

J.W. SPENCE — G

D

The Souters' Feast

1   The souter's wife she bare a son
Tant tearie orum
An at the feast there was great fun
Thee oddil an thee orum.

2   Souters they came doon frae Turra
An souters came frae Elgin o' Murray.

3   Souters came frae Peterhead
Wi fent a teeth in a' their heid.

4   Souters came frae Auld Deer
An some o' them was gey an queer.

5   A muckle hypal haveless loon
Frae the Fite Steen cam hytern doon.

6   An ullfart skyple came frae Creeman
A perfect scunner to the wummen.

7   Fan a' men thought they were a' come
A cripple breet cam doon frae Drum

8   Riding on an auld mear
The apron was his riding gear.

9   Sine they were a' set to their cheer
The best bit o' an auld mear.

10   But when wi' feastin they were foo
The cripple breet began to spew.

11   First he spewed the rack strap
An after that the batter caup.

12   Eleven lasts upon a string
An after that an ellisin.,

13   A bunch o' birse, a ball o' wax,
An sharpit knives five or sax.

14   An fan they thought he was a clean
He spewed a turkas an a steen.

15   Fan thinkin' noo that a' was clear
Up came the steel an' a' the gear.

JOHN MILNE — G

E
Tanty Eerie Orum

1   The sooters cam fae Aiberdeen
       Tanty eerie orum
    .   .   .   .
       Thee odle an' thee orum.
    Etc., etc.

2   After they thocht that a' was clear
    Oot cam a steel and a' the gear.
    And after they thocht that a' was deen
    Oot cam a muckle sharpin' steen.

Mrs MARGARET GILLESPIE — D

F

1   There wis a sooter had a soo
       Ti-yow-dil-ilti-orum.

Rev. JOHN CALDER — G

McGINTY'S MEAL-AN-ALE

A

McGinty's Meal-an-Ale

1 This is nae a sang o' love na nor yet a sang o' money
It's naething very peetyfu' an naething very funny
Bit there's Heelan Scotch Lowlan' Scotch Butter Scotch an' honey
If there's nane o them for a' there's a mixter o' the three
An there's nae a word o beef-brose sowans sautie bannocks
Nor o' pan cakes an' pess eggs for them wi' dainty stammacks   [Easter
It's a' about a meal-an-ale that happent at Balmannocks
McGinty's meal-an-ale far the pig gaed there tae see.
    They war howlin' in the kitchen like a caravan o' tinkies
    Aye an some wis playin ping-pong an tiddley-widdley-winkies
    Far up the howe or doon the howe there never wis sic jinkies
    As McGinty's meal an ale far the pig gaed there tae see.

2 McGinty's pig hid broken lowse an wan'ert tae the lobby
Far he open shivt the pantry door an cam' upo' the toddy
An' he gaed kin'ly tae the stuff, like ony human body
At McGinty's meal-an-ale far the pig gaed there tae see.
Miss McGinty she ran butt the hoose, the road wis dark an' crookit
She fell heelster-gowdy ower the pig, for it she never lookit
An' she leet oot a skyrl wid a' paralyst a teuchit
At McGinty's meal-an-ale far the pig gaed there tae see.

3 Johnny Murphy he ran aifter her, an owre the pig was leapin'
Bit he trampit on an ashet that wis sittin' fu' o' dreepin'   [serving plate
An he fell doon an' peelt his croon, an' couldna haud fae greetin'
At McGinty's meal-an-ale far the pig gaed there tae see
For the pantry skyelf cam' ricklin' doon an' he wis lyin kirnin   [rattling, mixing
Amon' saft soap, piz-meal, corn floor an' yirnin   [rennet
Like a gollach amon' tricle bit McGinty's wife wis girnin   [beetle
At the soss upon her pantry fleer an' widna lat 'im be.   [soggy mess

4 Syne they a' ran skyrlin tae the door bit fan' that it wis tuggit
For aye it heeld the faister aye the mair they ruggit
Tull McGinty roart tae bring an aix he widna be humbuggit
Na nor lockit in his ain hoose, an that he'd lat them see.
Sae the wife cam' trailin wi' an aix an' throu the bar wis hacket
An' open flew the door at aince sae close as they war packet
An' a' the crew gaed tum'lin oot like taties fae a backet
At McGinty's meal-an-ale far the pig gaed there tae see.

5 They hid spartles they hid tatie chappers troth they warna jokin'
An' they said they'd gar the pig claw far he wis never yokin'
Bit be this time the lad wis fou an' didna care a dokin'
At McGinty's meal-an-ale far the pig gaed there tae see.
O there's eely pigs an' jeely pigs, an pigs for haudin' butter   [oil jars; jam jars
Aye bit this pig wis greetin' fou an tum'lin in the gutter
Tull McGinty an' his foreman trailt 'im oot upon a shutter
Fae McGinty's meal an ale far the pig gaed there tae see.

6 Miss McGinty took the thing tae hert an' hidet in her closet
An' they rubbit Johnny Murphy's heed wi' turpenteen an' roset
An' they harlt him wi' meal-an-ale ye really wid suppose't
He hid sleepit in a mason's troch, an' risen tae the spree.
O weary on the barley bree an' weary fa' the widder
For it's keegerin amon dubs an' drink they gyang na weel thegidder   [mixing up
Bit there's little doot McGinty's pig is wishin' for anidder
O' McGinty's meal-an-ales far the pig gaed there tae see.

GEORGE BRUCE THOMSON — G

B

McGinties Meal and Ale

1 There is nae a sang o' love, na nor yet a sang o' money
It's naething very fine na nor naething very funny
It's a Lowland Scotch, Highland Scotch, Butter Scotch an' honey
If it's nae ane o' a' that it's a mixture o' the three.
There wis nae a wird o' beef brose, soans, nor sautee bannaks
Na for pancakes, nor paste eggs for them wi' dainty stammacks
It was a' aboot a meal and ale it happened at Balmanay
McGintie's meal and ale far the pig got on the spree.
They were howlin in the kitchen like a caravan o' tinkies
Some wis playin' ping pong an tiddlee, widdlee winkies
Far up the howe nor down the howe, there never wis sic ginkies
As McGintie's meal and ale whaur the pig got on the spree.

2 Oh McGintie's pig had broken oot and wandered tae the lobby
An open shoved the pantry door, and cam upon the toddy
An he took tae the stuff, just like ony human body
At McGintie's meal and ale far he first got on the spree.
Miss McGinty she ran ben the hoose, the road was dark and crookit
She gaed hilster gowdie owre the pig, for it she never lookit
But she loot oot a yell wid hae terrified a teuchit
At McGinty's meal and ale far the pig got on the spree.

3 Sin they a' ran scirlin tae the door and fan that it was ruggit
An' aye the mair they tried it 'twas aye the harder rugit
Till McGinty roared tae bring an axe for he wadna be humbugit
Na nor lockit in his ain hoose, an that he'd lat them see
So Miss McGinty she cam wi' an axe an' through the bar was hakit
Ilka ane o' them cam rumblin oot like taties frae a bakit
At McGinty's meal and ale far they a got on the spree.

4 There wis spurtles, there wis tatie chappers, troth they warna jokin'
And he said he'd gar the pig claw tho it was never jokin'
But it wis greetin' fou an didna care a dockin
At McGinty's meal and ale far it first got on the spree.
There was hie sows and ream pigs an pigs for haudin' butter
An' bit this pig wis roarin' fou an rowin in the gutter
Till McGinty an' his man trailed him hame upon a shutter
Fae McGinty's meal and ale faur he first got on the spree.

5 Miss McGinty took the thing tae hert an hidet in her closit
But they rubbit James Murphy's heid wi' turpentine an rosit
An' they harled him wi' meal an' ale till ye railly wad supposit
He'd sleepit in a mason's trough in reason o' the spree.
Weary's the barley bree an weary o' the weather
An kiggerin' amon duds an' drink gang nae weel thegither
But I've nae doot McGinty's pig's wishin for anither
O' McGinty's meal and ale faur he first got on the spree.

JAMES MORRISON — G

MIDDLETACK CLIACK

1   My comrades and acquaintances attend unto my tale,
    And I will write a verse or two about a meal and ale,
    If you be doubtful where it was, the farm was Middletack,
    It was held not long ago, I'll certify the fact.

2   Although I am a miller lad I was invited there
    To be one of the company that I might get a share,
    And when we were all gathered out of us there was not few,
    We made a lively company as ever I did view.

3   The master is a generous man and he deserves great praise
    Prosperity be to him then and many happy days,
    For he was liberal wi' his stores, that did keep up the glee,
    Though far above our company, he was aye frank and free.

4   His meal and ale an' ither drink enlivened us at once,
    And when we got the lasses out we did commence to dance,
    There was so many charming maids, I can't describe them all
    But I will tell you who was thought the chief ones at the ball.

5   The housemaid was the flower of it she did outshine them a'
    Though not with any gaudy dress, for she was not too braw,
    Nor had she any ornaments about her yellow hair,
    It was her natural beauty that made her the belle there.

6   Mary Taylor is her name, a lovely girl is she,
    And ane that I could never doubt a virtuous maid to be
    She was so charmin' to my eyes, that it was my design,
    To ask if she was promised yet or if she would be mine.

7   Barbara Walker comes in noo, she was the second there,
    It was not thought the rest of them could with this two compare,
    And as for Marget Morrison, her equal there was few
    Though it be for a decent lass that I'm referring noo.

8   Jane Whyte she did eclipse them all if it had been for length
    I think she would have stood the test if it had been for strength.

9   Miss Bisset was a charming maid she cam' doon frae Greenhill
    She is as good a songster as e'er need try their skill
    I heard her sing some excellent songs including "Johnnie Sangster"
    O he had been a worthy chiel, besides a gallant bandster.

10   There were more pretty charming maids, I now must leave them all,
    And bring in Willie Barclay, he is so very tall,
    I am not certain of his height, he is six feet and more
    But he is such a spacious chiel the girls do him adore.

11   But Jamie Tham I can't omit, he must be put in here,
    For he had many droll remarks and stories that were queer,
    He carried ale and stronger drink an' gae the folk fu' thirsty,
    But yet I think his special feat was singing "Cripple Kirsty".

12   Wi' singing and wi' dancin' we charmed a' the folk,
    And thus we did keep up the glee till after three o'clock,
    And then we wished each ither well, wi' many happy days
    The party then did separate with three cheers and hurrahs.

Mrs JAFFRAY — D

THE HARVEST HOME

1 Come all ye jolly lads and lasses
    Ranting round in pleasure's ring
    Join with me tak' up the chorus
    And wi' mirth and glee we'll sing.
       Blithe and merry hae we been
       Blithe and merry let us be
       Mony a merry night we've seen
       And mony mair we hope to see.

2 We came nae here for wardle's gear
    Nae warldly motive did us draw
    But we came here to fit the fleer
    And dance till we be like to fa'.

3 Noo minstrels screw your fiddles up
    And see if they be right in tune
    And gie us "Donald kissed Katie
    Down among the camowine".   [camomile

4 Wha wid see the bonnie lasses
    A' sae handsome trig and braw
    Them to please wha wid refeese
    To wint their sleep an hour or twa.

5 The craps secured frae wind and rain
    Stands in the stackyard snug and dry
    Boreas' blast may rage in vain
    We'll whistle while it's going by.

6 Now the harvest works are owre
    The fields are bare, the yards are fu'
    And we unto the ploo repair
    And for another crap pursue.

7 He that first does weary here
    A dosent fleep we will him ca'   [feeble lout
    But he that's hinmost in the fleer
    We'll judge him chief amang us a'.

8 Now we're a' here sae happy met
    Floating round in pleasure's stream
    We winna flit till Phoebus' licht
    Be shining out wi' morning beam.

JOHN MOWAT — G

KIRN SONG

1   There's Robbie Burns, altho' he be dead,
     And the green turf spread over his head,
     He was the lad that could handle the ploo,
     And enjoy himsel' at oor kirn aye true.

2   Some drink to ladies, and some drink to lairds,
     But here is to the farmers wi' their big corn yairds,
     Wi' their big cornyairds and their big barn fu',
     Gie us a' a wee drappie to weet our moo.

JONATHAN GAULD — G

AULD WARRACK'S PLOUGH FEAST

A
Warrack's Plough Feast

1 Auld Warrack made a plough feast,
    Ye never saw sic fun;
    An' mony a lad and lass came there
    To see the play begun.
    It happened at Drumallachie,
    Upon the banks of Don.

2 If ye wad favour me this day,
    It's never be forgot,
    An' gin yer nowte come owre the brae,
    We'll turn them round the Pot.

3 Some held on, an' some held in,
    An' some o' them did ca',
    But Brockie in the furrow fit,
    He gart the wyner thraw.

4 Some got sprots, an' some got sauchs,
    An' some got raips o' straw;
    Auld Bruntie owre in Sinnahard,
    He made a link or twa.
    There's Sandy Hunter on the brae,
    I troth he'll mak' a rhyme.

5 Auld Warrack he took aff his bonnet,
    It was to say the grace;
    An' a' the sins an' wives he had,
    It's them he did confess.

6 Some got breid an' cheese their fill,
    An' some got breid for a';
    But the herdie got a dish o' want,
    An' that was warst ava.

Rev. GEORGE WILLIAMS — D

B
Warrack's Plough Feast

1 At the yokin' of auld Warrack's plough
    The neighbours a' came roun.

2 Auld Bruntie owre in Sinnahard,
    He made a link or twa,
    And that was a' the soume they had,   [plough chain
    The rest was made o' straw.

ALEXANDER CALLAM — D

THE COUNTRY ROCKIN'

1   It has often been alloo'd that the best o' human life
    Is the hours o' social harmony when free frae party strife
    When freenship smiles and love beguiles mang lads an' lasses
    These joys we only find when assembled at a country rockin'.
       Whack-fal-al-de-al etc.

2   When the gudeman frae the fire bids us frankly venture ben
    In hamely sangs an' social joys a nicht wi' him tae spen'
    The welcome kind attracts each mind we need na ither friendly token
    When we join the honest social core assembled at a country rockin'.

3   Noo since we're cheery met for a nicht o' social joy
    Let every care be banished for that wad oor peace destroy
    When freenship smiles an' love beguiles at sangs we'll hae a hearty yokin' [contest
    And we'll chat the lays o' Robbie Burns wha first described the country rockin'.

4   And when we tak oor hameward road, it's no taen sair amiss
    Tho frae some bonny smilin' face we steal a wee bit kiss
    Her hert tae move and tell oor love in vows that ne'er will be broken
    Till in some biggin' o' oor ain we'll hae a herty country rockin'.

JAMES CHEYNE — G

DECEMBER CAM'

1   December cam' the twenty fift
Accordin' to the aul' time
When frosty win's blew i' the drift
It was a bitter caul' time.

2   The maiden she wad clim' the crook
O' soot to clean the lum
And by misfortun' slipt her fit
And lichtit on her bum
I' the fire that nicht.

3   The maiden then she beuk the breid
An' scour't the hoose fu' clean
The cheers an steels they got a doak
And a' tae task were ta'en.

4   Reekin' het, an' butter't weel,
We got them frae her ain han',
Fu' sweet that nicht.

5   A great bombard o' caups an' cogs
Cam' rowin frae the pantry
The dainty diece got mony a shog   [jog
Frae crookit rungs o' rowantree.

6   This happen't a' the day afore
By way o' preparation
For sic a day.

Mrs RETTIE — G

637

THE TWELVE DAYS OF CHRISTMAS

1   The second day of Christenmas my true love sent to me
Two pipers playing,
Three geese a-laying
Four ladies dancing
Five gold rings
Three French hens
Two calling birds
One turtle dove
A partridge an' a pear tree.

WILLIAM WALKER — G

638

HERE'S TO YE A' AND A HAPPY NEW YEAR

1   Here's tae the lassie that never gets fu'
Here's tae the lassie that aye proves sae true
Here's tae the lad that's aye fill'd in beer
Here's to ye a' and a Happy New Year.

2   The old year has gone and the new year has come
With pleasure to plenty and sorrows to some
So I'll toss o'er this glass and I'll drink it with cheer
For a health tae ye a' and a Happy New Year.

Miss ANNIE SHIRER — G

639

GET UP GUDEWIFE

Get up gudewife and shak' your feathers,
Dinna think that we are beggars;
We're only bairns come oot to play:
Rise up and gie's oor Hogmanay.

GAVIN GREIG — G

640

OUR FEET'S CAULD

Our feet's cauld, our sheen's thin,
Gie's a piece an' lat's rin.   [piece of food

ALEXANDER ROBB — G

641

WE ARE A' QUEEN MARY'S MEN

1 This is guid New Year's Even-night,
     We are a' Queen Mary's men,
   And we've come here to claim our right,
     And that's before oor Lady.

2 Auld man, gae tae your ale-in-vat,
   And hand us here twa pints o' that.

3 Guid-wife, gae to your pork-ham,
   And cut it large and cut it roond,
   Be sure you cut no your big thoom.

4 Here's tae the ane wi' the yellow hair,
   She's in the hoose and we maun hae her.

5 I wish yer kye may a' weel thrive,
   And every ane a guid calf.

6 I wish your mares weel in their boal,
   And every ane a stag foal.

7 I wish your hens may a' weel thrive,
   And every ane lay three times five.

8 I wish yer geese weel fae the hill,
   And every ane twelve at her heel.

9 Be ye maids, or be ye nane,
   Ye'll a' be kissed or ye gang hame.

J.A. FOTHERINGHAM – G

519

BESUTHIAN

A

The Thiggin' Song.

1   The aul' year's deen an' the new's begun,
    Besoothan, besoothan,
    An' noo the beggars they have come,
    An' awa' besoothan toon.

2   Rise up, gweedwife, an' binna sweer,
    An' deal your charity to the peer.

3   It's nae for wirsel 't we stan' for,   [ourselves
    Bit seekin' charity for the peer.

4   Ye'll tak' th' peck bit nae the muttie,
    An' deal your charity lairge an' lucky.

5   Yer door is open an' we'll come in,
    An' we'll return wi' little din.

6   In meal an' money gin ye be scant,
    We'll kiss yer lasses or we want.

ISAAC TROUP — G & D

B

1   The auld year's oot an' the new's come in,
     Besuthian, besuthian,
    An' the beggars are begun to ging,
     An' we're aye besuthian toun.

2 Rise up, goodwife, an' be not sweer,
    Besuthian, besuthian,
  An' deal your charity on the peer,
    An' we'll aye besuthian toun.

3 We beg for meal an' we beg for maut,
    Besuthian, besuthian,
  An' we beg for money to buy wir saut,
    An' we're aye besuthian toun.

4 Fae you that's young an' in yer prime,
    Besuthian, besuthian,
  Fae you we'll be expeckin' bawbees,
    An' we'll aye besuthian toun.

5 Gin yer ale be at the barm,
    Besuthian, besuthian,
  We'll tak' a drap to haud us warm,
    An' we're aye besuthian toun.

6 If o' meal or money ye be scant,
    Besuthian, besuthian,
  We'll kiss yer lasses or we want,
    An' we're aye besuthian toun.

7 Oor sheen are made o' aul' Norse hide,
    Besuthian, besuthian,
  Oor feet are caul', we canna weel bide,
    An' we're aye besuthian toun.

ALEXANDER HARDY — G & D

C

Thiggers' Song

1 The gweed New Year it is come in,
    Be soothing be soothing.
  An' noo the beggars begin to rin
    Be soothing be soothing.

2 It's nae for oorsel's that we stan' here
    Be soothing, be soothing
  It's seekin' charity for the peer
    An' awa be soothing toon.

3 Oor sheen are made o' auld horse hide
    Be soothing be soothing
  Alas! my taes I canna bide
    Be soothing be soothing.

4 Rise up guidwife an' binna sweer
    Be soothing be soothing
  An' deal yer charity to the peer
    Be soothing be soothing.

5 Ye winna fill yer cog no mutty
    Be soothing be soothing
  But fill yer big pail large and lucky
    Be soothing, be soothing.

6 Johnnie Baxter an' his wife
    Be soothing be soothing
  For they hae a'most lost ther life
    An' awa be soothing toon.

7 For want o' meat an' for want o' claes
    Be soothing be soothing.

JAMES PIRIE — D

D

1   The auld year's out, and the new's in,
     Be soothan! Be soothan!
  An' a' the beggars are begun,
     An' we'll a' be soothan toun.

2   Rise up, gudewife, an' dinna be sweere,
  Bestow your charity on the peer.

3   If meal or money wi' ye be scant,
  We'll kiss your lasses ere we want.

4   If your ale be at the barm,
  We'll tak' a drink to had us warm.

5   The back o' my house's thacket wi' rye,
  I canna sing mair, my throat's so dry.

6   My sheen they're made o' an auld horse hide,
  My feet's sae cauld, I canna langer bide.

Rev. GEORGE WILLIAMS — D

E

The maiden o' Millegin she gangs sae braw,
    A soothin, a soothin,
Till never a penny had she awa,
    An' awa' be Soothin toun.
She hes neither coo nor hog,
    Be soothin, be soothin;
Bit a bonny daem and a dainty dog,
    An' awa' to Soothin toun.
Rise up, good wife, and dinna be sweer,
An' deal yer charity to the peer,
    Be soothin', be soothin',
An' gin ye dinna lift yer han',
We'll mak ye sure o' a verse o' wer sang,
    An' awa' be Soothin toun.
For the tailor he ance gaed ower the score, [went beyond the bounds
An' put the back o' the breeks afore,   of reason
    An' awa' be Soothin toun.

Rev. GEORGE WILLIAMS — D

YE GAE BUT TO YOUR BEEF-STAN'

Besuthan

Ye gae but to your beef-stan',   [beef-barrel
Ye cut a collop baith lairge and lang,   [slice of meat
And see that ye dinna cut your han',
And see that ye dinna cut your han',
And aye Besuthan toonie;
By Bairnsdale and Coventry,
And awa by Rillanatoonie. —
Hogmanay!

Miss BELL ROBERTSON — G

THEY SELL'T HIS TEETH TO TEETHE A RAKE

A

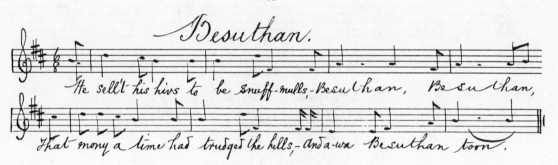

ALEXANDER ROBB — G

B

1 They sell't his teeth to teethe a rake,
   Besuthian, besuthian
Which mony a nicht had teem't the hake,
   An' awa besuthian toon.

2 They sell't his ribs for riddle rims,
His rumple banes to be claes pins.   [rump

3 The blacksmith bocht his iron brogues,
His carcase feasted the tanner's dogs.

JAMES CHEYNE — G

THE RAM O' DIRRAM

A

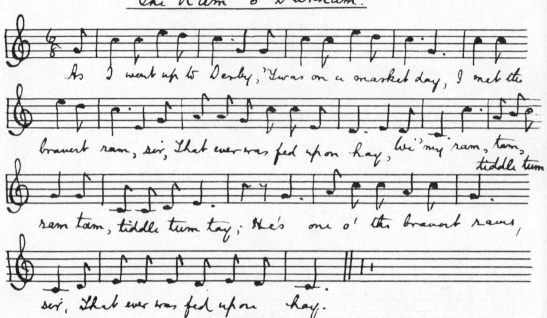

The Ram o' Durham.

1. As I went up to Derby
   Twas on a market day
   I saw the bravest ram sir
   That e'er was feed upon hay.
      Wi my ram tam tiddle tum
      Ram tam tiddle tum tye
      He's one of the bravest rams sir
      That ever was feed upon hay.

2. He hid four feet to gang on
   An four feet to stan
   An ilka foot i't this ram hid
   Wid hae cover'd an acre o land.

3. The horns 'it this ram hid
   They reach'd up to the moon
   A man went up in December
   An he didna come back till June.

4. The teeth that this ram hid
   They were like a hunter's horn
   An every meal i't this ram took
   It ate five bolls o corn.

5. The ram it had a back sir
   That reached up to the sky
   The eagles bigget their nests on't
   For I've heard the young ones cry.

6. The w'oo that was upon his back
   Twas scarcely man could reach't
   Bit the eagles bigget their nests in't
   An the ministers stood an they preach'd.

7. The tail that this ram hid
   Wis fifty mile a'n an ell
   And it was saul' at Derby
   To ring St Andrew's bell.

8. The man that killed the ram sir
   Wis up to his eyes in blood
   An the boy that held the bason
   Wis wash'd away in the flood.

9. The blood o this wonderful ram sir
   It ran for a mile an mair
   An it turn'd the millar's wheel sir
   As't hid never been turn'd before.

10 The man that own'd the ram sir
   He must have been very rich
   An the man that sings this song sir
   Must be the son of a witch.

11 Now if you don't believe me
   An think I'm telling a sham
   You may go up to Derby
   An there you'll see the ram.

Mrs MARGARET GILLESPIE — D

B

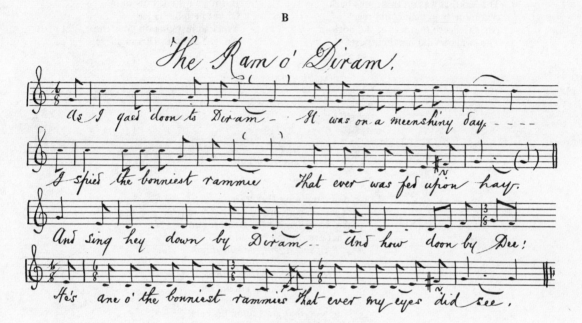

ALEXANDER ROBB — G

C

The Ram o' Dirrim

1 I went doon thro Dirrim
   'Twas on an ancient day
   I saw one o' the bravest rams sir
   Cam trippin alang the way.
   Hey doon to Dirrim
   An' in thro Dirrim Duree
   I saw one o' the bravest rams sir
   That ever my eyes did see.

2 He had four feet to gang on,
   An' ither four to stan' on,
   An every fit that this ram gaed
   Wad a covered an' acre o' lan'.

3 The head that was on this ram sir
   Wad a cairret a regiment o' men
   An' the tongue that was in this ram's head
   Wad a dinèd the same.

525

4   The teeth that was in this ram sir
    Wad a hadden a bushel o' corn
    An the one that was at the reet o' them
    Wad a been a fine tootin' horn.

5   The horns that was on this ram's head
    Was twenty cubits high
    An' the eagles biggit their nests in them
    For I heard the young ones cry.

6   The 'oo that was on this ram's back
    Was more than man could reach
    An' the fleece that was at the bottom
    The swallows did big their nests.

7   The one that sticket this ram sir
    Was droont amang his blood
    An' the one that held the basin
    Was cairrit awa wi' the flood.

8   The tail that was on this ram sir
    Was a hundred yairds an' an ell
    You'll send it doon to Dirrim
    To ring St Andrew's bell.

9   But if you think I be jokin'
    Or yet be tellin' a lee
    You can just ging on your three fitet mare
    An' gae doon to Dirrim an' see.

Miss F. GRANT — D

D

The Ram o' Dirram

1   As I cam in by Diram Dee
    'Twas on a moonshine day
    An' there I spied the greatest ram
    That ever mine eyes did see.
      An sing diram, an sing diram
      An' sing diram dolder ree
      He was the greatest ram sir
      That ever mine eyes did see.

2   The woo that grew upon his back
    Made fifty packs o' claith
    An for to make a lie sir
    I would be very laith.

3   The horns that grew upon his head
    They were so very high
    The eagles biggit their nests in them
    For we heard the young ones cry.

4   The tail that hang ahin this ram
    Was fifty fadom an' an ell
    An it was sold at Diram Dee
    To ring the market bell.

5   The man that killed this ram sir
    The boy who held the tub
    An the people looking on sir
    Were swept away with his blood.

JOHN MILNE — G

E
The Ram o' Dirram

1   He had four feet tae stand upon,
    And ither four tae gang upon,
    And he was the bravest ram, sir,
    That ever mine eyes did see.

2   The man that killed that ram, sir,
    Was drooned amon' the blood,
    And the boy that held the basin
    He was washen awa' in the flood.

3   And gin ye dinna believe me, sir,
    Or doubt what I've said tae you,
    Ye can tak' Dorman's three-fittet mare,
    And ride on and see it's true.

Miss ANNIE SHIRER — G

ROBIN'S TESTAMENT

A

1 Ye will tak' my twa bonnie e'en,
  That eest to blink sae bricht;
  Ye'll gie them to yon shewster lass,   [seamstress
  To save her o' candle licht.

2 Ye will tak' my bonnie nib,   [beak
  That eest to pickle the corn;
  And gie it to yon little herd,
  To be a tootin' horn.

3 And ye will tak' my twa bonnie wings
  That eest to spread sae wide;
  And ye'll hae them to St. Mary's Kirk,
  To cover her sunny side.

4 And ye will tak' my twa bonnie legs,
  That eest to walk sae trig;
  And ye'll hae them to yon burn bank
  For pillars to the brig.

5 And ye will tak' my bonnie tail
  That eest to cock so fine;
  And ye'll gie it to yon bonnie bride,
  To be her weddin' goon.

6 Ye will tak' your ten owsen,
  And trail me to the hill;
  And pairt sma' and sair a'
  That hungry may get their fill.

7 When Robin had his testament made,
  And had nae mair to say,
  By cam' a greedy gled,
  And snappit him away.

ALEXANDER ROBB — G

B

The Robin.

I will leave my bonny nib That had ees't to pick the cor-n,
(To replat) fiddle diddle jinkum, my fiddle diddle jinkum jeerie,
An' I'll leave it to yon scholars, It'll be to them a
Thon jinkum flinkum, pay doo day, Thon dainty dum a
Fine & Refrain
hor-n. Wi' my fiddle diddle jinkum, My
deerie.

1 I will leave my bonnie nib
   That had ees't to pick the corn,
   An' I'll leave it to yon scholars,
   It'll be to them a horn.
        Wi' my fiddle diddle jinkum,
        My fiddle diddle jinkum,
        My fiddle diddle jinkum jeerie,
        Thon jinkum flinkum, pay doo day,
        Thon dainty dum a deerie.

2 I will leave my bonny heid,
   It is baith lang an' sma',
   An I'll leave it to yon scholars,
   It'll be to them a ba'.

Mrs LYALL — D

C

Robin Sick and Wearie

1 As I cam' in by yon sea stran',
   And doon the water sae wearie,
   And there I saw him little Robin
   Was sittin' on a breerie.   [brier
        Fadle dadle didirie dan,
        Finkim dinkim dearie,
        Fadle dadle didrie dan,
        Robin sick and wearie.

2 It's I wad mak' my testment here,
   Guidman, gin ye hear me.

3 It's ye tak' aff my bonnie neb
    It used to pickle the corn,
    And ye gie it to some bonnie boy
    To be a sounding horn.

4 Ye tak' aff my bonnie head,
    It is sae bonnie and sma',
    And ye gie't the Queen and her Maries
    To be a tossing ba'.

5 And ye tak' aff my bonnie wings
    That used to flap sae wide,
    And ye hae them to Marykirk
    To cover the sunny side.

6 Ye tak' aff my bonnie legs,
    They are sae bonnie and trig,
    And ye hae them to the wan water
    To be stannerts to the brig.

7 And syne ye yoke your ten owsen,
    And trail me to the hill,
    And ye tak' oot my sma' thairms   [intestines
    Lat the birdies get a fill.

Miss BELL ROBERTSON — G

D

Robin's Testament

1 Robin was the sickest bird
    That ever yet did fly
    And he would have his testament made
    Before that he should die.
        And sing, fiddly linkum, dinkum, dinkum
        Fiddly linkum darie,
        Sing hitherie, titherie, tando
        Robin's sick and weary.

2 Ye'll tak my bonnie e'enikies
    That showed me a' the licht
    And ye'll gie them to some sewster dame
    To hain her candle licht.

3 Ye'll tak' my bonnie nibbikie
    That pickit a' the corn
    Ye'll gie it to some aul' guidman
    To be a tootin horn.

4 Ye'll tak my bonnie wingikies
    They're o' the purple brown
    And ye'll gie them to some sewster dame
    To mak' a bridal goon.

5   Ye'll tak' my bonnie leggikies
    They are sae neat and trig,
    And ye'll gie them to some mason lad
    For arches to a brig.

6   When Robin had his testament made
    And ready for to die
    By cam' a greedy gled
    And fuppit him away.

J.W. SPENCE — G

E
Robin's Testament

1   Ye'll tak my little nibbickie
    That picket a' the corn
    And gie it to some aul' goodiedee
    To be a tooting horn.
       Fiddlum, dinkum, dinkum dinkum
       Fiddlum dinkum deerie.
       Hitheray, titheray tae
       Robin sick-a-weary.

2   Ye'll tak my little wingikies
    That eest tae flap sae wide
    And gie them to St Mary's kirk
    To hap the sunny side.

H. DUNCAN — G

THE HAUGHS O' GARTLY

1 Lang Lowrie o Bucharn
He wis there wi's tree o' arn   [alder stick
He said he wid them a' govérn
Upon the Haughs o' Gairtly.

ALEX MACDONALD — D

THE CUSHNIE WINTER SPORTS

1 Dauvid Ferries, that skeelie auld man,   [skilled at healing
Was doctor till the doctor cam'.
They didna gyang, but I fear they ran
On the nicht o' Fastern's even.

2 Wha was there but Effie Milne,
She swore she wad the laddie kill,
Gin she got him aboot the mill
On the nicht o' Fastern's even.

3 Effie Milne we maunna affront,
Or Willie Forbes'll gie's a dunt,
An sae we sanna touch upon't,
On the nicht o' Fastern's even.

4 Rachie hersel' she did declare,
She wadna gyang to the wreaths nae mair,
For fear o' getting her .   .   . laid bare,
On the nicht o' Fastern's even.

Rev. GEORGE WILLIAMS — D

649

TO MEN

A

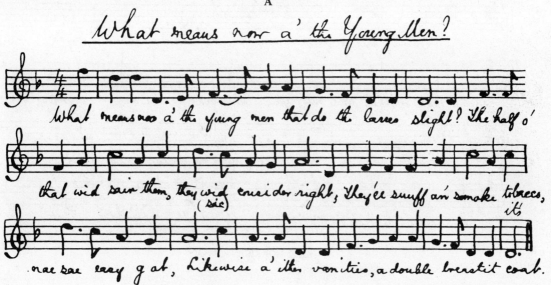

What means now a' the Young Men?

What means noo a' the young men that do the lasses slight? The half o'
that wid sair them, they wid (sic) consider right; They'll snuff an' smoke tobacco, it's
nae sae easy gat, Likewise a' ither vanities, a double breastit coat.

1   What means noo a' the young men that do the lasses slight?
    The half o' that wid sair them, they wid consider right;
    They'll snuff an' smoke tobacco, it's nae so easy got,
    Likewise a' other vanities, a double breastit coat.

2   They maun hae their pump shoes jist newly come fae France,
    An' nackets in their pocketies, to reesle fan they dance,
    Although their sark be tweedled cotton, a linen neck abeen,   [twilled
    A ribbon black gaes roon' their hat, an' wow but fa's like them!

3   They'll tak ye to a tavern, an' call a herty pint,
    An' they'll tak oot a snuff-box wi' a siller joint;
    They'll curse an' they'll swear by the nations all abroad
    That they could kiss their wedded wife upon the walking road.

4   But then when they get mairrit, oh then comes a' the sorrow,
    The hoosie it's to big, an' the siller it's to borrow;
    They'll pit ye in a ricky hoose, an' lat ye greet your fill;
    So, lassie, gin ye brew weel, ye'll drink the better ale.

CHARLES EWEN — D

B

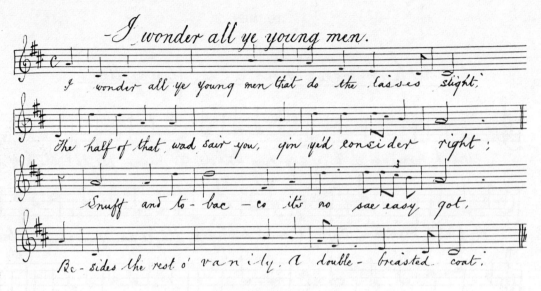

I wonder all ye young men.

I wonder all ye young men that do the lasses slight;

The half of that wad sair you, gin ye'd consider right;

Snuff and to-bac-co it's no sae easy got,

Be-sides the rest o' vanity, a double-breasted coat.

Miss K. MORRICE – G

C

To Men

1　I winner what a' the young men mean that does the lasses slight
　　The half o' that wid sair them gin they wid consider right
　　They're snuffin' their tobacco, it's nae sae easy got
　　Besides some ither vanities, a dooble breasted coat.

2　Their doobe shanled pumps in their lasses e'en do glance
　　And tackets in their pocketies to reesel when they dance.
　　Although their shirt be tweedlin coorse a linen neck abeen
　　Wi' ribbons black aboot their hats and vows wha's like them.

3　They'll tack them to a tavern and there they'll call a pint
　　They'll pull o'ot a snuff-box wi' a siller joint
　　They'll curse and they'll swear by their nations all abroad
　　That they could coort their wedded wives all on the walkin' road.

4　But the apple tree buds bonny, it buds on every side
　　And when young men a-wooin goes they're puffèd up with pride
　　They're puffèd up with pride and they'll gar the siller flee
　　They'll mak the bonnie lasses think that the Lowden hoose is free.

5　But ah when ye are merrit O' then begins the sorrow
　　The hoose it is tae build the siller is tae borrow.
　　They'll set ye doon in a ricky hoose and lat ye greet your fill
　　So lassie gin ye brew weel ye'll drink the better ale.

Source unrecorded – G

D

Oh What Do All the Young Men Mean

1   Oh what do all the young men mean that do the lasses slight
    One half of it would do would they consider right
    They curse and they swear, by the nations all around
    That they wouldna court a bonnie lassie in the walking ground.

2   It's snuff and tobacco is nae sae easy got
    Likewise some other vanities, a double breasted coat.

J. SIM — G

I'M NOW TWENTY-TWO

1   I'm now twenty-two and a good-looking chiel,
     I've on a new suit frae the heid to the heel;
     My tie's made of satin, my watch-chain of gowd,
     I walk like the gents with a swaggering showd.

2   I never wear tackets, you may think it wrang,
     My boots are all elastic, and squeak when I gang;
     I've a ring on my finger, but auld Baubie Rose
     Says, It wad set me far better if it hang on my nose.

3   Lang, lang hae I laboured to rear a moustache,
     On hair oil I hae spent aboot twa pounds o' cash;
     But nature has made me a good-lookin' chap,
     It's gien me some hair, but a gey sober crap.

4   I try to speak proper to old and to young,
     But their braid Buchan words stick like glue to my tongue;
     When I mean to say "meat" I'm sure to say "maet",
     For my half-Buchan English oft gars me look blate.

5   I doot my auld mither has surely mista'en,
     For dressin' and coortin' has a' been in vain;
     The weel-tochered maidens they're unco weel watched,
     Forbye they are saucy and no to be catched.

6   The lasses in Rora they are a' fu' o' pride,
     I shifted my grun and gaed doon to Langside;
     I oiled my moustache, and put on my best tie,
     But the limmers rin aff when they see me draw nigh.

7   They bid me get books and advise me to read,
     But books I detest, and hae deen a' my days.
     What's knowledge and books to compare wi' braw claes?
     A vain man's a fool Auld King Solomon said.
     Nae mair I'll rin aifter ilk weel-tochered maid,
     But I'll try and put wisdom into my heid.

8   Experience has taught me and opened my e'en,
     And see sic a puir silly gowk as I hae been;
     I've ta'en their advice, and see mysel' noo, —
     To folly and flattery a last lang adieu!

Mrs TAYLOR (Rora) — G

651

JAMIE'S BRAW CLAES

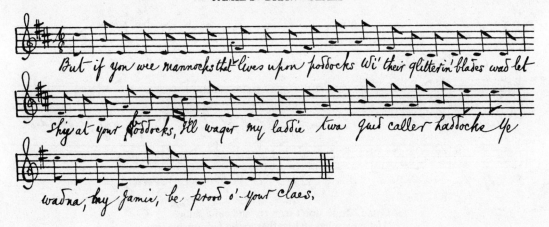

But if yon wee mannocks that lives upon poddocks Wi' their glitterin' blades wad let
shy at your poddocks, I'll wager my laddie twa guid caller haddocks Ye
wadna, my Jamie, be proud o' your claes,

1   Oor son Jamie was a kin' o' a queer ane
    He wad gang richt or wrang to the grand volunteerin'
    We a' kent fu' brawly withoot ony spierin'
    It wasna for fechtin' but jist for the claes.

2   He got on a suit and oh, how the callant
    Cam' stroodin' and stridin' into oor bit dwallin'   [strutting
    And doon thro' the fleer I thocht I had fallen
    To see oor puir laddie sae proud o' his claes.

3   Auld grannie i' the neuk wi' her black cuttie smokin',
    And wi' her auld fit aye the cradle was rockin'
    Thocht noo to hersel', It's a' far past jokin'
    When laddies like Jamie hae gotten sic claes.

4   But if yon wee mannocks that lives upon poddocks   [little men; frogs
    Wi' their glittering blades wad lat shy at your boddocks
    I'll wager my laddie twa guid caller haddocks
    Ye wadna, my Jamie, be proud o' your claes.

ALEXANDER ROBB — G

COME, DEAR, DON'T FEAR

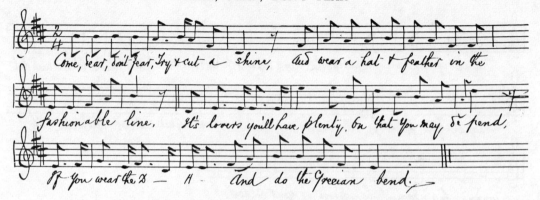

1 Come, dear, don't fear, try and cut a shine,
  And wear a hat and feather in the fashionable line.
  It's lovers you'll have plenty, on that you may depend,
  If you wear the D — H — and do the Grecian bend.

JAMES ANGUS – G

653

JEAN PIRIE

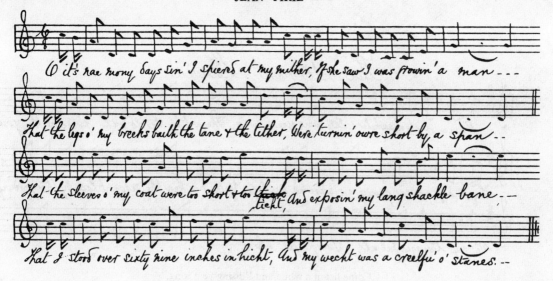

1   O it's nae mony days sin' I spiered at my mither,
       If she saw I was growin' a man
       That the legs o' my breeks baith the tane and the tither,
       Were turnin' owre short by a span
       That the sleeves o' my coat were too short and too ticht,
       And exposin' my lang shackle bane
       That I stood over sixty nine inches in hicht,
       And my wecht was a creelfu' o' stanes.

JOHN QUIRRIE — G

THE SERVAN' LASSES

A

The Servant Lasses.

Come listen awhile & I'll sing you a song, The wit of the old & the pride of the young;

They're a' grown sae gaudy as sure as my life, Ye'll nae ken the servant lass by the goodwife.

Wi' my twiggie fal al, Twiggie fal al ee

1   Come listen a while and I'll sing ye a song,
    The wit o' the auld and the pride o' the young,
    They're a' grown sae gaudie, as sure as my life,
    Ye'd scarce ken the servan' lass by the guidwife.   [from
        Wi' my twiggie fal la,
        Fal diddle a.

2   It's nae farmer's dochter, nor tradesman's indeed
    For what I'm about to sing my new creed,
    It's o'or servan lasses, they a' ging sae braw,
    They wad ootstrip their mistresses by far and awa.

3   Between sax and seven young miss gaes to school
    Before you discern it she's wise or a fool,
    And there she must learn to read and to write,
    Till she's fit for a lawyer or something sic like.

4   When schooling is over to service she goes,
    For the greed o' high wages as you may suppose,
    An' then she sets out wi' a white muslin gown,
    An' a bonnet wad hide the moonlicht fra a town.

5   Doun frae her bonnet there hings a bit silk,
    Like fat my auld minnie had syein' her milk,
    I know it is useful for beauties to grace,
    That it hides a' the wrinkles o' tar in their face.

6   She curls up her hair like a water dog's tail,
    An' rows it in paper as roun' as a snail,
    Wi' that an' the veil hangin' doon o'er her e'en
    There's fint a bit wrinkle ava to be seen.

7   It's then she sets out like a ship in full sail,
    Wi' sax seven flowers about her gown tail,
    An' gin she should happen to g'bye ony men
    They'll say one to another, O what is she yon?

8 Sunday about she maun gang to the church,
But what she hears there she widna min' much,
The psalms nor the text she would scarce min' upon,
But she min's weel to say, "Fatna bonnie chiel's yon?"

9 To balls, fairs, and weddings she'll rant an' she'll rove,
An' at ilka meeting she'll get a new love,
An' wi' her gallantin' all three is gae roun'
When her apron gets up and her bonnet comes doun.

10 When some o' her sweethearts hears that she is wrong,
In this same country they'll nae tarry long,
Awa to America or sic a like trick,
An' Missie, peer thing, gets the wheep shaft to lick.

11 Then she's confined like a cow on the grass,
The bonnet's shoved aff and the whole gaudy dress,
An' noo at the cradle when the wee one does roar,
She greets at the thing that she looch at afore.

12 I am an auld bachelor forty an' three,
This sangie I made for to keep me in glee,
This sangie I made for the fun o' the thing,
But my throat's growin' sair and I'm no fit to sing.

WILLIAM WALKER — G

B

The Braw Servant Lasses.

Ye braw servant lasses I'll sing you a song, The wit o' the auld & the pride o' the young,
They're a' grown sae dainty as sure as my life, Ye scarce ken the servant lass by the goodwife.

1 Ye braw servant lasses, I'll sing ye a song,
The wit o' the old and the pride o' the young.
They're a' grown sae dainty, as sure as your life,
Ye scarce ken the servant lass by the goodwife.

2 Between six and seven young miss goes to school,
Afore they weel ken if she's wise or a fool,
And there she does learn for to count and to write,
Till she's fit for a lawyer or something siclike.

3 When schooling is over to service she goes,
It is for high wages as you may suppose,
The first of it is for a white muslin goon
And bonnet wad haud the meenlicht frae a toon.

4   At balls and at concerts she'll rant and she'll rove,
       At every new meeting she finds a new love
       And wi' her gallantin' ere three years gaes roon,
       Her apron gaes up and her bonnet comes doon.

5   And when her true lover does hear she is wrang,
       Into the same country he'll no tarry lang,
       But awa' to America – oh! sic a trick
       And leave the puir lassie the whip shaft to lick.

6   Now she is confined like a cow to the grass
       Her bonnet's laid up and her high dainty dress,
       The cradle does rock while the bairnie does roar,
       And she greets at the thing that she laucht at before.

MAGGIE WATT – G

C

JAMES ANGUS – G

D

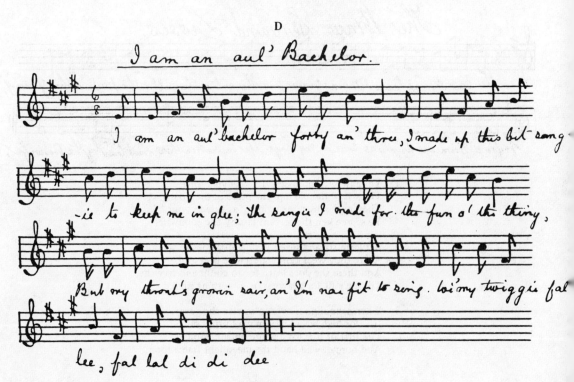

Mrs LYALL – D

542

E
The Servan' Lasses

1   Ye decent auld women I'll sing you a sang
     To the wit o' the auld an' the pride o' the young
     They're a' grown sae gaudy as sure as my life
     You'll nae ken the servan lass by the gweedwife
        Wi' my twigie ful ee ful addie ee.

2   It's no fairmers' daughters or tradesman's indeed
     For which I intend to sing my new creed
     It's oor servan lasses they're a' grown sae braw
     They ootstrip their mistress by far an' awa.

3   Btween six an' seven young miss goes to school
     Before ye can tell if she's wise or a fool
     An' there she must learn to read an' to write
     Or she's fit for a lawyer or something sic like.

4   When schoolin' is over to service she goes
     For greed of high wages as you may suppose
     The first of it goes on a white muslin goon
     An' a bonnet wad keep the moonlight fae a toon.

5   An' doon fae her bonnet there hings a bit silk
     Like what my auld grannie had seyin her milk
     I own it is usefu' the beauty to grace
     For it hides a' the wrinkles that is in her face.

6   She curls her hair like a water dog's tail
     Rolled up in a paper as round as a snail
     Wi' that an' the veil hingin doon owre her een
     There's never ae wrinkle ava to be seen.

7   An' noo she's rigged oot like a ship in full sail
     Wi' sax seven flounces aboot her goon tail
     The vera first Sunday the buckle gangs on
     Ane says to the ither "Oh! what has she on."

8   For Sunday aboot she must go to the church
     But what she hears there she will no mind it much
     The text nor the psalm she will no mind upon
     But she'll mind very well what her neighbours had on.

9   At balls an' at weddin's she'll rant an she'll roar
     At every new meetin' she gets a new love
     But wi' her galantin or three years gae roon
     Her pride that was up it gets a tak doon.

10   When some of her sweethearts know that she is wrang
     Unto the same country they'll no tairry lang
     But rin to America O sic a trick
     An' Missie puir thing gets the wheep shaft to lick.

11   An' noo she's confined like a coo on the girss
     The bonnet's laid by wi' the hale gaudy dress
     The cradle she rocks while the wean does roar
     An' she greets at the thing that she leuch at afore.

12 I am an' auld batchelor forty an' three
   I made up this bit sangie to keep me in glee
   The sangie I made for the fun o' the thing
   But my throat's growin sair an' I'm nae fit to sing.

Mrs LYALL — G & D

F

The Servan' Lasses

1   Ye daecent old women I will sing you a song
   The wit of the old and the pride of the young
   For they're a' grown so gaudy as sure as my life
   That you will scarce ken a servant frae a guidwife.
      Wi my twigie fall la fall-all de-die da
      Wi my twige fall la fall-all-de die dee.

2   It's no farmer's daughter nor tradesmen indeed
   In which I intend to sing my new creed
   For the servant lasses they're a' grown so braw
   That they outstrip their mistress by far and away.

3   Between six and seven young miss goes to school
   Before that you know if she is wise or a fool
   For to learn to count and to write
   Till she is fit for a lawyer or something siclike.

4   When schooling is over to service miss goes
   For the greed of high wages as ye may suppose
   And the first of it goes for a white muslin gown
   And a bonnet wid keep the moonlight from the town.

5   And down from the bonnet there hangs a bit silk
   Like what my auld granny had for sien her milk
   I am sure it is useful from beauty to grace
   For it hides a' the wrinkles that are in her face.

6   She curls up her hair like a water dog's tail
   Rowes up in a paper as round as a snail
   Wi' that and the veil hanging down owre her brow
   And there's scarcely a wrinkle ava to be seen.

7   Now she's rigged out like a ship in full sail
   Wi' six seven flounces around her gown tail
   The very first Sunday the buckle goes on
   Says the one to the other Jeck, what is she yon.

8   Sunday about she must go to the church
   And what she hears there she winna mind much
   The text and the Psalms she winna mind upon
   But she'll mind very well what her neighbour's got on.

9   At balls, fairs and weddings she'll rant and she'll rove
   At every new meeting she'll get a new love
   And wi' a' her gallivanting till three years go round
   The belly goes up and the bonnet goes down.

10 Now she is confined like a cow on the grass
The bonnet laid by and the whole gaudy dress
And she rocks at the cradle while the wee one does roar
And greets at the thing that she laughed at before.

11 While some of her sweethearts knows that they're wrong
In the same country they'll no tarry long
But run off to America oh sik a rik
And missie poor thing gets the fop shaft to lick.

12 I am an old bachelor three score and three
I made up this sangie to keep me in glee
I made up this sangie for the fun of the thing
My throat's grown sair and I am no fit to sing.

Source unrecorded — G

G
The Servan' Lasses

1 Come, listen awhile and I'll sing you a sang,
The wit o' the old and the pride o' the young,
They're a' grown sae gaudy, as sure as my life,
Ye wid scarcely ken the servan' lass by the goodwife.
Wi' my twiggie fal a thi fal di dee da.

2 Atween six and seven young miss goes to school,
Before you discern she's wise or a fool;
And there she maun learn to read and to write,
Till she's fit for a lawyer or something siclike.

3 When school is over, to service she goes,
For greed o' high wages, as ye may suppose,
The first that she goes in a white muslin goon,
An' a bonnet wid haud the moonlicht fae a toon.

4 Seen doon fae her bonnet there hings a bit silk,
Like what my aul' granny had seyin' her milk,
I know it is useful her beauties to grace,
For it hides a' the wrinkles that are in her face.

5 She curls up her hair like a water-dog's tail,
Rowed up in a paper as roon' as a snail,
So wi' that and the veil hingin' over her e'en,
The feint a wrinkle ava' 's to be seen.

6 But now she's set oot like a ship in full sail,
Wi' six seven flaunces roon' her goon tails,
And when she is going by ony man,
They say one to another, "Oh what is she on?"

7 Sunday aboot she maun gang to the church,
And what she hears there she winna min' much,
The text nor the psalms she winna min' on,
But she min's weel to say; "Fat a bonny chiel's yon?"

8   At balls, fairs, and weddin's she'll rant and she'll rove,
And ilka meeting she'll get a new love;
But wi' her gallant air three years come roon',
Her apron gets up and her bonnet comes doon.

9   When some o' her sweethearts hears that she's wrong,
In that same country they winna tarry long;
They rin to market, Oh, sic a trick,
And missy, poor thing, gets the whip-shaft to lick.

10   But now she's confined like a coo on the grass,
Her bonnet's laid aff and that whole gaudy dress;
She sits at the cradle while the wee een does roar,
And greets at the thing that she leuch at afore.

CHARLES EWEN — D

H
The Servan' Lasses

1   Oor servan' lasses are a' grown sae braw
They ootstrip their mistress by far and awa
Between six and seven young miss goes to school
Before you would know she was wise or a fool.

2   And then she is learned to read and to write
For she's fit for a lawyer or something sic like
When schooling is over to service she goes
It is for high wages as you may suppose.

3   The first of it goes for a new muslin goon
And a bonnet wad keep the meenlicht frae the toon
Doon frae the bonnet hings a bit silk
Like fat my auld granny had for sying her milk.

4   Wi' that and a veil hinging owre her e'en
And never a wrinkle ava to be seen
Oor servan' lasses as sure as my life
Ye'd ne'er ken the servan' lass frae the guidwife.

5   But as the time it goes in and the sissons come roon
Up goes the apron and the bonnet comes doon.

J.B. SINCLAIR — G

AYE WORK AWA

1 Help yersel's whaur ere ye gang an aye work awa
    Mang the simmer sunshine and the cheerless winter snaw
    Never lippen tae yer frien's, tho' they may loudly blaw,
    Help yersels whaure'er ye gang an aye work awa.
      Aye work awa my friens O aye work awa
      Help yersels whaure'er ye gang an' aye work awa.
      Aye work awa my friens O aye work awa
      Help yersels whaure'er ye gang an aye work awa.

2 Fortune favours them wha work aye wi' a busy haun' ·
    Folk'll ne'er win forrit if they at the fire-en' staun';
    Look afore ye tak' the loup in mickle things an' sma',
    Tak things in a canny way but aye work awa.

3 Dinna speak unkindly words aboot the words ye ken
    Never let a bitter ane anither's ear gae ben
    Lifeless folk are fautless but there's nane without a flaw
    Kindly speak o' neighbours then an aye work awa.

4 Never say that ye're ill used though prood folk pass ye by
    Want o' sense mak's witless folk aft haud their heids owre high
    Dauner on, ne'er fash yer thoom wi' sic like folk ava',   [stroll; pay no heed
    Warsel on fu' cheerily an' aye work awa.   [wrestle

5 Keep a calm sough, never let your tongue wag up and doon   [keep quiet
    Empty girnels are aye sure to gie the loodest soon';
    When ye hear o' ither's quarrels, while they scrape and craw
    Mang them be't, be aye your word an aye work awa.

6 Life a' through is jist a fecht e'en to the very grave
    Better life abune is promised to the leal and brave
    Let us fecht wi' faithfu' herts and we owercome it a'
    Help yersels whaure'er ye gang an aye work awa.

JAMES ANGUS — G

I'M A WORKIN' CHAP

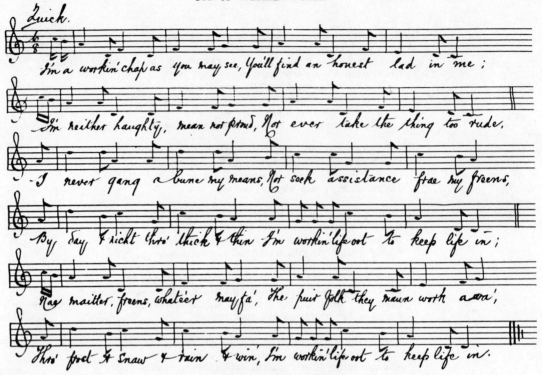

1   I'm a workin' chap as you may see,
You'll find an honest lad in me;
I'm neither haughty, mean nor proud,
Nor ever take the thing too rude.
I never gang abune my means,
Nor seek assistance frae my freens,
By day and nicht thro' thick and thin
I'm workin' life oot to keep life in;
Nae maitter, freens, whate'er may fa',
The puir folk they maun work awa',
Thro' frost and snaw and rain and win',
I'm workin' life oot to keep life in.

JOHN ORD – G

PUNCTUALITY

1 Certain fidgety folks we have all of us met,
   Who are famous for being too soon
   When invited to dinner at two o'clock
   They're sure to turn up about noon
   Punctuality's all very proper I know
   And all hurry and worry I hate
   So it always happens wherever I go
   I'm exactly ten minutes too late.
      Punctuality's all very proper I know
      And all hurry and worry I hate
      So it always happens wherever I go
      I'm exactly ten minutes too late.

2 If I jump on a nigger, or ride on a horse
   To be nicely in time for the train
   I'm half in a fever and quite in a fuss
   To think that my efforts are vain
   I arrive at the station and look at my watch
   I find it's five minutes to eight
   And then I discover it's five minutes past
   And I am ten minutes too late.

3 Some time ago I fell deeply in love
   I courted in verse and in prose
   She gave me a lock of her hair and a glove
   So I made up my mind to propose.
   But a cab drove away as I knocked at the door
   And her answer decided my fate
   My rival was there just five minutes before
   And I was ten minutes too late.

4 On my numerous afflictions I need not prolong
   No one but myself rightly knows
   For this trouble has haunted me all my life long
   And shall haunt me I fear to its close
   When I reach the last stage of my earthly career
   And I lie in a critical state
   All the medicines and physics the doctors prescribe
   I'll take them ten minutes too late.

Miss LIZZIE CRIGHTON — G

THE CLOCK

1   Its hands of old had a touch of gold,
And its chimes ring still the sweetest;
"Tick, tick," it said, "quick, quick to bed,
For nine has given warning,
You'll never hae health, nor you'll never hae wealth,
Gin ye dinna rise in the mornin'."

Mrs LYALL — D

THE DROOSY CHIEL

A

Rise, Jock, rise!

Rise, Jock, rise! the mornin' bells are ringin', Lyin' snorin'
i' yer bed, ye'll never, never thrive; Rise, Jock, rise! the
mornin' bells are ringin', Lyin' snorin' i' yer bed at half-past five!

Mrs MARGARET GILLESPIE — D

B

The Droosy Chiel

1   Hoo are ye a' the night my freens? I trust ye're keeping well
    I hae nae doot but that you'll think that I'm a droosy chiel
    I hae been droosy a' my days since ever I was born
    My wife declares her voice is broke wi' cryin' in the morn.
       Rise, Jock, rise, the bells they a' are ringing
       Lying in your bed I'm sure you'll never thrive
       Early in the morning continually she's singing
       Johnnie are you waukin' man, it's half past five.

2   I was droosy there the ither day while stanin' at my wark
    When a' at ance awa I gaed asleep as soond's a tap
    My maister he was gaun his roonds and me he chanced to spy
    He quietly cam' slippin' up and in my ear did cry:

3   I'm waukened at the half hoor so as I'll hae lots o' time
    But I can never manage in afore it's hauf past nine
    An' a' the wee kids in the wark whenever me they spy
    They a' stand roon me in a band and this is what they cry.

T.S. TOWERS — G

660

THE GUID COAT O' BLUE

A

The Guid Coat o' Blue

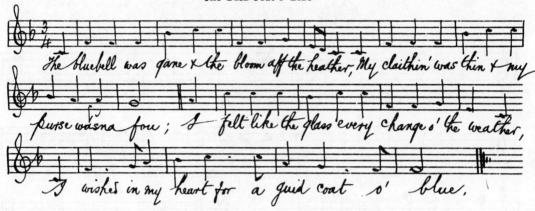

1 The bluebell was gane and the bloom aff the heather,
   My claithen was thin and my purse wasna fou.
   I felt like a gless ilka change o' the weather
   And wished in my heart I'd a guid coat o' blue.

2 Then fair fa' my wifie sae thrifty and kindly;
   As sune as she kent o' the wind piercin' thro',
   She's gane to the wabster and fittet me finely   [weaver
   And laid roon my shoulders a guid coat o' blue.

3 Then fair fa' the tailor, our ain honest Sandy;
   He's gien me braw room in't, he ever cuts true
   I'm nae clippet aff·like a daft idle dandy
   But happit and tosh in my guid coat o' blue.

4 Noo daft dreary winter may rant, rage and rustle,
   And frae her hail graneries wild tempests brew.
   I care na for her nor her snaw blasts a whistle
   For weel lined wi' plaidin's my guid coat o' blue.

5 Nae mair will I dread the cauld blasts o' Ben Ledi
   Or sigh as the ice covered Ochils I view
   I may hae been cauld but for ance I am tidy
   Sae gausy and tosh in my guid coat o' blue.   [smart

6 But weary fa' pride, for it's never contentit
   Ilk ane maun be dressed noo in fine Spanish woo'
   The warld was better at first when I kent it
   Wi' lang plaidin hose and a guid coat o' blue.

7 Lea's me on the Scotchmen, mine ain honest sailor
   Lea's me on auld fashions, I lauch at the new.
   A fig for the fellow wha's made by the tailor!
   Gie me sense and worth and a guid coat o' blue.

8   We fret ower the taxes, and taxes we've mony
     The meal is while's dear and we've ill gettin thro'
     But daft silly pride is the warst tax o' ony
     They'll no be content wi' a guid coat o' blue.

ALEXANDER ROBB — G

B
The Coat o' Blue

1   Some chaps wad hae a score o' coats,
     But I have only two;
     I wear my jacket all the week,
     And on Sunday my coat o' blue.

2   We complain o' haein' taxes, and taxes we hae mony;
     And meal aften dear, and we're ill winnin' throu;
     But daft silly pride is the warst tax o' ony —
     Was never content wi' a guid coat o' blue.

3   Fair fa' the tailor, our ain honest Sandy,
     He's gien scouth room in't, he ever cuts true   [plenty
     Like nae daft idle dandy
     I'm unco weel pleased wi' my guid coat o' blue.

Miss ANNIE SHIRER — G

THE CUDDY

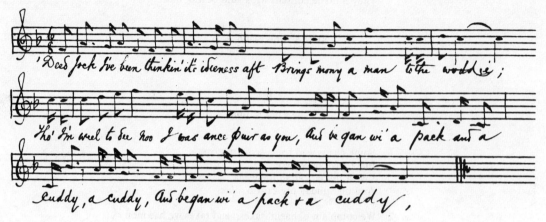

'Deed Jock I've been thinkin' it's idleness aft Brings mony a man to the wuddie; Tho' I'm weel to dee noo I was ance puir as you, And began wi' a pack and a cuddy, a cuddy, And began wi' a pack + a cuddy,

1 Deed Jock, I've been thinkin' it's idleness aft
That brings mony a man to the wuddy
Tho I'm weel to dee noo, I was ance puir as you
An' began wi' a pack an' a cuddy.

2 Folks sneered and they laughed to see us gae by
For sometimes my claes were fu' duddy
But clean at the skin, I was makin' the tin.
Losh, who could gang braw wi' a cuddy?

3 Sometimes we gaed sooth, sometimes we gaed north
Up bye roads that aft times were muddy
But altho' we gaed far, altho we gaed near
There were aye bits o' cakes for the cuddy.

4 We aye had a e'e that's my cuddy and me
But oh it was a douce little body
For to get a drap ale ay and maybe a gill
And there were aye bits o' cakes for the cuddy.

5 But I've droppit my wanderin ways noo for a shop
And to plenish a hoose is my study
For a bonnie wee wifie has lippened her lifie
Wi' me and my douce little cuddie.

6 Twa three years hae gaen by and we hae deen weel
We've got bairnies baith sonsy and ruddy
Oh it's pleasin' to see wi' gleg laddies e'e
Lauchin' wild owre the pleased little cuddie.

7 Freens tak my advice, guide weel what ye get
Watch weel when the tide's at the floodie
If a stout heart ye hae ye may climb a stiff brae
Blithely ending like me and my cuddy.

ALEXANDER ROBB – G

662

JEAN FINDLATER'S LOON

1   The winter was lang an the seed time was late
An' the caul month o' March sealed John Findlator's fate;
She dwin'd like a snaw wreath till some time in June   [for "He"; wasted away
Then left Jean a widow wi ae raggit loon.
Derry down down hey derry down.

GEORGE RIDDELL – G

PADDLE YOUR OWN CANOE

1 I've travelled about a bit in my time
   And of troubles I've seen a few
   But found it better in every clime
   To paddle my own canoe.

2 My wants are small, I care not at all
   If my debts are paid when due;
   I drive away strife in the ocean of life
   While I paddle my own canoe.

3 Then love your neighbour as yourself
   As the world you go travelling through
   And never sit down with a tear or a frown
   But paddle your own canoe.

4 I have no wife, to bother my life
   No lover to prove untrue
   But the whole day long, with a laugh and a song
   I paddle my own canoe.

5 I rise with the lark, and from daylight to dark
   I do what I have to do
   I'm careless of wealth, if I've only the health
   To paddle my own canoe.

6 It's all very well to depend on a friend
   That is, if you've proved him true
   But you'll find it better by far in the end
   To paddle your own canoe.

7 "To borrow" is dearer by far than "to buy"
   A maxim though old, still true,
   You never will sigh, if you only will try
   To paddle your own canoe.

8 If a hurricane rise, in the midday skies
   And the sun is lost to view
   Move steadily by with a steadfast eye
   And paddle your ain canoe.

9 The daisies that grow in the bright green fields
   Are blooming so sweet for you
   So never sit down with a tear or a frown
   But paddle your own canoe.

Miss LIZZIE CRIGHTON — G

664

WE'RE A' CUTTIN'

For we're a' cuttin'
Cut, cut, cuttin',
For we're a' cuttin'
Our passage thro' this world.

Mrs MARGARET GILLESPIE — D

665

SWEEP YOUR OWN DOOR CLEAN

1   I hate to hear folk talk about other folks affairs
And think that no one in this world has got a way like him
About some trifling matter they are having a great adoo
But with patience wait, till once they're done and turn to them and say:
Don't speak harshly oh, let it be your plan
Don't be proud and pass remarks about your fellow man
But pass them by and never speak about what you have seen
Don't say ill of your neighbour, sweep your own door clean.

2   It's little that some folks should ken, for what they ken they tell
And all the time they're bletherin and tellin' on them sell.
If they'd keep their tongues between their teeth you'll find it's true I say
The man who keeps his own door clean has got enough to do.

3   Don't judge a man by what he wears for if you do you're wrong
For in my lifetime many a man I've seen going struggling hard along
Although he brought to poverty he's not been brought to shame
Though hunger stares him in the face whiles no the man's to blame.

Source unrecorded — G

666

THE SLIPPY STANE

A

The Slippy Stane

To the tune of 56 *The Laddie wi' the Tarry Trews* Ab

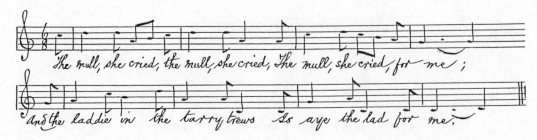

The mull, she cried, the mull, she cried, The mull, she cried, for me;
And the laddie in the tarry trews Is aye the lad for me.

JAMES ANGUS — G

B

The Slippy Stane

1 Wade canny through this weary world and guide your steps wi' care
  And never dae your neighbour wrang but aye dae what is fair
  Folk fa' and never rise again wha never fell before
  There's aye a muckle slippy stane at ilka body's door.
      There's aye a muckle slippy stane at ilka body's door.

2 And should your neighbour chance to slip O dinna pass him by
  But lend a hand to lift him up and dinna let him lie
  Some day the case may be your ain altho' ye've wealth in store
  There's aye a muckle slippy stane at ilka body's door.

3 There are slippy stanes where'er ye gang in palace, hut, or ha'
  And ye maun watch and nae gang wrang or owre them ye may fa'
  For kings and emperors hae fa'en and nobles mony a score
  There's aye a muckle slippy stane at ilka body's door.

Source unrecorded — G

C

The Slippery Stane

1 Gin your neebor chance to fa' you maunna pass him by;
  Lend a hand; help him up, dinna let him lie;
  For maybe ye may chance to fa', as they've been mony a score,
  For there's aye a muckle slippery stane at ilka body's door.

Source unrecorded — G

558

WHEN FORTUNE TURNS THE WHEEL

A

J. NAAMAN – G

B

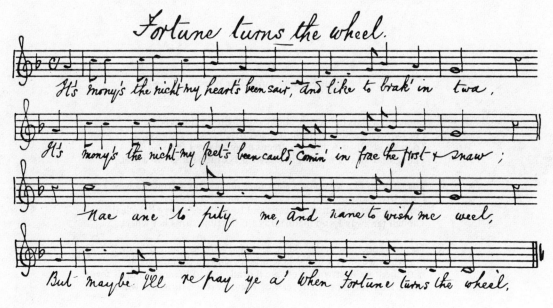

Mrs FOWLIE – G

C
When Fortune Turns Her Wheel

1 Come, fill a glass, let's drink about; this night we'll merry be
For harmony and friendship free likewise my comrades ye
To meet ye all aince mair, my freen's a sacred joy I feel
Though far away I now maun stray till Fortune turns her wheel.

2 The changes of a comrade's state ne'er makes true friendship less
For a true Caledonian's heart feels warmest for distress
For I hae met some trusty freens and to me they've aye been leal
Though far away I now maun stray till Fortune turns her wheel.

3 It's not vain clothes, nor gold, he says that's the estimate of man
For when we meet a friend in straits we shake a friendly han'
With them we'll sit with them we'll drink and to them our minds reveal;
And friends we'll be whatever way blind Fortune turns her wheel.

4 But oh, I loved a bonnie lass, and her I'll justly blame;
For when hard fortune frowned on me she denied she knew my name
But falsehood by remorse is paid and to her I'll never kneel
I'll sweethearts find, baith fair and kind when Fortune turns her wheel.

5 Some o' my aince pretendin' freens if freens I may them call
Proved false and turned their backs on me when mine was at the wall.
But in this glass I'll let it pass I'm sure I wish them weel
If my hard fate on them await may Fortune turn her wheel.

6 Adieu, ye hills of Caledon, likewise sweet Avonsdale,
For friendship binds the strongest ties love tells the softest tales
Adieu my freens and comrades here I ken ye wish me weel,
And I may yet can pey my debts when Fortune turns her wheel.

Mrs THOM — G

D
When Fortune Turns Her Wheel

1 Come fill a glass let's drink about this night we'll merry be
For harmony and friendship free likewise my comrades ye
To meet ye all ance mair my freens a sacred joy I feel
Though far away I noo maun stray till Fortune turns her wheel.

2 The changes of a comrade's state neer makes true friendship less
For a true Caledonian's heart feels warmest for distress
For I hae met some trusty freens and to me they've aye been leal
Though far away I noo maun stray till Fortune turns her wheel.

3 Tis not vain clothes nor gold he says that's the estimate o' man
For when we meet a friend in straits we shake a friendly hand
With them we'll sit with them we'll drink and to them our minds reveal
And friends we'll be whatever way blind Fortune turns her wheel.

4 But O I loved a bonnie lass and her I'll justly blame
   For when hard fortune frowned at me she denied she knew my name
   But falsehood by remorse is paid and to her I'll never kneel
   I'll sweethearts find baith fair and kind when Fortune turns her wheel.

5 Some o' my aince pretendin freens if freens I may them call
   Proved false and turned their backs when mine was at the wall
   But in this glass I'll let it pass I'm sure I wish them weel
   If my hard fate on them await may Fortune turn her wheel.

6 Adieu ye hills o' Caledon likewise sweet Avondale
   For friendship joins the strongest ties love tells the softest tale
   Adieu my freens and comrades here I ken ye wish me weel
   And I may yet can pay my debts when Fortune turns her wheel.

D.R. McKENZIE — G

E

When Fortune Turns the Wheel

1 There is a lad aboot this place O sair is he to blame
   For when misfortune fell on me he denied he knew my name
   And though he kens I liked him weel to me he would not yield
   But maybe I'll repay him back when Fortune turns the wheel.

2 Mony a nicht my heart's been sair and like to brak in twa
   Mony a nicht my feet's been cauld comin' in frae frost and snaw.
   But there was none to pity me nor none to wish me weel
   But maybe I'll repay them back when Fortune turns the wheel.

3 Here's to my intended friends my foes I may them ca'
   For they did turn their backs on me when mine was at the wa
   I take the wine glass in my hand and drink and wish them weel
   And maybe I'll repay them back when Fortune turns the wheel.

New Pitsligo lady — G

UP A TREE

A

1   I had friends in great variety,
They courted my society,
They came to dine and drank my wine,
And shook my hand with glee;
Now I may wait till Whitsuntide,
For when they see me on the Clyde,
They pass me on the other side,
Now I'm in poverty.

Miss BELL ROBERTSON — G

B

1   Once I could drive my four-in-hand,
With money too at my command,
Could do the grand, you'll understand,
How foolish I hae been.
I may walk from now till Whitsun
And when they see me on the glide,
They'll pass me down the other side,
Because I'm up a tree.

WILLIAM STEPHEN — G

A SHILLIN' OR TWA

A

1 While cautious and canny we slip ourselves thro'
This wearisome warld just as other folks do,
May we aye frae our pockets be ready to draw,
Coming clink frae our pockets a shilling or twa.

JAMES ANGUS — G

B
A Shillin' or Twa

1 The poor man in business, by fortune unblest,
Is forced to appear on the bankruptcy list,
His chairs and his tables are a' ta'en awa,
And it's a' for the want o' a shillin' or twa.

Mrs RETTIE — G

IF BUT ONE HEART BE TRUE

1 There's mony a freen we a' may meet in bright and prosperous days
Who when adversity draws near their confidence betrays
Yet hopefully and cheerfully our courage we'll renew
If but one heart be true to us, if but one heart be true.

Miss ANNIE SHIRER — G

671

OH DINNA QUARREL THE BAIRNIES

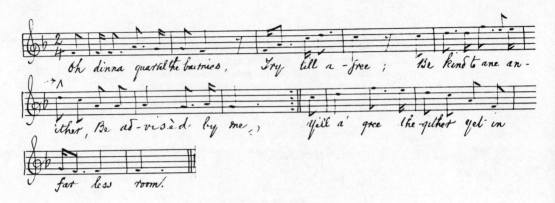

Oh dinna quarrel the bairnies, Try till a-gree; Be kind to ane anither, Be ad-visèd by me, Ye'll a' gree the-gither yet in
far less room.

1 Oh dinna quarrel the bairnies, try till agree;
Be kind to ane anither, be advisèd by me.
Oh dinna quarrel the bairnies, try till agree;
Be kind to ane anither, be advisèd by me.
Ye'll a' gree thegither yet in far less room.

JAMES GREIG — G

672

BEHAVE YERSEL'

1 Behave yersel, behave yersel'
Behave yersel afore folk
Whate'er ye do when oot o' view
Be carefu' mind afore folk.

2 Can I behave, can I behave,
Can I behave afore folk
For weary fa your sleekit sel'   [sly
Gars me ging gite afore folk.   [mad

Mrs DUNCAN — G

673

I DON'T THINK MUCH OF YOU

A

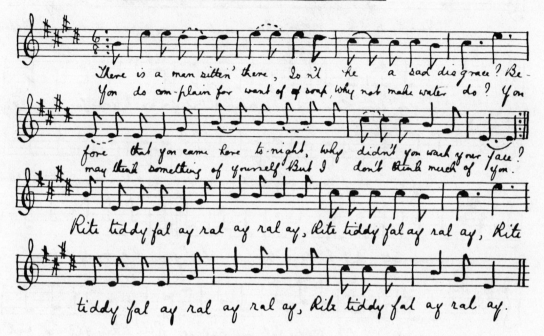

There is a man sittin' there.

There is a man sittin' there, Isn't he a sad disgrace? Before that you came here to-night, why didn't you wash your face?
You do com-plain for want of of soap, why not make water do? You
may think something of yourself But I don't think much of you.

Rite tiddy fal ay ral ay ral ay, Rite tiddy fal ay ral ay, Rite
tiddy fal ay ral ay ral ay, Rite tiddy fal ay ral ay.

Mrs MARGARET GILLESPIE — D

Song No. 673

B

There is a man sittin' there.

There is a man sittin' there, isn't he a sad disgrace? Before

that you came home tonight why didn't you wash your face? You do com-

plain for want of soap, why don't make water do? You may think somethin'

of your-self, but I don't think much o' you. Rite tiddy fal ay ral

ay ral ay, Rite tiddy fal ay ral ee, Rite tiddy fal ay ral

ay ral ay, Rite tiddy fal ay ral ee.

Mrs GREIG – D

C

1   Now I think I'll cut my stick and not say any more
    I see some ladies sitting there I didn't see before
    I know they want to speak to me and what it is I know
    But ladies I'm a married man so I don't think much of you.

Mrs DUNCAN – G

TO COONT MY KIN AN' PEDIGREE

To coont my kin an' pedigree it shows you're scant o' grace
But ye are like Melchisedeck we dinna know your race
An' ye were come o' noble blood, some cause ye had to blaw,
But we do think ye spell the name that finishes the law.
The filthy stuff that ye composed saired you for saiven weeks
But I composed the half o' this or I got on my breeks.
The half o' this is nae your ain that ye hae sent to me
An't hadna been a pedlar chiel that's gleyed upon an e'e.
I would think little o' mysel an' I had been at squeel
To apply to ony pedlar lad or ony packman chiel.

CHARLES MURRAY — D

AE NIGHT LAST OOK FAN GROWING LATE

1   Ae night last ook fan growing late
    The sin far west the Craigie
    A chiel came flaught bred up the gate   [spread-
    Upon a Highland stagie.   eagled

2   I think Is this guager? — Na.
    And fan the chiel cam nearer
    Says — Here's a letter — ha-ha-ha
    Pull out and pay the bearer.

3   Nae haste says I, took up my hand
    Came owre the shalt a rattle
    Tak that and cam the gate you came
    Deil pay you with a pattle.
                          [put on my spectacles

4   I saddled my snout, the seal gart flee
    To read with vir I yokkit   [vigour
    I prayed, I cursed, I leuch a' three
    . . . for me, I maist chockkit.

5   And sae I might to get sic snipes   [gibes
    And yet would try to banter
    A student playin the college pipes
    Wi' my twalpenny chanter.

6   Ye ar witcht an war, an war can be
    Wae worth me but I think it
    For an you look for wit fae me
    Depend upon 't ye're blinket.   [bewitched

7   And yet I'm prood, na that's a sin
    I'se only ca it saucy
    That I've a scholar i' my kin
    That caes my lingae gausie.   [impressive

8   But is it really truth you speak
    Or are ye only funnin
    And drawin' Willie through the reek
    Wi' your Collegiate cunnin?

9   But an ye mock me ony mair
    Depend upon 't I'll flyte ye
    For caim a dog against the hair
    He'll turn about and bite ye.

10   And after a' when I refleck
    Ye may be speakin' true, man
    And even shawin some respeck
    To your auld Buchan plooman.

11   Now I maun lay an' ly behyne
    Fan ye're far far afore me
    For if I mint my meer to speak
    Ye'll bid the Devil smore me.

12   But I'se hae done in time to come
    And sign my renunciation
    The critics syne may cla their bum
    For want of occupation.

13   The plooman then may . . . or hope
    Whichever way he can do
    And dight his arce wi' every scrape
    That ever he put his hand to.

14   Now fare ye weel my best o' friens
    In Ryme fareweel for ever
    If ony ither stoits atween's
    We il giet the longest liver.

WILLIAM WALKER — G

O MUCKLE DEIL FAT HAS COME O' YE

1 O muckle deil fat has come o' ye
   When we hae sic a grab to gie you   [crowd
   A pretty grab o' thieves an witches.
   Her liars and clackying bitches   [chattering
   Ye'll let them stick until the hang
   Ye loosy bitch ye'll loss your fang   [catch
   But ye man tauk them a' at once
   For stealing our strays and stanes.

2 Shame fo you than ye slip the rogue
   That sta my mither's lugey couge
   But ye maun come and tak them wi' ye
   Ye'll sit off at hook and crook
   Till ye hae them in your black mooly
   Yee'l nae leave them in middle state
   For fear they back might fin the gate
   And though sometimes they're in a hurry
   You'll not leave them in purgatory
   But hae them to immediate station
   The dirtiest corner in all your nation.

3 Wi' hay and stray stap up their bums
   And cram them hard wi your black thums
   Syne win their wishes about their pow   [wind
   An' pit them fairly in a low
   An' wi het lime ye'll roast them red
   That they stay frae the house o' guid.
   I think their hips deserves a herdin
   For stealin rapes we used for girden
   We never saw the like before
   For they wid the .   .   .   . guid
   For they sta wood to make a door.

4 Now deil do your duty right
   And take the villains frae our sight
   And gin ye chance tae come oor way
   Ye'se nae be treat wi sups o' fye   [whey
   Tho I should hirple on my crutch   [hobble
   Or gaily help of some old witch
   Ye's get guid whisky till ye leave it
   Tho I gae fort as far's Glenlivet.   [for it

5 Now harvest folk take no offence
   To wish you ill wad be nae sense
   Be honest still be chased and leel   [chaste
   Ye maunna fear the muckle deil
   I take a saxpence in my pouch
   And owre tae Brewer Megull scout
   I'll step fu tentie and fu cannie   [cautiously
   For fear that I should anger Nannie.

6   My ryme is done and sae fareweel
     Guid health to ilka honest chiel
     Fa sorra is't that made this ryme
     An fa committed sic a crime
     That gentle folk they are a farson
     Guid faith I think it's bin the parson
     But oh my troth I dinna think it
     Or that it had bin the linket
     The learnt folk they hae sic grammar
     That they can neither sit nor stan er.

7   I doubt it's been that marchand chiels
     Ye widna true fa acs like fools   [believe who acts
     For whiles they hae but nought ado
     For right sair for all the three.
     Fegs maybe been that souters
     That cruzlie rossety fouters   [arrogant resinous slackers
     But nae doubt it's been my gutcher   [grandfather
     A chiel they call him Donald Boutcher
     I really think it's my belief
     That he wad sell better sells beef.

WILLIAM WALKER — G

MOSSIE AND HIS MEER

A

Mossy and his Meer.

I, Mossy was a cunning man A little mare did buy; For winking and for jinkin There were few could her come nigh; She was as cunning as a fox, As cunning as a hare, And I will tell you by and bey How Mossie catch'd his meer. Wi' my fal lalla lal de deedum fal de deedum day, Wi' my hirrum dirrum dowdum deedum, hirrum leedum day.

Mrs MARGARET GILLESPIE — D

B

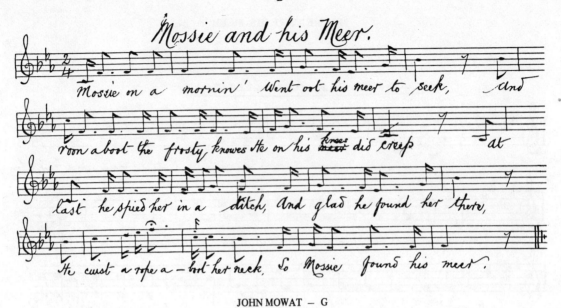

Mossie and his Meer.

Mossie on a mornin' Went oot his meer to seek, And
roon aboot the frosty knowes He on his knees did creep At
last he spied her in a ditch, And glad he found her there,
He cuist a rope a—boot her neck, So Mossie found his meer.

JOHN MOWAT — G

C

Mossy an's Meat.

GEORGE RIDDELL — G

THE WICKED CAPTAIN

1   As taut a craft was the Nancy
As ever the wild waves bore,
And a goodly sight was her sails of white
As she swept the wind before.

2   And as gallant a crew she had on board
As ever sailed the sea;
But the captain of the Nancy,
Oh, a wicked man was he.

3   An angry frown was on his brow,
And an oath on his bearded lip,
And he was loved by never a one
Of all who sailed the ship.

4   And let the wind blow high or low,
The night be foul or fair,
The voice of the wicked captain
Was never raised in prayer.

5   Not long had the Nancy been to sea
When the captain he fell ill,
God laid his hand on the sinful man,
And the wicked tongue was still.

6   The fever burned on his aching brow,
And gnawed at his heart within,
Yet never a prayer to the God above
Did he pray, that man of sin.

Miss ANNIE SHIRER − G

THE GLEAD

1 It happened once upon a time
It was early in a spring
A glead was hatched near by a wood
For mavis used to sing.   [thrush

2 His mother soon did him forsake
And left him there to scrawel   [scramble
And he was at the point to die
For hunger, and for cold.

3 A friend stepped in at that great need
And brought him owre to Mains
And he's returned him little thanks
For a' his care and pains.

4 His fathers they grew up so fast
His tail was right canty
Ye wadna seen a silkier glead
Though you had counted twenty.

5 He was not long into his nest
Till he found out his station
So he wad try to cross the breed
And end in fornication.

6 He's blotted out the tenth command
And says it's not worth minding
If he's got corn and hay to sell
The laws they are not binding.

7 His winnings they's grown so big
He thinks not worth his pains
To stretch them out and take a plight [pledge, bond
Upon the town o' Mains.

8 He's gart the ladies a' remove
Right seer against their will
For he has gotten a bigger farm
His greedy greedy claws to fill.

9 But the bodie a have gotten hillts
To keep them same thing cheery
And left the rubach to the glead   [rubbish
To scrape till he be weary.

10 There is a hay ruck stands on the hill
Bears witness for the sachen
I wish it may rot or blaw away
And syne he will try destraction.

11 But I'll put in my word again
I think it is wantin
We'll peel him bare as he came there
And set him to the plantin.

12 And gather wives in we . . .
Wi fingers long and sma
And they will make him wee behind
For the driving them awa.

13 But I hope the days recommanding fash
Guests will be granted
When muckle farmers they will brack
And leger be wanted.

14 Now fare weel ye greedy gled
We thank for your pains
And wish you never clear and great
Upon the town of Mains.

15 And so the glead, the great glead
The scamfering of Mains
We wish him muckle toil and pains
For a' your gread and pains.

WILLIAM WALKER – G

BOUND FOR GLORY NOO

1   A carter really saved, you think, is surely something new
      Wha loves the Lord and hates the drink yet praise his name 'tis true
      For since the Lord has taen me up I'm never never fou
      The horse I used to kick and whup I clap and care for noo.
          Then up my mates and praise the Lord, it's grand to ken it's true
          Tho' only common carter chaps we're bound for glory noo.

2   The police kent me far and wide when drink set me aflame
      And mony a row I raised ootside and mony a shine at hame
      I used to gang an unco length, hoo far nae man can tell
      I spent my means and time and strength to curse and kill mysel.

3   Withoot an oath I couldna speak, I served the devil grand
      And yet wi' a' I had the cheek to think I was a man.
      But noo frae every evil word his grace can keep me free
      And every day I praise the Lord for what he's done for me.
          I canna tell ye a' I feel but this I ken is true
          Tho' but a common carter chap I'm bound for glory noo.

Miss ANNIE RITCHIE — G

681

THE GUISE O' TYRIE

1   O wat ye how the guise began,
The guise began, the guise began
O wat ye how the guise began
The guise began at Tyrie.
Lady Tyrie and the laird o' Glack
They baith o' them lived in the Slack
Between the twa there was a pack
To enter cripple Andrew.

JOHN MILNE — G

682

TAMMY CHALMERS

A

Tammy Chalmers

1   Oh, why left I the kirk that patronage gae me
And why left I the manse I got withoot a fee
Wi' its bonnie glebe so green and violets on the lea
Oh wae worth Tammie Chalmers, he's fairly diddled me.

2   And ilka year the godly folk did some fine present bring
And under me my simple flock did flourish prosperously
Oh wae worth Tammie Chalmers he's fairly diddled me.

3   Oh, here nae Sabbath bell awakes the Sabbath morn
For neither bell nor belfry does this bothy kirk adorn
But rotten kirks for sarkin faur stane and lime sud be   [covering
Oh wae worth Tammie Chalmers he's fairly diddled me.

4   They say there's balm for every woe and cure for every pain
But nocht can bring my bonnie glebe and stipend back again
My wife she's broken-hearted wi' grief I'm like to dee
O wae worth Tammie Chalmers he's fairly diddled me.

Miss BELL ROBERTSON — G

B

1   But lath and rotten sarkin where stane and lime should be
Wae worth you Tammie Chalmers for ye've fairly diddled me.

Rev. JOHN CALDER — G

576

683

THE WIDOW'S CRUISIE

Doon by Tough an Tullynessle
Aye the wifie wi her vessle
At Kildrummy an' at Towie
Aye the wifie an' her bowie
Towie an' Glenbucket tee
He tell't the story aff wi glee
He took a turn doon by Keig
An' tell't the story aff fu gleg
Took a turn up by Tough
An' at the bowie loot a sough
His hearers a' kent weel aneuch
That he was but a gawpie
But he turned the bible owre an' owre
An' tried the Psalms o' Dauvid
But there was something hearse aboot's throat
Or gruppit in his grauvit.   [caught, cravat
But he said
Sin I am to conclude my story
I'll wish you safely into glory
Of otherwise ye shall hae plenty
An' meal an' eelie to be yer dainty.

CHARLES MURRAY — D

684

BETTY MULL'S SQUEEL

1 She taul's aboot Judas and said he was coorse,
    Bit a braw stock was Aul' Abraham;   [fellow
    She thocht his graifstane was aye to be seen
    On a knap up abeen Kaper-naum.   [knoll

Miss HELEN BRUCE — G

685

THE SOLDIER AND THE SAILOR

A

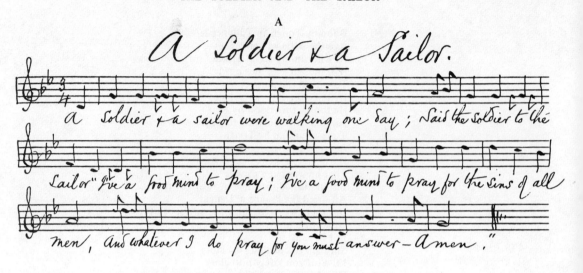

A Soldier & a Sailor.

A soldier & a sailor were walking one day; Said the soldier to the sailor "I've a good mind to pray; I've a good mind to pray for the sins of all men, And whatever I do pray for you must answer — Amen."

1   A soldier and a sailor were walking one day
     Said the soldier to the sailor I've a good mind to pray
     I've a good mind to pray here for the sins of all men
     And whatever I pray for ye must answer Amen.

2   They walkèd together till they came to a tree
     Said the soldier to the sailor This my pulpit shall be
     And while I do pray here for the sins of all men
     Whatever I do pray for, ye must answer Amen.

3   The first thing I'll pray for, I'll pray for strong beer
     And if we get one glass we must have a good cheer
     And if we get one glass oh may we get ten
     May we never want good liquor. Said the sailor Amen.

4   The next thing I'll pray for I'll pray for all wives
     That they may live happy all the rest of their lives
     And if they get one man oh may they get ten
     May they never want a good one. Said the sailor Amen.

5   The next thing I'll pray for I'll pray for our Queen
     That she may live happy and long may she reign
     And if she gets one man oh may she get ten
     May she never want a good one. Said the sailor Amen.

6   Ye squires dukes and earls ye make a fine show
     Ye captains and colonels and generals also
     For ye rob off the back and the bellies o' puir men
     May the muckle, muckle deil tak them. Said the sailor Amen.

JAMES GREIG — G

B

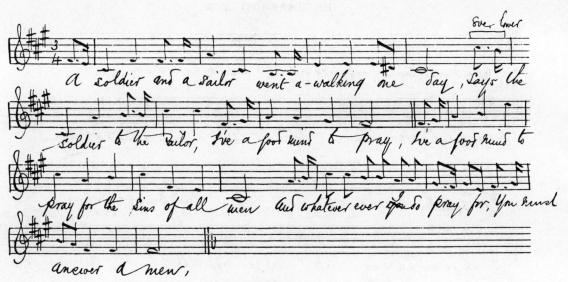

JOHN QUIRRIE – G

C

1   A soldier and a sailor were walking one day
     Said the soldier to the sailor "I've a good mind to pray

     . . . .
     Whatever ye do pray for ye must answer Amen."

2   The next thing I'll pray for, I'll pray for good wives
     That we may live happy all the rest of our days
     An' if ye get one wife we'll maybe get ten
     May we never, never want good wives. Quo' the sailor, Amen.

Source unrecorded – G

THE UPPERMOST TUB

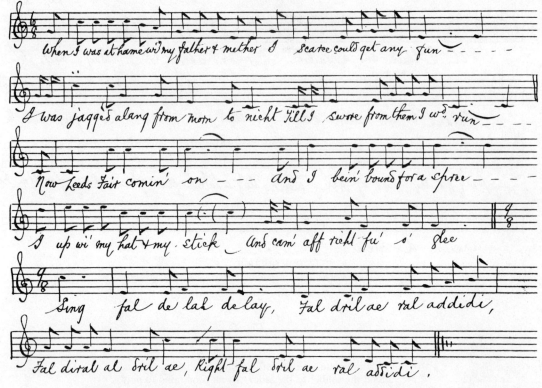

1 When I was at hame wi' my father and mither I scarce could get any fun,
I was jaggèd along from morn to nicht, till I swore from them I would run.   [joggled
Now Leeds Fair comin' on, and I bein' bound for a spree,
I up wi' my hat and my stick and cam' aff richt fu' o' glee —
Sing Fal de lal de lay, fal dirrel ae ral addidi,
Fal dirrel ae dirrel ae, right fal dirrel ae ral addidi.

2 Next I went intil a kirk I was never in a kirk a' my days,
I didna ken how to get on because I didna know their ways
But I gaed awa' staggerin' in and a fellow comes in at my back,
Gie's me a toss wi' his stick, says, Young man tak' aff your hat.

3 I gaed awa and sat doon on a seat, and I chanced for to look up above,
And I sees a lad come staggerin' in, paps down in the uppermost tub.
In comes anither efter him, a comical lookin' blade,
He sat doon in the lowermost tub and mocked every word that the lad in the
                                                uppermost tub said.

4 Wi' this the lad in the uppermost tub says, Come let us sing,
Wi' this the lad in the lowermost tub made a' the hoose to ring.
Some sang well, others did grunt and groan,
Every man sang what they will, but I sang Bob and John.

5 When prayin' and singin' was over, and the folks all gone away,
I went up to the lad in the uppermost tub and axed what was to pay.
Oh nothing at all says he; By gum, says I, but you're fair,
So I up wi' my hat and my stick, and cam' whistlin' doon the stair.

WILLIAM LAWRENCE — G

FIFTEENTH PSALM

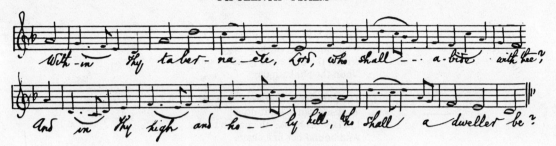

1   Within Thy tabernacle, Lord,
     Who shall abide with thee?
     And in Thy high and holy hill,
     Who shall a dweller be?

P.R. GORDON — G

COVENANTERS

WILLIAM REID — G

THE PRESBYTERIAN CAT

1   An active Presbyterian cat,
     While watching for her prey,
     Within the house she caught a mouse
     Upon the Sabbath day.

2   The parson being grieved sore,
     That such an act was done,
     Laid by his book, the cat he took,
     And bound her in a chain.

3   O ye wicked crater
     And blood-shedder, said he,
     Are ye to bring to ill this day
     My holy wife and me?

4   But since it's woe, we'se haud it so,
     For blood for blood sall pay;
     They hanged her hie upon a tree,
     The parson sang a psalm —

5   Blest is the man that has a kist,
     And bread and cheese therein;
     Curst is the man that claws himsel',
     And rives aff a' the skin.

Miss BELL ROBERTSON — G

THE AULD WIFE AND HER CATTIE

A

B

There Was an Auld Wifie

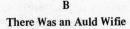

1   There was an aul' wifie, she clippit her cattie
    For takin' a moosie on Christenmas day,
    But I wite the body she paid for that,
    For the half o' her cattie was clippit away.

Mrs MARGARET GILLESPIE — D

OUR ORANGE FLAGS MAY GANG TO RAGS

1   The other day as I did stray
Where Flora gay displays her treasure
Each field in bloom with rich perfume
My heart amused beyond all measure
As I did stray close by a shade
Where streamlets played in sweet meander
I heard a cry as I drew nigh
"Ah let us die or we surrender".

2   I stood and gazed, some time amazed,
To hear so strange a declaration
But then this song ere it was long
Was changed into a conversation.
Dear Billy lad, the case is bad
It puts me mad with pure vexation
To think that we content can be
Or bear to see emancipation.

3   The news I hear, I greatly fear
Will drive me fairly to distraction
Since popish Dan I understan'
Again has won the Clare election
Forbid that we should ever see
The ministry of great Brittania
Becoming slaves to popish knaves
And to their graves sent by old Granyer.

4   Now she's broke loose, she will be croose
For her old truce she's broke asunder
Our Limerick tie she will deny
But let us die or we surrender.
May the auld Deil take partial Peel
Why did he yield to popish Donnell
And Wellington who laurels won
How fast he's run to join O'Connell.

5   But now we're late they have us beat
By numbers great throughout the nation
They're ten to one I understand
And they'll command emancipation.
Our Orange flags may gang to rags
Our drums like kegs lie in a corner
Or else sound shrill on ilka hill
To praise their bill and popish honour.

Source unrecorded — D

THE LAST SPEECH AND DYING WORDS OF THE AULD KIRK OF TURRIFF

1 On Hallow'een fan bonfires blinket
  An' boodies roun' folk's hallens genkit   [spirits played hide and seek
  An' murther'd ghosts bout murders clinkit
  Their iron ruckles   [chains
  An' fettered fiends thro loanings linkit
  Wi' their hapshackles.   [chains

2 Fan ghaists an goblins deils an' brownies
  Like sma flecks flock'd 'bout country townies   [for "sna", snow
  An' niffered shargers like baboonies   [exchanged children
  Girn'd by the fire
  An' water wraiths like Shetland ponies
  Brawl'd thro' the mire.

3 Fan Spunkie sparkit o' the knows   [will o' wisp
  And Kelpie yelpit i' the hows   [water horse
  An' witches, warlocks, wirricrows
  Played up their farces
  Wi' elfin candles in red lows
  In a' their a——es.

4 Fan satyrs, sylphs, an' nimble fairies
  Play'd seek and hide like fudding hairies   [frisking hares
  Wi' ridden hags, yeclep'd night-maries   [called
  That grip folks kinkin   [spluttering
  Till baith their back and side maist sair is
  Hauf wa'ak, hauf winkin'.

5 Twas on that night that I right eerie
  That darksome, dismal night and dreary
  Go'd o'er the knowe to seek my mearie
  Ayont the whins
  The bonfires lamping far and near aye
  Like shot o' guns.

6 I took a turn 'bout Cosie's Knowe
  An' coming up the quarry howe
  The horned howlet gae a wow   [owl
  Aboan my heid
  My riggin divot frae my pow   [bonnet
  Crap aff wi' dread.

7 My tremblin' knees forgat to ben
  My hair stood bolt upon its en'
  An' whaur I was I did na' ken
  Nor fat to dee
  For I could neither fack nor fen'   [take respite; shelter
  Nor fecht nor flee.

8 Gaen gateward to the Brig o' Hell
  Sic panic fear athwart me fell
  That fan I try'd to sain my sell   [bless
  My tongue camsterie   [unmanageable
  Ae Paternoster wad na tell
  Nor Av' Marie.

9 I was come ha'lens up anent   [halfway; alongside
  Auld Rector Mitchell's monument
  Needin' my staff an' a' my tent
  To keep o' my leg
  Lat never unco face nor kent
  Get sic a fleg.   [fright

10 The rising moon o'er Latchacook
  Shone o' the auld kirk's nearest nook
  Fat sees I crawlin' up the jouk
  But a grim spector
  That wid a fley'd wi' ae bare look   [put to flight
  Ane stout as Hector.

11 Guid guide's. He was a fearsome chiel
  A' clad wi' wings frae neck to heel
  A lang sharp scythe an' glittering steel [for "o'"
  His arm did wield
  A sand glass an' a cutler's wheel
  Glanced on his shield.

12 He had na mon' nor hose, nor e'en [for "mou", mouth; for "nose"
  But a' the holes far they had been;
  An' for a belly – he had nane
  Nor yet intimmers   [entrails
  An a' his ribs, and hurkle banes,   [thigh bones
  Like auld kilnsimmers.   [kiln beams

13 A sna' while beard hang down his breast [for "white"
  Twa horn'd neive in length at least
  Syne he was sic a glutton beast
  His hungry maw
  Whate'er can in't nae count he keist [for "cam"; was not particular
  But ate up a'.

14 He'd ae peculiar property
  Coming or gaen ye might him spy
  But fan he was just hard in by
  He did na kythe   [was not visible
  Nor stood he eir but ance to try
  To sharp his scythe.

15 Thinks I, Fat is he seekin' here?
  But sooth I was some fley'd to spear
  Yet howsomever I crap near
  Withouten spearing
  Inquisitive ye may be seer
  To ken his errand.

16 Now he had heard that the Auld Kirk
  Was ferrial grown, and wid na wirk [unhallowed
  And he cam skouking up kirk   [sneaking
  To mak her testment
  Syne scoop her e'en wi' his lang dirk
  And shut her casement.

17 First to the bell-house he cried ben
  A quorum o' auld warld's men
  Ane wi ane ink horn an' a pen
  They ca'd him Johnny
  Fat mair was this? I'm seek I ken
  Aye – "Testimony".

18 There was ane "Tam – Antiquity"
   An' ane "Univer – Sality"
   Anither chee'd it seemed to me   [chield, man
   They a well kent
   Came ben and joined the ither three
   They ca'd "Consent".

19 Into the bell-house they sat down
   An spy'd a' ferlies roun' an roun'
   Says "Tam" There's mony a quean an' loun,
   Has here been shriven
   That wore Skeerfirs day's sackin gown   [for "Skeer Thursday's", Maundy
   True Fastern's Even.   [for "Frae"   Thursday's

20 An yonder i' the meikle door,
   The fanter's bink is to the fore   [for "fauter's", penitent's; bench
   In my time I've seen mony a score
   Their penance dree
   But we'll see fat we've met here for
   An' lat that be.

21 Wi' that the Auld Kirk gae a groan
   An' after that a dreary moan
   An' sighed an said Oh hon! Oh hon!
   I'm like to fail
   Tak ye your pen my auld man John
   And write my tale.

22 Lang on the hillock I have been
   And mony alterations seen
   Now sin my days are near han' done   [nearly
   Afore I fail
   Some o' my former deeds I mean
   In brief to tell.

23 Like mony a gude auld warld's dame
   I wot na weel how auld I am
   But far back i' the rolls o' fame
   My name ye'll see
   Tho' wha first rear'd my Gothic frame
   Has scaped me.

24 My education i' my youth,
   Was plain an' simple ae fauld truth   [uncomplicated
   Gley'd error wi' Erastian mouth
   Here was na' bred
   Nor schismatick devoid o' truth
   Set up his trade.

25 I bade my bairns ten precepts heed
   Taught them a short substantial creed
   The scripture lessons I did read
   An' fan we pray'd
   The Glore and Paternoster guid
   We sang and said.

26 Their duty was composed i' two
   Strong active verbs *believe* and *do*
   An' suffer what would not eschew
   Without a sin
   And do as they'd be done unto
   By fraimt an' kin.

27 My bishop and my sovreign baith,
    Obediently I lived beneath
    Folk that had gear did them bequeath   [for "then"
    Some share to me
    They thought na then toom handed faith
    Was piety.

28 Braid Buchan's dame an' Cummine height,   [for "Ann"; called
    To God and me (this Kirk) bequeathed
    The land frae Knockieburn straight
    To Cowan's How
    My borders ran on left and right
    An threeple plough.   [triple ploughland

29 Aboot this time ane ca'd the pope
    At Rome set up a trantlin shop   [trinket
    His bulls and briefs they ran clean scope
    Wi' his epistles
    To furnish ilka fool and fop
    Wi' rattlin whistles.

30 An' I being now a gaudy dame
    Frae Rome new fashions daily came,
    Saints, reliques, images, oh shame
    I did adore
    More legendary tales than them
    I sprattled o'er.   [scrambled

31 But yet I war'd my gear fu' weel
    Twelve beedman I gave claith and meal
    To mony a stranger a nicht's beil   [shelter
    Some boys I bred
    On my expenses at the school
    Strange tongues to read.

32 At length some folk began to grudge
    I did o'er mony idlers lodge
    Syne on my doctrines they sat judge
    And strange to hear
    My mind o' doctrine fause to purge
    They gripp'd my gear.   [seized

33 And now I was I wat na fat
    Was sometimes this and sometimes that
    Till our guid king the mastery gat
    O' factious fools
    Syne he my fauts did regulate
    By scriptural rules.

34 About this time my patron Hay
    Ga'd up wi' Huntly to Strathspey
    There gar'd the Kirk's head elder fley
    At fam'd Glenlivat
    Nae Presbyterian then was I
    Ye may believe it.

35 Next came a race o' hectrin saints   [hectoring
    Wi' solemn leagues and covenants
    They learn'd my bairns like the ants
    Nae king to heed
    Ca'd them that own'd them malynants   [for "malignants"
    An' shed their bleed.

36 Fan this quixotic race was out
    They turned loyal and devout
    I had some fauts ye needna dout,
    But fat'l ye say?
    Aince mair I turned my mind about
    Fat lasts for aye.

37 To Presbetrie sma love had I
    Till Mitchell did my rights invade
    Against my bairns' will he made
    Me change profession
    Twas only force that ever sway't
    Me to this notion.

38 This hunner year an' mair I've been
    Just what yoursels hae heard an' seen
    Haaf black, haaf white, haaf foul, haaf clean
    I've made a fashion
    To nabble on and keep the mean   [go steady
    Ca'd moderation.

39 An' doctor, noo a word or twa   [for "dochter"
    Wi' you. Ye're stately neat an' braw
    Exceeding far yer auld mamma
    But faith I red
    Ye'll hae enough ado for't a'
    To be as guid.

40 Wi' prayer they laid my first foundation
    Auld folk ca'd that a consecration
    And aye on me they had some notion
    O' sanctity
    Hence twas that tho' I changed profession
    They stuck by me.

41 Round my wa's foot lies many a saint
    Now, doctor, baith o' this ye want
    An' acts o' kings o' parliament
    Are nae sae sicker
    As the auld law o' use and wont
    Fan parties bicker.

42 Gin ye for parties preach and pray
    Or greedy seek owre muckle pey
    Turn careless o' your family
    Or proud and saucy
    Ye'll aiblens share the fate some day
    O' Piscopacy.

43 Heigh where ye stan' there an' look down
    Wi stately pride o'er my cott-town
    Wi' tourin' steeple, brazen crown
    Sae fair and ruddy,
    But mind, I dinna fear yer frown
    Ye're near the woody.

44 Noo, doctor, do as weel's you can
    And strive to end as I began
    Reform upon the grand auld plan
    Pure orthodox
    Free frae the foul Geneva stain
    Or spots o' Knox.

45 Quo Tam "I hear a cockie crawin'
A signal that I maun be drawin'
An' yon's Aurora's horn daw'in,
Ayont Blairmormon'
An drunken Phoebus clears his lawin'
Wi' Luckie German."

46 Wi' that Tam lifted the foot stane
Time took the altar a' his lane
John gripp'd the Bible for his frien'
Syne ane an' a'
Without good day or yet good e'en
Fast trudg'd awa'.

A. RETTIE — G

693

QUEEN JEAN

A

1 Oh women, oh women, oh women, cried she
   You'll send for my mother, she'll come and see me.

2 They sent for her mother who instantly came
   What ails you my daughter, you look pale and wan.

3 Oh mother, oh mother, oh mother, cried she
   You'll send for King Henry, he'll come and see me.

4 They sent for King Henry, who instantly came
   What ails you my lady, you look pale and wan.

5 King Henry, King Henry, King Henry, cried she
   You'll send for a doctor to come and see me.

6 He sent for a doctor who instantly came
   What ails you my Queen you look pale and wan.

7 Oh doctor, oh doctor, oh doctor, cried she
   Ye'll open my left side and see fat ails me.

8 She wept and she wailed, she fell into a swoon
   Till they opened her left side and a young prince was found.

9 She wept and she wailed, she wrung her hands sore
   But the pride of Old England will flourish no more.

10 Black was the kitchen and black was the hall
   And black was the aprons that hung on them all.

11 And black were the women attending Queen Jean
   But bonnie King Henry lay weeping him lane.

Miss BELL ROBERTSON — G

B

1 We have sent for etc.
   And they are by your bedside,
   Queen Jeannie, Queen Jeannie,
   Your eyes they look red.

Miss BELL ROBERTSON — G

FAT'LL I DEE AN MY DEARIE DEE

A

Oh me! fat'll I dee!

Oh me! fat'll I dee! I'le dee fan my dearie dees; Oh me!

fat'll I dee! I'le dee fan Jeannie dees.

Miss ELIZABETH GREIG — D

B

1 Fat'll I dee an my dearie dee,
   Fat'll I dee an my dearie dee?
   I'll put on the kettle and mak' a sup tea,
   And comfort my hert an my dearie dee.

Source unrecorded — G

695

OH, GIN YE WERE DEID, GOODMAN

1 Oh, gin ye were deid, goodman,
   An' a green sod on your heid, goodman,
   I wid waur my widowheid
   Upon a rantin' Hielan'man.

Mrs MARGARET GILLESPIE — D

THE SON OF A SEVEN

The son of a seven's a miser
Although he be charity rolled
Like a doctor he'll clamp up your body
Like a cobbler he'll stick up your sole.

When you come into my shop you'll find all my little alls tricked up against the wall so that there's not a scraping of a jelly pot nor a pennyworth of ointment but what you must pay down twopence. But weel out I never heed that when once I get hold of the

Fal dree lal dreel tweedledum
Fal dreel al dreel ee
Fal dreel tweedle
Fal dreel dreedle-ee.

One Mr Bobie the Censer
Sent for me one day in great haste
Lest death took him out of the way, sir,
And then into German he went.

I sent him a powder for sleeping
A few hours after he'd teen't
He went to his bed and he slept sir
But believe me he never waked again.

Well I went over next morning to see how my dose had squat and met a servant maid in the close with a long long face. Ho, ho, says I to my-sel there's no use for a doctor so I was going to retire. Walk upstairs, doctor, said she. So I walked upstairs and saw my old friend on a table with a long white robe over him and his younger brother in a window weeping. Very sorry, says I'm Bobie for your brother's sudden exchange. Oh never heed that. Give us your bill, doctor. Oh never heed the bill, said I. Consider how your brother's lying there. Oh never heed that. We are grass and here today and away tomorrow. Give us your bill, doctor. So I gave him off a bill about as long's my staff: some alacapaine, roots, some horses a dish, and the powder of julip etc. But reediet I never heeded the bill when once I got hold of the

Fal dree lal dreel tweedledum
Fal dreel al dreel ee
Fal dreel tweedle
Fal dreel dreedle-ee.

Miss BELL ROBERTSON — G

MACPHERSON'S RANT

A

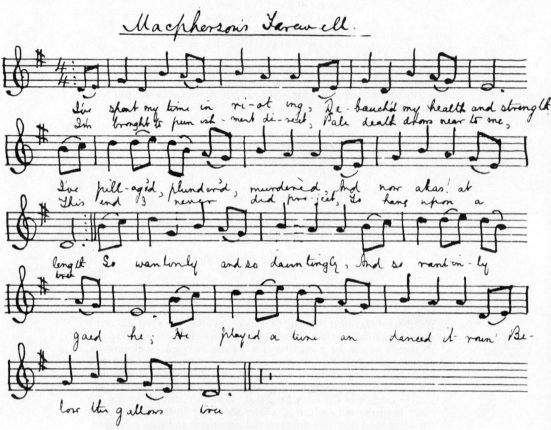

Macpherson's Farewell.

1 I've spent my time in rioting, debauched my health an strenth
   I've pillaged plunder'd an murdered and now alas at length
   I'm brought to punishment direct, pale death draws near to me
   This end I never did project to hang upon a tree.
       So wantinly an so dauntinly an so rantinly gied he   [defiantly
       He played a tune an he danced it roun below the gallows tree.

2 He took his fiddle in his hand an three times round went he
   There wis nean o them his fiddle tak an he brak her o'er his knee
   He took his fiddle in his hand an dashed her to a stone
   Said There's nean on earth shall play on thee when I am dead an gone.

3 The laird o Grant that Highland saint o might and majesty
   He pled the cause for Peter Broun an let Macpherson dee
   But Braco Duff in rage enough he first laid hands on me
   An if that death did not prevent I would avenged be.

4 No man on earth that draweth breath more courage had than I
   I dared my foes unto their face and would not from them fly
   Fareweel my friends an comrades a', fareweel my wife an bairns
   There's nae repentance in my breast for the fiddle's in my arms.

Mrs MARGARET GILLESPIE and GEORGE F. DUNCAN — D

B

Macpherson's Rant

To the tune of version A

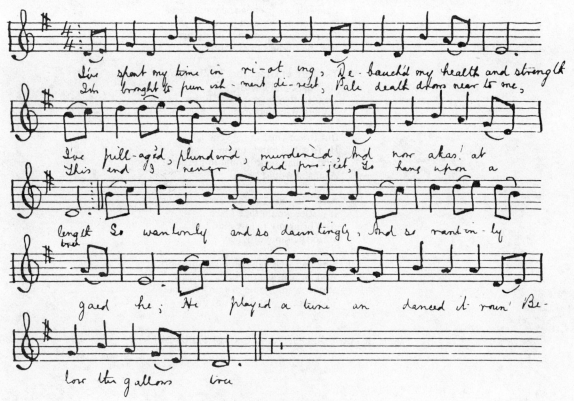

1   Farewell ye prisons dark an strong
    The wretch's destiny
    Macpherson's time will not be long
    On yonder gallows tree.
        Sae rantinlie an sae wantonlie
        Sae dauntinlie gaed he
        He played a tune an danced it roun
        Below the gallows tree.

2   Oh what is death but parting breath
    On mony a bludy plain
    I've daur'd his face and in this place
    I scorn him yet again.

3   Take off this bands from off my hands
    An bring to me my sword
    There's nae a man in a' Scotland
    But I'll brave him at a word.

4   I've lived a life o sturt an strife   [violence
    An I die by treacherie
    It burns my heart I must depart
    An not avenged be.

5 He's taen his fiddle in his hand
    An broke it o'er a stone
    Said There's nene on earth shall play on thee
    When I am deed an gone.

6 Farewell my friends and comrades a'
    Farewell my wife an bairns
    There's nae repentance in my breast
    For the fiddle's in my arms.

7 The laird of Grant that highland saunt
    His might and majesty
    He pled the cause o Peter Brown
    An lets Macpherson dee.

8 But Braco Duff in rage enough
    He first laid hands on me
    And if that death would not prevent
    Avenged would I be.

9 As for my life I do not care
    If justice would take place
    And bring my fellow plunderers
    Unto the same disgrace.

10 Now farewell light thou sunshine bright
    And all beneath the sky
    May coward shame distain his name
    The wretch that dares not die.

Mrs MARGARET GILLESPIE AND GEORGE F. DUNCAN – D

C
Macpherson's Rant

1 . . . .
   . . . .
He played the cards wi' Peter Broon
And loot Macpherson dee.

ARTHUR BARRON – G

D

Macpherson's Lament.

JOHN MOWAT – G

E

Macpherson's Rant.

Oh some's come here to see me dee, And some to buy my fiddle;

But afore that I wad pairt wi' her I'd brak' her thro' the middle.

Sae rantin'ly, sae wantonly, Sae dauntin'ly gaed he;

He played a spring & danced it roon Below the gallows tree.

Miss H. RAE – G

F

Macpherson's Rant.

Ye'll tak' these bands from 'off my hands, And bring to me my sword, And there's nae a man in a' Scotland But I'll brave him at a sword.

JOHN JOHNSTONE – G

G

Macpherson's Rant

1   Some cam' here to see me hanged,
And some to buy my fiddle.
But afore that I wad part wi' her
I'd brak her thro' the middle.

A. CAMPBELL – G

ROSEN THE BEAU

A
Rosin-de-bow

I've travelled the wide world o-ver And now to another must go

I know there's hot quarters awaiting To welcome old Rosin the Beau

To welcome old Rosin the Beau --- To welcome old Rosin the Beau --

For I know there's hot quarters awaiting To welcome old Rosin the Beau.--

1   I've travelled this wide world over
     And now to another must go
     For I know there's good quarters awaiting
     To welcome old Rosin-de-bow
        To welcome old Rosin-de-bow O, O,
        To welcome old Rosin-de-bow
        For I know there's good quarters awaiting
        To welcome old Rosin-de-bow.

2   When I'm dead and laid in my coffin
     The ladies will all want to know
     Just slip up the lid of the coffin
     Let them look at old Rosin-de-bow.
        Let them look at old Rosin-de-bow, O, O,
        Let them look at old Rosin-de-bow
        Just slip up the lid of the coffin
        Let them look on old Rosin-de-bow.

3   You'll get me a dozen brave fellows
     And stand them all round in a row
     Let them drink out of half gallon bottles
     To the name of old Rosin-de-bow
        To the name of old Rosin-de-bow, O, O,
        To the name of old Rosin-de-bow
        Let them drink out of half gallon bottles
        To the name of old Rosin-de-bow.

4   You'll get this dozen brave fellows
     And let them all staggering go
     And dig a deep hole in a meadow
     And in it toss Rosin-de-bow
        And in it toss Rosin-de-bow, O, O,
        And in it toss Rosin-de-bow
        And dig a deep hole in a meadow
        And in it toss Rosin-de-bow.

5   Then get me a pair of good tomb-stones
Place one at my head and my toe,
And do not neglect to scratch on them
The name of old Rosin-de-bow
    The name of old Rosin-de-bow, O, O,
    The name of old Rosin-de-bow
    And do not neglect to scratch on them
    The name of old Rosin-de-bow.

6   When I'm dead and laid out in the country,
A voice you will hear from below
Crying Bring me good whiskey and water,
To be drink to old Rosin-de-bow
    To be drink to old Rosin-de-bow, O, O,
    To be drink to old Rosin-de-bow
    Crying Bring me good whiskey and water
    To be drink to old Rosin-de-bow.

7   I feel that grim tyrant approaching
That dread and implackable foe
Who spares neither age nor condition
Nor even old Rosin-de-bow
    Nor even old Rosin-de-bow, O, O,
    Nor even old Rosin-de-bow
    Who spares neither age nor condition
    Nor even old Rosin-de-bow.

8   Noo the last fareweel o' my country,
I mean noo to let you all know,
So fare ye weel, Scotland and Ireland,
And away goes old Rosin the Bow
    Away goes old Rosin the Bow -ow, ow,
    Away goes old Rosin the Bow
    So fare ye weel, Scotland and Ireland,
    And away goes old Rosin the Bow.

Mrs MARGARET GILLESPIE and Rev. JAMES B. DUNCAN — G & D

B

JAMES WILL — G

THE SCOTS PIPERS

1   I'll hae nane o' yer mournin' an' weepin',
    Fin ance that I'm deid an' I'm gone,
    Convene me a score o' Scots pipers
    Tae play my corpse up the kirk loan.

2   When Davie wis young an' his tykie
    Herdin' his sheep on the ley,
    It wis at the sin side o' a' ykie
    An' there he first learnt tae play.

3   Fin Saul was possessed wi' a deevil,
    He callèd for David his son,
    An' played him a chairge o' remeaval
    An' soon't him tae hell wi' his drone.

4   A blast fae the . . . .

ALEXANDER SIM — G

700

THE TERM

A

The Term, or The Deein' Plooman

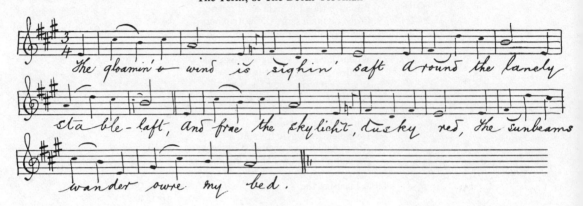

The gloamin's wind is sighin' saft around the lanely stable-laft, And frae the skylicht, dusky red, The sunbeams wander owre my bed.

Miss BROWN – G

B

The Term, or The Dying Ploughboy

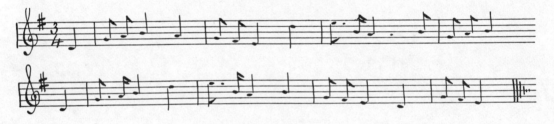

GEORGE WILSON – G

C

The Term

1 The glowing wind is sighin' saft
Around the lonely stable laft,
And frae the skylight dusky red
The sunbeams wander o'er my bed.

2 The doctor left me words o' cheer,
But something tells me death is near;
My time on earth has no been lang,
But noo's the term and I maun gang.

3   Ah me it's but a week the morn
      Since I was weel and hairstin' corn;
      As fu' o' health, as blithe and strong
      As ony ane in a' the throng.

4   But something in my breast gaed wrang,
      A vessel burst and bluid oot sprang;
      And ere my sun was in mid-skies
      I laid me doon nae mair to rise.

5   Farewell my nags, my bonnie pair,
      I'll never yoke nor lowse ye mair;
      Farewell my plough, wi' you this hand
      Shall turn nae mair the fresh red land.

6   Farewell my friends and parents dear,
      My voice again ye'll never hear;
      Farewell for aye thou setting sun;
      My day is o'er, my work is done.

7   I've served my master weel and true,
      And well-done work I daurna rue,
      But forbye I micht hae striven
      To win the fee and arles o' Heaven.

8   O has my Master got my name,
      And shall I get a welcome hame?
      Thou who dost help in need afford,
      Receive me to thy service Lord.

SAM DAVIDSON — G

D

The Dying Plooman

1   The gloomy winds were sighing soft
      Around yon lonely stable loft,
      And while the sun was in the skies,
      You laid me down, nae mair to rise.

2   The doctor left me in very good cheer,
      But something tells me death is near;
      My time on earth will no be lang,
      And noo's the time that I maun gang.

3   'Tis only but a week the morn
      Since I was weel and hairstin' corn,
      As full of glee and mirth and fun
      As anyone amongst the young.

4   Something aboot my hert's gane wrang,
      A vessel burst, and the blood ootsprang;
      And while the sun was in the skies
      You laid me doon, nae mair to rise.

5   Farewell my nags, my dandy pair,
      I'll never yoke nor loose you mair;
      Farewell my ploo, wi' you this han'
      I'll never turn o'er nae mair fresh lan'.

6   I've served my maister weel and true,
      And weel deen wark I'll never rue;
      But for all that I should have striven
      To gain the fairest realms of Heaven.

7   Farewell my friends and comrades dear,
      My voice again you'll never hear;
      And fair tae you, yon setting sun,
      My day is o'er, my work is done.

Miss LIZZIE INGRAM — G

BURNS'S FAREWELL

1 Come near tae me Jean, come close tae my side
  Come kneel and pray wi' me, oh,
  That the widow's God may saften the road
  For my helpless bairns and thee oh.
  My heart is now fu' o' love that's Divine
  Yet strong is my love for thee oh
  He who tempers the wind to the wee shorn lamb
  Will baith husband an' father be oh.

2 My sun slowly sets this sweet summer eve
  Oh I'm loath to leave them an thee oh
  Yet I see through the gloom fast gatherin roon
  Kin' freens wha will succour gie oh.
  She has come to his side as when first his young bride
  Her airms aroon him twine oh
  My true love she cried I richt fain wad hae died
  But maun bide wi' mine and thine oh.

3 She has clasp'd his cauld hand and kiss'd his cauld lips
  Mute grief is sair tae dree oh,
  But a lock o' his hair on her widow'd breast to wear
  True love can never dee oh.
  Late and ear' she'll toil and spin, their daily bread to win
  Tho frugal it maun be oh
  An' his presence hoverin' near her patient soul will cheer
  While she waits for Heaven's decree oh.

4 They hae laid him to rest in St Michael's kirkyard
  That martial mournfu' train oh
  An' the wee birdies wild a requiem sing
  Aroun' his lowly headstane oh
  Now his name has a shrine in ilka true heart
  That kens the "Mither Tongue" oh
  And the glory and fame o' Scotia's sweet Bard
  Will resound till the crack o' doom oh.

E. RENNIE — G

THE TESTAMENT

1 Farewell my wife, my joy in life, I freely now do give thee
    My whole estate with all my plate, being just about to leave thee
    A piece of soap an auld cairt rope, a frying pan and kettle
    A broken pail a thrashing flail, an iron wedge and beetle.

2 Two painted chairs, nine warding pears, with an old dreeping platter
    A bed of hay on which I lay, an old saucepan for butter.
    A large mug, a twa-quart jug, a bottle full of brandy,
    A looking-glass to show your face, you'll find it very handy.

3 There's as guid a musket as ever blew a pound of shot and ballast,
    A leather sash and calabash, my powder horn and wallet,
    An auld sword blade, a garden spade, a hoe, a rake, a ladder,
    My wooden pen and cluster pin, my cluster pipes and bladder.

4 There's a chappin dish, an old stock fish, if I be not mistaken,
    A pound of pork, a broken fork, a knife without a handle.
    A peck of meal, a spinning wheel, and half a pound of bacon,
    A lusty lump twa-quarter junt and half a farthing candle.

5 My greasy hat, an old tom cat, a yard and half o' linen,
    A pot of grease and woollen fleece, in order for the spinnin'
    A small tooth comb, an old birk broom, a candlestick and hatchet,
    A coverlet strapped down with red, a bag of rags to patch it.

6 My pouch and pipes, twa oaken tripes, an oaken dish well carven,   [for "oxen"
    My little hog and spotted dog, and twa young pigs just starvin'.
    This is my store, I have no more, I freely now do give thee,
    My years is gone, my days is run, and so I think to leave thee.

7 But since I die, my dear, don't cry, for I've left thee my riches,
    Another spouse comes by-and-by, with money in his breeches.
    So fare ye well, my dearest Nell, I find I now must leave thee,
    But since that I've left you so weel, my dear don't let it grieve thee.

Mrs RETTIE — G

THE MILLER'S WILL

A

1   There was a miller had three sons
    And he did call them one by one
    Before to them the mill he would give
    They must tell him first how they are to live.
      Wi' ma fal da dee, lal da daldy-dee.

2   He called upon his oldest son.
    O son, said he my gless is run
    Before to thee the mill I give
    You must tell me first how you are to live.

3   O father said he my name is Jeck
    Of every bushel I will take a peck
    And of all the corn that I do grind
    It's a good living I will find.

4   O son, says he you're a silly lad
    You've scarcely gotten half the trade
    The mill to you I could never give
    For by honesty no man can live.

5   He called upon his second son
    O son says he my gless is run
    Before to thee the mill I give
    You must tell me first how you are to live.

6   O father says he my name is Ralph
    Of every bushel I will take the half
    Of all the corn that I do grind
    It's a good living I will find.

7   O son say he you're a silly lad
    Ye've scarcely gotten half the trade
    The mill to you I could never give
    For by honesty no man can live.

8   He called upon his youngest son
    O son says he my gless is run
    Before to thee the mill I give
    You must tell me first how you are to live.

9   O father says he I'm your youngest boy
    And of taking mooter is all my joy
    Of all the corn that I do lack
    I'll take it all and forswear the sack.

10   O son, said he, you're the only lad
    The rest o' your brothers hasn't got half the trade
    The mill's be yours the old man cried
    Then closed his eyes and so he died.

JOHN LAWRENCE — G

B

1   There was a miller who had three sons
      He called them to him one by one
      To see which of them was the greatest thief
      That he might have the mill in chief.
       Hal de dal lal, hal de dal lal.

2   He called unto him his eldest son,
      Says: I am old and my days are done,
      By what means do you intend to live
      If I to you the mill do give?

3   Oh, says he since my name is Jeck
      From every bushel I'll take a peck
      By this means I intend to live
      If ye to me the mill do give.

4   You are my son, the old man said,
      But you do not know the half of trade,
      By this means no one is fit to live,
      So the mill to you I will never give.

5   He called unto him his second son,
      Says, I am old and my days are done,
      By what means do you intend to live,
      If I to you the mill do give.

6   Oh, says he, since my name is Ralph,
      From every bushel I'll take a half,
      By this means I do intend to live,
      If ye to me the mill do give.

7   You are my son, the old man said,
      But you do not know the half of trade,
      By this means no one is fit to live,
      So the mill to you I will never give.

8   He called unto him his youngest son,
      Says, I am old and my days are done,
      By what means do you intend to live,
      If I to you the mill do give?

9   Oh, says he, I'm your youngest boy,
      And taking moulter is all my joy,
      Before that I a good living lack
      I will take it all and forswear the sack.

10   You are my son, the old man said,
      Your brothers know not the half of trade,
      The mill's be thine, the old man cried,
      With that he closed his eyes and died.

Source unrecorded — G

C
The Miller's Three Sons

1 There was a miller who had three sons,
He called them to him one by one,
To see which o' them was the greatest thief,
That he might have the mill in chief.
    Lal de dal, lal, lal de lal lall.

2 He called unto him his eldest son
Says I am old and my days are done
By what means do you intend to live
If I to you the mill do give.

3 Oh says he since my name is Jeck
Frae every bushel I'll take a peck
By this means I intend to live
If ye to me the mill do give.

4 You are my son the old man said
But you do not know the half to trade
By this means no one is fit to live
So the mill to you I will never give.

5 He called unto him his second son
Says I am old and my days are done
By what means do you intend to live
If I to you the mill do give?

6 Oh says he since my name is Ralph
Frae every bushel I'll take a half
By this means I do intend to live
If ye to me the mill do give.

7 You are my son the old man said
But you do not know the half of trade
By this means no one is fit to live
So the mill to you I will never give.

8 He called unto him his youngest son
Says I am old and my days are done
By what means do you intend to live
If I to you the mill do give.

9 Oh says he I'm your youngest boy,
And taking mouter is all my joy
Before that I a good living lack
I will take it all and forswear the sack.

10 You are my son the old man said
Your brothers know not the half of trade
The mill's be thine the old man cried
Wi' that he closed his eyes and died.

WILLIAM FORSYTH — G

704

OH THE MILLER HE STOLE CORN

A

1   When bold King Edward ruled the land,
      He ruled it like a king,
      And he turned his three sons out of doors
      Because they could not sing.

2   The first he was a miller,
      The second he was a weaver,
      The third he was a little tailor boy,
      Three thievish rogues together.

3   The miller he staw meal,
      And the weaver he staw yarn
      And the little tailor boy he stole broadcloth
      To keep those three rogues warm.

4   The miller was drowned in his dam,
      The weaver was hung wi' his yarn,
      And the deil ran awa' wi' the little tailor boy,
      Wi' his broadcloth under his arm.

Mrs GREIG – G

B

The little Tailor Dick.

Victoria rules the nations, She is a mighty queen; Three sons of yore she turn'd to the door, Because they could not sing.

1   Victoria rules the nations
   She is a mighty queen,
   Three sons of yore she turned to the door,
   Because they could not sing.
      Because they could not sing
      Because they could not sing
      Three sons of yore she turned to the door
      Because they could not sing.

2   The first he was a miller,
   The second he was a weaver,
   The third he was a little tailor
   And they thought him wondrous clever.
      And they thought him wondrous clever
      And they thought him wondrous clever
      The third he was a little tailor
      And they thought him wondrous clever.

3   But the miller he stole corn
   And the weaver he stole yarn
   And the little tailor an' he stole broad cloth
   For to keep these three rogues warm.
      For to keep these three rogues warm
      For to keep these three rogues warm
      And the little tailor an' he stole broad cloth
      For to keep these three rogues warm.

4   The miller was drooned in his dam
   The weaver was hung in his yarn
   Auld Nick cut his stick wi the little tailor Dick
   On the broadcloth under his arm.
      On the broadcloth under his arm
      On the broadcloth under his arm
      Auld Nick cut his stick wi the little tailor Dick
      On the broadcloth under his arm.

ANDREW WALKER — D

C
King Arthur

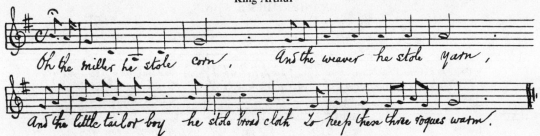

Oh the miller he stole corn, And the weaver he stole yarn, And the little tailor boy he stole broad cloth To keep these three rogues warm.

G.K.C. – G

D

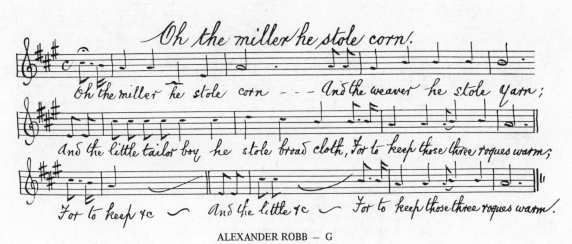

Oh the miller he stole corn.

Oh the miller he stole corn — — — And the weaver he stole yarn; And the little tailor boy, he stole broad cloth, For to keep these three rogues warm; For to keep &c And the little &c For to keep those three rogues warm.

ALEXANDER ROBB – G

E
The Miller's Sons

1 There was a miller and he had three sons
  And three little rogues you'll see
  The first was a miller, the second was a weaver
  And the third was a little tailor boy, boy
    The third was a little tailor boy.

2 The miller he stole corn
  And the weaver he stole yarn
  And the little tailor boy he stole broad cloth
  For to keep these three rogues warm.

3 But the miller he drowned in his dam
  And the weaver he hanged in his yarn
  Old Nick played stick with the little tailor boy
  And the broadcloth under his arm.

WILLIAM DUNBAR – G

611

GRANDMOTHER'S CHAIR

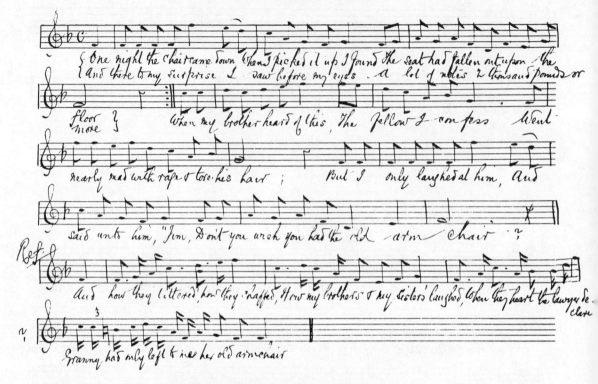

1   One night the chair came down, when I picked it up I found
The seat had fallen out upon the floor
And there to my surprise I saw before my eyes
A lot of notes, two thousand pounds or more.
When my brother heard of this, the fellow I confess
Went nearly mad with rage and tore his hair;
But I only laughed at him, and said unto him, "Jim,
Don't you wish you had the old arm chair?"
     And how they tittered, how they chaffed,
     How my brothers and my sisters laughed,
     When they heart the lawyer declare
     Granny had only left to me her old armchair.

Miss JEANNIE CRICHTON − G

BE KIN' TO YER NAINSEL, JOHN

A

Be kin' tae yer nainsel, John.

There's three speens i' the creel, John, There's three speens i' the creel, John,

Gie the tane to the lassie, an' the tither to the laddie, An' the cuttie tae yer nainsel, John.

Sae be kin' tae yer nainsel, John, Sae be kin' tae yer nainsel, John.

We're a-wearin' awa' tae the Lan's o' the Leal, Sae be kin' tae yer nainsel, John.

1 There's three speens i' the creel, John,
  There's three speens i' the creel, John,
  Gie the tane to the lassie, and the tither to the laddie,
  And the cuttie tae yer nainsel, John.
      Sae be kin' tae yer nainsel, John,
      Sae be kin' tae yer nainsel, John,
      We're a-wearin' awa tae the Lan's o' the Leal,
      Sae be kin' tae yer nainsel, John.

2 There's three kye i' the byre, John,
  There's three kye i' the byre, John,
  Gie the tane to the lassie, and the tither to the laddie,
  And the quaikie tae yer nainsel, John.   [quey, heifer

3 There's three cairts and three ploos, John,
  There's three cairts and three ploos, John,
  Gie the tane tae the lassie, and the tither tae the laddie,
  And the tither tae yer nainsel, John.

4 There's thirty acres o' ploo'd lan', John,
  There's thirty acres o' ploo'd lan', John,
  Gie the tane to the lassie, and the tither to the laddie,
  And the quaikie ter yer nainsel, John.

5 Ye'll mak' a drink tae me, John,
  Ye'll mak' a drink tae me, John,
  Wi' a wee bittie butter, and a little puckle succar,
  And a wee drap o' a dram, John.

6 It's I'm ingaun tae leave ye, John,
  It's I'm ingaun tae leave ye, John,
  Sae be kin' tae the lassie and be kin' tae the laddie
  And be kin' tae yer nainsel, John.

7   Now my wife she's dead and gone,
Now my wife she's dead and gone,
But I maun hae anither, I've plenty for to keep her,
And be kin' tae my nainsel, John.
Sae be kin' tae yer nainsel, John,
Sae be kin' tae yer nainsel, John,
We're a-wearin' awa' tae the Lan's o' the Leal,
And be kin' tae yer nainsel, John.

Mrs JAFFRAY (Mintlaw) — G

B

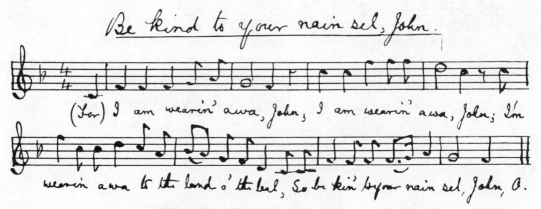

Be kind to your nain sel, John.

I am wearin awa John
I am wearin awa John
I'm wearin awa to the land o the leel
And be kind to yere nainsel John O.

1   Ye'll heat anither drink to me John O
Ye'll heat anither drink to me John O
Wi a wee bit o' butter an a little puckle succor
An a little wee drappie o a dram John O.
For I am wearin awa John
For I am wearin awa John etc.

2   There is three speens in the creel John
There is three speens in the creel O.
Gie the te'en to the laddie, gie the tither to the lassie
Keep the little cuttie speenie to yersel John.

3   There's three kye in the byre John
There's three kye in the byre John
Gie the ane to the laddie an the tither to the lassie
Keep the little hummle couie to yersel John.

4   There's three steels in the hoose, John
There's three steels in the hoose, John
Gie the teen to the laddie, gie the tither to the lassie
Keep the three-leggit steelie to yersel, John.

Mrs MARGARET GILLESPIE — D

C

O be kind to yer nainsel John
O be kind to yer nainsel John
Wi' a wee bittie butter and a wi pickle sugar
O be kind to yer nainsel John.

1   There is thirty acres o' good lan
    There is thirty acres o' good lan
    There's the corn to the lassie an' the bere to the laddie
    An' the tatties to your nainsel John.
        So be kind to your nainsel John etc.

2   There's three horse i' the stable
    There's three horse i' the stable
    There's ane to the lassie an anither to the laddie
    An the stallion to your nainsel John.

3   There's three nout in the byre
    There's three nout in the byre
    There's ane to the lassie an anither to the laddie
    An the stirkie to your nainsel John.

4   My wife's dead an' gone
    Ah my wife's dead an' gone
    I must have anither, I've got plenty to keep her
    An' be kind to my nainsel John.

ANDREW WALKER — D

615

D

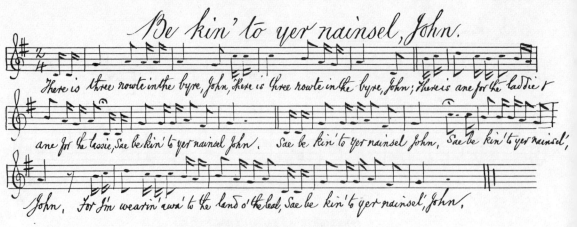

Be kin' to yer nainsel, John.

1   There is three nowte in the byre, John,
     There is three nowte in the byre, John,
     There is ane for the laddie and anither for the lassie,
     And the stirkie to yer nainsel, John.
       Sae be kin' to yer nainsel, John,
       Sae be kin' to yer nainsel, John,
       For I'm wearin' awa' to the land o' the leal,
       Sae be kin' to yer nainsel, John.

2   There is three horse in the stable, John,
     There is three horse in the stable, John,
     There is ane for the laddie, and ane for the lassie,
     And the styagie for yer nainsel, John.

3   There is three sheep in the faul' John,
     There is three sheep in the faul' John,
     There is ane for the laddie, and ane for the lassie,
     And the lambie for yer nainsel, John.

JAMES BREBNER – G

E

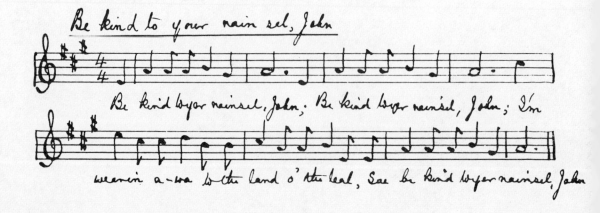

Be kind to your nain sel, John

Be kind to your nain sel, John,
Be kind to your nain sel, John,
I'm weerin' awa to the land o' the leal,
So be kind to your nain sel, John.

1   Mak a drink to your nain sel, John,
    Mak a drink to your nain sel, John,
    Wi' a wee bit butter and a wee puckle sugar,
    And a wee wee drappie o' a dram.

2   There's three speens in the drawer, John,
    There's three speens in the drawer, John,
    There's een to the laddie and anither to the lassie,
    And a cutty to your nain sel, John.

Mrs PETRIE — D

F
Be Kin' To Yer Nainsel, John

I'm wearin' awa', John,
Like snaw fin' it's thaw, John,
I'm wearin' awa' to the land o' the leal.

1   Fy, gar heat a sup drink, John,
    Fy, gar heat a sup drink, John,
    Heat it wi' butter and meal,
       For I'm wearin' awa', etc.

2   Gie Jock the coo, John,
    Gie Jean the quey, John,
    Keep the calf to yersel'.

3   Gie Jock the yowe, John,
    Gie Jean the hog, John,
    Keep the lammie to yersel'.

4   Gie the lad the cup, John,
    Gie the lass the plate,
    Keep the riven dishie to yersel.

5   Aye be kin' to yer nainsel, John.

Miss BELL ROBERTSON — G

G
Be Kin' To Yer Nainsel', John

1   There is three spunes in the creel, John,
There is three spunes in the creel;
There is ane for the laddie and anither for the lassie,
And the auld kail cutty for yer nainsel', John;
       Sae be kin' etc.

2   There's three poun' in the bank, John,
There's three poun' in the bank;
There's ane for the laddie, there's anither for the lassie,
And all the owerplus to yer nainsel, John.

Mrs MARGARET STRACHAN — G

H

1   There's hennies in the hen hoose, John,
Gie the hennies to the lassies and the duckies to the laddies
And keep the cockies tae yer nainsel John.
       Sae be kin' tae yer nainsel, John,
       For I'm wearin' awa' tae the lan' o' the leal,
       Sae be kin' to yer nainsel, John.

2   Mak' a drink tae yer nainsel, John,
Tak' a wee bittie butter, and a wee lickie sugar,
And a wee wee drappie o' a dram.

Miss ANNIE SHIRER — G

I
Be Kin' To Yer Nainsel, John

1   Be kin' to yer nainsel, John,
Mak' a drink to your nainsel, John,
Wi' a wee bittie butter, an' a wee pickle succar,
An' a little wee drappie o' a dram.

Mrs RETTIE — G

J

Heat anidder drink t' me, John,
Wi' a wee bittie butter, and a little puckle succar,
An' be kin' t' yer ain sel, John.

Source unrecorded — G

347 **THE BARNYARDS O' DELGATY**   Cf. Kennedy No. 242. Greig chooses this song to open his first study in Ob. of Ploughman Songs, and begins with some general remarks. "[Specimens of the Harvest Song] might, in a general way, fall under our present heading of 'Ploughman Songs'; but we apply the term, in a more restricted way, to that kind of ditty which recounts the experiences of a farm-servant while fulfilling his half-yearly engagement at some 'toon.' Its form is largely stereotyped. It deals mainly in characterisations. It characterises the farm and the farmer, fellow servants, male and female, the horses, the work, and sometimes the food. Nor is this always done 'in complimental mood.' The references to the master especially are often quite caustic. Sometimes the food forms matter of sinister comment, in which case the mistress or the housekeeper may get dragged in. Fellow servants of the male sex are usually handled by the singer in a kindly enough way. The treatment of the female members of the establishment varies a good deal. As a rule it does not err on the side of chivalry. Sometimes indeed the allusions call for expurgation at the hands of those who would seek to introduce the ditties to modern readers or hearers." (G, Ob. 4)

Greig then gives a composite song text and adds: "'The Barnyards o' Delgaty' is one of our most popular Buchan songs, and its vogue has been considerably extended of late by the singing of Mr A. Milne, Maud, our best platform exponent of the old-time ministrelsy. Versions of the words vary as usual. Singers make changes from time to time, and sometimes a new verse gets introduced. Such things happen with all traditional songs. There is a song 'Jock o' Rhynie' sung to the same tune as 'The Barnyards o' Delgaty,' which is usually treated as a separate ditty; but Mr J. M'Allan, Shevado, gives me a version [A] which connects the two into one song – the Rhynie part being simply another bit of our hero's experiences when he

> Steppit up by Benachie,
> And left the Buchan gentry.

I can well believe that this is the original way. The Rhynie episode appears as 'Linten Lowrin' (another form of the refrain) in Ford's *Vagabond Songs and Ballads*, pp. 207-8, and in *Songs of the North*, 1.134-6, in the latter collection with the tune, but in a corrupt version which overlays its original pentatonic character. The tune is associated with several other songs." (G, Ob. 4)

"[Mr John Milne] says:– 'I see in the *Observer* [i.e. Ob. 4] the song beginning 'In New Deer parish I was born' leading into 'The Barnyards o' Delgaty.' The way that I remember to have heard, the same beginning led into 'Jock o' Rhynie.' The author was by some said to be one Jamie Riddel. But evidently there is some mistake, as another song begins –

> Jamie Riddel is my name,
> The truth to you I'll never deny;
> In Cairnie parish I was born,
> I learned the Gaelic in Strathspey.

I have heard 'Assist me all ye Muses' attribute[d] to the same author.' Yes, there is some confusion about the songs referred to, as I pointed out in my article. I have got them in various shapes and connections, and it is not likely that we shall ever be able to 'redd it up.' There is a tradition that the hero who turns up at Rhynie was a kind of runaway from Buchan, and this inclines me to connect the two episodes into one song." (G, Ob. 7, 14 January 1908)

Greig also quoted in Ob. 9 the opinion that the songs were separate expressed in a letter from Mrs Corbet; see note to 348 "Jock o' Rhynie". There is a further mention of the song in Ob. 20 where Greig says: "[The Rev. John Strachan] refers to the song 'The Barnyards of Delgaty.' As far as I can gather it had been written in the early part of last century." The farm of Barnyards on the estate of Delgaty is a mile north-east of Turriff (see map).

A   Gm 3.4c; a) Gw 10.109-10, b) Gw 12.58-61. "September 1907. Heard when a boy." (Gm) In Aa part of stanza 5 is written and deleted after stanza 9, and stanzas 5-6, which appear opposite the main text, were apparently written after the rest of the text.
B   Gm 3.1a; Gw 43.95-7. "September 1907. Cadence also given by William Forsyth, Durie, Mintlaw, eighty-five in June 1908. Heard mother sing it when he was a boy." (Gm) At 6.2, "harrows" is altered from "harness."
C   Dm 103a. At Dm 104, Duncan indicates that Mrs Gillespie sang this to the same tune as she sang 348 "Jock o' Rhynie". "Same words as Mr Greig (*Folk-Song in Buchan*, pp. 70-1), but with other chorus. Mrs Gillespie, December 1905." (Dm) One stanza is given in Dm:

> As I gaed in by Netherdale,
> At Turra market for to fee,
> I met in wi' a fairmer chap
> At the barnyards o' Delgaty
> *Lim fal lay, fal lairil laddy,*
> *Lim fal lay, fal lairil lee.*

The *Folk-Song in Buchan* version has "Frae" in l. 4 and, as chorus, has:

> *Liltrin adie toorin adie,*
> *Liltrin adie tooral ee.*

D   Gm 1.39c. January 1906.

E   Gm 4.33c. Acknowledged in Ob. 140, 16 August 1910.

F   Gm 3.66a. February 1908.

G   Gm 1.39a. 1905.

H   Gm 2.143c. September 1907.

I   Gm 3.145c. Acknowledged in Ob. 56, 22 December 1908.

J   Gm 3.117a. July 1908.

K   Gm 1.38a. 1904. A bracketed "3" above the "4" of "1904" perhaps indicates that the year should be definitely or tentatively given as 1903. "Cf. 'Mary Jamieson' [from Miss Annie Ritchie], and 'My bonnie is over the ocean'. Cf. some ways of refrain with 'Roy's Wife'." (Gm)

L   Gm 1.39b. December 1905.

M   Gm 1.38b. 1904.

N   Gm 2.56b. "Communicated by William Walker, 65 Argyle Place, per Scott Skinner, Aberdeen. November 1906." (Gm)

O   Gw 1.57-9. Stanza 3 is bracketed and the following revisions of words and spellings are indicated: 4.1 doup (rump), 4.2 fite (white), 4.4 yockin' (yokin'), 5.3 moat (mote) 5.4 Fyls nathing but (And aye the tither), gilp (jilp), 6.2, 4 There's mony a bonnie lassie there … Wad make me welcome to his lair (Mony's the bonnie lass I see … And winkin' [*replacing deleted* smilin'] owre the pews to me).

P   Gw 61.72-3.

Q   Gw 1.44.

348   **JOCK O' RHYNIE**   Cf. Norman Buchan, *101 Scottish Songs* (Glasgow and London, 1962), p. 83 "Rhynie". See map for the location of Mains of Rhynie. Greig notes in Ob. 20 that the octogenerian William Forsyth told him "that he remembers as a boy hearing his mother sing 'Jock o' Rhynie.' This would carry the song back say to 1830." The farmer at Mains of Rhynie was John Gordon from the 1830s to his death in 1859, but in 1851 he had retired and his son, Robert, was doing the active farming. (Cen. E.B., Rhynie, 1851; Register of Deaths)

"From Mrs Corbet, New Deer, I have a most interesting communication. She says:– 'I see in the issue of Tuesday last some reference made to the name of the hero of "Jock o' Rhynie," some supposing that it was "Jamie Riddel." My grandmother often spoke of him, as she knew him well, and she always called him Jock Riddel. She said he was born on the farm of Craigmill, which is half-way between New Deer and Maud, and presently occupied by Mr Farquhar. I don't remember all the particulars about the hero, but he went to London and was for several years employed at the House of Parliament. While there a fire broke out and he rushed into the burning building and secured a box which contained some valuable papers. By this he was so severely burned that he lost his eyesight; and he afterwards received an annual allowance from the Government during the remainder of his life. I may mention that "Jock o' Rhynie" and "Bogieside" are both by the same author, but am of opinion that he was not the author of the "Barnyards o' Delgaty," but rather that the author of that song has borrowed a good many of the verses belonging to "Jock o' Rhynie," with a few alterations.' All this is very interesting indeed, and I have to thank Mrs Corbet for her kindness in communicating the valuable information." (G, Ob. 9, 28 January 1908)

Duncan wrote to Greig on 1 February 1908 saying: "Your last correspondent's statements (and Mr Milne's [see note to 347 'The Barnyards o' Delgaty']) about the song beginning, 'In New Deer pairis,' etc. ending in 'Jock o Rhynie' and being different from 'The Barnyards' agree with my own information. 'Jock o' Rhynie' is, however, a misnomer: it names, not the hero and narrator, but the farmer at whose 'place' he was – a man well-known, or rather notorious, and still well remembered by older people. I have a quite distinct song [349 'The Praise o' Huntly'] under the name, in which the narrator is a woman engaging with him. It came from the Huntly way originally." (2732/26/28) Duncan notes the results of his investigations into this song in Dw. "Mr William Anderson, formerly of Wellhouse, told me that he remembered 'Jock o' Rhynie' coming to the Alford markets and that a song had been composed about him. That might be about the middle of the nineteenth century. Mr Alexander Mackay gives the following further details. His father had been feed with Jock. He was farmer at Mains of Rhynie, and his name, he thinks, was John Gordon; but he was generally known as Jock o' Rhynie. Of the song Jock is said to have remarked that it was not true that his work was 'ill to work', but that they might have truly said that 'Rhynie's work was very hard'. Mr Mackay's father often spoke about the song as connected with Jock; and Mr Mackay's mother, still alive, states that the writer of the song was a man called Buchan. (Is this, however, a mistaken inference from the line, 'Buchan laddie, come awa'?) The following stories were told about him. He knew how many rounds of ploughing there were on every field in his farm, and once, when he came home after a business, he remarked that all had gone right when he was away except that he missed a round of all the three ploughs; and that had been really one bad night that they had stopped! One night, on a Saturday, he said to a man that he might have finished, and the answer was: 'There's seven days in next week, and they're a' coming this way' (a characteristic farmservant story!). On another occasion, a boy remarked that he was not able [to] keep up with the others in filling carts, because he had a small spade; and Jock said: 'Weel, laddie, ye'll need to fill it the fuller'." (Dw 5.56-7)

A   Dm 103a; Gillespie 373-4. "From father and mother, also Mrs Bog of Artamford. Noted 1905. Tune also sung to same name by Archibald Knowles. It appears in *Songs of the North*, 1.134-6, as 'Linten Lowrin'. That form of the refrain I never heard, but seem to remember 'Li/ten'. The various forms have probaby come from 'Liltin' owre an' owre an' addie' – all having meaning but the last word, a more close to it. The tune in *Songs of the*

620

North suggests arrangement. Verses from that volume in Ford, p. 207-8. Cf. [477] 'The Weaver Lad'; [581 'Donald Blue' I]." (Dm) Duncan originally had a note: "Called also 'The Barnyards o' Delgaty'." but this is deleted. "Not sure if this is complete." (Gillespie) Duncan has made a few alterations to the text as first written: *title* "Rhynie" for "Rynie", 1.3 "doot" for "dout", 2.3 "ill" for "ull", 3.3 "they're" for "their" (Duncan's reading has been adopted here), 3.4 "ava" for "of a'", 7.4 "be" for "come", 8.3 "She" for "An".

B Dm 427b. "Noted 30th July, 1908." (Dm)

C Gm 2.16b. "Version – James B. Duncan." (Gm)

D Dw 1.144-6. "From her mother in girlhood. Noted 17th June, 1908. Mrs Taylor afterwards remembered the following verse, and thinks it comes in as verse 2. [Text, st.2.] She was not sure about the proper position of words here given as verse [8]. One is inclined to think that this verse and verse [10] ought to stand together at the end of the whole. Mrs Taylor recognised the common tune when sung to her as being the one she knew. [12.2] also sung:– 'I've spent my time in mirth and glee'." (Dw)

E Gw 51.8.

F Gw 37.15.

G Gw 5.112v.

349 **THE PRAISE O' HUNTLY** "Referring to the 'Jock o' Rhynie' matter, I am glad to be able, through the kindness of my friend, the Rev. J.B. Duncan, to give the following song which embodies the fragment printed last week as well as a verse or two which I once got from Mr J.W. Spence. The occurrence of 'The Buchan gentry' both in this song and in 'The Barnyards o' Delgaty,' as given in Ob.4, helps to confirm our impression that the hero in the two ditties is the same man." [Text] (G, Ob. 146) Duncan suggests in a letter to Greig that it was a woman who was feed in this song (see note to 348 "Jock o' Rhynie"). See map for the location of Huntly and Mains of Rhynie.

A Dm 459a; Wallace 22-3, Dw 5.161-2. "From James Reid, Liggerdale, thirty years ago. Noted 26th August 1908." (Dm) "Noted September 1908. Could there be any connection in authorship between this and the song [348] 'Jock o' Rhynie' [D]? 10.1 'see': perhaps should be 'discern', as the rhyme would suggest. Mr Garioch's version [C] has 'I'm not a fool nor yet a bairn'." (Dw) In Wallace, Duncan had queried the same point, wondering whether "learn" at 10.2 should be "hae" to give a partial rhyme with "see" but he added "But he has not heard this".

B Gm 5.15b; a) Gw 3.41, b) Gw 10.108v. August 1905. (Gm)

C Dm 322c; Garioch 26, Dw 4. 75. "From his father in boyhood. Noted 29th July 1907." (Dm) "Can't remember more." (D, Garioch) At 3.3 "about your farm" is given as an alternative to "sow your corn". In Dw, Duncan gives "on" in place of "and" at 3.2.

D Dm 103b. "Learnt in Huntly. Noted September 1906. Two syllables, perhaps 'fae him,' apparently wanting in third line. The hold gave impression of a ¾ measure, thus:

𝅘𝅥𝅭 𝅘𝅥𝅮

There is no relation to preceding song ('Jock o' Rhynie'), except that the 'Jock' is probably the same. It is of a man meeting with him. (Later note.) The words are, it now appears, from 'The Praise o' Huntly' [A]; but the air does not appear the same." (Dm)

E Gw 57.40-1. 5.4 "It": MS "I". There is a line beside st. 5 marked with a query, presumably indicating a doubt as to whether the stanza belongs to this song. "From the same source [as 364 'Benton'] I have got a part of a song connected with 'Jock o' Rhynie.' The hero of 'The Barnyards o' Delgaty' [Ob. 4] is in some versions taken away to Rhynie, the last stanza of the following fragment occurring in the course of that song – a stanza which can hardly belong to the same ditty as the preceding four, being metrically different. There seems to be a connection of some kind between the songs, the characters, and the incidents; and we should be glad if anyone could help to 'redd it up.'" (G, Ob. 145)

F Gw 1.54. The stanzas are also published in Milne, p.8.

G Gw 6.33.

350 **TIRED O' WORKIN' LYAUVIE'S BRAES**

Misc. 158. "From her mother. No more words; and these are said to have been substituted by a servant boy (at least, the local references), to express his own experience. 'Lyauvie's' = Lawfold in Rayne; 'Imphm's toon' = an old farm house he had to go to for attendance on cattle, as some distance." (D, Misc.) Lawfold, in the parish of Rayne, is north-west of Inverurie.

351 **DARRAHILL** "This is another ploughman ditty. None of the versions which we have got is complete, and we should be thankful to have a complete copy, or any verses additional to what we give." (G, Ob. 133) "Mr Johnstone [New Deer] adds an interesting note in reference to 'Darahill.' He says:– 'My mother was engaged there one harvest and gathered corn both on that farm and also on Smithyburn, and the words 'Like ye ken' was a very common expression of the farmers when she was there." (G, Ob. 135) Darrahill (see map) and the adjacent Smithyburn are in the parish of Foveran. The farm in Turriff referred to in the note to F is called Darra.

A   Gm 4.65c.

B   Gw 10.53-4. August 1907. At 3.1 the alternative reading "keerious" is written above "curious". 5.1 "thing": MS "think".

C   Gw 56.62-3. "From one who gets *Buchan Observer*, Johannesburg." (Gw)   "From 'One who gets the *Buchan Observer*,' Johannesburg, per the Editor, comes a version of 'Darahill.' It corresponds in the main with what we gave in [Ob. 133], but the following helps us at a certain point:– [Text, st. 4]. Maggie Dickie who 'makes the brose' recalls the kitchie-lass in 'The Barnyards o' Delgaty' with – [Text, st. 5, 3-4]. And the last verse is thoroughly characteristic – [Text, st. 6]." (G, Ob. 143, 6 September 1910)

D   790.1/3/4. "Got from James Mackenzie of Ellon in Johannesburg in 1890." C.M. (790.1/3/4)

E   Dw 5.113-4.

F   Gw 5.113. The heading is "Darahill (near Turriff)" with "s?" inserted after "Dara".

352   DARRA

Dm 423a; Argo-Duncan 12-3, Dw 3.145. "Mixo-Lydian. Heard among farmservants. Noted 13th September 1907. Verified 16th July, 1908. The meaning of the chorus seems to be that 'Darra' was in the habit of using the expression 'Fa? man, fa' (= who?), since, according to a later stanza he was known in Aberdeen as 'aul' *Darra fa*'. 'Darrahill' is in Foveran." (Dm)   "2.3 'hamlicky' = 'hammock'. St. 5: second half of verse seems to be wanting. He states that Darrahill is near Aberdeen." (D, Argo-Duncan)

353   ELLON FAIR   See map for the location of Ellon.

A   Gw 18.97-9. "We now give a local song which records the experiences of an 'orra loon' at the feeing market. For the copy I am indebted to Mrs Bruce, Foveran, who says that it was in the way of being sung some forty years ago, although she is not sure if the version she sends is complete." (G, Ob. 26, 26 May 1908) Greig also thanks Miss Helen Bruce for writing out and sending the song.

B   Gw 27.17. "[Miss Bell Robertson] contributes a note on 'Ellon Fair' [Ob. 26], in which she says the piece was written by the late John Ker, well known as a rhymer. For verse 4 she gives a correction – [Text, st. 1] The following are given as additional verses – [Text, sts. 2-3]." (G, Ob. 34, 21 July 1908) See also note to 365 "Frae the Martimas Term" where the spelling "Carr" occurs for this author's name.

354   ELLON MARKET   Cf. "Ellon Market" from William Mathieson in the archive of the School of Scottish Studies, SA 1952/1/B20-2; MS 1.28.

A   Dm 467c; 998/7/3/39, Dw 1.173-4. "Learnt from farm servant, called John Christie, who was much about Belhelvie. He was in middle life, near fifty, when he was with the Philips, nearly ten years ago." (D, 998/7/3/39) "Noted 7th September 1908. The air is of course the chorus of 'The boatie rows', first half unvaried, and with third line a good deal varied, and fourth but slightly changed from first strain. It might have come from imperfect recollection, but Mr Philip stated that it was sung to him as here given." (Dm)

B   Gw 21.108-9. Acknowledged in Ob. 29, 16 June 1908.

C   Gw 3.81.

355   SOUTH YTHSIE   See map for the location of the farm, South Ythsie. "I am pleased to be able to assign to its author another local song. 'South Ythsie,' long popular in our district, was composed by Mr William Forsyth about the middle of last century when as a young man he was engaged on the farm. While no doubt several of the expressions used in this class of song are more or less common property, it will be seen that [378] 'Guise o' Tough' must have borrowed a good deal from 'South Ythsie.' Many of our readers will be glad to have our copy of Mr Forsyth's song got from himself and kindly communicated by Miss Forsyth. The tune is given as the same as that of 'Keith o' Netherthird.' I have heard it capitally sung by Mr James Murison, Doghillock. The author, now halfway through the eighties, resides at Durie, Mintlaw; and when we also remember that the author of 'The High Rocks of Pennan' lived to be a nonagenarian, we can see the force of the old toast – 'Health and Song!' – [Text.]" (G, Ob. 21) "When on a visit lately to my good friends of olden days at Millhill, Old Deer, I had, among other happy experiences, the pleasure of meeting Mr William Forsyth, Durie, author of the song 'South Ythsie' [Ob. 21]. Mr Forsyth, although fully half-way through the eighties, is still wonderfully hale. He sang to me two or three tunes, and has kindly promised to send me complete copies of the words. His memory is still very clear, and as it extends far back into last century his recollections of songs are valuable. He told me, for instance, that he remembers as a boy hearing his mother sing 'Jock o' Rhynie.' This would carry the song back say to 1830. I was also considerably impressed when he told me that he had lately noticed in the papers the death, at the age of sixty odd years, of the 'little boy' mentioned in his own song." (G, Ob. 52) Although Forsyth claims to have written the song in 1851 (see note to C), none of the named characters are on the census record of that year (Cen. E.B., Tarves, 1851), and the number of male servants is five as opposed to seven listed in the song. Not until the 1870s was this number reached. (Cen. E.B., Tarves, 1861, 1871, 1881). The farmer for much of the second half of the nineteenth century was James Hay (see 386 "Swaggers" and 387 "Nethermill"). (V.R. Aberdeenshire, 1859 to 1901.)

A   Gm 3.71c. March 1908. Acknowledged under the title "The Song of South Ythsie" in Ob. 18, 31 March 1908.

B   Gm 1.95b. January 1906.

C Ob. 21. Greig acknowledged receiving this version in Ob. 19, 7 April 1908. He says there: "Last week I mentioned that a correspondent had favoured me with a copy of 'South Ythsie,' [see A] and now I am greatly pleased to hear from Miss Forsyth, Durie, Mintlaw, who communicates the very interesting information that the song was composed by her father, Mr William Forsyth, when he was at South Ythsie in 1851. Miss Forsyth points out, what we had observed, that several verses in 'Guise of Tough' (printed in [Ob. 4]) are borrowed from 'South Ythsie'; but honour to whom honour is due; and we hope on an early date to print the latter song from the authentic copy, which Miss Forsyth has kindly transcribed for us."

356 **SLEEPY TOON** For the location, see map. The farm was officially named Christ's Kirk, with Sleepytoon appearing as the title after 1870. Adam Mitchell, named in the song, was farmer from the 1840s to 1858. (Cen. E.B., Kennethmont, 1851; V.R. Aberdeenshire, 1855, 1859) "Another [ploughman song from John Ord besides 359 'Ye're Now on Bogieside' and 366 'Netherthird'] commenced:– [Text F]. 'Sleepy Town' is I think in the neighbourhood of Fyvie." (G, Ob. 102)

"In [Ob. 123] we gave an incomplete version of 'Sleepytoon;' and now we are able to give a complete copy [E] kindly forwarded by Mr J.W. Spence, Fyvie." (G, Ob. 127) "In [Ob. 123], we gave a bit of 'Sleepytoon,' and in [Ob. 127] we printed what, from its length, we took to be a complete version of the song. It would seem, however, that there is no saying when we have a complete copy of things that from their construction and style may run on to almost any length. My friend, the Rev. Mr Duncan, has kindly supplied a copy of 'Sleepytoon' which is well on to twice as long as the version we gave. Besides, as Mr Duncan points out, there are considerable differences in individual lines between the two versions. Under the circumstances we think it best to print Mr Duncan's copy entire. – [Text A.] Referring to the song Mr Duncan says:– 'It belongs to the Vale of Alford as the local allusions show. The song is still well known here to those familiar with such things, and I have three separate records of it. Some years ago I made somewhat full enquiries about the reputed author. The results are more trustworthy than is usual in such cases. I had always heard it attributed to a man popularly known as "Poet Clark," and at last hunted up his residence in the upper part of the parish of Keig. I found, however, that he had left the place, and had died in a son's house in Glasgow in January 1907. He was then between seventy and eighty years old. Recently I made a record of the song from an old man who had been a farm servant along with Clark, had learnt the song from himself, and had often heard him sing it, and also speak about the "making" of it. His full name was William Clark, and his earliest residence, as far as known to my informants, was in the parish of Alford. He was a farm servant, and latterly a general labourer. His old fellow servant spoke of him as "awfu' leernt." I tried to find out about any other compositions, but did not trace any. The popular name indicated their existence, and a woman who knew him spoke of him having many such, and even liking to teach them to her children. Clark had been a servant at Sleepy Toon, which is in the parish of Kennethmont. The time referred to must have been when he was quite young, as one of my versions which also came almost directly from himself goes back to 1854. The name of the farmer is "Adam Mitchell" in all my versions. It seems to have been the actual name, but the farm has changed hands several times since then.' We may say that the name, as given by Mr Spence, was the same, although we did not [in Ob. 127] print it in full. Mr Duncan adds that he has always found the song sung to a version of 'Jack Munro'." (G, Ob. 133)

A Dm 434c, Harper 42; Gw 56.71-8, Dw 1.107-11. "Dorian. Noted by Mrs Harper from Mr James High, Ferniebank, Monymusk. June, 1908. Mr High (Choirmaster Cluny Episcopal Church) heard this from William Tough. It was his *one* song; and in earlier days 'Willie's song' was heard on every occasion when he was present at any social gathering. He is now about seventy, living at Hill of Balrach, Monymusk; but 'he is not to be drawn to sing it' now. (Mrs Harper) Mrs Harper wrote the air on G, correcting the sharp where F occurs in eighth bar, and noting that 'the flat seventh is very prominent'. The omission of the sharp, however, brings out its character as Dorian. [B] might be written in the same way, being, however, without the distinctive note." (Dm) Duncan has deleted the words "an old farm servant at 'Sleepy Toon' itself" after "William Tough". Mrs Harper comments with reference to the length of the last note in the first line of music that "Mr High said there was great emphasis on the 'That'." (Harper 42) Dw has the following variants in words and consonants from the Gw text printed: 1.3 meal (meat), 2.4 slippery (sliddery), 4.1 to fee (fee), 5.1 me 'ill agree (I agree), 5.2 get (have), 5.3 bid (bids), 9.4 To (For to), 14.4 fae (frae), 15.1 we (he = we?), 16.1 was determined (were determined on't), 17.2 we (ye), 18.2 scoondrels (deevils), 24.1 And (But), 24.3-4 He bann'd and swore at us and ca'd us / Twa most cursed scampts (May the deevil get you to himsel' / For twa infernal scamps), 27.1 But the term (The term time), 28.1 Martimas (Martinmas).

B Dm 251b; Mackay 2.20-2, Dw 5.28-31. Duncan indicates at Dm 252 that Alexander Mackay sang this song to the same tune as "When first I was a little wee Boy". "Noted 13th March, 1907." (Dm 252) "Alexander Mackay. Sleepy Toon, he states, is in the parish of Kennethmont, not far from Auchline. The song, Mr Mackay adds, was made by William Clark, who lived not long ago (speaking of 1907) at Pond Cottage, Castle Forbes, and may be living there still. Mr Mackay had met him not more than two years ago. He lived earlier above Shannoch in the land of Culfork [to the west of Alford], in a small house not now existing. He was a farmservant, and was engaged at Sleepy Toon. Latterly he put broom on houses, and did other such jobs. He was an uncle of the man William Knowles, who is now a postboy at the hotel. Mr Mackay knew a brother of the Knowles mentioned in the song, who informed him that it was his brother that was meant. William Clark was known as 'Poet Clark', and had a lot of 'doggerel verses'. Mr Mackay has many a time heard the song from his boyhood; it was sung in farm kitchens. The above is all he ever heard sung, whether complete or not.

"Thursday, 23rd July, 1908. I have today been at Pond Cottage, Keig, and learnt that 'Poet Clark' died in Glasgow in the house of a son in January, 1907. He lived in one end of the cottage, Mrs Tough, with her husband, who was Keig and Whitehouse postman, occupying the other. (Mrs Tough's husband died about the same date, and she is now post master in Keig, going up towards Brindy.) Mrs Tough to some extent attended on William Clark, though not paid for it. She states that he had a lot of verses, which he would repeat; but many of them were rather 'profane'. He liked to teach them to the children, though he avoided doing it when she was present. Her mother, who, she said, 'was a serious woman,' then reproved him for his tendency, and it was amusing to hear them together. He would have been between seventy and eighty when he died; but 'he was not good to himself when he had money,' spending it on drink. He didn't like to ask, and he had fallen behind with his rent, with which circumstance Mrs Tough seemed to connect his leaving, though another person told me that he was in the habit of leaving for Glasgow in the winter season. Mrs Tough stated that he had been a farmservant, but latterly did labouring work, when he did work at all." (Dw)

C Gm 3.210a; Gw 50.100, 102, Ob. 123. "Part got from John Johnstone, New Deer, and part from Charles Walker, Brucklay." (Gw) Stanzas 7-8 are not in Gw and are taken from Ob. where Greig comments, "From Mr A. Milne, Maud, I have got the following version, part being contributed by Mr John Johnstone, New Deer, and part by Mr C. Walker, Brucklay. As it is still incomplete, we hope that readers who can supplement it will come to our rescue. The tune as sung by Mr Milne is what we have been in the way of calling 'Jack Munro.'" The tune in Gm was received from Alex Milne.

D Dw 3.112-6. "Charles Ewen, Street, Tough, (poorhouse), 20th April, 1910. He is eighty-one years old, and has lived in Monymusk, and afterwards in the Alford district. He learnt the song from the author, 'Poet Clark' himself, when he was 'about the house' with him at Cairnballoch, which was a few years before the death of MacConachie, the farmer there. (Say about – years ago [the period is left blank]). Clark sang the song himself to the tune of 'Jack Munro' to which Charles Ewen also sings it; and he had often heard Clark speak about making it, but never heard him say anything about the circumstances of its composition. Clark had lots of rhymes, but he doesn't know any others of them. Clark was 'awfu' leernt' and 'was a terrible billy to write letters about law'. But 'drink put him all wrong'; 'he was not a weel-livin' lad'. This version is not materially different from [A], except that there verses 10-27 are additional, and there are slight differences of order in the stanzas. Curiously enough verse 10 is one of the stanzas in that version said to have come from Charles Ewen. Mr Mackay's much shorter version [B] varies much more from both, and the last stanza has no corresponding verse in either." (Dw)

E Gw 54.14-8.

F Gw 46.112. Acknowledged in Ob. 102, 16 November 1909; see note to 359 "Ye're Now on Bogieside".

357 **THE SCRANKY BLACK FARMER** Cf. a version sung by William Milne in the archive of the School of Scottish Studies, SA 1952/52/A4. "The record which we have of the words of this song is quite possibly incomplete. The place-names in the fourth verse seem to have got a bit mixed up. This kind of thing is of quite common occurrence in traditional ditties with local allusions, when they wander out into the world. To the singer who may not know the original personnel and geography of the song one name is as good as another. He will even at times manufacture place-names that never were on any map. 'The Scranky Black Farmer' is superior to most songs of its class, some lines being unusually felicitous. There is distinct melody in –

Wi' him I engagèd a servant to be,
Which makes me lament I went far frae the sea.

The tune, of which I have some five records, is a very fine old Dorian – one of the best I know." (G, Ob. 89) The farmer is named as William Ironside at Gm 2.23d and as Daniel Skinner at Gm 1.80c. William Ironside farmed at Earlsfield till 1863 and Daniel Skinner from then until 1882. This information and details about life on the farm from the farmer's point of view are given in the posthumously published *Autobiography of Daniel Skinner. Farmer. Earlsfield* (Inverurie, 1929). Skinner was dark, as can be confirmed from a photograph in the possession of Mr Alexander Bruce, Aberdeen, and therefore fits the title. See map for the location of Earlsfield.

A Gm 2.23d; Gw 61.81-2. June 1906.

B Gm 1.80b; Gw 2.1-2a. November 1905. "Uncertain here and there." (Gm) At 3.2 "various countries" appears to have been altered from "Yarrows country" at the time of writing, and there are a number of revisions apparently made later: *title* "Scrankie" for "Skrankie", 3.3 "and" for "Keen", 4.3 "victuals" for "wages", 5.3 "wind" for the first "rain", 6.1 "time" for the first "day", 6.2 "go home" for "be going", 8.2 "Leathha'" for "Leathhall".

C Gm 1.80c. April 1906. Greig has attached to the words "Scranky black fairmer" the note "Skinner was his name".

D Gm 1.44a. 1905.

E Gm 2.22d. August 1906.

F Dw 1.140-2. At 10.2 Duncan has the note: "'Leith-ha''? or in preceding line 'all'?". "From her mother. I have not the tune from any other source, but one is given by Mr Greig (and a very striking one) in the *Rymour*

Club Miscellanea 1.23. Noted 17th June, 1908. Mr Greig's words are considerably shorter. Mr Alexander Mackay, Alford, states that this song was composed with reference to a man of the name of Ironside in Earlsfield, and that it was attributed to Poet Clark (see [note to 356 'Sleepy Toon' B]). But as this attribution to Clark seems to have been common with other songs in the district (for example 'Drumallachie') it must remain very doubtful." (Dw)

G   Gw 57.33-5. Acknowledged in Ob. 145, 20 September 1910.

358   **THE GREEDY GLED O' MAINS**   The main title is editorial.

Gw 1.56-7. John Milne published this song in 1901 (Milne, p. 9) and commented: "[This song] was popular in the first thirty years of the [nineteenth] century. 'The Mains' mentioned was Mains of Pitfour, as I learned from my mother, who knew its history." See map for the location of Mains of Pitfour.

359   **YE'RE NOW ON BOGIESIDE**

Gw 46.111. Cf. Ord, p. 281 "You're Now on Bogieside".The main title is editorial, on the model of Ord's title in his printed version which gives "you" not "ye" in the text. "Superintendent John Ord, Glasgow, who has been contributing a number of notes on some of the songs which have already appeared in our column for supplementary use, writes me as follows:– 'I think one more attempt might be made to recover a few more of the genuine ploughman's songs before the end of the series, and amongst others the following are a few of those most popular:– [Text. The others quoted are 366 "Netherthird" B and 356 "Sleepy Toon" F.]'" (G, Ob. 102, 16 November 1909)

360   **THE BARNS O' BENEUCHES**   "From tragedy [232 'The Fire of Frendraught'] we pass to comedy. Contrasts afford relief, and help towards a balanced judgment on life and its problems. We have here another specimen of the Ploughman Ditty – a rustic satire, which for smartness is distinctly above the average of its class. Our copy has been contributed by Mr J. Wight, Balthangie. Although we have no record of the tune we may safely take it that it is an adaptation of 'Johnnie Cope.'" (G, Ob. 142) The farm of Barnyards of Badenyouchers, Fordyce (see map), had Alexander Kemp as overseer in 1871 but not in 1881 (Cen. E.B., Fordyce, 1871, 1881). This song of his departure is therefore from the 1870s. The highland shepherd referred to may be Neil McDonald of Fortingall, Perthshire (Cen. E.B., Fordyce, 1871).

A   Gm 3.27c.

B   Gw 41.79-81. The reading "if you can" at 7.3 is taken from an uncatalogued set of songs from John Wight among Greig's papers. In Gw this wording has been replaced by "ane and a'", caught from the preceding line. Acknowledged in Ob. 57, 29 December 1908.

361   **MAINS O' ELRICK**   See map for the location of Little Elrick.

Misc. 51. "Noted 1905 from Mrs Gillespie. A fragment of a doggerel song made about 1855. The queen visited Haddo House that year, and the servants at Little Elrick were angry because they received no holiday, the grieve, a certain George Chessar, being on bad terms with his mistress, the farmer, so that the matter was not mentioned between them. The servants took revenge by working on Sabbath, while the people passed to church, a fact alluded to in this verse. The air is a curious compound: the first half is the second line of 'The Banks o' Claudy' [as recorded from George F. Duncan, Mrs Gillespie and myself], and the remainder ends poorly, but is probably intended to imitate Psalm Tune style." (D, Misc.)

362   **REID HOOSE**   The title is editorial.

Gw 49.35.

363   **THE BENTON CREW**   The four brothers Benton referred to in the note to the next song are William, Joseph, John and James, who farmed at Harthill in Whitehouse (indicated on the map), Cattie in Whitehouse, Mosside in Alford, and Airlie in Keig, all in the vale of Alford, from 1874 to 1890 (V.R., Aberdeenshire, 1873 to 1891).

Gm 3.178c; Gw 43.66. Acknowledged in Ob. 87, 10 August 1909. See note to 364 "Benton".

364   **BENTON**   "We have here another specimen of the Ploughman ditty – and an exceedingly good one. Our copy was got quite recently from a kind helper on Donside [Mrs Sim]." (G, Ob. 145, 20 September 1910) "[Mr James M. Taylor] contributes a note on 'Benton,' given a fortnight ago [in Ob. 145]. His direct acquaintance with the locale of the song enables him to make his note very full and informing. He has heard the song sung in his native district; and it is not very old. From Mr Robb, New Deer, I once got a fragment of a song 'The Benton Crew,' and I can now see that it refers to the same man, or men, there being four brothers of the name, all with the same kind of reputation among farm-servants." (G, Ob. 147) "In Aberdeenshire Bantam becomes 'Banton' hence Banton and Banton- cock – a spirited barnyard fowl of small size, much given to fighting." John Ord (Ord, p. 239)

Gw 57.45-9.

365 **FRAE THE MARTIMAS TERM**

Gw 27.17. In Gw this fragment is written immediately after 353 "Ellon Fair" B (which is said in Ob. 26 to be by John Ker) and is headed: "A couplet from another song by John Carr." (Gw) The title is editorial.

366 **NETHERTHIRD** This fragment and the following one may belong to the same song, but, in the absence of overlapping material, it is not possible to be certain of this.

A Gm 3.136a.
B Gw 46.112. Acknowledged in Ob. 102, 16 November 1909; see note to 359 "Ye're Now on Bogieside".

367 **NETHERHA'** See note to 366 "Netherthird".

Gm 1.165b, Argo 3.13-5. April 1906. (Gm) In Gm, "Auchterless" is given in brackets after the title. In Argo, the title is "Netherthird, Auchterless", which gives some support to the idea suggested above that this fragment belongs to the same song as the preceding one, and "Drumdelgie" also appears in brackets, probably as an indication of the tune.

368 **THIS IS HALLOWEVEN** Cf. *Rymour Club Miscellanea*, 1.177.

Gm 2.4b. July 1906. "'Clout the Cauldron'. Commonly sung before the Term by those leaving their places." (Gm)

369 **THE GLASS MARKET** Markethill to the north of Haugh of Glass (see map) was "for centuries the site of Glass market" (James Godsman, *Glass, Aberdeenshire, The Story of a Parish*, Aberdeen, 1970, p. 198 and end map).

Gm 1.95c. January 1906. "Noted in C in Rev. George Birnie's copy." (Gm)

370 **BRANNAN FAIR O' BANFF**

Dm 50b. "Heard it from earliest recollections. Noted 1905. The song described those that used to appear at the fair, but then all gone, with other sights of the day. Mrs Gillespie says the time referred to was that of her grandfather, from whom she heard of 'Cocker'. She remembers one other verse:–

> An' for to carry on my sang,
> There was lyin' at Castle Panton there
> Geordie Raeburn an' Willie Beer,
> But noo I see they're wantin there.

The tune is probably older." (Dm) Duncan has deleted "fair" before "day" and attached the note "A place in Banff so called" to the words "Castle Panton".

371 **THERE WAS A FAIR**

Misc. 131. "Noted by Mrs Harper from same source as last [i.e. 'Through the moss and through the muir' from Mrs Greig and Miss Elizabeth Greig], August 1907. Cf. [611 'Hey the Bonnie Breistknots']." (D, Misc.)

372 **JOHN BRUCE O' THE FORNET** Cf. *Kerr's "Cornkisters" (Bothy Ballads)* (James S. Kerr, Glasgow, 1950), pp. 12-3 "Auld Jock Bruce o' the Fornet". "I have three copies of this song, and they differ but slightly from each other. The inference from this is that the song must be comparatively recent – a conclusion which certain known circumstances confirm. Two of the copies give the right name of the place where the redoubtable John Bruce lived; while the third [D] has given it a twist into 'Corner,' a reading which we are prepared to adopt [in the text printed in Ob.] for reasons that will occur to sensible people. The ditty is superior to most productions of its kind, and we can understand the writer having the reputation among his fellows of being 'a bit of a poet.' Men who have got the rhyming gift are found in all classes of the community; but while your baker or postman writes verse as innocuous as it is transcendental on 'Spring' or 'The Flower of Ugieside,' the rhyming ploughman 'makes up' a stroud on 'Mains o' Beyont,' in which he castigates the farmer and flicks his fellow-servants in lines that make no pretence to literary finish but speak straight, and plain, and strong. The former effusions may rejoice for a week in print in the Poets' Corner, but are straightway forgotten by all except their authors. The ploughman ditty, so far from being printed, may not even be written down; but it is picked up by ear by other ploughman lads, travelling ever outward until some fifty years after it may be picked up anywhere over the north-east of Scotland, to be printed at length, with annotation, in a special column, and ultimately mayhap to find a place in a printed volume of native minstrelsy. This may appear strange, but it is instructive. It shows, for one thing, that a note of sincerity and conviction may give vogue and life to a very humble composition, while no amount of mere literary pretension will save a piece that is lacking in these qualities." (G, Ob. 133) John Bruce farmed South Fornet in the parish of Skene from 1870 to 1885 (V.R., Aberdeenshire, 1869 to 1871). See map for location.

A Gm 4.160b.
B Gw 45.77-80. "From one of my cousins, ten years ago. He has the tune also." A.S. (Gw) Acknowledged in Ob. 101, 16 November 1909.

C   Dw 3.103-5. "Written for Mrs Lyall by a girl in the Skene district, about June, 1911. The writing is not very accurate, and some liberty may safely be used in transcription. Obvious errors have been corrected. *Later note*. A week or two later (3rd March, 1911) Mrs Lyall furnished the following additional details. The song was written for her by a girl Barbara Rae, whose father was foreman at Fornet about twelve years ago: she lives in Lyne of Skene. Mrs Lyall communicated with the man referred to in the song as foreman, and named Leslie, who has now a farm about a mile from Lyne of Skene; and his information as to the authorship was that "they all had a hand at the making up of it. But it was William Ligertwood who was the moving spirit, and it was said that he had a good education." (Dw) Mrs Lyall adds in a letter to Duncan (998/16/134):– "We looked the old ledger [Mr Lyall being a shoemaker (Duncan's note)], and Mr Lyall finds Ligertwood was at the Fornet in the summer of 1871. His father was a general merchant in the Methlick district. Ligertwood is now dead, but I cannot tell you when." "Afterwards she said that she noticed it was sung to 'Johnnie Cope'. 6.2 'suit': 'sit'?" (Dw)

D   Gw 44.80-4. Stanzas 2 and 4 are given separately at the end, the first being marked "Second verse". It replaces an incomplete version of stanza 2 which lacked line 2. "Miss Bell Robertson, New Pitsligo, sends me [a copy of] 'John Bruce' (kindly contributed by a lady friend)." (G, Ob. 26, 26 May 1908) "I got a copy of this one for Mr Greig. A girl got it for me so I know nothing beyond what I told him at the time." (Robertson, *Song Notes*, 1.36)

E   Gw 3.63-6. "E. Forsyth per George Bruce-Thomson." (Gw) At 6.4 an alteration to "Bruce" from "Birnie" in the same hand appears to be a correction of a miscopy.

F   Misc. 150; Dw 1.168-9. "Air – 'Johnnie Cope'. Noted from R. Reid, shoemaker, Kemney, 30th July, 1908. Heard by him in his shop about ten years ago. Only first strain of air used." (D, Misc.)

373   **BRUNTIE'S**   In Ob. 178, Greig gives text B with the title "Auld Luckie" and with "Bruntie's" at 1.2 indicated only by "B —'s" and adds the following remarks. "Another specimen of the Ploughman ditty – and an extra good one. As we have already claimed, these ditties are the most individual and characteristic productions that the modern folk-muse can show. They are always marked by sincerity, and utterance at once direct and forcible. The farm-servant knows his own mind, and speaks it with freedom and force and absolute candour. He has neither affectation nor reticence, and herein lies his strength. The foreman in our song makes a good appearance. His sallies illustrate the wit and humour of the farmyard – frequently more ready and clever than people would believe who are not familiar with the farm-servant class. Our copy of the song [B] was got from Mr A. Fowlie, New Deer. It bore the name of the farm where Auld Luckie lived and reigned, but we have judged it best to keep in the background anything that might lead to identification, although we know nothing of the place or characters." The farm of Bruntyards Gamrie, Banffshire (see map), was farmed by Mrs Annabella Duff (Auld Luckie) the widow of the former farmer, James Duff, from 1883 to 1893 (V.R., Aberdeenshire, 1881 to 1894). The song was reputedly written by a local poet called Shaw (see note to 401 "Pitgair").

A   Gm 3.51b.

B   Gw 13.80-3. January 1908. At 3.3 the letter "o" is written above the "a" of "na" in both cases.

374   **TOCHINEAL**   Cf. Ord, p. 353. See map for the location of the farm. The heading is given as "Tochineal. (Cruickshank?)".

Gw 46.113.

375   **MONYMUSK**   Cf. Ord, p. 68, "Rural Courtship". The title is editorial. The farm is Lethenty in the parish of Tullynessle and Forbes (see map). The song was probably composed before 1876 when the farmer Robert Wilson died and left the farm to his daughter. The full song relates the attempts by a farm servant to court his sweetheart by entering her bedchamber at night.

A   Gm 4.133b.

B   Gw 47.65. This was published among Annie Shirer's contributions to the *Rymour Club Miscellanea* at 2.55 as a separate item with the title "The Old Maid's Lament". There are the following verbal variations: 1.3 The servant lassie aye gets the lads (That servant lassies a' get lads), 1.4 Fin (And).

376   **BETWEEN STANEHIVE AND LAURENCEKIRK**   "Poor chap – I'm sure he has our sympathy. I have got two or three versions of the words. In one copy [A] St Ives is given for Stanehive, which renders the geography pretty loose. The tune which I have got is a variant of 'Erin's lovely home.'" (G, Ob. 49)

A   Gm 1.78c. "November 1905. 'Erin's Lovely Home' [from Mrs Clark]. See ['Bredalbane' from the Rev. John Calder]." (Gm)

B   Gw 55.58-60. "From Mr Andrew Dunbar." A.S. (Gw) See note to E.

C   Gw 9.84-6, 43.61-3. A question mark queries the sense of the latter part of this line at Gw 9.85. The copy in Gw 43 has the following verbal variations: 1.1 did fee (fe'et), 1.2 to work (that), 1.3 His foremost horses for to work (To work his foremost horses), 3.3 master (mother), 6.4 aye (a').

D   Gw 18.100-2.

E   Gw 55.60. Following B is the note "Have heard it begin [Text E]." A.S.

377 **THE BOTHY LADS O' FORFAR** Cf. Norman Buchan and Peter Hall, *The Scottish Folksinger* (London and Glasgow, 1973), pp. 24-5 "Tattie Jock".

A Ob. 151. "This genuine specimen of the Bothy Ballad has been forwarded, along with some other pieces, by my friend Mr James M. Taylor, Aberdeen, who got them from an old farm-servant acquaintance. As Mr Taylor points out, the reference to Botany Bay helps to fix the age of the song." (G, Ob. 151, 8 November 1910)

B Ob. 36. "Mr M'Kenzie mentions a Fife song which he would like to get a copy of. It deals with the time when men were sent to Botany Bay, and the following are the opening verses:– [Text]." (G, Ob. 36, 4 August 1908)

378 **THE GUISE O' TOUGH** Cf., for tune, Norman Buchan and Peter Hall, *The Scottish Folksinger* (London and Glasgow, 1973), pp. 120-1. "We have room for only one other specimen of the ploughman song; but it is one of the best of its class, and when sung never fails to 'take'." (G, Ob. 4) The song refers to the farm of Guise in the parish of Tough (see map).

A Gm 1.75b; Gw 1.113-5. October 1905. (Gm) 5.4 "ging": MS "gig", 7.4 "gard": MS "gad". At 8.2 "throw" is an alteration of "through" in Gw.

B Gm 4.183a. "Also to [384] 'Drumdelgie' and 'Ellon Fair'." (Gm)

C Gw 58.45-8, Argo 2a.9-13. The following readings are from Argo; the Gw readings are shown in brackets: 13.2 Jamieson's (Jamieson is), 17.3 And any (And if any). Acknowledged in Ob. 154, 22 November 1910.

379 **GEORDIE WILLIAMSON**

Gw 48.79-81. "Have heard several long versions of this song." A.S. (Gw) After the title there is the note: "(cf. 'Guise o' Tough')". At 9.4 a carat mark is inserted before "devil".

380 **I LEFT INVERQUHOMERY** See map for the location of Inverquhomery and Auchmaliddie.

Gw 10.59. August 1907.

381 **NEWHILLS** The main title is editorial. In Ob. 92 Greig gives A with the title "Newmill", the first line as "It was to Newmill, ayont the hills," and the name of the farmer indicated only by "Mr B.", and comments, "I may say that I altered the first line a little for a good purpose." The place he calls Newmill is actually Newhills near Sclattie Mill in the parish of Newhills, now on the outskirts of Aberdeen City (see map). Greig adds the following comments. "My copy of this song – words and tune, I also owe to Mr A. Robb, New Deer. We have here an illustration of the caustic vein which often runs through ploughman ditties. It is the farm-servants' way of stigmatising places where they consider themselves to have been ill used. We may mention that the place here referred to is not in this part of the country. The tune is in the Dorian mode, the rhythm suggesting some kind of affinity with an old strathspey." (G, Ob. 92) The song is no later than 1889 for Max Gregor gives a version of the song as from the singer "Blin' Bob" [Duncan M'Kinley] who died in that year. (Max Gregor, *Life of "Blin' Bob"*, Aberdeen, 1889)

A Gm 1.91b; Gw 5.6-9. May 1906.

B Gm 3.17b. September 1907.

C Dm 94c. "Dorian. From James Davidson, farmservant, Burnside, Carnousie, in seventies. Noted from Mrs Gillespie and George F. Duncan, 1905. A farm-servant song. This is not the first verse, which is not remembered." (Dm)

D Gw 46.37-40. There is no indication of source, but possibly this text should be assigned to Alexander Robb on the grounds of its similarity to A, of which it may be a second copy.

382 **STRALOCH**

Gw 55.23.

383 **ON THE 16th O' OCTOBER**

a) Ob. 153, b) Gw 56.108. "The Rev. Dr Forrest, Lonmay, sends me a copy of some lines that were found written on the walls of the men's chaumer at Crichnalade in the parish of Fyvie, more than fifty years ago. As a specimen of rustic verse they are well worth preserving." (G, Ob. 153) "Rev. Dr. Forrest. Found in chaumer at Crichnalade, Fyvie." (Gw)

384 **DRUMDELGIE** Cf. Ord, pp. 209-11. "One of the best known songs in the north-east is 'Drumdelgie.' Versions of it vary so much that it is not easy getting a satisfactory reading of the song; but the following may be taken as a fair average version. – [Composite text of fourteen stanzas following the sequence of A.] The air to which 'Drumdelgie' is sung does duty for several other ditties, e.g. [452] 'The Miller o' Straloch,' and is about the best known folk-tune which we have in the north. Nor is it confined to Scotland. Indeed its distribution is the widest of all the folk-tunes I have yet tried to trace. It is well known in England, and also in Ireland; and I find it in a Welsh collection of old airs. And as if this wasn't enough, I find it in the *National Choir* [2.4] claimed by an amateur fiddler as his own original composition!" (G, Ob. 4) The large farm of three hundred acres was created at

Drumdelgie in 1838 (Gordon Castle, Rental and Factors MS., 1815 to 1862, GD 44, SEC 53). It was farmed from then till 1860 by William Grant and thereafter by his son William, when it was enlarged to six hundred acres (V.R., Aberdeenshire, 1860) and the male workforce increased from eight to sixteen, which is beyond that indicated in any version of the song (Cen. E.B., Aberdeenshire, 1851, 1861). A George Bird appears in versions collected by James Carpenter in the 1930s (Carpenter). Bird was seventeen in 1851 (Cen E.B., Cairnie, 1851) and would have been employed from 1846 at the earliest. Ian Carter in *Farmlife in Northeast Scotland, 1840-1914* (Edinburgh, 1979), p. 44, notes in regard to Drumdelgie, that "after 1850 plough oxen became much less common on large farms". See map for the location of the farm.

A   Gm 1.163d; Gw 4.104-7. April 1906. (Gm) At 6.3 "through" is deleted before "some". At 11.3 a wavy line over the "o" of "not" apparently indicates a pronunciation of "o" as in "note".

B   Gm 1.48a; Gw 3.56-8. "1904. Gavin Greig junior caught from J. Sinclair, Alehousehill. Cf. Petrie No. 106. Cf. 'The Felons for our land' in *Four Irish Songs*. O'Neill No. 589 'Boys from Mullingar'. *Old Welsh Airs* [i.e. Nicholas Bennett, *Alawon fy ngwlad. The Lays of my Land* (Newtown, 1896)], 2.116. When with second strain cf. 'John Grumlie'." (Gm) The word "caught" replaces deleted "got".

C   Dm 70c; Walker 32, Dw 3.18. "Heard in farm service. Noted September 1906. Compare [452 'The Miller o' Straloch' C]. The tune occurs in Petrie's *Irish Airs*, essentially the same, without name, No. 106. 'Banchory's Lands' [from Isaac Troup] is another version of this air; also [317 'The Wee Toon Clerk' E]; 'The Lass o' Everton' [from Mrs Lyall]." (Dm)

D   Gm 4.183a; Gw 43.98-9. "Mr J. Angus, Peterhead, sends me some verses of a song which was given in [Ob. 4] under the title of 'Drumdelgie,' by which name it is known in the north. Mr Angus's version localises the ditty as 'Glenbervie.' This is interesting." (G, Ob. 93, 21 September 1909)

E   Gm 2.98b. October 1906.

F   Gm 2.73d. August 1906.

G   Gm 1.48b. 1905.

H   Gm 1.48c. 1905.

I   Gm 1.49d. January 1906.

J   Gm 1.193c. "Cf. No. Petrie 106." (Gm) This is No. 62 of the set of tunes received from Riddell. It is among the airs Riddell heard played by "Auld Jeck" [John Ritchie]; see note to 471 "Wi' the Apron On" D. Cf. George Riddell, "Five Old Airs, with Notes", *Rymour Club Miscellanea*, 2.188-92.

K   Gm 2.105a. "November 1906. Uncertain." (Gm)

L   Gm 1.3b. The title "Drumdelgie" has an attached note: "Near Huntly". "Ploughman lilt. Not same as Buchan version – q.v. p. –." (Gm) Greig has left his intended page reference blank.

M   Gm 1.6c. "1905. See [L]. Cf. [677 'Mossie and his Meer' C]." (Gm)

N   Gm 2.103a. "Communicated by David Thomson per Scott Skinner. November 1906." (Gm) Greig has attached to the last line, Violet Davidson's version, the comment: "Noted in C major, but with notes – 'Flat third' and 'Try C minor'."

O   Gw 13.75-9. January 1908. (Gw) "Mr A. Fowlie, Ironside, has kindly handed me a budget of songs to copy – mostly as sung by his neighbour Mr Glennie. One of these, 'Drumdelgie' contains one or two verses which I have never seen before, and which I am very glad to get." (G, Ob. 10, 4 February 1908)

P   Gw 22.53-6.

Q   Gw 39.21-4. Acknowledged in Ob. 82, 6 July 1909.

R   Gw 61.74-6.

S   Gw 1.53. At 1.2 "crack" is written "cracks" with "s" deleted.

T   Argo-Duncan 19, Dw 3.150. "From the same schoolboy as the preceding [i.e. from Duncan Shearer]. Compare the underlined readings with a similar fragment, containing the same two verses [C]. The second reading may be the correct one; but the first is a very amusing corruption for: 'There's a *fairmie* up in Cairnie, *It's* kent both far and wide, *To be the* high Drumdelgie,' etc." (Dw) In Argo-Duncan, at 1.4 "Deveron side" replaces deleted "Ythan side".

U   Gw 3.92.

385   **THERE'S A SET O' FARMERS HERE ABOUT**   The title is editorial.

Gw 57.102. "From mother." (Gw) "This song and the following [392 'Potterton' B] were popular in mother's girlhood and were a protest of servants against the treatment they got." (Robertson, *Song Notes*, 2.13) Acknowledged in Ob. 161, 10 January 1911.

386   **SWAGGERS**   Cf. the version sung by John Strachan in the archive of the School of Scottish Studies, SA 1952/25/ B21. "'Swaggers' is a satirical song, as may be gathered from the opening verses. – [Text B, sts. 1-2.] The song was sung to me by Mr A. Murison, Wellhowe, to the tune which we have already referred to as 'The Parks of Keltie.'" (G, Ob. 4) "In an early article [Ob.4] we gave a specimen verse or two of 'Swaggers,' and we now print the song in full. It is very popular in this part of the country. We have seen that the ploughman ditty is always more or less of a satire. 'Swaggers' is caustic to a degree. One must remember, however, that in these diatribes we hear only one side of the question. Were farmers to 'make up' songs about their servants we should doubtless get pictures of the Ploughman Laddie somewhat different to those which folk-song provides – contributed as these

latter almost always are by the laddies themselves. 'Swaggers' is sung to a variant of 'The Briar Bush,' one of the commonest tunes which we have." (G, Ob. 138) James Hay, nicknamed "Swaggers", was the farmer at Newmill in the parish of Auchterless, and at Nethermill, the location of the next song (Cen E.B., Auchterless, Tarves, 1851 to 1871). See map for the locations of Newmill and Nethermill.

A   Gm 3.4a; Gw 19.46-51, Argo 23.12-6. The following readings are taken from Argo; the Gw readings are shown in brackets: 3.3 my (the), 11.2 pad (haud), 12.2 in (gin). September 1907. (Gm)

B   Gm 2.87b; Gw 7.38-42. August 1906. There are several alterations to st.1: l.1 "through" for "thro'", l.2 "gaun" for "gyaun", and l. 3 "lauch, lauchin'" for "lauch-lauchin'". At 3.3 and 10.3 alternative readings are given: "ilka country show" for "a' the country shows" and "for we've got oor freedom noo" for "for we're oot o' the tyrant's clutch".

C   Gm 1.144c, Gw 3.92. March 1906. "Cf. 'Bonnie Briar Bush'." (Gm) In Gw the variant "Sae stately and sae slow" from Arthur Barron is noted opposite 1.2

D   Gw 35.7-10. Acknowledged in Ob. 71, 13 April 1909.

E   Gw 41.84-8. The following readings are taken from an uncatalogued set of songs from John Wight among Greig's papers; the Gw readings are shown in brackets: 9.4 cairts (cairt), 17.1 raips (neeps), 17.3 Say (Says). Acknowledged in Ob. 57, 29 December 1908.

F   Dw 1.169-70. "This is incomplete, of course. It is from a manuscript of Mrs Beaton, Turriff, which she had received from a Miss Margaret Porterfield, Turriff, about ninety years old, who had at one time been a servant. Received in summer of 1908." (Dw)

G   Gw 7.37v-41v. "From *People's Journal* correspondent 21 November 1908." (Gw)

H   Misc. 104. "Air – 'The Brier Bush'. William Duncan (1906): remembers it as a farm-servant song, much sung in his boyhood, about fifty years ago, in Buchan. 'Swaggers' was the nickname of an Auchterless farmer. Cf. partial uses of this air in ['Young Johnny Doyle' from Mrs Gillespie and 'The Banks o' Ugie' from Robert Alexander]." (D, Misc.)

I   Gw 61.73-4.

387   **NETHERMILL**   "This song is claimed by our octogenarian friend, Mr William Forsyth, Mintlaw, who also composed [355] 'South Ythsie'. Swaggers has another ditty all to himself [386 'Swaggers']." (G, Ob. 179) James Hay farmed at Nethermill in the parish of Tarves up to 1878 (V.R. Aberdeenshire, 1878, 1879), although his sister, Jannet, was resident (Cen E.B., Tarves, 1871). See also note to the previous song.

Gw 21.73-7. Acknowledged in Ob. 31, 30 June 1908, among pieces sent by Miss Forsyth that had been composed by her father. "By William Forsyth, Durie, Mintlaw, circa 85." (Gw) At 13.3 "tee" replaces deleted "deen".

388   **I'VE SAIR'D WI' MEN**

Gw 1.65-6. In Milne, p. 10, John Milne mentions that these stanzas came "after an introduction". At 3.1-2 Milne has: "At Upper an' at Lower Mill, at Raxton, an' St Eithan".

389   **CAMELOUN**   Cf. the version sung by William Mathieson in the archive of the School of Scottish Studies, SA 1952/18/A4. See map for the location of the farm. "'Cameloun' is well known. It is a characteristic specimen of the ploughman song, and contains some vigorous stanzas. Mr J.W. Spence, Fyvie, gives the author's name as R. Cooper. The air, which I first noted from Mr Spence's singing, is in what we call the Dorian or Ray mode, ending on the second note of the ordinary scale. Tunes of this kind are very old and produce a striking effect on the modern ear." (G, Ob. 16) "The tune, which we have got associated with another song [349 'The Praise o' Huntly'], is a Dorian, with some of its intervals softened by the introduction of passing notes. The last line of the melody lends itself to bucolic intonation and inflection more perfectly than any other succession of notes which we have ever come across in folk-tune." (G, *Folk-Song in Buchan*, p. 74) The tune that Greig published in *Folk-Song in Buchan* is not identical with any of the ones given here but the last line to which he refers is the same as that of A.

A   Gm 1.51a; a) Gw 3.39-40, b) Gw 16.22-5. "By R. Cooper." (Gw 16) "July 1905. 'Johnnie Cope'. Cf. 'Jack Munro'." (Gm)

B   Gm 1.51c. 1905.

C   Gm 1.51d. April 1906.

D   Gm 3.161b.

E   Gw 3.38v-40v. At "ken" in 4.1 there is a note: "'clean' (Dr. Nicol, Alford)"; cf. version F.

F   Gw 3.39v. At 1.2 and 1.4 alternative spellings are given: meat (mate), and Eat (ate).

390   **JAMIE BROON**   James Brown and his son, of the same name, farmed at Hilton of Culsh in the parish of New Deer (see map) from the 1850s to the 1890s.

Gm 1.104c. "December 1905. Words of *quite* recent origin. Hilton of Culsh." (Gm)

391 **THE WEARY FAIRMERS**   Cf. Ford, pp. 202-4. The title is editorial.

A   Gm 2.140b; Gw 10.86-8. "September 1907. [677 'Mossie and his Meer' C]." (Gm)   September 1902. (Gw) "= 'The Weary Farmers', Ford's *Vagabond Songs and Ballads*, p. 202." (Gw)

B   1.40b.

392 **POTTERTON**   See map for location.

A   Gw 47.64. "Was one of my father's songs, altho this verse or two was all I could remember." A.S. (Gw) These stanzas were published among Annie Shirer's contributions to the *Rymour Club Miscellanea*, stanza 1 under the title "Hard Driving" at 2.109, and stanzas 2-3 under the title "In Derision of Masters" at 2.110. There are the following verbal variations: 1.2 There was (There's), 1.3 It was (But it's), and (or), 1.4 And – Come, lads, yoke. (Or else "Yoke! yoke!"), 3.4 yer (a). In Gw the stanzas run continuously but are without stanza numbering or title.

B   Gw 57.103. Acknowledged in Ob. 161, 10 January 1911. Greig refers to it there as "characteristic and happy". See also note to 385 "There's a Set o' Farmers Here About".

393 **COME A' YE BUCHAN LADDIES**

Gw 3.91. "Dr. Mitchell – remembers hearing it sung about his first Aikey Fair. Also recalls the fact that there was a song composed about 'The Bloomer Ball' at Artamford by one Reid. – Thinks Laing late of Fadliedykes might remember – as being one of the company. March 1906." (Gw)

394 **THERE'S NAE LUCK AT TULLO'S TOON**

Misc. 97. "Fragment from William Duncan; sung in markets from broadsheet in his boyhood." (D, Misc.)

395 **THE GOODMAN'S SONG**   A comparable song beginning "Baulky lands mak's girsy corn" is put in context by an introductory note in "The Aucht-Owsen Plough", *Rymour Club Miscellanea*, 3.186-7: "The 'gaadster' (goadman) and the ploughman whistled to encourage the team, and the following are the words of a favourite tune."

Gw 11.100. December 1907.

396 **MAINS O' BOYNDIE**   See map for location.

Gw 1.51-2. At 3.2 "their" was later altered to "there"; Milne, p. 7, has "here" in this line and "the foreman" at 2.4. John Milne in introducing this song version in 1901 in Milne, *Buchan Folk Songs*, comments (p.7): "Mill of Boyndie, Banff, was, in the beginning of the nineteenth century, one of the largest farms in the North-East, and was known and famed as a go-ahead place. Although not in Buchan nor Aberdeenshire, it was so near that Buchan lads generally formed part of its staff of hands, as young men of energetic disposition were always anxious and eager to put in a period of service at so famous a place. What would farm servants now think of the system which then prevailed, as handed down to us in a song, which is pretty well authenticated? My grandfather was one of the lads who served on the farm."

397 **MAINS O' CULSH**   See map for location.

Gm 2.89b; Gw 7.43-5. August 1906. (Gm, Gw)

398 **LAMACHREE AND MEGRUM**   "Sometimes a ploughman song deals with a series of places at which the singer is understood to have served. 'Lamachree and Megrum' may be given as an example. – [Text C, sts. 1-6.] This song is given, along with many other specimens of local ministrelsy, in Mr John Milne's *Buchan Folk-Songs*, a most interesting and suggestive booklet. I have heard a song, [397] 'Mains o' Culsh' with the same enigmatical refrain and sung to the same tune. The tune is in the old Dorian mode, and Mr Riddell of Rosehearty points out to me its affinity with one of the measures of the old Strathspey 'Johnnie Jigammy'."(G, Ob. 4)   "The air is a Dorian, with a tendency to mix the modes." (G, *Folk-Song in Buchan*, p. 71)

A   Gm 1.40a. Greig gives references to 677 "Mossie and his Meer" C (from George Riddell) and "Johnnie Jiggenny" from George Riddell.

B   Dm 258a. "Often heard, but not a song of his own. Noted 13th March, 1907. The refrains are interesting as suggesting significance rather than manufactured words, as usual; and the second nearly coincides with refrain ['Auld grey Megrum'] in *Rymour Club Miscellanea* 1.22 'Lamachree and Megrum' [a composite text contributed by Greig, with a tune nearly identical with A]. The next verse is:

> I speir'd at her, fat did she mean,
> *Mornin' an' aiberlin;*
> She said her bakin case was deen,
> *Mallachree's Maigrim.*

The rest is stated to be not presentable. The tune is the same as the 'Lamachree and Maigrim', and is the same song." (Dm)

C   Gw 1.54-6. John Milne published the first six stanzas in 1901 in Milne, pp. 8-9; the text there has "boun's" (= bounds), not "loons", at 6.2. See map for the location of Auchtydure.

D   Gw 13.16-7. Acknowledged in Ob. 8, 21 January 1908.

E   Ob. 6, 7 January 1908.

399   **MARAFRAY**   The location is near Montrose.

Gw 11.77-8.

400   **SOWENS FOR SAP**   "The words and tune of the above song were got from Mr A. Robb, New Deer. The verses are distinctly vigorous. The 'owrecome' –

> Sowens for sap at oor New Tap
> Ye'll find it winna do –

seems to mean that at this particular place nothing will pass muster which is not up to the proper mark. The tune is that of 'The Parks o' Keltie,' an air which is in extensive use among traditional singers." (G, Ob. 92)

Gm 1.166a; Gw 5.55-7. "May 1906. 'Keltie'." (Gm)

401   **PITGAIR**   "This is [a] Banffshire song, and of comparatively recent date. Pitgair is a farm in the parish of Gamrie [see map], and the characters referred to – the chief ones at least, can be identified. The song, unsurpassed among local pastorals for simplicity and natural truth, is said to have been written by a man named Shaw, who was long beadle at Alvah and had considerable local reputation as a rhymer and as a character. The air to which it is sung is a very common one, and belongs to a type of melody with a characteristic cadence in the AEolian mode that seems to have got naturalised in the North." (G, Ob. 51) "We do not as a rule set much store by traditions as to authorship. When they merely give us the name of a man otherwise unknown, even should the information be true, we have got *vox et praeterea nihil*. But Shaw is credited with other local songs, such as [316] 'Mrs Greig of Sandlaw' and 'Lucky Duff' [373 'Bruntie's']. The air does duty for several other songs and ballads, and belongs to a type very common in this part of the country. We consider it one of the most beautiful of our traditional melodies, the cadences being particularly fine. In general outline it bears some resemblance to 'My love's in Germany.'" (G, *Folk-Song in Buchan*, p. 75) "It seems that [Shaw] published a booklet of verse. Mr Ord says he once had a copy, but gave it away, and never got it back. He remembers some of the songs that were in it, and has heard Shaw himself sing some of them; but never 'O Charlie, O Charlie,' adding, however, that he never heard anyone dispute Shaw's claim to it, and calling attention to the fact that Shaw's own name occurs in the song." (G, Ob. 102) The "old Andrew Kindness" mentioned in the song is likely to be the man of this name who was sixty-six in 1881. Isabella Gray, also mentioned, was thirty-four in the same year. (Cen E.B., Gamrie, 1881) Greig notes at Argo 3.13 that "Spence senior [i.e. Thomas Spence] knew Shaw etc. Colliehill and A. Kindness".

A   Gm 2.65a; Gw 7.46-8. "August 1906. Learned at Northfield of Gamrie, 1869." (Gm)

B   Gm 1.145a; Gw 4.14-5. "March 1906. See Christie 1.80 second strain, and 1.276." (Gm) Greig also gives cross references to the tunes of "Lord Thomas of Winesberrie" in the Appendix of George R. Kinloch's *Ancient Scottish Ballads* (London, 1827), and "Lord Aboyne" in R.A. Smith's *The Scottish Minstrel* (Glasgow and Edinburgh, 1820-4), 4.6-7, and gives an internal reference to Gm 1.129 where the following deleted verse occurs at the foot of the page:

> Noo Annie Scott ye'll pit on the muckle pot,
> And ye'll mak' them porridge o' plenty
> Three hungry herbs and they're comin' frae Pitgair,
> And they're used wi' poverty and scanty.

C   Gm 1.145b, Argo 10.19-20. April 1906. (Gm)

D   Dm 7a; Gillespie 618. At Dm 28, Duncan lists "Pitgair" among the songs Mrs Gillespie sang to the "Binorie" tune given, and adds: "Noted 1906. Heard at Redburn, Byth. [Text, st. 1 without 'ye' in l. 2 and with 'owre' not 'to' in l. 3.] It is a local Buchan song. Cf. *Folk-Song in Buchan*, pp. 74-5 (words same)." (Dm 28)

E   Gm 1.189b. "For the above air we have evidently the term of 'My love's in Germany'." (Gm) This is No. 48 of the set of tunes received from Riddell.

F   Dm 346b. "AEolian. Noted by Mrs Harper from her mother. August 1907. Farther words remembered:– 'You, Missie Pope, ye'll sit in the parlour neuk,/ And keep a' the men fae the smokin'.' See [D]. This is nearest the other version of air sung to 'The Rantin' Laddie' [from Mrs Gillespie]." (Dm)

G   Gw 1.50. This version was published in Milne, p. 7; the Milne text has "leader" not "forman" at 3.1.

402   **LIKEWISE WE HAE A HOOSEMAID**   The title is editorial.

Gw 38.73. At 2.2 "ee" is written above the "oo" of "toothless".

403 **OOR FAIRM TOON** Cf. *Tocher* 5 (No. 36-7), 423-4. "This piece of lively and humorous verse was communicated by Mr Jaffray, Lonmay. The author, Mr Laird, hails from the Memsie quarter. The song is evidently modelled on the lines of 'Oor Kailyard,' and intended to be sung to the same tune, which, it may be pointed out, is just a variant of 'The Parks o' Keltie' already referred to [cf. note to 400 'Sowens for Sap']." (G, Ob. 92)

A   Gw 10.60-2. August 1907. "Composed by Laird, Memsie." (Gw)
B   Gm 1.105c. "May 1906. Tune 'There grows a bonnie brier bush'." (Gm)

404 **THE LOTHIAN HAIRST** Cf. *Tocher* 1 (No. 7), 209. "The 'Lothian Hairst' is another popular harvest song belonging to the north, although its name may be a little misleading at first. ... The tune to which this song is sung is in what we call the Dorian mode and must be very old. I have noted it from a number of people – the song being widely sung." (G, Ob. 3) "This is a real bothy song, and is said to have been written about sixty years ago by a Highland lassie, one of a band of Deeside harvesters to the Lothians, where grain cutting began several weeks earlier than in the far North. The 'rules' referred to in the song as well as in the recollections of many of our rural population are all against the charges recently made by a writer, who claimed that in the reaping hook days and later in the days of the scythe, bands of harvesters of both sexes occupied bothies indiscriminately." (John Ord, "Byways of Scottish Song" in *The Weekly Welcome*, 16 October 1907.)

A   Dm 255a; Mackay 2.36-7, Dw 5.52-3. "From a maid-servant at Asloun twenty-four years ago. Noted 13th March, 1907. There is considerable affinity with [152 'The Plains of Waterloo' A] in the first three lines; they may even be versions of one tune. It is identical with tune in *Rymour Club Miscellanea* 1.25, except in the second half of second (long) line: the second half is also wanting there. Cf. 'Caroline o' Edinburgh Toon' [from Alexander Mackay]." (Dm) "4.4 'tumes': does not know the meaning; only it means that he kept them free from harm." (D, Mackay)
B   Gm 1.57b; Gw 16.19-21. 1905. (Gm) In Gm Greig gives a cross-reference to [160] "The Duke of Athole's Nurse" [C]. 10.2 "boat": MS "brat".
C   Gm 3.36b; Gw 4.87v-9v. September 1907. (Gm) November 1906. (Gw) C is written opposite G and is confined to variations from it; the sections printed in square brackets are from G. There are also a few scattered words given opposite the corresponding points in G: G 1.2 on Shawfield shore, G 2.1 maister, G 2.4 Sae bravely as he led the squad, G 5.3 Come fill your glass.
D   Gm 2.8a. August 1906. "Robson" in the ascription is altered from "Naaman".
E   Gm 1.56c. January 1906.
F   Gm 1.57a. 1904.
G   Gw 4.88-90. The heading is "The Lothian Hairst (a and b)" with reference to this version and C which is written opposite.
H   Gw 46.76-8. "T. Roger. Sung by John Quirrie, assisted by Fred Wallace, East Huich, Crimond." (Gw) Acknowledged in Ob. 105, 14 December 1909, where Greig mentions that the song as sung by John Quirrie was forwarded to him by T. Roger.
I   Gw 20.9-11. Copied May 1908 from a farm servant's manuscript book supplied by Sam Davidson. The blanks in the text apparently represent illegible words in the source. At 4.2 "sleep" replaces deleted "bed".
J   Gw 22.41-3.

405 **THE HARVEST SONG** Cf. E.B. Lyle, *Andrew Crawfurd's Collection of Ballads and Songs* (Edinburgh, 1975–), No. 51 "The Faughhill Shearing". "['The Harvest Song'] is a somewhat quaint and primitive production, and deals with an order of things that has largely passed away, no department of farm work having been so revolutionised during the past hundred years as harvesting has been. It is all the more pleasing to have olden times revived as they are in this simple and unpretentious ditty." (G, Ob. 98)

Gw 14.24-6. "Mother got it from an old farmer. He sang it at the meal and ale. He was old when she was young." (Robertson, *Song Notes*, 2.45) At 6.7, "Faur" [= Where] is written beside "Far".

406 **THE BAND O' SHEARERS** Cf. Ford, pp. 196-7. "['The Band o' Shearers'] is attributed to Robert Hogg, who was a nephew of the Ettrick Shepherd, and lived in the earlier part of last century. The versions, however, which we came across – oral and printed – are so many and differ so widely that we doubt if Robert Hogg was the author of the *original* one. This doubt is strengthened by the study of the song itself; and altogether we are pretty strongly inclined to put the original 'Band o' Shearers' back into the 18th century at least. The tune to which I have heard it sung in the north is different from the one given in the *National Choir* and in Ford's *Vagabond Songs and Ballads*." (G, Ob. 3)

A   Dm 471b; Wallace 52-3, Dw 6.13-4. "Noted 26th August 1908. Only last line of [B] coincides with last line of chorus here; and if they were once the same, they have gone far apart. It is also different from Ford's tune, p. 196." (Dm)
B   Dm 238b; 998/7/3/10, Dw 2.61. "Dorian. Learnt in Skene fifty-five years ago from an old Highlandman. Noted 19th December 1906. Mode doubtful; it has suggestions of a modern air, as well as ancient modal tendencies. Words from Mrs Gillespie, also in Ford, p. 197. Mrs Gillespie [see version F] gives air of 'Johnnie Cope'. Ford's melody has a slight resemblance." (Dm) "Another verse wanting." (D, 998/7/3/10)

C   Dm 483a. "Noted 26th November 1908. Name used – 'The Band o' Shearers'. The syncopation in lines 1 and 4 was quite distinct." (Dm)

D   Gm 3.60b. "This is all I can remember of a song very popular some fifty years ago." W.W. (Gm)

E   Gm 1.68c. August 1905. "Ford, p. 196. Cf. 'Jeannie's Bawbee'. Rogers, p. 274, and broadsides." (Gm)

F   Misc. 85; Gillespie 398-9. In Misc. this song is included in the group sung to the air of [125] "Johnnie Cope". "Mrs Gillespie (1905): sung by James Buchan. Chorus repeats music. Words, with variations, in Ford, p. 197; but tune is different. He states that the words are by Robert Hogg, a nephew of the Ettrick Shepherd. [B] is in words a considerably altered version, with still another tune. The second strain of 'Johnnie Cope' was not sung." (D, Misc.) At 4.1 "aye" was altered from "I" at the time of writing. "Probably not complete." (D, Gillespie) "A different tune sung to this in Glasgow 1868." William Walker (Gillespie)

G   Gw 24.36-7. At 3.3 "slyly" is altered in MS from "slowly".

H   Gw 46.114-5. "Per John Ord." (Gw)

407 JOHNNIE SANGSTER "'Johnnie Sangster' has for long been the most popular of our northern Harvest Songs. … The song is attributed to William Scott of Fetterangus, who was born in 1785. He went to Aberdeen as a youth to learn his trade – that of a tailor, after which he proceeded to London, returning once more to Aberdeen, where he remained for a number of years. His next move was to America, but ultimately he returned to spend the evening of his days in his native parish of Old Deer. In 1832 he published a volume – *Poems, chiefly in the Buchan dialect*. Scott's muse is mainly bucolic. He is indeed our local Theocritus, and also, in some ways, a kind of Scottish Bloomfield. His pictures of rural life in some of its rougher and more sordid aspects are often most graphic and convincing. In song as well as in poem he draws freely on his early experiences of country life. 'The Hirdie' [429 'The Herd Laddie'], another of his songs, is perhaps as well-known as 'Johnnie Sangster.' … The air to which 'Johnnie Sangster' is sung is an old Strathspey tune known as 'Johnnie Lad.' I noted it from the singing of Mr W. Farquhar, Breakshill, Mintlaw, some years ago." (G, Ob. 3, 17 December 1907) "My friend, Mr William Walker, Aberdeen, author of *Bards of Bon-accord* – that best and most thorough of county anthologies, from which the facts given about William Scott of Fetterangus in [Ob. 3] were taken – kindly informs me that 'Johnnie Sangster' does not appear in Scott's *Poems and Songs*. This does not, of course, destroy Scott's claim to the song, but leaves it to rest on tradition." (G, Ob. 4) Greig adds in "Some Buchan Songs. No. 2 'Johnnie Sangster'", *Aberdeen Buchan Association Magazine*, No. 12 (March 1914), 3-4, as reprinted in a separate pamphlet, pp. 4-5: "'Johnnie Sangster' is not in Scott's published volume of verse, but the song may very well have been written after that book was published, for it deals with a phase of agricultural life and work distinctly later as to date than anything introduced in the bucolic part of *Poems*. Scott died about 1850."

A   Gm 1.19a; Gw 2.71-4, Argo 20.9-11. 1903. (Gm) Greig copied the following tune immediately after A for the purpose of comparison:

He identifies it as a reel from *Middleton's Selection of Strathspeys, Reels etc.* arranged by Peter Milne, and refers also to *Davie's Caledonian Repository*, 2.47. At the foot of the page he adds: "Note by Rev. James B. Duncan on 'Jock Sangster'. 'This local song, of which you spoke, was known to Mrs Gillespie, but she recalls only the chorus [see C].'". The following alterations were made to the song as first written: refrain l.2 "shafe" to "sheaf", 2.1 "farder" to "forder", 3.1 "gae" to "gie", "Foo" to "Hoo", 3.4 "straw" to "strae", 4.2 "trowsers" to "trousers", 4.3 "As" to "But as", "we" to "they", "down" to "doon", 6.3 "wudna wuss" to "widna wish", 7.2 "feeding" to "feedin'", 7.4 "thick" to "theek", "craddle" to "cradle", 8.3 "these" to "this", "settle" to "sattle". One alteration, of "rufts" to "tufts" at 7.4 has been accepted into the text. The second "o" given here in the following words may have been written on top of an earlier "u" or "w": 1.4 "oot", 2.2 "cloods", 3.2 "Foo", 6.4 "doon", 7.2 "hoose". A note attached to the final stanza runs: "Got afterwards from William Farquhar. – Is it meant as epilogue to song? If so must be intended to be spoken."

B   Gm 1.18c. December 1905.

C   Dm 39c. At Dm 40, Duncan lists "Jock Sangster" among the songs sung to the air "Johnny Lad" as sung by Mrs Gillespie and adds: "Mrs Gillespie – noted 1905. Local. Chorus:– [Text]. See *Rymour Club Miscellanea* 1.21." (Dm)

D Harper 30, Dw 1.66-7. "No tune given, but the tune always used as noted [for C]." (Dw) "Mrs Jaffray says this was sung in Rathen district about the fifties." M.H. (Harper) At 1.4 "sheaf" was first written "sheef".

E Gw 64.17-20.

F Gw 1.62-3. The following alterations were made to the text as first written: 2.1 "our" to "oor", 2.2 "tobaco" to "tobacco", 2.3 "man" to "maun", 2.4 "buisy" to "busy", and 3.4 "a" to "the". At 1.2 "sarest" has an "i" inserted after "e"; probably it was meant to follow "a". The second "o" in "cloods" and "oot" in 2.2 may have been altered from "u".

408 **THE HAIRST O' RETTIE** Cf. "The Hairst o' Rettie" sung by Charlie Murray on *Scottish Tradition* 1 "Bothy Ballads" (Tangent Records, TNGM 109). See map for the location of Rettie. "Since [the period of the composition of 409 'The Boghead Crew'] the reaper and binder have revolutionised the harvest field. It is quite clear that much of the old social feeling and happy intercourse has gone as being incompatible with the modern conditions of work. Most people, we fear, will think that the poetry of the harvest field also is gone; but that something may be made even out of the mechanical reaper is evident from the following clever and spirited ditty which I first heard sung by Mr J. Quirrie, Craigston, to a tune which is pretty generally known as 'The Parks o' Keltie' and is near akin to 'The Brier Bush.' The version of the words here given [B] was got through Mr A. Milne, Maud. [Text.] Good for singer, song, and subject!" (G, Ob. 3) "In connection with ... 'The Hairst o' Rettie,' I have an interesting communication from my friend Mr John S. Rae, the Bard of Banffshire. He says 'It may interest you to know that 'The Rettie Hairst' by Park refers to my brother 'Willie Rae'; and the Spence – J.W. Spence, Fyvie – is a far-off twig of the same heather.' There is here a lot in little. First as to Mr Rae himself. Born on the 25th January, 1859, the hundredth anniversary of Burns' birthday, our friend could hardly fail to be himself a poet; and he is one, of true note and high achievement. He appears in Volume 3 of Edwards' *Modern Scottish Poets*; and in 1884 he published his *Poems and Songs*, a volume which I secured on its first appearance and found full of fine and inspiring verse. It was only last autumn, however, that I had the pleasure of meeting the poet, when, under the wing of my good neighbour Mr George Watt, Whinhill, and some Cuminestown friends, I was driven over country to Burngrains. There we were most hospitably entertained by Mr and Mrs Rae, seniors and juniors, and enjoyed our outing to the full. The poet himself I found one of the most interesting men I have ever met, with a strain of lofty mysticism in his many-sided nature. With wide literary sympathies and modern outlook he combines a deep interest in and knowledge of the old minstrelsy, and from him and his worthy helpmeet I noted down several old songs. (I never like to miss a chance!) Now my readers will remember how, in 'The Hairst o' Rettie,' 'Willie Rae' is described as a kind of genius at his work. This I can well understand when I learn that he is a brother of the Bard; and to show further how hereditary is native ability I may mention that a daughter of Mr John S. Rae follows her father in paths poetic, and that by-and-by he may have to look to his laurels! Then Mr Rae gives Park as the author of 'The Hairst o' Rettie.' When dealing with the song I omitted to state that Mr Quirrie who first sang it to me mentioned that it was written by William Park, blacksmith. I am glad now to have Mr Rae's confirmation of this information. Mr Quirrie sang another song of Park's composition – 'Whitehills Harbour.' Very interesting too is Mr Rae's reference to Mr J.W. Spence, for Mr Spence has been one of my best helpers in my folk-song work." (G, Ob. 7) The hero of the song, Willie Rae, was grieve at Rettie in the years 1889 to 1892 (V.R., Banffshire, 1888 to 1893).

A Gm 2.67a. August 1906. "'The Parks o' Keltie'." (Gm)

B Gw 11.9-12. Manuscript alterations have been accepted into the text; original readings are given in brackets. Title: o' (of), 1.1 ay (I), Maks (Makes), 2.2 to (the), o' (oh), 2.4 nor (and), 5.1 straught (straight), 5.3 shavies (shaveies), straught (straight), 6.4 Tak' (Tak).

409 **THE BOGHEAD CREW** See map for the location of Boghead. "[This] song, which has a considerable vogue locally, I got from Mr A. Robb, New Deer. It takes a bit of memory to carry compositions of this length in one's head; and in this respect the exponents of our older minstrelsy put to the blush most of those who go in for modern compositions; for, while the former will sing songs and especially ballads of almost interminable length, which, as likely as not, they may never even have *seen* in print or writing, the latter will hardly embark on a song of three or four verses without the printed sheet to refresh their memories. The tune, too, I noted from Mr Robb's singing; and I have also got versions of it from Mr A. Barron, Mains of Whitehill, and Mr J.W. Spence, Fyvie. It is a good specimen of the old-time melody. 'Johnnie Sangster' and 'The Boghead Crew,' though considerably separated as to date, both belong to the old order of things when the scythe held sway on the harvest field. In those days the hairst rig was the scene of some of the happiest experiences of the rural year. Scythers, gatherers, bandsters, and rakers were associated in the work. Besides the regular farm-hands there were others – mostly local tradesmen and cottars' wives, engaged for the season. An eager happy spirit was abroad; everybody was in high good humour. Moving over the field in a body, the busy workers had many opportunities for friendly word and merry sally. Acquaintanceships then formed often ripened into life-long partnerships. The 'Boghead Crew' comes in just about the end of this order of things." (G, Ob. 3)

"I have a letter from an old pupil, Mr James Mitchell, Boyndlie, giving some interesting information about 'The Boghead Crew.' He says:– 'It was composed by Mr James Trail, Mossend Cottage, Boyndlie. The harvest of 1872, when he was at Boghead, he awakened one night and composed the whole song before he fell asleep again. He told me several of the names were altered and there are five verses omitted.' Mr Robb, New Deer, has also communicated the name of the author. The alteration of names in the song illustrates what we have once and again referred to – the tendency to variation in things that are handed about orally. It applies to many things besides songs, and really cannot be avoided. After all, however, in this particular case it does not matter so very much. Those who know the characters will keep the names right; and for those who don't know the characters one name is as good as another. As to the omission of verses, I may say that I had two or three more than I gave [sts. 22 and 25 in A], but that in songs with personal allusions one has sometimes to exercise a little sub-editing discretion when they come to be printed. My correspondent also informs me that Mr Trail has several more songs which he thinks would be well worth publication. I am communicating with Mr Trail about these [see note to 410 'The Kiethen Hairst'].'" (G, Ob. 5) "One who calls himself 'An Old Servant' sends me a copy of the 'Boghead Crew,' for which I thank him. He says he was at Boghead two years and was also brought up beside it. His version contains the two or three verses which I omitted; but as Mr Trail himself quite approves of the omission we need not re-open the matter. In justice to the author, however, let it be said that there is really nothing wrong with the verses in themselves." (G, Ob. 7, 14 January 1908)

A   Gm 1.83b; Gw 4.108-14. May 1906. (Gm) At 16.4 "guid" is written after deleted "fine". There are a few alternative readings or revisions, apparently added later: 1.3 "I left the parish of Longside", 2.1 "weather" for "mornin'", 14.2 "does" for "did", 15.4 "blade" for "blades", 24.4 "breid and" for "flint for", 26.4 "cam'" for "come". The stanzas which do not appear in Ob., 22 and 25, are marked for omission.

B   Gm 1.44c. 1905. "See [10] 'Greenland' first strain – [L]." (Gm)

C   Gm 2.75c.

D   Gm 3.144b. Acknowledged in Ob. 56, 22 December 1908.

410   **THE KIETHEN HAIRST**   See map for location. "I have a letter from Mr Trail, Boyndlie, author of the 'Boghead Crew,' to whom reference was recently made [in Ob. 3, see notes to 409]. Unlike many other writers of verse, Mr Trail possesses, as Mr Mitchell assured me he did, the highly commendable virtue of modesty, and would rather underrate anything he has written. Merit, however, is of many degrees; and while men like Burns claim highest honours for their supreme achievements, the man who writes a song that secures and maintains for a generation even a local reputation deserves recognition. Mr Trail sends a copy of another of his Harvest songs, 'The Kiethen Hairst.' It is pretty much on the same lines as the 'Boghead Crew.'" (G, Ob. 7, 14 January 1908)

Gw 13.9-12.

411   **THE ARDLAW CREW**   See map for the location of Mid Ardlaw. "'The Ardlaw Crew' belongs to a class of song of which we have already given a number of specimens. These ditties of farm life constitute the most genuinely native part of our popular minstrelsy. They may not amount to much as poetry; but there is an air of sincerity and conviction about them that makes for force and vitality. Further, they illustrate local life and language better than any other kind of song or ballad which we have. 'The Ardlaw Crew' may be taken as a very good specimen of this type of ditty. Our copy of the words comes from the author, Mr Gordon M'Queen, Aberdour, per Mr John Mowat. As the song is of quite recent origin we have taken the liberty to soften one personal allusion. The air we take to be that of 'Jack Munro,' so commonly sung to ditties of this kind." (G, Ob. 92) The personal allusion referred to is in the second half of stanza 21 which Greig prints as:

> And wi' sae mony hungry mou's,
> She's aften busy bakin'.

Gw 23.22-8. August 1908. "Gordon McQueen (per John Mowat)." (Gw) Acknowledged in Ob. 37, 11 August 1908.

412   **THE NORTHESSIE CREW**   See map for the location of North Essie. "My old neighbour, Mr James Ewen, now in the St Fergus district, sends me a harvest song, 'The Northessie Crew,' which was composed last summer. When, like 'The Boghead Crew,' it gets taken up and sung over Buchan, we shall have pleasure in printing it as a full-fledged song. Meantime we pick a few of the verses by way of specimen. – [Text.]" (G, Ob. 16, 17 March 1908)

Ob. 16.

413   **MY PLOUGHMAN BOY**

Gw 20.64-5. In the title "My" is altered to "The" in Gw. Copied May 1908 from a farm servant's manuscript book supplied by Sam Davidson.

414   **THE JOLLY PLOUGHMAN LAD**

Gw 5.12-3.

415   **THE CARSE O' POMMAIZE**   Cf. *Tocher* 2 (No. 12), 157, and McNaughtan No. 420 *The Carse of Pommaize* (Poet's Box, Glasgow, 14 April 1877). "'The Carse o' Pommaize' is an exceedingly popular ditty. I have some half-dozen records of it, and also a broadside version. I take [this title] to be the original one, although there are several variants – 'Carse o' Braemise,' 'Arland's, Arline's, or even Ireland's fine braes.' I have records of two different

tunes to the song. One seems to be a set of 'Villikins and his Dinah,' bringing in the flat seventh. The other is a variant of the tune I have got to 'The Forsaken Lover'." (G, Ob. 118)

A   Gm 3.13b; Gw 10.114-5. September 1907. (Gm)
B   Gm 4.121c. Acknowledged in Ob. 158, 20 December 1910.
C   Gm 2.81c. August 1906.
D   Gw 48.10-3. 1.4, 2.4 "Arland's": MS "Atland's". Acknowledged in Ob. 109, 11 January 1910.
E   Gw 1.111-2.
F   Gw 20.7-8. At 5.1 "go" and "kneel" are altered in Gw from "gaed" and "kneeled". Copied May 1908 from a farm servant's manuscript book supplied by Sam Davidson.
G   Gw 37.88-90. Acknowledged in Ob. 60, 26 January 1909. This song was among those collected by William Cheyne in the Turriff district and forwarded to Greig by James M. Taylor.
H   Gw 29.96-7.

416   THE PLOUGHMAN CHIEL AND THE PLOUGHMAN LADDIE

Gm 2.58c. August 1906.

417   THE WOODS OF RICKARTON   See map for location.

A   Gm 1.163c; Gw 16.52-5. April 1906. (Gm)
B   a) Gm 3.196a, b) 4.171a, c) 4.177c. "Also 'Banks of Claudy', and 'Tarves Rant'." (Gm 3) "Also to 'Tarves Rant'." (Gm 4.171a) "5 January 1913. Second record." (Gm 4.177c)
C   Gw 23.95-8. November 1908. "A characteristic ploughboy song. Heard it frequently sung in Fyvie parish in 1889, when this copy was got." (Gw) The word "she" in 11.4 is editorial. The line runs: "If so feel so inclined" and "(they'll)" is written above "feel so". Acknowledged in Ob. 54, 8 December 1908.

418   WE ARE ALL JOLLY FELLOWS THAT FOLLOW THE PLOUGH   Cf. Roy Palmer, *Everyman's Book of English Country Songs* (London, 1979), No. 3 "All Jolly Fellows that Follow the Plough". "We have taken the above ditty [version B] from a ballad leaflet kindly sent by Mr James Angus, Peterhead. As it seems to hail originally from England we print it for purposes of comparison with our northern ploughman songs, of which we have already given many specimens. Along with a general likeness, we note some points of difference between the English ploughman and his northern brother. The former says –

> When six o'clock comes at breakfast we meet,
> And beef, bread, and pork, boys, so heartily, eat;

while the latter reports as follows:–

> Syne after workin' half an hour
> To the kitchen each one goes;
> It's there to get oor breakfast,
> Which is generally brose.

If it is safe to found on a single specimen of the southern ploughman ditty, we should also say that the relations between master and servant appear to be more cordial across the Border than they are with us, judging from the general tone of our local ploughman songs." (G, Ob. 158)

A   Dm 216a; Walker 31, Dw 3.18. "Learnt at home. Noted September 1906. This, and [209] 'Lord Ronald' [F and G], as also 'The Emigrant's Farewell' [from Jonathan Gauld], are all varying forms of the air known as 'Villikens and his Dinah', which appears to have been as common in Scottish folk-song as in English. Compare *Folk-Song Journal* 1.172. See [211 'Villikens and his Dinah' A]." (Dm)
B   Ob. 158.

419   THE LAD WHA HAUDS THE PLOO

Gw 39.42-4. Acknowledged in Ob. 82, 6 July 1909.

420   THE FYVIE PLOUGHMEN   "Fyvie may be expected to have its ploughman songs. One of these sounds the praises of the ploughman. The sentiments are good, although the verse is at times a little lame. ... It is sung to the same tune as [152] 'The Plains of Waterloo.'" (G, Ob. 16)

A   Gm 1.23a; Gw 1.21-4. 1904. (Gm)
B   Gm 1.22b. "Arthur Barron from John Milne, October 1905." (Gm)
C   Gw 20.40-2. Copied May 1908 from a farm servant's manuscript book supplied by Sam Davidson.
D   Gw 47.60-3. "From one of my cousins and if I could get him at home, he would give you a hearing of the tune." A.S. (Gw)
E   Gw 37.76-8. Acknowledged in Ob.60, 26 January 1909. This song was among those collected by William Cheyne in the Turriff district and forwarded to Greig by James M. Taylor.

421 **HARROWING TIME**   Cf. the version sung by John Strachan in the archive of the School of Scottish Studies, SA 1952/25/A1. "'Harrowing Time' is sung to the tune which does duty for 'Drumdelgie,' 'The Miller of Straloch,' and some other ditties." (G, Ob. 71)

A   Gm 3.127a; Gw 17.48-9. "Noted by L. Crighton, Bonnykelly. July 1908." (Gm)
B   Gm 3.143b; Gw 28.43.
C   Gm 3.208c.
D   Gm 4.146a.
E   Gw 30.44-6. "Heard at meal and ale." B.R. (Gw) Robertson apparently did not recall a precise source, commenting in Robertson, *Song Notes*, 2.41: "I do not know about this one."
F   Gw 11.109-11. January 1908. "Air – 'The Miller o' Straloch'." (Gw) Acknowledged in Ob. 7, 14 January 1908.
G   Gw 48.41-3.

422 **THE PLOOIN' MATCH**   "Our copy of 'The Plooin' Match' has been kindly supplied by Mr A. Milne, Maud, who sang it, with great applause, at a recent Agricultural function in New Deer. I do not know where the song came from, or who made it up. As sung by Mr Milne it brought in the names of a number of local celebrities, to the great amusement of these gentlemen and their friends. What the original names (if the song has been transplanted) may have been we do not know, but when these are lost sight of, then any names will do. In this way, the song could be adapted to different localities. Mr Milne sang it to the tune of 'Whistle owre the lave o't.'" (G, Ob. 163)

Gw 59.20-4. At 6.4, 7.4, and 8.4 "plooman" is given in the MS but is altered to "ploomen" in the first two cases. "Per Alex Milne, Maud." (Gw)

423 **THEN SOME WI PINS**   The main title is editorial.

Gw 1.59. "Ploughman song deals with ploughman life – its occupations and interests. A ploughing match for instance may inspire its rough-and-ready muse. – [Text, sts. 1-4]." (G, *Folk-Song in Buchan*, p. 44)

424 **THE TYRIE PLOOIN' MATCH**

Ob. 161. "From a copy of a song on a local ploughing match, furnished by Mr J. Burnett, Whitehill, I would extract a few verses. – [Text.] The rhyme is dated 1866, and bears the name of William D. Jeffrey, who was born in the parish of Fyvie in 1845, and after trying various jobs in earlier years turned shoemaker at length, and settled near Old Meldrum. He died in 1892. Jeffrey wrote a good deal of verse, improving as time went on, until he secured recognition as a local bard of considerable merit." (G, Ob. 161) Omissions are indicated following stanzas 2 and 5. The song was acknowledged in Ob. 161, 10 January 1911.

425 **AH, SMILER LAD**

Ob. 66. "Mr John Mowat, Craigmaud, is cordially thanked for a kind communication enclosing a piece of verse – a ploughman's address to his horse when suppering him after a ploughing match. The match took place at Tyrie Mains about 1812, and the ploughman in question was said to come from Rora. The piece is not a song, but it is so good and seasonable that we must try to find room for as much of it as possible. – [Text.]" (G, Ob. 66) See also note to 426 "The Inverquhomery Ploughing Match".

426 **THE INVERQUHOMERY PLOUGHING MATCH**

Ob. 166. "From Mrs Moir, Ellon, comes a newpaper cutting of a poetical account of a ploughing match held at Inverquhomery [see map] so long ago as 1867. It bears the name of John Sim, whom I take to be the individual to whom [425] 'Ah, Smiler Lad' was attributed. An extract will show the style of the piece. – [Text.]" (G, Ob. 166, 21 February 1911) "A correspondent has kindly supplied a note on the John Sim referred to in our last article as the author of some lines on a ploughing match. He was miller at Mill of Inverquhomery for a number of years. He held a ploughing match annually, and regularly put an account of it with the names of the prize-winners into rhyme, and sent it to the *[Buchan] Observer*, where his effusions were in the way of appearing." (G, Ob. 167)

427 **DALMUIR PLOUGHING MATCH**   Cf. McNaughtan No. 565 *Dalmuir Ploughing Match* (Poet's Box, Glasgow, 12 June 1858). The air is given as "Villikins and his Dinah". "In one or two of our earlier articles we gave a selection of ploughman songs, but there is such a wealth of this minstrelsy that we may make another dip into it. The ploughing match is a great institution about this season of the rural year, and the rustic muse may be expected to have its say on the subject. The song which we give hails from the south-west of Scotland. The verses are marked by a certain air of natural sincerity. About the tune I do not know, as I have never heard the song rendered by any singer. I should be glad of any information about it." (G, Ob. 65, 2 March 1909)

Gw 9.64-70. In 12.4 "at" is altered from "on" in the MS.

428 **HAWKIE**   Cf. *Rymour Club Miscellanea*, 3.180, "Ca' Hawkie", and Robert Chambers, *Popular Rhymes of Scotland*, new edition (Edinburgh and London, [1870]), p. 24.

> Gw 44.38. "Now you will see that as she won't go herself she is to be *ca'd*. But gin she winna ca she is to be *drawn* or led and gin she'll neither lead nor ca like Robbie's soo, why she must be *dreeld*." B.R. (Gw)

429 **THE HERD LADDIE**   Cf. William Scott, *Poems, chiefly in the Buchan dialect* (Aberdeen, 1832), pp. 20-1 "The Hirdie". "When writing about [407] 'Johnnie Sangster' [in Ob. 3 we mentioned] 'The Hirdie' as another of William Scott's songs. While his claim to the authorship of the former ditty must, as far as we know, be left to rest on local tradition, 'The Hirdie' can be attributed to him with all confidence, since it appears in his published book of *Poems and Songs*, an incomplete copy of which I have on loan from Mr Walker, Brucklay. The song has long been a favourite, and no wonder: it is such a pleasing picture of young life, and so full of fine natural touches. It is usually sung to a lively tune in jig rhythm known as 'The Hills of Glenorchy.' It was first sung to me by Mr Brebner, Aucheoch." (G, Ob. 6)

A   Dm 46a; Alexander 1.6-9, Dw 3.36-8. "Learnt in Culsalmond some sixty years ago. Noted September 1906. Mr Alexander learnt this from a travelling character, partly deranged, who had been in better circumstances, by name Charles Farquharson. Tune [C] has not much resemblance beyond identity of rhythm. The bar is here divided differently, and this might have been used in [C]: there is not much to choose between them." (Dm) October or November 1906. (Alexander)   There are deletions at 3.1 and 7.2 of a second "n" in "Jeannie" and "d" of "And". In shorthand "breid" is indicated above "bread" at 1.5 and "Thus" above "This" at 5.1 and Duncan has written "approbation" above "a probation" at 2.4.

B   Dm 438c; Wallace 17-8, Dw 5.154-7. "Noted 4th August 1908. [A, B, and C] all have the same rhythm, but little else in common except in the fourth line (before repeat) which so far coincides in all." (Dm)   "Noted September, 1908." (Dw)

C   Dm 43c; Gillespie 32-5. "Noted 1905 by George F. Duncan from Mrs Gillespie and himself. From father. Robert Chree also sings this practically the same. Sung to 'The Laird o' Cockpen' by Miss Elizabeth Greig: noted by Mrs Harper August 1907 [cf. note at Misc. 134]." (Dm)   "Copied by George F. Duncan from Mrs Gillespie, 1905. Incomplete." (D, Misc.)   At 3.3 "sides?" is written above "sidies" and at 4.4 "licht – G. [i.e. George]" is shown as an alternative to "fa'". At 6.3 "tae" is deleted before "to".

D   Gm 2.68b; Gw 9.71-3. March 1907. (Gm)   At 8.3 "for" is altered from "far" in the MS.

E   Gm 1.122d. "March 1906. Last half of a verse. Sung by 'Goval'." (Gm)

F   Gm 1.55b. "Words by William Scott, Fetterangus. See *Poems*." (Gm)   On the tune, Greig first noted "Air said by Arthur Barron to be 'The Hills o' Glenorchy'" and then crossed out the middle section leaving only the words "Air 'The Hills o' Glenorchy'" and added references to Colin Brown, *The Thistle* (London and Glasgow, 1884), p. 136 "The Braes o' Glenorchy" and Frank Kidson, *Traditional Tunes* (Oxford, 1891), p. 98 "Coupshawholme Fair".

G   Gw 53.75.

430 **JOCKY AND HIS OWSEN**   Cf. Walter Gregor, *Notes on the Folk-Lore of the North-East of Scotland* (London, 1881), pp. 195-6, where there is the following statement. "The fields in many districts were unfenced, and the cattle had to be tended, 'hirdit.' The 'hird' used a stick for driving the cattle – 'a club.' If possible the club was of ash. This was because, if it had to be used, which was often done by throwing, it was believed that it would break no bones, and would not injure the beast if struck. In some districts this club was ornamented with a carving representing 'Jockie's plew.' Tradition has it that at one time there was in use a plough drawn by thirty oxen. This plough was made of oak, of great strength, and with one stilt, having a cross piece of wood at its end for the ploughman to hold it by. Its work was lately to be seen on many moors in the broad curved ridges that went by the name of 'Burrel Rigs.' The carving on the 'hirdie club' was very simple; it consisted of notches cut in a small piece of the club, smoothed for the purpose, to show in what way the oxen were yoked. 'Jockie,' as the ploughman was called, was represented by a cross, as well as the two oxen before the last four. Here is the order in which the oxen were yoked:–

> Twa afore ane,
> Three afore five,
> Noo ane an than ane,
> An four comes belive,
> First twa an than twa,
> An three at a cast,
> Double ane an twice twa,
> An Jockie at the last.

In other districts the 'hird' carved in notches merely the number of cattle in the herd, giving the bull, if there was one in the herd, a cross." For a description of how the oxen were yoked, see John B. Pratt, *Buchan* (Aberdeen, 1858, repr. 1981), p. 18.

> Gw 62.55. "In the old herding days the number of the owsen were cut out in notches on the herd's club in the order that they are set down in the rhyme, with a figure of Jocky at the end." Mrs Rettie (Gw)

431 **HERDIE DERDIE** Cf. Walter Gregor, *Notes on the Folk-Lore of the North-East of Scotland* (London, 1881), p. 196. Gregor adds, following the note given with the previous song, "Here is a rhyme those who watched the cattle used to repeat at the top of their voice on seeing each other's cattle wandering:–

> Hirdie, dirdie,
> Blaw yir horn,
> A' the kye's amo'the corn.
> Here's ane, here's twa;
> Sic a hird a nivir saw,
> Here aboot or far awa,
> . . . . . dings them a'.

The name of the 'hird' whose beast was straying was added in the last line. The last line sometimes took the form:–

> Deel blaw the hirdie's plaid awa."

Ob. 159.

432 **COWAYE**

Gw 5.106. "Communicated by Rennie, Monymusk (76) who was a herd in boyhood." (Gw) The heading is "Cry of one herd to another". "Cowaye" = come along; see SND "come" I.1(2).

433 **THE MUIRLAND FARMER** Cf. Rogers, p. 74, "The Muirland Farmer" by Andrew Scott. "This excellent song, which is sometimes called 'The Sma' Farmer' was written by Andrew Scott (1757-1839), on whom a note was given … in connection with another of his songs [73] 'Simon and Janet.' It is pleasing to find a lyric of distinct literary merit, like 'The Muirland Farmer,' adopted by the traditional singer, although one result of such attention always is that the name of the author drops out of sight. The song is printed in Whitelaw's *Book of Scottish Song*, and in Rogers' *Modern Scottish Minstrel*. It is directed to be sung to the tune of 'The rock and the wee pickle tow.' I have recorded the tune from the singing of Mr Robb, New Deer, and Mrs Jaffray, Mintlaw, and both records [B and C] represent variants of the air in question." (G, Ob. 122, 12 April 1910) In Ob. 124, Greig notes that Miss Bell Robertson "says that 'The Muirland Farmer' was a great favourite of her father's".

A Dm 234a; Alexander 2.5-7, Dw 3.69-70. "Learnt in Culsalmond fifty or sixty years ago. Noted December 1906. The words of this, under the title, 'The Gude Farmer', appear in Whitelaw, p. 94, and are stated to be by A. Scott, and to have been written to the tune of 'The Rock and the Wee Pickle Tow'. The air here has affinities with that tune as given by Johnson, No. 439, but is not very close to it. It is still farther from other forms of air for that song; see [474 'The Wife and Her Wee Pickle Tow' A, B, and E]." (Dm) January or February 1907. (Alexander) The music indicates the use of eight-line stanzas, but the text in Alexander is in four-line stanzas as given here. As Duncan notes, one half stanza is wanting, and, since there is no indication of where the blank should come, the setting out as in Alexander has been retained. At 10.1 "auld mither" is given as an alternative to "granmither".
B Gm 1.115b; Gw 5.1-3. "May 1906. 'Wee Pickle Tow'." (Gm) "Whitelaw, *Scottish Songs*, p. 94." (Gw) The following alterations are made in the MS: 1.3 "i'" for deleted "in" or "wi", and 4.1 "spence" for "spruce".
C Gm 4.4b; Gw 52.16. "With variants from printed copy." (Gw)
D Gw 1.99-102. At 2.1 "slopin'" in the manuscript replaces an originally written "slapin" and at 5.1 "an'" is given as an alternative to the dash.

434 **THE BEAUTY OF BUCHAN** "This lament was communicated by Miss Bell Robertson, who says it was sung by her grandmother. It may thus belong to the latter part of the eighteenth or the earlier part of the nineteenth century. The song refers to the disappearance of sheep from Buchan – presumably owing to the progress of cultivation. It has evidently been inspired by 'The Flowers of the Forest,' and, quite naturally, is sung to that tune." (G, Ob. 52)

Gw 13.46-8. January 1908. "A song of her grandmother's, who died 1837. Bell Robertson's father born in 1800. Sung to 'Flowers of the Forest.'" (Gw) "It was one of my mother's. She got it from her mother. It was after the hills were brought under cultivation and sheep put away to make room for cattle." (Robertson, *Song Notes*, 2.26) At 3.3 a revision of "they're cracked wi'" to "to crack wi'" has been accepted into the text.

435 **DEPRESSION** "We have heard Mr Mowat sing another song [besides 439 'A Song of Welcome'] which gives a picture of the agricultural situation as it would have been in the seventies of last century when the word 'Depression' came into vogue. The tune of the song is 'The Lass o' Glenshee.' It may be added that in general spirit and intention as well as in measure and tune 'Depression' recalls 'The High Rocks of Pennan.'" (G, Ob. 147)

Gm 3.4b; Gw 19.23-5. "September 1907. Heard about 1850." (Gm) The dashes in 3.2 do not appear in Gw but have been taken from Ob. 147.

436 **THE FROSTIT CORN**

Gw 29.110-1. "Tune 'Johnnie Cope'." (Gw)

437 **THE THRESHERMAN** Cf. Roy Palmer, *Everyman's Book of English Country Songs* (London, 1979), No. 23 "The Jolly Thresherman".

   A Gm 1.135a; Gw 3.99-100. March 1906. (Gm, Gw) Johnson No. 372 different tune. *Folk-Song Journal* 1.79." (Gm) At 2.1 "park?" is offered instead of the word "work" which is repeated in the following line.

   B Gm 3.136c.

   C Gm 2.73b. "August 1906. See [John Broadwood,] *Sussex Songs* No.14." (Gm)

   D Gm 2.148b. "Mrs Stevenson per Superintendent Ord, September 1907."

   E Gw 41.54-5. "Per William Scott." (Gw)

   F Gw 3.98v.

438 **LORD FIFE** This song concerns James, fourth Earl of Fife, who lived from 1776 to 1857. "I got this song, words and tune, from Mrs Cruickshank, Greciehill. I do not know to which Lord Fife it refers; but it is very pleasing to find that there have been landlords who could call forth such whole-hearted admiration. Were all our estates in the hands of men of this type the land question would not give much trouble. The tune to which 'Lord Fife' is sung is a set of 'The Briar Bush,' an air that is used for a lot more songs." (G, Ob. 147) "Miss Bell Robertson is able to tell us that the peer alluded to was the Good Earl James, the grand-uncle of the duke [Alexander William George (1849-1912), first Duke of Fife] – an ideal landlord and idolized by his tenants. This information is also given by Mr John Mowat." (G, Ob. 149)

   A Gm 4.16b; Gw 54.71-4. 11.4 "M. and W.": "M and W.U." (Gw), "M and double U" (Ob. 147). Words acknowledged in Ob. 126 and 129, 10 and 31 May 1910; music acknowledged in Ob. 130, 7 June 1910.

   B Ob. 160. "Referring to the song on Lord Fife [Ob. 147], Mr Gauld says he has heard a variant of verse 8 – [Text]." (G, Ob. 160)

439 **A SONG OF WELCOME** The song as composed for Alexander George Fraser (1785-1853), sixteenth Lord Saltoun. "I have heard Mr John Mowat, Craigmaud, sing a song, 'Lord Saltoun,' which was composed and rendered as a welcome home to the great man who bore the title at the time. I find that I have a note of the tune but not of the words." (G, Ob. 147) "[Mr John Mowat] favours me with a copy of the song on Lord Saltoun to which we referred [in Ob. 147]. He was grand-uncle to the present laird [Alexander William Frederick Fraser (1851-1933), eighteenth Lord Saltoun] and the song was made up on his home-coming after the battle of Waterloo. – [Text] Mr Mowat adds that there are good lairds to be got yet, and gives the following personal testimony, which speaks right well for landlord and tenant both:– 'I have been under three lairds, and I have not a bad word on any of them'." (G, Ob. 149, 18 October 1910) Greig had formerly acknowledged receiving the words of "Our noble lord's come to the North" in Ob. 37, 11 August 1908.

     Gw 23.51-2, 58.77-8. 1.2 "Florth" = Philorth; see map for location. The copy in Gw 23, which is headed "Philorth" has the following verbal variations: 1.3 join (pain), 4.2 Frenchmen there (the French), 5.3 bravely (brawly), 5.4 weary (cheery).

440 **THERE'S TILLYDEASK** See map for the location of Tillydesk.

     Gw 1.66. John Milne published this fragment in Milne, p. 10, commenting: "I have forgotten what the theme was". In Milne, "reask" is given in place of "reast" (1.1) and "taps" in place of "capes" (2.4), and lines 1.3-4 run: "An' a' the water o' that toons / Rins doon upon Ardgrain".

441 **MULLNABEENY** See John Milne's note quoted with 442 "Sa Up and Rise". Greig observes in Ob. 167 that Mill o' Boyndie "was a farm of even more importance than Mr Milne gives it credit for, as [D] shows [with its reference to 'twenty pair']." See map for the location of Mill of Boyndie.

   A Gm 3.112c; Gw 17.109-10. 2.2 "It": MS "I". Words and music acknowledged in Ob. 31, 30 June 1908.

   B Gm 2.51a. July 1906.

   C Gw 4.25.

   D Ob. 167, 28 February 1911.

442 **SA UP AND RISE**

     Ob. 163. "Mr John Milne, Maud, sends me an interesting communication concerning a local song, from which I quote:– 'Mill of Boyndlie [a slip, as Greig notes in Ob. 167, for Boyndie], by Banff, was a famed farm in the beginning of last century. My grandfather was a servant for some years at that time at the farm, and I can remember him giving details of how matters went on. The farmer was a Mr Milne, who tried to get the most and best work out of his horsemen (some fourteen pairs) by reesing them up rather than grumbling and quarrelling with them. He was always first up, and instead of knocking at their chaumer door to waken them after 4 a.m., he went round among the houses singing a cheery lilt of a song telling the joys to be derived from first-class farm-work, workmen, and working-gear. I can now only remember the chorus, as I only heard snatches of it when a boy. – [Text.] Perhaps if you were to quote these two lines in your notes you might elicit more from some of your correspondents.'" (G, Ob. 163, 24 January 1911)

443 **THE BRAES O' BROO** "This is a popular song. There is a good deal of difference in the versions which one gets. The original would seem to be fairly old, but later hands have brought it up to date by references to modern inventions. The version which in the main I follow [A] was got from Mr William Watson, New Byth. I have heard the ditty sung to different tunes." (G, Ob. 65)

A Gm 3.159c; Gw 40.34-5. Notes in Gw in William Walker's hand refer to John Bell's *Rhymes of Northern Bards; being a curious collection of old and new songs and poems, peculiar to the counties of Newcastle upon Tyne, Northumberland, and Durham* (Newcastle upon Tyne, 1812) where the song "The Ploughman" at page 237 has stanzas on the washing of the ploughman's clothes like the last stanza in A. At 4.1 "ye" is an editorial addition in line with the surrounding stanzas. Acknowledged in Ob. 67, 16 March 1909.

B Dm 102a; Gillespie 327-9. "From Mary Duffus, servant, about 1850. Noted 1905." (Dm) "All I can remember." M.G. (Gillespie) "'It seems nearly complete.' (Mrs G.) Later she remembered the verse about 'the braes o' Broo' in Mr Greig's version [Ob. 65]." (D, Gillespie)

C Gm 3.101a; Gw 21.41-2. May 1908. (Gm, Gw) Music acknowledged in Ob. 28, 9 June 1908.

D Gm 4.64c.

E Gm 3.11c. September 1907.

F Gw 42.103. Acknowledged in Ob. 67, 16 March 1909.

G Gw 27.54.

444 **IT WASNA SAE**

Gw 25.97. "I got it from an elderly woman with whom I was working when I was a girl." (Robertson, *Song Notes*, 1.11)

445 **THE PLOOMAN LADDIE** Cf. Norman Buchan and Peter Hall, *The Scottish Folksinger* (London and Glasgow, 1973), p. 129 "Plooman Laddies". "The tune of 'The Ploughman Laddie,' of which I have got two records, is the same as that to which 'The Rigs o' Rye' is sung." (G, Ob. 130)

A Dm 302a; Dw 1.99. "Mrs Lyall, from her mother. Noted 4th June, 1907. This is a version of [277 'The Beggar's Dawtie' A and E], and is interesting as containing the flat seventh not only in the tune (as the version 'The Rigs o' Rye' [from Mrs Greig]) but also in cadence. For others, see [277 'The Beggar's Dawtie' D, from Mrs Greig, and F, from Mrs Lyall]. Mrs Gillespie remembers this as sung by mother." (Dm)

B Gm 2.148c; Gw 10.94-5. September 1907. (Gm, Gw)

C Gm 4.65a, Gw 46.91. See note to 446 "My Love's a Plooman".

D Gm 2.9c. May 1906. Acknowledged in Ob. 28, 9 June 1908. Greig mentions that the tune was noted down by Miss Milne.

E Gw 51.29-31. "From K. Morrice." A.S. (Gw)

F Gw 12.4.

446 **MY LOVE'S A PLOOMAN**

Gm 4.65b; Gw 46.91. At Gw 46.91 this stanza is followed by the two stanzas of 445 "The Plooman Laddie" C and the three stanzas are treated as a single song under the title "The Ploughman Laddie" with the source indicated as "M.S.", i.e. Mrs Sangster. When Greig published a composite version of 445 "The Plooman Laddie" in Ob. 130, he began it with this stanza. This brought a response from Mrs Sangster and Greig states in Ob. 135: "[Mrs Sangster] says that the first verse 'My love is a ploughman and follows the plough, etc.,' is another song altogether from 'I mith hae gotten the gairner o' yonder tree, etc.,' although they were combined in our version. The songs are different, she says, and have different tunes." The tunes of the two songs as taken down from the singing of Miss Sangster occur together on the same page of Gm 4.

447 **THE PRAISE OF PLOUGHMEN** Cf. the version sung by Mrs Martha Reid in the archive of the School of Scottish Studies, SA 1955/50/A1. Greig printed texts from John Mowat of "The Praise of Ploughmen" and 632 "The Harvest Home" in Ob. 164 and followed them with the comment: "The above two songs ... were written by John Anderson, farmer, Upper Boyndlie, about the middle of last century, or perhaps somewhat earlier. In [Ob. 21] we gave two of his songs, 'The High Rocks of Pennan,' and 'Boyndlie's Braes,' with a note on the author, as supplied by Miss Bell Robertson. We then recorded our impression that these two pieces were all that now remained of Anderson's poetical work; but Mr John Mowat, Craigmaud, has been able to supply us with copies of the two additional songs above printed. As regards the former of the two, 'The Praise of Ploughmen,' I may mention that some four or five years ago I got from Mr A. Robb, New Deer, a record of the tune [A] with the first verse. My fellow worker, Rev. Mr Duncan, once informed me that he had got similar words, but with a different tune. Mr Mowat promises to let me hear his tunes when we meet, when, in the case of the first song at least, interesting comparisons can be made." (G, Ob. 164) "Referring to the two songs, 'The praise of ploughmen' and 'The Harvest Home' which we gave in [Ob. 164] as the composition of John Anderson, Boyndlie, Miss Bell Robertson says that they must have been written before 1841, the date of another song of his, 'Boyndlie's Braes,' and advances strong reasons for this conclusion. This helps to get over a difficulty which was raised when Mr A. Robb gave me a part of the

song [A] as learned from his mother who, born in 1822, heard it sung in the Crimond market when she was a young girl. If the song in question is Anderson's it could hardly have been written later than 1830." (G, Ob. 166)

A Gm 2.13a; Gw 52.73-4. "June 1906. James B. Duncan similar words – different tune."(Gm) "Sung in a Crimond Market when his mother, born in 1822, was a very young girl." (Gw)
B Gw 59.51-4. "By John Anderson, Upper Boyndlie. From John Mowat." (Gw) When giving this version in Ob. 164, Greig corrects "to" to "the" in 8.1.
C Gw 12.57.
D Misc. 87. The song is listed among those sung to the air of "Johnnie Cope". "Each stanza describes the various occupations, and finishes as above. Mrs Gillespie, from Mary Duffus; common among farmservant[s]. Air only first strain." (D, Misc.)

448 **THE PAINFUL PLOUGH** Cf. Lucy E. Broadwood and J.A. Fuller Maitland *English County Songs* (London, 1893), pp. 126-7 "The Painful (or Faithful) Plough". "Painful" has the sense "laborious".

A Gm 4.143a.
B Gm 1.187b. "['The Fause Lover' from Mrs Gordon.]" (Gm) This is No. 41 of the set of tunes received from Riddell. The heading is "The Ploo, or Sally Monroe" and Greig gives a cross-reference to [23 "Sally Munro" C].
C Gw 60.18-23. At 2.2 there is a query after "inaurate".
D Gw 63.67-70, 62.77-80. The copy in Gw 62 has the following verbal variations: 2.2 being (living), 3.4 bread (brand), 4.4 those (these), 5.1 streets (street), 5.3 Appear (*space left for missing word*), 5.4 This cakes (These bakers), 6.4 ploo (ploos), 7.2 They're a benefit (They've a' brought).
E Gw 56.43-5, 42.41-3. "Tune 'The Irish Boy'. T. Roger – Calls it a Berwick song." (Gw 56) The copy in Gw 42 has the following verbal variations: 1.2 through (though), 2.1 ours (our), 2.3 these (their), 2.4 much (such), 3.3 weren't (wasn't), 4.2 ploughs (plough), 4.3 Indies (India), 4.4 These (There), 5.4 their (the).

449 **THE LADDIE THAT HANDLES THE PLOO** Cf. the version sung by Ella Scott in the archive of the School of Scottish Studies, SA 1960/168/A15. "The intimate connection of folk-song with life and work is shown by the number of ditties that deal with trades and occupations. Most of these have their champions, but 'the laddie that handles the ploo' is the general favourite. His calling is treated as the one on which all others depend – a view of things for which a good deal can be said. ... The air I have got to 'The laddie that handles the ploo' is a variant of 'Logan Braes,' one of the most widely distributed tunes which we have." (G, Ob. 107)

A Gm 4.45b; Gw 40.57-9. At 4.1 "brook" is deleted before "dist". Words acknowledged in Ob. 78, 1 June 1909, and music in Ob. 143, 6 September 1910.
B Gm 2.72b, Argo 18.10-1, Gw 61.40. The Gw text has "millert" in place of "miller" and does not include the last two lines.
C Gm 1.59c. "1905. Cf. 'When the kye comes hame', 'Ilka blade o'grass' and 'Castles in the air'. 'Logan Braes', 'Greenland', etc. Cf. 'My heart [it] is sair' [from Duncan]." (Gm)
D Dm 390b. "From an uncle, Francis Roy. Noted 7th November 1907. The air is a version of 'My He'rt it is sair' [taken down by George F. Duncan]; see note [to that song version]. Mrs Gillespie remembers this as sung by 'Betty Mitchell'." (Dm)
E Gm 2.113b. June 1907.
F Lyall 1.9-10, Dw 4.86. 3.3 "little": MS "litte". "From Miss Elsie Davidson. Not one of her father's. She has heard this song sung at a concert." (D, Lyall) "Mrs Lyall's own form of the chorus is somewhat different; see [D]. She had heard it from an uncle, from whom she received the tune. 2.1 'wa'': 'wall?'" (Dw)
G Gw 28.1-3. At 2.1 "plane" is altered from "plain". Acknowledged in Ob. 36, 4 August 1908.
H Gw 46.109-10. July 1908. Acknowledged in Ob. 37, 11 August 1908.
I Gw 30.63. "That was popular in my young day. I do not know where or when I got it." (Robertson, *Song Notes*, 2.42)
J Ob. 160.

450 **COME, ALL YE JOLLY PLOOBOYS** The main title is editorial.

Dm 471a, 458b; Wallace 19-21, Dw 5.158-60. "Dorian. Learnt about thirty years [ago] from a Lumphanan shepherd. Noted 26th August 1908. This is a version of the air set to ''Twas in the month of August' [from Robert Chree] and 'Drumallachie' [as sung by Robert Chree to the ''Twas in the month of August' tune and as sung by Alexander Mackay], cf. especially second version of the latter) and [253 'The Braemar Poacher' B]; also 'The hat my father wore' [from William Wallace]." (Dm) "2.2 'for': confirms it as 'for'." (D, Wallace)

451 **COMMEND ME TO THE PLOOMAN** Cf. Kinsley No. 205 "The Ploughman".

Gm 1.141a. "March 1906. David Herd, *Ancient and Modern Scottish Songs* (Glasgow, 1869), 2.144-5. Cf. 'Wee German Lairdie'. 'When the King comes'. 'Boyne Water'? Cf. 'Green grow the rashes' and 'Blyther Blythe'." (Gm) Greig refers to Peter Buchan's *Ancient Ballads and Songs of the North of Scotland* (Edinburgh, 1875), 2.52, drawing attention by a line in Gm to the similarity to 1.3-4 of the lines in "Nathaniel Gordon": "Cast aff the wet, put on the dry, / Come to your bed my deary". He also gives cross-references in Gm to the following tunes: *The Gesto Collection of Highland Music*, compiled and arranged by Keith Norman MacDonald (1895), p. 118 "The Battle of the Boyne", Johnson No. 464 "O May thy morn", Thomas D'Urfey, *Wit and Mirth: or Pills to Purge Melancholy* (London, 1876), 5.112 "A Song", O'Neill No. 128 "The Banks of Banna", Frank Kidson, *Traditional Tunes* (Oxford, 1891), p. 22 "The Dowie Dens of Yarrow", and Lachlan MacBean, *The Songs and Hymns of the Gael* (Stirling, 1900), No. 27 "O Theid Sinn – Away, Away".

452　**THE MILLER O' STRALOCH**　Cf. the version sung by John Strachan in the archive of the School of Scottish Studies, SA 1952/26/A6. "The various trades that find place in the economy of rural life get due attention at the hands of the folk-songist. It is usually a case of defence or glorification. The miller is a special favourite. Sometimes he speaks for himself. 'The Miller of Straloch' has evidently borrowed some ideas from a fellow-craftsman of earlier date." (G, *Folk-Song in Buchan*, p. 28) "Straloch is a property to the north-west of Newmachar Station. The 'owre-word' [refrain] of the song is evidently borrowed from the 'Miller of Dee.' The tune is an exceedingly common one. It is sung to 'Drumdelgie' and quite a number of other dities." (G, Ob. 41)

A　Gm 2.25a; Gw 5.103-4. This is possibly the song called "The Miller" which was acknowledged in Ob. 26,26 May 1908.

B　Dm 399c; Lyall 1.45, Dw 4.92. "This is one I remembered of my uncle's, Francis Roy, Lumsden. My mother remembered the second verse." Mrs. L. (Lyall) "Noted 17th April 1908. Called 'I'm a little wee millertie'." (Dm)　"No more was remembered." (Dw)

C　Dm 70b; Gillespie 271. "From Mary Cruickshank, servant about fifty years ago. Noted 1905. Compare with ['Drumdelgie' from Mrs Walker]. The last lines (metrical) are the same." (Dm)　At 1.2 "Straloch" is altered from "Strawloch".

D　Gm 1.48d. "Rev. James B. Duncan 1905. Cf. [384] 'Drumdelgie' [B, G, H]." (Gm) The figure "5" in the date replaces deleted "4".

E　Gw 23.99-101. "November 1908. A song with a fine swing." J.W. (Gw) Acknowledged in Ob. 54, 8 December 1908.

F　Gw 16.58-60.

453　**MERRY MAY THE MAID BE**　Cf. Johnson No. 123 "The Miller". In Ob. 56, Greig notes: "From Mr James M. Taylor, Aberdeen, I have received a number of interesting things. Returning on the Miller [Ob. 41], he gives an old song that appeared in the *Charmer* about 150 years ago.", and Greig then quotes the first four lines.

Dm 196b; Gillespie 503-4. "From mother. Noted 1906. Called also 'The Miller'. For words see Herd, 2.70, and for their history (first verse traditional, the rest by Sir John Clerk of Pennycuik, Baron of Exchequer, 1751) see Stenhouse, p. 120, and Whitelaw, *Songs*, p. 178. Johnson (No. 123) sets to a different tune, now sung (since Graham's *Songs*) to 'Mary Morison'. (Dm)

454　**THE DUSTY MILLER**　Cf. Johnson No. 144 "Dusty Miller" and Kinsley No. 201.

A　Dm 119c; Gillespie 508. "From 'Betty Mitchell', who sang it all: noted 1905. The [tune as given] would be more correctly written (as sung) in 4/4 time. Each bar would then have a crotchet added to last note, except third bar, which would end thus:–

In Johnson, No. 144, but tune considerably different. The other half of verse there is –

> Hey, the dusty miller, And his dusty coat,
> He will win a shilling, Or he spend a groat. (First words).

Air (nearer Johnson's) in William Chappell, *Old English Popular Music*, ed. H. Ellis Wooldridge (London and New York, 1893), 2.166. See Glen, p. 41. Cf. 'The Comet' [from Mrs Greig]." (Dm)

B　Gm 1.16b. "Petrie Nos. 343 and 344. Communicated by William Forbes, Newark, Ellon, who says the tune is certainly old, but in its present form not more than three hundred years old. Hardie's set [C] he thinks has been altered from above by a strathspey player accustomed to close his tunes in that style. William Forbes cannot find his song book for words but gives the following from memory. [Text, with 'Hey .. gets a dusty miller' and 'Lease me on .. till her' marked 'first measure' and 'Dusty was his coat ... frae the miller' marked 'second measure as in second four bars above'.] Tune was sung lower than above setting." (Gm)

C　Gm 1.16a. "Ancient dance. Communicated by James Hardie, prize strathspey player and violin maker (117 Nicholson Street, Edinburgh). Relative of James Strachan (Drumnagarrow)." (Gm)

D　Gw 36.75. "My father's sister used to sing this one to me." (Robertson, *Song Notes*, 2.5)

455　**THE CROOK AND PLAID**　Cf. *Lyric Gems*, 2.228-9, Ford, pp. 58-61, and Rogers, pp. 389-90. "'The Crook and Plaid' was written by Henry Scott Riddell (1798-1870) who, starting life as a shepherd, took by-and-by to study, and ultimately became minister of Teviotdale, in the south of Scotland, from which position, however, ill-health compelled him to withdraw, after a few years' incumbency. His early experiences gave him an intimate and first-hand knowledge of pastoral life, which he uses to good effect in his songs. In a MS. autobiography [as quoted in Rogers, p. 366] he gives some interesting reminiscences of those early days. – 'We had gone to what pastoral phraseology terms "an out bye herding" in the wilds of Eskdalemuir. Here we continued for a number of years, and had, in this remote, but most friendly and hospitable district, many visitors. Among others who constituted part of the company of these days was one whom I have good reason to remember – the Ettrick Shepherd. This was about the time when Hogg began to write, or at least to publish: as I can remember from the circumstance of my being able to repeat the most part of the pieces in his first publication by hearing them read by others before I could read them myself. It may perhaps be worth while to state that at these meetings the sons of farmers, and even of lairds, did not disdain to make their appearance, and mingle delightedly with the lads that wore the crook and plaid. At these happy meetings I treasured up a goodly store of old Border ballads, as well as modern songs; for in those years of unencumbered and careless existence I could, on hearing a song, or even a ballad, sung twice, have fixed it on my mind word for word.' – All which is fine and inspiring. 'The crook and plaid' is now to all intents and purposes a traditional song. Quite lately I had a letter from a gentleman in Aberdeen, who, quoting a fragment of the song, asked if I could help him to get a copy, as he had for long tried in vain to lay hands on the complete song. There is another and older version of 'The Crook and Plaid' but Riddell's song deserves to hold the field. Christie prints a mixed version. The tune which he gives is pretty much the same as that given in *Lyric Gems* and Ford's *Vagabond Songs and Ballads*. The tune which we have recorded is somewhat different in the earlier part, but comes into line when the refrain is reached. Riddell achieved another success in 'Scotland yet' – one of the best patriotic songs which we have." (G, Ob. 106)

A Dm 82b; Gillespie 473-4. "Learnt first from Mary Duffus, servant. Noted 1905. This varies from [B] not only in time but in details of notes. Other versions, also varying considerably, are in Ford, p. 58, and Christie, 2.264; yet all are undoubtedly from the same original. Compare also with above air. The words which Ford gives are by Henry Scott Riddell; but see note to [B]. The first line is nearly identical with air in the *Folk-Song Journal*, 1.214." (Dm) There are alterations of "lilies" to "lily" (3.1) and "keen" to "ken" (5.4). At 5.1 "the gloman" follows the deleted words "the flowers".

B Dm 83a, 998/7/4/22, Dw 2.153-4. "From a note book; written [by George F. Duncan] in 1885 from memory chiefly. Learned originally from Robert Mackie, Craiglug, 1873-4." (Dw) "See [A] and note. The version of words of which this is the first verse, is not Riddell's. There are five verses, the first three similar to Christie's first three (from tradition and a chap-book), the fourth neither in Christie nor in Ford, and the fifth having connection with Ford (from Riddell)." (Dm)

C Dm 302c. "From her mother. Noted 4th June, 1907. Called 'The Shepherd Laddie' by Mrs Lyall." (Dm)

D Gm 1.141c. "March 1906. A.R. sings to same tune 'For the bonnie ship the Diamond etc.' [11 'The Diamond Ship']. See Ford. Christie 2.264. Refrain same." (Gm)

E Gm 4.185a.

F Gw 6.88. The stanza is headed "Fragment".

456 **THE COUNTRY CARRIER** Cf. Frank Purslow, *The Wanton Seed* (London, 1968), p. 27.

Gm 2.23b. July 1906.

457 **JIM THE CARTER LAD** Cf. Kennedy No. 228. "'Jim the Carter Lad' is English and comparatively modern; but it has become traditional, and as such is well known in the north. It is a cheery lay with a healthy sentiment. My copy of the words has been supplied by Mr James Angus, Peterhead. I have a record of the tune [A] got a year or two ago from Mr A. Robb, New Deer. It is English in character, as one would expect." (G, Ob. 99)

A Gm 2.21d; Gw 5.102. June 1906. (Gm)

B Gw 45.46-8. Acknowledged in Ob. 99, 2 November 1909.

C Gw 41.76-8. At 5.2 "weary" is written in brackets after deleted "carry". Acknowledged in Ob. 57, 29 December 1908.

458 **THE TOLL BAR**

Gm 3.83c. April 1908.

459 **BOYNDLIE ROAD** "Last week [in Ob. 7] we gave [460] 'The Buchan Turnpike,' and now Miss Bell Robertson, New Pitsligo, sends me another 'Road' song. We give a few verses of the homely rhyme. – [Text, sts. 1-4]" (G, Ob. 8, 21 January 1908)

Gw 14.112-3. February 1908. St. 7 is preceded by the comment: "There is another verse, but I think it belongs to the other ('Buchan Road' [i.e. 460 'The Buchan Turnpike']) and got mixed." B.R. (Gw) "A song of Jamie Rankin's. He used to sing it and the other one." (Robertson, *Song Notes*, 2.47)

460 **THE BUCHAN TURNPIKE** In Ob. 7, 14 January 1908, Greig gave a text of "The Buchan Turnpike" commenting: "Here in the year 1908 we print the song in honour of the centenary of the event which it commemorates." His text (11.2) named the author as "Jamie Shirran frae New Deer", but Duncan, in a letter to Greig of 25 January

1908, identified the author as John Shirran: "I think the song on the making of the road was made by *John* Shirran, who lived near George Park's place, in a small farm called Sandbrigs, on the other side of the old New Pitsligo road – afterwards occupied by *Robert* Park. He was dead before my time, but I have heard much about his force of character, his sometimes eccentric sayings and doings, and his rhymes. I remember other two men in that district that sang the song, besides my father, and the name they sang was *John* Shirran, and all understood it to be the work of the well-known rhymer. I have had some experience of how slippery these traditions are; but in this case the evidence is more satisfactory than usual, and there seems to be no opposing claimant. The Christian name might easily go wrong, and 'New Deer' no doubt refers to the parish, not the village." (2732/26/27)

"The turnpike, as every Buchan man knows, starts from Peterhead, runs through the villages of Longside, Mintlaw, and New Pitsligo, and on through a rather bare stretch of country to Macduff and Banff. Between Brucklay Station and New Pitsligo it runs for a bit along the borders of New Deer and Strichen parishes, in the former of which lived the redoubtable Johnnie Shirran, who, as author of the ditty, has taken care to weave his "*fecit*" into it. The nondescript crew of aliens, described in [A, st. 2], brought trouble to the native dwellers near the road, as indicated in a fragmentary verse [E, st. 2] recently recovered from another singer. The author, John Shirran, lived at a small farm called Sandbrigs, a little to the south of the road, and within a mile of Whitehill, in the Parish of New Deer. ... The song is illustrative and instructive. The old ballad took rise in the natural desire to keep alive the memory of some notable happening, and the humbler folk-song of more recent days had a similar beginning. And look how well the plan has worked! For fifty years after the making of the Peterhead and Banff road, while folk-song remained a living force, Buchan people were not allowed to forget about the event; and even to-day, after the lapse of more than a century, quite a number of people in our locality know about the making of that road from the commemorative song and from no other source of information whatever. Indeed, not even from Pratt's *Buchan* can the date of the event be got, let alone a record of the achievements of Chiel Chalmers and the other fellows! ... Of the tune to which 'The Buchan Turnpike' is sung I have got three records. Varying more or less from each other, they are all versions of a tune which, for identification, we may call 'Johnnie Cope', although it has to be pointed out that this well-known tune of the books is itself but one set of a much older traditional tune from which all the variants derive." (G, "Some Buchan Songs. The Buchan Turnpike" in *Aberdeen Buchan Association Magazine* No.11, January 1914, 2-4, as reprinted in a separate pamphlet, pp. 4-7) The progress on the turnpike can be traced in *The Aberdeen Journal*; see, e.g., 3 Oct. 1804, 4.1 (Peterhead end to be begun), 29 June 1808, 1.5 (New Pitsligo section open), and 15 Aug. 1810, 1.3 (whole line "nearly compleated").

A   Gm 3. 184c; Gw 7.17. Greig notes at Gm 3.22 that John S. Rae sang "Buchan Road" to "Johnnie Cope".

B   Gm 4.33b. Acknowledged in Ob. 140, 16 August 1910.

C   Gw 7.15-7.

D   Gw 1.49-50. The first three stanzas were published in Milne, p. 6.

E   Misc. 106-7, Gw 61.83. "The reference is chiefly to the making of the Peterhead and Banff Turnpike, the second verse referring to the questionable character of the navvies. Mrs Gillespie; sung by father, Murison of Wellhow, and James Cruickshank. It was always understood that the composer [*replacing deleted* "writer"] of the words was John Shirran, who lived at Sandbriggs before Robert Park, and died there at an advanced age probably about the forties. Mrs Gillespie had seen him. He was a man of considerable force of character. Mr Greig has met with the song, set to a different tune. William Duncan remembers the following as succeeding [*replacing deleted* "following"] the first two lines:– [Text F]. Greig in Gw 61 gives stanza 2 of Duncan's text and the following note: "*John* Shirran, the author, lived at Sandbrigs, before Robert Park, and died there at an advanced age, probably about the forties. A man of considerable force of character. Was the author of several other ditties."

F   Misc. 107. See note to E.

461   **THE SMITH'S A GALLANT FIREMAN**   Cf., for tune, *Kerr's First Collection of Merry Melodies for the Violin* (James S. Kerr, Glasgow, n.d.), p. 4, and, for words, Edwards, seventh series, pp. 197-8. "One of the best songs ever written to a dance tune is 'The Smith's a gallant fireman,' by John Harrison, who, born in Forglen in 1814, was in early life a farm servant, and afterwards so improved himself and his lot as to secure important appointments in the service first of Blackie and Son and then of William Mackenzie – two well-known publishing houses. The late William Carnie, Aberdeen, in his *Reminiscences* [2.90-2] tells the story of the origin of the song – 'Calling one day upon Harrison in Edinburgh and getting upon things vocal, he asked me if I knew an auld fiddle spring 'The Smith's a gallant fireman.' Fine that: had danced to it a hundred times in Highland barn and Lowland laft. Handing me a bit of manuscript he said – Would this thing suit the music? The 'thing' was instanter sung and resung, when the author, pleased with his brain-birth, exclaimed – 'Man, Carnie, I never thocht it was so good: tak' it and sing't to our friends in Aberdeen.' He presented me with the copyright, and I have fulfilled his wishes a thousand times.' This was in 1862. Harrison died in Liverpool in 1889." (G, Ob. 73)

A   Gm 1.1a.

B   Gw 56.38-40.

C   Misc. 23. Duncan notes, "Tune well known", and adds that it was sung to the following songs in his collection: "Jenny dang the weaver", "Dinna think, bonny lassie", and "Willie Buck had a coo". He also gives a reference to the discussion of the tune in Glen, p. 230, under "Dinna think bonie lassie I'm gaun to leave you".

462 **JOHN BUCHAN, BLACKSMITH**

Gw 63.33-7. The author, William Lillie, is indicated at the end by his initials. At 9.1 "luck" replaces deleted "work". At Gw 63.24 the piece is listed under the title "To John Buchan, Blacksmith, concerning his plough".

463 **THE MASONS**   Cf. the version sung by John Mowat in the archive of the School of Scottish Studies, SA 1960/155/ A8. "It is interesting to see how the various trades are treated in traditional song. The Mason is a special favourite, and there are several ditties in his praise. 'The Mason Lads,' Miss Bell Robertson tells me, was popular in the earlier part of the last century, and is still pretty well known in the north-east. It is a great song of my friend Mr Mowat. I have several versions of the words, and they do not vary greatly. Of the tune I have three records. Two of these [A and C], got from Mr Mowat and Mrs Finnie, New Deer, agree pretty closely. The third [E], contributed by Mr G. Riddell, Rosehearty, under the title 'From the Seatown to the Newtown,' is somewhat different. Variants of the air, which is a specially fine one, are associated with several other songs." (G, Ob. 40)

A   Gm 3.18a; Gw 19.11-4. September 1907.
B   Gm 3.158c; Gw 28.108-11. "Heard at Aberdour fifty-three years ago." (Gm) At 4.3 "turrets" is written above "struts" and at 7.8 "for" is given in brackets and should perhaps be omitted. Acknowledged in Ob. 63, 16 February 1909.
C   Gm 2.74b; Gw 12.17v-20v. June 1907. (Gm) This text is written opposite F and shows variations from it; the words in square brackets are taken from F. Besides the stanzas printed, there are some smaller variations from F which are given here in brackets: F 1.3 road so beautiful and clear (bridge most beautiful and rare), 4.1 sodger lads since (our soldiers for), 4.2 Since they have gone to India to fight (They've gone unto the Indias to face), 4.3 keep (free), the foe (our foes), 4.4 sodger lads (soldiers), 5.2 much (do), 5.3 goldsmiths; silversmiths (silversmiths; goldsmiths), 5.4 die (have died).
D   Gm 3.88b. April 1908.
E   Gm 1.184d. This is No. 31 of the set of tunes received from Riddell.
F   Gw 12.18-21.
G   Gw 27.79-80. "Above song was very popular before Bell Robertson was born. One old man she knew sang it – he was a fine singer." (Gw) "This was a song of James Ross's and he sung it with life." (Robertson, *Song Notes*, 2.22)

464 **THE BONNIE MASON LADDIE**   "The above lyric – short and sweet, was communicated by Miss Bell Robertson. There is another song with the same title [see 465] which will be found in Whitelaw's well-known *Book of Scottish Song*." (G, Ob. 40)

Gw 27.77-8. "I got that [from] a schoolfriend, Maggie Fowlie, now Mrs John Iverson, Strichen." (Robertson, *Song Notes*, 2.22).

465 **THE MASON LADDIE**   Cf. Whitelaw, *Songs*, p. 119 "The Mason Laddie".

A   Dm 39c; Gillespie 281-2. At Dm 40, it is stated that Mrs Gillespie sang "The Mason Laddie" to the same tune as she sang "Johnny Lad". "Noted 1905. Learnt at school from Isa Clerihew, who received it from her grandfather:– [St. 1]. See Whitelaw, p. 119." (Dm) Alterations to the text as first written are given in brackets: 1.3 in (an'), 1.4 was (wash), gine (gin), 3.1 sho'el (sheel), 4.2 chaptioner fo (captioner tho), enough (aneuch), 5.1 rubs on the shoon (shows rotten sheen), 5.2 gingles on the loom (gigs on his lum,). At 6.1 "smeethe" replaces a heavily deleted word, perhaps "try".
B   Gm 3.102c. Acknowledged in Ob. 28, 9 June 1908.
C   Gw 3.80. "Whitelaw, *Scottish Songs*, p. 119." (Gw)

466 **FREEMASONS' SONG**

Ob. 156. "[This] is another of the Freemason Songs contributed by Mr James M. Angus, Peterhead." (G, Ob. 156)

467 **THE FREEMASON KING**   Laws Q 39 *The Building of Solomon's Temple*. "Freemasonry is a subject about which not much can be said. Outside the magic circle there is comparative ignorance, and inside there is reticence. Its inner history cannot well be got at, since those who don't know can't tell, and those who could tell, won't. Freemasonry, as the song shows, is carried back – imaginatively at least to Solomon and his Temple. Some masonic enthusiasts indeed, in searching for the origin of their craft, get away back to the building of the Tower of Babel, or even to the time of Noah and the Ark. But, whatever the origin of the masonic idea, the organisation of the craft, as we know it, must be comparatively modern. What chiefly interests us, however, is the fact that Freemasonry has its minstrelsy. Burns, it may be remembered, was a Freemason, and when he contemplated leaving his native land, wrote a Farewell to the Brethren of Tarbolton Lodge, to be sung to the air of 'Guidnicht and joy be wi' ye a'.' A couple of stanzas may be quoted:–

> Adieu! a heart-warm fond adieu;
> Dear brothers of the mystic tie,
> Ye favourèd, enlightened few,
> Companions of my social joy.
> Tho' I to foreign lands must hie,
> Pursuing Fortune's slidd'ry ba',
> With melting heart and brimful eye,
> I'll mind you still, tho' far awa'.
>
> Oft have I met your social band,
> And spent the cheerful, festive night;
> Oft, honoured with supreme command,
> Presided o'er the sons of light;
> And by that hieroglyphic bright,
> Which none but craftsmen ever saw,
> Strong Memory on my heart shall write
> Those happy scenes when far awa'.

This illustrates what we have already said in regard to Burns's lyrics – that they are not just folk-song, being too literary for the average man. He may enjoy hearing them sung by a good vocalist; but when he starts to sing himself he wants something less ideal and more 'hame-owre.' – Of 'The Building of the Temple' we have two records – one got some years ago, and the other quite recently." (G, Ob. 148, 11 October 1910)

A   Dm 330a; Garioch 20-1, Dw 4.68-9. "From William Forbes in Balchimmie, whose family came from Cromar (born about 1781). Learnt about 1845. Noted 29th July 1907. Christie, 2.274, mentions that an air given (a version of the tune [recorded with 'Donald's Return to Glencoe' from Mrs Gillespie and 'Allan Maclean' from Robert Alexander]) was 'sung in Morayshire to a long Masonic Ballad called "The Building of Solomon's Temple", of which he has a copy, but does not consider it worth being preserved' in his book. Probably this is the same ballad." (Dm) "No more remembered." (D, Garioch)

B   Gw 11.72-5. November 1907.

C   Ob. 148. It is possible that C, which appears only in Ob., is a composite text drawing to some extent on B, but it may be independent. The fresh source is probably the one referred to by Greig in Ob. 147: "[Miss Bell Robertson] sends me a copy of 'The Building of Solomon's Temple,' which she has secured from a friend. We hope to print it soon.".

D   Dw 1.129. "Mrs Johnstone, Bogie: it was sung by her father, New Deer parish, fifty years ago: he was a mason. She thinks the tune was the same as Mr Garioch's [A]. She states that the remainder describes the work done, hewing, building, etc." (Dw)

468   **THE RULES OF MASONRY**   The main title is editorial. "Mr Angus contributes the above song, expressing his confidence that it is over two hundred years old." (G, Ob. 155)

Ob. 155.

469   **THE COMPASS AND SQUARE**   "This song also [in addition to 470 'The Sons of Levi'] has been contributed by Mr Brown. The tune is 'Jocky the Ploughboy'." (G, Ob. 155)

Gw 58.5-7.

470   **THE SONS OF LEVI**   Cf. Sharp No. 363 and the slip McNaughtan No. 2467 *The Sons of Levi* (Poet's Box, Glasgow, 4 April 1874).

Gw 58.1-4. "This song has been contributed by Mr Brown. Of the first verse he can give only the refrain, which, I may say, is in the alternative form that makes allusion to David. The tune of the song is 'The Mason's Word – Keep your mouth shut.'" (G, Ob. 155) Greig's comment indicates that F.R. Brown knew of, but could not remember, a stanza before the stanza 1 given here. In the Poet's Box version, the "knights of Malta" stanza is the second and the first has the following wording:

> Come all ye craftsmen that do wish
> To propagate the grand design,
> Come enter into this bright temple
> And learn the craft that is sublime;
>> *For we are the true born sons of Levi,*
>> *Few on earth to us compare,*
>> *We are the root and branch of David,*
>> *That bright and glorious morning star.*

471 **WI' THE APRON ON** Cf. the broadside Madden 8, No. 37 *Adam in the Garden* (J. Pitts, Seven Dials, n.d.). "The Brotherhood of Gardeners trace their craft to a still earlier source [than the masons, as discussed in connection with 467 'The Freemason King']. Beginning in the Garden of Eden, they are, as regards antiquity, quite beyond competition, and take precedence of all other crafts. They have also their minstrelsy." (G, Ob. 148)

A   Gm 1.143a; Gw 4.55-6. March 1906. (Gm, Gw) "(Mason Song) is written after the title. Emendations are suggested with queries at 1.4 and 2.3: "his" for "her" and "Eden" for "Eve". Greig comments in relation to this text in Ob. 153: "One can hardly profess to understand this; and unless some Mason come to our rescue I fear the matter must remain, for us at least 'greatly dark.'" When giving st.1 in Ob. 40, Greig replaced "went" in the first line with "woned".

B   Gm 2.114b; Gw 56.10. June 1907. (Gm)

C   Dm 106a; 998/2/15. "Pentatonic. From 'Johnny Rainy' some fifty years ago. Noted 1905. 'Johnny Rainy' was a half-witted character, who lived in New Pitsligo, whose sister carried besoms for sale. He used to come to Affath in early days for harvest work, and regularly sang several songs. (He was no relation of 'Sanny Rainy', Strichen.) Air in Riddell, as played by 'Auld Jeck', only with a second strain, probably a later addition." (Dm) Note before st. 2: "All I can remember more of. This is the last half of a verse." M.G. (998/2/15)

D   Gm 1.194a. This is No. 63 of the set of tunes received from Riddell. It is included in a group of airs Riddell heard played by 'Auld Jeck' and Riddell's note places this song in its Masonic context: "The following airs [at Gm 1.192-4] were learned by the writer in early youth, from the playing of an old man, who rendered them with great spirit on the fife. For many years 'Auld Jeck' supplied music for what has always been the greatest pageant in the world to the youth of this district – The Rosehearty Mason's Walk – which from time immemorial has taken place at Auld Yule. The writer has never happened to see any of the airs in print and has reproduced them exactly as they were played by 'Auld Jeck'." G.R. (Gm) Riddell identifies Auld Jeck as John Ritchie in *Rymour Club Miscellanea*, 2.190.

E   Gw 27.40.

472 THE PLUMB AND LEVEL

Dw 1.129. "Also [like 467 'The Freemason King' D] from her father: masonic song. Tune not remembered, but not the same as the other one I have with this chorus. 2.4 'and the bit': 'in a bit'?"(Dw)

473 THE FREE GARDENER

A   Dm 224c; Alexander 1.35, Dw 3.58. "Dorian. From Culsalmond: often heard among the gardeners at Newton House. Noted September 1906. 'Old Adam was a Gairdener.' So called by Mr Alexander; but this is not really the first verse. Full words [in B], where the name is 'The Free Gardener'. No doubt, it was a trade song, used at the making of 'free gardeners'. The tune may be written AEolian or Dorian, but seems more natural in the latter mode." (Dm) October or November 1906. (Alexander)

B   Dw 2.36-7. "From her early note-book, this being dated April, 1867." (Dw)

474 THE SPINNIN' O'T

"Miss Bell Robertson sends me two or three interesting items of minstrelsy, among which is an introductory verse to 'The spinnin' o't' which I have never come across in any version of the song which I have hitherto seen. – [Text.]"(G, Ob. 60)

Gw 36.56.

475 SPINNING RHYME

Cf. Robert Chambers, *Popular Rhymes of Scotland*, new edition (Edinburgh and London, [1870]), p. 384 "Song of an Old Woman at her Wheel".

Gw 23.5.

476 THE WIFE AND HER WEE PICKLE TOW

Cf. *Lyric Gems*, 2.234-5, and *The Scottish Works of Alexander Ross*, ed. Margaret Wattie (Edinburgh, 1938), pp. 141-6.

A   Dm 279b; Gillespie 547-9. "From father. Noted 7th April, 1907." (Dm) "Partly from father, Mrs Duncan (Craigculter), Betty Mitchell, and Mrs Imlah (Delgaty)." (D, Gillespie) Duncan made the following alterations to the text as first written: 7.2 surcoat (sarkets), 7.3 raper (wrapper), 8.1 cloutet (clootet), 8.3 ruff (rough), 10.1 parlins (pearlins), 10.3 gine (gin), 12.2 wire (oor), but (beet). At 7.3 and 8.4 the "s" of "cast" and the "ee" of "fee" are replacements by Duncan of heavily deleted letters. In the text as first written, false starts have been deleted at 9.4 and 12.1: "An how get we th" and "They never".

B   Dm 279c; Alexander 2.40, Dw 3.99. "From his mother sixty years ago. Noted 29th April, 1907. These two versions of the air [A and B] are not materially different from each other; but they vary considerably from the versions in Johnson, No. 439, and also from [E]. The tune goes back to the seventeenth century; see Glen, p. 197. The words are old too, but the form in Johnson is from an improved version by Ross of Lochlee, of which an abridged edition was published in Herd, 2.92, and used in the *Museum*. The second half here is not in Herd or Johnson; and the rest is from the old form." (Dm) January or February 1907. (Alexander) "The [four-line] verses are given singly [in Alexander]; but 1 and 3 are first halves of stanzas, and 2 is a second half."(Dw)

C   Gm 3.39b. October 1907.

D   Gm 1.113a. "February 1906. Johnson No. 439 – *very* different." (Gm)

E   Dm 282a, Walker 19. "Learnt from her grandfather. Noted September 1906. There was no second strain here."
(Dm)

477 **THE WEAVER LAD**   Cf. Andrew L. Fenton, *Forfar Poets* (Forfar, 1879), pp. 61-2 "Tammy Traddlefeet" written
by David Shaw.

Dm 366a, Harper 38, Dw 1.90-1. "Noted by Mrs Harper from her mother, August 1907. The first two lines
of air are a variant on [348] 'Jock o' Rhynie' [A]." (Dm)   "The words sounded like what I have written although
I don't know the meaning of some of them." M.H. (Harper) "1.3 'read': specially noticed by Mrs Harper, but
she understands it means 'thread'."(Dw)   In *Forfar Poets*, the last lines in the first stanza run:

> Wi' waft an' warp, an' shears sae sharp,
> My rubbin' bane, my reed an' haddles,
> Sae nimbly as my shuttle flees,
> While up an' down tramp the traddles.

The following are dictionary definitions of the rather obscure technical words the lines contain. Rubbing bone:
A bone used to rub cloth in order to hide blemishes in the weave. (SND)   Reed: A weaver's instrument for
separating the threads of the warp and beating up the weft, formerly made of thin strips of reed or cane, but
now of metal wires, fastened by the ends into two parallel bars of wood. (OED)   Heddles: The small cords
or wires, with the shafts suspended from them, through which the warp is passed in a loom, and which raise
and sink a proportion of the threads alternately so as to allow the passage of the shuttle bearing the weft. (SND)

478 **O, MITHER, ONYBODY!**   Cf. *Whistle-Binkie* (Glasgow, 1890), 1. 147-8, "O Mither! Ony Body" written by
Alexander Rodger; the air is given as "Sir Alex. M'Donald's Reel".

Gw 34.32. "Have heard the first verse sung since ever I can remember but never heard anyone sing the whole.
Got it from a chap-book." B.R. (Gw)   Greig gives only the first stanza and notes: "She gives the rest as per
A. Rodger's version." At Gm 2.96b, he gives the title and notes: "*Whistle-Binkie* 1.147, Sir Alex. McDonald's
Reel". Acknowledged in Ob. 45, 6 October 1908.

479 **THE SHOEMAKER**   Cf. John Stokoe and Samuel Reay, *Songs and Ballads of Northern England* (Newcastle-on-
Tyne and London, 1893), pp. 114-5 "The Shoemaker".

Dm 355d. "Noted by Mrs Harper from her sister, Miss Elizabeth Greig, August 1907. Heard about New Deer."
(Dm)

480 **MY LOVIE WAS A SHOEMAKER**

Dm 314a. "Heard from Mrs Watt (Affath), Mrs Birnie (Artamford), and Miss Michael. Noted 25th June, 1907.
The first line coincides with 'Loch Eroch Side' ('The Lass o' Gowrie'), Johnson, No. 78. The words are stated
to be a chorus, but the music for the verses is the same. Cf. 'My Love's a gallant Shoemaker' [from Elizabeth
Greig]." (Dm)

481 **THE SHOEMAKER AT HIS LAST**

Gm 2.26c. The marks above the first line of music indicate a hammer accompaniment, as Greig notes.
"Communicated by Scott Skinner (William McC. Smith?). Aged couple. 'The Way to Wellingtown' – old
Northumbrian ditty." (Gm)   Greig refers to John Stokoe and Samuel Reay, *Songs and Ballads of Northern
England* (Newcastle-on-Tyne and London, 1893), p. 48 "Sair Fyel'd Hinny".

482 **THE COBBLER**

Gw 17.74-6. At 1.4 "in" replaces some deleted letters which appear to read "alon". "Composed by William
Reid, shoemaker, Peterhead, and I am unaware of its ever being in print. To the tune 'Cruiskeen Lawn'. Mr
Reid died five or six years ago." (Gw)   Acknowledged in Ob. 33, 14 July 1908.

483 **DICK DORBIN THE COBBLER**   Cf. Kennedy No. 222 "Fagan the Cobbler".

A   Dm 110a; Gillespie 350-1. "Heard from Alexander Murison, Wellhow, and others. Noted 1905. Also noted
from Mrs Walker, Wartley, and to same tune, September 1906. Her chorus a little different – in words. The
song was always sung with the accompaniment of beating with the right hand representing the hammer, and
as if on the lapstone in the left hand, keeping time to music. This was during chorus, a direct beat being given
on the hand at *hob-bob*, etc., and the left hand being turned round at each stroke on singing – *Rite tooril*, etc.
During the verse the singer seemed to sew, taking the shoemaker's long draw of the stitches. The first line
of air is identical with first line of Johnson, No. 452 ('My father has forty good shillings'); the remainder
different." (Dm)

B   Dm 110a; Walker 64. See note to A.

C   Gw 43.105-6. Acknowledged in Ob. 93, 21 September 1909.

484 **THE BOATMAN'S DANCE** Cf. George Henry Davidson, *Universal Melodist* (London, 1847-8), 1.21 "Dance, Boatman, Dance", and the second song in the broadside Madden 11, No. 38 *The Broken Hearted Gardener. Dance de Boatmen.* (E. Hodges, Seven Dials, n.d.).

> Dm 502a; Gillespie 502. "3rd September, 1909. The alternatives in fourth and fifth lines, with letters noted above, are from my own memory. I remember hearing the tune, with this verse, very often." (Dm) "1.4 'O'io' = Ohio. No more remembered." (D, Gillespie) The equivalent to 1.4 in the broadside version is: "And beating down the river Oio".

485 **THE BONNIE FISHER LASS** Cf. *Tocher* 3 (No. 20), pp. 146-7. "There are not many traditional songs dealing with fisher folk; and as for fisher folk themselves they do not seem to have any old minstrelsy dealing with their special calling and interests. If they have we have failed to recover any specimens. The words of 'The bonnie fisher lass' were got from Mrs A. Fowlie, New Deer; and I have a record of the tune as sung by Mr Sam Davidson, Tarves. It resembles 'Scarborough Banks'." (G, Ob. 153)

A   Dm 450a; Bain 2-3, Dw 4.10-1. "From his mother twenty years ago. Noted 22nd August 1908."(Dm) "3.1 'missels' = 'mussels'." (Dw)
B   Gm 1.26c. "1904. Cf. [20 'Scarborough Banks' C]."(Gm)
C   Gm 4.176c.
D   Gw 10.111-3.

486 **A KING CANNA SWAGGER** Cf. "Beggars and Ballad Singers" at pp. 4-7 of the chapbook BL 11606.aa.24:42 *A Garland of New Songs* (M. Angus and Son, Newcastle, n.d.). The title is editorial.

> Gw 31.13.

487 **COME ALL YE TRAMPS AND HAWKERS** Cf. Kennedy No. 358 "Tramps and Hawkers". Hamish Henderson mentions in the notes to the record *Come A' Ye Tramps and Hawkers* (Collector Records, JES 10) that the song "is reputed to have been composed by 'Besom Jimmy', a much travelled Angus-born hawker of the last century". The main title is editorial.

A   Gm 4.172a.
B   Gw 43.34-6. Acknowledged in Ob. 90, 31 August 1909.

488 **THE BEGGING** Cf. Kennedy No. 217 "A-Beggin' I Will Go". "One characteristic feature of our Scottish life in bygone days was the presence and potency of the beggar. The progress of social economics has led to the abolition, in theory at least, of begging; but in former times the Gaberlunzie had place and recognition afforded him in the social system, and, as real or, more frequently, supposititious, became the subject of many a ballad and ditty. 'The Beggin' Trade' is a very popular song, and we have noted it a lot of times. In Durfey's *Pills*, an English collection published about the beginning of the 18th century, there is a song, 'There was a Jovial Beggar,' which has the same refrain as our northern ditty and resembles it in one or two of the verses [see Thomas D'Urfey, *Wit and Mirth: or Pills to Purge Melancholy* (London, 1876 reprint), 3.265-6]. The tune, however, is quite different. Our tune is characteristic and full of go." (G, Ob. 30).

A   Dm 142c; Gillespie 121-5. "Mrs Gillespie and my own memory. From James Duncan who learnt from Alexander Campbell, servant, Affath, in or about 1860. Noted 1905. Ford, p. 270, has a different air, with little in common but the rhythm. He attributes the words to [Alexander] Ross of Lochlee." (Dm) "Commas that appear in the manuscript at 1.1 after "O" and at 2.4 after "room" have been omitted. Duncan made the following alterations to the text as first written: 2.1 and 7.4 "puoke" to "pyock", 3.2 "gare" to "gar", 9.4 "lowner" to "lower", 14.4 "fue" to "fu", 17.2 "away" to "awa", 18.3 "poer" to "place". At 16.3 "the theevil" is Duncan's alteration of a partially obscured reading, perhaps "they thavel".
B   Gm 1.76a; Gw 1.89-91. October 1905.
C   Gm 1.117b. April 1906.
D   Gm 3.16c. September 1907.
E   Dm 430c. "Noted 17th July 1908. William Duncan gives this as learnt from a James Anderson, near Whitehill of Strichen by John. It differs in first musical line from version of Mrs Gillespie [A]. All three agree in refrain." (Dm)
F   Gm 1.126c. March 1906.
G   Gm 4.93a.
H   Gm 1.184a. This is No. 28 of the set of tunes received from Riddell.
I   Gm 2.31b. July 1906.
J   Dm 315c. "Mode? Learnt many years ago. Noted June 1907. See [A]. There is little in common between them, except in the chorus. Mr Christie was not quite sure of the air of first line, but was confident of the rest." (Dm)
K   Gm 3.194b.
L   Gw 28.24-9.
M   Gw 27.60-3. "Heard forty years ago. Had forgot she had it." (Gw) "A neighbour of ours used to sing it." (Robertson, *Song Notes*, 2.21) Acknowledged in Ob. 37, 11 August 1908. Stanzas 12-4 included by Robertson

in a letter to Duncan (*Letters to Duncan*, 3 October 1914) have the following verbal differences: 12.3 And pour (And I'll pour), 12.4 the (that), 14.2 never (seldom).

N   Gw 10.12-5. July 1907. At 11.2 "A' stappit" is given in brackets beside "An stap it".

O   Gw 41.13-5. Acknowledged in Ob. 30, 23 June 1908.

P   Lyall 1.11-3, Dw 4.88. "One of Miss F. Grant's. She does not remember [this word replaces deleted 'mind'] in particular who she learned it from. It was 'weel kent' she says." Mrs L. (Lyall) "Mrs Lyall did not receive any tune." (D, Lyall) "2.2 'Or': 'I'll'?" (Dw)

Q   Gw 37.55-8. At 2.1 "the" is deleted before "some".

R   Gw 28.24v.

489   **BUY BROOM BESOMS**   Cf. John Stokoe and Samuel Reay, *Songs and Ballads of Northern England* (Newcastle-on-Tyne and London, 1893), pp. 20-1 "Buy Broom Buzzems".

A   Gm 3.86b. April 1905.

B   Misc. 67. The second half of the verse is given with the music. "Beginning of air forgotten. William Duncan, noted 1906. From a song book published by the late Andrew Stewart of *The People's Friend*: the songs were said to be, some old, some new, many for children. This is not probably old, but William Duncan had heard it long before seeing it in the book." (Dm)

C   Gw 3.69. "Tune?" (Gw)

D   Gw 36.82. "That was a song of mother's. I knew it always." (Robertson, *Song Notes*, 2.9)

490   **THE SCAVENGERS' BRIGADE**   Cf. "The Scavenger Brigade" beginning "It's mysel' a dacent Irish lad arrived fae Donegal" sung by John Strachan in the archive of the School of Scottish Studies, SA 1952/26/B13.

Gw 37.102.

491   **THE PLOUGHBOY'S DREAM**   Cf. *Folk Songs collected by Ralph Vaughan Williams*, ed. Roy Palmer (London, 1983), No. 94. "I got this song – words and tune, from Mr A. Barron, Mains of Whitehill, a year or two ago. It is quite possibly of English origin, but the excellent lesson which it inculcates of kindness to horses tells as well in Buchan as in any other agricultural district; and just now, when some of our young chaps may be becoming horsemen, the song may help to remind them of their duty towards the animals committed to their charge." (G, Ob. 54, 8 December 1908)

Gm 1.47a; Gw 1.25-7. 1905. (Gm)

492   **THE AULD HORSE'S LAMENT**

A   Gm 3.96a; Gw 21.18-20. Acknowledged in Ob. 26, 26 May 1908.

B   Gm 2.72c. July 1907.

C   Robertson, *Letters to Duncan*, 3 October 1914. Robertson says in her letter: "I see in the notes [in Ob. 26] mention of 'The Old Mare's Lament' [A]. I never remember to have heard one with that title but I have a bit on an 'Old Horse's Lament'. I have likely given it but will again. It may intrest you but it is not old but tells of what is too comon."

493   **THERE LIVES A MAN IN ARDES TOWN**   The main title is editorial.

Gw 25.59. "That was a song of mother's. I do not know where she got it." (Robertson, *Song Notes*, 1.7)

494   **THE AULD MAN'S MEAR'S DEID**   Cf. Ford, pp. 280-2, and Kinsley No. 585.

A   Dm 138a; Gillespie 444-5. "From mother. Noted 1905. Tune in Johnson, No. 485, and Ford, p. 280 (nearly the same) is quite distinct from this. According to Stenhouse, inferring from a passage in Allan Ramsay, both words and air were the composition of Patie Birnie, fiddler of Kinghorn, in seventeenth century, whose portrait exists. See Robert Chambers, *Songs of Scotland Prior to Burns*, p. 143, where Johnson's tune is also given. The tune here given I have heard often, and never any other. It is in Christie, 1.194 (also note 293), with considerable differences." (Dm) The following alterations, shown in brackets, were made by Duncan to the text as first written: 1.2 ho'ts (hots), 2.1 feircie an (fercie in), 2.2 whugloch (whitloch), 2.3 breuk (brook). Opposite 1.4, apparently with reference to "jade", he has the note "Also 'vyaig' = *vagabond*?".

B   Gw 44.13. "Bell Robertson's mother's way." (Gw) "Was a song of mother's. I do not know where she got it." (Robertson, *Song Notes*, 1.19) Acknowledged in Ob. 95, 5 October 1909.

495   **DUNCAN MACKALLIKIN**   Cf. McNaughtan No. 717 *Duncan M'Callochan* (Poet's Box, Glasgow, 23 February 1878). The air is given as "There cam' a young man to my daddie's door". Ford, p. 45, quotes a verse of this song in connection with a related song called "Duncan M'Callipin".

Dm 143a; Gillespie 259-62. "Noted from my own memory. Mrs Gillespie confirms. From Mr Jamieson, music teacher New Pitsligo. Ford, p. 43, gives a quite different tune, and a different version of the words, which are by Peter Forbes, gardener about Dalkeith in the beginning of the nineteenth century. Ford mentions this version. Called also 'Tranent Wedding'. This air is essentially the same as one called 'Bung Your Eye' in Henry Noltie's 'Violin Airs' (MS.), 1815." (Dm)

496 **TRUSTY**

      Gw 63.38-44. At 2.3 "bite" replaces deleted "like".

497 **TAM GIBB AND THE SOO**   Cf. Middleton, 1.44-6 "Tam Gibb and the Sow". "I do not know the author of this popular ditty, although it might well have been written by some member of the *Whistle Binkie* group of song-writers. I have seen it on a ballad leaflet. The tune which I have recorded once or twice recalls the air to which 'Tooral-ooral' – a funny song of last generation, used to be sung." (G, Ob. 162)

   A Gm 2.93a. August 1906.
   B Gm 1.58a. 1905.
   C Ob. 162. The indication "(Spoken)" is editorial.
   D Gw 35.67-70.

498 **JOHN FOX**   "This spirited ditty, which was communicated by Miss Bell Robertson, is well worth preserving. It is written with considerable force and insight, and is marked throughout by an agreeable play of fancy. The local allusions are interesting. Sawney Riddell, referred to as 'the carlie on the hill,' was the author of the piece, which must have been written in the earlier part of last century, when the depredations of the fox had to be reckoned with. Katie, mentioned in the previous verse, was a sister of Jamie Rankin, well known as the blind singer who supplied Peter Buchan with much of the material for his *Ballads*. Miss Robertson mentions 'Malcolm's Barn' as another piece composed by Riddell." (G, Ob. 103)

      Gw 14.99-102. February 1908. "Composed by Sawney Riddell 'the carlie o' the hill'. Composed another piece – 'Malcolm's Barn'. 10.3 'Katie's door': Katie Rankin, a sister of Jamie's." B.R. (Gw) At 14.2 "tod" replaces deleted "fox". At 12.3 the reading "left till him" is taken from Ob; Gw has "I left – him" with "ill" inserted above the dash. "I learned that one from Margaret Johnstone." (Robertson, *Song Notes*, 2.47)

499 **FATHER FOX**   Cf. Sharp No. 333 "The Fox and the Goose" and Christie, 2.278-9 "The Tod".

   A Gm 1.139b. March 1906.
   B Gm 1.139c. March 1906.
   C Harper 29. "Another song of Mrs Murdoch's was 'Father Fox' but I don't suppose it is of any use to you. I remember we got it to sing at school so it is likely a modern composition. I have the words from Mrs Jaffray and I remember the tune if you want it. [Text.]" M.H. (Harper)

500 **THE HARE'S LAMENT**

      Gw 63.49-55.

501 **FIN WE GANG UP TAE LONDON**

      Gm 2.57c; Gw 64.10. July 1906. (Gm)

502 **O JANET BRING ME BEN MY SUNDAY COAT**   Cf. William Scott, *Poems, chiefly in the Buchan dialect* (Aberdeen, 1832), pp. 199-202 "A Reform Kiss". The song is printed in eight-line stanzas with a chorus "Bow-ow-ow, fal-al-de-radie-adie, bow-ow-ow" and the tune is given as "Bow-ow-ow". The main title is editorial.

      Gw 38.69-70. 4.4 "their": MS "they're".

503 **THE BERWICK FREEMAN**

      Gw 45.14-6. Acknowledged in Ob. 97, 19 October 1909.

504 **THE HILLS O' GALLOWA'**   Cf. R.A. Smith, *The Scottish Minstrel* (Glasgow and Edinburgh, 1820-4), 6.29 "The Hills o' Gallowa".

   A Misc. 128; Dw 2.166, 998/7/4/31. "Manuscript of George F. Duncan (1875), from father, with whom it was a very favourite song. Words by Thomas Cunningham (Whitelaw, p. 115). Air, a version of 'The Lea Rig', a little different from Graham, 1.142. Noted here, because I have not seen it in any collection, with tune; it made an excellent song." (D, Misc.) At 2.3 in 998/7/4/31 "softly" replaces deleted "sweetly".

   B Gm 3.70a. March 1908. Greig acknowledges receiving the words of this song from John Mowat in Ob. 67 (16 March 1909) and Ob. 155 (29 November 1910).

505 **THE LAND OF THE WEST**   Cf. *Songs of Rory O'More, No. 5. "The Land of the West"*, written and composed by Samuel Lover (J. Duff and C. Hodgson, London, [c. 1840]).

      Misc. 54; Gillespie 446-7. The tune was first taken down as Æolian with doh = G but was revised to Dorian with doh = D (as given here). "Mrs Gillespie, from James Masterton. In Robert Chambers's *Songs of Scotland Prior to Burns*, p. 219, a song of this name is said to be a modern Irish song derived from the tune of 'The Rock and the Wee Pickle Tow'. The first line of this is nearly the same. This air, however, does not seem modern; it is Dorian, and should have been so written. (Later) The words, as now given by Mrs Gillespie, are by Samuel Lover." (D, Misc.) In 1.4 the word "love" follows "west" in Gillespie but is deleted there and does not occur in Misc. with the music. There are the following alterations, shown in brackets: 2.4 resplendant (resplendent), 4.3 Thare (There), 5.1 doth (do).

506 **HAININ'S WAAL** "'Hainin's Waal' is the composition of my musical friend, Mr Frank Gilruth, Dumfries. It is an engaging lyric, reminiscent of actual things, and recording genuine feelings. Many songs fail to make popular appeal because the subject is imaginary and the feelings affected. Here we have the central note of sincerity; the working out is concrete and convincing; and the whole is set in an atmosphere of fine natural feeling. Mr Gilruth's song is set to an air which he says is an adaptation of a strathspey well known in his native district of Gartly, where Hainin's Waal is situated. Being a lively 'spring' it goes well with the subject. I am much interested to find that it has clear affinities with our popular 'Barnyards of Delgaty' tune, otherwise known as 'Lintin Lowrin.'" (G, Ob. 164) See map for the location of Haining's Well.

Gw 59.48-50. At 2.1 "croon" replaces deleted "toon".

507 **THE HILL O' CALLIVAR** See map for the location of Coiliochbhar Hill.

Gm 2.136c; Gw 10.65-6. August 1907.

508 **LOCHNAGAR** Cf. Sharp No. 509 "Loch na Garr".

Misc. 124. "Noted 21st August 1907. Learnt long ago, but does not remember where, tho' it must have been in youth. The air of course is not folk-song, but is different from the ordinary one." (D, Misc.)

509 **MOUNTBLAIRY** See map for the location of Mountblairy.

Gw 40.100. Acknowledged in Ob. 78, 1 June 1909.

510 **MONQUHITTER'S LONELY HILL** See map for the location of Auchry.

Gw 4.81-2.

511 **THE TARLAND LAWS** See map for the location of Tarland.

Gw 57.82-5. "The song entitled 'The Tarland Laws' relating to a rude and boisterous period was written by the late William Thomson, farmer in Glack of Migvie in Tarland or Cromar district. The song was at one time very popular in Upper Deeside." J.G. (Gw)

512 **THE BODIES O' THE LYNE O' SKENE** See map for the location of Lyne of Skene.

998/7/3/33. The text given here is taken from a broadside printed by A. King and Co., Aberdeen. It contains only this song and ascribes it to W. Chisholm. Duncan adds the note: "Chisholm was a wandering packman, or pedlar, carrying odds and ends. He lived in the Lyne o' Skene. He died between 1862 and 1864. He was a weaver originally, belonging to Paisley or Kilmarnock, and came north about the fifties. He had written other things, but Mr Lyall does not know about them. The rhyme is not sung in the district, but the tune is some well-known one." (D, 998/7/3/33)

513 **AUL' MELDRUM TOON** The main title is editorial. For the sub-title and opening stanza, cf. the song "Cruel was my father" of which Greig received a version from Miss H. Rae. See map for the location of Old Meldrum.

Gw 39.6-7.

514 **THE DEN O' AULDBAR** Cf. Alan Reid, *The Bards of Angus and the Mearns* (Paisley, 1897), p. 524, "The Den of Aldbar". "Aldbar is near Brechin in Forfarshire. Mr Alan Reid in his *Bards of Angus and the Mearns* gives the song as the composition of John Archer, who was a worker in the mills of Blackiemill, near Brechin, and speaks of it as being popular in that district some sixty or seventy years ago. As showing how songs come to be adapted to different localities I may mention that my friend Mr J. Milne, Maud, got a version of the song from a local singer in which 'Aulmaud' had been substituted for 'Aldbar.' The air, which is the same as that of 'The Banks of Inverurie' [Ob. 11], I have noted from the singing of my friend the Rev. John Calder, M.A., Crimond." (G, Ob. 28) The text in Ob. and one given at Gw 9.89-90 are taken from Reid.

Gm 2.58b. "August 1906. 'Banks of Inverurie' [from John Quirrie]." (Gm)

515 **PETERHEAD**

Gw 18.3-4. April 1908.

516 **O CANNY AN' CUTE MEN YE'LL MEET BY THE DEE** The title is editorial, derived from line 1.

Gw 1.71.

654

517 O UGIE THO NAE CLASSIC STREAM The title is editorial, derived from line 1.

Gw 1.74.

518 ROTHIEMAY

Gw 40.94-9. Acknowledged in Ob. 78, 1 June 1909.

519 THE GIRLS O' AIBERDEEN

Gw 32.84-5. March 1909. "Picked it up somewhere. Used to sing it in New Zealand as far back as 1860. Never heard any other body sing it. Who wrote it?" A.H.D. (Gw) Greig responds to the question with the comment "?A.H.D.!" suggesting that the contributor may also have been also the author. He implies this also in his comments in Ob. where he drew attention to the song three times and made a special effort to discover if it had any traditional currency. "Our Buchan litterateur, Mr A.H. Duncan, Monyruy, sends me a racy communication, enclosing a copy of 'The Girls o' Aiberdeen,' a song which he used to sing in New Zealand in early days. Mr Duncan says he knows nothing of author or source, and as I have never come across the song before, I have sent it on to my friend Mr William Walker, Aberdeen, to see if he can help us. Meanwhile I would offer our versatile friend sincere thanks for his kind attention." (G, Ob. 68) "Mr Walker, Aberdeen, writes me in reference to 'The Girls o' Aiberdeen,' contributed by Mr Duncan, Monyruy. He says that he does not identify the song, but thinks it very like the work of John Imlah, a well-known songwriter who belonged to Aberdeen and flourished about the middle of last century. Imlah, Mr Walker says, contributed his songs far and wide, and it may be one of those he did not live to put into book form. He adds that the tune would be a guide, as Imlah, being a musical man, had his songs always set to very taking airs. I hope to get the tune from Mr Duncan. We are much indebted to Mr Walker for his kind contribution. The song will be given next week, to see if any reader knows anything about it; failing which, we may say that we have an alternative hypothesis as to the origin of the lyric, of which we have already given a hint both to Mr Duncan and to Mr Walker." (G, Ob. 69) In Ob. 70, after giving the text, Greig adds: "This is the song to which we have referred in [Ob. 68 and 69], as communicated by Mr Duncan, Monyruy. Being specially anxious to trace the song, I hope that any reader who may chance to know anything about it, or to have heard it anywhere, will kindly communicate the information."

520 THE TOON O' ARBROATH Cf. the broadside L.C. Folio 70, p. 6 *Toon of Arbroath* (Poet's Box, 10 Hunter Street, Dundee). Greig's composite text in Ob. 136, which has three stanzas corresponding to those in B and C, has the reading "sleep my last sleep aneath the Roon O" at 3.8. "'The Town o' Arbroath' belongs to the class of songs that are reminiscent – giving utterance to tender recollections of home and childhood. The class bulks largely in Scottish Song, doubtless because our countrymen, owing to the poverty of their own land, are so often driven to seek a living elsewhere. These songs, however, are not very old; for emigration which has produced them is a comparatively recent movement. One of the earliest of these lyrics, as it is still, in our opinion, the best, is Robert Gilfillan's 'Oh why left I my hame?' [see Rogers, p. 259] written in the earlier half of last century. 'The Town o' Arbroath' is an exceedingly good song, sincere and unaffected. Although written by a native of the town, it does not appear, so far as we have noticed, in that excellent anthology, *The Bards of Angus and the Mearns*, by our distinguished friend Mr Alan Reid of Edinburgh. This tends to confirm our impression that the career of the song has been mainly traditional. It has found its way north, and I have made two or three records of it in Buchan. The great feature of Arbroath is its Abbey, now in ruins, which was founded in 1178 by William the Lyon, and dedicated to S.S. Mary and Thomas a Becket. 'Auld Thomas' thus became the patron saint of the town. 'The Roon O' is a large circular aperture at one end of the Abbey – once a window, and still a marked feature of the immense and picturesque ruins. 'The Town o' Arbroath' is sung to a most engaging melody, comparatively modern in structure, with an echo of one or two tunes which we have heard." (G, Ob. 136)

A   Gm 1.83c. "Mrs Parley, who heard an old man (a native of Brechin) sing it. November 1905. Cf. 'Flow gently sweet Afton' and 'Road to Dundee'."(Gm)

B   Gw 2.30-1.

C   Gw 26.106-7. In the first line of the refrain "all" is deleted before "auld". Opposite "I propose" is "With a kiss then we sealed it", opposite "Down" is "Seaton's", opposite "Scotland – Then" is:

> I'll sail for auld Scotland
> And live in the hame that I left lang ago
> And when life's journey is over I'll die quite contented
> And sleep my last sleep aneath the roon O.

521 MY HEART'S IN THE HIGHLANDS Cf. Johnson No. 259 and Kinsley No. 301.

Dm 99b; Gillespie 354. "From Mrs Duncan, Craigculter, William Smith (Gamrie) and others. Noted 1905. The words sung are Burns's (first verse old); but this is not the tune in Johnson, No. 259, or in Graham, 3.114. Old words (from Sharpe) in Graham. Another version (from Peter Buchan chiefly) in Christie, 2.180, with still another tune, traditional in Buchan. (Sharpe's words in Stenhouse, p. *313). Compare this tune with ['The Waukin' o' the Claes' from Mrs Gillespie]: see note there. It might be written Dorian; but the progressions rather suggest minor with transition note. The last line of this tune (and of ['The Waukin' o' the Claes' from Mrs Gillespie], also of 'The Banks of the Spey' [from Robert Alexander]) occurs in Christie, 2.90." (Dm)

522 **THE HIGHLANDS! THE HIGHLANDS!**

Gw 34.31. "From her mother." (Gw)

523 **MY NATIVE HAME**

Gw 4.83-4. "Air. 'Go bring my guid auld harp once mair.'" (Gw)

524 **THE BONNETS O' BLUE**

Gw 28.6-8. July 1908. (Gw)

525 **THE LAND O' CAKES** Cf. *Lyric Gems*, 2.172 "The Land o' Cakes" by John Imlah.

Misc. 175; Dw 6.62. "10th November, 1911. Learnt thirty-five years ago: source forgotten. He never saw it in print, or heard it sung by any other. Obviously modern." (D, Misc.) In Misc. in r. 1 "sang" is an alteration of "song" and Duncan notes the pronunciation of the last two words as "ashbens queever".

526 **BANNOCKS O' BARLEY MEAL** Cf. Ford, pp. 142-4.

A Dm 42b. Duncan indicates at Dm 41 that Mrs Gillespie sang "Bannocks o' Barley" to the air recorded from John Duncan for "The Lass o' Glenshee". He adds: "Mrs Gillespie – 1905. Words in Ford, p. 142, but his tune must be different, having a chorus. An older song in Johnson, 'Bannocks o' Bear Meal', No. 475, and in Hogg, but with different tune. [Text]." (Dm 41) "'Bannocks o Barleymeal' same as Ford." (Gillespie 558)
B Gw 10.70-2. August 1907. At 2.5 "'mang" replaces deleted "mid". Acknowledged in Ob. 123, 19 April 1910.

527 **HIGHLAND HEATHER** Cf. *Lyric Gems*, 2.49.

Gw 34.60, 27.50. "Never heard more." B.R. (Gw) "I got that one from my brother James." (Robertson, *Song Notes*, 2.19) "My brother used to sing it." (Robertson, *Song Notes*, 2.36) Acknowledged in Ob. 47, 20 October 1908.

528 **THE HIGHLAND LAD**

Gm 3.129b; Gw 17.60.

529 **DUNCAN MACINTOSH**

Gm 1.81a; Gw 2.3-4. November 1905. (Gm) At 2.3 "lasses" is written "lassies" with "i" deleted.

530 **LAUCHIE** Cf. "Lauchy" sung and spoken by John Mowat in the archive of the School of Scottish Studies, SA 1960/155/A5.

A Gw 23.41-50. Acknowledged in Ob. 37, 11 August 1908. In the second prose passage, the archive recording has "Lord" before "Duke o' Argyle" and "Soid" in Gw is evidently a miscopy.
B Misc. 5. "Tune, 'Tullochgorum'. From father. Noted 1905." (D, Misc.)

531 **THE HILLS O' TRUMMACH**

Misc. 122. "The tune is 'The Braes o' Mar'. No more words known. It is said to have been sung by a Highlandman in the church of Kintore when others were singing the Psalm tunes. From Mr F. Christie, 5th June, 1907." (D, Misc.)

532 **THE SONG OF THE EMIGRANT** Cf. *The Scottish Song Book for Tenor* with notes by Alfred Moffat (Bayley & Ferguson, London, n.d.), pp. 76-7 "The Song of the Emigrant" by Hamilton Corbett.

Gw 6.96-7. The item is crossed out in Gw.

533 **MY HIELANT HAME**

Gw 26.108-9.

534 **THE HIGHLAND SHORE** Cf. the broadside Madden 24, No. 395 *The Irish Shore* (Haly, Cork, n.d.).

A Gm 1.82d; Gw 5.51-4. May 1906. (Gm) At 5.1 "me" replaces deleted "wi'".
B Gw 27.97-9.

535 **THE LAND O' AMERICA** "The following fragment is interesting in view of the present rush to Canada. – [Text A.] Strangely enough, Miss Bell Robertson, in a communication just to hand, quotes a fragment of this song as recalled by a similar stanza in [77] 'The Recruiting Sergeant' [Ob. 176]. [Text B, st. 1.] Another fragment recorded

some time ago seems to belong to the same ditty – [Text B, st. 2]." (G, Ob. 179, 30 May 1911)

A   Gw 62.66. "Heard sung at St Combs seventy years ago." (Gw)
B   Gw 49.111, Ob. 179.
C   Gw 27.104. "I do not know how I learnd the bits of that song. Everyone sang it but I got the verse with ['The women there they nakit rin'] in it from my brother James." (Robertson, *Song Notes*, 2.24)

536   **THE NEW PLANTATION**   Christie gives the air of "The New Plantation" with "Sweet fa's the Eve" at 2.256, remarking: "The Air, 'The New Plantation,' was sung to an Emigrant's song, the words of which the Editor was unable to procure". "We have here a song of the early emigrant, and, like all effusions of that kind, it is charged with a melancholy note. The colonists feel from home. Everything is strange; and the New Plantation does not fulfil their expectations. All they now want is to get back to old Scotland again. Things are much changed now, as the depleted howes of Buchan abundantly testify. Our copy of 'The New Plantation,' which is incomplete, was contributed by Miss Bell Robertson." (G, Ob. 132)

Gw 27.102-3. "I got it from Margret Johnstone at a meal and ale when I was about fourteen." (Robertson, *Song Notes*, 2.24) This was the same meal and ale at which Robertson heard 153 "Waterloo"; see note to that song.

537   **AWA' TAE CYPRUS**   "This is evidently a Glasgow ditty, and comparatively recent. I have a record of the tune contributed by Mr. A. Barron, Mains of Whitehill. It bears some resemblance to 'Hame, dearie, hame.'" (G, Ob. 132)

A   Gm 2.20a. "December 1906. Cf. ['Hame, dearie, hame' from Arthur Barron and Miss Annie Ritchie]." (Gm)
B   Ob. 132.

538   **THE NABOB**   Cf. R.A.Smith, *The Scottish Minstrel* (Glasgow and Edinburgh, 1820-4), 6.41 "When Silent Time Wi' Lightly Foot" written by Susanna Blamire. "At this season of the year many old friends meet again; and a time of reunion is a time of reminiscence. The past lives once more while "fond memory brings the light of other days around us." – Auld Lang Syne! What magic is in the word, and how its meaning grows on us as we advance in life. All the world knows that glorious Anthem of Humanity which Burns gave us. Can any social gathering of Scotsmen break up without singing it? There is, however, another song with this burden which should be better known than it is. It was written by Susanna Blamire, who was a contemporary of Burns, and although born in Cumberland wrote several Scottish songs. I have heard it sung with true feeling by Mr George Milne, Auchreddie, New Deer, to a fine old air which seems to have been the original tune of Auld Lang Syne. [Text.] The pathos of such a situation is moving. Happily it is not the lot of many of us to pass through an experience of this kind when all the changes that the years have wrought burst on us at once; yet never can we gather at this festive season without noting some break in the circle – without missing some face once so familiar and so welcome. And so it is ever 'joy touched with sorrow.'" (G, Ob. 5, 31 December 1907)

A   Dm 228b; 998/7/4/49, Dw 2.175. "Manuscript of George F. Duncan, written from father's singing, 1875. The words are by Susanna Blamire, and appeared first in the *Scots Magazine*, in [February] 1803, 'to the tune of "Auld Langsyne".' The present air, however, seems a remodelling of the tune above under modern musical feeling, rather than a Dorian form. Neither words nor music therefore are true folk-song, though they were sung traditionally, and are included for comparison here. For full words see Chambers's *Cyclopedia of English Literature* (1902), 2.801. The verse here given from the traditional singing is a little different. Cf. also [Stenhouse, "Additional Illustrations", Part VI], p. 521. 'The Nabob' is the original name; 'The Traveller's Return' was the one father used." (Dm)   "George F. Duncan, from father's dictation in 1875. Compare however with Mrs Gillespie's version [F], originally from the same source." (Dw)
B   Gm 1.136a. "March 1906. 'Shepherd on the hill' [from J.W. Spence]." (Gm) Greig gives cross-references to Johnson No. 413 "Auld lang syne" and R.A. Smith, *The Scottish Minstrel*, 3.66-7 "Shall Monarchy Be Quite Forgot".
C   Gm 3.192b.
D   Dm 229a. "Learnt not many years ago: not sure where. Noted 21st February 1907. A modification traditionally of the arrangement in [A]. No chorus in this version. Mr Mackay's name was 'The Nabob, or The Wanderer's Return'. The words of first verse are in the changed form sung." (Dm)
E   Gillespie 155-8. At 2.2 deleted "Where" precedes "Ilk", and at 3.1 "met" has been altered from "meet".
F   998/7/3/57. This version is enclosed with a letter to Duncan dated 10 October 1906 from Jessie H. McDonald, who says: "I enclose the words of a song sent me by a cousin of my father's. ... She is about sixty years of age, so the song must be a fairly old one."

539   **AULD YULE**   The piece was printed in the *Aberdeen Buchan Association Magazine* No. 17 (January 1916), pp. 4-6, with the heading "'Auld Yule,' by Forbes" and also reprinted from that source as a separate pamphlet in an edition of twelve copies. The introduction and commentary on the poem in the magazine, signed Z, runs as follows:

"The following excerpts from a lengthy poem in manuscript which came into our possession many years ago, depict with graphic force the feelings of those who clung to the old forms of our popular festivals, and lament the seeming hopelessness of their persistence. From certain phrases which occur in the poem, we have no doubt of its belonging to the 'Nor' East' of Aberdeenshire. In the form we now have it, it seems to have been the work of two writers, for in a note given at the end of its 238 lines, it is said '175 were Forbes's and 63 Allan's'. Who Forbes was we cannot surmise, but 'Allan' was probably Hugh Allan, tailor at Cuminestown, author of the well-known 'Auld Kirk o' Turra', a kindred effusion [see 692 'The Last Speech and Dying Words of the Auld Kirk of Turriff']. Though we have never met with a copy of 'Auld Yule' in print, it very likely was printed, as after the title, given above, it has a kind of dedication 'to those choice spirits whose door is ever open to the oppressed, the following poem is respectfully inscribed'. It is well worth noting among our local effusions. The adoption of the Gregorian Calendar (*New Style*), to correct the cumulative deficiencies in the Julian Calendar (*Old Style*), came late into England and Scotland, and was resented much by the common people. It was adopted in England in 1758, when eleven days were omitted after the 2nd September, so that what should have been the 3rd, was counted the 14th. The year 1800, which was a leap year (old style) was made a common year, thus making a total of twelve days' difference between the new and old styles of reckoning. In Scotland, in outlying districts the old style was kept up as regards popular festivals (Yule and New Year's Day particularly) till within living memory. The poem before us is a lament for the passisng of Auld Yule, who is personified as an old wandering outcast, met by the author:– [Text, sts. 1.1-6, 2.1-6]. So he unburdens his mind of the 'waefu' tale' by giving a varied account of how he fared as the guest of 'great an' sma'' in the rural life of byegone years, thus:– [Text, sts. 3-7]. Such through the various grades of rural life had been the custom, but 'the guise is altered noo' sighs the drooping figure of Auld Yule. The beer has grown thin – 'senseless trash', for the new malt tax has risen from *one* to '*four* crowns the bow', and 'nane a'maist can pay't'. The Seceders, an extreme flank of puritan Presbyterians, had so preached down and proscribed Yule festivities – suffering 'none to make good cheer or be merry according to the old custom'; and then came the last straw:–

> Their Kalendar ance mair is chang't,
> The waefu' *Auchteen Hunder*,
> Has a' their Rack'nings sae derang'd
> They'll never cour the wonder.

So the figure of the houseless, hopeless wanderer, Auld Yule, moans out that 'like the Hermit ...' [Text, st. 16]. So saying, 'Auld Yule' vanished 'like vapour' before the eyes of the astonished poet."

Gw 33.41-54. The Gw text appears to have been copied, directly or indirectly, from the manuscript used in the magazine article. At the head is written "'Auld Yule' by Forbes. To those choice spirits, whose door is ever open to the oppressed the following poem is respectfully inscribed." A query at "oppressed" probably indicates difficulty in reading the writing in the source. 4.13 "dogs": MS "days"; 5.12 "pass": MS "puss". At 8.1 "sair" replaces deleted "said" and at 17.4 "house" is altered from "hause". At the end is written: "Notes on the poem written on the margin and foot of page evidently by the writer:– Line 44 [4.2. *Space left blank.*]. 148 [11.8] 'Bred the turn' brought about the change. 170 [13.2] 'A crazy hand'. = the seceders first introduced the observance of Yule. [The word 'Easter' written before Yule is bracketed for deletion.] 182 [13.14] 'To this deficient hour'. A common phrase in Aberdeenshire meaning 'up to the present time'. 200 [15.4] 'ither wicked rogue'. The alteration betwixt the old and new style introduced in 1800 by adding a day to the former difference betwixt them – and thus confusing the usual method of calculating by the first Tuesday of every month which regulates the fairs etc. 234 [17.10]. 'By help o' barkin' dogs'. He followed the sound of dogs barking at their homes which [*space left blank*] out of these bogs. 238 lines – 175 Forbes's, 63 Allan's (evidently lines contributed by different authors)." In Gw the lines are divided into stanzas by spaces but the stanzas are not numbered.

540 **THE AULD HAT** Cf. James Maidment, *Scotish Ballads and Songs* (Edinburgh, 1859), pp. 134-41 "Luckidad's Garland", beginning "Since my old hat was new, it is / About fourscore of years". "The words of the song were supplied by Mrs Milne, Auchreddie. In Crosland's *English Songs and Poems* there is a ditty on somewhat similar lines ['Time's Alteration' in T.W.H. Crosland's *English Songs and Ballads* (London, 1902), pp. 100-3], as the following stanza will show:–

> When this old cap was new,
> 'Tis since two hundred year;
> No malice then we knew,
> But all things plenty were;
> All friendship now decays
> (Believe me, this is true);
> Which was not in those days
> When this old cap was new.

The tune of our northern song, a copy of which comes from Mr Lawrance, Lonmay, is in the old Dorian mode. It seems to have some affinity with the tune to which the ballad of [326] 'Young Allan' is sung." (G, Ob. 101)

A Gm 1.138a; Gw 10.31-3. "March 1906. Cf. 'Drumalachie'." (Gm)
B Gm 2.132c. August 1907.

541 **I AM NOW A POOR AULD MAN IN YEARS**   Cf. Frank Purslow, *The Foggy Dew* (London, 1974), p. 95 "When This Old Hat Was New" beginning "I am a poor old man, come listen to my song", and the broadside Madden 8, No. 1158 *The Old Hat* (J. Pitts, Seven Dials, n.d.).

Gw 28.17.

542 **THE HAPPY DAYS OF YOUTH**   Cf. Rogers, p. 259 "The Happy Days o' Youth" by Robert Gilfillan. "We have here another specimen of the traditional song showing traces of an origin more or less literary. I have two records of the words, and the tune I noted some time ago from the singing of Mrs Clark, late of Brucklay. It bears some resemblance to the old air called 'The Bridegroom Grat,' which is sometimes sung to 'Auld Robin Gray.' It suits 'The Happy Days of Youth' admirably." (G, Ob. 82) "Speaking of Robert Gilfillan (1798-1850) [see note to 520 'The Toon o' Arbroath'], I may say that I have just discovered that 'The happy days o' youth,' given in [Ob. 82], was written by him. We find that our copy wanted a verse, and besides, as was to be expected, varied here and there from the original, but not to any serious extent." (G, Ob. 136)

A   Gm 1.79a; Gw 2.85-6. "November 1905. Some uncertainty. Not always sung same way. Cf. 'When the sheep are in the fauld'."(Gm)
B   Dm 370b; 998/7/3/40, Dw 5.126. "Isaac Troup, learnt in youth. Noted 11th September 1907. From end of first line to beginning of fourth, this air is clearly similar to 'Aul' Widow Graylocks' [from Mrs Gillespie], first half. The first line also is nearer to the old air of 'Auld Robin Gray' than 'Widow Graylocks'; see G.F. Graham, *The Popular Songs of Scotland*, revised by J. Muir Wood (Glasgow, 1887), pp. 246-7. Somewhat fuller words in [C], where double stanza suggests tune of same length, corresponding to 'Widow Greylocks'." (Dm) The words are from George Troup.
C   Dw 2.38. "From her early note-book, this being written in 1867." (Dw)
D   Gw 19.91-2.

543 **THE FARMER'S INGLE**   Cf. *National Choir*, 1.272 "The Farmer's Ingle" beginning:

> Let Whigs triumph, let tyrants rage,
> Let poets sing their patron's praise,
> Let Turks tak' wives, and priests live single,
> But my delight's at a farmer's ingle.

A   Gw 23.70-1.
B   Dw 6.69. "Mrs Halley, at Port Elphinstone, in 1911. Received from her mother. Tune forgotten, as well as the rest of the song." (Dw)

544 **THE WIND AND THE SNOW**   The title is editorial.

Gw 49.38.

545 **WHEN THE DAY IS ON THE TURN**

Gw 45.49.

546 **A WIFE AND A BIGGIN O' YER AIN**

Gw 53.10-1. "From the chap Clark I mentioned." A.S. (Gw) Acknowledged in Ob. 126, 10 May 1910.

547 **BOGIE'S BANKS AND BOGIE'S BRAES**

Alexander 2.19A, Dw 3.80-1, Misc. 111-2. "The air is 'Corn Riggs'. A Rhynie song, heard sung by a Miss Muirden in Auchindoir. Noted from Mr Alexander, December, 1906." (D, Misc.) January or February 1907. (Alexander) The spelling "faur" (= where) in the third line of the chorus is taken from Misc. where the first stanza and chorus are given in Duncan's hand; Alexander has 'for'.

548 **THE AULD MAN'S SANG**   Cf. Graham, 3.68-9 "O! Why Should Old Age So Much Wound Us, O?" by John Skinner.

A   Dm 478c; Lyall 2.31-2, Dw 4.124. "Mrs Lyall, from her mother, who learnt it from *her* grandfather. Noted 26th November 1908. This, though considerably different from [B], is still farther apart from the air in Graham. In Skinner's *Poems* (ed. 1809, p. 70), it is indicated that a repeat is to be made from 'How happy,' etc., which would seem to indicate that he had no second strain, as in Graham." (Dm) "One of my mother's." Mrs L. (Lyall)
B   Dm 193c. "From father. Noted 1906. The words are by Skinner, but the tune is a version of 'Dumbarton's Drums': Johnson, No. 161; Robert Chambers's *Songs of Scotland Prior to Burns*, p. 369; Graham, 3.68. For its history see Glen; and for the form in the Skene MS. Graham 3.182. This version is considerably different from these. The song was written by Skinner to 'Dumbarton's Drums,' and is accordingly set to Johnson's version by Graham; but may not the version here given, being current in Buchan, be the one really intended by the poet? See farther [note to A]. The present air is more closely related to 'The Blathrie o't,' Johnson

No. 33, especially in the second half; and it is noticeable that one version of this song is said to be sung to 'Dumbarton's Drums' (Stenhouse, p. 32). 'The kye comes hame' is also a version of the same (Glen, p. 68)." (Dm)

C   Gm 4.40b. Acknowledged in Ob. 143, 6 September 1910.

D   Gw 1.45. The fragment is crossed out.

549   **HAPPY ROON' THE INGLE BLEEZIN'**   Cf. John Wilson, *Wilson's Edition of the Songs of Scotland* (London, [1842]), pp. 176-8 "Happy We Are A' Thegither" or "Happy Friendship".

> Misc. 174. "23rd October 1911. No more words remembered. Not an old song, evidently. Air for verses same as for chorus. (Learnt from his mother thirty years ago.)" (D, Misc.)

550   **THE PRESENT TIME IS OORS**

> Gm 3.158b; Gw 40.23-5. Acknowledged in Ob. 63, 16 February 1909.

551   **THIS CRONIES O' MINE**   Cf. Ford, pp. 92-5 "A Cronie o' Mine" written by Alexander Maclagan. "This song – one of the best things ever achieved in the vernacular, was written by Alexander Maclagan, who was born at Bridgend, Perth, in 1811, and died in Edinburgh, in 1879. A plumber to trade, Maclagan found time to cultivate literature, meeting with success sufficient to induce him, in the latter part of his life, to devote himself almost entirely to this line of effort. The merit of his poetry was recognised by Lord Jeffrey and other distinguished contemporaries, and he was awarded a Civil List pension. Besides 'A Cronie o' Mine,' he has written several other excellent songs, – 'My Auld Granny's Leather Pouch,' 'Auld Robin the Laird,' 'Hurrah for the Thistle,' and 'We'll hae nane but Hieland Bonnets here.' Some of them have been set to original music. The tune to which 'A Cronie o' Mine' is sung bears some resemblance to 'The Auld Gairdner.' The song is an excellent one for social gatherings, the chorus making irresistible appeal to the company to join in. My friend, Mr A. Milne, Maud, declaims the ditty with such effect that he has got to sing it, as the Yankees would say, *just every time*, with the result that it is about as well known in this part of the country as 'Auld Lang Syne.' Mr Milne frequently gives additional zest to the song by springing upon his audience some other 'Cronies,' who enjoy the joke of having to listen to a good-humoured description of themselves." (G, Ob. 119)

> Dm 224b; Alexander 1.27-9, Dw 3.51-4. "Learnt in youth in Culsalmond. Noted September 1906. Words in *Whistlebinkie*, 1.239 (ed. 1890) – 'The Smiddie', by Alexander MacLaggan, Edinburgh. They have got a little altered; e.g. it is 'this *cronie*', applied to blacksmith alone. It is there said to be set to 'The Days of Langsyne'. It is also in Ford, p. 92, 'A Cronie o' Mine'; but the tune is quite different." (Dm) October or November 1906. (Alexander) At 1 r. 1 "*Nor*" replaces deleted "*As*", and at 4.2 "or heed" is written beside "heid". 10.3 "'sieved' = money abstracted." (Dw) Despite Duncan's gloss, perhaps derived from Robert Alexander, the sense of "sieve" here, as noted in the *Scottish National Dictionary*, is actually "to make full of holes like a sieve ... by sparks of hot metal from an anvil". In the second line of the refrain Dw gives "ca' on" and Duncan notes that this was what he had written (with the music) although the text written by Mr Milne (Alexander 1) had "call them".

552   **SAE WILL WE YET**   Cf. Walter Watson, *Poems and Songs, chiefly in the Scottish dialect* (Glasgow, 1853), pp. 70-1 "Sit Down, My Crony", Whitelaw, p. 267, and Ford, pp. 256-8 "Sae Will We Yet" to the air "A Wee Drappie O't", Ford, pp. 181-2. "Watson's best known song is 'We've aye been provided for and sae will we yet,' which I can remember the late David Kennedy singing with fine heartiness. Mr Ord [in a private communication mentioned earlier in Ob. 129] gives the following as Watson's original version:– [Four stanzas as in Watson 1853]. In Whitelaw's *Book of Scottish Song* we find the following additional verses:– [Three stanzas]. Whitelaw's collection was published in 1844, ten years before Watson's death, and the song, with the extra verses is given as Watson's without qualification. This inclines one to think that the addenda may have been written by the author himself; but, inasmuch as in the final edition of Watson's works the song appears without the addenda, they must have been either withdrawn by the author, or discarded as spurious." (G, Ob. 129)

A   Dm 275b. "Noted 7th April 1907. Words in Ford, p. 256, but the tune referred to is different from either [A or B]. See Ford for authorship of words." (Dm)

B   Dm 275c. "From father. Noted 7th April, 1907. Mrs Gillespie thinks this was the more common. It is a version of [143] 'The Wearin' [o'] the Green': cf. [258 'Brannon on the Moor' B]. Mr Alexander sings the words to 'The Wearin' o' the Green'." (Dm)

C   Alexander 2.41, Dw 3.100. January or February 1907. (Alexander) The opening lines of st. 2 were first written: "Success to Old England, and long live the Queen / . . . subjects, an long may she reign"; these lines are deleted. At 3.1 "ploo" is altered from "plough".

553   **MY AIN FIRESIDE**   Cf. broadside copies of the song of this name beginning "Come, my lads, let's mount and go": Madden 16 No. 536 *My ain Fireside. Pilot! 'Tis a Fearful night.* (J. Ross, Newcastle, n.d.) and McNaughtan No. 1743 *My Ain Fireside. No. 2 Version.* (Poet's Box, Glasgow, 27 June 1874).

A   Gm 1.118a. February 1906. "White Cockade." (Gm)

B   Gw 41.51-3. 1.3 "a paid" (= all paid) is indicated beside "afraid" and is obviously intended to replace it. At 1.4 "my" is preceded by deleted "yer", and at 2.8 "a'" is altered from "aye".

554   KITTYBREWSTER   See map for location.

Gw 29.80-3.

555   THE ALE-WIFE   Cf. Christie, 1.190-1 "The Ale-wife and her Barrel".

A   Gw 43.75. At 2.4 "haud" is altered from "hand". "[Mrs Rettie] sends me a bit of a song which her grandmother used to repeat – [Text]." (G, Ob. 12, 18 February 1908)

B   Gw 46.54.

556   CRIPPLE KIRSTY   Cf. Middleton, 1.28, and the first song in the broadside Madden 16, No. 588 *Cripple Kirsty. The Unco Bit Want.* (n.p., n.d.). "Being a parody, and an exceedingly happy one, of 'Maggie Lauder,' it is of course sung to the same tune." (G, Ob. 170)

Gw 33.98-100. "Tune 'Maggie Lauder'. As sung by Hugh Gallanders, a fiddling neighbour of ours 1846-1850 at our fireside amusements. I have never come across this in print and never heard it sung but by Hughie." W.W. (Gw)   3.2 "Lanrick wise": the two printed texts mentioned have the reading "Lanraik-ways" which is at present also obscure.

557   A WEE DRAP O' WHISKY   Cf. the broadsides Cambridge University Library Sel.295 *Ballads* No. 26 *Hearts of Oak. We'll Hae a Drap Mair.* (Walker, Durham, n.d.) and Madden 24, No. 579 *One Drop More* (J. and M. Baird, 20 Paul St., [Dublin], n.d.)

A   Gm 3.162b; Gw 40.11-2. Acknowledged in Ob. 77, 25 May 1909.

B   Gm 4.166b.

C   Gw 11.33. November 1907. "Taken down from a thirsty soldier." (Gw)

558   THE HIELAN' HILLS

Gm 2.134c; Gw 10.46. August 1907. (Gm)

559   JOHN BARLEYCORN   Cf. Sharp No. 247 and Kinsley No. 23.

Gw 57.24-6. There is a note in Gw in William Walker's hand: "Burns' text (four verses omitted)". Walker also clarifies the obscurity of 8.1 by writing in "wasted o'er"; the whole line in Kinsley runs: "They wasted, o'er a scorching flame,".

560   A WEE DRAPPIE O'T   Cf. Ford, pp. 181-3. "This is a well known ditty which, like the former one, hovers between the book-song and the folk-song. While it praises good-fellowship it is, as Ford remarks, rather a temperance than a drinking song. The author does not seem to be known. The tune is the same as that which is sung to 'Sae will we yet'." (G, Ob. 144)

A   Gm 2.107b; Gw 9.11-2. January 1907. (Gm)   William Walker has written in opposite stanza 1 the readings "canker" for "burden" (1.2) and "We'll be happy wi a friend" for "We're aye happy wi' oor frien'" (1.4).

B   Gillespie 518-9; Misc. 19-20. This is included in Misc. in a group of songs sung to the tune "Lochleven Castle". "From Robert Mutch, apprentice with father in fifties. The tune was the 'Lochleven Castle' form. Ford, p. 181, has a different tune." (D, Misc.)   The form of the refrain is indicated after stanza 2 as: "Chorus and repeat last two lines". At 3.1, 3.2, and 4.4 "met" is written "meet" with the second "e" deleted. At 1.4 and 2.4 Duncan has deleted "our" and written "owre" above.

C   Gw 24.38-40. 2.4 "wi' a": MS "wi' it".

561   WHEN JONES' ALE WAS NEW   Cf. Roy Palmer, *Everyman's Book of English Country Songs* (London, 1979), No. 117 "When Jones's Ale Was New" and Ford, pp. 273-7 "When John's Ale Was New".

Gm 4.145a. The title is editorial. There is a note under "Jones'" in William Walker's hand: "?Joan's (old broadsheet ballad)".

562   COME, LANDLORD, FILL A FLOWING BOWL   Cf. *The Scottish Students' Song Book*, new edition (London and Glasgow, n.d.), pp. 186-7.

Misc. 49, 52. "Heard from William and Alexander Mavor, Whitehill. It seems modern and English. But cf. the following ['The Whore's March']." (D, Misc.)   St. 1 is given on page 49 with the music and st. 3 appears below it with the heading "Another verse". The stanza given here as 2 is added at the foot of page 52 with the note: "Above is another verse coming before the one on page 49 after the air."

563   THE COVE THAT SINGS   Cf. the broadsides: McNaughtan No. 535 *The Cove Wot Sings* (Poet's Box, Glasgow, 27 November 1852) and Madden 10, No. 141 *I'm one of the Chaps Wot Sings. Tuck Out.* (J. Catnach, 2, Monmouth-

court, 7 Dials, [London], n.d.). The Poet's Box copy names the air as "He was the boy could do it" and indicates that the line equivalent to 7.7 here: "How much to pay, landlord? said I" is spoken.

A   Gm 2.84a. July 1907.
B   Gw 45.20-4. Acknowledged in Ob. 97, 19 October 1909. 2.1 "Seven": MS "Leven".

564   **TAK' ANITHER GILL**   The title is editorial.

Gw 62.81, 63.71. The text in Gw 63 has the following variant readings: 1.3 "my boys", 1.4 "For fient", 2.1 no "frae".

565   **I'LL TAKE THIS GLASS INTO MY HANDS**   The title is editorial.

Gw 56.95. This is given as the second of "Two Toasts" in *Rymour Club Miscellanea*, 2.108-9. There are the following verbal differences: 1 hands (hand), 2 I cannot (There's none can), 4 lying on (on), know not (kenna).

566   **THE SNUFFER'S TOAST**

Gw 56.6. "Communicated by F. R. Brown, Paisley, as heard from a Bourtie character named Charlie." (Gw)

567   **SNUFFER'S GRACE**

Gw 56.7. "Same source as [566 'The Snuffer's Toast']."

568   **TOBACCO PIPES AND PORTER**   The title is editorial.

Gw 49.112. This is given in *Rymour Club Miscellanea*, 2.108, as one of "Two Short Songs" which were "said or sung by persons unwilling or unable to comply with repeated requests". The words "can" and "could" appear in the fourth line in place of the two occurrences of "will".

569   **THERE WAS FIRST GUID ALE**   Cf. *Rymour Club Miscellanea* 1.175 "Speyside Brewing Rhyme" which is stated to be "descriptive of a 'broust' of home-brewed ale, and the declining qualities of the product", and Robert Chambers, *Popular Rhymes of Scotland*, new edition (Edinburgh and London, [1870]), p. 392 "Different kinds of malt liquor". The title is editorial.

A   Gw 32.112. The heading is "Rhyme".
B   Gw 14.114.

570   **GLENDRONACH**   The title is editorial.

Ob. 62. "[Mrs Rettie] refers to a recollection she has of her father repeating a panegyric which the Rev. James Simmie, minister of Rothiemay in the early part of last century, composed on the Glendronach Distillery. She can recall only a part of the refrain – [Text]." (G, Ob.62, 9 February 1909) See map for the location of Glendronach.

571   **TAM BROON**   Cf. Kennedy No. 283.

Dm 414a; Troup 1.37-8, Dw 5.94-5. "Noted 29th June 1908." (Dm) "From his father. He speaks of it as [a] very old song. 1.1 'jeck' = knave (Mr Troup). I did not find this meaning of jeck or jack in Jamieson or Warrack, though it is quite clear here. *Chorus.* Mr Troup states that this was acted with four persons round a table, the singer signalling to each of the four in succession." (Dw)

572   **I'VE GOT A SHILLING**   Cf. Sharp No. 344 "The Jolly Shilling" and Opie No. 480.

A   Misc. 79; Alexander 2.12-3, Dw 3.74-5. "Mr Alexander, September, 1906; from a painter working at Newton house fifty years ago. But it seems English and modern." (D, Misc.) January or February 1907. (Alexander) The refrain is given as with the music in Misc.; in Alexander it is:

> *No pot nor pint shall grieve me*
> *Nor no false girl shall deceive me*
> *Rolling home, rolling home rolling ho-o-me*
> *As I go rolling home.*

B   Gw 38.51-2. "Our good friend the Editor has had a sederunt with Mr William Spence, Peterhead, securing from him several song records for which I am very much indebted. ... 'The Ramalie,' and 'The Shilling' – a capstan song – were heard sung by Greenland sailors many years ago." (G, Ob. 70, 6 April 1909)
C   Gw 44.53. Acknowledged in Ob. 93, 21 September 1909. After the complete first stanza, there is the note: "It goes over all the change, and when the last 2d is reached, 'There's a penny for to spend, there's a penny for to lend, / But nothing to take home to the wife." "This one I learned from the Ross girls but my aunt, my father's sister, used to sing it though she had but a few words." (Robertson, *Song Notes*, 1.32)

662

573 **JOCK GEDDES** Cf. Middleton, 1.107-9 and *Tocher* 4 (No. 25), pp. 44-5. Middleton mentions that it was a *People's Friend* prize song.

Gw 56.51-4. "Sung by D. Lawson senior, Logie. Per T. Roger." (Gw) At 1.3 "'im" replaces deleted "ye". St. 6 r. 2 "soo": MS "coo". "Sandy Campbell" at 6.1 is a taboo name for a pig; see *Tocher* 3 (No. 20), 151. Acknowledged in Ob. 51, 17 November 1908.

574 **THE DRUNK MASON**

Gw 34.86-9. "I do not know this one." (Robertson, *Song Notes*, 2.37) 5.3 "Maggie": the mare in Burns's poem "Tam o' Shanter".

575 **THE DRYGATE BRIG** Cf. *Whistle-Binkie* (Glasgow, 1890), 2.252-4 and *Lyric Gems*, 2.55-6 "The Drygate Brig" written by Alexander Rodger. "'The Drygate Brig' appears in *Whistle Binkie* as the composition of Sandy Roger, to whom we have once or twice referred as one of our best songwriters of the earlier half of last century. The Drygate Brig is in the north-east district of Glasgow. In *Lyric Gems* the song is set to the same tune as 'The Battle of Sheriffmuir' – an old Highland reel known as 'The Cameronian Rant'; and this is the tune to which I have heard it sung by Mr J. Quirrie, Craigston." (G, Ob. 162) The main title is editorial.

Gm 2.92a; Gw 46.35-6. September 1906. (Gm) The title in Gm is "On Monday nicht". "'The Drygate Brig', by A. Rodger. Whitelaw, p. 173." William Walker. (Gw)

576 **THE TARVES RANT** "'The Tarves Rant' is well known in our locality, and I have recorded it several times, the versions agreeing pretty closely. Certain references in the song prove it to be a comparatively recent production. As a study of the farm-servant 'out of the yoke,' it is one of the best things we have. The superior critic may despise such productions as being mere 'strouds' [rubbishy verses]; but touches like what we have in verses 3 and 7 of 'The Tarves Rant' [as E 7 and similar to E 3] are more intimate and illuminating than reams of pastoral poetry of the conventional type. No kind of minstrelsy, indeed, is more loyal to fact and truth than the ploughman song. Its purely literary value may be slight; but what it loses in inspiration it gains in sincerity and conviction. I have a record of the tune [A] from Mr Sam. Davidson, Tarves, and it appears to be a variant of an air which I have got to 'The banks of sweet Dundee.' In one version of the words I find a refrain which seems to show that the tune employed was a set of 'Jack Munro.'" (G, Ob. 81) See map for the location of Tarves.

A Gm 2.80a; Gw 7.29-34. August 1906. (Gm and Gw)
B Gm 3.82b. March 1908. Acknowledged in Ob. 19, 7 April 1908.
C Gm 4.171a. The tune headed "Riccarton" is marked "Also to 'Tarves Rant'."
D Gw 18.105-9.
E Gw 20.71-3. Copied May 1908 from a farm servant's manuscript book supplied by Sam Davidson.
F Gw 26.77-82.

577 **ROBIE AND GRANNY** Cf. Sharp No. 318 "Robbie and Grannie". A tune headed "Robin and Granny" sent to Greig by Miss Lucy Broadwood for inspection and comment is copied at Gm 3.35b.

Gw 57.71. "'Robie and Grannie' is one of our humorous old ditties. The above version was got from a Donside correspondent, and is incomplete. We hope some reader may be able to give us a fuller one. The ditty, I may say, has also been found in England." (G, Ob. 161) The song had been acknowledged in Ob. 145, 20 September 1910.

578 **TAKE IT, BOB** "From Mr Ironside, Bonnykelly, I have received a copy of the words of 'Take it Bob.' The tune, which I got from Mr Ironside some time ago, is set to one or two other ditties, such as 'Tak' it Man,' and appears to be traditional. It may originally have been a jig. 'Take it Bob' is modern and has been published. It makes a very good song of the humorous type – [Text, st. 1]. One verse achieves humour of an intense if somewhat grim order – [St. 3]." (G, Ob. 8, 21 January 1908)

Gm 3.45b; Gw 13.22-4. January 1908. (Gw) 3.3 "people" is taken from Ob.; Gw gives "heard round" without any sign of omission.

579 **TAK IT, MAN, TAK IT** Cf. Ford, pp. 15-7 "Tak' It, Man, Tak' It" written by David Webster. "The song, 'Tak' it, man, tak' it,' may be taken as a kind of an apology for the miller. It has been popular over the main part of lowland Scotland for a couple of generations. The words were written by David Webster, a minor poet of considerable repute, who was born in Dunblane in 1787 and died at Paisley in 1837. Like so many more of the bardic clan he was rather unsteady in his habits. The tune, as I have noted it from Mr A. Barron, Mains of Whitehill, is in 9/8 rhythm, and suggests an affinity with 'Patie's Wedding.' The song is often rendered with an accompaniment to represent the sound of the clapper, produced by beating on a table with elbows and fists, or using an empty brose-caup for the purpose." (G, Ob. 41)

A Gm 1.59a. 1905. "Cf. 'Patie's Weddin'." (Gm) "The Cogie" is given as an alternative title. R.1 "Then": MS "The"; r. 4 "cragie": MS "bragie". In r. 2 and 3 "cogie" is altered from "bogie" and "yill" from "gill".
B Gw 24.61-4. "Composed by D. Webster." (Gw) "Same as in Whitelaw's *Scottish Songs*, p. 248." William Walker. (Gw)

580 **ALE AND TOBACCO** Cf. Kennedy No. 274 "Here's To the Grog".

Gm 1.163b. April 1906.

581 **DONALD BLUE** Cf. Ford, pp. 48-9, and Ord, pp. 52-3. "'Donald Blue' has long been a popular ditty. Like other lays with an 'in the mornin'' owreword, it sings to a variant of 'Johnnie Cope.'" (G, Ob. 77)

A Dm 74c; Gillespie 456-7. At Dm 73, Duncan notes that Mrs Gillespie sang "Donal' Blue" to the same tune as she sang "Peggy in the Mornin'", and adds: "From Alex Imlah, Woodhead, Delgaty, in sixties. Noted 1905. George F. Duncan also remembers from R. Mackie. [The pairs of words shown in italics are linked by slurs.]

> My name's Donal Blue, an' ye ken me fu' weel,
> *Strake me* canny wi' the hair, I'm a quaet, simple chiel,
> But *gin ye* raise my bleed, I'm as roch's the verra deil;
> Wi' a claught *o' yer* noddle in the mornin.
>> But *gin ye* raise my bleed, I'm as roch's the verra deil;
>> Wi' a claught *o' yer* noddle in the mornin.

Ford, p. 48, says it is sung to 'Johnnie Cope'."(Dm) The changes indicated in brackets were made after the text was first written: 1.2 Gine (Gin), 1.3 gine (gin), 4.4 nocket (knocket), 5.2 Gine (Gin), 6.1 I (He), my (his), 9.3 keen (ken). The word "claught" (1.4) has the various senses "blow" and "clutch" in the different versions.

B Gm 3.49c.

C Dm 75a. "Noted from William Duncan 1906. As sung by W. Duguid, farm servant, about 1870. See [tune A]. They are not independent, yet not mere versions. The second half is *identical* with [that] tune, (Mrs Petrie's form) [see 'Peggy in the Mornin''], except penultimate note; yet the first portion of this (third metrical line) is an exact imitation, a fourth higher, of its own first line, which is different from the other tune. The A sharp is quite distinct, and indeed enters into that imitation."(Dm)

D Gm 4.168a. "Another way very like 'Johnnie Cope'."(Gm)

E Gm 4.46a; Gw 40.61.

F Gm 1.94a. "December 1905. 'Johnnie Cope'. *Folk-Song Journal*, 2.287. Cf. ['Peggy in the Mornin'' from Miss Annie Ritchie and Mrs Stuart]." (Gm)

G Gm 4.146b.

H Gm 4.117c. Acknowledged in Ob. 147, 4 October 1910.

I Dm 478a. "Mrs Lyall, from her mother. Noted 26th November 1908. The tune is another version of [348] 'Jock o' Rhynie' [A and B]; also [the first two lines of 477 'The Weaver Lad']. Mrs Lyall had not heard of 'Jock o' Rhynie'; but the first lines and refrain rather suggest it."(Dm)

J Gm 1.191c. "See [347 'The Branyards o' Delgaty', D, G, K, L, M]." (Gm) This is No. 57 in the set of tunes received from Riddell.

K Gw 24.14-7.

L Gw 48.37-40. Acknowledged in Ob. 112, 1 February 1910.

M Gw 36.29, Robertson, *Letters to Duncan*, 28 September 1914. In Gw 36, the lines appear directly after a fragment of another song on page 28 which is headed "Donald Blue" and begins "In Union Street". In her letter, Robertson comments: "I remember a verse of 'The Smith's Drunken Wife' not in the verson given [i.e. in Ob. 77]." The first line appears there as: "Now the smith he is blest we guid a sober wife".

582 **THE DRAP O' CAPPIE O** Cf. Johnson No. 297. "The song recalls 'The Wicked Wife,' and 'The Wife in the Wether's Skin.'" (G, Ob. 177)

A Gm 4.95c. The alternative title "Deevil's Buckie" is given in brackets.

B Gm 3.38c. October 1907.

C Gw 58.26-8. Acknowledged in Ob. 177, 16 May 1911.

583 **O, FOO WILL I GET HAME** Cf. "I'm Aye Drunk, I'm Seldom Sober" sung by Andra Stewart on the record *Folksongs & Music from the Berryfields of Blair* (Prestige/International 25016).

A Dm 414b; Troup 1.39, Dw 5.96-7. "From his brother. Noted 29th June 1908. This is a version of the air 'Blythe, blythe and merry was she' [from Mrs Gillespie]. The refrain especially closely corresponds. The first words turn out to be a corruption of '*Aqua vitae's* in my head' (Latin pronounced Scotch wise)! See [B]." (Dm) "1.2 Mr Troup first sang this, 'Brandy cost me fowr and nine,' and this is given [with the music]; but he afterwards gave ['Brandy rumbles in my wime'] as the original form, stating that the other was the change he had made himself, because he did not like to sing the original form, and hence took the changed version. Learnt from his brother, Alexander Troup. He had no explanation to give of the strange first line; but William Duncan, believes that Mrs Duncan, of Craigculter, sang this song, and that her first line began thus:– 'Acky wyti's in my heid, brandy's rummlin' in my wime.' Obviously this means 'aqua vitae', though curiously enough, it employs the *English* pronunciation of the Latin words, not the Scotch. But the most interesting thing is that it furnishes an explanation of Mr Troup's strange first line. 'Ask my feet and then' is thus revealed as a corruption of 'aqua vitae's in', though it is curious that now it is the Scotch pronunciation of the Latin that is employed. See a few more of Mrs Duncan's words in [Dm] 491." (Dw)

B   Dm 491a. "Dorian. From my own recollections. Noted 5th March 1909. It was sung by Mrs Duncan, Craigculter. Mrs Gillespie also remembers it, but was less sure of the air. 'Wity' has long *i*, implying the English pronunciation of *Aqua vitae*; while the corruption of 'Ask my feet an'' [A] implies the Scotch. Mrs Gillespie remembers also the following verse:–

> I got a shillin fae a frien'
> To buy a new sark to my sin,
> The drooth it gaed sae near my he'rt
> Till hame wi' it I couldna win." (Dm)

The line completed in shorthand runs: "An brandy's rum'lin in my wime".

584   HOOLY AND FAIRLY   Cf. Johnson, No. 191 and Whitelaw, *Songs*, pp. 29-30.

A   Dm 278c; Gillespie 532-4. "As sung by father, also Mrs Imlah, Woodhead, Delgaty. Noted 7th April, 1907. The song is in Johnson, No. 191, but the tune is different, and the words too in part. These words correspond with what Stenhouse gives as the older form; repeated in Whitelaw, p. 29. Probably it would be better in 9/8 time."(Dm)   The words "seem to" are deleted before "correspond". The word "hooly" was later altered to "heely" throughout, and there are the following other alterations: 2.1 Gerrie (Gairrie), 4.4 wifie (wife), 6.4 gine (gin), wifie (wife), 7.4 gine (gin), 11.3 cuckle (cuckold), 11.4 wifie (wife). "Crummie" and "Gerrie" (2.1) are the names of cows. A and B are versions of the anonymous form of the song given at Whitelaw, *Songs*, p. 29.

B   Dm 339a. "Mode? Noted by Mrs Harper from her mother, August 1907. See [A]. Source of this same as last air ['The Duke o' Gordon's Three Daughters' which Mrs Greig heard from her grandmother, Mrs Stuart, Auchmaleddie]. Mrs Harper gives 'First she drank "hooly"' – no doubt a slip of the singer for 'Crummie'. This air is nearer Johnson's, No. 191, though not identical."(Dm)

C   Gillespie 529-30. A note at the end runs: "This is not father's 'Hooly and Fairly.' I will give it you later on [see A]." Duncan later gave Mrs Gillespie's source for this version, adding: "From Mary Kindness, Turriff". There are the following alterations to the text as first written: 1.4 wifie (wife), r. 2 gine (gin), 2.2 ditin (dichtin), 5.1 waring (warring), 6.2 upraidd (upredd). The words "bandies" (7.2) and "doited" (8.2) are alterations that have been accepted into the text, the original first word being perhaps "bardies" (as in Whitelaw) although the "r" is heavily deleted, and the original second word not being fully legible. The C version is the form of the song by Joanna Baillie given at Whitelaw, *Songs*, p. 30.

585   JOCK AND MEG   Cf. the slip L.C. Folio 70, p. 142 *The Week After the Fair* (n.p., n.d.), and "The Haill Week o' the Fair" sung by Jamie Taylor on *Scottish Tradition* 1 "Bothy Ballads" (Tangent Records, TNGM 109).

A   Gm 2.15d; Gw 5.79-81. "June 1906. Cf. 'Crook and Plaid', Christie 2.264."(Gm)   At 6.1 "harm" is written above deleted "hoose(?)".

B   Gm 4.112a, Bm 223c; Gw 58.72-4. Acknowledged in Ob. 154, 22 November 1910. At 2.4 "done" is altered from "deen". The B, C, and D tunes were copied into Bm (which contains copies of Child ballad tunes) through a mistaken connection with 263 "Jock the Leg and the Merry Merchant" (Child No. 282). Duncan notes in Bm: "'Jock and Meg' is not connected here."

C   Gm 3.55b, Bm 222b. February 1908.

D   Gm 4.82a, Bm 222c.

E   Gw 55.46-9.

F   Gw 44.108-11. Acknowledged in Ob. 57, 29 December 1908.

G   Gw 13.84-6. January 1908. (Gw)   Acknowledged in Ob. 10, 4 February 1908.

H   Gw 53.37-8. "From Mrs Ingram, Methlick." Annie Shirer. (Gw)

I   Gw 37.109-10.

J   Ob. 7. "In [587] 'Johnnie, my man' we had one partner of the home bringing it to ruin with drink. In 'Jock and Meg' the candle is lighted at both ends, and the conflagration is at once lurid and rapid. Husband and wife of course rail at each other. – [Text, sts. 1-2.] Some glimmering hope of reformation appears at the end. – [Text, st. 3.]" (G, Ob. 7, 14 January 1908)

K   Gw 45.50. "I noticed a localised version of a Glasgow Music Hall song of fifty years ago. In it the word 'Brindle' was substituted for 'Bridewell' i.e. jail. One verse of the original runs as follows:– [Text]." J.O. (Gw)

586   THE BARLEY BREE   "'The Barley Bree' has been communicated by Mr James Thomson, Blackhill, who says that he never heard but one man sing it, and that was nearly sixty years ago. It cannot be much older than that, as the teetotaler is a comparatively modern emergence. It seems to have been written by some minor bard with a fair amount of literary skill. The tune, my correspondent says, is 'There's nae luck aboot the hoose.'" (G, Ob. 153)

A   Ob. 153.

B   Ob. 156. "Referring to 'The Barley Bree' [in Ob. 153] Miss Robertson says that it is taken from a Temperance song-book published some fifty years ago, and she gives the following additional lines:– [Text]." (G, Ob. 156)

587 **JOHNNIE, MY MAN** Cf. *Tocher* 1 (No. 1), 16-7 "Johnnie My Man". "Dealing with current folksong one has to remark not only the comparative absence of the drinking ditty but the actual presence of the 'temperance' lay. Plenty of sermons will be preached against intemperance at this season, but we do not think that any appeal from the pulpit would have more effect than the following traditional ditty, which is widely known and sung. [Text.]" (G,Ob. 7, 14 January 1908) In a note without tune at Gm 4.148, Greig mentions that the "butcher in Fetterangus" sang "Johnny My Man" to the tune "Lass o' Glenshee".

A   Dm 115a; Gillespie 149-50. "From Mary Cruickshank, servant, fifty years ago. Noted 1905. Words only in Ford, p. 327. Second half of air is only repetition." (Dm) The changes shown in brackets were made after the text was first written: 1.1 no (nae), on (o'), 3.1 no (nae), mind (wyme), 3.4 going (goin'), 4.2 no (nae), 4.3 ammend (amend), 5.1 no (nae), 8.1 ain fireside (fireside). At 4.2, the word "are", which is inserted before "gone", is accepted into the text.

B   Gm 3.149c; Gw 42.95-6. At 1.1 "are" replaces deleted "do".

C   Gm 1.67b; Gw 1.28-30. "August 1905. Cf. 'Here awa'."(Gm) 1.1 "ye": MS "yo".

D   Gm 4.71a.

E   Gm 3.1b. September 1907. Alternative notes and phrases are indicated in sol fa; doh = A.

F   Gm 3.32b. "From John Fox, 122 M'Lellan St., Glasgow, who heard the song when pretty young." (Gm)

G   Gm 2.72a. July 1907.

H   Gw 22.6-8. At 1.3 "Yer" is altered from "Ye're", at 4.3 "again" is deleted following "return", and at 7.4 "e'en" replaces deleted "hame".

I   Gw 50.92-4.

J   Gw 6.101-2.

K   Gw 60.67-8. A version of this song contributed by Annie Shirer, either K or L, is acknowledged in Ob. 164, 31 January 1911.

L   Gw 51.73-4. "From a Mr John Dick, twenty-five years ago. He is now in Fraserburgh and is a fine singer by ear." A.S. (Gw)

M   Gw 38.96-7.

588 **COME HAME TO YER LINGLES** Cf. Whitelaw, *Songs*, p. 334.

Dm 62a. At Dm 61, Duncan notes that Mrs Gillespie knew the tune she sang for "Jock Robb" as that of "Come Hame to yer Lingles" "but [she] does not remember the words except that these were repeated as in ['Jock Robb'], and that it is a wife pleading with a husband to 'come hame' from drinking. He is a shoemaker, the 'lingles' being 'roset-en's':– [Text]. See Whitelaw's *Songs*, p. 334."

589 **FIN YE GANG AWA JOHNNIE** Cf. Middleton, 1.29-30 "When You Gang Awa' Johnnie".

a) Gw 37.111-3, b) Gw 40.69.

590 **THE BRAW BLACK JUG**

A   Dm 239c; 998/7/3/10, Dw 2.66. "Learnt at Kinaldie about 1855 from a young man of Banff. Noted 19th December 1906. In William Chappell, *Old English Popular Music*, ed. H. Ellis Wooldridge (London and New York, 1893), 2.179, there is a song from broadsides, having some affinity in words. Its chorus is, 'O good ale, thou art my darling, and my joy both night and morning', and one verse corresponds with lines 3 and 4 here and two lines of another verse. The air has no connection. Mrs Gillespie had heard it sung by William Calder, blacksmith at Artamford." (Dm) At the end of st. 4, "etc." is an editorial addition. 1 r. 2 *"darling"*: MS *"drling"*. The word "night" in this line is a later insertion by Duncan.

B   Gw 45.8. Acknowledged in Ob. 95, 5 October 1909.

591 **AUL' SANNERS AN' I** Cf. R.H. Cromek, *Remains* (London, 1810), pp. 95-6 "My Kimmer and I".

A   Dm 379c. "From James Mackay at Boyndlie. Noted 25th September 1907." (Dm)

B   Dm 355b. "Noted by Mrs Harper from her mother August 1907. The air is a version of [211] 'Villikens and his Dinah': see [A], with references." (Dm)

592 **THE DROUTHY SOUTERS**

A   Gm 4.107b.

B   Gm 1.149a. March 1906. "Sung by 'Whitebog'." (Gm)

593 **GOOD ALE** Cf. Kinsley No. 596 "O gude ale comes etc.".

A   Dm 375a; Argo-Duncan 5-6, Dw 3.139. "Learnt from a farmservant fully twenty-six years ago. Noted 13th September 1907. Air a version of the tune appearing with 'Hynd Horn' [from Miss Jemima Milne] and 'Logan Braes' [from George Innes], 'My he'rt it is sair' [as noted by George F. Duncan] and 'The Donside Lassie' [from George Garioch]. There is a chorus, but the air of it is the same." (Dm) "He thinks these are the whole of the words." (Dw) 2.3 "'He': sic; I?" (Dw)

B Gm 1.187c. This is No. 42 of the set of tunes received from Riddell. There is a note copied from Riddell's manuscript along with the music: "Also sung to other words. The air is akin to 'Logan Water'." (Gm) Greig adds: "See Mr Duncan's version and Christie 2.252" and also refers to Henry T. Whyte (Fionn), *The Celtic Lyre* (Edinburgh, 1898), No. 2.

594 **THE DRUNKARD'S RAGGIT WEAN** Cf. *National Choir*, 1.206-7 "The Drunkard's Raggit Wean" written by J. P. Crawford.

 Gm 2.78a. June 1907. "'Castles in the air.'" (Gm)

595 **WATTY AND MEG** Cf. Robert Ford, *Vagabond Songs and Ballads of Scotland* (Paisley, 1899-1901), 1.115-24 "Watty and Meg" by Alexander Wilson.

 Gm 3.203c.

596 **REFORM AND WHIGS** George Outram, *Lyrics Legal and Miscellaneous*, 3rd ed. (Edinburgh and London, 1874), pp. 70-2 "The Reform Bill".

 Gw 43.42-5. Although unascribed in Gw, this may perhaps be identified as the version sent by William Watson which Greig acknowledged in Ob. 93, 21 September 1909. "Tune = 'The Quaker's Wife'. Notes at the beginning and end run: "Outram's *Poems*" and "Printed in Outram's volume". 2.3-4 "sort the coo ... sort the nation": feed the cow .. set the nation to rights.

597 **WEARY ON THE GILL STOUP**

A Gm 2.17a; Gw 12.37-8. "June 1906. Cf. 'O Gin that I were mairrit' – 'Byways of Scottish Song' [in *The Weekly Welcome*] 19 June 1907." (Gm)

B Alexander 2.19, Misc. 47. "From Mr Alexander, September 1906, and William Duncan, February 1906. Above are Mr Alexander's words: no more remembered." (D, Misc.) January or February 1907. (Alexander) In the first two lines of the refrain in Alexander, "stoup" is written "stoups" with the final "s" deleted. In Misc., the title is "Weary fa' [on] the Gill Stoup". Duncan lists this among the songs to be sung to the tune "Robin Tamson's Smiddy".

598 **ALWAYS ON THE SPREE**

 Gm 2.82b. July 1907.

599 **THE FILLIN' O' THE PUNCHBOWL WEARIES ME**

 Dm 139c. At Dm 140, this item from Mrs Gillespie is noted as being sung to the tune of "He's a Bonnie, Bonnie Laddie That I'm Gaun Wi'" from the same singer. "Noted 1905. Often sung." (Dm)

600 **WAE BE TO THAT WEARY DRINK, JOHN ANDERSON, MY JO** For discussion of "John Anderson my Jo" songs, see Kinsley No. 260.

A Garioch 30-1, Dw 4.74-5. "Learnt from young Samuel Dunn at Ininteer fifty years ago. It is evidently a modern product of the temperance movement such as was common fifty years ago. The tune of course is 'John Anderson, my Jo'."(Dw) The close is given as in Dw; Garioch has after "Jean" in 5.3 the direction "[*spoken, and join*]" and does not give the alternative "John" in the last line.

B Gw 53.51.

601 **JOHN BARLEYCORN, MY JO**

 Gw 17.77-81. "The above was composed by the late George Barron, shoemaker, at one time working at Auchnagatt, who I have been told composed his poetry when drunk and swore at it when sober." A.M. Insch. (Gw)

602 **THE TEETOTAL MILL** Cf. John Ashton, *Modern Street Ballads* (London, 1888), pp. 45-7 "Hurrah for Father Mathew's Mill" and the broadsides McNaughtan No. 2589 *The Teetotal Mill* (Poet's Box, Glasgow, 5 September 1857) and Madden 17, No. 332 *The Teetotal Mill. I'll Warm Yer*. (n.p., n.d.). "With the intention of giving a hearing to all sides of the question we follow up the two songs which countenance conviviality ['A Cogie o' Yill' (as in Ford, pp. 329-30) and 560 'A Wee Drappie O't'] with one which recommends total abstinence. In Ashton's *Modern Street Ballads* the song is 'Father Mathew's Mill,' and this we take to be the original designation of the wonderful place, Father Mathew having probably been a priest who had undertaken a crusade against drink. Some singer, to make the thing more intelligible to the general hearer, had substituted the epithet 'Teetotal' for 'Father Mathew's.' Besides being more readily intelligible to the present generation the substituted word is better for vocal purposes. The word 'shot' in the next to last verse means 'credit.' I have heard 'The Teetotal Mill' declaimed with great spirit by Mr James Greig, New Deer, to the tune of 'Villikins and his Dinah.'" (G, Ob. 144) "Miss Bell Robertson, referring to 'The Teetotal Mill,' reminds me that Father Mathew was an Irish priest who distinguished himself by

his crusade against intemperance, during the thirties and forties of last century. His fame seems to have been phenomenal, and his influence quite extraordinary. My correspondent says that Robert Gray Mason who wrote [604] 'The Clear Caul' Water' was contemporary with Father Mathew and thought it a great honour to ride in his carriage." (G, Ob. 147) On Father Theobald Mathew (1790-1856) and the Reverend Robert Gray Mason (1797-1867), see Brian Harrison, *Dictionary of British Temperance Biography* (Sheffield, 1973), p. 87.

Ob. 144.

603 **NANCY WHISKY** Cf. Kennedy No. 279. Greig prints a composite text in Ob. 90 under the title "The Dublin Weaver" and comments: "It is gratifying to find a song like this, with so good a moral, enjoying a wide and enduring popularity. We have already had occasion to point out that folk-song rarely lends itself to the glorification of drinking but rather discountenances it; and inasmuch as the testimony of folk-song on all questions bearing on the morale of the people carries the greatest weight, we are entitled to maintain that on the subject of drink the popular conscience has been, and is, wonderfully sound. As showing how the central idea of this particular song is recognised, we may mention that it is often named 'Nancy Whisky.' We have recorded two tunes for it, one of them a Dorian having affinities with a number of other folk-tunes."

A   Gm 3.2b; Gw 19.8-10. September 1907. (Gm)
B   Gm 3.149b; Gw 32.44-6. Acknowledged in Ob. 59 and 64, 19 January and 23 February 1909. 2.4 is preceded by a deleted line: "Till Nancy Whisky had me beguiled".
C   Dm 90a; Gillespie 301-2. "From father and mother. Noted 1905. Called also 'The Dublin Weaver,' or 'I am a Weaver.' The ballad is named by Christie (2.128) in connection with a different air. The melody appears (essentially) in Riddell's *Airs*, called 'Two Brothers in the Army.'" (Dm) The following revisions shown in brackets were made by Duncan to the text as first written: 1.2 a weaver to my trade (a ro-ch and a rakish blade,), 2.1 fifteen (seventeen), 2.2 has been (was), told (paid), 2.3 on (down), 3.1 up (down), 3.3 I will (I'll), 4.4 my heart (had me), 6.3 Fifty (Thirty), 6.4 quickly (down), 8.1 O Nancy's sister I chanced to spy (Nancy's sister did me decoy), 8.4 all that (all), and stanza 7 is heavily altered to:

> I put may hand into my pocket
> And all the money was well paid down,
> And all remainèd to buy my clothing,
> But all remainèd was but one crown.

Duncan notes: "The corrections are from John Duncan, April, 1908, from whom Mrs Gillespie learnt the song. There was a final verse expressing some kind of repentance." (D, Gillespie)
D   Dm 246c; Mackay 1.24, Dw 4.167-8. "Learnt in Clatt twenty-seven years ago. Noted 21st February 1907. Mrs Gillespie had also heard this tune. The rhythm of this might be still better expressed as 9/8." (Dm) "5.4 'a naked scale': that is, a sixpence (Mr Mackay)." (Dw)
E   Gm 4.72b.
F   Gm 1.160a. April 1906. "'False Mallie' [from Alexander Robb]. 'I will set my good ship in order'." (Gm)
G   Gm 2.51b. July 1906.
H   Gw 24.1-3.
I   Gw 41.67-9.
J   Gw 53.63-4. "From my uncle." Annie Shirer. (Gw)
K   Gw 37.107. Acknowledged in Ob. 76, 18 May 1909.

604 **THE CLEAR CAULD WATER** "This ditty has been communicated by Miss Bell Robertson, with the information, got from her father, that it was composed by a mason of the name of Robert Gray, who was a popular temperance lecturer about the Forties of last century. She says that it was a treat when sung by Willie Ross, a local singer of a bygone generation, to whom my correspondent frequently refers as a capital exponent of the native minstrelsy. Besides 'The Clear Cauld Water' we have had other ditties which show that the folk-singer is often an earnest advocate of temperance." (G, Ob. 175) "The author of 'The Clear Cauld Water' should have been given as Robert Gray Mason. By an inadvertence the surname was detached and treated as the name of his trade." (G, Ob. 177) See also note to 602 "The Teetotal Mill".

A   Dm 55d. "From Robert Mackie, Craiglug, Carnousie. Noted by me September 1905. George F. Duncan states that the song was sung by Robert Mackie's grandfather, who died at a great age, and must have sung it about the beginning of the nineteenth century. The song heard from others also. The tune is Gaelic; see *Lyric Gems*, 2.51." (Dm)
B   Misc. 101. At line 1, "auld wives" is given as a variant. "Air – 'The Lea Rig'. See Johnson, No. 49. Mrs Gillespie, from father; also William Duncan, who gives 'ale wives,' as heard by John Davidson, New Deer." (D, Misc.)
C   Gm 4.158b.
D   Gw 34.65-6, Ob. 175. Acknowledged in Ob. 47, 20 October 1908. "Her father says it was composed by Robert Gray – mason – a temperance lecturer who was rather popular among the 'forties'. A treat when sung by Willie Ross." (Gw) 2.3 "alewives": Gw "alewines", Ob. "ale-wives"; 4.2 "intemperance": Gw "temperance", Ob. "intemperance".

605 **SCOTCH MEDLEY**   There is some similarity to the first song in the chapbook L.C. 2853: 13 *The Scots Medley. To which are Added, The Land of Shilelah, Maggy Lauder, and Bessy Bell and Mary Gray* (William Scott, Greenock, n.d.). The chapbook song, which begins "As I cam' in by Calder fair", also consists of song titles, some of which are the same, but it appears to be a separate composition.

  Gw 43.100-4. Acknowledged in Ob. 93, 21 September 1909. 8.3 "Loupin": MS "houpin".

606 **FY, LET'S A TO THE BRIDAL**   Cf. Johnson No. 58.

  Dm 160c; Gillespie 246-9. "From Mrs Birnie, Artamford. Noted 1905. For words see Robert Chambers's *Songs of Scotland Prior to Burns*, p. 146. Only the words here, which are a chorus, are not in the printed versions. The tune is different, being an adaptation of ['Oh, but my Lovie she's little, she's little' from Mrs Gillespie]; Chambers's is from Johnson, No. 58." (Dm) A few clarifying alterations made by Duncan to the text as first written have been accepted: 4.4 "shangie" for "shaggie", 4.7 "Maudie" for "Maddie", 5.5 "pearlins" for "parlins", 7.6 "skink" for "sink", and 8.2 "mull" for "will".

607 **THE WEDDING**   Cf. John Stokoe and Samuel Reay, *Songs and Ballads of Northern England* (Newcastle-on-Tyne and London, 1893), pp. 24-6 "The Skipper's Wedding". "This riotous ditty was communicated some time ago by a gentleman who said that he had heard it sung in Buchan more than forty years ago. Quite lately I heard a bit of it sung by a local gentleman. The tune is Irish, and is known as 'The night before Larry was stretched.' It is sung in 9/8 rhythm, full of 'go,' and well adapted to the song. In *Songs of Northern England* there is a ditty 'The Skipper's Wedding,' which is set to the same tune." (G, Ob. 151)

  A   Gm 1.54c; Gw 4.29-33. "James Morrison M.A., Dunbeath. January 1906. Also sent 'My wife has ta'en the gee.' Got words from Mr. M. Heard in Buchan forty years ago. Johnson No. 383." (Gm) Greig also gives a reference in Gm to "The Skipper's Wedding" in *Songs and Ballads of Northern England*, pp. 24-6. "G. Morrison M.A. (late of Udny)." (Gw) Opposite 9.7 "Got fun wi' the mixin' o' legs" is written "Got fun wi' the ploy ye may ken" and it is this form that appears in the text as printed in Ob. 151.

  B   Dm 238a; 998/7/3/10, Dw 2.59-60. "Dorian. Learnt from his father in Fetteresso sixty years ago. Noted 19th December 1906. *Note*. This might be better on two sharps. The air has affinities with [616 'Patie's Wedding' A], which are closest in second strain." (Dm) "He states that two verses are missing." (Dw)

  C   Gw 62.100-1.

608 **CUTTIE'S WEDDIN'**   Cf. Norman Buchan, *101 Scottish Songs* (Glasgow, 1962), p. 122.

  A   Gm 1.52b. 1904. The sources referred to by Greig in his note shown here with the music are *Davie's Caledonian Repository* (James Davie, Aberdeen [c. 1830-40]), 2.76 "Coutie's Wedding" and *Middleton's Selection of Strathspeys, Reels etc.* arranged by Peter Milne (London and Glasgow, n.d.), p. 7 "Cuttie's Wedding". Greig also gives a reference to Peter Buchan's *Ancient Ballads and Songs of the North of Scotland* (Edinburgh, 1875), 1.250-1.

  B   Gm 2.18b. "Strathspey, – old." (Gm)

609 **THE TINKERS' WEDDIN'**   Cf. Ford, pp. 1-4 "The Tinklers' Waddin'". "This lively ditty was written by William Watt, about whom, in connection with another song of his, 'The House o' Glenneuk,' in [Ob. 96], we gave a short note [see 280 'The Pedlar and his Pack']. The tune is an adaptation of a pipe strathspey, the flat seventh, so difficult for the modern vocalist to intone, coming in with characteristic effect. The song is well and widely known. We have heard it sung by a genuine tinker – a high compliment surely to the author." (G, Ob. 102) Greig gives the text in Ob. as it appears in Ford.

  A   Misc. 121; Gillespie 216. "Noted from Mrs Gillespie, 25th June, 1907; from Mary Sinclair (sister of Mrs John Johnstone) when Mrs Gillespie was about fifteen years old (about 1857). See Ford, p. 1: this is a shorter air, containing the essential parts of his. The chorus, 'Dirrim a doo,' etc. was sung to same music; no second strain. Cf. ['Ae Morn last ook as I gaed oot; or, The Rantin Hielan'man' from Mrs Gillespie]. The tune to 'Kempy Kane,' No. 33 in William Motherwell's *Minstrelsy: Ancient and Modern* is partly the same as this." (D, Misc.) "See Ford, p. 1; the following shows Mrs Gillespie's differences:– (1) 'waved upon the green.' 'to hae' (for 'to haud'). Chorus:– 'Drim a doo a doo a doo, drim a doo a daddy O / Drim a doo a doo a doo, Hurrah,' etc. (after each four lines). (2) 'daft' (for 'wild') 'that' (for 'wha') 'marchin order.' Not quite sure of second half: thinks it different. (3) Thinks second line different. 'There was beef.' 'There was *pinches*' (so pronounced in north = 'muckle wime' of ox). 3 'caul coo-heel.' 'caller jeel.' (4) 'whangs o' baps'. Lines 7 and 8 different. (5) Thinks lines 3 and 4 and 9 and 10 different. In line 2 'sic a splore.' (6) First half different; second remembered, but not thought quite the same. (7) The same. (8) Remembered." (D, Gillespie)

  B   Gm 3.100b.

610 **THE DONSIDE WEDDING**

  Gm 4.144b. The title is editorial.

611 **HEY THE BONNIE BREISTKNOTS**   Cf. Johnson No. 214 "The Breast knots" and Ford, pp. 303-6.

Misc. 22; Gillespie 422-4. "See Johnson No. 214 (a different tune) and Ford, p. 303 (different from Johnson). Words by Ross of Lochlee. Cf. [371] 'There Was a Fair'." (D, Misc.) The word "leipit" at 6.3 is glossed in Gillespie as "overheated".

612 **O WHA'S AT THE WINDOW**   Cf. Graham, 2.60-1 "O Wha's at the Window, Wha, Wha?".

Gillespie 561. Duncan has written beside the title: "tune not entered: see below" and at the foot of the page: "Not traditional: words by A. Carlisle; music by R.A. Smith. See Graham 2.61."

613 **THE ROAD TO PETERHEAD**   In Ob. 52, Greig prints the B text and comments: "'The Road to Peterhead' was sent to me some time ago by A.D., but I know nothing about its origin or authorship. The little I have heard about the piece would seem to put it well back in the last century. Quite possibly the author is known, as his versification raises him a little above the average local rhymer. The phrase 'A country shearer by the Scot' is explained by my correspondent as 'a divider of meat.' I shall be glad to have any information about the song or the writer. I got a copy of the tune from Mr George Riddell, Rosehearty, who thinks it a variant of 'John Anderson, my Jo.' At several points it recalls 'Ythanside,' the stanza of which has the same metrical structure. I should not wonder if the two tunes had derived from the same original."

A   Gm 3.85b. April 1908. "Cf. 'John Anderson my Jo,' and some variants of 'Ythanside'. 'The Irish Girl' [from J.W. Spence]." (Gm)

B   Gw 15.1-7. Acknowledged in Ob. 13, 25 February 1908. A note at the end runs: "'A country shearer by the Scot' meant a divider of meat." In the word "country" the letter "r" is underlined and brackets are added above, perhaps indicating that the letter was not present in the source and that the word there read "county". The word "meat" is underlined and a question mark is added. Two textual revisions that appear in Ob. 52 are written in brackets at the ends of the relevant lines: 6.7 "pen" for "pains" and 15.2 "life doth last" for "do last". The words "was a" at 4.3 are given here from Ob.; there is a gap in the line in Gw.

C   Gw 63.6-7. "Lines by William Lillie, on visiting a Penny Wedding at Sandhole, Longside. (Fragment in pencil, written by D. Scott, about 1860.)" (Gw) Before st. 4 is the note: "On another piece of paper." The song is listed among the pieces by Lillie by the title "Penny Wedding" at Gw 63.8.

614 **SHEELICKS**   "This song is the composition of my friend Mr George Thomson, New Deer, and is one of several which he has written – all clever to a degree and marked by a humour as irresistible as it is original. To hear them sung by the author himself is a memorable treat. We have known such a performance break all local records in the matter of bringing down a house. Although never hitherto printed these songs have got about and abroad, until I begin to get records of them from singers at a distance. It is well that the versions of them should be correct, and I am glad to be able, through the courtesy of the author, to print 'Sheelicks' from his own manuscript. Presuming on a continuance of Mr Thomson's kind favours, I hope to be able to give some more specimens of this unique song cycle." (G, Ob. 134)

3088/11, Gw 57.1-5. The text is given from the manuscript which Thomson gave to Greig, which includes a note after the title: "Tune – 'The Deil amon the tailors'." The copy in Gw has "fiddle *fiddle* gaed the fiddle", "*in* a riddle", and "*to* his cross-eyed pet" in the refrain, and "Faistern Even" at 4.6. Acknowledged in Ob. 13, 25 February 1908.

615 **GORDON O' NEWTON'S MARRIAGE**   The song celebrates the marriage of Alexander Gordon of Newton, b. 1804, and Sarah, eldest daughter of Alexander Forbes, which took place on 20 February 1844. (*The House of Gordon*, ed. John Malcolm Bulloch, Aberdeen, 1903-12, 2.489.) See map for the location of Newton.

Dm 287a; Alexander 1.35-6, Dw 3.58-9. "Learnt soon after its composition. Noted 29th April, 1907. Words composed by an Alex. Moir, gamekeeper at Newtoon (an earlier note says 'forester') about 1848 or 1850, when the marriage took place. It was sung at the tenants' dinner. The air is a *third* version of the tune set to [538] 'The Nabob' [A and D]. Lines 5 and 6 of words are from a different verse." (Dm) October or November 1906. (Alexander) 2.1 home: "hame?" (Dw)

616 **PATIE'S WEDDING**   Cf. Johnson No. 383 "Patie's Wedding".

A   Dm 221b; Alexander 1.15-7, Dw 3.43-4. "Learnt in Culsalmond in boyhood. Noted September 1906. Words in Herd, 2.188. Johnson has it, No. 383, but the tune has little resemblance to this, beyond the rhythm. As a traditional tune, Mr Alexander's is of unusual character, and was noted and tested with special care. Compare with tune of [607 'The Wedding' B]." (Dm) October or November 1906. (Alexander) At 2.8 Duncan has altered "berries" to "berry".

B   Dm 274a. "Learnt in Banffshire. Noted 1905. The words were only partially remembered: those given are Herd's. No chorus was sung. See also [607 'The Wedding' B].

C   Gm 1.188b. This is No. 45 of the set of tunes received from Riddell. "Johnson No. 383." (Gm)

D   Gm 2.98c. October 1906.

E   Gw 3.101. March 1906. "Got rest from G.M. [see 607 'The Wedding' A]." (Gw) A note "Herd 2.188" is added in Walker's hand.

617 THE WATERS OF DEE Cf. C.H. Morine, *Maver's Collection of Genuine Scottish Melodies*, Volume 1 (Glasgow, 1865), No. 227 "The Water o' Dee".

Gw 34.13-4. 1.2 "en'": MS "'en". "Sung by a girl who was servant to mother when we were children." B.R. (Gw) The pencilled note "Maggie Johnstone" on 12v apparently identifies the girl. Acknowledged in Ob. 57, 29 December 1908.

618 THE CANTIE CARLIE Cf. the chapbooks L.C. 2787: 14 *The Canty Carlie, or the Ravelled Bridal of Auchronie* (Aberdeen: Printed for A. Keith, Long Acre, and W. Gordon, Upperkirkgate, n.d.) and L.C. 2862: 18 *The Canty Carly, or the Raveled Bridal of Auchronie* (Peterhead: Printed by P. Buchan for A. Keith, and W. Gordon, Aberdeen, n.d.). "The following ballad, gleaned verse by verse many years ago from the lips of a generation now no more, was, for the greater part of a century, one of the most popular songs of the countryside, and in great demand at merry-makings among the rustic population. The subjects of this celebrated marriage, which took place at Auchronie, parish of Kinellar [see map], in 1767, were James Glennie (the 'Cantie Carlie'), a crofter there, and Isobel Grant ('Bellie') a native of Granton, though long resident in Aberdeen. Isobel, who outlived her spouse for half-a-century, died at Auchronie sometime about 1834, and was noted in one of the local newspapers of the time as being better known as 'Bellie Grant, the heroine of the song, "The Cantie Carlie."'" The son, mentioned towards the end, was Alexander Glennie, the only offspring of the union – he too lived at Auchronie, and died unmarried in 1853, at the advanced age of eighty-five. The Rev. Gavin Mitchell, D.D., who married them, was locally reputed to be the author of the ballad." (William Walker, *A Garland of Bon-Accord*, p. 24)

"['The Cantie Carlie'] is a piece of extraordinary length – the longest thing in fact which we have ever heard sung. ... As a specimen of local literature of a bygone day 'The Cantie Carlie' is distinctly interesting. It is understood to have been the work of a Buchan professional gentleman and to be at least a century old. The tune, as I have heard it sung by Mr William Watson, New Byth, and others, is a familiar highland air, which is found associated with other ditties of a similar lively type." (G, Ob. 174, 25 April 1911)

A   *A Garland of Bon-Accord* (Privately printed in an edition of 35 copies, Aberdeen, 1886), pp. 24-37, Gw 19.52-68. "From *A Garland of Bon-Accord*." (Gw) "Last week I gave from the recollection of Mrs Rettie, Millbrex, a verse of 'The Cantie Carlie' [F] to see if any reader could help us to the rest of the song; and I am delighted to report that a copy has been supplied – words and tune, by Mr Jno. R. Trail Hill, Peterhead, from *A Garland of Bon-Accord*, privately printed for subscribers some twenty years ago. It is a long and rollicking rhyme extending to some forty verses. The tune seems to have been adapted from an old reel." (G, Ob. 17, 24 March 1908) The tune does not appear in Gm and is reproduced here from the *Garland*; the text is also taken directly from the *Garland* since the Gw 19 text is inaccurately copied from this source.

B   Gw 19.51v-67v. "William Watson, New Byth, per William Cumming, New Byth, May 1909. Note. – William Watson got 'Cantie Carlie' from his father – one of two men who learned it from the author, parish minister about Crimond or St. Fergus – about beginning of last century." (Gw) The words "Crimond or St. Fergus" are deleted by bracketing and a later note states: "afterwards revised to 'Longside'". This text is written opposite A and shows differences from it. Words from A included here to indicate position are given in square brackets. "[Mr William Watson has] furnished me with a number of very interesting variants of 'The Cantie Carlie', a long and characteristic ballad of local life, of which some time ago we got a version from a Peterhead gentleman, as it appears in *A Garland of Bon-Accord*, a privately printed collection. Mr Watson learned the ballad from his father, who got it from the author, a Buchan professional gentleman. I am much indebted to Mr Watson for providing the records [of several songs listed], and to Mr William Cumming, M.A., for making a note of them." (G, Ob. 77, 25 May 1909) No tune from William Watson appears in Gm although Greig mentions (see headnote) that he had heard him sing it.

C   Dm 87b; Gillespie 656. "*Cetera desunt*. For 'langen-gird' see 'lagen-gird' in Jamieson: Mrs Gillespie's explanation was the same. Also called 'The Canty Carlie'." (D, Gillespie) In John Jamieson's *Etymological Dictionary of the Scottish Language* (1841) under "lagen-gird" the sense of "to cast a laggen-gird" is given as "to bear a spurious child" (cf. SND *to cast a laggin-gird*, to bear an illegitimate child). At Dm, Duncan lists "The Wanton Carlie" from Mrs Gillespie among the songs sung to the tune of "Bonny Glasgow Green" from the same singer. At Dm 137, he adds st. 2 under the title "Ye needna be sae saucy, Bell" as another song to the same tune, commenting: "This is sung to first half of tune. No more remembered. – 'Lyangin' is the projecting part of the staves of a cog or tub, below the groove that holds the bottom. The 'lyangin gird' is the lowest gird: when it is slackened or 'cast', as in dry weather, the tub or cog leaks. Hence the figurative use here. Mrs Gillespie. 3rd March 1909. Heard at home." He later comments: "Afterwards remembered as 'The Wanton Carlie'" and adds a cross-reference to Dm 88.

D   Gm 4.4a; Gw 52.26. Acknowledged in Ob. 123, 19 April 1910.

E   Gw 41.19-20. The word "fragment" is written below the title. Acknowledged in Ob. 30, 23 June 1908.

F   Ob. 16. "[Mrs Rettie] remembers a few verses of a song which, although not sure about it, she thinks was called 'The Cantie Carlie.' I quote a verse and will be pleased if any reader can supplement Mrs Rettie's recollections." (G, Ob. 16, 17 March 1908)

619 THE WEDDING OF BALLAPOREEN Cf. George Henry Davidson, *Universal Melodist* (London, 1847-8), 1.105, and the second item in the broadside Madden 14, No. 506 *Paddy's Wedding. The Wedding of Ballyporeen* (Phair, Westminster, n.d.). "This is a popular ditty in the north, although it is quite clearly 'composed' and modern.

The tune, known by the name of 'Ballymona Orah,' is full of go and abandon, and well suits the rollicking verses." (G, Ob. 47)

A   Misc. 129-30, Harper 37-8, Dw 1.91. "Noted by Mrs Harper from her sister, Elizabeth Greig, August 1907. Mrs Gillespie remembers it to different air. It is evidently Irish, and the words 'composed,' not traditional, as well as the air. I find it, without any note of source, in Davidson's *Universal Melodist* (London, 1848), 1.105, but with different tune, under the title, 'The Wedding of Ballyporeen.' The above stanza [st. 1] appears, with natural differences, but with two additional lines before these. There are ten stanzas of this length." (D, Misc.)

B   Gm 3.10a; Gw 12.1. September 1907. (Gm) In Gw, the title is "Ballaporeen," and "confessed" appears instead of "composed" in line 2. There is also an additional line given separately: "There was Shielah and Laura the genius".

C   Gm 1.101b. January 1906. "Words from James Greig." (Gm) Greig's note could mean either that he had the words from James Greig (possibly version D) or that he intended to ask for them.

D   Gw 24.94-101. "Tune 'Bally Mona Orah'." (Gw) There are queries at "eunich" (2.3) and "shines" (7.5) and a few verbal alternatives are written in, as shown in brackets: 1.4 sang (song), 2.7 swear (stare), 2.8 weddin' (wedding), 3.4 group (troop), 4.7 Gainns (Ginnes), 5.1 to (for to), 6.8 rattle (wallop), 7.5 shines (shins), 9.3 did (they'd). The following two lines equivalent to 5.5 are given on the facing page:

> And if I survive and thrive, sirs,
> The very first christening I have, sirs.

620   **THE HAUGHIES O' INDEGO**   See map for the location of Indego.

Scottish Notes and Queries, 4.119, November 1890, Dw 2.99, Lyall 2.26-7. "From *Scottish Notes and Queries*, 4.119, sent by the Rev. George Williams." (Dw) The text in Lyall is also copied from the printed source. The piece in *Scottish Notes and Queries* is signed G.W., Thornhill, and a note before the song runs: "During a recent visit to Aberdeenshire I gleaned the following fragment of a ballad which still lingers in the memories of some of the inhabitants of the Howe o' Cromar, where Indego is situated. My own impression is that the ballad has reference to the period of 'The Trubles,' possibly to 1645, when contingents were gathering to the Battle of Alford, in the near neighbourhood. In the hope that some one may be able to complete the ballad, or throw additional light on its circumstances, I subjoin the verses as repeated to me." In Dw, Duncan quotes the passage except for the last sentence and observes: "But the verses given seem to me much more like the celebration of some kind [of] gathering for sport or merry making. No tune mentioned. The words do not suggest the ballad style of the seventeenth century." 1.2 "sky": probably for "sky setting" = nightfall.

621   **CADGER BRUCE**   See map for the location of Baldyvin.

790.1/3/9. This song, which follows a version of 628 "The Ball at Davidson's", is headed "Another McCombie", i.e. another piece composed by Peter McCombie (see note to 628 B). At the end Murray has added the note: "Another clue to the date. 'Cadger Bruce' was the first of the Bruces of Keig probably the great grandfather of Dr Simpson at the Brig of Alford. Cadger Bruce, according to gossip would sell dulse to the country folk and after he got their money remark 'They're nae ill dulse only the doggie fulpit [whelped] i' the cairt this mornin'.' The result was the dulse was thrown back in the cart and was sold again. Keen business instincts the cadger had, but many a high placed family has had its fortune founded on worse practices than that." The title is editorial.

622   **DUBBIENEUK**

Gw 1.61.

623   **MARY GLENNIE**

Gm 1.133a; Gw 3.98. March 1906. (Gm and Gw) "Local ditty – about a ball in the Ironside district, dealing with local characters – perhaps twenty-five years ago." (Gm) Opposite the first two lines of verse, Greig has written "Smith" with a question mark, possibly as a suggested alternative to "Glennie". In Gw the stanza is headed "Local Ball".

624   **JEAN DALGARNO**

Gw 1.61.

625   **THE SINGING CLASS**   The title is editorial. The two fragments on this theme are given together here but it should be noted that, although they may be parts of the same song, it is not possible to be certain of this on the present evidence.

A   Gw 34.117. "I am amused to think nothing could happen but there must be a song about it. Sometimes 'twas just a list of people who were at it with remarks about them complimentary or otherwise; but it was sung by all and sundry till something else happened; then another had to be got and the former one was forgot. I remember one I have heard bits of about a singing class – [Text]." B.R. (Gw)

B   Misc. 113-4. "Other words associated [with 626 'The Auchnairy Ball' A] seem rather to describe a singing class: – [Text]. Music of the 'Auchnairy Ball' not remembered; but [the words of 'The Singing Class' B] are associated with the air of 'Hame Cam Oor Goodman' [as sung by Mrs Gillespie]." (D, Misc.) Duncan gives an asterisk at the first line and attaches the note: "'Mary Roger' (Auchnairy's wife) is also mentioned." For the tune "Bangor" see Lachlan MacBean, *The Songs and Hymns of the Gael* (Stirling, 1900), p. 85. Its effect is also noted in the psalmody rhyme sung to it (*Rymour Club Miscellanea* 1.38):

> The high, high notes o' Bangor's tune
> Are very hard to raise,
> And trying hard to reach them gars
> The lasses burst their stays.

626 THE AUCHNAIRY BALL

A   Misc. 113-4. "A composition of Johnnie Willox, Fridayhill. One verse remembered:– [Text]." (D, Misc.) See also note to 625 'The Singing Class' B.

B   Gw 34.116v.6v-7. "Another [in addition to 625 'The Singing Class' A] was about a dance. One verse was [Text]. All this shows a prevailing trait – the fondness for singing." B.R. (Gw)

627 LANNAGAN'S BALL   Cf. Middleton, 2.96-7 "Lannigan's Ball".

A   Gm 1.141b. "April 1906. Kind of chorus." (Gm) Greig gives a reference in Gm to "Lannagan's Ball" on page 36 of *Kerr's First Collection of Merry Melodies for the Violin* (James S. Kerr, Glasgow, n.d.).

B   Gm 2.1c. June 1906.

628 THE BALL AT DAVIDSON'S

A   Dm 3c. At Dm 4, Duncan lists this fragment with the title "The Murlin and the Creel" among the songs sung to the tune of "Errol on the Green" [from Mrs Gillespie] and comments: "Noted January 1906. Not the first verse, but no more words remembered." In what is apparently a later note he adds: "Occurs in a rhyme by Peter McCombie, Boghead, 'the Rhymer of Tough' – 'The Ball at Davidson's'."

B   790.1/3/6. "I got the following from an old man John Murray (my grand uncle) Woodend, Alford, in the early eighties." Charles Murray. (790.1/3/6) The above note may refer to the complete collection of songs given together but certainly applies to this one which comes first. Murray notes concerning it: "The author said to be Peter McCombie, Boghead, Tough, known as 'The Rhymer of Tough'" and "'Jamie o' the Isle' in the 'Ball at Davidson's' was I think an Alford minister".

629 THE SOUTERS' FEAST   Cf. Norman Buchan, *101 Scottish Songs* (Glasgow, 1962), p. 1, Peter Buchan, "Secret Songs of Silence" (Harvard College Library MS 25241.9*), pp. 1-4, and Hamish Henderson, "*At the Foot o' Yon Excellin' Brae*: The Language of Scots Folksong", in *Scotland and the Lowland Tongue*, ed. J. Derrick McClure (Aberdeen, 1983), pp. 115-6. "Humour is not a strong feature of traditional minstrelsy. Our old ballads are nearly all serious, with a distinct tendency towards the tragic. Now and again in ballad and song we encounter humorous touches, and occasionally meet with a ditty which deals avowedly with the fun of something; but for the comic song pure and simple we must come down to quite recent days. 'The Souters' Feast' is about as humorous a folk-song as we have ever come across. The situation and the idea may not be original; but the song as we have it is clearly local, and seems to belong to central Buchan – the Maud district, we should say, judging from one kind of evidence or another. It can be traced back for a couple of generations at least, although it does not appear to be old. In a MS. collection of songs made by Peter Buchan between the years 1825 and 1830 there is one called 'The Souters' Feast.' Mr William Walker, Aberdeen, is able to give us the first verse. –

> There cam' a Souter out o' Oyne.
>   Tum, cerry, avum;
> Ridin' on a muckle preen,
>   Sing cidi, uptum, avum.

For the rest of the song we should have to go to Harvard University, U.S., where the MS. is now lodged; but we have reason to know that Peter's version would not make for edification though we had it. The latter part of our ditty recalls the predicament of the Souter in 'The Turnament,' a poem writen by William Dunbar, the greatest of our early Scottish poets. The combat is between the Tailor and the Souter; and Mahoun, who superintends the lists, is greatly troubled with the nervousness and cowardice of the combatants. The Souter advances into the field.

> Quhen on the telyour he did luke,
> His hairt a littill dwamying tuke,
> He mycht nocht rycht upsitt;
> In to his stommok wes sic ane steir,
> Off all his dennar quhilk he coft deir
> His breist held deill a bitt,

To comfort him or he raid forder,
The Devill of knychtheid gaif him order;
For sair syne he did spitt,
And he about the Devill's nek
Did spew agane ane quart of blek;
So knychtly he him quitt.

The tune [to] which 'The Souters' Feast' is sung seems to be made up of melodic phrases taken from 'Maggie Lauder,' although it is just possible that it may be an independent variant of that air. I first heard the song sung by Mr Brebner, Aucheoch, at a Burns' supper at Maud a good few years ago. Its vogue is being revived, and just last week I was pleased to hear it rendered at a concert by Mr James Brebner, junior." (G, Ob. 12, 18 February 1908)

A   Gm 3.69d; Gw 55.20-1. March 1908. (Gm)
B   Gm 1.55a; Ob. 12. "1 March 1905. Phrases of tune all found in 'Maggie Lauder'." (Gm)
C   Gm 4.164b.
D   Gw 1.84-5.
E   Misc. 26-7. "Mrs Gillespie, who thinks the song referred to the 'sooters' of Turriff, celebrated for their strength, and the coming of rivals from Aberdeen to fight them." (D, Misc.)
F   Gw 10.44.

630   **McGINTY'S MEAL-AN-ALE**   Cf. Norman Buchan, *101 Scottish Songs* (Glasgow, 1962). "A fortnight ago [in Ob. 134] we had the pleasure of giving an authentic copy of [614] 'Sheelicks,' by Mr George Bruce Thomson, New Deer; and we are now glad to be able to follow it up with another song from Mr Thomson's rare cycle, printed from his own manuscript. The reference to the treatment of the tune, we may say, is one of the author's own jokes, and need not be taken too seriously." (G, Ob. 136)   Greig is here commenting on the note which follows the song title in Ob.: "Tune – 'Roxburgh Castle', adapted (and ruined)." The note is also present in Thomson's manuscript (3088/11). See map for the location of Balmannocks.

A   3088/11, Gw 57.6-11. The music is derived from MS 3088/11, where it appears in sol fa notation. The original has a rest following the C on the first beat of the first bar; an alternative with a repeated C is given in order to accommodate the words of the first verse. The final C of the verse (bar 32) has been shortened from the original two beats to one, so as to fit the time signature. The words "Aye" and "Far" at the beginning of lines 2 and 3 of the chorus are included here from the words given with the music as they are required to fit the tune; they do not occur in the full texts given in either manuscript. In 3088/11, there is the following note after the first stanza: "Here also I had intended a pig made of drab cotton and stuffed with hay or something, maudlin laugh on his face etc. but it never came off." At 3.1, Gw has "Young Murphy" instead of "Johnny Murphy".
B   Gw 39.11-4. Acknowledged in Ob. 82, 6 July 1909.

631   **MIDDLETACK CLIACK**

Harper 31, Dw 1.68-70. "This is a song composed by a John Sim, miller, Rathen in 1860. Mrs Jaffray was at the feast. Middletack is the name of a farm in Rathen [see map]." M.H. (Harper) "Tune – 'Castles in the Air.'" (Dw)   At 11.1, Dw indicates that "Tham" is pronounced "Tam". "Cliack" or "clyack" is the word for the last sheaf of corn to be cut and also has the sense, as here, of the celebration at the end of harvest.

632   **THE HARVEST HOME**   Greig observes in Ob. 164 where he prints this song that it was written by John Anderson, farmer, Upper Boyndlie; see note to 447 "The Praise of Ploughmen".

Gw 59.55-7. "Miss Bell Robertson offers some helpful remarks on the songs of John Anderson which lately appeared in our column. Her suggestion of 'trig' for 'big,' as applied to the lasses in 'The Harvest Home,' seems to the point." (G, Ob. 168)

633   **KIRN SONG**

Gw 11.56. "Jonathan Gauld – as above [i.e. per Superintendent Ord]." (Gw)   "Fragment" is written beside the title.

634   **AULD WARRACK'S PLOUGH FEAST**   In a letter to Duncan of 16 January 1906 (998/7/2/1), the Rev. George Williams says: "I presume you have picked up 'Auld Warrack's Plough Feast'. ... I had 'The Plough Feast,' as far as known, printed some twenty years ago in the 'Free Press.'" *Letters to Duncan from the Rev. George Williams* (998/7/2/1-2). The main title is editorial, taken from this letter. William Warrack (born at Towie) was farmer at Mains of Towie in 1851, when he was aged sixty-eight. (Cen. E.B., Towie, 1851; V.R. Aberdeenshire, for the year ending Whitsunday 1860.)   See map for the location of Mains of Towie.

A   *The [Aberdeen] Weekly Free Press*, 25 July 1891, p. 5, col. 7, 998/7/3/71, Dw 2.96-7, 114-5. The following item headed 'Warrack's Plough Feast./ An Auld Sang.' appeared in *The [Aberdeen] Weekly Free Press* of 25 July 1891:

"Forty or fifty years ago there was a song, well known in Kildrummy, Towie, and Leochel-Cushnie, called 'Warrack's Plough Feast.' It is evidently old, and describes a custom now obsolete. The editor of the *Weekly*

Free Press will be pleased to receive contributions with a view to the more perfect presentation of this fragment, which, we presume, was never before printed, but which may linger still in the memory of the older inhabitants of these parishes:– [Text, sts. 1-3, with spaces indicated between the stanzas, which have the notes between sts. 1 and 2: 'Hole i' the ballad.', and between sts. 2 and 3: 'Another hiatus'. The word 'Pot' at the end of st. 2 has an explanatory footnote 'The Pot o' Drumallachie.'] Another version is –

> Brockie an' the fit in fur,
> They gart the wyner thraw.

Hereupon the 'soum' [plough chain] seems to have broken; and, as our old friend pithily remarked, 'there was a terrible splatter for nae eese.' To mend the broken gear [Text, st. 4, with 'Another gap.' marked at the end]. The yoking ended, the feast began – [Text, st. 5]. Here follows a verse of the grace, not reproduced – [Text, st. 6]. It ought to be possible to rescue this song from oblivion, and so to illustrate the social condition of a generation that is past and well-nigh forgotten." The item is signed "W." and, in letters to Duncan of 16 and 18 January 1906 (998/7/2/1-2), the Reverend George Williams identifies himself as the writer, saying: "I presume you have picked up 'Auld Warrack's Plough Feast'. ... I had 'The Plough Feast,' as far as known, printed some twenty years ago in the *Free Press*."

In a follow-up letter dated 18 January 1906, Williams gives Duncan the text in a rather different form from the one he sent to the newspaper, which apparently draws on B, to which he refers. This letter runs:

"Here is all I know of the 'Plough Feast.' It was recited to me a score of years ago by late John Leys, Kirkton of Cushnie. It hardly ranks as a song –

> Auld Warrack made a plough-feast,
> Ye never saw sic fun –
> It happen'd at Drumallochie,
> Upo' the banks o' Don.
> At the yokin' o' auld Warrack's plough,
> The neibors a' cam' roun',
> An' mony's the lad an' lass was there
> To see the play begun.

> (Invitations were issued.)

> If ye wad favour me this day,
> It's never be forgot;
> An' gin yer nowte come owre the brae
> We'll turn them roun the Pot.

> (Operations commenced)

> Some held on and some held in
> An' some o' them did ca';
> But Brockie in the fur-afit,
> He gart the wyner thraw.

> (The 'thraw' of the thrawn wyner resulted in a broken soam.)

> Some got (fir) and some got sprots,
> An' some got raips o' strae,

> (Conjectural –

> To try an' men' the broken soam
> An' en' the wark that day.)

> . . . .

> There's Sandy Hunter on the brae,
> I' troth he'll mak' a rhyme.

> (At the supper table)

> Auld Warrack, he took aff his bonnet,
> It was to say the grace,
> An' a' the sins an' wives he had
> 'Twas them he did confess:

> I never had a lawfu' wife,
> Nor yet a lawfu' son;
> But I fell foul o' Maggie Thows
> An' sair't I do bemoan.

(Mr Warrack's moral character suffers nothing by the rest of his grace being awanting.)

> Some got bread and cheese their fill,
> An' some got bread for a';
> But the hirdie got a dish o' want
> An' that was warst ava'.

(See *Aberdeen Free Press* 19-9-'91) Surely some other lines of this spirited ballad might be recovered, if some of the older people of Towie were interviewed."

B   *The [Aberdeen] Weekly Free Press*, 19 September 1891, p. 5, col. 7, 998/7/3/71. In his second letter to Duncan, Williams gives a reference to a letter which appeared under the heading "Warrack's Plough Feast" in *The [Aberdeen] Weekly Free Press* of 19 September 1891. It was written from Windsor, Ontario, Canada, on August 28, 1891 and runs:

"Sir, – In your paper of July 25th ult., you publish fragments of an auld sang called 'Warrack's Plough Feast.' Your correspondent says it is evidently old, but he doesn't give it age enough. It is seventy or eighty years old. When I was a boy, my mother often repeated snatches of it, and many of them remained in my memory for many years. Now they are mostly all gone.

"Your first stanza is as I would put it, with the addition of these two lines:– [Text, st. 1]. As to the breaking of the soume, or rather the mending of it, what remains in my memory is – [Text, st. 2].

"My mother also repeated pieces of other poems of Sandy Hunter's; one ran:– 'At the white yetts they held a court martial suppose it was late, etc.'

"A word as to Sandy Hunter himself. He seems to have been a bit of a character if the impression left on my mind, from what I heard of him, be correct. He is said to have made love to one of the lasses at Glenkindy in these terms – 'Od, lassie, if ye had a pouch I would ripe it, and if ye had a box I would tak' it, for it's seven years sin' I liket you, though I never tauld you till noo.' There was a Charles Hunter lived up in Glenbucket about the same time who might have been a brother, who had a very high esteem for his wife, and frequently praised her to his servants in language like this – 'Gweed faith, noo, Jock Gauld, it will pit a trick on you to get a wife like my Mary.' – I am, etc. Alex. Callam.

"P.S. – Excuse an old fellow of eighty-four. – A.C."

635   THE COUNTRY ROCKIN'

Gw 29.112-3.

636   DECEMBER CAM'

Gw 38.12-3. "Mrs Rettie, Millbrex, sends me a very interesting consignment of minstrelsy [including] a rhyme about Yule, which was written, my correspondent thinks, by an Inverkeithney man, an Episcopalian, as a kind of satire on the way Presbyterians held Christmas. It commences thus – [Text, st. 1]." (G, Ob. 59, 19 January 1909) "[Mrs Rettie] gives me another verse or two of the 'Auld Yule' rhyme which have recurred to memory since her last communication." (G, Ob. 60, 26 January 1909) In Gw after the first stanza is the prose comment: "Description of preparations – house-cleaning etc. before Yule", and "(And the sowens)" is written before 4.1.

637   THE TWELVE DAYS OF CHRISTMAS   Cf. Sharp No. 334 "The Twelve Days of Christmas". The title is editorial.

Gw 33.15. "I remember a fragment of an old song which my mother used to sing to us. It was mainly an enumeration of the gifts which a lover sent to his lass at Christmas. I[t] began with the first day of Xmas. and every succeeding day (second day of Xmas., third day of Xmas. and so on) which also enumerated all before stated. – [Text.] Pleasant tune." W.W. (Gw)

638   HERE'S TO YE A' AND A HAPPY NEW YEAR   The title is editorial.

Gw 61.32.

639   GET UP GUDEWIFE   Cf. *Tocher* 2 (No. 12), 121, and Robert Chambers, *Popular Rhymes of Scotland*, new edition (Edinburgh and London, [1870]), pp. 165-6. The title is editorial.

Ob. 5. "The last day of the year brings thoughts and reflections from which we cannot well escape whatever our circumstances may be or whatever we may chance to be engaged in. The folk-songist, too, feels the spirit of the season and to the occasion must tune his lyre. To the young the season suggest joy and keen expectancy. We can remember how on the last night of the year we used to sally forth to serenade the neighbouring houses with – [Text]. And the appeal was generally successful, few goodwives having the heart to send the young serenaders away empty-handed. We hardly think this custom is in vogue as it once was. Our young people are so well looked after with Christmas trees and treats of one kind or another that they do not need to forage for themselves as children long ago had to do." (G, Ob. 5, 31 December 1907) In line 1, the word "feathers" refers to a feather bed.

640 **OUR FEET'S CAULD** Cf. Robert Chambers, *Popular Rhymes of Scotland*, new edition (Edinburgh and London, [1870]), p.166, and *Rymour Club Miscellanea*, 3.135. The title is editorial.

Gw 61.77.

641 **WE ARE A' QUEEN MARY'S MEN** Cf. *Tocher* 3 (No. 20), 142-3.

Gm 4.40a; Gw 53.90-2. "Per J.A. Fotheringham, Orkney." (Gw) In stanza 3, the first line of the refrain follows line 1 and the second follows line 3. At 6.1 "beul'" is given below "boal" and at 7.1 "hens" replaces the deleted word "herds". Acknowledged in Ob 132 and 143, 21 June and 6 September 1910.

642 **BESUTHIAN** Cf. *Scottish Notes and Queries* 1 (1888), 163. This song and the custom with which is was associated were the subject of correspondence in the *Aberdeen Free Press* in October 1906 and both Greig and Duncan copied texts from the newspaper. The correspondence began with a query letter by J. Alexander printed on 18 October (p. 5, col. 3). This is headed "Old Song Wanted." and runs:

"Sir, – As I have been collecting information of the customs, etc., of days gone by in rural Aberdeenshire I have been told that up to the dawning of the 19th century bands of young men called at the farms in their immediate vicinity, collecting oatmeal or cash, which was distributed amongst the poor. When they arrived at a farm they joined in singing a ballad, a song which ran something like this:–

> The aul' 'ear's deen an' th' New's begun,
> Besoothin, besoothin!
> An' noo th' beggars they hae come
> An' we're aye besoothin toun.

Could any reader supply me with a full text of this ballad? – I am, etc., J.A."

On 26 October (p. 10, col. 1), another letter from Alexander was published, this time headed "An Old Song." It includes texts A and B and runs:

"Sir, – I have been able to secure two versions of the old song I asked your readers to supply, one by your correspondent Mr Isaac Troup, and another kindly sent me some years ago through the editor of the *Weekly Free Press* by Mr Alexander M'Hardy, Dunpheil, Corgarff. Both versions are evidently parts of the same ballad as it had been sung in two different parts of the county of Aberdeen.

"As was the case with many of the folk songs, the rhyme is of little account. If the words could be made to 'clink' with the music, it was of no consequence whether they 'rhymed' or not. The chief value of the ballad lies in the fact that it was sung by the young men who 'begged' for the poor on New Year's Day. As one old man said to Mr Troup, when they had sung the last verse, that in which it is asserted 'We'll kiss yer lasses or we want' – 'Sic a steer there wis in th' hoose wi' th' lasses flingin' by their wheels, an' rinnin' skirlin'!' No doubt they would when a band of young men invaded the house intent on kissing the girls since they could get neither 'meal nor siller.'

"I cannot give any explanation of the refrain 'Besoothan,' nor of 'Besoothin toun.' There must have been some meaning attached to them, and it would be interesting to know what some of your readers who have antiquarian knowledge, or some understanding of philology, have to say about it. I believe the 'muttie' was an old measure. There may still be seen, I suppose, a peck measure with the bottom at a certain depth. On turning over the measure you found that between the bottom edge of the staves and the bottom of the measure there is space which might be a different measure from the peck. And so it is, for in this one measure you have both the peck and the muttie, the bottom being so placed within the staves that formed the circumference of the circular measure as to have a measure at both ends.

"I may be allowed to reproduce the old song as supplied to me by the two gentlemen above. First we shall give Mr M'Hardy's version:– [Text B]. Mr M'Hardy seems to have some recollection of a concluding stanza, which began –

> Let health, an' wealth, an' a' abide,
> Besuthian, besuthian,

but he stops there, which I regret. Here is Mr Troup's version of the ballad:– [Text A]. From these two versions a tolerably full copy of the ballad may be made up, I think. I am, etc., J. Alexander, Ythan Wells, Insch. October 25, 1906."

A response to Alexander's query about the meaning of the refrain came in the following letter which appeared in the *Aberdeen Free Press* of 27 October 1906 (p. 3, col. 4), most of which was copied at Gw 8.39.

"Sir, – 'Besuthian' in the refrain of this old song appears to me as a corruption of the Anglo-Saxon word 'Theowian' – to serve; and the verb 'Be' as a prefix – Be-theowian – meaning, be serving. Then 'An' awa,' a contraction of an' we'll a'; and 'toun' a corruption of roun'. Apply this to Mr Troup's version of the rhyme [A] and it would run thus:–

> The aul' year's deen an' the new begun,
> Be servin'! Be servin'!!
> An' noo the beggars they have come;
> An' we'll a' be servin' roun'.

Rise up gweed wife, an' benna sweer;
Be servin'! Be servin'!!
An' deal y'er charity tae the peer;
An' we'll a' be servin' roun'.

The last verse would make this explanation more pat –

In meal an' money gin ye be scant;
Be servin'! Be servin!!
We'll kiss yer lasses (servan's) or we want;
An' we'll a' be servin' roun'.

– I am, etc., T."

Duncan himself wrote in to the *Aberdeen Free Press* on 27 October and his letter was published under the heading 'The New Year Begging Song.' on the 29th (p. 3, col. 8). He comments that Mr J. Alexander "may be interested in a third version of the song he has given" and quotes most of the text and the accompanying notes given by Walter Gregor in *Notes on the Folk-Lore of the North-East of Scotland* (London, 1881), pp. 160-2. He comments: "It will be observed that this version, allowing for the inevitable variants of traditional songs, corresponds to parts of both the versions already given [A and B]. The last stanza, and one I have not quoted [Gregor's st. 3], are independent; and the alternate refrain ['An awa b' mony a toon'] dispenses with the enigmatical word 'b'soothan.' Dr Gregor offers no explanation of this word either in text or glossary; and I would suggest that the variety of such meaningless words in refrains and choruses is so great that one is hardly entitled to expect a meaning, especially in view of its being more generally used than in this one song."

A Dm 371c; *Aberdeen Free Press*, 26 October 1986, p. 10, col. 1, Gw 8.29v-30v, Dw 2.53. "Noted 11th September 1907. Used in 'thigging' or begging for the poor at the New Year season. 'Besoothin' is pronounced with 'th' as in 'thon' [i.e. as in 'those']. Also called 'Bezoothin.'" (Dm) The Gw and Dw texts are both derived from the *Aberdeen Free Press*, and parts of Alexander's letter (see note above) are copied or summarised at Gw 8.32-3. Duncan remarks in Dw that Mr Troup referred him to this newspaper for the words in his version.

B *Aberdeen Free Press*, 26 October 1906, p. 10, col. 1, Gw 8.30-1, Dw 2.73. See note at the head of the song.

C 998/7/3/53, Dw 2.54-5. "Thiggers' Song. The word thigger was a name applied to a common beggar in early statutes, and was subsequently applied to any person who went about receiving a supply not as a common beggar, but as giving people an opportunity of manifesting their liberality. There were thiggers who spent a day collecting meal and money for a poor neighbour. Previous to the passing of the Poor Law Amendment Act of 1845 the poor and necessitous in every parish depended upon private charity for support. In many cases small allowances were given by Kirk sessions, but the chief support was private charity. It was no uncommon thing in the winter season to see a company of men with bags on their backs traversing a country parish collecting meal for a poor neighbour. The parish minister and some others gave money. In this way two or three bolls of oatmeal and small sums of money were collected. Sometimes the thiggers were accompanied by a fiddler, and a reel was danced in a farm kitchen or in front of the house. The thiggers' object was to infuse good humour in the people they visited. They had a characteristic song which was slightly altered to suit particular circumstances. The name of the participant of the charity was always introduced into the song. [Text.] N.B. The above does not complete the song, but I am unable to give more. J.P.

"Another kind of thiggers solicited charity for their own behoof. It was quite common within living memory to see a hillside crofter thigging seed corn. He represented that his own corn had not come to maturity or had been damaged by frost. The loss of a cow or a horse was also represented as a reason for soliciting support. Thiggers of this sort did not confine their operations to their own parishes, and were not always known, and the statements of a person not known had to be taken on trust. Some of them carried petitions headed by well known persons, but many of them had no petition or credentials of any kind. James Pirie, 15, Academy St, Elgin, 8th February 1907." J.P. (998/7/3/53)

D *Banffshire Journal*, 12 November 1889, p. 6, col.4, 998/7/2/5, Dw 2.71. The Rev. George Williams sent copies of versions D and E to Duncan. His source for D was a letter headed "Folk-Lore in Strathdon" in the *Banffshire Journal* which runs:

"Mr Editor, – In answer to the wish of a Grange Minstrel in the *Banffshire Journal* of October 29th, I have collected the following verses, which were sung fifty years ago by the young men of our Strath when going the round of our district collecting meal and money for the poor and distressed about the New Year, and often I have seen five or six bolls of meal and two or three pounds of money collected in an afternoon, to be distributed to the most necessitous:– [Text]. Another stanza was generally added about the party or parties the collection was made for, but it was various, and, in most instances, of indifferent composition.

"If you think it worth a corner in your valuable paper, I shall be very happy to see it in print, as I do not think that ever it has been honoured with printers' ink before. – Your kind attention to the above will oblige, J.F., Corgarff, November 7, 1889."

There is a footnote glossing "barm" (4.1) as "yeast".

E William Cramond, *The Parish of Grange: lecture delivered in the parish church of Grange* (Printed at *The Banffshire Journal* office for the author, 1895), pp. 17-8, 998/7/2/5, Dw 2.72. "Copied from Cramond's *Grange Parish*, I think – (about 1890)." G.W. (998/7/2/5) Cramond quotes a passage concerning the custom and the song published by Andrew Halliday Duff in "Auld Yule; or, Christmas in Scotland", *National Magazine* 3 (1858), 198-9, and adds: "Here is another version sung at Braco:– [Text]." Williams's text is evidently an inaccurate copy of this.

643 **YE GAE BUT TO YOUR BEEF-STAN'**   The main title is editorial.

Gw 57.114. "Sung by a man who came through Rosehearty begging when Bell's grandmother was a lassie circa 1775. He ended by shouting 'Hogmanay!'." (Gw) In Ob. 161, Greig gives the first seven lines and adds the note: "After singing the rhyme the man cried 'Hogmanay!'."

644 **THEY SELL'T HIS TEETH TO TEETHE A RAKE**   The main title is editorial.

A   Gm 3.117b. August 1908. (Gm) Acknowledged in Ob. 34, 21 July 1909.
B   *Aberdeen Free Press*, 27 October 1906, p. 3, col. 4, Gw 8. 37-9. This song was published in the *Aberdeen Free Press* in a letter which formed part of the series noted under 642 "Besuthian". The text and a prose comment in Gw were copied from this source. The whole letter runs:
      "Sir, – I have been interested in the correspondence re the old song with 'Besuthian' as a refrain. The word seems to have been in common use among our old ballad and song composers, as it was common to our northern shires in days gone by. There is another song with the same refrain, 'Besuthian,' which I have heard sung with great gusto in the farm kitchens and bothies thirty years ago. The following are one or two verses; possibly some one may be able to fill in the blanks. It refers to an old crofter or wandering tinker who had lost his horse, and the song goes on to tell how they disposed of his remains. [Text B.]
      "These are just snatches of the song from memory, but it shows that they, as I have said, used 'Besuthian' pretty freely in thae auld warl' days. – I am, etc., James Cheyne. Charleston Dairy, Crown Street. October 26, 1905."

645 **THE RAM O' DIRRAM**   Cf. Opie No. 129, and Sharp No. 325 "The Derby Ram".

A   Dm 142b; Gillespie 438-40. "From John Cruickshank, Redburn, Byth. Sung by many others. Noted 1905. It is pronounced 'Doram.' Words only in Ford, ('Ram o' Bervie'), p. 124. It was often sung." (Dm) There are alterations at 3.1 from "it" to "'it" and at 3.4 from "untill" to "till".
B   Gm 3.81a. February 1908.
C   Lyall 1.31-3. "Miss F. Grant. Not sure who she heard it from." Mrs. L. (Lyall) "Mrs Lyall did not receive any tune." (D, Lyall)
D   Gw 1.82-3.
E   Gw 53.87.

646 **ROBIN'S TESTAMENT**   Cf. Robert Chambers, *The Songs of Scotland Prior to Burns* (Edinburgh and London, 1880), pp. 240-2 "Robin Redbreast's Testament".

A   Gm 3.139c; Gw 56.15-6. Words and music acknowledged in Ob. 46, 13 October 1908.
B   Dm 390c. "Mrs Lyall, from her mother. Noted 7th November 1907. A nursery song. Farther verses remembered:– [Text, st. 2]. Another speaks about leaving his 'legs to Mary Kirk, they'll help to bear her up' ['she being lame,' said Mrs Lyall; but no doubt it [is] 'St. Mary's Kirk']. This is the same as 'The Robin's Testament' in Chambers's *Songs* (from Herd, 2.166): given also in Whitelaw and Gardner's collections [see Whitelaw, *Songs*, p. 569, and *The Songs of Scotland*, new and revised edition (Alexander Gardner, Paisley, n.d.), pp. 24-5]. His version is conjectured by Chambers, from local allusions, to belong to the seventeenth century. It has, however, nothing in common with these verses, except the idea and a little in the first verse of this." (Dm)
C   Gw 25.81-2. 3.2 "It: = that." (Gw) Acknowledged in Ob. 26, 26 May 1908.
D   Gw 54.40-1. At st. 6, the beginning of the refrain is given and in this case it opens with "Sing" not "And sing".
E   Gw 39.100. 1.3 "to some": MS "to the some".

647 **THE HAUGHS O' GARTLY**   See map for the location of Gartly.

998/7/3/12, Dw 2.89. "Part of another rhyme has cropped up which you may know. It is a description of a New Year game of shinty. It was sung, as you will observe, to the tune of 'The Haws of Cromdale'." (A. Macdonald in a letter to Duncan of 17 November 1906, 998/7/3/12) Macdonald notes that "Bucharn" is "in Gartly".

648 **THE CUSHNIE WINTER SPORTS**   See map for the location of Cushnie.

998/7/2/2, Dw 2.98. "During the course of a very hard and long winter, men and women met near Mains of Cushnie to enjoy an hour's fun – tobogganing – more than a hundred years ago. A song was composed about it. I give fragments." (George Williams in a letter to Duncan of 18 January 1906, 998/7/2/2) Williams notes: "a bad accident" before st. 1 and gives "wan?" as an alternative to "cam" at 1.2. Between sts. 1 and 2 he has the note: "Jean Adam had her skin torn badly and they ran to *Monymusk* for a doctor!" and he explains that it was "for writing the song" that Effie Milne "swore she wad the laddie kill" in st. 2. The gap in 4.3 is indicated by square brackets. "No tune was mentioned, but it suggests the very frequent 'Johnnie Cope.' Later Mr

Williams said that he heard the song from his Uncle James, and the tune seemed uncommonly like the 'Haughs o' Cromdale,' but his uncle was no great singer." (Dw)

649 **TO MEN**   "This is pretty hard on the young men of the snuff period; and yet we believe there are critics who, making the necessary changes, would be prepared to apply it to lots of present-day young men. Some of the readings in the text of the song [C] we are not quite sure about, and should be glad if any reader could correct or supplement our version. The tune [B] was taken down a few weeks ago from the singing of Miss K. Morice, Kininmonth. It is a variant of a fine old air which is found attached to several other songs." (G, Ob. 150)

A   Dm 503a; Dw 3.111. "20th April, 1910. The tune is that of 'The Sheffield Apprentice,' etc.: see [the version of 'The Sheffield Apprentice' from George F. Duncan, Mrs Gillespie and myself]. It is very near the variants from George F. Duncan." (Dm)   3.4: "explained as meaning that they would be good to her." (Dw)   Probably the reference in 2.2 is to "nacket" in the sense of "a quantity of snuff made up in a ball-shaped or cylindrical form, a small roll of tobacco" (SND). The balls would rattle against each other ("reesle") in the young men's pockets when they danced.

B   Gm 4.55a. Acknowledged in Ob. 143, 6 September 1910.

C   Gw 42.92-4.

D   Gw 50.33. "Heard in Porter Fair thirty years ago. From Blind Bob." (Gw)

650 **I'M NOW TWENTY-TWO**

Gw 51.70-2. "Got from an old lady [Mrs Taylor] at Rora, who says it was written by one Gibb, who resided at Longside, fifty years ago." A.S. (Gw)

651 **JAMIE'S BRAW CLAES**

Gm 2.109b; Gw 9.97. "May 1907. 'Hills of Glenorchy.'" (Gm)   The title is the one given with the music; Gw has "Jamie and his Claes". At 4.1 the reference is to the French, presumably at the period of the Napoleonic War.

652 **COME, DEAR, DON'T FEAR**

Gm 4.121a.

653 **JEAN PIRIE**

Gm 2.71a. August 1906. "Words from *People's Journal* twenty-six years ago." (Gm)

654 **THE SERVAN' LASSES**   "Time and again we have had masters and mistresses criticised from the servants' point of view; here servants themselves, or one class of them at least, get overhauled, and the handling is by no means gentle. Satire always tends to go to extremes: indeed, to be effective, it must perforce exaggerate; and, when directed against a class, it is bound to do injustice to many individual members of that class. The reference in the song to a certain phase of rural life need not be objected to. The satirist is but dealing with matters of common observation and knowledge, and it must be admitted that he enforces the moral of the situation with very considerable effect. The [line 'And she greets for the thing that she lauched at afore'] could hardly be bettered. In this matter, however, as in many others, the last word of all remains with Burns. –

> Then gently scan your brother man,
> Still gentlier sister woman;
> Tho' they may gang a kennin wrang,
> To step aside is human;
> One point must still be greatly dark,
> The moving why they do it;
> And just as lamely can ye mark
> How far perhaps they rue it.
>
> Then at the balance let's be mute,
> We never can adjust it;
> What's done we partly may compute,
> But know not what's resisted.

The tune of 'The braw servan' lasses,' as I have got it, is that of 'The Hills of Glenorchy.'" (G, Ob. 98)   Greig did not include in Gm a tune from the butcher in Fetterangus but he notes at 4.147b that he sang "The Braw Servan' Lasses" to "Hills o' Glenorchy".

A   Gm 3.132b; Gw 31.23-6. "Circa 1880. ?'Carrickfergus'." (Gm)   "Sung in a bothy at Portlethen by a young lad with great gusto – and much applause. 1893." W.W. (Gw)   At r. 1 *twiggie* is corrected from *triggie* in Walker's hand, and at 8.1 "church" is written above "kirk".

B   Gm 1.107c; Gw 3.67-8. "February 1906. 'Hills of Glenorchy.'" (Gm)

C   Gm 3.189c.

D   Dm 295b. "Mrs Lyall, from her grandfather (Auchterless) fully thirty years ago. Noted 4th June, 1907. Air a variant version of [293 'Paddy in Glasgow' B] and [282 'The Exciseman in a Coal Pit']. Mrs Lyall states (later) that the name should be 'The Servan' Lasses', and that it is not about a bachelor. Full words afterwards obtained [see E]: this verse is only the last." (Dm)

E   Lyall 2.1-4, Dw 4.107-9, Gw 19.80-3. At 2.4 the query "*screed?*" is written after "creed" and at 9.1 the query "*rove?*" is written above "roar". At 6.3 "een" replaces deleted "face". In Dw, Duncan queries whether "Or" at 3.4 should be "Ere" and "unto" at 10.2 "into." "The source is not mentioned, but I do not think it was her own memory." (Dw) "[Mrs Lyall] sends a copy of 'The Servan' Lasses' – a song at once clever and full of wise admonition. I may mention that I have a record of the song made more than two years ago; but I am very glad indeed to have Mrs Lyall's version, as it is much more complete. My correspondent adds that she has sung the air to my collaborator, the Rev. Mr Duncan. I shall be interested to discover whether it is the same as the one I recorded." (G, Ob. 22, 28 April 1908) The Gw text has the following verbal variants, shown in brackets: 7.3 gangs (gaes), 9.3 or (ere), 11.4 that she (she).

F   Gw 26.70-3. At 6.3 the rhyming word "e'en" is suggested in brackets after "brow".

G   Dw 3.121-3. "The tune was not noted, but he sang it, and it was apparently the same tune as Mrs Lyall's [D]." (Dw) At 6.4 Duncan comments on "is": "sic: 'what *has* she on'?".

H   Gw 18.113-4. "Sung by John Rennie sixty years ago, in New Pitsligo. He was at college but his mind gave way. I got hold of this from an old body." J.B. Sinclair. (Gw) Acknowledged in Ob. 23, 5 May 1908.

655   **AYE WORK AWA**   Cf. *Whistle-Binkie* (Glasgow, 1890), 1.489-90 "Aye Work Awa'" written by Joseph Wright.

Gw 38.77-80. Acknowledged in Ob. 68, 23 February 1909.

656   **I'M A WORKIN' CHAP**

Gm 3.32a. "Per favour of Superintendent Ord. October 1907." (Gm) Ord prints a full text in his *Bothy Songs and Ballads*, pp. 51-2. "This song resembles somewhat our modern music hall ditties. I picked it up, both words and tune, upwards of twenty-five years ago from the singing of an old friend, whom I have lost sight of for many years, and Mr. James B. Allan, A.L.C.M., Glasgow, has arranged the music for the benefit of the readers of the *Welcome*. I submitted the song to Mr. Gavin Greig M.A., the ex-president of the Buchan Field Club, who is perhaps the highest authority on folk song in Scotland, and he states that the tune is undoubtedly old, but that in his opinion the words are modern." John Ord "Byways of Scottish Song" in *The Weekly Welcome*, 15 January 1908.

657   **PUNCTUALITY**

Gw 17.63-5.

658   **THE CLOCK**

Misc. 152; Lyall 2.41, Dw 4.133. "Learnt by her mother from an innkeeper at Glen of Wartle, who had it pasted on his clock." (D, Lyall) "Mrs Lyall, from her mother. Noted 11th August 1908. It may have been a popular song; but neither words nor music suggest 'folk-song.' No more words remembered (except two lines; see [Dw 4.133]." (D, Misc.) The text is printed here as in Misc. with the music. In Lyall and Dw, the first two of these lines are given as the beginning of a second stanza; stanza 1 concludes with the remaining four lines but opens:

> The old, old clock of the household stock,
> Is the bonniest thing an the neatest.

659   **THE DROOSY CHIEL**

A   Dm 201a. "Sung by James Davidson, farmservant, Burnside, Carnousie, about 1870. Noted 1906. Mrs Gillespie had heard this also in Banff. There were more words than these." (Dm)

B   Gw 46.9-10. For tune, see No. 12 in Towers' song manuscript, Edinburgh University Library Gen. 767.11.

660   **THE GUID COAT O' BLUE**   Cf. *Whistle-Binkie* (Glasgow, 1890), 2.130-1 "My Guid Coat o' Blue" written by John Paterson; the air is given as "The Lass o' Glenshee".

A   Gm 2.59b; Gw 1.14-7. July 1906. (Gm)

B   Gw 53.69. The ascription is uncertain. A version from Annie Shirer is acknowledged in Ob. 107, 28 December 1909.

661   **THE CUDDY**   Cf. Middleton, 1.113-4, and Thomas Denham, *Poems and Snatches of Prose* (Aberdeen, 1845), pp. 96-9. "'The Cuddy,' which has now a fair vogue as a traditional song, appears [at pp. 55-6] in *The Aberdeenshire Lintie*, a collection of lyrics by local bards [edited by T.C. Watson] which was published in 1854, a second edition being issued just last year. The ditty was written by Thomas Denham, a bard of Bon-accord, who flourished about the forties, and was a contemporary of Peter Still and William Thom. He had gifts literary, musical, and histrionic,

but was too fond of conviviality to succeed in life. 'The Cuddy' was one of the songs which the late William Carnie, of Aberdeen, helped to sing into popularity. It is set to the air of 'Last May a braw wooer.'" (G, Ob. 109, 11 January 1910)

> Gm 2.19a; Gw 5.84-6. "June 1906. 'Last May.'" (Gm) In Gw, William Walker has added the note "See Denham's *Poems*." A text at Gw 10.18-20 was copied from *The Aberdeenshire Lintie*.

662 **JEAN FINDLATER'S LOON** Cf. Middleton, 1.76-7, and William Anderson, *Rhymes, Reveries, and Reminiscences*, 2nd ed. (Aberdeen, 1867), pp. 5-8 "Jean Finlater's Loon". "'Jean Findlater's Loun' has long been a popular ditty in the north. It was written by William Anderson (1802-1867), a bard of Bon-Accord, who after a turn at one or two occupations at length joined the Harbour Police, rising to the rank of lieutenant. He contributed verse to the *Aberdeen Herald*, and published a volume of poetry *Rhymes, Reveries, and Reminiscences* in 1851. 'Jean Findlater's Loun' appears [at pp. 74-6] in the *Aberdeenshire Lintie*, a collection of local verse first issued in 1854. From Mr George Riddell, Rosehearty, I once got a copy of a tune to which the ditty is sung. It is a variant of 'Dick Turpin,' with the well-known 'Derry-down' tag." (G, Ob. 173)

> Gm 1.185c. This is No. 34 of the set of tunes received from Riddell.

663 **PADDLE YOUR OWN CANOE** Cf. *Paddle Your Own Canoe* written and sung by Harry Clifton (Hopwood and Crew, London, c. 1890).

> Gw 17.68-70.

664 **WE'RE A' CUTTIN'**

> Misc. 94. "Mrs Gillespie (1905): from W. Birnie, Artamford. It does not seem traditional." (D, Misc.) Duncan gives this fragment in Misc. as one of the songs sung to the tune "We're a' noddin'", *Lyric Gems* 2.233.

665 **SWEEP YOUR OWN DOOR CLEAN**

> Gw 4.68-9.

666 **THE SLIPPY STANE** Cf. *National Choir* 1.339. The song is said there to be by James Hendrie and to have been first published in *The People's Friend* in 1875. See also Edwards, eighth series, pp. 248-9, where Hamilton Nimmo is named as the author. In Ob. 111, Greig gives the song as in Edwards and comments: "A reader has expressed a wish to see the above song, and we are very pleased to print it. It was written by Hamilton Nimmo (1836-1892), a well-known vocalist, who used to tour the country with his entertainments of Scottish song and ballad. He wrote several songs – words and music. One of his best efforts is 'I'm lying on a foreign shore,' which is widely known and sung. Unfortunately he got drawn into a lawsuit over the copyright of 'The Crookit Bawbee.' The decision went against him. He had to pay £5 of damages to the pursuer – not such a big matter; but the expenses attending the defence of the case amounted to some £1200. Fine thing law – for some people! Poor Nimmo was forced into bankruptcy. But happily a substantial legacy came his way through the death of a rich relative, which enabled him to pay his creditors in full, and once more look the whole world in the face. 'The slippery stane' has a considerable vogue, although, as usual in the case of songs of this kind, the name of the author has pretty much dropped out of sight."

A   Gm 4.171b.
B   Gw 18.95-6.
C   Ob. 121. "The reader at whose request 'The Slippery Stane' was inserted [in Ob. 111] writes to say that he would be additionally obliged if we would print the following verse, and ask if anyone could complete it, as, he says, it is supposed to be the original – [Text C]." (G, Ob. 121) This verse corresponds to stanza 2 in the *National Choir* version.

667 **WHEN FORTUNE TURNS THE WHEEL** Cf. the slip McNaughtan No. 832 *Fortune Turns the Wheel* (Poet's Box, Glasgow, 15 August 1874). "This is a popular ditty, having a considerable circulation as a broadside. The tune which I have got for it seems to have affinity with the tune to which [152] 'The Plains of Waterloo' is sung." (G, Ob. 88)

A   Gm 2.8b. August 1906.
B   Gm 2.141b. September 1907.
C   Gw 22.89-91.
D   Gw 28.12-4. Acknowledged in Ob. 36, 4 August 1908.
E   Gw 39.64-5. "Pitsligo lady per Bell Robertson." (Gw) Acknowledged in Ob. 82, 6 July 1909.

668 **UP A TREE** Cf. the slip McNaughtan No. 2732 *Up a Tree* (Poet's Box, Glasgow, 18 December 1875).

A   Gw 34.55. The stanza is headed "Fragment". The words "on the Clyde" and the last line are underlined. "I don't know about this one." (Robertson, *Song Notes*, 2.36)
B   Ob. 63. "Mr William Stephen, Lonmay, would like a copy of a song of which he remembers only bits. One

of these is:– [Text]." (G, Ob. 63) "To Mr George Cadger, Peterhead, I am much indebted for a copy of the words of 'Up a Tree,' which I am sending to the gentleman who asked for them, together with the tune. Mr Cadger tells how he used to sing the song long ago to an old man who had once been wealthy but had come down in the world. When the poor chap got fuddled, as he often did, he would have 'Up a Tree,' with the result that he grat like a bairn." (G, Ob. 66)

669 **A SHILLIN' OR TWA** Cf. Ord, pp. 388-9, and the slip McNaughtan No. 2411 *A Shilling or Twa* (Poet's Box, Glasgow, 28 April 1877).

A Ob. 140. "Mr James Angus, Peterhead, sends me an incomplete copy of 'A Shilling or twa.' The song begins – [Text]. We may say that the song was given by Mr John Ord in *Weekly Welcome* some time ago from an old broadside; but we shall be happy if any reader can supply us with a traditional version." (G, Ob. 140, 16 August 1910)
B Gw 13.92. February 1908.

670 **IF BUT ONE HEART BE TRUE** The title is editorial.

Gw 49.38. 1.1 "we": MS "wi'".

671 **OH DINNA QUARREL THE BAIRNIES** The title is editorial.

Gm 4.37b. September 1908.

672 **BEHAVE YERSEL'** Cf. *Lyric Gems*, 2.130-1 "Behave Yoursel' Before Folk" and "The Answer" by Alexander Rodger.

Gw 37.106.

673 **I DON'T THINK MUCH OF YOU** Cf. Frank Purslow, *Marrow Bones* (London, 1965), p. 18 "Compliments Returned". The main title is editorial.

A Dm 378c. "Mrs Gillespie, from A. Mavor. Noted 25th September 1907. Mrs Gillespie gives words additional:– [Text, st. 2]. The song seems of the modern Music Hall type." (Dm)
B Dm 354a. "Noted by Mrs Harper from her mother's singing, August 1907. Heard by Mrs Greig in Cluny. The tune is given in the measure of Mrs Harper's manuscript, but seems rather to suggest 6/8 time, with longer note at end of each line." (Dm)
C Gw 37.53.

674 **TO COONT MY KIN AN' PEDIGREE**

790.1/3/8. "Another fragment of McCombie's [see note to 628 'The Ball at Davidson's' B]. Apparently there was something of the nature of a 'flyting' between him and another rhymer whose name was Milne. At that time Milne was the name of the hangman which explains the reference to 'finishing the law.' If there is a record of the hangman this would help to fix the date – if it is worth while doing so. [Text.] It looks as if the pedlar had got the rival rhymer to help him to get a bit of his own back." Charles Murray. (790.1/3/8) In line 8, Murray first wrote "illegible" before "chiel" and then deleted this and inserted "pedlar". William Walker has noted: "?Sanders Laing c. 1820-30" at this line and "Johnnie Milne?" at line 4. Line 2: see *Hebrews* 7.3.

675 **AE NIGHT LAST OOK FAN GROWING LATE** The title is editorial.

Gw 63.27-9. 8.1 "is it really": MS "is really". At 4.4 and 13.1 the dots indicate spaces in Gw. The initials "W.L." are given at the end, identifying William Lillie as the author.

676 **O MUCKLE DEIL FAT HAS COME O' YE** The title is editorial.

Gw 63.56-9. There is no division into stanzas in Gw. The dots at 3.10 indicate a space in the manuscript line.

677 **MOSSIE AND HIS MEER** Cf. Ford, pp. 39-42. "This satirical ditty must be fairly old. Peter Buchan gives it in his *Gleanings* (1825); and Ford, who prints it in his *Vagabond Songs and Ballads*, traces it back to the middle of last century, at which time it was considered an old song. The political touch in the last verse seems to carry the ditty back to Jacobite times. The tune, which I have recorded once or twice, is a Dorian of a very pronounced type." (G, Ob. 171)

A Dm 122b. "Dorian. Mrs Gillespie, from Katie Steven, dressmaker, New Pitsligo. Noted 1905. In Riddell's 'Airs' [see C], with this name. Words and air (with very slight differences) in Ford, p. 39." (Dm) "See Ford, p. 39; the following shows the differences:– (1) Verse the same, but chorus thus:–

Hey doo a dadden um, hey doo a dee,
Hey doo a dadden um, dadden um a dee;

or thus:– '*Wi' my fal lalla lal de deedum,*' etc., as in [Dm]. (4) 'That' for 'wha'. (5) 'Fae the ell'. The words as above were sung by Alex. Imlah, Woodhead of Delgaty. Tom Murdoch and Katie Stephen (New Pitsligo) sang a different form in which the relations of men and women were compared to how 'Mossie catch'd his meer' – not very delicate, it seems. It may be the older form, from which the present was made as a Jacobite song. The two forms of chorus probably from Katie Stephen and Tom Murdoch." (D, Gillespie 202)

B   Gm 3.181b. Acknowledged in Ob. 95, 5 October 1909.

C   Gm 1.179d. This is No. 11 of the set of tunes received from Riddell. "Dorian mode. Ford, p. 39." (Gm) Greig also gives references to Henry T. Whyte (Fionn), *The Celtic Lyre* (Edinburgh, 1898), No. 44 "Mairi Laghach – Winsome Mary", "Johnnie Cooper" from Alexander Robb, "Winsome Mary" from Charles Walker, and 398 "Lamachree and Megrum" A.

678   THE WICKED CAPTAIN

Gw 53.88-9.

679   THE GLEAD   The title is editorial.

Gw 63.45-8. 15.2 "Mains": MS "mouns", which seems likely to be a miscopy of "Mains". The initials "H.H.I.S." appear at the conclusion of the piece.

680   BOUND FOR GLORY NOO   The title is editorial.

Gw 49.73-4. In 3 r. 1 "what" is deleted before "a'". "From Miss Ritchie, Causewayhill." A.S. (Gw)

681   THE GUISE O' TYRIE   Cf. William Walker, *The Bards of Bon-Accord* (Aberdeen, 1887), pp. 70-2. "The church and religion as such have practically no place in folk-song, which indeed in relation to religion as to love is largely pagan. If ecclesiastical matters are to receive attention at its hands they must as a rule come into the arena of local incident lending itself to satirical comment. The disputed settlement of the Rev. Andrew Cant as minister of the parish of Tyrie gave occasion to an effusion of this kind. – [Text.]" (G, *Folk-Song in Buchan*, p. 33) In *The Bards of Bon-Accord*, Walker gives a version of seven stanzas, of which the one given here is the first, and comments: "The following snatch of a humorous song is said to have been written on the appointment of Andrew Cant, the well-known covenanting leader, to his first charge. The parish of Pitsligo had been recently erected by a partition of the parish of Aberlour, and Alexander Forbes, first Lord Pitsligo, had built a suitable church, and, in the exercise of his right as patron, appointed Mr. Cant, at that time tutor in his family, to the new pulpit. The news of this appointment was received with considerable disapprobation in the adjoining parish of Tyrie, the lands of which, for the most part, belonged to members of the Pitsligo family – and out of this discontent sprang the song. ... Evidently the lady Fraser got rather rough usage from tongue and hand of 'the muirland wives' for her support of the budding 'apostle of the Covenant'; but how Elphinstone of Glack got mixed up in it, we have been unable to explain. The 'Slack' (line 6) is probably one of the winding glens known as The Slacks of Cairnbanno in New Deer." On Andrew Cant and the religious and historical background, see William Watt, *A History of Aberdeen and Banff* (Edinburgh and London, 1900), pp. 232-4, 261-4, and Ian B. Cowan, *The Scottish Covenanters 1660-1688* (London, 1976).

Gw 1.41-2. John Milne published the fragment in Milne, p. 3.

682   TAMMY CHALMERS   This song is a satiric treatment of the Disruption of 1843 when, under the leadership of Dr Thomas Chalmers, approximately a third of the ministers of the Church of Scotland resigned their offices and endowments and formed the Free Church. See Thomas Brown, *Annals of the Disruption*, new edition (Edinburgh, 1893), especially ch. 15 "Leaving the Manse", ch. 22 "Temporary Places of Worship", and ch. 24 "The Sustentation Fund", and Andrew L. Drummond and James Bulloch, *The Scottish Church 1688-1843* (Edinburgh, 1973), ch. 12.

A   Gw 27.1-2.

B   Gw 10.42.

683   THE WIDOW'S CRUISIE

790.1/3/10. Line 1: "Doon" replaces deleted "Up". Murray has the heading: "I find this amongst my notes as if it were also McCombie's [see note to 628 'The Ball at Davidson's' B] but I don't think it is. I think there are many variations but this may be of interest for comparison." At line 12 he has the note: "See the other fragment 'The cock was but a gawpie' [i.e. line 4 of 'Janet she cam' doon the gait' also in 790.1/3/10]." William Walker has added the comment: "About a minister who preached always when in a strange pulpit the same sermon on the text – 'the widow's cruisie'." See 1 *Kings* 17.8-16. The title is editorial.

684   BETTY MULL'S SQUEEL

Ob. 29. "To Miss Helen Bruce, Foveran, I am indebted for copies of [354] 'Ellon Market,' and 'Betty Mull's Squeel.' Betty's seminary is understood to have been in the Belhelvie district, and her teaching seems to have been of the true dame-school order." (G, Ob. 29, 16 June 1908)

685 **THE SOLDIER AND THE SAILOR**   Cf. Sharp No. 376 "The Sailor and the Soldier".

A   Gm 1.31a; Gw 6.59-61, 3.33-5. 1904. (Gm)   In Gw 6 "I" is altered from "y" at 2.4 and "all" is altered from "auld" at 4.1; Gw 3 gives "I" and "auld". At 3.3, 4.3, and 5.3 "oh" (as in Gw 3) is read in place of "o'". The text in Gw 3 gives stanzas 4 and 5 in the reverse order; verbal differences are shown in brackets: Title: The, the (A, a), 1.3 pray here (pray), 1.4 ye (you), 3.2, 3 if (while), 6.3 For ye (Ye), back (backs), o' (of).

B   Gm 2.52a. Greig has a question mark after the initials "J.Q.", querying the ascription to John Quirrie.

C   Gw 38.93.

686 **THE UPPERMOST TUB**

Gm 2.133a; Gw 10.36-8. August 1907. (Gm and Gw)

687 **FIFTEENTH PSALM**

Gm 4.132c.

688 **COVENANTERS**

Gm 3.9c. September 1907. The words "Psalm Tune" follow the title and there is a note: "Mr Cowan of Banchory brought the tune North from Dumfriessh with the information that it was a Covenanting tune.".

689 **THE PRESBYTERIAN CAT**   Cf. Ford, pp. 319-21 "The Cameronian Cat", and *Rymour Club Miscellanea*, 1.33, 231-2. The title is editorial.

Gw 44.54-5. "Mother had that one. Her father sung it to her. He died when she was only six." (Robertson, *Song Notes*, 1.32)

690 **THE AULD WIFE AND HER CATTIE**   Cf. *Tocher* 2 (No. 12), 121.

A   Gm 4.95b.

B   Misc. 95. This item is included in a set of songs sung to the air "Carrickfergus." "Mrs Gillespie (1905); sung by William Kirkton, carpenter with father. He also sang 'Carrickfergus' to words of its own. [Last line] supplied by Mr Harper, Schoolhouse, Cluny, [in the form 'For the half o' her cattie was eaten that day']." (D, Misc.) In a later note, Duncan adds that "Mrs Gillespie now gives" the last line in an "alternative form" with "clippit away" in place of "eaten that day".

691 **OUR ORANGE FLAGS MAY GANG TO RAGS**   R. Dudley Edwards gives an account of the political situation which was the context for this song in *A New History of Ireland* (Dublin, 1972), pp. 159-60: "[Daniel O'Connell] from about 1824 until his death in 1847 was the most notable Irish political leader. The reversal of Tory policy on the issue of Catholic emancipation can be ascribed to O'Connell's methods. Wellington, the victor of Waterloo, who became Prime Minister in 1828, was obliged to consider what would be the full consequences of a resort to force in Ireland over the Catholic question. The climax came when O'Connell was returned as member of parliament for Clare and at the bar of the House of Commons refused to take the declaration against transubstantiation and the anti-Catholic oath of allegiance. Tory feelings were aroused to an intense heat, but in their wisdom, Wellington and his home secretary and political heir, Sir Robert Peel, forced George IV to give way. In the United Kingdom as a whole, the feeling was that there should be no further delay in conceding emancipation. The Catholic Emancipation Act was passed in [April] 1829 and ended the restriction of parliament to Protestant members." At a new election on 30 July 1829, O'Connell was returned unopposed as M.P. for County Clare.

790.1/1/10. The title is editorial, taken from 5.5. The song text has the following marginal and interspersed comments, evidently intended to be included in performance: 1.2 Flora (Flora the goddess o' flooers), 1.6 meander (that's a crookit beem), 2.4 conversation (a dialogue atween twa as it were), 2.5 Billy lad (William the 4th), 3.3 popish Dan (Daniel O'Connell), 3.4 *Again* has won the Clare election (He was twice elected for the Co. Clare but couldna haud a seat.), 4.2 old truce (the truce signed), 5.5 Our Orange flags may gang to rags (I wadna like to see't. There's only ae Orangeman in Inverewen [?]. I was made an Orangeman in the County o Cork in the year saxteen an' I'm a freemason tee and ye ken well they'll tak' naebody for a freemason or an Orangeman either that's nae soond in body and mind.).

692 **THE LAST SPEECH AND DYING WORDS OF THE AULD KIRK OF TURRIFF**   Cf. Hugh Allan, *The Auld Kirk of Turra's Testament* (John Wilson, Aberdeen, 1863) and *The Auld Kirk o' Turra's Testament to Her Daughter (the Present Parish Church)* (*Banffshire Journal* Office, Banff, 1917). Besides these two separately published pamphlets, which contain different versions of the poem, another text was published in *Scottish Notes and Queries*, second series, 6 (1905), 183-5, and comments in *Scottish Notes and Queries*, second series, 7 (1905-6), 12 and 27-8, include variants from manuscript sources. The Gw text, which is stated to be "From Rettie's manuscript copy", is an independent version and its twelfth stanza is not found in the other texts mentioned. Hugh Allan was a tailor in Cuminestown in the parish of Monquhitter who was said to have composed several songs as well as this poem. His stance here is that of a member of the Episcopal Church of Scotland. The poem relates to the building of the new parish church of Turriff in 1794.

Gw 33.55-73. There are the following notes after the text in Gw. (The line references have been changed to accord with the numbered stanzas in the printed text; Gw does not have stanza numbers and the references there are given by the line of the poem.) "1.2 'Hallans': Little hall, a small porch placed in country houses outside the door. 'To gink': To play at 'leet-bo' or hide and seek. 1.6 'Hapshackles': Coverings for the wrist. The wrist is called in Aberdeenshire the shackle bone – that is the bone where shackles or cuffs are placed. 'Hapshackles' made of hasps or secured by a chain and padlock as the entrances of jails commonly are. 2.3 'Niffer'd shargers': Children changed by the fairies who took away the healthy child and left one of their own brood cankered and diminutive in the extreme. 2.5, 3.2 'Water wraiths,' 'Kelpies': Two distinct spirits – the one yelps or barks like a dog, the other assumes the form of a small horse who entices the unwary to mount him, runs off and drowns them in the water. At other times he will assume the shape and size of a loaf of bread or other small necessary article lying on the ground as if dropped by accident, which being picked up and put in the pocket by a person about to ford the river he swells to such an enormous size as sinks them to the bottom. 3.1 'Spunkie': Will-o'-the-wisp. 3.5 'Elfin candles': —. 4.4: 'Kinkin': The diaphragm, from 'kink' a short kind of hysterical laugh, hence 'kinkhoast' =chincough [whooping cough]. 6.1 'Cosie's howe' (margin): A small glen hard by Turriff belongs to Cosmo Morrice, vintner (in the verse 'Cosie's Know'). 6.5 'Riggin divot': A bonnet. 8.1 'Brig o' Hell': A bridge so called in the village of Turriff. 8.6 'Av' Marie': Ave Mary. 10.3 'Crowlin': Different from crawling – means the feeble efforts to walk made by decrepit age. 12.6 'Kiln sunners' [for 'simmers']: Beams on which the flooring of the kiln is laid; being continually exposed to heat and smoke they are much the colour of a mummy. 14.4 'He didna kythe': Made no impression on the outward sense. 24.3 'Erastian': Prelacy was the bugbear of the Covenanters. 34.3 'Head elder fley': Argyle. 35.3 'Like the ants': The ants celebrated for their republican, as the bees are for their monarchial, form of government. 45.1 Luckie German: The German Ocean."

Two mid-line commas which affected the sense have been omitted, at 13.2 after "neive" and at 27.5 after "na". In the first case there is a space after the comma, perhaps indicating that it was felt that a word was missing before "in length at least". The method of measuring referred to is well described by James Gammack in *Scottish Notes and Queries*, second series, 7 (1905-6), 27: "the 'horn'd nive' is the hand closed firmly and having the thumb set up at full length: two of these on end measured the beard".

693 **QUEEN JEAN** Child 170 *The Death of Queen Jane.* "Of this ballad Child published nine versions, partly English and partly Scottish; and three more have since been printed in the *Folk-Song Journal* (2.221-3, 3.67-8). The reference is to Jane Seymour, queen of Henry VIII, and the birth of Prince Edward. She died twelve days after the birth; and it seems 'there was a belief that severe surgery had been required' [Child 3.372-3], though for that there is no good authority, and the story of the ballad is really without foundation. It is of some interest to note that our version [A], learnt in Aberdeenshire some sixty years ago, corresponds stanza by stanza up to 8 in general meaning, though by [no] means in the details of the lines, with a version received from singing at the other end of Scotland (Kirkcudbright) and forwarded to Child (his version E). It is curious that the correspondence extends even to the omission of an introductory stanza, found in some form in all other versions, and to the following effect (Percy [Child A]):–

> Queen Jane was in labour [full] six weeks and more,
> And the women were weary, and fain would give o'er.

The Kirkcudbright version does not go farther; but our closing stanzas have their parallels in meaning, though not verbally, in other versions. The variation mentioned in Miss Robertson's note [B] is not in any version yet recorded." (D, *Last Leaves* MS, 790.6/2/6) Greig added the note: "Cf. 'Cockpen.'" to his copy at Gm 2.155 of the tune "Queen Jeanie" from George R. Kinloch's *Ancient Scottish Ballads* (London, 1827).

A Gw 27.5-7, Bw 1.71. Acknowledged in Ob. 34, 21 July 1908. "Miss Bell Robertson, learnt about sixty years ago from two girls." (D, *Last Leaves* MS, 790.6/2/6) "I never heard 'Queen Jane' complet, only bits from the Ross girls and from a tinker boy." (Robertson, *Letters to Duncan*, 4 August 1915)

B Gw 27.7, Bw 1.71-2. The following note by Bell Robertson follows A in Gw: "A tinker boy that used to come in to my father's had another version, but I never could make it out, but when she asked them to send they said – [Text]." Line 4 "bedside" : MS "beside".

694 **FAT'LL I DEE AN MY DEARIE DEE** The title is editorial.

A Dm 347c. "Noted by Mrs Harper from her sister, Miss Elizabeth Greig, August 1907." (Dm)

B Gw 55.30. "Laird o' Cockpen." (Gw) Another fragment at the bottom of the same page "Geordie's frank and Geordie's free" is given as from "Miss Greig – from her mother" and the note may possibly apply to this fragment also.

695 **OH, GIN YE WERE DEID, GOODMAN** Cf. Johnson No. 409.

Misc. 99. "Air – 'Green grow the rashes.' Mrs Gillespie; sung by father. See words in Herd, 2.207 ('I wish that you were dead, goodman.'). For a different air see Graham 3.132, and Johnson, No. 409 (= 'There was a lad')." (D, Misc.)

696 THE SON OF A SEVEN

Gw 27.34-6. "Had gone out of fashion in Bell Robertson's day; but was popular when her father was young, who used to say it as a nursery rhyme." (Gw) The first "bill" in the second prose passage replaces deleted "skill". In the expressions at the end of the two prose passages: "But weel out I never heed" and "But reediet I never heeded", it seems likely that "weel out" and "reediet" are miscopies, possibly of the same source word or words. The items listed in the bill in the second prose passage include elecampane and horse radish.

697 MACPHERSON'S RANT Cf. Johnson No. 114 "McPherson's Farewell", Kinsley No. 196, and James Maidment, *Scotish Ballads and Songs* (Edinburgh, 1859), pp.29-34.

A Dm 169b; Gillespie 569-70. "MS. of George F. Duncan, noted from father in 1885." (Dm) In Gillespie, "old way" is written beside the title.

B Gillespie 524-6, Dw 2.167. "The above is from father, but is apparently partly from Burns. Mrs Gillespie gave the following stanza at an earlier date as coming just before No. 5:

> He took his fiddle in his hand,
> And three times roun' went he,
> There wad neen o' them his fiddle tak,
> And he brak her owre his knee.

But see [A] for older words." (D, Gillespie) Duncan copied at Dw 2.167 a text of five stanzas written by George F. Duncan (998/7/4/35) as derived "from father, 1885", but notes: "This is simply Burns's form. Compare with Mrs Gillespie's first form [B], which contains this and older words. It would seem now, however, that father simply sang Burns's song." There are the following divergences from the text in Kinsley: 1.4 On yonder (Below), 3.2 bring (gie), 3.3 no (not), 5.1 thou (and), 5.3 distain (be on), 5.4 dares not (fears to).

C Gm 1.130b; Gw 3.96. "Christie 2.266." (Gm)

D Gm 3.181a. Acknowledged in Ob. 95, 5 October 1909.

E Gm 3.43a. November 1906.

F Gm 4.74a. A pencil note gives a cross-reference to "Broomhill's Bonnie Daughter" from John Johnstone.

G Gw 3.96.

698 ROSEN THE BEAU Cf. Sharp No. 230 "Rosin the Beau".

A Gm 3.100c, Misc. 10-1; Gillespie 151-4. "Mrs Gillespie; from John Duguid: noted 1905. Is it modern and English? Given, words and music, in William Alexander Barrett's *English Folk-Songs* (Novello, London, [1891]), No. 53, as 'Rosin the *Beau*' (?)." (D,Misc.) In the words of stanza 1 given with the music in Misc., "good?" is written on both occasions beside "hot" and Duncan notes: "The alternative words were both in use." In Gillespie, the text at first consisted of seven stanzas, and stanza 8 was added later in Duncan's hand, with the attached note: "Above verse is the last, added by Mrs Gillespie at a later date. Mrs Gillespie states that the song was always sung with the words – 'Rosin-*de*-Bow'." He altered the title to "Rosin the Bow" as well as using this form in the stanza he wrote. The last three lines of stanza 8 are not written out but are indicated by "etc.". The Gm music, which was received by Greig from Duncan, is identical with the music given in sol fa in Misc.

B Gm 1.54a. 1905. "Cf. 'Geordie Downie' from [George Bruce Thomson]." (Gm) "Bow" was altered to "Beau" both in the text and in the title.

699 THE SCOTS PIPERS

Gw 62.102. At 3.4 "his" is written below "the" and appears to be intended to replace this word.

700 THE TERM Cf. *Lilts o' the Lea-Rig* by a Herd Loon [Robert H. Calder] (Brechin, 1900), pp. 37-8 "The Deein' Plooman". "Looking through a manuscript book of songs kindly lent by a farm servant, I have just come on one called 'The Term' which moves me deeply. It is in fact one of the most touching pieces of verse I have ever come across. – [Text C.]" (G, Ob. 26) "Referring to 'The Term,' or 'The Dying Ploughboy' [Ob. 26] – Miss Brown, New Deer, informs me that she used to hear it sung by a farm-servant who was in their employment at Bonnykelly some sixteen years ago. He said that the verses were composed by a young fellow who died under the circumstances referred to at a farm in the Aberdour district, and that the lad gave copies to all his fellow servants of whom Miss Brown's informant was one. If this be so, it greatly intensifies our regret that a life so promising should have been cut short 'ere its sun was in mid-skies.'" (G, Ob. 29)

"I am greatly pleased to have got the question of the authorship of 'The Term' [Ob. 26] definitely settled. For this I am indebted to my learned friend Mr A. Macdonald, M.A., Durris, who communicates the information that the lyric was written by the Rev. R.H. Calder, M.A., minister of Glenlivet, and appears under the title of 'The Deein' Plooman' in his *Lilts o' the Lea-Rig*, a small volume of verse published in 1900. Mr Macdonald very kindly sends me a look of the book. All this is to me very interesting indeed; for the author, who is a brother of the Rev. Mr [John] Calder of Crimond, was a classmate of my own both at the Old Aberdeen Grammar School under Dr Dey, and at the University. We knew him as a poet in those days, and I have since then come across a number of his pieces in Edwards' *Modern Scottish Poets* and in *Life and Work*. Much of Mr Calder's poetical work reaches a high level; but 'The Deein' Plooman' is one of the best things he has written and is indeed one of the best things of its kind *ever* written. It will live. I am sure my readers will join with me in offering Mr Macdonald our best thanks for letting us know to whom we owe a lyric that has impressed us all so very much." (G, Ob. 32, 7 July 1908) A text copied from *Lilts o' the Lea-Rig* appears at Gw 20.114-5.

A   Gm 3.113a. June 1908. (Gm) Acknowledged in Ob. 31, 30 June 1908. See note to C.

B   Gm 3.110b. June 1908.

C   Gw 20.29-30. Copied May 1908 from a farm servant's manuscript book supplied by Sam Davidson. At the end of the text is the query: "?Author". The following note is written on the facing page, Gw 20.29v: "Miss Brown, Backhill, Bonnykelly, says that some sixteen years ago they had a servant (?Maclennan) then about thirty, who gave them a copy of 'The Term', saying that it was composed by a young fellow, a farm servant at Tillyquhairn near Aberdour, in the circumstances detailed in the song, and that he gave a copy to all his fellow servants, of whom Maclennan was one. Miss Brown has a recollection of the general way of the tune."

D   Gw 47.98-9. "From Miss Lizzie Ingram. These two [i.e. this song and the preceding one, 316 "Mrs Greig of Sandlaw" B, from William Ingram] they had among them for fifty years." A.S. "Cf. with original, to illustrate traditionary variation." (Gw)

701   **BURNS'S FAREWELL**

Gw 56.1-2. "E. Rennie, Milladen. Original." (Gw)

702   **THE TESTAMENT**

Gw 9.55-8. February 1907. At 3.1 "bullet" is given in explanation of "ballast" in brackets after that word.

703   **THE MILLER'S WILL**   Cf. Kennedy No. 232 "The Miller's Last Will". "The miller of folk-song figures in many an escapade – more breezy, as a rule, than respectable. More frequently indeed than any other member of the rural community is the miller depicted as a bit of a rake. On another side too – that of honesty, he is often assailed with bantering insinuations if not more overt charges. These things, however, are not to be taken as affecting the reputation of the trade as a whole for probity and fair dealing. [Text.] This song, which is known all over the country, appears to hail originally from the south. I have a record of the tune [A] from Mr J. Lawrence, Lonmay, which is also sung to 'The Apprentice Sailor Boy,' and is well known in England." (G, Ob. 41)

A   Gm 2.53c; Gw 7.5-7. July 1906. (Gm) "'Sailor Boy.'" (Gm)

B   Gw 7.4v-6v.

C   Gw 43.55-7.

D   Gw 47.4. "From Mr William Dunbar. I have also heard his father sing it." A.S. (Gw)

704   **OH THE MILLER HE STOLE CORN**   Cf. Sharp No. 322 "The Three Sons".

A   Gm 1.147c; Gw 3.113, 4.6. March 1906. (Gm and Gw 3)

B   Dm 494d; 998/7/3/18, Dw 2.78. "From Miss Jessie H. McDonald, Alford, 1906 (her own notation). She received it from Mr Andrew Walker, Alford. The air is another version of 'The British Grenadiers'. See ['The Banks o' Clyde' from Mrs Greig and Mrs Gillespie]." (Dm) In the words with the music written by Miss McDonald (998/7/3/18), the first line has "nation" not "nations". In Dw, Duncan queries at 1.1: "'nations': should this be 'ocean'?" and notes concerning the refrain: "Apparently sung to the same music as the verse."

C   Gm 2.18d. "*Weekly Herald*, G.K.C., Drum. Cf. [562 'Come, Landlord, Fill a Flowing Bowl']." Gm)

D   Gm 3.39c. October 1907.

705   **GRANDMOTHER'S CHAIR**   Cf. Michael R. Turner and Antony Miall, *Just a Song at Twilight: The Second Parlour Song Book* (London, 1975), pp. 229-32 "Grandmother's Chair" written and composed by John Read.

Gm 3.85a. April 1908.

706   **BE KIN' TO YER NAINSEL, JOHN**   Greig appealed for versions of this in Ob. 112: "Can any of our readers kindly help us with the following songs:– 'Be kin' to yer nainsel, John,' and 'Aul' Widow Greylocks?' Versions, complete or fragmentary, of either or both, will be greatly valued." Two weeks later he began to publish responses.

"The other song we asked for [besides 'Aul' Widow Greylocks'] was 'Be kin' to yer nainsel', John'; and Miss Bell Robertson gives her recollections of it as sung by her mother and aunt, premising that the song appears to be a parody on 'The Land o' the Leal':– [Text F]. In this way she goes over the beasts and articles in the house, always telling him to give away the best and keep the worst, but still every now and again bidding him be kind to himself, for she is wearin' awa'. The Rev. John Strachan, M.A., Cruden Rectory, also sends me a very interesting communication, in which he quotes from the Life of Thomas Smith, a Cruden boy, who rose to be a Judge of the Supreme Court of Pennsylvania. Writing of 1762, the biographer [Burton Alva Konkle] says:– 'Thomas was now seventeen years old, and his mother has left record that he was "always a good and kind lad" to her, and in later years she used to hum over one of what he said was his favourite songs:–

> Be kind to me as long as I'm here,
> I'll maybe wear awa' yet.'

'The Land o' the Leal' was written in 1798, and it is quite likely that Lady Nairne got a hint from some older song like the one to which the above couplet belongs. We are greatly indebted to our correspondents for their kind contributions, and trust that others who can will add their quota of help and give us any recollections they may have of these 'wearin' awa'' songs." (G, Ob. 114, 15 February 1910)

"['Be kin' to yer nainsel, John'] raises some very interesting questions. ... The Rev. Mr Duncan, Lynturk, informs me that he has one or two versions of the song – the refrain being – [Text B, as with music]. He says:– 'At least one of my versions goes back a hundred years or more. In this case, the suggestion of parody is the first and most obvious, but there are difficulties.' Yes, there are difficulties. Miss Robertson's – 'Fy, gar heat a sup drink, John' [F], is older than Lady Nairne's day. But here again we must call a halt meantime." (G, Ob. 116)

"We return to 'Be kin' to yer nainsel, John,' and 'Aul' Widow Greylocks.' – *Re* the former song, Miss Bell Robertson favours me with some further recollections. She says that her mother knew Lady Nairne's song, or part of it, but that when she wished to put a child to sleep she always sang the other. The tune was the same, and so was the refrain. She began –

> I'm wearin' awa', John,
> Like snaw fin' it's thaw, John,
> I'm wearin' awa' to the land o' the leal,
> Fy, gar eat a sup drink, John,
> Heat it wi' butter and meal, etc.

My correspondent says that she never heard her mother say where she got her version of the song, but she feels sure that her aunt had got hers from her mother who would have been a girl about 1780. Miss Robertson refers to the controversy that once arose (and has been repeated since) as to the authorship of 'The Land of the Leal,' some people claiming it for Burns, and she recalls that one correspondent referred to the earlier song about the unmanly John." (G, Ob. 119) See also William Montgomerie, "The Land o' the Leal", *Scottish Studies* 3 (1959), 201-8.

A Gm 4.1a; Gw 52.1-3. April 1910. (Gm) "Although we have had a good deal to say about this song of late I print the above version entire, because it is the most complete I have yet got. It has been supplied by Mrs Jaffray, Mintlaw. The tune to which she sings it is the same as what I recorded from the singing of Mr Brebner, Aucheoch." (G, Ob. 122)

B Dm 55a; Gillespie 306-7. "Mrs Gillespie – learnt from her step-grandmother, Mrs Duncan, Craigculter. Noted 1905. This verse [with the music] is the chorus, but is sung first. The next words are –

> Ye'll heat anither drink to me, John, O;
> Ye'll heat anither drink to me, John, O;
> Wi' a wee bit o' butter, an' a little puckle sucker,
> An a wee, wee drappie o' a dram, John.

The third metrical line given to the [C] tune borrows the third line here – inappropriately." (Dm) "Mrs Duncan, Craigculter, from whom the song came (or rather from 'Jean Strachan,' her mother) sang all the first *eight* lines as chorus. A good deal wanting." (D, Gillespie) The text in Gillespie indicates that the four "heat anither drink" lines were sung as chorus, with the "wearin awa" lines as the opening stanza. The bracketed "For" Duncan gives with the music has been taken here to mean that the word was not included in the lines as sung at the beginning of the song. At 3.3-4 "ane" is altered to "teen" and "hummle" to "crummie".

"Mrs Gillespie states that she heard the song from her step-grandmother nearly sixty years ago, and that it was sung to father as a child by his stepmother's mother – say about 1822, when she was already advanced in years, being known as 'aul' Jean Strachan.' Most probably she had learnt the song long before: old people usually sang only songs learnt in youth. That would take the song back to the end of the eighteenth century. Now Lady Nairne's 'The Land o' the Leal' goes back to 1798, and contains these coincidences with this:– (1) the use of the expression 'the land o' the leal' for heaven; (2) the *combination* of this with the words 'I am wearin awa,' (3) the address to the husband as 'John' and (4) the use of all these in an address from a dying wife to her husband. Even the first coincidence could hardly be accidental, and the union of the four accidentally is impossible. Then the dates exclude the supposition of this folk-song borrowing from Lady Nairne's words, if that were otherwise probable; and the alternative is that she took the expressions above from the popular song, being struck with their beauty, and gave them a more serious setting. That was in harmony with her ordinary practice. It is true that she does not mention this when stating the origin of the song ('I wrote it merely because I liked the air so much'); but that was in old age, and she might have forgotten, or thought the circumstance unimportant, as the practice was so common. But this discovery of the suggestion of Lady Nairne's song, and the origin of its most striking expression, is exceedingly interesting, though no editor has known of it. See Robert Ford's *Song Histories* (Glasgow and Edinburgh, 1900) on 'The Land o' the Leal' [pp. 110-24], where the known facts are stated with reference to the song. (Compare [note on 'Aul' Widow Greylocks' at Dm 256].)" (Dm 56)

C Dm 55c; 998/7/3/17, Dw 1.178. "Mr Andrew Walker, Alford. Noted by Miss Jessie H. McDonald 1905." (Dm) "This [st. 4] is the last verse, but Mr Walker is not sure of the order of the others. There may be more verses in it. Dictated by Mr Walker to Miss Macdonald. December, 1905." (Dw) In 998/7/3/17 Duncan observes: "The first verse as received from Mrs Gillespie: then as follows: [Text, written by Jessie McDonald]." In Dw, he gives as opening stanza:

I am wearin' awa, John,
I am wearin' awa, John,
I'm wearin' awa to the land o' the leal,
So be kin' to your nain sel, John, O.

D   Gm 3.205b; Gw 50.31-2. In Gw there is a note at the end: "So with implements etc." Words and music acknowledged in Ob. 116.

E   Dm 55b; Dw 6.46. "Mrs Petrie – learnt from her mother. Noted 1906." (Dm)   "Chorus repeated after each succeeding verse. No more remembered. Noted September, 1911." (Dw)

F   Ob. 114, 117, 119.

G   Gw 50.34. "Supplementary verses to 'that very old song.'" (Gw)   Acknowledged in Ob. 119, where Greig comments that "my correspondent takes the song to be very old – an opinion in which I concur."

H   Gw 49.111, 104. Stanza 1 is given at Gw 49.111, and stanza 2 and the refrain are given at Gw 49.104 with the comments: "Heard by A.S." and "Fragment picked up when young." A.S. Stanza 1 is quoted in Ob. 121, and stanza 2 in Ob. 123; see note to J.

I   Ob. 123.

J   Ob. 123. "The following approximations [to I and A 5] have been supplied:– [Texts H 2 and J.] The former is sent by [Miss Annie Shirer], and the latter by an anonymous correspondent, who says it was the refrain which her mother used to sing to the ditty." (G, Ob. 123)

INDEX OF TITLES

INDEX OF SINGERS/SOURCES

Hutcheon, A.	557C
Ingram, Mrs	585H
Ingram, Miss Lizzie	700D
Insch, A.M.	482, 601
Ironside, James	578
Jaffray, Mrs	407D, 499C, 631
Jaffray, Mrs (Mintlaw)	433C, 618D, 706A
Jaffray, John	351B, 380, 403A, 526B
Johnstone, Mrs	467D, 472
Johnstone, John	347E, 356C, 460B, 581H, 585D, 697F
Knowles, Archibald	406B, 590A, 607B
Lawrence, John	703A
Lawrence, William	540B, 563B, 686
Lawson, D.	573
Leask, J.	515
Littlejohn, Miss	560A
Lorimer, William	603I
Lyall, Mrs	350, 445A, 449D, 452B, 455C, 476, 548A, 581I, 646B, 654D, 654E, 658
MacDonald, Alex	496, 647
Mackay, Alexander	356B, 398B, 404A, 538D, 603D
Mackie, James	492A
Massie, W.	384A, 389C
McAllan, John	347A
McBoyle, J.	449B, 492B, 587G
McDonald, Miss Jessie H.	538F
McKenzie, D.R.	377B, 524, 667D
McQueen, Gordon	411
Melvin, Mr	391B
Michie, Angus	585G
Milne, Mrs	437A, 445D, 463D, 540A
Milne, Alex	347M, 398A, 408B, 422
Milne, George	538B, 616E
Milne, John	347O, 347Q, 349F, 358, 376D, 384S, 388, 396, 398C, 401G, 407F, 421F, 423, 440, 442, 443F, 460C, 460D, 516, 517, 548D, 622, 629D, 645D, 681
Milne, Mrs John	616B
Mitchell, Dr	393
Mitchell, Miss Kate	378C, 585B
Moir, Mrs	426
Morrice, Miss K.	445E, 649B